ECONOMIC SURVEY OF LATIN AMERICA, 1962

ECONOMIC SURVEY OF LATIN AMERICA, 1962

THIS SURVEY WAS PREPARED IN THE
DEPARTMENT OF ECONOMIC AFFAIRS OF
THE PAN AMERICAN UNION

PUBLISHED FOR THE

ORGANIZATION OF AMERICAN STATES

BY

THE JOHNS HOPKINS PRESS, BALTIMORE

330.98
Ec 74
1962

© 1964, THE JOHNS HOPKINS PRESS
BALTIMORE, MARYLAND 21218
PRINTED IN THE UNITED STATES OF AMERICA
LIBRARY OF CONGRESS CATALOG CARD NO. 50-3616

THIS SURVEY WAS PREPARED BY THE SECRETARIAT OF THE ORGANIZATION OF AMERICAN STATES, WHICH ALONE IS RESPONSIBLE FOR ITS CONTENTS. THE SECRETARIAT WISHES TO EXPRESS ITS GRATITUDE TO THE ECONOMIC COMMISSION FOR LATIN AMERICA (ECLA) FOR THE CO-OPERATION RECEIVED DURING THE PREPARATION OF THE SURVEY.

CONTENTS

PART I
THE LATIN AMERICAN ECONOMY AND THE ALLIANCE FOR PROGRESS

Chapter 1.
LATIN AMERICAN EXPORTS AND
THE MARKETS FOR BASIC PRODUCTS...................... 1
   Economic Activity in the Industrialized Countries.................... 1
   The International Market for Basic Products........................ 10
      Sugar... 16
      Bananas.. 19
      Cacao.. 24
      Coffee.. 25
      Wheat.. 35
      Corn... 38
      Meat... 39
      Cotton... 49
      Wool... 53
      Copper... 54
      Lead and Zinc.. 58
      Tin.. 61
      Silver.. 64
      Petroleum.. 65
   Total Exports and Their Geographic Structure....................... 68

Chapter 2.
LATIN AMERICA'S CAPACITY TO IMPORT,
AND ITS BALANCE OF PAYMENTS............................ 74
   Total Capacity to Import, Its Utilization, and the Net Balance of Payments 74
   Noncompensatory Capital Movements................................ 85

v

vi   CONTENTS

  Official Loans and Grants.................................... 88
  Private Capital.. 101
  Compensatory Financing of the Balance of Payments.............. 112

Chapter 3.
TOTAL PRODUCTION, CAPITAL FORMATION,
AND MONETARY DEVELOPMENT............................ 120
  Variations in Total Product and Capital Formation................ 120
  Monetary Developments...................................... 127
    Money supply trends..................................... 128
    Factors of Monetary Expansion............................. 129
    Balance of Payments and Price Pressures..................... 133
    Fiscal Pressures... 137
    Bank Credit to the Private Sector.......................... 140
    Institutional reforms..................................... 143

Chapter 4.
THE MANUFACTURING SECTOR............................. 146
  General Development of Manufacturing.......................... 146
    Current Consumer-Goods Industries........................ 150
    Paper Industry... 151
    Chemical Industries...................................... 157
    Petroleum Refining...................................... 161
    The Cement Industry.................................... 165
    The Iron and Steel Industry.............................. 167
    The Motor-Vehicle Industry............................... 174
    Tractor Production...................................... 179
    Shipbuilding... 181
    Industrial Machinery and Equipment....................... 183

Chapter 5.
THE EXECUTION OF ECONOMIC PROGRAMS
UNDER THE ALLIANCE FOR PROGRESS...................... 185
  Development Planning....................................... 185
    Progress Achieved in Plan Formulation..................... 186
    Growth Targets: Output, Capital Formation, and the Balance of Payments... 191
    Measures to Reduce Structural Imbalance.................... 201
  National Programs of Agrarian Reform.......................... 209
    The General Pattern of Recent Agrarian Reform Programs...... 211
    The Experiences of Individual Countries..................... 222
  Tax Reform.. 235
    Increased Tax Receipts................................... 236
    More Equitable Distribution of the Tax Burden.............. 241
    Tax Incentives to Investment.............................. 242
    Improved Tax Administration.............................. 243

PART II
CHARACTERISTICS AND DEVELOPMENT OF THE CENTRAL AMERICAN PRODUCTIVE STRUCTURE

INTRODUCTION.. 249
  Objectives and Principal Results of the Investigation................... 249
  The Problems of Small Countries and Their Application to the Central American Situation.. 257

Chapter 6.
STRUCTURE, RECENT DEVELOPMENT, AND PROSPECTS OF CENTRAL AMERICAN EXPORTS................ 263
  Pattern and Development of Exports................................ 263
    Coffee.. 268
    Bananas.. 271
    Cotton... 275
    Wood.. 280
    Meat.. 280
    Sugar.. 284
    Cocoa... 288
  Prospects in 1963–67 for Exports Outside of Central America........... 290
    Assumptions... 291
    Projections.. 295
  Projection of the Value of Central America's Major Primary Product Exports in 1967... 296
    Coffee... 296
    Bananas.. 303
    Cotton... 306
    Wood.. 311
    Meat.. 312
    Sugar.. 315
    Cocoa... 317

Chapter 7.
PRINCIPAL CHARACTERISTICS AND DEVELOPMENT OF THE CENTRAL AMERICAN PRODUCTIVE STRUCTURE......... 319
  Structure of the Production of Goods and Services................... 319
    Structure of the Output by Major Sectors of Economic Activity...... 319
    Structure of the Economically Active Population and of Productivity by Sectors... 330
  Manufacturing Structure.. 334
    Potential of Industrial Growth and its Components................. 334
    Structure and Development of the Industrial Output............... 338

viii CONTENTS

    Recent Development in the Production of Selected Products and Per Capita Production and Consumption Levels...... 347
    Industrial Employment and Capital Structure; Productivity and Capital Intensity...... 354

Chapter 8.
EVOLUTION AND STRUCTURE OF CENTRAL AMERICAN IMPORTS AND PROSPECTS FOR INTRA-CENTRAL AMERICAN TRADE...... 372

    Changes in Import Volume...... 372
    Changes in the Composition of Imports...... 374
        Foodstuffs (SICT Section 0)...... 378
        Chemical and Pharmaceutical Products (SICT Section 5)...... 380
    Changes in Sources of Imports...... 385
        Renewal of Trade with Europe and Japan...... 387
        Variations in Prices Paid by Central America...... 388
        Sectoral Relative Prices...... 389
        Import Substitution...... 392
        Direction of Investments...... 393
    Intra-Central American Trade...... 394
        Reciprocal Food Imports...... 408
        Reciprocal Textile Imports...... 411
    Prospects for Inter-Central American Trade...... 415
        Factors Delaying Reciprocal Trade and the Integration Program...... 416
        Replacement of Overseas Imports and Reciprocal Trade...... 419

Annex.
CENTRAL AMERICA: OVERSEAS AND RECIPROCAL IMPORTS IN 1961, IN APPROXIMATE RELATION TO REPLACEMENT POTENTIAL...... 424

LIST OF TABLES

1-1 United States: Variations in Certain Components of the Gross National Product...... 3
1-2 Indices of Industrial Production in Certain Developed Countries...... 5

1-3 Canada: Variations in Certain Components of the Gross National Product.. 6
1-4 United Kingdom: Variations in Certain Components of the Gross Domestic Product.. 7
1-5 Imports of Industrialized Areas: Total World and from Latin America. 9
1-6 Basic Products: Prices on the International Market for Selected Commodities, Annual Averages, 1960–1962; Quarterly Averages, 1962 and 1963.. 11
1-7 Latin America: Value, Volume, and Unit Price of Foreign Trade, 1960–1963... 12
1-8 Centrifugal Sugar: World Production, by Principal Regions.......... 17
1-9 Centrifugal Sugar: Stocks in Principal Exporting Countries.......... 18
1-10 Sugar: Production and Exports of Selected Countries............... 20
1-11 Centrifugal Sugar: Exports of Selected Latin American Countries, by Principal Regions of Destination............................... 21
1-12 Bananas: Exports of Latin American Countries, Value and Volume.. 23
1-13 Bananas: Imports of Selected Countries, by Region of Origin........ 26
1-14 Cacao Beans: Production, Consumption, and Stocks................ 28
1-15 Cacao Beans: Production and Exports of Selected Countries......... 29
1-16 Cacao Beans: Exports of Selected Countries, by Principal Region of Destination... 30
1-17 Green Coffee: World Production, Stocks, and Exports............... 31
1-18 Total United States Green Coffee Imports, by Country of Origin.... 31
1-19 Coffee Beans: World Imports, by Selected Countries and Regions.... 32
1-20 Green Coffee: Exports of Selected Latin American Countries, by Principal Region of Destination.................................. 33
1-21 Green Coffee: World Production and Exports, by Country and Region 36
1-22 Green Coffee: Value and Volume of Exports of Latin American Countries 37
1-23 Wheat: World Production and Stocks in Selected Countries......... 38
1-24 Wheat and Wheat Flour: Exports, by Principal Region of Destination 40
1-25 Corn: World Production, by Selected Regions and Countries........ 42
1-26 Corn: Exports of Selected Countries, by Principal Region of Destination.. 44
1-27 Corn: Stocks in Selected Exporting Countries on January 1 of Each Year.. 46
1-28 European Economic Community: Imports and Exports of Beef and Cattle on the Hoof.. 46
1-29 United Kingdom: Total Meat Imports, by Country of Origin....... 47
1-30 United States: Imports of Beef and Cattle on the Hoof, by Origin.... 48
1-31 Cotton: World Stocks, Production, and Consumption.............. 49
1-32 Cotton: Production and Exports of Selected Countries.............. 51
1-33 Cotton: Exports of Selected Countries and Regions, by Destination... 52
1-34 Wool: Consumption of Virgin Wool in Selected Countries.......... 53
1-35 Wool: Stocks in Principal Exporting Countries at the Beginning of the Respective Commercial Year................................... 55

1-36	Wool: Export of Principal Producer Countries, by Region of Destination.	56
1-37	Copper: Production, by Country of Origin.	57
1-38	Copper: Consumption in Selected Countries and Total World Consumption.	57
1-39	Unwrought Copper: Exports and Imports of Selected Countries.	58
1-40	Lead and Zinc: Stocks in the United States and the United Kingdom.	59
1-41	Lead and Zinc: Production, by Selected Countries and Total World Production.	60
1-42	Lead and Zinc: Latin American Exports.	61
1-43	Tin: World Production and Consumption, 1960–1962.	62
1-44	Tin: Imports of Selected Countries.	63
1-45	Soviet Union: Tin Exports and Imports.	64
1-46	Silver: World Production, by Selected Countries.	65
1-47	Crude Petroleum: World Production, by Selected Countries.	66
1-48	Crude Petroleum and Petroleum Products: Exports of Latin American Countries.	68
1-49	United States: Foreign Trade in Crude Petroleum and Petroleum Products.	69
1-50	Latin America: Exports, by Principal Regions of Destination, 1960–1962.	70
1-51	Latin American Intraregional Exports, 1960–1962.	73
2-1	Latin America: Total Capacity to Import, 1961 and 1962.	76
2-2	Latin America: Total Capacity to Import and Principal Contributing Factors, 1960–1962.	78
2-3	Latin America: Capacity to Import, Imports, and Balance-of-Payments Position, 1960–1962.	79
2-4	Latin America: Current Capacity to Import, Imports, and Balance on Current Account, 1960–1962.	81
2-5	Latin America: Net Balances on the Main Accounts of Foreign Payments, 1960–1962.	87
2-6	Latin America: Total Flow of Capital, 1960–1962.	87
2-7	Latin America: Composition of Noncompensatory Capital Movements, 1960–1962.	89
2-8	Latin America: Composition of Official Capital Receipts and Grants from the United States Government, 1960–1962.	90
2-9	Latin America: Grants by the United States Government under the American Aid Program and Public Law 480, Title III, 1960–1962.	92
2-10	Latin America: Loans Authorized and Net Disbursements by the Agency for International Development, 1960–1962.	94
2-11	Latin America: Loans Authorized and Net Disbursements under the Social Progress Trust Fund, 1960–1962.	95
2-12	Latin America: Composition of Official Capital Receipts from International Agencies, 1960–1962.	96
2-13	Latin America: Loans Authorized and Net Disbursements by the Inter-American Development Bank, 1961–1962.	97

CONTENTS xi

2-14 Latin America: Loans Authorized and Net Disbursements by the International Bank for Reconstruction and Development, 1960–1962   98
2-15 Latin America: Net Flow of Official Capital from Japan and OECD Member Countries, Excluding the United States, 1960-1962.......   99
2-16 Latin America: Net Flow of Official Capital from Japan and OECD Countries Other than the United States, by Recipient Countries...   100
2-17 Latin America: Direct Investments and Transactions in Securities by United States Private Capital, 1960-1962......................   102
2-18 Latin America: Net Inflow of United States Private Capital for Direct Investment, 1960-1962..   103
2-19 Latin America: Private Export Credits Guaranteed by the Governments of the OECD Member Countries, Excluding the United States, 1960-1962...   107
2-20 Latin America: Net Flow of Guaranteed Private Export Credits.....   107
2-21 Latin America: Short-Term Assets of the Private Sector Reported by Banks in the United States, 1960-1962.......................   109
2-22 Latin America: Foreign Debt Servicing in Selected Countries in 1962.   111
2-23 Latin America: International Reserves and Compensatory Balance of Payments Accounts, 1960-1962..............................   112
2-24 Latin America: Net Annual Variations in the Debt with the International Monetary Fund, 1960—March, 1963.....................   114
2-25 Latin America: Compensatory Loans by the Export-Import Bank of Washington, 1960—March, 1963............................   115
2-26 Latin America: Movement of Compensatory Accounts of the Balance of Payments, 1960-1962......................................   117
2-27 Latin America: Movement of Compensatory Accounts of the Balance of Payments in 1962..   118

3-1 Changes Over the Preceding Year in the Total Agricultural and Manufacturing Gross Product and in Fixed Investments in 1961 and 1962   122
3-2 Latin America: Fixed Capital Formation by Sectors and the Inflow of Direct Private Investment, 1961 and 1962.....................   125
3-3 Latin America: Percentage Changes in Money Supply, 1957-1963....   128
3-4 Latin America: Major Factors of Monetary Expansion in 1962.......   130
3-5 Latin America: Ratio of Public to Private Sector Credit Extended by the Banking System, 1961-1963..............................   133
3-6 Latin America: Indices of Exchange Rate and Price Trends after Major 1958-1959 Exchange Rate Adjustments........................   135
3-7 Latin America: Percentage Changes in Cost of Living Index, 1957-1963   137
3-8 Latin America: Percentage Change in Banking System's Net Claims on Government, 1961-1963.....................................   138
3-9 Latin America: Bank Credit to the Private Sector in 1961 and 1962...   141

4-1 Latin America: Manufacturing Growth, by Country and by Selected Industrial Products, 1957-1962................................   148
4-2 Latin America: Growth of the Traditional Industries in Five Selected Countries, 1957-1962..   152
4-3 Latin America: Production of Cellulose Pulp, Paper, and Cardboard, 1957, 1960, 1961, and 1962...................................   153

4-4 Latin America: Caustic Soda and Sulphuric Acid Production, 1957, 1960, 1961, and 1962 158
4-5 Latin America: Petroleum Refining, 1957, 1960, 1961, and 1962 163
4-6 Latin America: Cement Production, 1957, 1960, 1961, and 1962 166
4-7 Latin America: Production of Pig Iron, Raw Steel, and Finished Steel in 1957, 1960, 1961, and 1962 169
4-8 Latin America: Motor Vehicle Production, 1957, 1960, 1961, and 1962 175
4-9 Latin America: Tractor Production, 1957, 1960, 1961, and 1962 180

5-1 Development Plans Prepared or in Preparation 188
5-2 Planned Growth of Gross Domestic Product and the Necessary Investment, Compared with the Magnitudes Realized in 1961 and 1962 ... 192
5-3 Recent and Projected Contribution of Foreign Capital in Seven Countries 194
5-4 The Financing of Planned Investment, Compared with Recent Realized Investment 198
5-5 Planned Foreign Trade 202
5-6 Planned Annual Increases in Production, by Sectors, in Five Countries. 204
5-7 The Distribution of Planned Investment by Sectors 206
5-8 Summary of Some Major Features of Agrarian Reform Laws Passed since August, 1961 216
5-9 Progress in Implementing the Agrarian Reform Legislation Passed since Punta del Este 224

6-1 Central American Exports, by Country of Origin, 1955–1962 264
6-2 Commodity Distribution of Central American Exports, 1955–1962 265
6-3 Value, Volume, and Unit Value of Central America's Major Primary Product Exports, 1955–1962 266
6-4 Central American Exports, by Destination, 1955–1962 267
6-5 Share of Coffee in Central American Export Receipts, 1955–1962 268
6-6 Central American Coffee Exports: Total and by Country of Origin, 1955–1962 269
6-7 Central American Coffee Exports, by Destination, 1955–1961 270
6-8 Position of Central American Coffee in Major Markets, 1955–1961 ... 272
6-9 Central American Coffee Exports to Western Europe, by Country of Destination, 1955–1961 273
6-10 Share of Central American Coffee in Imports of Major European Countries in 1961 273
6-11 Share of Bananas in Central American Export Receipts, 1955–1962 .. 274
6-12 Central American Banana Exports: Total and by Country of Origin, 1955–1962 275
6-13 Central American Banana Exports by Destination, 1956–1961 276
6-14 Share of Cotton in Central American Export Receipts, 1955–1962 276
6-15 Volume and Value of Central American Cotton Exports, Total and by Country of Origin, 1955–1962 277
6-16 Central American Cotton Exports, by Major Markets, 1955–1962 278
6-17 Total Cotton Imports and Share of Central America in Selected Markets, 1955–1962 279

6-18 Share of Major Markets in Cotton Exports of Major Central American Producers, 1955-1962................................. 279
6-19 Central American Wood Exports, Total and by Country of Origin, 1955-1962.. 281
6-20 Central American Wood Exports, by Destination, 1955-1961........ 282
6-21 Central American Meat Exports, Total and by Country of Origin, 1955-1962.. 283
6-22 Central American Meat Exports, by Destination, 1955-1961......... 285
6-23 Central American Sugar Exports, Total and by Country of Origin, 1955-1962.. 286
6-24 Raw Cane Sugar Spot Price, 1955-1963......................... 287
6-25 Central American Sugar Exports, by Destination, 1955-1962........ 287
6-26 Volume and Value of Central American Cocoa Exports, 1955-1962.. 289
6-27 Costa Rican Cocoa Statistics, 1955-1962......................... 290
6-28 Costa Rican Cocoa Exports, by Destination in 1961................ 290
6-29 Projected Trend in Value of Central America's Major Primary Product Exports Outside of Integration Area in 1962-1967............... 294
6-30 Projection of Volume of Central American Coffee Exports to the United States in 1967... 298
6-31 Projection of Volume of Central American Coffee Exports to Western Europe in 1967... 299
6-32 Summary of Projection of Central American Unroasted Coffee Exports in 1967.. 301
6-33 Projected Trend in Volume of Banana Imports from Central America in Major Markets in 1962-1967............................. 304
6-34 Summary of Projection of Central American Banana Exports in 1967. 305
6-35 Central American Cotton Production Statistics, 1955-1963, and Projections for 1967.. 307
6-36 Summary of Projection of Central American Raw Cotton Exports in 1967... 310
6-37 Summary of Projection of Central American Wood Exports in 1967... 313
6-38 Projected Volume of Central American Exports of Beef in 1967...... 314
6-39 Summary of Projection of Central American Meat Exports in 1967... 315
6-40 Summary of Projection of Central American Sugar Exports in 1967.. 317
6-41 Summary of Projection of Costa Rican Cocoa Exports in 1967....... 318

7-1 Central American Isthmus: Structure of the Combined Output of the Countries of the Area, Excluding and Including Panama, by Sectors of Economic Activity, 1950, 1955, and 1960..................... 321
7-2 Central American Isthmus: Structure of the Product, by Major Sectors of Economic Activity of the Six Countries of the Area, Separately, 1950 and 1960... 323
7-3 Central American Isthmus: Growth Rate of the Various Sectors of Economic Activity in the Consolidated Gross Product of the Area, Excluding and Including Panama, 1950-1955, 1955-1960, and 1950-1960... 324

7-4 Central American Isthmus: Growth Rate of the Total Product and Per Capita Growth Rate for the Six Countries of the Area, 1950–1955, 1955–1960, and 1950–1960.. 326
7-5 Central America and the World: Changes in the Structure of the Product of Selected Countries, Grouped According to Development and Size, 1950.. 328
7-6 Central American Isthmus: Structure of the Economically Active Population in the Six Countries and in the Area as a Whole, Excluding and Including Panama, 1950–1960 (or 1961).................... 331
7-7 Central American Isthmus: Consolidated Structure of the Manufacturing Output of the Countries of the Area, Excluding and Including Panama, 1955... 340
7-8 Central American Isthmus: Structure of the Manufacturing Product of the Six Countries of the Area, by Country, 1955................... 344
7-9 Central America: Consolidated Structure of the Manufacturing Product of the Five Countries, 1953 and 1958: Growth by Groups and Lines of Industry, 1953–1958.. 346
7-10 Central America: Growth in the Combined Production of Selected Industrial Products between 1953 and 1961...................... 348
7-11 Central America and Other Areas of the World: Per Capita Production of Selected Products, 1960..................................... 351
7-12 Central America and Other Areas of the World: Per Capita Apparent Consumption of Selected Products, 1960........................ 352
7-13 Central America: Manufacturing Output and Employment of Four Countries, Total and by Country, 1955 and Other Years near 1955 360
7-14 Guatemala: Structure of Employment and Added Value in the Manufacturing Component of the Industrial Sector, 1953 and 1957...... 362
7-15 Central America: Structure of the Relative Productivity of Labor in the Combined Manufacturing Sector of Four Countries, 1955...... 363
7-16 Costa Rica and Honduras: Structure of Existing Fixed Capital and Capital Intensity in the Manufacturing Sector, by Industrial Groups and Branches, 1957.. 366
7-17 Costa Rica and Honduras: Relative Capital Intensity and Relative Productivity, by Industrial Groups and Branches, 1957........... 368

8-1 Volume of Imports in Central America, Selected Years.............. 373
8-2 Central America: Indices of Physical Volume of Imports............. 377
8-3 Central America: Percentage of Imports by SICT Sections.......... 378
8-4 Central America: Imports of Food Products....................... 382
8-5 Central America: Imports of Chemical and Pharmaceutical Products.. 383
8-6 Central America: Origin of Imports.............................. 386
8-7 Industrialized Countries: Indices of Unit Values of Exports.......... 388
8-8 Annual Rates of Increase for Wholesale Prices of Selected Groups of Industrial Products in the United States, the Federal Republic of Germany, and Japan, 1950–1961..................................... 390
8-9 Central America: Difference in Import Value of Chemical Products, by Suppliers and Selected Periods................................. 390
8-10 Central America: Imports by SICT Sections and Selected Sources 1953, 1957, 1961... 391

8–11 Central America: Difference in Import Value of Machinery and Automotive Equipment, According to Origin.......................... 392
8–12 Central America: Difference between 1953–1957 and 1957–1961 in Value Imported from the United States and Other Sources by Chief Components of SICT Sections 6 and 8.......................... 393
8–13 Central America: Reciprocal C.I.F. Imports, by SICT Sections, 1955–1962.. 397
8–14 Central America: Reciprocal Imports, by Groups of Countries and Selected Years.. 404
8–15 Central America: Value of Intra-Central American Imports by El Salvador, Guatemala, and Honduras, by Sectors and Industries of Origin in 1957 and 1961.. 406
8–16 Central America: Intra-Central American Imports by El Salvador, Guatemala, and Honduras, by Food Industry of Origin in 1957 and 1961.. 409
8–17 El Salvador: Trade in Textile Products with Guatemala, 1961....... 415
8–18 Central America: Manufacturing Plants Recently Completed or under Construction and Planned for 1963.............................. 419

SYMBOLS USED

Three dots (...) indicate that data are not available or are not separately reported.

A dash (—) indicates that the amount is nil or negligible.

A minus sign (−) indicates a deficit or decrease.

A stroke (/) indicates a crop year or fiscal year; e.g., 1954/55.

A full stop (.) is used to indicate decimals.

Use of hyphen (-) between two dates (e.g., 1950–54) normally signifies an annual average for the calendar years involved, including the beginning and end years. "to" between the years indicates the full period; e.g., "1950 to 1954" means 1950 to 1954 inclusive.

References to "tons" indicate metric tons; and to "dollars," United States dollars, unless otherwise stated.

Totals do not necessarily correspond to the sum of their components, because of rounding.

An asterisk (*) is used to indicate figures partially or wholly estimated.

The term "billion" signifies a thousand million.

PART I
THE LATIN AMERICAN ECONOMY AND THE ALLIANCE FOR PROGRESS

CHAPTER 1

LATIN AMERICAN EXPORTS AND THE MARKETS FOR BASIC PRODUCTS

ECONOMIC ACTIVITY IN THE INDUSTRIALIZED COUNTRIES

Economic expansion continued in the industrialized part of the world in 1962, although the degree of expansion was quite different in each region. In the countries that had been affected by a slight recession in 1960/61,* economic activity recovered in the first half of 1962. Although this movement slowed down in the second half of 1962 and the first quarter of 1963, the increases for the year as a whole in the various countries were generally higher than those for the previous year. The opposite occurred in the European Economic Community, where the rate of growth of economic activity continued to decline; the annual percentages of increase in the national product of the various countries of the Community were lower than those for 1961 and much lower than those during the accelerated expansion of 1959/60.

The over-all demand increase in the industrialized regions contributed to the progress of imports from the underdeveloped areas. However, the intensity of this phenomenon varied a great deal from one industrial country to another, not only because the rates of growth of the total expenditure were not the same in the various countries but also because the component parts of that expenditure did not increase in the same manner everywhere. In addition, in certain countries specific factors affected the amount of purchases from the developing regions.

United States. In the United States, the recovery of economic activity, begun after the 1960/61 recession, continued in 1962 and the first half of

---

* For a list of date styling and certain symbols used in text and tables, please see the page "Symbols Used" in the front matter of this book.

1963; but it tapered off in the second half of 1962. The real gross national product, which had increased 7.7 per cent in the first quarter of 1962 and 6 per cent in the second quarter of that year over the levels for the same quarters of 1961, grew only 4.7 per cent and 3.1 per cent in the last two quarters.[1]

This relatively small increase in the volume of the total demand was essentially the result of the increase in private consumption expenditures and investment by business. The change in consumption expenditures reflected simultaneously a constant increase in expenditures for services, the import content of which is insignificant, and a strong recovery in purchases of durable goods, which were 8.6 per cent higher than in 1961. Purchases of automobiles increased 20 per cent over the previous year, reaching a particularly high level in the last quarter of 1962. Moreover, the gross formation of private capital increased 9.5 per cent over 1961 but did not reach the high proportion of gross national product attained in 1955 and 1959. Its most dynamic component was investment in fixed capital, which increased 13 per cent over the previous year, while construction and the policy of private enterprise regarding stocks progressed at an uneven rate. In effect, private business increased its reserves of goods in the first two quarters of 1962, in the expectation of a strike in the steel industry, and then maintained them at a relatively constant level, so that the increase in stocks for the whole year was slightly above that for 1961. This fact is particularly important because it had an unfavorable effect on the volume of imports from the lesser developed countries.

Parallel to the increase in private consumption expenditures and investments by private enterprise, a slightly higher rate of growth was noted in governmental expenditures than in the previous year. In addition, the volume of exports rose 3.9 per cent instead of 1.6 per cent in 1961; but this phenomenon did not have any appreciable effect on the level of economic activity, since foreign sales constitute a marginal element in United States total expenditures.

The recovery to a relatively satisfactory rate of total demand helped stimulate production, especially *industrial production*. Actually, in the second half of the year, industrial production did not increase at the same accelerated rate as in the first half, and the rate of increase continued to diminish in the first half of 1963. However, the total increase for 1962 was 8.3 per cent, as compared with only 0.8 per cent in 1961, and in the

---

[1] These percentages were computed on the basis of the seasonally adjusted index of volume of the gross national product at 1954 prices (see Table 1–1).

TABLE 1-1. United States: Variations in Certain Components of the Gross National Product

(Billions of dollars at 1954 prices)

Period	GNP	Personal consumption expenditures				Government purchases of goods and services	Gross domestic formation of private capital[b]	Exports of goods and services	Imports of goods and services
		Durable goods	Nondurable goods	Services	Total				
1960	440.2	42.2	141.4	114.7	298.3	79.8	60.7	24.9	23.4
			(Indices: preceding period = 100.0)						
Years									
1961	101.7	98.6	101.3	104.1	102.0	105.3	95.2	101.6	100.4
1962	105.3	108.6	103.6	104.3	104.6	107.0	109.5	103.9	109.4
Quarters[a]									
1961 I	98.4	92.0	100.6	104.5	100.9	104.8	75.0	108.0	94.1
II	100.4	96.0	100.0	103.7	100.9	104.1	91.9	98.0	95.0
III	102.4	99.8	101.8	104.0	102.3	103.5	103.1	99.6	102.9
IV	105.9	106.2	103.0	104.4	103.9	109.1	114.9	101.1	109.7
1962 I	107.7	113.1	103.9	104.3	105.3	108.1	126.6	101.5	111.7
II	106.0	108.0	104.1	104.3	104.8	107.1	113.4	108.6	113.6
III	104.7	106.9	103.5	104.2	104.2	108.6	103.3	104.4	108.6
IV	103.1	107.2	103.0	103.8	103.9	105.0	98.0	100.4	104.0

[a] Seasonally adjusted quarterly totals at annual rates.
[b] Includes gross domestic formation of fixed capital plus changes in stocks.

Source: U.S. Department of Commerce, *Survey of Current Business*, February, 1963.

first half of 1963 it continued growing at an annual rate of nearly 4 per cent (see Table 1–2).

Progress in manufacturing industry was considerable (8.5 per cent higher than in 1961) and was even greater in basic metals and in the other metals industries whose activity is directly connected with the automobile industry. Expansion was also rapid in the chemical industries and, although to a lesser degree, in the textile industry. Production in the foodstuff industries increased at the same rate as during the previous year. This distribution of the percentages of growth of the various industrial sectors undoubtedly favored the expansion of imports of minerals and hydrocarbons, which are traditionally supplied largely by certain Latin American countries.

Canada. In Canada, in general, the recovery was more or less the same as that of the United States. The gross national product increased 6.2 per cent in 1962 as compared with 2.6 per cent in 1961 (see Table 1–3). The various components of total expenditure increased in widely differing proportions. Governmental expenditures increased more slowly than in the previous year (3.3 per cent in 1962 as compared with 4.6 per cent in 1961), and the same phenomenon was noted with respect to the volume of exports of goods and services, which increased 4.4 per cent in 1962 as compared with 7.5 per cent in 1961. The increase in consumer expenditures was scarcely more rapid than in previous years, since the expansion in purchases of certain durable goods (automobiles) was counteracted by the decrease in the rate of growth in service expenditures. In contrast, very rapid progress was made in the gross formation of private capital, which rose 14 per cent in 1962 as compared with the previous year, when it declined slightly. This renewal of activity in private investment resulted essentially from the increase in purchases of capital equipment, while stocks remained near the relatively low level of 1961.

United Kingdom. In the United Kingdom, the measures adopted by the Government in July, 1961, in order to meet the crisis in external payments and to reduce the pressure of domestic demand on productive capacity had halted the increase in the gross domestic product at the end of 1961. In the first half of 1962, some recovery was noted, but it was of short duration, since the economic expansion was again interrupted in the last quarter. In short, the gross domestic product for 1962 as a whole scarcely reached a level above that of 1961.

TABLE 1-2. Indices of Industrial Production in Certain Developed Countries

(Indices: previous period = 100)

Period	United States	Canada	EEC	Belgium Luxembourg	France	West Germany	Italy	Nether-lands	European Free Trade Association	United Kingdom
Years										
1961	100.8	103.1	106.4	104.6	104.8	105.5	109.9	101.3	101.5	100.8
1962	108.3	107.5	...	105.9	...	104.7	111.0	103.8	...	100.0
Quarters[a]										
1961 I	93.4	97.0	107.1	97.7		108.5	109.0	106.5	101.5	100.8
II	99.2	102.3	106.4	106.9		106.1	109.4	100.0	102.2	101.5
III	103.4	106.2	104.6	104.6	104.6	104.4	109.8	100.0	102.2	100.0
IV	109.6	107.7	105.6	109.4	105.1	103.2	115.0	101.2	100.0	99.2
1962 I	112.4	109.3	105.5	111.1	106.2	102.1	113.5	101.8	100.7	99.2
II	109.2	109.1	105.5	101.4	105.5	104.7	110.6	103.1	100.7	100.0
III	106.5	107.3	106.0	105.8	105.5	105.8	108.4	105.2	101.4	102.3
IV	104.0	105.0	105.3	104.3	105.4	102.0	106.5	103.7	101.5	100.8
1963 I	103.5	105.5		101.0	100.5	101.9	105.4	100.5		97.4
II	105.0	...		...	...	...	...	...		...

[a] Seasonally adjusted.

Source: OECD, General Statistics, March, 1962.

TABLE 1-3. Canada: Variations in Certain Components of the Gross National Product

(Millions of dollars at 1957 prices)

Period	GNP	Consumer expenditures for goods and services	Government expenditures for goods and services	Gross domestic formation of private capital[b]	Exports of goods and services	Imports of goods and services
1960	34,144	22,357	6,255	6,576	6,884	8,020
(Indices: preceding period = 100)						
Years						
1961	102.6	103.2	104.6	90.9	107.5	101.2
1962	106.2	103.7	103.3	113.8	104.4	101.3
Quarters[a]						
1961 I	98.4	102.0	104.1	78.7	99.9	97.7
II	103.0	103.5	106.1	91.0	110.0	98.7
III	103.6	103.7	102.6	95.2	108.7	103.4
IV	95.0	103.5	105.7	100.7	111.9	105.0
1962 I	108.5	105.9	101.1	115.6	105.9	102.1
II	106.3	103.6	107.5	110.6	105.9	105.4
III	106.0	102.2	103.5	127.2	101.8	101.7
IV	104.7	103.1	101.2	103.5	104.1	96.4

[a] Totals seasonally adjusted quarterly at annual rates.
[b] Includes gross domestic formation of fixed capital plus variations in stocks.
Source: Canadian Statistical Review, April, 1963.

Actually, the rate of growth of almost all the components of total demand decreased (see Table 1-4). This trend was not very significant in the area of private consumption, since, although the expenditures for nondurable goods and services increased at a lower rate, there were more substantial increases in the purchases of certain durable goods, especially automobiles. Government expenditures increased less than in the past, and the same was true of exports. Above all, gross capital formation decreased by 5.8 per cent, compared with the 1961 figure. The vigorous growth in public investment, which increased 5 per cent over 1961, did not compensate for the sharp reduction in private investment in fixed capital, which in the last quarter of 1962 was 18 per cent less than the previous year. Moreover, the pronounced quarterly variations in stocks represented only a slight increase for the year as a whole.

As is natural under such conditions, the expansion of industrial production was interrupted. In the first five months of 1963, it remained stationary at the level reached in the same period of the preceding year. In

TABLE 1–4. United Kingdom: Variations in Certain Components of the Gross Domestic Product

(Millions of pounds at 1958 prices)

Period	GDP	Consumer Expenditures				Current expenditures of the government	Gross domestic capital formation[b]	Exports of goods and services	Imports of goods and services
		Durable goods	Nondurable goods	Services	Total				
1960	24,616	1,474	12,747	2,313	16,534	3,850	4,717	5,093	5,578
			(Indices: previous period = 100)						
Years									
1961	102.9	95.4	102.3	102.1	101.7	105.8	101.1	103.1	99.9
1962	100.1	104.7	101.0	101.3	101.3	102.2	94.2	101.3	101.7
Quarters[a]									
1961 I	102.6	88.5	103.8	101.6	102.0	106.4	105.7	102.5	106.1
II	103.6	98.6	102.2	102.9	102.0	104.8	104.1	104.2	100.4
III	103.9	99.2	102.0	102.2	101.8	108.2	99.5	103.8	97.1
IV	101.6	96.2	101.4	101.5	101.0	103.7	95.6	101.9	96.2
1962 I	99.0	96.1	100.1	99.5	99.7	102.9	90.0	98.2	95.5
II	100.8	100.5	101.3	101.8	101.3	104.4	94.2	102.1	100.4
III	100.2	104.2	100.9	101.6	101.3	102.8	99.3	101.9	106.2
IV	100.1	119.2	101.6	102.2	103.1	98.8	93.2	102.8	105.1

[a] Seasonally adjusted quarters.
[b] Includes gross domestic formation of fixed capital plus variations in stocks.

Source: Central Statistical Office, *Monthly Digest of Statistics* (London), March, 1963.

1962, only the chemical industry registered a relatively favorable rate of growth. In all the other sectors, production remained stationary (manufacturing industry) or declined (metallurgical and textile industries).

European Economic Community. In the European Economic Community, the rate of growth of the economy continued to decline. In fact, the gross national product increased only 4.5 per cent in 1962, while in 1961 it had increased 5.2 per cent and in 1960, 7.1 per cent.

The causes of this unusual development have been fully analyzed in reports by the Community Commission and are therefore mentioned here only briefly.

On the one hand, foreign demand ceased to stimulate the economic cycle, since Community exports increased little from 1961 to 1962. The renewal of economic activity in the United States was actually insufficient, and that of Great Britain did not last long enough to compensate for the impact of previous recessions on world trade. In addition, the developing countries could not further increase their purchases from the European Common Market because of their difficult foreign payments situation and the less liberal policy of the Six regarding medium-term financing of exports.

On the other hand, certain components of the domestic demand progressed less rapidly than in the past. First of all, the gross formation of fixed capital rose only 5.5 per cent in 1962, compared with a rise of 9 per cent in 1961. Actually, the more rapid expansion of public investment was sufficient to make up for the decrease in private investment, for which there were various causes, such as the results of the last recession in the United States; the not too favorable outlook for exports to the underdeveloped countries; the sharp increase in production capacity; the decline in profits resulting from higher wages and salaries that were not always matched by a real improvement in productivity; and credit restrictions in certain countries. In the second place, the trend in inventories did not contribute to an expansion of total demand, despite a small increase in the stocks of raw materials at the end of the year.

The moderate expansion of demand contributed to lowering the rate of growth of the total industrial production of the Community, which increased only 5 per cent in 1962, as opposed to 7 per cent in 1961. However, this occurred only in France and Germany; in Belgium, Netherlands, and Italy, progress was somewhat greater than in the preceding year. In the first quarter of 1963, the rate of expansion of most of the countries of the Community continued to decline.

The behavior of several sectors of the industrial activity was quite diverse. Expansion was relatively weak in certain basic industries (iron and steel, nonferrous metals industries), in those producing capital equipment, or those that are affected by a structural trend toward recession (extractive industries). In contrast, there was a sharp increase in the chemical and electrochemical industry and in certain sectors of the production of durable goods. In the Community, as in the United States, 1962 was an excellent year for automobile production, which increased 15 per cent, compared with 2 per cent in the preceding year.

It is clear that the decline in the rate of growth of exports—only 1 per cent in the first quarter of 1963—domestic demand, and industrial production could endanger the long-term expansion of Community purchases abroad, especially from the developing countries.

Despite these dangers in Continental Europe and the uncertainties of the economic cycle in other industrialized countries, 1962 was generally characterized by an increase in imports by the more developed areas (see Table 1–5).

TABLE 1–5. Imports of Industrialized Areas: Total World and from Latin America (Monthly Averages)

Period	United States Total	United States Latin America	European Economic Community Total	European Economic Community Latin America	European Free Trade Association Total	European Free Trade Association Latin America
1960 (millions of dollars)	1,221.0	291.8	2,467.7	151.2	1,923.4	106.3
(Indices: previous period = 100)						
Years						
1961	98.0	90.0	108.6	99.8	102.0	92.2
1962	113.2	106.7	111.2	117.1	104.5	104.1
Quarters						
1961 I	88.6	95.1	107.4	99.9	105.7	102.4
II	90.2	82.0	111.0	103.3	103.5	93.0
III	103.3	86.7	106.6	97.0	100.0	87.3
IV	111.3	96.9	109.1	99.0	99.0	85.9
1962 I	115.9	104.6	113.4	115.4	102.7	99.9
II	118.2	105.1	108.4	118.6	103.7	107.8
III	110.3	107.3	111.6	119.4	107.0	115.8
IV	109.2	110.1	111.0	115.0	106.3	113.2
1963 I	99.5	93.6	105.1	104.1	...	...

Source: OECD, Foreign Trade, Series A, December, 1962, July, 1963.

THE INTERNATIONAL MARKET FOR BASIC PRODUCTS

The year 1962 brought about a halt in the downward trend of recent years for many Latin American export products.[2] In the first half of 1963, a marked increase began to be noted in several markets, including sugar, cacao, and wool, while the rise in the price of silver continued (see Table 1–6). If the total index for export prices continued to decline, it was because the two most important products of the region either remained stationary (petroleum) or continued to decline and did not become stabilized until the first quarter in 1963 (coffee).

In 1962, the impact of price changes even caused a slight fall, but this was not reflected in the income from exports in the region, since the volume exported increased markedly. Thus, the value of exports rose for the first time above the 1957 level and exceeded the 1961 level by more than $500 million, or about 7 per cent.

In short, the increases in prices of manufactured products caused the terms of trade of the region to remain stationary in 1962. The analysis of specific products that follows will illustrate the degree to which this is the result of opposing trends in several products and countries (see Table 1–7). The preliminary estimates for the first and second quarters of 1963 point to the possibility of some improvement in the terms of trade, although, as will be shown later, continued improvement for certain products is uncertain.

The study of the problem relating to exports of basic products continued actively in the various international agencies that have been examining the subject. At the regional level, activities in this field were concentrated chiefly on implementing resolutions adopted by the Inter-American Economic and Social Council at its 1961 and 1962 meetings. These activities included the following:

1. A meeting of the Group of Experts on the Stabilization of Export Receipts was held in the first quarter of 1962. At that meeting, the bases of a proposal for the establishment of an international fund for the stabilization of export proceeds were adopted.[3] This proposal was submitted to the United Nations Commission on International Commodity Trade for consideration, and that Commission decided to assign a technical working group to examine the proposals of the OAS Group of Experts and of the United Nations Group of Experts.

[2] For a detailed analysis of the market trends in these products between 1957 and 1961, see OAS/ECLA *Economic & Social Survey of Latin America, 1961* (Washington, D.C., 1962).

[3] *Final Report of the Group of Experts on the Stabilization of Export Receipts* (OEA/Ser.H/X.3, Doc. 7).

TABLE 1-6. Basic Products: Prices on the International Market for Selected Commodities, Annual Averages, 1960–1962; Quarterly Averages, 1962 and 1963

Commodity	Market	Unit	1960	1961	1962	1962 I	1962 II	1962 III	1962 IV	1963 I
Crude sugar	F.O.B. New York	U.S. ¢ per lb.	5.35	5.36	5.56	5.51	5.56	5.57	5.61	5.96
Crude sugar	F.O.B. world free market	U.S. ¢ per lb.	3.10	2.91	2.97	2.44	2.64	3.11	3.74	6.03
Chilled meat (Argentina)	London	d. per lb.	29.0	27.4	28.5	29.7	28.6	30.3	26.7	—
Copper	London	£ per l.t.	246	230	234	233	234	234	234	234
Tin	London	£ per l.t.	797	888	897	954	915	856	863	853
Silver	New York	U.S. ¢ per oz.	91.4	92.4	107.8	102.7	101.8	106.7	119.9	124.2
Wool (Uruguayan, 58–60's, clean basis)	Boston	$ per lb.	0.95	0.88	0.97	0.90	0.98	1.00	1.00	1.50
Coffee (Santos No. 4)	New York	U.S. ¢ per lb.	36.6	36.0	34.0	34.1	34.4	34.0	33.3	33.4
Coffee (Manizales)	New York	U.S. ¢ per lb.	44.9	43.6	40.8	42.5	40.4	40.2	39.9	39.9
Cacao (Bahía)	New York	U.S. ¢ per lb.	26.6	22.4	21.3	21.2	20.9	21.2	22.1	26.2
Cotton (Mexican, Matamoros S.M.1 1/16w)	Liverpool	U.S. ¢ per lb.	29.4	30.2	29.3	29.7	29.6	28.7	28.6	29.8
Cotton (São Paulo type 5)	Liverpool	U.S. ¢ per lb.	26.3	28.0	26.7	27.9	26.6	25.7	26.2	26.7
Cotton (Peruvian Pima No. 1)	Liverpool	U.S. ¢ per lb.	46.2	42.7	40.0	41.8	40.0	38.6	38.4	39.4
Corn "La Plata" (Argentina)	C.I.F. London	d. per lb.	21.6	21.1	20.8	21.0	21.0	20.3	21.1	—
Lead	London	£ per l.t.	72.1	64.2	56.3	59.5	59.3	52.2	54.2	54.9
Zinc	London	£ per l.t.	89.3	77.8	67.5	69.5	68.3	64.9	67.1	69.6
Wool (Argentina, 40–36's, clean basis)	Boston	$ per lb.	0.80	0.77	0.66	0.72	0.67	0.63	0.64	0.73
Bananas	United States	$ per cwt.	6.48	6.29	6.03	6.29	6.16	5.41	6.27	—
Crude petroleum (35.0–35.9, gravity API)	F.O.B. Venezuela	$ per bbl.	2.80	2.80	2.80	2.80	2.80	2.80	2.80	2.80
Wheat (Argentina, "up-river")	C.I.F. London	d. per lb.	24.7	25.8	25.9	25.8	26.2	26.1	25.1	24.6

Sources: United Nations, *Boletín Mensual de Estadística*; FAO, *Boletín Mensual de Economía y Estadística Agrícolas.*

TABLE 1-7. Latin America: Value, Volume, and Unit Price of Foreign Trade, 1960–1963

(Indices: 1961 = 100)

Period	Exports			Imports			Terms of Trade
	Value	Unit price	Volume	Value	Unit price	Volume	
1960	98	101	97	97	100	97	101
1961	100	100	100	100	100	100	100
1962	107	99	108	104	102	102	97
1961							
I	100	100	100	92	99	93	101
II	101	101	100	98	101	97	100
III	98	101	97	103	101	102	100
IV	100	98	102	108	101	107	97
1962							
I	107	102	105	98	102	96	100
II	107	101	106	99	102	97	99
III	106	97	109	107	102	105	95
IV	106	97	109	110	102	108	95
1963							
I	109	98	111	91	102	89	96
II	...	101	...	...	102	...	99

Notes: The unit prices for exports, with the exception of the figures for Peru and Venezuela, have been computed on the basis of the figures for value and the Laspeyres *de quantum* indices of the Monetary Fund, thereby obtaining Paasche indices for 16 countries. The unit values for imports are based on figures for nine countries. The quarterly variations for these nine countries were obtained by making an adjustment on the basis of the unit value of world exports of manufactured products shown in the June, 1963, edition of the above-mentioned *Bulletin*.

The 1963 export indices show the variations in the international quotations for 16 principal products, weighted according to their exported value in 1961. These variations were incorporated in the last quarter of 1962.

Sources: Official information in the cases of Peru and Venezuela; in the others, information published by the United Nations in *Monthly Bulletin of Statistics* and by the International Monetary Fund in *International Financial Statistics*. Although mentioned in the sources, Cuba is not included in this table.

This development was noted particularly in the *United States* whose imports rose 13.2 per cent over the previous year, whereas they had decreased 2 per cent in 1961 over those for 1960. However, the imports coming from Latin America increased to a lesser extent than those from the world as a whole, and so the Latin American proportion of foreign purchases made by the United States dropped slightly (from 21.9 per cent in 1961 to 20 per cent in 1962). Imports from the Dominican Republic, Ecuador, Chile, and Venezuela increased, while those from certain other countries, such as Peru and Brazil, declined.

The increase in imports was smaller in *Canada* than in the United States as a result of the devaluation of the Canadian dollar (May, 1962) and of the levying of temporary surcharges on imports in the second half of the year. A similar development occurred in the countries of the *European Free Trade Association,* with the difference that imports by those countries from Latin America increased more rapidly than from the rest of the world (see Table 1–5).

In the *European Economic Community,* the expansion in foreign purchases continued to rise, despite the slower economic growth. In 1962, imports increased 11.2 per cent, as compared with 8.6 per cent in 1961. This growth did not affect raw materials because the drop in prices did not induce buyers to increase their stocks. However, it affected considerably finished industrial products and foodstuffs. It should be noted, however, that purchases of foodstuffs were heavy, especially in the first half of 1962, as a result of the poor harvests in 1961 in several European countries, but that in the second half of 1962 they declined, as the 1962 harvest was particularly good in those countries. Therefore, it is likely that the more rapid increase in imports by the Six resulting from purchases of foodstuffs will be of short duration. At its Eleventh Meeting, the United Nations Commission on International Commodity Trade decided that, in view of the prospects for a possible solution of the problem through the action adopted by the International Monetary Fund on compensatory credits [4] and the difficulties in adopting any of the proposed stabilization solutions, it would not recommend any of them to the governments for approval for the time being.[5] This naturally does not exclude the possibility that the Latin American countries may continue considering the desirability and possibility of creating such a fund as the one proposed on a regional basis; however, the OAS also decided to postpone any action until the efficacy of the Fund's new policy can be evaluated in practice.[6]

2. The IA-ECOSOC Special Committee on Basic Products held its first meeting from July 16 to August 15, 1962, at which time it examined various aspects of the situation of the international commodities markets,

---

[4] See International Monetary Fund, *Financiamiento compensatorio de las exportaciones.*

[5] United Nations, Economic and Social Council, Commission on International Commodity Trade, *Report of the Eleventh Session,* April 29—May 10, 1963 (Doc. E/3763).

[6] See Doc. UP/G.35/2, Pan American Union, Washington, D.C., 1963.

especially with respect to those subject to discriminatory restrictions and tariffs by the countries of the European Economic Community. The Committee recommended that the IA-ECOSOC set up Action Groups for meat and bananas to make overtures to the countries of the Community in order to eliminate or reduce restrictions placed on the imports of these products from Latin America.[7] On the basis of these recommendations, the First Annual Meeting of the Inter-American Economic and Social Council at the Ministerial Level in October, 1962, approved the establishment of Action Groups for meat, bananas, and cacao, as well as a special group of experts to examine the problems of marketing sugar at the Hemisphere and world levels.[8]

3. The Committee to negotiate the elimination of restrictions on coffee consumption, established by the IA-ECOSOC by a resolution annexed to the Punta del Este Charter, held several meetings in the first half of 1962, at which the nature of the restrictions applied by the countries of the European Economic Community to coffee imports from Latin America was studied and a plan of action was adopted. By virtue of the recommendations of this Committee, the Secretary General of the OAS made overtures to the member countries of the Community requesting the elimination or reduction of such restrictions; these efforts were supported jointly by the governments of all the member countries of the OAS through their diplomatic representations to the EEC.

4. The Meat Action Group held its first meetings in December, 1962. First, it examined the draft regulations on the beef market, which had been pending approval by the Council of Ministers of the EEC, and then it studied the implications the entry of the United Kingdom into the Community would have for Latin American exporters.[9]

With respect to the first point, the Group pointed out that the draft regulations could have restrictive effects on Latin American exports of beef to the Community, but that such effects could be reduced if the so-called "guiding prices" and the corresponding "sluice-gate prices" were fixed at levels close to the lowest prevailing prices in the Community at the time. Accordingly, the Group decided to promote consultation at the governmental level with the authorities of the EEC regarding the draft regulations. The approval of the regulations has been

---

[7] *Final Report of the First Meeting of the Committee on Basic Products* (Washington, Pan American Union, August 16, 1962).

[8] First Annual Meeting of the Inter-American Economic and Social Council at the Ministerial Level, *Final Report* (Washington, D.C., 1963).

[9] See First Annual Meeting of the IA-ECOSOC at the Expert and Ministerial Levels. *The Effects of the European Economic Community on the Latin American Economies* (OEA/CIES/Doc. 10).

postponed because of the disagreement that developed among EEC members regarding the suspension of negotiations with the United Kingdom.

5. The Banana Action Group held its first meetings in Janaury, 1963, and made a detailed examination of existing regulations on imports of bananas in several European countries, especially in the markets of France, Italy, and the United Kingdom, where quantitative or other restrictions on imports of Latin American bananas are the most severe. A document prepared by the Secretariat, *The Impact of Trade Restrictions in Europe on Latin American Banana Producers,* was submitted and discussed during recent meetings of GATT; this was the first time that GATT had concerned itself extensively with this product. In another significant event, brought about through the support of OAS member countries, the Commodities Committee of the FAO, at its meetings in May, 1963, agreed to ask the Secretariat of the FAO to prepare a study on the banana-market problems and at the same time to ask the Director of the FAO to call a meeting of the Ad Hoc Banana Group to consider said study at the beginning of 1964.

6. The Cacao Action Group, whose meetings were held in March, 1963, concentrated its efforts on an analysis of the preliminary draft of the international agreement prepared by the FAO Cacao Study Group, especially in a discussion of certain aspects of this preliminary draft about which there has not been price unanimity among the Latin American countries. This Group's final report incorporated a declaration by Ecuador proposing certain rules in relation to export quotas and the election of directors; however, these did not obtain the unanimous approval of the delegates to this meeting. The Cacao Group agreed to hold a second meeting before the meeting of the conference convoked by the United Nations Secretary General to negotiate the International Cacao Agreement, scheduled for the end of 1963.

7. The Group of Experts on Sugar, which was charged with studying the sugar-marketing problems at the hemisphere and world levels, held its meetings between the end of April and the middle of July, 1963. This Group's final report will be submitted to the member governments before the meeting of the authorities charged with formulating the sugar policy, which is scheduled for the end of 1963.[10]

8. The activities of the various commodity groups were examined by the IA-ECOSOC Special Committee on Basic Products at a second

---

[10] For further details regarding the above developments, see IA-ECOSOC Special Committee on Basic Products, *Final Report of the Second Meeting,* Doc. CIES/Com. VIII/17, Rev. (Washington, D.C.), August 21, 1963.

meeting (August 5–12, 1963), during which the Committee agreed to give its full support to the work carried out and to recommend that it be intensified. Other topics examined in detail by the Committee included the activities of GATT; trade relations with the European Economic Community; the position of the member countries with respect to the United Nations Conference on Trade and Development; and the policy of compensatory credits announced by the International Monetary Fund at the start of 1963. (See footnote 10.)

Sugar

The quotations for raw sugar on the free-world market declined in the first quarter of 1962 to the lowest levels recorded since 1941; later there began a slow recovery which picked up a certain momentum in the final months of 1962. Nevertheless, the average 1962 price, which was 2.98 cents (United States) a pound, was barely 2.4 per cent above the 1961 average price, which was 2.91 cents a pound.

However, in the first months of 1963 the recovery process continued, and in the course of a few weeks prices exceeded those for previous years, including the maximum prices reached during the Suez crisis in the first half of 1957. At the end of May, 1963, the quotations on the New York market for sugar going to the free market had already risen above 11.0 cents a pound, the maximum figure for any previous period, as compared with the maximum price of 4.64 cents at the end of December, 1962. After reaching a maximum of 13.5 cents a pound, the quotations began to decline slowly at the beginning of the second half of 1963.

The radical change that occurred in the market conditions was due basically to the declining trend in production in the two preceding years and the prospects for a greater shrinkage in stocks for the free-market area in 1963. If the figures for world production are studied, it is seen that the reduction last year was only 5.3 per cent with respect to the maximum level reached in 1960/61. However, in examining production figures by region, it is noted that the drop in production in Western Europe—the most important importing region in the free-market area—was 26.4 per cent in the period under discussion, while Cuban production dropped 33.5 per cent in the same period (see Table 1-8). That is to say that although the drop in world sugar production has not been exceptionally great, sugar trade in the free-market area has declined considerably. The countries where sugar production has continued to increase (Philippines and the Latin American countries, with the exception of

TABLE 1-8. Centrifugal Sugar: World Production, by Principal Regions

Region	(Thousands of metric tons) 1959/60	(Indices: 1959/60 = 100.0)		
		1960/61	1961/62	1962/63*
Cuba	5,860	115.5	82.2	76.8
Other Latin American Countries	8,586	99.1	102.3	107.7[a]
All of Latin America	14,446	105.7	94.1	95.1
Western Europe	7,967	135.5	105.0	99.8
Eastern Europe and Soviet Union	9,401	110.9	116.4	112.9
Africa	2,646	90.3	106.7	112.1
Taiwan	798	118.8	90.7	95.2
Philippines	1,387	94.9	105.8	117.0
Australia	1,271	107.3	107.0	141.4
Total world production	50,084	110.5	103.5	104.6

[a] Colombia had no exports in 1960. In 1961 it exported 46,000 tons; in 1962, 65,700 tons.

Sources: Estimates by F. O. Licht, reproduced in International Sugar Council, *Statistical Bulletin; Press Summary* (London), September 14, 1962; April 3, 1963.

Cuba) ship their exports to the preferential market of the United States, and the same thing has occurred with the countries that supply the preferential market of the United Kingdom, chiefly Australia.

Added to the impact of the drop in production in certain exporting regions and the increased import requirements of Western Europe are the effects of a substantial drop in stocks in most of the exporting countries. It should be stressed again that the changes that have occurred in the level of stocks in Cuba have been one of the most important factors in the recent price development. The Cuban sugar stock, which previously amounted to more than one million tons, dropped at the end of 1962 to 91,000 tons (see Table 1-9). A sharp drop in the stocks of countries such as Argentina, Mexico, Peru, and others outside the Latin American region is also noted.

On the United States market, 1962 quotations for sugar imports remained at levels slightly above those for the previous year, although the premium prices granted by this market over free-market prices dropped sharply at the end of the year, owing to a more rapid increase in prices in the free-market area. It should also be noted that in the last months

TABLE 1-9. Centrifugal Sugar: Stocks in Principal Exporting Countries[a]

Country	(Thousands of short tons) 1959/60	(Indices: 1959/60 = 100.0)		
		1960/61	1961/62	1962/63*
Argentina	142	264.1	246.5	62.0
Brazil	572	106.6	67.5	105.4
Colombia	24	154.1	304.2	145.8
Mexico	456	110.1	67.8	35.3
Peru	96	116.7	40.6	48.9
Cuba	1,222	89.5	84.1	7.4
Australia	171	119.3	117.5	81.9
Philippines	249	125.7	50.6	70.7
Taiwan	141	70.9	66.0	92.2
Total of countries enumerated	3,265	105.0	82.4	48.2

[a] At the start of the respective production year.

Source: U.S. Department of Agriculture, *Foreign Agriculture Circular,* April, 1963, FS-1-63.

of 1962 circumstances arose that had a very temporary effect on United States market prices, due to the fact that the supply shortage that was noted at the end of the first quarter of 1963 still prevailed. These circumstances were (1) the so-called Cuban crisis of October, 1962, and (2) the increased demand for imports in order to provide a stockpile in anticipation of the longshoreman strike which did occur at the end of the year. The rapid rise in prices in the free-market area affected the price level in the United States market. Nevertheless, the increases in this market have been smaller, and consequently the prices of imported sugar in the United States have not included a premium, but rather a discount, with respect to prices on the free-world market since February, 1963.

United States sugar legislation was amended in the middle of 1962. Even though the system of basic import quotas assigned by country was retained, each government was authorized to suspend quotas for countries with which it does not have diplomatic relations (at present, Cuba). Unused quotas are pooled to form a global quota and are assigned to other countries, but the imports thus redistributed are subject to a duty equal to the difference between United States market prices and world free-market prices. Since this legislation went into effect, imports charged against the basic quotas assigned by country have been subject to a duty equal to 10 per cent of the total fixed duty for imports charged against the global quota.[11] This percentage of the duty on imports charged against the basic quotas would rise to 20 per cent in 1963 and to 30 per cent in 1964 (always based on the complete duty levied on imports charged against the global quota).

As established, the effect of the operation of these duties is to decrease the margin of preference enjoyed by Latin American sugar exports to the United States market over exports to the rest of the world. However, the development of the world free-market at the end of 1962 and the beginning of 1963 has, for the time being, reduced the significance of these duties. The exclusion of Cuba from the United States market acted as a stimulus to increase production and the exports of a good number of Latin American countries. Actually, production in the rest of Latin America increased in the last two years by 3 and 5 per cent, respectively (see Table 1–10). Total exports declined by 2 per cent in 1961 and 18 per cent in 1962. This is chiefly a reflection of the decreases that had occurred in Argentina, Brazil, Mexico, the Dominican Republic, and Peru, which furnished the largest percentage of the region's exports.

The geographic distribution of Latin American sugar exports underwent important changes in the last two years which, as has already been pointed out, were caused by the exclusion of Cuba from the United States market. Part of the import quota that had been allocated to Cuba was redistributed to other Latin American countries. When these countries increased their exports to the United States, they decreased those they shipped to the free-market region (in this case, the rest of the world). At the same time, Cuban trade shifted toward the market of the Soviet Union, the countries of Eastern Europe, and Continental China (see Table 1–11).

Bananas

Banana prices in the most important markets for Latin American exporters have exhibited different tendencies in the past three years. In the United States, which absorbs most of the Latin American exports, there was a moderate but persistent decline accompanied by a slight decline in the total volume of imports. In the Federal Republic of Germany—the second largest market for Latin American bananas—the

[11] For example, if in 1962 the existing premium between the United States market prices and world free-market prices had been 2 cents per pound, the duty on imports charged against the global quota would be 2 cents per pound and the duty on imports charged to the basic quotas would be 0.2 cents per pound.

TABLE 1-10. Sugar: Production and Exports[a] of Selected Countries

Country		(Thousands of metric tons) 1959/60	(Indices: 1959/60 = 100.0)		
			1960/61	1961/62	1962/63*
Argentina	Production	991	86.1	71.4	82.2
	Exports	113.0	165.1	88.5	
Brazil	Production	3,052	106.8	110.9	110.9
	Exports	854.8	87.1	56.0	
Colombia	Production	336	108.3	122.0	125.0
	Exports	—	[b]	[b]	
Costa Rica	Production	60	116.7	153.3	158.3
	Exports	20.4	148.0	137.2	
Cuba	Production	5,860	115.5	82.2	76.8[c]
	Exports	5,634.5	113.8	91.1	
Dominican Republic	Production	986	88.5	91.5	101.4
	Exports	1,099.1	72.2	77.0	
Ecuador	Production	488	108.2	131.3	145.1
	Exports	14.2	335.9	457.7	
El Salvador	Production	51	96.1	125.5	129.4
	Exports	10.9	126.6	183.5	
Guatemala	Production	71	116.9	174.6	176.0
	Exports	6.1	114.7	442.6	
Haiti	Production	60	123.3	116.7	108.3
	Exports	30.1	131.9	116.3	
Mexico	Production	1,620	92.0	95.5	101.8
	Exports	462.4	132.3	75.7	
Nicaragua	Production	64	98.4	128.1	120.3
	Exports	34.9	80.2	106.0	
Peru	Production	807	99.0	94.2	104.1
	Exports	513.7	107.5	97.3	
Subtotal	Production	8,586	99.1	102.3	107.7
	Exports	3,159.6	98.1	80.9	
Total Latin America	Production	14,446	105.7	94.1	951.0
	Exports	8,794.1	108.2	87.4	

[a] In all cases the exports are for the second calendar year mentioned in each column heading.

[b] Colombia had no exports in 1960. It exported 46,000 tons in 1961 and 65,700 tons in 1962.

[c] Later data indicate an even sharper drop, and it is considered probable that the crop will yield no more than 2.9 million tons.

Sources: International Sugar Council, *Statistical Bulletin*, September 14, 1962; April 3, 1963.

TABLE 1-11. Centrifugal Sugar: Exports of Selected Latin American Countries, by Principal Regions of Destination

Exporting country		United States	European Economic Community	European Free Trade Association	Soviet Union and Eastern Europe[a]	Japan	Others	Total
Brazil	1960 (1,000 tons)	103.4	130.1	49.8	10.2	288.3	273.0	854.8
	1961 Index[b]	283.6	6.0	67.1	—	89.7	55.6	87.1
	1962 Index[b]	349.6	—	76.3	—	7.3	21.2	56.0
Cuba	1960 (1,000 tons)	1,948.6	315.3	215.6	2,260.0	204.6	690.3	5,634.5
	1961 Index[b]	—	24.1	66.7	212.0	206.9	141.8	113.8
	1962 Index[b]	—	12.6	72.9	162.1	210.9	121.3	91.1
Dominican Republic	1960 (1,000 tons)	424.9	102.2	348.9	—	84.8	138.3	1,099.1
	1961 Index[b]	81.1	2.5	67.9	—	131.1	71.1	72.2
	1962 Index[b]	192.9	4.4	—	—	10.5	9.2	77.0
Mexico	1960 (1,000 tons)	382.4	43.1	4.1	—	—	32.8	462.4
	1961 Index[b]	159.7	—	—	—	—	3.0	132.3
	1962 Index[b]	91.6	—	—	—	—	—	75.7
Nicaragua	1960 (1,000 tons)	34.9	—	—	—	—	—	34.9
	1961 Index[b]	80.2	—	—	—	—	—	80.2
	1962 Index[b]	106.0	—	—	—	—	—	106.0
Peru	1960 (1,000 tons)	285.4	15.8	49.9	—	80.6	82.0	513.7
	1961 Index[b]	191.3	6.3	4.0	—	3.1	—	107.5
	1962 Index[b]	175.2	—	—	—	—	—	97.3
Total six countries	1960 (1,000 tons)	3,179.6	606.5	668.3	2,270.3	658.3	1,216.4	8,599.4
	1961 Index[b]	57.3	14.4	62.3	211.0	120.8	101.2	106.3
	1962 Index[b]	64.9	7.3	29.2	161.4	70.1	74.7	85.3

[a] Includes Continental China.
[b] Indices: 1960 = 100.0.

Source: International Sugar Council, *Statistical Bulletin.*

average 1960–62 prices were practically stable, despite the fact that the monthly averages showed rather sharp fluctuations. Latin American exports to that country in 1962 reached a level similar to 1960 but dropped 4.5 per cent from the volume in 1961.

These developments in the markets of the two countries that absorb most of Latin American banana exports justify the concern with which the immediate outlook for the foreign market of this product is being viewed in these countries. In the case of the United States, all of whose imports come from Latin America and are free of restrictions and duties of any kind, the problem is related to changes in consumer habits, which are diminishing the per capita consumption; supply restrictions and price increases have played no part in this development. Rather, banana prices have remained relatively stable for long periods and in recent years have tended to decline. The problems are more complex in the case of the European markets. In some cases, the Latin American product faces quantitative restrictions and discriminatory practices, while in others the level of tariffs makes the price of the fruit to the consumer excessive. Furthermore, bananas were practically the only tropical product excluded from the reductions in the common external tariff of the European Economic Community for imports from "third countries," whereas the "duty-free quota" authorized for imports of the Federal Republic of Germany from countries not members of the Community remained unchanged.[12]

This means that the highly discriminatory treatment given imports coming from Latin America was not liberalized with respect to bananas as it was for other tropical products.

These problems of Latin American banana exports to the European countries, particularly the countries of the Community, were studied by the Banana Action Group—created by the Inter-American Economic and Social Council—at meetings of the Group held at the beginning of 1963. In the conclusions adopted by the countries making up this Group (Costa Rica, Ecuador, United States, Honduras, and Panama),[13] it was pointed out that the present structure of the European banana markets is unfavorable to the development of Latin American production. The opinion was expressed that existing regulations can have a negative effect of considerable magnitude on the income derived from these exports. At the same time, the conclusions indicate that the restrictions adopted will reduce consumption levels and will lead to complete exclusion of the

[12] However, both in 1961 and 1962, as a special dispensation, the Community granted West Germany an increase in the amount of this quota.

[13] Delegates from Brazil, Colombia, and Nicaragua participated as observers.

TABLE 1-12. Bananas: Exports of Latin American Countries, Value and Volume[a]

Country		1960	1961	1962
			(Indices: 1960 = 100.0)	
Brazil	Value	4.6	82.6	...
	Volume	241.9	103.1	...
Colombia	Value	13.7	102.9	77.4
	Volume	209.9	107.1	79.9
Costa Rica	Value	20.3	103.0	103.9
	Volume	225.5	91.3	106.5
Dominican Republic	Value	11.2	100.9	...
	Volume	180.4	90.1	...
Ecuador	Value	88.9	91.0	94.7
	Volume	1,149.1	93.8	90.8
Guatemala	Value	19.9	82.4	42.7
	Volume	251.3	81.9	42.8
Honduras	Value	28.7	116.0	119.2
	Volume	379.5	117.5	105.0
Panama	Value	18.2	109.9	96.2
	Volume	263.3	115.6	100.0

[a] Value in millions of dollars; volume in thousands of tons.

Sources: IMF, *International Financial Statistics*, and additional information obtained from statistical publications of the countries concerned.

more efficient producers from some of the most important European markets.[14]

In most of the Latin American countries, the volume of banana exports dropped in 1962 from previous years, but due to a lack of complete statistics on production, the extent to which these exports reflect a decrease in production or a contraction in foreign demand cannot be measured accurately (see Table 1-12). In certain markets, such as that of the United States, it is obvious that the contraction in demand must have been the cause of the reduction in imports, since in this country, as already stated, there are no quantitative restrictions or duties on such

[14] See *The Impact of Trade Restrictions in Europe on the Banana Producing Countries of Latin America* (Washington, D.C., March 11, 1963) (UP/G. 27/12. Rev.).

imports. In the European markets, the situation is different. In countries such as France, Italy, and the United Kingdom, the Latin American producers are practically excluded from the market because of the preferential treatment granted to other suppliers (see Table 1–13). In other importing countries (Belgium, Netherlands, Austria, and Switzerland), purchases from Latin America continued to increase, but the volume of their total imports is relatively small, compared with that of the other European countries mentioned above.

Cacao

After a decline that lasted three years and in 1962 brought the price of cacao beans to the lowest levels recorded since 1949, the market began to recover in the first months of 1963 as a result of the change that occurred in the general outlook for production and consumption.

The period of price decline reflected principally the sharp growth in world production between 1958/59 and 1960/61. In the same period, consumption expanded less than production and, to a certain extent, represented only a recovery from the 1957/58 decline. Consequently, during the period 1958/59–1960/61 very large stocks were accumulated, chiefly in the consumer countries. However, in the past two years, although world production remained above the 1959/60 level, there was a downward trend with respect to the maximum volume reached in 1960/61. Moreover, since expansion in consumption continued at a higher rate than in the two preceding years, a deficit of approximately 77,000 tons between world production and consumption is predicted for 1962/63. Between 1958/59 and 1961/62, an excess of world production over total consumption was recorded (see Table 1–14).

Within this general picture, the position of the Latin American countries was particularly critical during the 1960/62 period, since, in some, added to the effects of the drop in cacao prices was a contraction in production, especially in Brazil, the chief cacao exporter of the region (see Table 1–15). Accordingly, both Latin American production and exports developed quite differently from the trend observed in the African countries. Although there has also been a certain decline in production in the African countries in the last two years, the total volume continues to be considerably higher than that of 1959/60.

The decrease in Latin American exports was due primarily to a decrease in exports to the United States and secondarily to a decrease in exports to the European Economic Community and countries having centrally planned economies (see Table 1–16). Since the decrease in exports to those regions was due to smaller stocks in the Latin American countries and not to a contraction in foreign demand, African exports of cacao to the above-mentioned regions increased substantially.

The possibility of concluding an international cacao agreement continued to be discussed in 1962. The Cacao Study Group held its Fifth Meeting (Switzerland, May, 1962) and studied the draft agreement prepared the year before by a group of experts. However, at these meetings, as well as in others held later by the Executive Committee of the Study Group, it was decided merely to continue the preparatory work and to postpone until the middle of 1963 [15] the decision to hold an international conference to negotiate the Agreement.

Coffee

The decline in international prices for green coffee, rather moderate in 1960 and 1961, continued in 1962 and did not appear to halt until the first months of 1963, despite certain events that pointed to greater firmness of the market and a relative degree of stability in the foreign prices for this product. In fact, world production in 1960/61–1962/63 remained at much lower levels than in 1959/60, and in the producing countries both consumption and exports increased slightly in the past two years. However, the accumulation of stocks continued at an increasing rate, since, in absolute terms, total production continued to exceed the demand of domestic consumption and export demand, despite recent drops (see Table 1–17). Thus, at the beginning of the 1962/63 commercial year, stocks were double what they were in 1959/60 and represented the equivalent of approximately two years of world exports.

The new International Coffee Agreement, which, it was hoped, would have a certain stabilizing effect on prices, does not appear to have helped alter the market behavior yet, although the last quarter of 1962 was already covered by the Agreement. It is clear, however, that this new agreement is, to a certain extent, a continuation of previous agreements, reinforced now by the participation of importing countries to give greater effectiveness to strict compliance with export quotas; accordingly, it does not constitute a completely new element in the market. Moreover, unlike the other international commodity agreements (sugar and tin, for example), the Coffee Agreement does not provide for a mechanism for altering export quotas in direct ratio to a certain price level, and so the quotas do not perform a strictly price stabilizing function but rather a

[15] See FAO, *Situación de los productos básicos 1963* (Rome, 1963).

TABLE 1-13. Bananas: Imports of Selected Countries, by Region of Origin

Origin	Importers	Belgium-Luxembourg	France	Netherlands	Italy	Fed. Rep. of Germany	United Kingdom	Austria	Switzerland	Canada	United States	Total
Brazil	1960 (1,000 tons)	—	—	—	1.0	—	4.7	—	—	—	—	5.7
	1961 Indices[a]	—	—	—	—	—	110.6	—	—	—	—	91.2
	1962 Indices[a]	—	—	—	—	—	110.1	—	—	...	...	—
Colombia	1960 (1,000 tons)	11.9	—	15.6	—	147.2	—	2.4	9.6	0.2	4.3	191.2
	1961 Indices[a]	109.2	—	128.2	—	110.0	—	91.7	117.7	—	79.1	110.8
	1962 Indices[a]	...	—	74.4	—	88.6	—	54.2	75.0	...	107.0	—
Costa Rica	1960 (1,000 tons)	—	—	—	—	—	—	—	—	23.3	256.3	279.6
	1961 Indices[a]	—	—	—	—	—	—	—	—	92.3	86.9	87.3
	1962 Indices[a]	...	—	—	—	—	—	—	—	...	95.1	—
Dominican Republic	1960 (1,000 tons)	4.2	—	7.9	—	56.4	3.5	1.0	4.4	3.6	77.3	158.3
	1961 Indices[a]	211.9	—	177.2	—	96.1	117.1	303.0	113.6	44.4	46.4	80.2
	1962 Indices[a]	...	—	206.3	—	114.2	105.7	660.0	259.1	—	26.0	—
Ecuador	1960 (1,000 tons)	22.5	—	12.4	—	200.6	—	21.2	19.4	68.1	615.1	959.3
	1961 Indices[a]	116.0	—	104.0	—	102.2	—	87.7	117.0	72.2	86.5	90.4
	1962 Indices[a]	...	—	103.2	—	98.3	—	77.8	78.4	...	113.7	—

	1	2	3	4	5	6	7	8	9	10	11
Guatemala 1960 (1,000 tons)	3.4	—	—	6.4	—	—	1.1	3.6	11.2	137.0	178.6
1961 Indices[a]	20.6	—	—	56.3	—	—	63.6	25.0	61.6	78.7	77.9
1962 Indices[a]	—	—	—	159.4	—	—	163.6	197.2	...	33.8	—
Honduras 1960 (1,000 tons)	5.9	—	—	6.3	15.1	—	0.4	2.4	20.9	291.6	342.6
1961 Indices[a]	59.3	—	—	57.1	86.0	—	175.0	58.3	202.9	124.3	124.7
1962 Indices[a]	...	—	—	73.0	53.0	—	650.0	154.2	...	112.6	—
Panama 1960 (1,000 tons)	—	—	—	—	—	—	—	—	41.5	255.5	297.0
1961 Indices[a]	[b]	—	—	[c]	[d]	—	—	—	96.1	96.8	97.7
1962 Indices[a]	...	—	—	[c]	[d]	—	—	—	...	78.6	—
Subtotal 1960 (1,000 tons)	47.9	—	—	48.6	435.2	1.0	8.2	26.1	39.4	168.8	1,637.1	2,412.3
1961 Indices[a]	109.6	—	—	113.0	104.5	—	113.4	97.7	104.8	95.7	92.3	95.8
1962 Indices[a]	...	—	—	117.7	100.1	—	103.7	110.3	113.2	...	95.6	—
Others 1960 (1,000 tons)	17.2	347.1	1.0	10.1	10.0	335.9	1.6	4.7	0.2	—	811.3
1961 Indices[a]	82.0	103.9	84.5	120.8	106.0	119.6	105.8	137.5	117.0	50.0	—	106.2
1962 Indices[a]	...	112.8	119.6	120.8	242.0	157.0	107.9	93.8	161.7	...	—	—
Total 1960 (1,000 tons)	65.1	347.1	85.5	58.7	445.2	344.1	27.7	44.1	169.0	1,637.1	3,223.6
1961 Indices[a]	102.3	103.9	118.2	114.3	104.6	106.0	100.0	106.1	95.6	92.3	98.5
1962 Indices[a]	...	112.8	155.2	118.2	103.3	107.8	109.4	118.4	...	95.6	—

[a] Indices: 1960 = 100.0.
[b] Imports of 300 tons in 1961.
[c] Imports of 800 tons in 1961 and 1,700 tons in 1962.
[d] Imports of 2,100 tons in 1961 and 2,700 tons in 1962.

Sources: Commonwealth Economic Committee, *Fruit Intelligence* (London), editions January–May, 1963; U.S. Department of Agriculture, *Foreign Crops and Markets*, various issues.

TABLE 1-14. Cacao Beans: Production, Consumption, and Stocks

(Thousands of metric tons)

	1959/60	1960/61	1961/62	1962/63*
Production[a]	1,045	1,172	1,131	1,109
Consumption[b]	939	1,041	1,110	1,186
Surplus or deficit	+106	+131	+21	−77
Stocks in consumer countries[b]	326	446	466	390

[a] According to the source cited below, the production figures were reduced 1 per cent for weight loss.

[b] The consumption figures refer to the calendar year and the stocks to the end of the second calendar year indicated in the column heading.

Source: Gill & Duffers, Ltd., *Cocoa Market Report* (London), May 6, 1963.

function of regulating competition among producers. Finally, since the accumulation of stocks has continued to increase, the market could in practice "ignore" recent drops in production.

From the standpoint of foreign demand, the development in the coffee market was more active, and this has been expressed in an increase of 6 per cent in 1962 world imports over those of the previous year. Most of this increase was due to United States imports, brought about, in part, by increased consumption and, in part, by an accumulation of stocks in that country in anticipation of a longshoremen's strike, which actually occurred at the end of December, 1962.[16] In connection with the increased import volume, and despite the fact that imports from Latin America shared in the increase, it should be noted that the rapid growth in imports from Africa continued to take place (see Table 1–18). In 1960, Latin America furnished 80 per cent of total United States imports, but this figure dropped to 75.8 per cent in 1962. In contrast, imports from Africa represented 17.3 per cent of the total imports in 1960 and 20.9 per cent in 1962. Imports by most of the European countries also reflected increases of varying percentages, especially those of the Federal Republic of Germany, while the imports of the countries having centrally planned economies dropped slightly (see Table 1–19).

It should be mentioned, with respect to imports by the Federal Republic of Germany, that it submitted a proposal to the Commission of the European Economic Community to replace the ad valorem duty

---

[16] Stocks of green coffee in the United States at the end of December, 1962, totaled 4 million bags, as compared with 2.8 million bags at the end of December, 1961.

TABLE 1-15. Cacao Beans: Production and Exports of Selected Countries[a]

Country	(Thousands of metric tons) 1959/60	(Indices: 1959/60 = 100)		
		1960/61	1961/62	1962/63[b]
Brazil				
Production	199	61.3	59.3	52.3
Exports	125.5	83.3	40.0	
Colombia				
Production	19	100.0	100.0	105.3
Exports	—	—	—	
Costa Rica				
Production	12	108.3	83.3	100.0
Exports	12.2	85.2	98.0	
Dominican Republic				
Production	42	88.1	85.7	92.8
Exports	26.4	44.3	73.8	
Ecuador				
Production	35	120.0	108.6	108.6
Exports	35.6	91.3	88.0	
Mexico				
Production	23	117.4	121.7	121.7
Exports	3.1	177.2	393.7	
Venezuela				
Production	14	85.7	85.7	85.7
Exports	8.0	122.7	131.3	
Other Latin America				
Production	14	100.0	92.8	107.1
Total Latin America				
Production	358	79.9	76.5	74.9
Exports	210.9	81.6	64.0	
Cameroon				
Production	64	110.9	118.7	114.1
Exports	58.9	99.0	83.8	
Ghana				
Production	322	136.3	129.5	125.1
Exports	307.6	133.9	139.1	
Ivory Coast				
Production	62	151.6	132.2	156.4
Exports	62.9	140.6	160.6	
Nigeria				
Production	157	126.1	123.6	110.2
Exports	159.5	117.1	124.0	
Other Africa				
Production	57	108.8	108.8	110.5
Total Africa				
Production	662	130.7	125.5	122.2
Exports[b]	588.9	126.6	131.8	
World Total				
Production	1,056	112.2	108.2	106.1
Exports	876.8	114.0	—	

[a] Production figures refer to the crop year, while those for exports refer to the second calendar year indicated in the column.
[b] Includes only those countries listed.

Source: Gill & Duffers, Ltd., Cocoa Market Report, (London), May 6, 1963.

TABLE 1-16. Cacao Beans: Exports of Selected Countries, by Principal Region of Destination

	Importers					
Exporters	United States	European Economic Community	European Free Trade Association	Soviet Union and Eastern Europe	Others	Total
Brazil						
1960 (Tons)	54,444	35,425	2,405	24,266	8,911	125,451
1961 Indices[a]	84.6	66.4	91.5	88.3	127.5	83.3
1962 Indices[a]	23.7	35.6	125.3	61.4	75.2	40.0
Dominican Republic						
1960 (Tons)	...	...	...	...	...	26,400
1961 Indices[a]	...	...	...	...	...	44.3
1962 Indices[a]	...	...	...	...	...	73.8
Ecuador						
1960 (Tons)	22,852	8,475	1,124	—	3,131	35,582
1961 Indices[a]	72.7	84.9	102.8	[b]	224.1	91.3
1962 Indices[a]	...	...	...	...	...	88.0
Venezuela						
1960 (Tons)	6,832	1,070	59	—	51	8,012
1961 Indices[a]	78.2	391.4	196.6	—	—	122.7
1962 Indices[a]	...	...	...	...	...	131.3
Cameroon						
1960 (Tons)	5,698	51,992	135	674	396	58,894
1961 Indices[a]	150.9	93.9	122.2	44.8	105.8	99.0
1962 Indices[a]	107.0	78.4	1,014.8	55.9	185.6	83.8
Ghana						
1960 (Tons)	58,110	125,972	57,689	34,492	26,383	307,646
1961 Indices[a]	243.9	119.1	103.6	69.2	124.8	133.9
1962 Indices[a]	196.8	119.2	116.4	147.6	144.1	139.1
Ivory Coast						
1960 (Tons)	13,443	42,156	485	4,603	2,206	62,892
1961 Indices[a]	168.7	140.0	676.5	—	158.3	140.6
1962 Indices[a]	263.4	136.6	342.7	—	288.9	160.6
Nigeria						
1960 (Tons)	34,696	64,094	40,647	11,582	8,473	159,493
1961 Indices[a]	196.6	97.3	126.2	—	58.5	117.1
1962 Indices[a]	181.9	115.8	120.3	4.4	130.1	124.0
Total						
1960						704,386
1961						115.2
1962						113.2

[a] Indices: 1960 = 100.0.

[b] In 1961, 524 tons were exported to this group of countries.

Sources: Commonwealth Economic Committee, *Tropical Products Quarterly* (London), March, 1963; Gill & Duffers, Ltd., *Cocoa Market Report*, (London), April 5, 1963, No. 159.

TABLE 1-17. Green Coffee: World Production, Stocks, and Exports (Commercial Year July–June)

	(Millions of bags of 60 kilos) 1959/60	(Indices: 1959/60 = 100.0)		
		1960/61	1961/62	1962/63*
Initial stocks	40.4	156.2	169.6[a]	200.2
Production	78.9	83.0	90.2	83.0
Total amounts available	119.3	107.8	117.1	122.7
Exports	43.8	101.4	103.9	...
Consumption in producer countries	12.5	101.6	106.4	...

[a] Reduced by 3 million bags distributed in Brazil.

Source: U.S. Department of Agriculture, *Foreign Agricultural Circular*, December, 1962, FCOF 4–62.

TABLE 1-18. Total United States Green Coffee Imports, by Country of Origin

Country	(Thousands of bags of 60 kilos) 1960	(Indices: 1960 = 100.0)	
		1961	1962
Brazil	9,261	92.6	98.2
Colombia	4,254	95.9	101.8
Costa Rica	271	136.1	142.1
Dominican Republic	403	65.3	103.7
Ecuador	317	63.7	116.4
El Salvador	416	140.1	202.6
Guatemala	798	118.9	121.2
Haiti	64	118.8	240.6
Honduras	332	43.4	48.2
Mexico	1,097	114.3	122.3
Nicaragua	170	132.4	111.8
Panama	16	37.5	5.0
Peru	347	110.1	134.6
Venezuela	345	99.7	78.6
Subtotal	18,091	96.5	105.0
Africa	3,824	119.7	133.7
Others	186	162.9	209.1
Total	22,101	101.0	110.8

Source: U.S. Department of Agriculture, *Foreign Agriculture Circular*, March, 1963, FCOF 1–63.

TABLE 1-19. Coffee Beans: World Imports, by Selected Countries and Regions

Country or region	(Thousands of bags of 60 kilos) 1960	(Indices: 1960 = 100.0) 1961	1962
Canada	995	112.5	119.3
United States	22,101	101.0	110.8
Western Europe	15,247	104.8	108.5
European Economic Community	10,479	103.4	106.0
Federal Republic of Germany	3,323	105.1	116.6
Belgium-Luxembourg	1,109	93.4	75.4
France	3,477	98.0	100.0
Netherlands	917	125.1	115.9
Italy	1,653	106.0	112.2
Free Trade Association	4,208	105.0	113.8
Austria	203	107.4	112.8
Denmark	698	104.2	111.5
Norway	483	93.2	106.8
Portugal	185	113.5	104.3
United Kingdom	919	106.4	125.6
Sweden	1,222	106.0	113.4
Switzerland	498	108.4	106.8
Other Western Europe[a]	560	130.2	115.5
Eastern Europe	861	133.1	128.3
East Germany	289	106.9	108.0
Czechoslovakia	133	174.4	136.1
Hungary	55	72.7	103.6
Poland	65	107.7	115.4
Soviet Union	319	155.2	150.5
Latin America[b]	602	118.8	108.8
Japan	178	141.6	133.1
Other Countries	2,392	103.3	104.8
Total World Imports	42,440	103.9	110.1

[a] Includes Spain, Greece, Turkey, and Yugoslavia.
[b] Includes Argentina, Chile, and Uruguay.
Source: George Gordon Paton, *Complete Coffee Coverage* (New York), March 4, 1963.

on imports of green coffee from third countries with a specific duty, thereby decreasing the proportionally more restrictive effect the ad valorem tariff has on imports of more expensive grades of coffee, but without injuring imports from the associated countries of the Community, since, in any case, such imports are duty-free. To date, no decision has been reached on that proposal.

The Latin American countries increased their exports to Western Europe and Canada, in some cases in larger proportions than shown in the import figures for those areas, while they decreased their exports to those countries having centrally planned economies, almost all of whose exports come from Brazil and Colombia (see Table 1–20). The figures for Latin American exports to the United States do not agree with the figures for United States imports in 1962, especially in the list by country.

TABLE 1–20. Green Coffee: Exports of Selected Latin American Countries, by Principal Region of Destination

Exporting country	United States	Canada	European Economic Community	Free Trade Ass'n.	Soviet Union & Eastern Europe	Other	Total
Brazil							
1960 (1,000 bags)	9,361	294	2,736	2,075	621	1,712	16,819
1961 Indices[a]	91.6	108.8	117.0	105.8	122.1	111.2	100.9
1962 Indices[a]	87.0	114.6	118.3	112.0	107.2	96.6	97.4
Colombia							
1960 (1,000 bags)	4,350	109	857	321	144	157	5,938
1961 Indices[a]	90.8	107.3	106.0	110.9	29.9	177.1	95.2
1962 Indices[a]	99.5	115.6	131.9	144.5	44.4	284.7	110.5
Costa Rica							
1960 (1,000 bags)	274	9	439	40	1	3	766
1961 Indices[a]	131.8	77.8	95.7	97.5	—	266.7	109.0
1962 Indices[a]	128.1	111.1	110.0	117.5	—	366.7	117.8
Dominican Rep.							
1960 (1,000 bags)	413	6	59	2	—	1	481
1961 Indices[a]	68.3	66.7	81.4	50.0	—	—	69.6
1962 Indices[a]	101.0	—	113.6	50.0	—	200.0	101.2
Ecuador							
1960 (1,000 bags)	323	1	190	16	—	9	539
1961 Indices[a]	59.1	200.0	90.5	43.8	—	100.0	70.7
1962 Indices[a]	115.5	100.0	83.2	50.0	—	111.1	102.2
El Salvador							
1960 (1,000 bags)	371	5	740	46	—	16	1,178
1961 Indices[a]	179.8	240.0	96.6	76.1	—	12.5	121.5
1962 Indices[a]	180.6	260.0	97.4	100.0	—	175.0	125.4
Guatemala							
1960 (1,000 bags)	825	4	427	58	—	15	1,329
1961 Indices[a]	96.0	150.0	85.7	124.1	—	126.7	94.4
1962 Indices[a]	90.4	200.0	143.3	148.3	[b]	640.0	116.8
Haiti							
1960 (1,000 bags)	60	—	296	33	1	4	394
1961 Indices[a]	141.7	—	79.4	75.8	—	75.0	88.3
1962 Indices[a]	231.7	—	114.5	93.9	—	125.0	130.5
Honduras							
1960 (1,000 bags)	149	—	70	17	—	22	258
1961 Indices[a]	89.3	—	55.7	41.2	—	140.9	81.4
1962 Indices[a]	100.7	[c]	107.1	23.5	—	163.6	103.1

(Continued)

TABLE 1-20 *Continued*

Exporting country	United States	Canada	European Economic Community	Free Trade Ass'n.	Soviet Union & Eastern Europe	Other	Total
Mexico							
1960 (1,000 bags)	1,128	16	160	36	1	43	1,384
1961 Indices[a]	118.3	100.0	65.0	77.8	—	2.3	107.2
1962 Indices[a]	115.6	106.3	45.0	158.3	—	16.3	105.3
Nicaragua							
1960 (1,000 bags)	188	1	170	2	—	—	361
1961 Indices[a]	111.2	100.0	79.4	100.0	—	[d]	96.7
1962 Indices[a]	100.0	100.0	84.1	50.0	—	[d]	93.6
Peru							
1960 (1,000 bags)	332	3	92	6	—	7	440
1961 Indices[a]	117.5	33.3	142.4	333.3	—	357.1	128.9
1962 Indices[a]	141.0	200.0	112.0	400.0	—	328.6	141.8
Venezuela							
1960 (1,000 bags)	359	—	33	16	—	—	408
1961 Indices[a]	97.8	[e]	118.2	93.8	—	—	99.5
1962 Indices[a]	71.6	[e]	133.3	93.8	—	[f]	78.2
Total							
1960 (1,000 bags)	18,153	448	6,270	2,668	768	1,988	30,295
1961 Indices[a]	95.5	108.7	103.9	105.1	104.3	114.7	99.8
1962 Indices[a]	96.7	116.3	114.6	116.5	95.7	116.9	103.7

[a] Indices: 1960 = 100.0.   [b] Exports of 4,000 bags in 1962.   [c] Exports of 1,000 bags in 1963.   [d] Exports of 2,000 and 5,000 bags in 1961 and 1962, respectively.   [e] Exports of 1,000 bags in 1961 and 1962.   [f] Exports of 2,000 bags in 1962.

Source: Pan American Coffee Bureau, *Annual Coffee Statistics* (New York), 1962.

The 9 per cent increase shown in the figures for 1962 United States imports from Latin America appears as only 1 per cent in the figures for Latin American exports to that country.[17]

The decline in world coffee production reflects, above all, the changes that have been occurring in Brazilian production; these have been aggravated by the decline in Colombian production and, at times, by that of other smaller producers (see Table 1–21). Most of the Latin American countries had registered increases in their exports, with Brazil the main exception, although, as has been stated, this was not due to a decline in production, since Brazil has large surpluses from previous harvests.

[17] The discrepancy is especially noticeable in countries such as Brazil, Guatemala, Costa Rica, and Mexico. This difference is due, in part, to the lag that occurred in recording the export and import statistics in the various countries and, in part, to the fact that the 1962 figures are only tentative. It is possible, however, that there are other causes that cannot be determined for the moment. Therefore the differences between Tables 1–18 and 1–19, on the one hand, and Table 1–20, on the other hand, should be noted.

However, although the volume of exports of most Latin American countries increased over the previous years, the drop in internal prices in 1962 was expressed in a decrease in the value of coffee exports, or in a lower increase than that recorded by the volume of exports. For the region as a whole, in 1962 the value of exports fell 2 per cent below that of 1961, despite an increase of 4.3 per cent in volume (see Table 1–22).

Wheat

World wheat production in 1962/63 stood 3 and 2 per cent higher, respectively, than the shortfall levels of the two previous years. Australia, Canada, and Western Europe led this recovery, while the production of both the United States and Argentina again declined (see Table 1–23).

Because of the reduction in the stocks of the principal exporters, owing to previous production drops, and the increase in the import needs of Western Europe—especially the Common Market—and Continental China, prices rallied slightly for Argentine wheat and much more markedly for Canadian and Australian wheat. In view of the recovery in production in the importing regions, it is to be expected that the rising trend in the world market will not continue.

At the beginning of the 1962/63 crop year, stocks in the United States were lower than in the two previous years, but they remained at levels slightly above those of 1959/60. It is estimated that 1962/63 production will be approximately 13 per cent less than that of the preceding year; but a decrease in exports is also anticipated, so that, on the whole, the change in total stocks may be very slight. Of greater importance—but with consequences as yet unpredictable—is the fact that United States wheat production controls will be eliminated in 1964, as a result of the defeat of the referendum conducted at the end of May, 1963, by the farmers of the United States. Since the elimination of production controls means also the elimination of the guaranteed prices at 80 per cent of parity, it is believed that a sharp drop in wheat prices on the domestic market is likely. Wheat prices on the export market are subject to minimum and maximum limits, fixed in the 1962 International Wheat Agreement,[18] so that the effect of an eventual drop in the domestic prices of the United States will not necessarily lead to a drop in export prices.

The largest export increases in both 1960/61 and 1961/62 occurred

---

[18] It should be mentioned in this connection that the Soviet Union participates as an exporting member in the new International Wheat Agreement, thereby somewhat strengthening the position of this Agreement in the regulation of the world wheat market.

TABLE 1-21. Green Coffee: World Production and Exports, by Country and Region[a]

Country or region	(1,000 bags) 1959/60	(Indices: 1959/60 = 100.0)		
		1960/61	1961/62	1962/63*
Brazil				
Production	37,000	59.5	75.7	54.1
Exports[b]	16,819	100.9	97.4	
Colombia				
Production	7,000	100.0	97.1	94.3
Exports[b]	5,938	95.2	110.5	
Costa Rica				
Production	800	131.2	121.2	116.9
Exports[b]	766	109.0	117.8	
Dominican Republic				
Production	460	81.5	97.8	87.0
Exports[b]	481	69.6	101.2	
Ecuador				
Production	475	105.3	126.3	136.8
Exports[b]	539	70.7	102.2	
El Salvador				
Production	1,475	91.5	122.0	96.6
Exports[b]	1,178	121.5	125.4	
Guatemala				
Production	1,400	92.8	108.9	110.7
Exports[b]	1,329	94.4	116.8	
Haiti				
Production	500	55.0	105.0	85.0
Exports[b]	394	88.3	130.5	
Honduras				
Production	300	75.0	96.7	108.3
Exports[b]	258	81.4	103.1	
Mexico				
Production	1,550	93.5	96.8	96.8
Exports[b]	1,384	107.2	105.3	
Nicaragua				
Production	325	136.3	121.5	135.4
Exports[b]	361	96.7	93.6	
Peru				
Production	375	110.7	160.0	173.3
Exports[b]	440	128.9	141.8	
Venezuela				
Production	410	103.7	85.4	109.8
Exports[b]	408	99.5	78.2	
Latin America				
Production	52,070	70.7	84.2	67.9
Exports[b]	30,295	99.8	103.7	
Africa				
Production	11,996	111.0	98.1	115.8
Exports[b]	10,879	103.8	114.9	
Total World				
Production	66,421	79.5	87.2	77.9
Exports[b]	42,658	102.2	107.2	

[a] Exportable production for commercial years July–June.
[b] Exports refer to the second calendar year indicated in the column.
Sources: U.S. Department of Agriculture, Foreign Agriculture Circular, March, 1963, FCOF 1–63. Paton, Complete Coffee Coverage, May 23, 1963.

TABLE 1–22. Green Coffee: Value[a] and Volume[b] of Exports of Latin American Countries

		(Indices: 1960 = 100.0)	
Country	1960	1961	1962
Brazil			
Value	713.0	99.6	90.2
Volume	16,819	100.9	97.4
Colombia			
Value	333.5	92.3	99.5
Volume	5,938	95.2	110.5
Costa Rica			
Value	45.4	98.9	103.1
Volume	766	109.0	117.8
Dominican Republic			
Value	22.6	61.1	88.0
Volume	481	68.0	105.6
Ecuador			
Value	21.9	65.3	95.4
Volume	539	70.7	102.0
El Salvador			
Value	76.7	91.5	83.7
Volume	1,178	121.5	125.5
Guatemala			
Value	78.6	88.0	86.8
Volume	1,329	94.4	116.8
Haiti			
Value	17.3	77.5	119.7
Volume	394	88.3	130.5
Honduras			
Volue	11.8	75.8	97.0
Volume	258	81.4	102.3
Mexico			
Value	71.7	100.0	100.7
Volume	1,384	107.2	105.3
Nicaragua			
Value	19.2	90.6	80.2
Volume	371	93.5	96.0
Total 11 countries			
Value	1,411.7	95.0	93.1
Volume	29,447	99.3	103.5

[a] Millions of dollars.
[b] Millions of bags.

Sources: Values: International Monetary Fund, *International Financial Statistics*. Volumes: Paton, *Complete Coffee Coverage*, May 23, 1963.

TABLE 1-23. Wheat: World Production and Stocks in Selected Countries

	(Thousands of metric tons) 1959/1960	(Indices: 1959/60 = 100.0)		
		1960/61	1961/62	1962/63*
Production				
United States	30,512	121.1	110.1	97.4
Canada	11,254	125.4	68.5	134.8
Western Europe[a]	42,665	92.8	88.2	110.6
Eastern Europe	13,955	92.7	97.1	97.4
Soviet Union	69,101	93.0	96.2	102.2
Australia	5,402	137.9	124.5	151.1
Latin America	9,386	83.2	94.6	...
Argentina	(5,837)	(67.8)	(87.4)	(83.9)
World Total	249,200	98.2	95.0	104.5
Stocks[b]				
Argentina	1,633	100.0	58.3	21.7
Australia	1,851	94.1	41.2	26.5
Canada	14,941	109.3	110.7	72.1
United States	35,244	101.5	108.9	100.8
Total	53,669	103.3	105.6	87.8

[a] Includes Yugoslavia.
[b] At the beginning of the crop year of each country.

Sources: FAO, *Boletín Mensual de Economía y Estadística Agrícolas;* U.S. Department of Agriculture, *The Wheat Situation*, February, 1963.

in the United States, Canada, and Australia; in 1961/62 they also occurred, in lower percentages, in Argentina and France (see Table 1-24). The Soviet Union was therefore the only exporting country that did not contribute to the increase in the world wheat trade. It should be noted, also, that the increase in exports was concentrated chiefly in those going to the EEC countries, Eastern Europe, and Continental China, with a considerable increase in 1961/62 in exports to Latin America, chiefly Brazil, whose production declined in 1961/62.

Corn

World corn trade represents a small proportion of world production. Most of the corn exports are concentrated in the United States, and most of the corn imports in the countries of Western Europe. The quotations for this product in the United Kingdom have fluctuated relatively little in the past three years, although a downward trend in that period has been evident, especially if the prices are compared with those for the

1950–57 period. The high level of stocks in the United States has undoubtedly affected this situation.

In 1961/62, world production remained almost at the same level as in the previous year, although there were significant changes in certain countries. Western Europe, and particularly Yugoslavia, the largest exporter in the region, registered considerable decreases. The production of Thailand, South Africa, and other countries in those areas increased moderately. The greatest expansion occurred in the Soviet Union. The production of the United States, the largest world exporter, dropped in 1961/62 and is expected to remain at almost the same level in 1962/63 (see Table 1–25).

There were certain increases in Latin American production, especially in Argentina, Brazil, and other minor producers. In this region, Argentina is the only exporting country of any significance, and although its production increased in the past two years, exports decreased in relation to the volume reached in 1959/60. Apparently the drop was caused by a decrease in the total production of other cereals owing to severe droughts, which made it necessary to hold back a part of the exportable balances of corn for domestic consumption.

The sharp rise in corn exports in 1961/62 in relation to previous years was caused by increased import requirements in the EEC countries and other countries of Western Europe. Another considerable part was derived from an increase in world exports to Japan. The United States, which almost doubled its exports between 1959/60 and 1961/62, supplied a large part of these increased needs.

Argentina was unable to profit from the expansion in the international demand for corn, and its exports to Western Europe and Japan have, in the past two years, been considerably below those of 1959/60 (see Table 1–26).

In the first quarter of 1963, the situation of the international corn prices continued practically the same as in the previous year. In the first half of the 1962/63 commercial year, United States exports continued at the high level of the previous year, and, although at the beginning of 1963 its stocks were lower than at the beginning of 1962, the volume of the stocks insures an adequate supply for the near future (see Table 1–27).

Meat

In 1962, the developments in beef prices on the international market showed certain erratic fluctuations. Within these fluctuations, in the first nine months of the year prices remained above those in the previous

TABLE 1-24. Wheat and Wheat Flour: Exports, by Principal Region of Destination

Exporters		European Economic Community	European Free Trade Association	Eastern Europe and Continental China	Latin America	Japan	Others	Total
Argentina	1959/60 (1,000 tons)	555.8	325.5	—	1,198.2	—	29.5	2,109.0
	1960/61 Indices[a]	71.0	86.0	—	91.9	—	451.5	90.5
	1961/62 Indices[a]	184.9	120.3	[b]	66.2	[c]	141.0	111.6
Australia	1959/60 (1,000 tons)	115.1	656.0	—	—	378.6	2,151.9	3,301.6
	1960/61 Indices[a]	504.2	128.6	[d]	—	94.4	96.0	153.0
	1961/62 Indices[a]	482.6	120.1	[d]	[c]	112.8	117.5	189.4
Canada	1959/60 (1,000 tons)	1,408.8	2,961.2	132.6	298.4	1,254.8	1,519.5	7,575.3
	1960/61 Indices[a]	145.0	95.3	934.2	104.5	122.7	92.2	123.5
	1961/62 Indices[a]	130.2	89.7	2,052.9	87.7	106.3	74.5	131.2
United States	1959/60 (1,000 tons)	723.5	786.3	723.9	2,145.1	109.2	8,500.8	13,788.8
	1960/61 Indices[a]	290.2	103.8	154.7	94.6	100.7	129.3	130.3
	1961/62 Indices[a]	260.5	134.6	64.5	131.4	111.0	144.8	141.8

France	1959/60 (1,000 tons)	510.7	227.8	—	59.6	—	957.2	1,755.3
	1960/61 Indices[a]	108.2	74.1	[f]	28.0	—	80.6	87.7
	1961/62 Indices[a]	118.9	116.6	[f]	43.3	—	78.8	105.6
Soviet Union	1959/60 (1,000 tons)	261.8	243.3	3,934.9	—	67.3	395.7	4,900.0
	1960/61 Indices[a]	240.8	192.5	52.8	[g]	81.0	29.0	75.0
	1961/62 Indices[a]	111.3	178.1	75.5	[g]	22.3	106.3	96.7
Subtotal	1959/60 (1,000 tons)	3,575.7	5,197.1	4,791.4	3,701.3	2,609.9	13,554.6	33,430.0
	1960/61 Indices[a]	176.2	103.8	118.3	102.5	109.9	114.2	118.2
	1961/62 Indices[a]	173.4	107.5	175.5	122.0	106.7	126.8	133.7
Total World Exports	1959/60 (1,000 tons)							36,049.9
	1960/61 Indices							114.6
	1961/62 Indices							130.9

[a] Indices: 1959/60 = 100.0.
[b] 98,700 tons in 1961/62.
[c] 700 tons in 1961/62.
[d] Exports of 1.2 and 1.95 million tons in 1960/61 and 1961/62, respectively.
[e] Exports of 1,700 tons in 1961/62.
[f] Exports of 29,400 and 200,100 tons in 1960/61 and 1961/62, respectively.
[g] Exports of 150,000 tons to Cuba and 186,200 to Brazil in 1960/61 and 330,000 tons to Cuba and 282,900 to Brazil in 1961/62.

Sources: FAO, *World Trade Grain Statistics*, 1959/60—1960/61; U.S. Department of Agriculture, *The Wheat Situation*, February, 1963.

TABLE 1-25. Corn: World Production, by Selected Regions and Countries

Country or region	(Thousands of metric tons) 1959/60	(Indices: 1959/60 = 100.0)		
		1960/61	1961/62	1962/63*
Western Europe	14,294	103.8	96.5	...
Eastern Europe	11,456	98.1	91.6	...
Soviet Union	12,020	155.6	200.2	...
United States	97,149	102.2	94.8	93.9
Asia	10,930	106.1	106.2	...
Africa	10,950	113.3	...	...
Latin America				
Argentina	4,108	118.1	127.1	...
Brazil	8,554	105.2	...	...
Mexico	5,563	93.5	100.0	...
Total World Production	207,700	103.1	102.7	...

Source: FAO, Boletín Mensual de Economía y Estadística Agrícolas, December, 1962.

year, but in the final months of 1962 there was a sharp price fall, which continued in the first quarter of 1963. In May, 1963, another price recovery began. However, the average price in the first four months of the year was almost 20 per cent below the level for the corresponding period of 1962.

From the standpoint of the Latin American exporters, certain circumstances created a climate of uncertainty in the immediate outlook for the foreign meat market: (1) the import regulations adopted by the countries of the European Economic Community and (2) the effects that would result from the eventual entry of the United Kingdom into the Community. To study the possible implications of this market development, the member countries of the Meat Action Group held a meeting in Buenos Aires at the end of 1962. During that meeting, it was agreed to encourage negotiation at the governmental level in the member countries of the Community so that the regulations finally adopted on meat imports would not have an excessively severe effect on Latin American exports.

In 1962, total Argentine exports were higher than in the two previous years, partially as a result of increased imports by the EEC, the United Kingdom, and Spain. In Uruguay, exports to other markets increased more, but there was also an increase in the total value. In the first quarter of 1963, there was a marked expansion in Argentine exports to

Great Britain and Italy, resulting partly from the drought in the exporting country; at the same time, British imports of refrigerated beef from Uruguay recovered.

Despite the increase in 1962, total imports of beef and other cattle on the hoof by the EEC countries did not remain at the 1960 level. This decline, which was relatively serious if the net imports of this group of countries is considered, was due chiefly to the expansion of French production and exports. However, this market development was not unfavorable to the Latin American exporting countries, since their total 1962 beef exports to the Community were higher than those in the two previous years [19] (see Table 1–28), due chiefly to the recovery of Italian imports. Italy not only increased its purchases from Argentina by almost 10,000 tons but also imported more than 3,000 tons from Brazil. However, it should be remembered that there is no assurance that the position of the Latin American countries in the Community market will remain unchanged in the immediate future, due to the fact that the common agricultural policy regulations on meat have not been effected as yet.

Total exports to the United Kingdom, which before 1962 had been the most important single market for Latin American exporters, increased considerably, although the 1960 levels were not reached, especially of beef imports. To a great extent, this decline in imports was due to an increase in domestic production. However, Latin American participation within that reduced import volume improved in relation to that of the United Kingdom's other suppliers (see Table 1–29). The continued increase in imports at the beginning of 1963 led to an official British statement that consideration was being given to the possibility of applying quantitative restrictions. If this were done, it could have very grave consequences for Latin American exporters.

The demand for imported meat continued to expand in the United States. This increased demand was chiefly for fresh, chilled, and frozen beef, items of trade in which Mexico alone among the Latin American countries has a share of any importance (see Table 1–30). This trade continued to expand rapidly in the first quarter of 1963. Imports from Argentina, Uruguay, and other Latin American exporters are primarily in the form of canned meats, whose total importation in 1962 declined in relation to the preceding year but continued at a higher level than in 1960. However, another of the important products in the meat trade—imports of cattle on the hoof—again showed a substantial gain, coming largely from Mexico.

[19] Latin American countries do not supply cattle on the hoof to the European Economic Community.

TABLE 1–26. Corn: Exports of Selected Countries, by Principal Region of Destination (Commercial Years July–June)

Exporting country		European Economic Community	European Free Trade Association	Canada	Japan	Other Asia (except Continental China)	Others	Total
Argentina	1959/60 (1,000 tons)	2,278.1	463.4	—	420.7	—	8.3	3,170.5
	1960/61 Indices[a]	62.6	28.7	—	66.5	—	680.7	59.8
	1961/62 Indices	75.0	29.2	—	42.9	—	2,754.2	71.1
United States	1959/60 (1,000 tons)	1,703.6	2,308.4	541.0	199.9	236.1	476.9	5,465.9
	1960/61 Indices	120.2	93.8	149.5	303.8	101.8	154.9	120.9
	1961/62 Indices	182.5	129.0	245.7	446.1	220.1	320.2	189.4
France	1959/60 (1,000 tons)	11.7	81.3	—	0.3	—	1.2	94.5
	1960/61 Indices	2,996.5	362.4	—	—	[a]	1,708.3	709.4
	1961/62 Indices	1,391.4	196.8	—	—	—	1,675.0	362.8
Yugoslavia	1959/60 (1,000 tons)	288.4	185.6	—	15.1	2.5	16.0	507.6
	1960/61 Indices	40.4	85.3	—	—	—	690.0	75.9
	1961/62 Indices	19.2	38.1	—	—	200.0	90.0	28.6

EXPORTS AND PRIMARY PRODUCTS' MARKETS 45

Thailand	1959/60 (1,000 tons)	—	—	223.7	51.2	4.8	279.7
	1960/61 Indices	—	—	182.4	142.4	—	185.5
	1961/62 Indices	—	—	143.8	398.2	91.7	210.6
South Africa	1959/60 (1,000 tons)	32.9	167.4	167.8	—	2.8	370.9
	1960/61 Indices	288.7	141.7	273.1	c	314.3	215.9
	1961/62 Indices	2,381.4	120.9	304.2	c	2,489.3	424.1
Total 6 countries	1959/60 (1,000 tons)	4,314.7	3,206.1	541.0	1,027.5	289.8	510.0	9,889.1
	1960/61 Indices	93.6	94.4	149.5	170.6	110.3	183.3	110.0
	1961/62 Indices	134.9	112.4	245.7	185.3	253.8	365.6	154.3
Total World Exports	1959/60 (1,000 tons)							10,870.0
	1960/61 Indices							11.3
	1961/62 Indices							166.0

Sources: FAO, *World Trade Grain Statistics,* 1959/60—1960/61; U.S. Department of Agriculture, *World Agricultural Production and Trade,* April, 1963.

^a Exports of 4,700 tons in 1960/61.
^b Exports of 37,900 and 59,200 tons in 1960/61 and 1961/62, respectively.
^c Exports of 1,600 and 7,000 tons in 1960/61 and 1961/62, respectively.

TABLE 1-27. Corn: Stocks in Selected Exporting Countries on January 1 of Each Year

Exporting country	(Thousands of metric tons) 1960	(Indices: 1960 = 100.0)		
		1961	1962	1963*
Argentina	1,397	45.4	81.8	63.6
United States	110,344	107.9	103.5	97.2
Total 2 countries	111,741	107.1	103.2	96.8

Source: U.S. Department of Agriculture, *World Agricultural Production and Trade*, March, 1963.

TABLE 1-28. European Economic Community: Imports and Exports of Beef and Cattle on the Hoof

Region	Beef (Thousand tons)			Cattle on the hoof (Thousand head)		
	1960	1961	1962[a]	1960	1961	1962[a]
A. Imports, by origin						
Belgium-Luxembourg	2	1	2	8	7	7
France	44	58	58	116	77	50
Federal Republic of Germany	14	3	4	—	—	—
Italy	—	—	—	—	—	1
Netherlands	32	17	27	42	133	55
Subtotal	92	79	91	166	217	113
Argentina	52	66	82	—	—	—
Brazil	4	3	5	—	—	—
Uruguay	14	9	7	—	—	—
Other countries	85	23	44	680	659	574
Total	247	180	229	846	876	687
B. Total exports[b]	122	137	200	225	273	166
C. Net imports, (A − B)	125	43	30	621	603	521

[a] The figures for Germany and Italy cover 11 months; those for Belgium-Luxembourg, 10 months.

[b] Including exports to the member countries of the Community.

Source: Commonwealth Economic Committee, *Intelligence Bulletin* (London), April, 1963.

TABLE 1-29. United Kingdom: Total Meat Imports, by Country of Origin

Country	(Thousands of long tons) 1960	(Indices: 1960 = 100.0)	
		1961	1962
Beef[a]			
Argentina	183.6	77.5	88.3
Brazil	0.8	157.3	168.6
Uruguay	32.6	61.9	52.4
Subtotal	216.9	75.4	83.2
Australia	64.6	49.8	54.1
New Zealand	23.2	74.4	50.3
Ireland	14.7	223.7	146.3
Other countries	33.3	125.5	235.7
Total	352.8	81.6	92.7
Lamb[b]			
Argentina	30.5	65.4	69.3
Chile	1.8	181.6	47.1
Uruguay	—	—	—
Australia	30.9	83.1	71.9
New Zealand	300.0	96.5	97.3
Others	12.0	69.3	134.2
Total	375.3	92.4	93.9
Canned Beef			
Argentina	19.8	116.8	129.5
Brazil	4.1	100.9	49.5
Paraguay	4.7	115.1	134.5
Uruguay	3.3	54.0	102.0
Australia	19.0	80.8	53.6
New Zealand	0.8	112.7	118.9
Ireland	9.2	94.1	62.8
Others	16.4	142.1	150.5
Total	77.3	106.9	102.1

[a] Beef and veal.
[b] Mutton and lamb.

Source: Commonwealth Economic Committee, *Intelligence Bulletin*, February, 1963; March, 1963.

TABLE 1-30. United States: Imports of Beef and Cattle on the Hoof, by Origin

Item and source	(Tons) 1960	(Indices: 1960 = 100.0) 1961	1962
Fresh, chilled, and frozen beef			
Australia	63,670	155.5	315.0
New Zealand	58,824	113.7	160.0
Canada	8,751	148.1	100.2
Ireland	23,763	128.7	126.9
Mexico	17,408	135.5	152.6
Others	15,075	98.0	159.3
Total	187,491	132.2	204.9
Beef, cured			
Canada	100	28.0	51.0
Argentina	557	74.3	43.8
Brazil	87	125.3	100.0
Paraguay	22	—	—
Uruguay	—	a	—
Others	90	173.3	135.5
Total	856	95.6	58.9
Beef, processed			
Argentina	2,448	154.4	180.3
Brazil	272	244.8	436.8
Paraguay	—	—	b
Total	2,720	163.4	207.7
Beef, canned			
Argentina	21,775	110.2	91.5
Brazil	3,911	147.6	153.2
Paraguay	4,021	105.8	96.6
Uruguay	4,400	139.6	171.7
Others	534	144.9	166.3
Total	34,641	118.1	110.4
Beef cattle on the hoof[c]			
Canada	273	183.1	182.4
Mexico	391	138.9	192.3
Total	664	157.1	188.2

[a] 111 tons.
[b] 48 tons.
[c] Thousands of heads.

Sources: Commonwealth Economic Committee, *Intelligence Bulletin*, March, 1963; U.S. Department of Agriculture, *Livestock and Meat Situation*, May, 1963.

Cotton

On the international cotton market, a relatively significant drop in world exports and a moderate price decline, especially for extra-long staple cotton, were noted. During the period 1959/60 to 1961/62, world production remained practically stable, but an increase of approximately 4 per cent is forecast for 1962–63. This probable increase, added to the stock increases of the importing countries in the two previous years, is one of the chief causes for the weakness of the market, especially during the second half of 1962. In addition, United States stocks, which had declined in 1960 and 1961, again increased in 1962; the same occurred in other exporting countries (see Table 1–31).

TABLE 1–31. Cotton: World Stocks, Production, and Consumption (Crop Years August/July)

	(Millions of bales)[a] 1959/60	(Indices: 1959/60 = 100.0)		
		1960/61	1961/62	1962/63*
Stocks				
United States	8.9	85.4	80.9	87.6
Other exporters	3.6	88.9	97.2	102.8
Importing countries	5.3	113.2	122.6	103.8
Subtotal	17.8	94.4	96.6	95.5
Centrally planned countries[b]	3.2	106.2	78.1	68.7
World total	21.0	96.2	93.8	91.4
Production				
United States	14.5	99.3	99.3	102.8
Other countries	16.7	113.8	116.8	125.7
Subtotal	31.2	107.0	108.6	115.1
Centrally planned countries[b]	16.0	87.5	86.2	86.2
World total	47.2	100.4	101.1	105.3
Consumption				
United States	9.0	92.2	100.0	91.1
Other countries	22.2	104.9	105.8	104.0
Subtotal	31.2	101.3	104.2	100.3
Centrally planned countries[b]	17.1	95.9	91.8	93.0
World total	48.3	99.4	99.8	97.7

[a] Bales of 478 pounds net weight.
[b] Includes Soviet Union, Continental China, and the countries of Eastern Europe.

Source: International Cotton Advisory Committee, *Cotton, Monthly Review of the World Situation* (Washington), April–May, 1963.

Nor have the developments in world consumption been very encouraging, since in 1959/60 through 1961/62 it remained practically stationary. However, within this world situation, the Latin American position has been improving in relation to both production and exports. Brazilian production, which continued its long-term recovery of recent years, despite a slight decline in 1962/63, is significant. The production of Mexico and Colombia increased substantially in the same year. The increased importance cotton has acquired in Central America, where, in recent years, it has become the second most important export product, is also significant.[20] The production of the Latin American countries as a whole has increased more rapidly than total world production (see Table 1–32). With respect to exports, it is interesting to note that, despite the 1960/61 and 1961/62 decline in world exports, Latin American exports increased in both periods, an increase to which practically all the countries in the region contributed.

The decrease in world exports occurred chiefly in the United States, Egypt, and Pakistan (see Table 1–33). The drop in exports coincides with a decrease in production in 1961/62 only in the case of Egypt. In the United States, production has remained relatively unchanged in the last three years. However, world production fluctuated significantly in 1959/60 and 1961/62. It can be concluded that the decrease in world exports was caused principally by decreased demand in the chief importing areas, which already had large stocks. This contraction in demand had already reached significant proportions in 1960/61 and acquired greater intensity in 1961/62 in the two European regional economic groups; in the same year it spread to Japan and to those countries having centrally planned economies (see Table 1–33). It should be noted, however, that in 1961/62 Latin American exports to the European Economic Community, countries with centrally planned economies, and other markets continued to be higher than in the two previous years, thereby compensating for the decline in exports to the European Free Trade Association, Japan, and the United States.

One thing which, in the near future, will have a definite influence on the progress of the cotton fiber trade is the Agreement on International Trade in Cotton Textiles, which was signed by a number of industrialized countries [21] and went into force in October, 1962, for a period of five years. This Agreement is an important instrument for regulating trade in a branch of the manufacturing industry that is in a stage of

[20] See Chapter 6 of this *Survey*.
[21] See United Nations Commission on International Commodity Trade, *Hechos recientes en materia de productos básicos,* Memorandum No. 44, 1962.

TABLE 1–32. Cotton: Production and Exports of Selected Countries

Country	(Thousands of bales of 478 lbs.) 1959/60	(Indices: 1959/60 = 100.0)		
		1960/61	1961/62	1962/63*
Argentina				
Production	430	130.0	116.3	116.3
Exports	31.1	246.0	456.3	—
Brazil				
Production	1,700	114.7	147.0	135.3
Exports	448.2	155.6	159.2	—
Colombia				
Production	310	99.3	113.9	121.0
Exports	31.4	379.9	460.2	—
El Salvador				
Production	140.0	132.1	185.7	...
Exports	112.7	123.4	186.1	—
Guatemala				
Production	65.0	146.1	223.1	...
Exports	52.0	144.2	221.1	—
Mexico				
Production	1,660	126.5	119.9	142.8
Exports	1,265.6	115.3	112.1	—
Nicaragua				
Production	130	115.4	196.1	...
Exports	114.8	121.0	209.1	—
Paraguay				
Production	20	175.0	250.0	...
Exports	5.0	400.0	700.0	—
Peru				
Production	643	86.6	100.8	93.3
Exports	544.7	116.8	134.1	—
Latin America				
Production	5,098	116.5	131.4	...
Exports	2,605.5	129.0	143.9	—
World Total				
Production	47,249	100.4	101.0	105.2
Exports	17,325	97.1	87.6	—
Latin American percentage of total world				
Production	10.8	12.5	14.0	—
Exports	6.6	20.0	24.7	—

Source: International Cotton Advisory Committee, *Cotton—World Statistics* (Washington), April, 1963.

TABLE 1-33. Cotton: Exports of Selected Countries and Regions, by Destination (Crop Year August/July)

Country or region		United States	European Economic Community	European Free Trade Association	Soviet Union and Eastern Europe[a]	Japan	Others	Total
Latin America[c]	1959/60 (1,000 bales)	83.5	951.5	322.1	79.0	764.7	347.7	2,548.5
	1960/61 Indices[b]	132.8	116.3	112.4	63.3	140.8	161.0	128.2
	1961/62 Indices	102.5	126.2	105.0	168.1	121.5	193.4	141.2
United States	1959/60 (1,000 bales)	—	2,291.7	882.4	71.2	1,755.0	2,181.3	7,181.6
	1960/61 Indices[b]	—	77.8	75.7	320.4	99.4	101.3	92.3
	1961/62 Indices	—	47.5	59.0	195.2	58.6	98.1	68.4
Other Countries[d]	1959/60 (1,000 bales)	112.4	922.4	390.4	1,341.2	255.5	541.7	3,563.6
	1960/61 Indices[b]	103.4	65.2	69.3	101.5	68.9	85.3	83.8
	1961/62 Indices	75.9	94.6	80.3	71.5	75.9	106.0	84.1
Subtotal	1959/60 (1,000 bales)	195.9	4,165.6	1,594.9	1,491.4	2,775.2	3,070.7	13,293.7
	1960/61 Indices[b]	115.9	83.8	81.5	109.9	108.0	105.2	96.9
	1961/62 Indices	87.2	75.9	73.5	82.5	77.5	110.3	86.6
World total	1959/60 (1,000 bales)	—	—	—	—	—	—	17,325.0
	1960/61 Indices[b]	—	—	—	—	—	—	97.1
	1961/62 Indices	—	—	—	—	—	—	87.6

[a] Includes Continental China.
[b] Indices: 1959/60 = 100.0.
[c] Includes Argentina, Brazil, Colombia, El Salvador, Mexico, Nicaragua, and Peru. The difference from the total for Latin America in the preceding table is due to the exclusion of Guatemala and Paraguay, for which figures on country of destination are not available.
[d] Other countries include Egypt, Pakistan, Syria, Sudan, and Turkey.

Source: International Cotton Advisory Committee, Cotton—World Statistics, April, 1963.

Wool

In the past two years, wool prices have varied somewhat, depending on the type of fiber. Prices for coarse wools, in general, dropped sharply, while those for fine wools, which had declined less sharply in 1961, rose to levels slightly above those of 1960.

These price tendencies appear to reflect chiefly qualitative changes in demand, since there have been no major changes in world production and consumption as compared with 1960. Figures for wool consumption in a representative group of countries show that, although there have been significant changes in the recent period among the various countries, total consumption has remained stable (see Table 1–34).

For several years now, competition between the cotton and wool industries and artificial fibers has been a factor restricting the expansion of consumption of natural fibers, and progress in research in recent years has improved even further the competitive position of artificial fibers

TABLE 1–34. Wool: Consumption of Virgin Wool in Selected Countries

Country	(Millions of pounds)[a] 1960	(Indices: 1960 = 100)	
		1961	1962
Federal Republic of Germany	151	99.3	97.3
Australia	74	87.8	98.6
Belgium	86	95.3	109.3
United States	415	100.7	105.1
France	301	100.0	96.7
Netherlands	22	95.4	100.0
Italy	198	94.4	100.5
Japan	301	116.3	106.3
United Kingdom	481	98.1	93.1
Sweden	12	91.7	83.3
Total 10 countries	2,041	100.8	100.0

[a] Clean basis.

Source: Commonwealth Economic Committee, *Wool Intelligence* (London), February, 1963.

by reducing market prices (the most recent reductions have been for rayon and orlon) and by improving the quality of the various fibers and the ways of using them in the manufacture of articles that previously contained natural fibers. For example, the rayon fiber being used now, unlike that of the past, does not shrink and has greater resistance, and its appearance remains unaltered after several washings. A new fiber of polypropylene is being used in the manufacture of rugs, curtains, sweaters, bathing suits, and other articles of clothing because it combines the qualities of wool and nylon. Rayon production in the United States, for example, increased from 314 million pounds in 1960 to 400.5 million pounds in 1961 (27.5 per cent), and it is estimated that it will reach 510 million pounds in 1962.

The International Wool Study Group, at the request of the Government of the United States, met in London in mid-December, 1962, to study the problems of the wool-textile industry. The meeting was exploratory in nature and did not adopt recommendations of any kind; however, it agreed to meet again at the beginning of 1964.[22]

The exports of the chief wool producers increased 4 per cent in both 1961 and 1962. However, in the case of Argentina and Uruguay, 1962 exports were lower than in the preceding year; this was reflected in an increase in the stocks of those two countries, but not in a significant proportion, because production dropped that year (see Table 1–35).

The distribution of exports by regions of destination shows that the increase in exports in the past two years was concentrated in the United States, the EEC countries, and Japan (included in "other countries" in Table 1–36). Exports to the Soviet Union—where production has been increasing—and to the countries of Eastern Europe decreased substantially, as did those to the United Kingdom and to other countries of Continental Europe, where the textile industry has been in a period of decline.

Copper

Price trends in the group of nonferrous metals varied considerably. New York prices for copper in 1962 remained at the level reached in the second half of 1961; that is, they continued to be lower than in 1959–60. Quotations on the London metals exchange also remained stationary at a level slightly above that of the preceding year, although in reliable trade circles it is maintained that this stability resulted largely from

[22] See United Nations Commission on International Commodity Trade, *Hechos recientes en materia de productos básicos,* Memorandum No. 45, 1962.

TABLE 1-35. Wool: Stocks in Principal Exporting Countries at the Beginning of the Respective Commercial Year[a]

Exporting country	(Millions of pounds) 1960	(Indices: 1960 = 100) 1961	1962
Argentina	50	50.0	60.0
Uruguay	30	36.6	50.0
Australia	31	112.9	96.8
New Zealand	10	100.0	100.0
South Africa	1	400.0[b]	100.0[b]
Total 5 countries	122	69.7	70.5

[a] To October 1 in Argentina and Uruguay and to July 1 in the other countries.
[b] To May 30.
Source: U.S. Department of Agriculture, Foreign Crops and Markets, World Summaries, September 27, 1962.

the purchases made by the Rhodesian Selection Trust. Actually, market conditions were not very satisfactory, and price stability was influenced somewhat by measures to reduce production, announced by the large producers in Africa, the United States, and Chile. Such announcements did not mean, however, an actual reduction in world copper production in 1962, as compared with the previous year, but it did constitute a decline relative to total installed productive capacity, which increased slightly more than 100,000 tons with respect to 1961.[23] World production of primary copper increased slightly in 1962 above the level of the two previous years, while consumption remained almost at the same level as 1961 (see Tables 1-37 and 1-38). Accordingly, stocks of refined copper in the importing countries at the end of 1962 had increased 16 per cent over the previous year.

Copper production in Chile increased in 1962, as compared with 1961, despite the reductions announced by the large mining concerns in that country. Peruvian production decreased, however, as a result of a strike of mine workers and because of the damage caused by a plant explosion. The total exports of these two countries showed the same trends as their respective production; that is, an increase in Chile and a decrease in Peru.

Imports remained rather stable, except in the case of Italy and Japan, which continued their vigorous industrial expansion. However, Japan

[23] See *American Metal Market, Supplement* (New York), January 14, 1963.

TABLE 1-36. Wool: Export of Principal Producer Countries, by Region of Destination

Exporting country		United States	European Economic Community	European Free Trade Association[c]	Soviet Union and Eastern Europe[d]	Others	Total
Argentina[a]	1959/60 (millions of lbs.)	69	103	53	27	28	280
	1960/61 Indices[b]	82.6	140.8	132.1	88.9	157.1	121.4
	1961/62 Indices	94.2	115.5	124.5	88.9	114.3	109.3
Uruguay[a]	1959/60 (millions of lbs.)	13	21	20	6	5	65
	1960/61 Indices[b]	169.2	233.3	325.0	83.3	180.0	230.8
	1961/62 Indices	146.1	161.9	155.0	200.0	240.0	166.1
Australia[a]	1959/60 (millions of lbs.)	39	495	327	139	396	1,396
	1960/61 Indices[b]	92.3	91.3	82.3	77.0	124.7	97.3
	1961/62 Indices	143.6	98.6	77.4	87.0	129.3	102.4
New Zealand[a]	1959/60 (millions of lbs.)	66	203	180	45	34	528
	1960/61 Indices[b]	107.6	94.1	93.3	62.2	155.9	96.8
	1961/62 Indices	125.7	123.6	100.5	22.2	152.9	109.3
South Africa[a]	1959/60 (millions of lbs.)	33	131	64	19	19	266
	1960/61 Indices[b]	103.0	113.0	117.2	21.0	89.5	104.5
	1961/62 Indices	145.4	131.3	101.6	21.0	142.1	118.8
Totals	1959/60 (millions of lbs.)	220	953	644	236	482	2,535
	1960/61 Indices[b]	100.0	103.3	100.5	71.2	128.0	104.0
	1961/62 Indices	123.2	111.6	92.5	72.4	131.7	108.0

[a] Crop years: October–September for Argentina and Uruguay and July–June for the other countries.
[b] Indices: 1959/60 = 100.0.
[c] Most of the amounts correspond to the United Kingdom.
[d] Includes Continental China.

Sources: U.S. Department of Agriculture, *Foreign Crops and Markets*, World Summaries, Dec. 28, 1961; Dec. 27, 1962.

TABLE 1-37. Copper: Production, by Country of Origin

Country	(Thousands of short tons) 1960	(Indices: 1960 = 100.0)	
		1961	1962
United States	1,092.5	106.1	112.0
Canada	439.3	100.0	105.9
Chile	586.6	102.9	110.1
Mexico	66.5	81.8	78.0
Peru	200.3	109.0	91.3
Republic of the Congo (Leopoldville)	332.9	97.4	97.0
Northern Rhodesia	635.3	99.7	97.6
Australia	117.7	82.2	92.4
Centrally planned countries	602.2	104.2	108.7
Total world production	4,541.6	102.3	105.7

Source: Yearbook of the American Bureau of Metal Statistics (New York), June, 1963.

TABLE 1-38. Copper: Consumption in Selected Countries and Total World Consumption

Country	(Thousands of short tons) 1960	(Indices: 1960 = 100.0)	
		1961	1962
United States[a]	1,279.7	111.4	118.6
Canada	117.6	120.6	128.8
France	261.0	102.9	103.0
Federal Republic of Germany	593.3	106.1	91.6
Italy	212.2	102.9	124.6
Netherlands	62.5	75.5	46.9
Belgium	96.5	97.1	76.4
Sweden	87.0	90.6	97.4
Switzerland	40.4	141.8	107.2
United Kingdom	617.6	94.4	93.9
Centrally planned countries	729.7	103.8	105.1
Total world production	4,843.7	104.6	104.0

[a] Primary and secondary copper.

Source: Yearbook of the American Bureau of Metal Statistics, June, 1963.

increased only its imports of concentrates, while its imports of refined copper declined appreciably (see Table 1-39).

Lead and Zinc

Prices for lead and zinc, which had been declining since the middle of 1957, dropped even further in 1962, despite increases of 4 and 3 per cent, respectively, in world consumption of the two metals. In 1962, the average prices for these metals on the London metal market were 12.3 and 13.2 per cent lower, respectively, than the 1961 levels. In the second half of 1962, they dropped sharply when British industrial expansion came to a halt. This weakness continued during the first quarter of 1963; but the prices for both metals began to rise in the second quarter, exceeding the

TABLE 1-39. Unwrought Copper: Exports and Imports of Selected Countries

Country	(Thousands of metric tons) 1960	(Indices: 1960 = 100.0)	
		1961	1962
Exporters			
Chile	512.8	105.7	109.8
Mexico	36.9	66.4	79.9
Peru	176.1	110.0	92.2
Northern Rhodesia	563.3	97.2	94.2
Republic of the Congo (Leopoldville)	149.4	—	—
Canada	303.1	89.1	98.8
United States	403.6	98.2	76.1
Importers			
United States	473.2	87.1	90.9
Belgium	274.5	101.0	90.3
France	206.6	107.8	109.7
Italy[a]	193.2	102.5	124.2
Netherlands	321.1	93.5	67.0
Federal Republic of Germany[a]	430.3	109.0	93.4
United Kingdom[a]	556.5	96.3	96.2
Sweden[a]	75.5	95.9	95.6
Japan[b]	59.4	175.6	70.2
Japan[c]	463.3	93.7	112.8

[a] Refined and blister copper.
[b] Refined copper only.
[c] Copper ore and concentrates, gross weight.

Source: British Bureau of Non-Ferrous Metals, *World Non-Ferrous Metals Statistics*, March, 1963.

levels for the corresponding period of 1962 by 3 and 11 per cent, respectively, for lead—whose drop in price had been greater—and for zinc.

In the United States market, which is protected by the quotas established on commercial imports of these two metals, zinc prices remained unchanged in the two years cited and lead prices dropped 12 per cent until October, 1962. Later, a trend toward price recovery was noted, which continued throughout the first half of 1963, partially influenced by the increased demand in the United States as a result of the high production level of the automobile industry.

Moreover, there was a certain reduction in stocks of the metals, particularly lead, whose world production registered certain increases between 1960 and 1962. Zinc production, although also higher in the past two years, increased at a slower rate (see Tables 1–40 and 1–41). The meetings of the International Lead and Zinc Study Group in 1962 did not result in an agreement to give greater effectiveness to the recom-

TABLE 1–40. Lead and Zinc: Stocks in the United States and the United Kingdom

Country	(Thousands of metric tons) 1960	(Indices: 1960 = 100.0)	
		1961	1962
Lead			
United States			
Smelters and refiners	277.4	102.2	77.3
Consumers	88.3	101.8	92.5
Total	365.7	102.1	81.0
United Kingdom			
Consumers	21.6	98.1	107.5
Others	50.3	110.9	69.1
Total	71.9	107.1	80.6
Zinc			
United States			
Producers	189.0	80.1	86.5
Consumers	66.0	139.7	112.8
Total	255.0	95.6	93.3
United Kingdom			
Consumers	20.5	100.5	86.1
Others	38.4	140.2	149.2
Total	58.9	126.2	127.1

Source: Yearbook of the American Bureau of Metal Statistics, June, 1963.

TABLE 1-41. Lead and Zinc: Production, by Selected Countries and Total World Production[a]

Country	(Thousands of metric tons) 1960	(Indices: 1960 = 100.0)	
		1961	1962
Lead			
United States	223.8	106.2	96.2
Canada	186.6	112.0	102.7
Argentina	23.6	114.2	121.9
Mexico	190.7	95.1	101.4
Bolivia	21.4	94.9	86.9
Peru	131.6	103.7	95.0
Total world production	2,299.8	102.1	105.6
Zinc			
United States	395.0	106.7	116.1
Canada	390.1	103.0	116.7
Mexico	271.4	99.1	92.3
Argentina	28.6	105.7	115.5
Peru	178.1	97.7	90.1
Bolivia	4.0	132.4	90.6
Total world production	3,215.0	101.8	104.4

[a] Metallic content of the ore production.

Source: *Yearbook of the American Bureau of Metal Statistics,* June, 1963.

mendations for production restrictions, up to now announced voluntarily and unilaterally by certain countries, but apparently without strict compliance.

In addition to increased demand, already mentioned as one of the factors that helped soften the trend toward price depression in the second half of 1962, the announcement made by the representatives of the Soviet Union before the International Lead and Zinc Study Group to the effect that in 1962 the Soviet Union would maintain its exports at lower levels than in 1961 also had an effect.[24]

In 1962, exports of lead and zinc from Mexico and Peru declined by a rather high percentage from the levels reached in 1961. With the exception of Mexican lead, the production of these metals in these two countries was less than that of 1961 (see Table 1-42).

[24] Soviet Union exports in 1960 and 1961 were: lead, 69,800 tons and 102,300 tons, respectively; zinc, 90,400 and 116,200 tons, respectively (*American Metal Market,* September 6, 1962).

Tin

Contrary to what happened to the metals examined above, the international tin market continued to be dominated by a situation in which consumer demand exceeded current production. This imbalance, which caused a substantial price recovery in 1961 after the decline of the previous three years, permitted prices to remain in 1962 at levels slightly higher than those for the previous year, even though the relative deficit in the stocks decreased considerably. As a matter of fact, whereas world tin production increased moderately between 1960 and 1962, total consumption declined in those two years (see Table 1–43). Even more significant, however, is the fact that world production in 1962 continued to be 16 per cent below that of 1956 and was exceeded by world consumption; this is why the market continued to show signs of an upturn in the first half of 1963.

One of the aspects of the international tin market that created an uncertainty regarding price outlook in 1961 and the first half of 1962—the decision of the Government of the United States to sell part of its strategic reserves—was finally cleared up in July, 1962, when the Congress of the United States authorized the sale of 150,000 tons of its reserves. According to official statements, this amount, the equivalent of one year's world production, will be sold over the course of several years and in a manner that will not disrupt the market. At the end of August, 1962, the Government of the United States announced that the total amount of tin that it would put on sale by the end of 1962 would be 3,000 tons, distributed at the rate of 200 tons a week. According to

TABLE 1–42. Lead and Zinc: Latin American Exports

Item and country	(Thousands of metric tons) 1960	(Indices: 1960 = 100.0)	
		1961	1962*
Lead			
Mexico	148.6	115.8	92.8
Peru	117.8	121.0	110.5
Zinc			
Mexico	408.5	105.1	85.5
Peru	157.8	130.9	113.0

Sources: Banco de Comercio Exterior, México, *Revista de Comercio Exterior;* Banco Central de Reserva del Perú, *Boletín Mensual.*

TABLE 1-43. Tin: World Production and Consumption, 1960-1962

Country	(Thousands of long tons) 1960	(Indices: 1960 = 100.0)	
		1961	1962
Production[a]			
Republic of the Congo	8.9	74.2	81.0
Nigeria	7.7	101.3	106.5
Indonesia	22.6	82.3	77.9
Malaya	52.0	107.7	112.7
Thailand	12.1	109.9	121.5
Bolivia	19.4	106.7	112.4
Total world production[b]	135.5	101.1	105.5
Consumption			
United States	51.5	96.5	103.7
France	11.2	90.2	100.0
Italy	4.6	113.0	117.4
Federal Republic of Germany	27.7	93.1	42.2
United Kingdom	21.8	92.7	98.2
Other Western European countries	14.1	114.2	99.3
Total world consumption[b]	167.7	98.4	93.6

[a] Metallic content of concentrates.
[b] Excludes centrally planned countries.
Source: International Tin Council, *Statistical Bulletin*, May, 1963.

preliminary reports, the amount actually sold was less than the fixed limit. However, the possibility that the amounts put on the market—which constitute a potential supply of great significance—may be altered by administrative decision has had a certain influence on prices, causing them to drop moderately in the second half of the year from those in the first half. In the first six months of 1963, the sales of tin from such reserves continued to be within the limits fixed in 1962, but later it was announced that in the third quarter of 1963, 400 tons a week would be put on sale; this increase was adopted at the suggestion of the International Tin Council.

In the United States, the stocks in the hands of tin consumers at the end of 1962 were substantially lower than at the end of the previous year. In the United Kingdom, stocks in authorized warehouses were only 4,000 tons, as compared with 16,600 tons at the end of 1958. Moreover, the Stabilizing Reserve administered by the International Tin Council exhausted its stocks in the first quarter of 1961 and therefore now has the necessary financial resources to participate in the market if it should become necessary.

Tin production and exports of Bolivia continued the process of recovery noted in the two previous years. The total exported in 1962 (almost 4 per cent higher than that of 1961) was affected adversely only by a rail strike in November that lasted twenty days.

The consumption decline referred to above was reflected in decreased demand in the importing countries. In the United States, decreased imports in the past two years were in ore concentrates, while imports in metallic tin increased moderately. This tendency, however, may change in the near future, since in the middle of 1962 Bolivia signed a contract to supply ore concentrates to the Texas refining plant.

In the principal European countries, 1962 imports showed a slight recovery over the low levels of 1961, but in most cases they continued to be lower than those of 1960 (see Table 1–44). The most important exception was the Federal Republic of Germany, whose 1962 imports were substantially lower than those for the two previous years.

TABLE 1–44. Tin: Imports of Selected Countries

Country	(Thousands of long tons) 1960	(Indices: 1960 = 100.0)	
		1961	1962
Concentrates[a]			
United States	14.0	63.6	38.6
Belgium	7.4	97.3	98.6
Netherlands	6.1	50.8	90.2
United Kingdom	24.8	89.9	70.2
Malaya	21.5	88.3	111.6
Total of these five	73.8	82.0	80.8
Metal			
United States	39.5	101.0	104.8
France	11.7	85.5	95.7
Federal Republic of Germany	28.0	94.6	39.6
Netherlands	2.2	100.0	113.6
Italy	4.6	106.5	102.2
Japan	11.7	102.6	99.1
United Kingdom	2.9	62.1	317.2
Total of these seven	100.6	96.7	91.2

[a] Metallic content.

Source: International Tin Council, *Statistical Bulletin,* May, 1963.

One of the aspects of the international tin market that should be examined is the role played by Soviet imports and exports. The large volume of exports from the Soviet Union was one of the factors that had a preponderant effect on the drop in international prices in 1958. Most of these exports went to Western European markets. In the years to follow, exports declined markedly; in 1962 they were scarcely a quarter of the volume attained in 1958. Although initially that was the result of the informal agreement between the International Tin Council and the Soviet Union to limit exports to the markets of Western Europe, the substantial drop in Soviet exports in 1961 and 1962 was the result of decreased imports of tin from Continental China by the Soviet Union (see Table 1-45). In 1962, Soviet tin exports to the rest of the world were reduced to a tenth of the volume attained in 1958.

Silver

Silver prices followed the rather significant course of nonferrous metals on the international market in 1962. In the 1950's, silver prices fluctuated only slightly on the New York market, owing to the intervention of the United States Treasury in the market of this metal. There has been a certain expansion in the use of silver for industrial purposes in recent years, but silver production has not increased to the same extent, due, in part, to the depression that has affected the mining production of copper, lead, and zinc, which furnished part of the total silver production (see Table 1-46). Increased commercial demand for silver in the United States in recent years made the "free stocks" (that is, stocks

TABLE 1-45. Soviet Union: Tin Exports and Imports

Item and region	(Thousands of long tons) 1958	1959	1960	1961	1962*
		(Indices: 1958 = 100.0)			
Imports					
Total[a]	19.1	107.3	91.6	58.1	...
Exports					
Eastern Europe	3.8	110.5	78.9	97.4	...
Other countries	18.1	75.1	45.9	10.5	...
Total	21.9	81.3	51.6	25.6	10.0

[a] Almost all from mainland China.
Source: International Tin Council, *Statistical Bulletin*, May, 1963.

TABLE 1-46. Silver: World Production, by Selected Countries

Country	(Millions of fine ounces) 1958	(Indices: 1958 = 100.0)		
		1960	1961	1962
Bolivia	6.0	81.7	65.0	83.3
Canada	31.2	109.0	100.0	99.4
Mexico	47.6	93.5	84.7	87.2
Peru	25.9	118.9	129.7	123.6
United States	35.7	112.3	118.5	89.6
Others	58.3	95.7	93.7	98.6
Total world production[a]	204.7	102.6	100.6	97.2

[a] Countries having a centrally planned economy not included.
Source: Handy & Harman, New York, *El Mercado de Valores* (Nacional Financiera México), February 11, 1963.

not required as backing for the money in circulation) of the Treasury drop from 222 million fine ounces in April, 1959, to 22 million in November, 1961. This caused the Government of the United States to suspend sales of silver from that month on; this meant an elimination of the "ceiling" price established by the Treasury in commercial transactions of this metal. Accordingly, silver prices began a spiraling process that continued practically uninterrupted until the first months of 1963. Simultaneously with the suspension of silver sales by the United States Treasury, the Government proposed to Congress certain amendments in the laws intended to eliminate (1) the price support that the Treasury maintains on silver produced in the United States and (2) the use of silver as a monetary reserve (except for the minting of coins).[25] In the course of 1962, no decision was adopted on these proposals, and therefore silver prices have been approaching (in the first months of 1963) the value of silver as a metal reserve for the "silver certificates" in circulation in the United States. Between December, 1961, and December, 1962, the average silver prices in New York rose from 103.3 to 119.9 cents per fine ounce, an increase of 16 per cent.

Petroleum

Prices for Venezuelan crude petroleum for export have been unchanged since 1960, even though on several occasions this price stability has been distorted by the granting of discounts from the producers' list prices.

[25] See *Economic Report of the President* (Washington), January, 1962.

This practice, which the Venezuelan producers followed rather freely in 1960 and 1961, has apparently been abandoned, owing partly to the opposition to it manifested by the Venezuelan Government and partly to the relative strengthening of demand for petroleum on the world market in the recent period.

World production of crude petroleum has continued to expand in practically all of the principal producing areas. In 1962, production rose 8 per cent over that of the previous year, chiefly in the Soviet Union, the Middle East, and Venezuela. United States production, subject to controls, has increased to a relatively minor extent in recent years (see Table 1–47).

In Latin America, with the exception of Venezuela, the greatest increase in production was in Argentina, permitting that country to increase its degree of self-sufficiency in petroleum products. There were small increases in other countries (Chile, Mexico, and Peru), while in Colombia —which has a small export surplus—Brazil, and Ecuador, production dropped. Production in the region as a whole increased 8.6 per cent (see Table 1–47).

TABLE 1–47. Crude Petroleum: World Production, by Selected Countries

Country	(Thousands of metric tons) 1960	(Indices: 1960 = 100.0)	
		1961	1962
Argentina	9,146	132.8	147.6
Bolivia	415	85.3	94.0
Brazil	3,871	117.4	111.1
Chile	945	127.7	156.6
Colombia	7,821	95.3	92.1
Ecuador	361	108.3	91.4
Mexico	14,125	107.7	114.7
Peru	2,530	101.5	114.6
Venezuela	188,045	102.2	111.9
Total	148,831	104.2	113.2
United States	347,121	101.8	103.4
Canada	25,827	115.1	131.6
Middle East	264,994	107.2	117.3
Soviet Union	147,900	112.2	125.8
Total world production	1,052,042	106.4	115.1

Source: Petroleum Press Service (London), January, 1963.

From the standpoint of the foreign market, the development in Venezuelan production and exports is the most significant. Venezuelan production in 1962 rose 9.3 per cent over that of 1961. Exports of crude petroleum and petroleum products increased 8 per cent between the two years cited (see Table 1–48). This result can be termed favorable if the conditions prevailing on the world market are taken into account. In fact, the restrictions on the importation of crude petroleum and petroleum products into the United States, a country that absorbs a large part of Venezuelan exports, have raised a barrier to the expansion of Venezuelan sales, if not in absolute terms, at least regarding its percentage share of the increased consumption. In this connection, it should be pointed out that import controls put into effect in the United States for 1963 tend to restrict importation even more by changing the formula that was used in fixing import quotas. From 1963 on, import quotas will be fixed at the equivalent of 12.2 per cent of domestic production of crude petroleum and natural gas, but imports from Canada and Mexico (which are not subject to controls) are added to controlled imports in computing the 12.2 per cent. Thus, theoretically Canada and Mexico may furnish constantly increasing proportions of imports, causing the quotas available for imports from Venezuela to decline.[26]

Another important aspect of the growing change in the international petroleum market is Soviet exports. The rapid expansion in that country's production (in 1961 and 1962 it exceeded Venezuelan production, becoming the second largest producer of crude petroleum in the world) has been accompanied by a definite effort to penetrate the markets of Western Europe. The most recent figures available on the volume of exports from the Soviet Union go only as far as 1961, but by then its total exports of crude petroleum and petroleum products were 155.5 and 93.6 per cent, respectively, higher than the figures for 1958.

Relatively speaking, the development of greatest significance within the Latin American region was that of Mexican exports, which were 39 per cent higher in 1962 than in 1961. This is a result of the exemption from the above-mentioned United States controls on imports from Mexico. Colombian and Peruvian exports, however, declined sharply in the last two years, due partly to the tendency for domestic consumption to grow more than production capacity.

[26] As shown in Table 1-49, Canadian production registered a high growth rate in recent years. In Mexico, expansion was much lower, and beginning in 1962 it established a maximum limit on exports to the United States. As a result, whereas the amount supplied by Canada increased from 11 per cent in 1960 to 21 per cent in 1962, that of Latin America dropped from 51 per cent to 44 per cent in the same period.

TABLE 1–48. Crude Petroleum and Petroleum Products: Exports of Latin American Countries

	Country	Units 1960	(Indices: 1960 = 100.0) 1961	1962
Venezuela:	Crude petroleum	116.2[a]	101.9	111.0
	Petroleum products	40.0[a]	105.5	111.3
	Total	156.2[a]	102.8	111.1
Colombia	Total	31,332[b]	87.9	77.6
Mexico	Total	2,256[c]	133.1	185.1
Peru	Total	786[c]	87.2	79.3

[a] Millions of cubic meters.
[b] Thousands of barrels.
[c] Thousands of metric tons.

Sources: Banco Central de Venezuela, *Boletín Estadística;* Departamento Nacional de Estadística, *Boletín Mensual* (Bogotá, Colombia); Banco de Comercio Exterior, México, *Comercio Exterior;* Banco Central de Reserva del Perú, *Boletín.*

TOTAL EXPORTS AND THEIR GEOGRAPHIC STRUCTURE

The total value of Latin American exports in 1962 increased 6 per cent over the figure for the previous year and for the first time exceeded that reached in 1957 (see Table 1–50). The study of the foreign market conditions of the chief export products appearing on preceding pages provides certain facts for determining the prevailing trends in the exportation of each of the countries; but undoubtedly, in addition to the external factors, there are other domestic factors that play an important role under certain circumstances. As has already been pointed out, generally it should be noted that in most cases the increased value of exports reflects increases in the volume of products exported more than an improvement in price level. Only in two cases, sugar and tin, was the improvement in foreign prices more important than the volume exported in the total contribution to the value of the exports of the various countries.

Thus, it is obvious that although the 1962 exports show a marked improvement over the conditions of the immediately preceding years, they have not yet recovered the dynamic growth trend of the years prior to 1956/57. This is particularly evident if it is noted that the over-all

TABLE 1-49. United States: Foreign Trade in Crude Petroleum and Petroleum Products

Item and country	(Millions of barrels) 1960	(Indices: 1960 = 100)	
		1961	1962
Exports			
Crude petroleum	3.1	103.2	58.1
Petroleum products	70.8	85.2	84.0
Total	73.9	85.9	82.9
Imports			
Crude petroleum	371.6	102.7	110.6
Petroleum products	292.5	108.7	119.0
Total	664.1	105.3	114.3
Origin of Imports[a]			
Colombia	14.8	67.6	58.1
Mexico	0.9	400.0	400.0
Venezuela	172.9	90.1	97.7
Latin America[b]	188.6	90.8	96.8
Canada	41.3	161.3	206.3
Middle East[c]	113.2	105.2	95.9
Others	28.5	86.3	121.7
Total	371.6	102.7	110.6
Percentage of Imports from:			
Latin America	50.8	44.9	44.4
(Venezuela)	(46.5)	(40.8)	(41.1)
Canada	11.1	17.5	20.7

[a] Imports of crude petroleum only. There is no information available on the origin of imports of petroleum products.
[b] In 1961 and 1962, includes 1.8 and 1.3 million barrels imported from Brazil.
[c] Includes imports from Iran, Iraq, Kuwait, Qatar, Saudi Arabia, and the Neutral Zone.
Source: American Petroleum Institute, *Annual Statistical Bulletin* (New York), April, 1963.

improvement that occurred in 1962 in four countries—Argentina, Mexico, Peru, and Venezuela—exceeded that of the region as a whole.[27]

Within this group of countries, the increase in the exports of Peru is a singular case. In 1960, large-scale exploitation of new copper deposits was begun; copper exports were three times the amount of the previous years. To that was added, in 1961 and 1962, the transfer of sales of sugar from the free market to the United States market, at higher prices.

[27] In absolute terms, these four countries obtained the largest increases. In relative terms, certain other countries obtained larger increases.

TABLE 1-50. Latin America: Exports, by Principal Regions of Destination, 1960–1962

Destination	(Millions of dollars) 1960	(Indices: 1960 = 100)		(Percentages of the total)		
		1961	1962	1960	1961	1962
United States	3,600	90.8	93.9	41.8	37.7	37.7
Canada	145	110.3	120.7	1.7	1.8	1.9
Western Europe	2,720	101.5	112.5	31.6	31.8	33.3
European Economic Community	1,580	101.3	114.6	18.3	18.5	19.7
European Free Trade Ass'n.	1,010	97.0	102.0	11.7	11.3	11.2
Other Western European Countries	130	138.5	169.2	1.5	2.1	2.4
Japan	240	141.7	139.6	2.8	3.9	3.6
Other Asian countries	36	197.2	161.1	0.4	0.8	0.6
Soviet Union	135	255.6	277.8	1.6	4.0	4.1
Eastern Europe	130	123.1	146.2	1.5	1.8	2.1
Continental China	41	185.4	243.9	0.5	0.9	1.1
Africa	75	101.3	122.7	0.9	0.9	1.0
Latin America	680	83.8	91.2	7.9	6.6	6.7
Others[a]	808	104.2	100.9	9.4	9.7	8.9
Total	8,610	100.7	106.8	100.0	100.0	100.0

[a] Most of these figures are for exports of crude petroleum from Venezuela to the Netherlands Antilles.

Source: United Nations, *Monthly Bulletin of Statistics*, June, 1963.

Moreover, there has been a considerable expansion in exports of fishery products in the past three years. Finally, the rise in silver prices in 1962 also increased income from exports of lead and zinc that year. This combination of substantial increases in the volume of exports of certain products and improved prices in others, which has occurred in practically no other Latin American country in recent years, explains the high rate of expansion in Peru's export value since 1958.

In Mexico, whose basic exports are not very different, in over-all terms, from those of Peru, the copper, lead, and zinc mines have not contributed to the increase in exports in recent years. The improvement in silver prices in 1962 was a stimulus to the exportation of silver, whose production had been dropping since 1958. Like Peru, Mexico benefited from the change that occurred in the United States sugar market, since its exports to that country increased substantially, along with exports of cattle on the hoof and petroleum products. Finally, cotton exports—which declined in 1960 and 1961—reached in 1962 the highest level in the past five years. Mexico, moreover, is one of the countries that has succeeded in increasing trade with other countries within the region, especially with some of the other members of the Latin American Free Trade Association (LAFTA).

Argentine exports, which declined in 1961 because of the substantial drop in grain production caused by a prolonged drought, recovered in 1962, reaching levels not attained since 1953. The principal export products of this country were not subject to excessive price fluctuations on the foreign markets in 1962, although at the end of that year and in the beginning of 1963 there were sharp drops in meat prices. Wool was the only important exception. To a large extent, the changes in the value of total exports have reflected changes in the volume of available surplus for export.

Finally, Venezuela is one of the few countries where the relative price stability of its principal export product—petroleum and petroleum products—has coincided with an increasing volume of production and exports, despite certain unfavorable aspects brought about by the conditions on the international petroleum market.

The trend in Latin American exports by principal region of destination showed certain changes in 1961–62, which were due largely to the interruption of trade between Cuba and the United States and the shift in Cuban exports to countries having centrally planned economies. This partially explains the reduction noted in exports to the United States and, at the same time, the increase in exports to the centrally planned countries. Other Latin American countries have also succeeded in expanding their exports to centrally planned countries, chiefly in products such as coffee, cacao, cotton, wool, and cowhides, although the absolute values continue to be relatively low [28] (see Table 1–50).

A significant development, however, is that of exports to the European Economic Community. In 1962, these exports increased markedly, as a result, as has already been seen, of the expansion—and in certain cases, the recovery—of sales of cotton, beef, corn, wheat, coffee, and certain other products. It is obvious, however, that the preferential arrangements with the African countries associated with the Community and the regulations of the common agricultural policy have not been completed and that, therefore, the expected restrictions have not yet been fully manifested.

In 1962, there was a 12 per cent increase in Latin American intraregional exports over those of 1961, representing a partial recovery from

[28] Both Argentina and Brazil, which supply about 85 per cent of non-Cuban Latin American exports to the Soviet bloc, sell three times as much to Eastern Europe as to the Soviet Union. Their sales to Continental China are insignificant by comparison.

the 1961 decline. However, within the totals for these last two years, there are certain changes that should be examined. First, the drop in 1961 reflected chiefly a decline in exports from Argentina and Venezuela, which, in turn, resulted from widely differing causes. In the case of Argentina, it was caused by a reduction in the exports of grain owing to a short harvest; and in Venezuela, a decrease in exports of petroleum and petroleum products owing to the disappearance of markets such as those of Cuba and Argentina.[29] Owing to the high proportion of Venezuelan and Argentine exports in the total regional exports (34 and 25 per cent, respectively, in 1960), the drop in these two countries affected considerably the total figures for the region, despite the fact that other countries—principally Brazil, Chile, and Mexico—increased their exports to the region in that year (see Table 1–51).

Argentine and Venezuelan exports recovered partially in 1962 from the decline of the previous year. The same thing happened to Peruvian exports, which exceeded substantially those of the two previous years. This situation, combined with the increases in the exports of Chile, Colombia, Mexico, Paraguay, and Uruguay, was the reason for the favorable result already mentioned in Latin American intraregional trade as a whole.

Of special interest is the development of LAFTA trade. Unfortunately, as yet only fragmentary data are available. In 1962, Latin American intraregional exports increased in seven of the nine member countries, the exceptions being Brazil and Ecuador. However, if account is taken of the fact that in Argentina the 1962 figures reflect only a partial recovery and that, to a certain extent, this is also true of Peru, it would appear that actually the expansion in Latin American intraregional exports has not yet acquired a sustained growth rate. However, it is significant that it is the LAFTA member countries that, in 1962, exceeded, as a whole, the 1960 figures. In short, exports from Mexico to Brazil increased considerably (from $1.8 million in 1961 to $7.6 million in 1962), a trend that apparently continued during the first half of 1963.[30]

In the Central American countries, trade with the rest of Latin America declined in 1962. An increase was recorded in intra-area trade, according to the over-all figures [31] (see Table 1–51).

---

[29] In Cuba, supplies from the Soviet Union replaced those from Venezuela; and in Argentina, expansion of domestic production decreased import requirements.

[30] See Banco de Comercio Exterior, México, *Comercio Exterior*, July, 1963.

[31] For a more detailed analysis of Central American intraregional trade, see Part II of this *Survey*, especially Chapter 8.

TABLE 1-51. Latin American Intraregional Exports, 1960–1962[a]

Country	(Millions of dollars) 1960	(Indices: 1960 = 100.0)	
		1961	1962
Argentina	171.1	65.8	89.2
Brazil	89.0	109.6	88.4
Chile	38.2	118.6	134.8
Colombia	8.9	105.6	125.8
Ecuador	9.1	91.2	68.1
Mexico	24.2	124.8	158.7
Paraguay	8.9	110.1	121.3
Peru	43.3	88.7	120.3
Uruguay	4.0	157.5	227.5
Subtotal	396.7	90.3	103.5
Costa Rica	4.8	104.1	79.2
El Salvador	12.6	119.8	103.2[b]
Guatemala	6.0	145.0	58.3
Honduras	12.9	89.9	121.7[b]
Nicaragua	4.1	87.8	114.6
Subtotal	40.4	108.9	100.7
Bolivia	8.4	78.6	83.3
Dominican Republic	0.8	175.0	187.5
Haiti	—	—	—
Panama	0.1	100.0	100.0
Venezuela	231.8	72.2	82.0[c]
Subtotal	241.1	72.8	82.4
Total	678.9	85.2	95.8

[a] The totals given in this table for 1961 and 1962 are slightly higher than those in Table 1-50 because they include revisions and estimates that came after the publication of the total figures for the region.

[b] Estimates based on nine months.

[c] Estimates based on seven months.

Source: United Nations, *Direction of International Trade.* The 1962 figures include certain estimates based on incomplete data.

CHAPTER 2

LATIN AMERICA'S CAPACITY TO IMPORT, AND ITS BALANCE OF PAYMENTS[1]

TOTAL CAPACITY TO IMPORT, ITS UTILIZATION, AND THE NET BALANCE OF PAYMENTS

Changes during 1962 in total capacity to import have varied so widely among individual Latin American countries[2] that most generalizations about the region as a whole can be dangerously misleading. Total for-

[1] The terminology and the tools of analysis used throughout this chapter are the same as those used and defined in detail in Chapter II of the *Economic Survey of Latin America, 1961* (Washington, 1962). The capacity to import is the algebraic sum of the export of goods, the net service balance, and the net balance of donations and noncompensatory capital movements. The net service balance includes remittances of profit and interest but excludes gross foreign exchange expenditures for transportation and insurance of imports. That is, the import capacity and the imports referred to in this chapter are on a c.i.f. basis. The expenditures for transportation and insurance in practice are inseparable from imports. In addition, for certain Latin American countries chronological series of f.o.b. import values are not available. While compensatory accounts are defined as financing operations carried out by monetary authorities for the exclusive purpose of equalizing the credits and debits of the balance of payments, the movements of noncompensatory (or autonomous) capital correspond to a commercial operation or a specific investment. More details on the composition of noncompensatory and compensatory movements are given later in this chapter (p. 85). According to the general definition given above, the difference between total capacity to import and actual imports represents the over-all deficit or surplus in the balance of payments. This deficit or surplus generally differs from the net balance on compensatory accounts, due to errors and omissions which would be related mainly to capital movements induced by speculative or extraeconomic motives. In some countries, however, overvaluation or undervaluation of exports, imports, or foreign tourism transactions seems to be another source of errors and omissions. Official data from the IMF's *Balance of Payments Yearbooks* include adjustments for contraband.

[2] Because of the lack of data on Cuba's balance of payments in 1960, 1961, and 1962, this country is not included in the analysis except where specific indication is made to the contrary.

eign exchange receipts from current and noncompensatory financial sources rose in 12 countries of the region between 1961 and 1962 (see Table 2–1); in nine—Bolivia, Colombia, Costa Rica, the Dominican Republic, Ecuador, Honduras, Nicaragua, Panama, and Peru—the rate of increase was particularly high. On the other hand, sharp declines in total capacity to import were recorded in Argentina, Brazil, and Uruguay. As a combined result of these different trends from one country to another, the total of Latin America's import capacity was lower in 1962 than in 1961, but the decline was less than 2 per cent, even if the rising negative errors and omissions item in the balance of payments is considered to be related mainly to the movements of noncompensatory capital.

There was, however, a considerable shift in the distribution of the region's foreign exchange receipts between current income and financial receipts. While Latin America's total exports rose by approximately 5 per cent, the net inflow of capital and donations registered a sudden downturn during the past year (see Table 2–2). The improvement in export trade, which took place in 15 out of 19 Latin American countries, was the main factor responsible for the strengthening of the total capacity to import in El Salvador, Mexico, Nicaragua, and Peru.[3] In some other countries—Colombia, the Dominican Republic, Ecuador, and Honduras—there were also favorable changes in the total net balance of donations and capital transactions. Only in Bolivia, however, did the rise in import capacity result almost exclusively from an increase in the net inflow of external financial resources. On the other hand, a net outflow of capital took place in Argentina, Haiti, and Venezuela in 1962. As a result, the import capacity of these three countries declined during the past year, in spite of the sizable increment recorded by their exports. Guatemala, Brazil, and Uruguay suffered from both a fall in their exports and a worsening in the capital account of their balance of payments; the latter two countries were those registering the greatest declines in import capacity.

Changes in the value of imports also differed from one Latin American country to another. In only four out of 19, however, was there a decline in 1962 over 1961 (see Table 2–3); and in only two of these—Argentina and Chile—could the drop be described as large. In the aggregate, Latin America's imports increased but slightly between 1961 and 1962.

For several consecutive years in the recent past, Latin America's overall balance of payments has shown a deficit. Since in 1962 there was a

---

[3] Due to an increase in the negative balance of errors and omissions, it is doubtful that capacity to import actually improved in Chile, although export value was greater than in 1961.

slight decline in the region's import capacity and an increase—also small—in its imports, the negative balance of external transactions rose in relation to 1961. It amounted to approximately 10 per cent of noncompensatory foreign-exchange receipts available for financing purchases abroad, against 7.5 per cent in the previous year. This worsening of the region's external disequilibrium mainly reflected the shift from a surplus to a deficit in Brazil's balance of payments (see again Table 2–3). In 1962 a total of nine Latin American countries registered imports in excess of noncompensatory foreign-exchange receipts. Moreover, although the nine remaining countries recorded surpluses in their 1962 balance of payments, only Peru enjoyed a truly favorable external position during the last three years.

Even though Brazil's deficit in 1962 was somewhat lower than in 1960, it represented no less than 30 per cent of total import capacity. The

TABLE 2–1. Latin America: Total Capacity to Import, 1961 and 1962

(Millions of dollars)

Country	1961	1962*
Countries whose total capacity to import increased		
Bolivia	86	114
Chile	530	556
Colombia	424	519
Costa Rica	100	114
Dominican Republic	108	195
Ecuador	105	142
El Salvador	120	129
Honduras	64	84
Mexico	1,658	1,894
Nicaragua	67	89
Panama	180	212
Peru	492	549
Countries whose total capacity to import decreased		
Argentina	1,239	1,059
Brazil	1,563	1,224
Guatemala	133	122
Haiti	47	41
Paraguay	59	52
Uruguay	190	140
Venezuela	1,185	1,133
Total for Latin America	8,350	8,368

(Continued)

TABLE 2-1 *Continued*

Sources and method of estimates: For 1961: International Monetary Fund, *Balance of Payments Yearbook*, Vol. 14. For 1962: Provisional balance of payments data from IMF's *International Financial Statistics*, August, 1963, and *Balance of Payments Yearbook*, Vol. 15, July and August, 1963. For 1963, for the following countries: Bolivia, Brazil, Colombia, Chile, Costa Rica, Dominican Republic, Ecuador, El Salvador, Guatemala, Haiti, Panama, and Paraguay. Figures for Honduras, Mexico, and Nicaragua are from those countries' reports to the IA-ECOSOC, October, 1963. In the case of Mexico, the revision covers 1960-62; for the others, only the 1961 and 1962 data are revised.

In estimating total capacity to import of the other countries— Argentina, Peru, Uruguay, and Venezuela—the following method was used: The value of imports was known, as well as the net balance of payments through the variations in the compensatory accounts, and the approximate value of the total capacity to import was obtained by subtraction. Next, by subtracting the values of commodity exports—which were also known—the over-all net balance for service and capital accounts was obtained. An estimate of the net service balance was made, taking into account the relative stability of this item, as well as the changes in the service transactions shown by the United States balance of payments with Latin America. Finally, the net balance for donations and noncompensatory capital accounts was calculated as a residual figure. These calculations were based on data from the IMF's *International Financial Statistics* and from the following nonofficial sources: *Economic Survey*, Buenos Aires, March, 1963, for Argentina; and *Memoria del Banco Central de Venezuela* for the year 1962 for Venezuela.

---

resumption of such a basically unfavorable trend in the Brazilian economy resulted from the downward inflexibility of imports and the fall in total import capacity. It is noteworthy that for three consecutive years imports have been almost constant, in spite of considerable differences in current internal conditions and in the annual rate of real economic growth. On the other hand, the chronic deficit on current account increased considerably because the great improvement registered by merchandise exports in the preceding year was not repeated (see Table 2-4). While in 1961 the freely fluctuating rates of exchange had helped to foster minor Brazilian exports, the introduction of a fixed rate in January, 1962, apparently had the opposite effect.[4] Furthermore, current

[4] See Bank of London and South America, *Quarterly Review*, April, 1963, page 82. The coffee export rate and the free rate were as follows (in cruzeiros per dollar):

	1960	1961	1962
Coffee export rate	90	135	182
Free rate	205	318	475

(IMF, *International Financial Statistics*, July, 1963.)

TABLE 2–2. Latin America: Total Capacity to Import and Principal Contributing Factors, 1960–1962

(Millions of dollars)

Country	Exports			Services			Net Balance of Non-Compensatory Capital Movement and Grants			Total Capacity to Import		
	1960	1961	1962*	1960	1961	1962*	1960	1961	1962*	1960	1961	1962*
Argentina	1,079	964	1,210	−27	−75	−104	337	350	47	1,389	1,239	1,059
Bolivia	55	60	62	−7	−5	−3	27	31	55	75	86	114
Brazil	1,270	1,405	1,214	−346	−236	−148	170	394	158	1,094	1,563	1,224
Chile	481	443	484	−110	−116	−94	73	203	116	444	530	556
Colombia	495	477	492	−39	−37	−27	59	−16	54	515	424	519
Costa Rica	87	83	90	4	6	1	11	11	23	102	100	114
Dominican Republic	163	138	173	−15	−15	−11	−19	−15	33	129	108	195
Ecuador	148	133	140	−41	−41	−37	21	13	39	128	105	142
El Salvador	103	119	136	−9	−12	−13	9	13	6	103	120	129
Guatemala	116	114	114	−5	−7	−8	33	26	16	144	133	122
Haiti	38	32	42	6	—	2	7	15	−3	51	47	41
Honduras	64	74	82	10	−3	−2	−1	−7	4	73	64	84
Mexico	739	804	899	542	565	632	122	285	264	1,403	1,654	1,795
Nicaragua	64	70	89	−8	−14	−21	9	11	20	65	67	89
Panama	102	116	133	34	52	61	24	12	18	160	180	212
Paraguay	37	44	40	−1	−2	−2	12	17	14	48	59	52
Peru	445	511	556	−55	−43	−53	−4	24	46	386	492	549
Uruguay	129	175	153	21	19	7	51	−4	−20	201	190	140
Venezuela	2,454	2,500	2,565	−671	−824	−879	−417	−491	−553	1,366	1,185	1,133
Total for Latin America	8,069	8,262	8,674	−717	−788	−699	524	872	293	7,876	8,346	8,268

Sources: See Table 2–1.

TABLE 2–3. Latin America: Capacity to Import, Imports, and Balance-of-Payments Position, 1960–1962

(Millions of dollars)

Country	1960				1961				1962*			
	Total capacity to import	Imports CIF	Net total balance	Errors and omissions	Total capacity to import	Imports CIF	Net total balance	Errors and omissions	Total capacity to import	Imports CIF	Net total balance	Errors and omissions
Argentina	1,389	1,249	140	4	1,239	1,460	−221	−11	1,059	1,350	−291	…
Bolivia	75	80	−5	3	86	82	4	−2	114	104	10	−14
Brazil	1,094	1,462	−368	−43	1,563	1,460	103	−2	1,224	1,475	−251	−137
Chile	444	540	−96	34	530	614	−84	−47	556	554	2	71
Colombia	515	542	−27	−15	424	580	−156	−9	519	586	−67	−3
Costa Rica	102	112	−10	−1	100	109	−9	−2	114	116	−2	6
Dominican Republic	129	97	32	−25	108	81	27	−41	195	152	43	−31
Ecuador	128	126	2	−4	105	117	−12	−3	142	133	9	3
El Salvador	103	123	−20	−2	120	109	11	−18	129	125	4	4
Guatemala	144	142	2	4	133	137	−4	−2	122	140	−18	1
Haiti	51	43	8	−6	47	42	5	−3	41	45	−4	−2
Honduras	73	73	—	−1	64	66	−2	−1	84	74	10	2
Mexico	1,403	1,455	−52	−26	1,654	1,431	223	−247	1,795	1,451	344	−240
Nicaragua	65	66	−1	−3	67	59	8	−2	89	79	10	−2
Panama	160	171	−11	5	180	200	−20	13	212	224	−12	11
Paraguay	48	50	−2	−1	59	55	4	−1	52	47	5	−6
Peru	386	368	18	−4	492	461	31	4	549	533	16	−3
Uruguay	201	229	−28	1	190	208	−18	−36	140	230	−90	…
Venezuela	1,366	1,305	61	−370	1,185	1,218	−33	−11	1,133	1,178	−45	…
Total for Latin America	7,876	8,233	−357	−450	8,346	8,489	−143	−417	8,268	8,596	−328	−482

Sources: See Table 2–1.

earnings from coffee exports diminished by approximately $80 million. Had Brazil's net inflow of capital been as large as in 1961, it would have sufficed to cover the deficit on current account, but it was actually much lower in consequence of the combined influence of a decline in foreign direct investment, heavy amortization payments of the external debt, and some capital flight.[5]

The most conspicuous feature of Uruguay's external position during the last three years has been a chronic and very large deficit on current account. Both the low level of receipts and the high level of expenditures have been responsible for this situation. In 1962, a new decline in exports raised the deficit up to approximately 43 per cent of the current capacity to import. At the same time, the capital account registered a growing outflow of funds, which was most likely caused in part by the basic disequilibrium affecting Uruguay's current foreign transactions. In any case, the balance-of-payments crisis tended to become aggravated in a cumulative way during the first months of 1963, and in May, for the second time within four years, the Uruguayan peso was devalued, this time by 50 per cent.

Argentina and Chile have also experienced recurrent and serious difficulties in their foreign payments, hardly less acute than those of Brazil and Uruguay. Argentina's export returns in 1962, however, exceeded not only their exceptionally low level of 1961 but also each of the annual figures since 1956. Since the stagnation of exports has been a basic weakness of the country's external position during the last decade, the experience of 1962 can certainly be regarded as favorable.[6] Moreover, a simultaneous decline in purchases abroad helped to reduce by more than two-thirds the negative balance on merchandise account (from $496 million in 1961 to $140 million in 1962). On the other hand, the net outflow of funds on capital account contrasted sharply with the huge inflow of external financial resources that took place in 1961. The improvement in the trade balance has its negative aspects, however, insofar as the downturn in imports resulted from an absolute decline in over-all economic activity and from a serious lack of liquidity within the country. For several years, as in the case of Brazil, a large portion of Argentine imports has been financed with short- and medium-term

[5] For more details on capital movement see below, p. 85.
[6] The official data used in this *Survey* may indeed underestimate the 1962 improvement considerably. Estimates based on the physical volume of Argentina's principal exports and on international market quotations indicate that exports may actually have grown by more than another $100 million. Likewise, it is presumed that the IMF unit value figures for 1962 incorporate this bias, which may be related to the valuation of exports after the March, 1962, devaluation.

TABLE 2–4. Latin America: Current Capacity to Import,[a] Imports, and Balance on Current Account, 1960–1962

(Millions of dollars)

Country	1960			1961			1962*		
	Current capacity to import	Imports CIF	Balance on current account	Current capacity to import	Imports CIF	Balance on current account	Current capacity to import	Imports CIF	Balance on current account
Argentina	1,052	1,249	−197	889	1,460	−571	1,106	1,350	−244
Bolivia	48	80	−32	55	82	−27	59	104	−45
Brazil	924	1,462	−538	1,169	1,460	−291	1,066	1,475	−409
Chile	371	540	−169	327	614	−287	390	554	−164
Colombia	456	542	−86	440	580	−140	465	586	−121
Costa Rica	91	112	−21	89	109	−20	91	116	−25
Dominican Republic	148	97	51	123	81	42	162	152	10
Ecuador	107	126	−19	92	117	−25	103	133	−30
El Salvador	94	123	−29	107	109	−2	123	125	−2
Guatemala	111	142	−31	107	137	−30	106	140	−34
Haiti	44	43	1	32	42	−10	44	45	−1
Honduras	74	73	1	71	66	5	80	74	6
Mexico	1,281	1,455	−174	1,369	1,431	−62	1,529	1,451	80
Nicaragua	56	66	−10	56	59	−3	68	79	−11
Panama	136	171	−35	168	200	−32	194	224	−30
Paraguay	36	50	−14	42	55	−13	38	47	−9
Peru	390	368	22	468	461	7	503	533	−30
Uruguay	150	229	−79	194	208	−14	160	230	−70
Venezuela	1,783	1,305	478	1,676	1,218	458	1,686	1,178	508
Total for Latin America	7,352	8,233	−881	7,474	8,489	−1,015	7,975	8,596	−621

[a] The current capacity to import is the algebraic sum of commodity exports and the net service balance such as defined in footnote 1, this chapter.

Sources: See Table 2–1.

loans (see Table 2–2). In 1962, payments made for the amortization of these credits, as well as remittances of profits and interest, exerted strong pressures on the availabilities of foreign exchange. Furthermore, the maintenance until April, 1962, of an overvalued exchange rate [7] and, later, the growing political instability certainly played a role in the flight of domestic and foreign capital.[8]

While Chile's exports increased much less than those of Argentina and only regained their 1960 level, the external transactions recorded on capital account show for 1962 a net inflow of funds much smaller than in 1961 (see again Table 2–2). The negative errors of the balance-of-payments data, moreover, record an increase from $47 million to $71 million between these two years. Insofar as these errors and omissions represent a flight of capital, it can be assumed that total import capacity actually did not increase but was practically the same in 1961. In any case, Chile's imports decreased considerably in 1962. Accordingly, the negative balance of external transactions was reduced by approximately one-half in relation to the previous year; this result was obtained in spite of a slight rise in the rate of economic growth. Still, this was the third deficit in three consecutive years, and it amounted to almost 13 per cent of total import capacity. Throughout 1962, the external value of the Chilean escudo fell sharply in the free market, which had been created at the end of 1961 for certain invisible transactions. From October onward, this devaluation extended to the official exchange rates applying to exports and imports. More recently, however, the latter rate has tended to stabilize at approximately 1.9 escudos per dollar, against 1.05 a year earlier.

Colombia and Venezuela also suffered from three consecutive balance-of-payments deficits in the last three years and had to devalue their national currencies during this period. In Colombia, however, the external disequilibrium affecting the economy was less acute and the devaluation of much smaller proportions than in Chile, as was also the rate of growth of GNP. Although the increase in Colombia's exports in 1962, and the decline in net payments for services (see Table 2–2), were both of limited

---

[7] The rate of exchange was as follows:

	1959	1960	1961	1962 1st q.	1962 2nd q.	1962 3rd q.	1962 4th q.
Pesos per dollar	83	83	83	83	135	129	134

In the first quarter of 1962 the Central Bank intervened massively on the foreign exchange market.

[8] To some extent the flight of domestic capital might have been carried out through the undervaluation of export returns referred to in footnote 6.

size, together they contributed to reduce noticeably the negative balance on current account. Moreover, the net inflow of private capital rose in the last year, and the balance of official capital movements turned from negative to positive, mainly because of an extension in the period of repayment of some heavy external debts and an increase in disbursements on authorized loans. While all these circumstances determined a decline in 1962 in the over-all balance-of-payments deficit, a downward adjustment of the external value of the Colombian peso was carried out in November as a more basic step toward external equilibrium. Within the framework of a multiple-exchange system, this devaluation mainly affected the selling and buying rates other than those applying to coffee exports.

In Venezuela, the partial devaluation of the bolivar goes back to mid-1960. Together with some direct trade restrictions, it has contributed considerably to the cutting down of the foreign deficit from the very high figures of 1959 and early 1960. As exports rose in 1962 and imports were somewhat lower than in 1961, the usual surplus on merchandise account amounted to $1,387 million, against $1,282 million the preceding year. The increase in gross export receipts, however, was almost completely offset by a corresponding rise in remittances of profits accruing from foreign direct investment in petroleum and mining. The flight of domestic capital apparently decreased considerably,[9] but, on the other hand, a rather large amount of disinvestment by foreign enterprises continued to take place in the petroleum sector.[10] Moreover, heavy repayments were made on loan accounts, mainly for the amortization of compensatory and short-term loans received in previous years. As a result, the net outflow of funds on capital account continued to be very large, and the balance-of-payments deficit—however small in relative terms—was practically the same as in 1961 (see Table 2–3).

In several other Latin American countries, the balance-of-payments positions, though not basically weak, have tended to be rather unstable from one year to another. Among these countries only one, Ecuador, devalued its currency during the 1960–62 period.[11] Honduras, Nicaragua, Panama, and Paraguay practically succeeded in balancing their foreign transactions in 1962. Bolivia, Guatemala, and Haiti, on the other hand, registered a worsening in their external positions in relation to 1961. For

---

[9] See *Memoria del Banco Central de Venezuela* for 1962, page 16.

[10] It may be, however, that misreporting of repatriated profits partly produced this result so that the capital outflow is overstated at the same time as the negative balance on service account.

[11] This devaluation was carried out in 1961.

several years, these three Latin American countries have relied heavily upon foreign grants for paying their imports. In both Guatemala and Haiti, the amount of such grants declined considerably in 1962. In Bolivia, official donations, as well as the net inflow of capital, actually increased in the last year. But these additional resources were not large enough to finance the extraordinary rise in imports, and the balance of payments of the country turned from positive to slightly negative. On the other hand, between 1961 and 1962, Costa Rica, the Dominican Republic, Ecuador, and El Salvador recorded a shift from a deficit to a surplus in their foreign payments. While in 1961 purchases abroad by the first three countries had failed to adjust downward to the fall in noncompensatory foreign-exchange receipts, in 1962 the reverse occurred: the increase in imports lagged behind the rise in import capacity. In El Salvador, the sustained growth of merchandise exports since 1960 has been the main factor responsible for reducing the foreign deficit in 1961 and determining a surplus in 1962.

Although Mexico's balance of payments has also been unstable during the last decade, the cycle of its fluctuations has tended to be longer than in the above-mentioned countries. In the long run, moreover, Mexico's external position has been much more favorable than that of other Latin American countries of comparable economic size, such as Argentina and Brazil. The last foreign-exchange crisis in Mexico occurred in 1954 and resulted in a devaluation of the peso. A period of strengthening of the balance of payments followed, but this trend was reversed from 1957 onward. During the last three years, however, a marked improvement has again taken place in the country's external position; the foreign deficit declined substantially between 1960 and 1961 and turned to a surplus in 1962. Among the positive factors contributing to this have been the increasing diversification of merchandise exports, the steady growth of tourism receipts, the large amount of foreign loans obtained from private and official sources, and the successes achieved in substituting imports by domestic production without causing strong inflationary pressures. On the other hand, erratic movements of foreign direct investment and domestic capital, increases in remittances of profits, fluctuations in agricultural output for export, and falls or stagnation in primary products prices have all had an adverse impact on Mexico's import capacity. In 1962, however, there was an upturn in cotton sales and the receipts from tourism continued to rise, while the value of imports was practically the same as in 1961. As a result, the current account of the balance of payments recorded a surplus for the first time since 1951. The positive balance of the external transactions on capital account, however, although relatively large, was smaller than in the previous year because loan disbursements from foreign sources were offset to some extent by an increase in the outflow of short-term capital over the last two years, during which period over-all economic growth also slackened.

This decline in the rate of development of total output may, in turn, be regarded as one of the factors in the improvement of the balance-of-payments position insofar as it has been responsible for the relative stagnation of imports.

Like most of the other Latin American countries, Peru was unable during the fifties to escape foreign-payments difficulties and avoid a loss in the external value of its currency. In the more recent past, however, its external situation has been exceptionally good. Three consecutive and large increases in Peruvian imports took place, beginning in 1960, without affecting the external equilibrium of the national economy. In fact, the rise in import capacity was large and steady enough to make it possible to obtain a balance-of-payments surplus in these three years. It must be pointed out that the financing of additional imports did not stem from an excessive rise in foreign indebtedness but rather from the upward trend of Peru's foreign-exchange receipts, caused, in turn, by the growth of increasingly diversified exports. Repayments on external loans were made regularly, and remittances of profits and interests did not show any substantial changes between 1960 and 1962. There was, however, some flight of Peruvian capital, particularly in mid-1962. This outflow of funds, which can be attributed mainly to noneconomic considerations, did not permanently affect Peru's external position adversely because of the rapid increase in foreign-exchange receipts. As far as the prospects for the near future are concerned, however, it is unlikely that exports will continue to grow at quite the same rate as in past years. In particular, the recent and very large increases in the sales of Peruvian fish meal, which started from a very low level in absolute terms, are not likely to continue indefinitely. There are, however, prospects of substantial increases in iron ore and potash exports.

NONCOMPENSATORY CAPITAL MOVEMENTS

The net flow of noncompensatory capital into Latin America recorded a downturn in 1962 after two years of successive increases. This decline in autonomous financial receipts[12] amounted to several hundred million dollars in absolute terms and reduced by more than three-fourths the 1961 figure (see Table 2–5). It explains, moreover, why the region's foreign deficit rose in 1962 in spite of a marked improvement in the current account of the balance of payments. The total flow of capital, including the changes in liabilities on compensatory accounts,[13] was substantially higher than the autonomous financial receipts during the last three years (see Table 2–6). Furthermore, in 1962 the net inflow of external resources on compensatory accounts was greater than on those of a noncompensatory nature and not much smaller than in the previous year. Nevertheless, the total flow of capital decreased by about one-half in relation to 1961.

Several important qualifications must be made, however, concerning the true meaning of these recent changes. As pointed out above, the overall figures for Latin America in fact cover divergent trends, as far as the various countries and items of the capital account are concerned. First, the fall in autonomous financial receipts of Latin America reflects primarily the unfavorable experiences of a few countries, such as Argentina and Brazil, which heavily influence the region's total. Second, the decline in the gross inflow of noncompensatory capital was of a lesser magnitude than the increase recorded by the gross outflow, which was considerable as a result of heavy amortization payments and a rise in the recorded flight of Latin American capital. Third, insofar as the errors

[12] Including donations. The data available at this time, as well as the method used in estimating the balance of payments of some countries (see footnote 1 of this chapter and the sources for Table 2–1), do not allow for separating donations from capital movement for Latin America as a whole. The decline indicated above and in Table 2–5 refers to the region's total, also shown in column 5 of Table 2–4 (net balance of capital movements and grants). Since private donations are relatively small and stable, it can be assumed that they did not contribute significantly to the over-all change in the net balance of capital movements and grants between 1961 and 1962. An estimate of private donations is given in Table 2–7, together with data on the composition of capital movements. Table 2–7 also includes official data on grants made by the United States Government. These grants represent almost the totality of the official donations made to Latin America.

[13] This total excludes assets on compensatory accounts, since they represent the reserves of international means of payments at the permanent disposal of the national monetary authorities. On the other hand, liabilities on compensatory accounts include deferred import payments. Indeed, the nonpayment of due commercial debts implies external financing, although it does not necessarily constitute a loan made voluntarily by the creditor country and certainly does not improve the external credit of the debtor country. As will be shown below (p. 112), this unorthodox method of financing a balance-of-payments deficit regained some importance in 1962.

TABLE 2-5. Latin America: Net Balances on the Main Accounts of Foreign Payments, 1960–1962

(Millions of dollars)

Item	1960	1961	1962*
Balance on current account	−881	−1,015	−621
Net over-all balance of noncompensatory capital and grants	524	872	293
Errors and omissions	−450	−417	−482
Compensatory accounts	807	560	810

Source: See Tables 2–2, 2–3, and 2–4.

and omissions have corresponded to unrecorded flight of financial resources, it must be added that in 1962 there was only a slight rise in the negative balance on this account. Last, the net inflow in 1962 of noncompensatory official capital and donations from the United States was practically the same as in 1961, and the financial contribution of international organizations actually increased.

TABLE 2-6. Latin America: Total Flow of Capital,[a] 1960–1962

(Millions of dollars)

Item	1960	1961	1962*
A. Net flow of noncompensatory capital and grants	524	872	293
B. Changes in total liabilities on compensatory accounts	845	521	396
Total capital, A + B	1,369	1,393	689

[a] For the definition of the total flow of capital, see footnote 13, this chapter.
Source: See Tables 2–1 and 2–2.

Loans and grants made by the United States Government now constitute the most important factor on the credit side of the capital account. This role had been played before by United States private capital, the importance of which has also recently tended to decline in absolute terms. Because of the lack of detailed data, movements of private and official capital from other sources, as well as the transactions related to Latin American capital, must be grouped under the residual item "other capital" (see Table 2–7). While the wide fluctuations in this item used to be partly the consequence of the erratic movements registered by Latin American private assets, its considerably negative balance in 1962 reflected also the heavy amortization payments made by Argentina and Brazil to creditor countries, especially in Western Europe, as well as a decline in the gross inflow of private capital from countries other than the United States.

Official Loans and Grants

The United States Contribution. While the United States' noncompensatory contribution in 1961 was characterized mostly by a very large increase in its amount in relation to the previous year, in 1962 it underwent changes mainly in its structure; in 1962 it totaled almost $500 million, practically the same as in 1961. There were, however, considerable increases in official grants and loan disbursements by the Agency for International Development (AID), and to a lesser extent by the Social Progress Trust Fund, and sharp declines in those made by the Export-Import Bank of Washington (EXIMBANK) and under Public Law 480 (see Table 2–8). Since AID is specifically designed to meet the needs of underdeveloped countries, its growing importance as a lending institution constitutes a positive step toward a sound financing of economic growth in Latin America.[14] Official grants, too, are a valuable contribution, especially when they provide basic resources to countries whose foreign-exchange receipts are not even sufficient to finance current imports of raw materials and essential consumer goods.

The recent changes, first in the amount, and then in the composition, of the actual flow of United States official capital into Latin America are part of the international program tending to give substance to the Charter of Punta del Este. Even if the compensatory credits are added, however, disbursements by the United States Government in 1962 still were substantially below the $1 billion level which is to be its average annual financial contribution to the Alliance.[15] Moreover, the net total disbursed under grants and noncompensatory and compensatory capital declined by approximately $130 million between 1961 and 1962 (see again Table 2–8). On the other hand, the total amount of official loans and grants authorized by the United States rose from $380 million in 1959/60 to $982 million in 1960/61, $1,100 million in 1961/62, and approximately $984 million in 1962/63.[16] An essential condition for a

---

[14] Low interest rates, amortization at long term (and in some cases in the currency of the debtor country), as well as a wide range of economic and social purposes, are the main features of the loans granted by the Agency for International Development.

[15] See speech by Secretary of the Treasury, the Hon. C. Douglas Dillon, on September 11, 1961, in Los Angeles cited in Inter-American Development Bank presentation to IA-ECOSOC Special Commission IV in San José, Costa Rica, July, 1963.

[16] Report of the First Annual Review of the Alliance for Progress, 87th U.S. Congress, Second Session, and unpublished information from the Agency for International Development.

further rise in the United States' official disbursements has therefore been laid down for the years to come. In turn, the fulfillment of other conditions—such as the improvement of administrative machinery and the implementation of structural reforms and development plans in the

TABLE 2–7. Latin America: Composition of Noncompensatory Capital Movements, 1960–1962

(Millions of dollars)

Item	1960	1961	1962
A. Grants and noncompensatory capital from the United States Government (net total)	245	504	492
B. Direct investments and transactions in foreign securities from United States private sources (net total)	189	195	3
C. Financial transactions with international institutions (net total)	5	−10	70
D. Other capital (net total)[a]	198	294	−152
E. Total noncompensatory capital and official grants (A + B + C + D)	637	983	413
F. Private donations (net total)	−113	−111	−120
G. Net over-all balance of noncompensatory capital and grants (E + F)	524	872	293

[a] The item "Other capital" includes noncompensatory private loans from the United States, noncompensatory transactions with other countries on private and official account, and short-term capital movements, including privately owned assets of Latin Americans.

Sources and method: Line A: United States balance of payments published by the U.S. Department of Commerce in *Survey of Current Business*, June, 1961; June, 1962; and June, 1963. In adding up grants and loans, the compensatory loans by the Export and Import Bank of Washington, the United States Treasury Department, and the United States subscriptions to the Inter-American Development Bank have been subtracted. The net disbursements under the compensatory loans totaled −$45 million, $256 million, and $142 million for 1960, 1961, and 1962, respectively.

Line B: U.S. Department of Commerce, *Survey of Current Business*, June, 1961; June, 1962; and June, 1963. The 1962 figure excludes a $75 million bond issue floated by the Inter-American Development Bank in the United States. See pages 101 and 106.

Line C: Figures taken from Inter-American Development Bank, *Annual Report*, 1961 and 1962; International Development Association, *Statements of Loans and Credits*, December, 1960, 1961, and 1962; IMF, *International Financial Statistics*, issues of February, 1961, 1962, and 1963, for the loans by the International Finance Corporation and by the International Bank for Reconstruction and Development.

Line D: Residual figures equal to: [E − (A + B + C)], see footnote [a] of this table.

Line E: Figures on this line are equal to "Net over-all balance of noncompensatory capital and official grants" (line G) minus "Private donations" (line F).

Line F: These consolidated figures for Latin America as a whole have been calculated from IMF's *Balance of Payments Yearbook* for each individual country for 1960 and 1961. The regional figure for 1962 is a preliminary estimate.

Line G: Taken from Table 2–6.

TABLE 2-8. Latin America: Composition of Official Capital Receipts and Grants from the United States Government, 1960-1962

(Millions of dollars)

Item	1960	1961	1962*
A. Official grants by the United States Government[a]	119	167	194
B. Loans by the Agency for International Development (net disbursements)	25	107	186
C. Loans from the Social Progress Trust Fund administered by the Inter-American Development Bank (net disbursements)	—	1	22
D. Loans under Public Law 480 (net disbursements)	28	78	33
E. Development loans by the Export-Import Bank (net disbursements)		113	32
F. Other official capital from the United States Government (net)	25	38	25
G. Total grants and noncompensatory capital from the United States Government (A + B + C + D + E + F)	245	504	492
Other Capital			
Compensatory loans by the Eximbank and the United States Treasury (net total)	−45	256	142
United States subscriptions to the Inter-American Development Bank	80	110	60
Net grand total taken from official U.S. balance of payments	280	870	694

[a] Excluding military grants.

Sources and notes on method: Line A: Figures taken from the United States balance of payments published by the U.S. Department of Commerce in *Survey of Current Business*, June, 1961; June, 1962; and June, 1963. Besides grants under the American Aid Program, this item includes grants under Public Law 480, Title I, as well as small amounts (approximately $13 million annually) of pension payments to Americans residing in Latin America. See Table 2-9, note [a].

Lines B and D: From the U.S. Department of Commerce, *Foreign Grants and Credits by the U.S. Government*, calendar years 1960 and 1961. The figure of line B for 1962 was taken from the U.S. Department of State, *Report on Country Loans by the Agency for International Development*, December 1962. The figure of line D for 1962 was taken from *Foreign Grants and Credits*, December 31, 1962, advance release. Figures of line D differ from those carried on AID's reports, mainly because the latter include some transactions which may be considered as grants and also are related to the dates of actual delivery of food products.

Line C: Inter-American Development Bank, *Annual Report*, 1961 and 1962.

Line E: Export-Import Bank of Washington, *Statement of Loans and Credits*, December 31, 1960, 1961, and 1962.

Line F: Residual figures equal to: [G − (A + B + C + D)].

Line G: See sources and method of Table 2-7, line A.

Under heading of Other Capital:

First line: Eximbank's *Statement of Loans and Credits*, December, 1960, 1961, and 1962, and U.S. Treasury Department, *Treasury Bulletin*, May, 1960 and 1961 and April, 1962 and 1963.

(Continued)

CAPACITY TO IMPORT AND BALANCE OF PAYMENTS 91

TABLE 2-8 *Continued*

Second line: Inter-American Development Bank, *Annual Report*, 1961 and 1962.

Third line: These figures were obtained by adding up lines 28, 29, and 38 of the United States balance of payments published by the U.S. Department of Commerce in *Survey of Current Business*, June, 1961; June, 1962; and June, 1963. Of course, these figures appear with minus signs in the balance of payments of the United States. These figures include additional items not carried in the AID report, principally pensions and other transfers, U.S. subscription to the Inter-American Development Bank, U.S. Treasury compensatory loans and residual.

recipient countries—could contribute to narrowing the present gap between authorizations and disbursements.[17]

The upward trend in total grants continued in 1962, essentially because the size of grants—as distinguished from loans—of agricultural surpluses under Public Law 480 was more than twice as large as in 1961[18] (see Table 2-9). As in 1960 and 1961, however, grants under the Foreign Assistance Act (which created the Agency for International Development and incorporated into the United States Legislation the Alliance for Progress programs) accounted for most of the total unilateral transfers from the United States Government. Although Bolivia, by far the main recipient country, obtained more assistance from this source than in 1961, the amount of such grants for Latin America as a whole decreased in 1962.

Along with the increase in its disbursements, the amount of loans authorized by AID rose considerably in 1962 (see Table 2-10). Both developments repeated the experience of 1961 and also of 1960. Likewise, the amount of disbursements continued to increase more rapidly than that of new authorizations, the former having passed from one-quarter of the latter in 1960 to almost one-half in 1961 and noticeably more than one-half in 1962. The actual flow of funds mainly benefited Argentina, Brazil, Chile, Colombia, and the Dominican Republic, all of which have suffered from a serious lack of foreign exchange during the past years.

---

[17] Naturally the disbursement rate depends to a considerable degree on the nature of the project to be financed. Large dams or irrigation projects, for instance, which may take five or even more years to finish, may imply a disbursement rate of only 20 per cent (or less) per annum. This should be kept in mind also with regard to the comparable figures given below for the international financial institutions (see below, p. 99).

[18] While Argentina, a food-exporting country, did not receive any assistance under this heading, Brazil, Colombia, and Mexico were the main beneficiaries, in absolute terms, of such donations. In the two first countries, agricultural production is still basically insufficient to cover domestic needs, and in the latter the volume of some crops has been experiencing rather wide fluctuations from one year to another.

TABLE 2-9. Latin America: Grants by the United States Government under the American Aid Program and Public Law 480, Title III,[a] 1960–1962

(*Millions of dollars*)

	1960		1961		1962	
Country	American Aid	Public Law 480[a]	American Aid	Public Law 480[a]	American Aid	Public Law 480[a]
Argentina	0.6	—	0.8	—	1.3	—
Bolivia	10.6	0.2	18.2	0.4	23.4	1.4
Brazil	9.0	2.3	6.9	5.2	10.3	8.4
Chile	4.9	9.0	19.5	8.6	10.5	3.4
Colombia	2.6	3.2	3.1	6.7	4.1	10.9
Costa Rica	1.2	—	1.5	—	1.8	—
Dominican Republic	0.1	—	—	0.1	0.4	2.7
Ecuador	2.8	0.4	3.0	1.0	2.8	1.7
El Salvador	1.1	—	1.3	0.1	1.8	1.6
Guatemala	10.9	0.3	10.8	0.4	4.0	1.0
Haiti	5.2	0.1	12.2	0.6	3.1	0.8
Honduras	2.2	0.2	2.8	0.2	3.1	0.2
Mexico	0.8	1.3	0.7	3.5	0.8	8.9
Nicaragua	1.1	—	1.4	0.3	1.5	1.1
Panama	1.6	0.2	2.9	0.2	3.9	0.5
Paraguay	2.6	0.8	2.2	1.2	2.1	0.4
Peru	2.8	2.2	2.3	3.1	2.3	2.0
Uruguay	0.1	0.2	0.1	0.3	0.1	0.4
Venezuela	0.1	—	0.2	—	1.1	1.1
Total Latin America	60.3	20.4	89.9	31.9	78.4	46.5

[a] Totals differ from Table 2-8, line A, because official donations by the U.S. Government also include some other items, such as grants under Titles I and II of Public Law 480, grants under the Peace Corps Program, Inter-American Highway, regional donations (especially for Inter-American and Central American organizations), and pensions paid to residents in Latin America. A detailed breakdown by countries is not available as far as these other grants are concerned.

Sources: For Public Law 480, Title III, grants, Agency for International Development, *Operation Reports;* for American Aid grants, Agency for International Development, *Country Finance Reports,* various years.

Among these countries, Chile, which in 1962 began to put into effect its development plan and some structural reforms,[19] received the largest share of AID's total disbursements.

In 1962, also, the Social Progress Trust Fund raised its disbursements to Latin America substantially above the level of 1961 (see Table 2–11). This $394 million fund[20] is administered by the Inter-American Development Bank (IDB), which in less than two years of existence, has author-

[19] See Chapter 5 of this *Survey*.
[20] It is expected that in the course of 1963 its resources will be augmented.

ized total loans of $320 million to all the Latin American countries,[21] Cuba and Haiti excepted. Most of the money has been earmarked for construction of housing for low-income groups (48 per cent), sanitation and water supply (32 per cent), and land colonization (15 per cent). While at the end of 1962 the Fund's disbursements stood at about 10 per cent of authorized loans, by August 31, 1963, this proportion had risen to almost 18 per cent.

The decline in 1962 in net disbursements by the Eximbank offset the increase in those made by AID (see again Table 2–8). It resulted from a reduction in gross disbursements and a simultaneous increase in amortization payments. For Latin America as a whole, gross disbursements amounted to $203 million and amortization payments totaled $133 million, against $213 million and $100 million, respectively, in 1961. These changes at the regional level reflected mainly the declines in the net flow to Brazil and Chile and, to a lesser extent, those to Colombia and Mexico. In Peru, amortization payments exceeded gross disbursements for the third consecutive year, but the net disbursements made by the Eximbank to Argentina increased by approximately $8 million. Moreover, the amount of authorized loans for the region as a whole rose from $137 million to $203 million. In 1960 also an increase in total authorizations took place, and it was followed by a substantial rise in net disbursements in 1961. Conversely, the decline in disbursements which occurred in 1962 was preceded by a reduction in authorization in the year before. Thus, the actual amount of financial assistance given by the Eximbank in the 1960–62 period has been characterized by wide fluctuations from one year to another.

The same can be said with respect to disbursements made under Title I of Public Law 480 (see again Table 2–8). This law makes it possible for the United States Government to grant and also to lend to underdeveloped countries part of the local currency proceeds obtained through the export of agricultural surplus. Both the sales [22] and loans are made in the national currency of the recipient country. Within Latin America, Brazil and Chile have in the past received the largest share of such

---

[21] By mid-1963 this total had risen to $348 million.

[22] For Latin America as a whole, total sales agreements were as follows (in millions of dollars):

	1960	1961	1962	Fiscal Years 1961/62	1962/63
Total sales agreements[a]	95.5	99.5	212.3	156.5	185.4

[a] These figures exclude such estimated amounts of the local currency proceeds to be spent by the U.S. Government in the recipient country.

Source: Agency for International Development.

TABLE 2–10. Latin America: Loans Authorized and Net Disbursements by the Agency for International Development, 1960–1962

(Millions of dollars)

	\multicolumn{8}{c}{Fiscal years}							

	1960		1961		1962*		1961/62		1962/63	
Country	Loans authorized	Net disbursements	Loans authorized	Net disbursements	Loans authorized	Net disbursements	Loans authorized	Net disbursements	Loans authorized	Net disbursements
Argentina	—	3.3	6.0	7.3	39.0	19.9	19.9	1.0	96.4	20.4
Bolivia	—	0.3	7.3	0.3	7.6	3.2	7.6	21.8	18.3	2.8
Brazil	—	—	65.0	50.0	16.9	24.8	74.5	81.8	62.9	26.9
Chile	10.5	0.5	108.2	30.3	40.0	56.6	140.0	66.4	35.0	89.8
Colombia	25.0	—	—	1.5	90.0	37.7	30.0	35.6	87.2	36.3
Costa Rica	—	0.5	8.6	0.7	—	4.4	—	3.9	10.6	3.0
Dominican Republic	—	—	—	—	27.1	16.8	25.0	11.6	2.1	12.8
Ecuador	—	5.3	10.7	6.6	18.7	8.8	13.0	12.6	13.3	6.2
El Salvador	—	—	1.6	—	0.8	—	—	1.3	16.6	0.3
Guatemala	11.0	3.5	—	—	—	1.4	—[a]	6.6	0.7	1.7
Haiti	0.3	0.6	0.3	2.9	2.8	1.0	—	9.2	2.8[b]	0.4
Honduras	2.8	1.7	1.3	2.7	0.6	1.6	—	6.7	4.1[c]	2.3
Mexico	—	—	—	—	20.0	—	20.0	0.8	—	2.0
Nicaragua	2.5	0.2	7.6	0.4	0.9	1.8	0.9	2.5	1.0	2.0
Panama	10.3	5.4	2.5	0.5	6.0	2.3	—	4.3	6.0	1.7
Paraguay	—	2.3	7.1	0.7	0.1	2.1	−0.7	2.4	—	2.8
Peru	29.5	—	1.0	0.1	12.8	−0.8	17.6	2.9	—	2.6
Uruguay	—	1.0	—	3.2	—	2.3	—	3.6	6.0	6.9
Venezuela	5.0	—	10.0	0.1	40.0	2.2	10.1	1.1	30.0	4.8
Total Latin America	96.9	24.6	237.2	107.3	323.3	186.1	357.9	276.1	393.0	225.7

[a] Less than $50,000.
[b] In process of being deobligated.
[c] Includes $0.6 million IAPSP funds approved in FY1962, but included as part of FY1963 program.

Sources: For 1960 and 1961, U.S. Department of Commerce, *Foreign Grants and Credits*, calendar years 1960 and 1961. For 1962, U.S. Department of State, *Report on Country Loans*, December, 1962. For fiscal year 1961 and 1962, Agency for International Development, *U.S. Foreign Assistance and Assistance from International Organizations*, July 1, 1945—June 30, 1962, and unpublished information from AID.

TABLE 2-11. Latin America: Loans Authorized and Net Disbursements under the Social Progress Trust Fund, 1960–1962

(Millions of dollars)

Country	Fiscal years					
	1961		1962		1961/62	
	Loans authorized	Net disbursements	Loans authorized	Net disbursements	Loans authorized	Net disbursements
Argentina	—	—	35.0	—	5.0	—
Bolivia	—	—	6.5	—	—	—
Brazil	4.1	—	46.7	2.4	47.0	—
Chile	13.7	—	9.3	1.9	18.7	—
Colombia	22.8	—	8.5	3.8	22.8	1.8
Costa Rica	3.5	0.4	—	1.5	3.5	0.5
Dominican Republic	—	—	6.5	0.5	—	—
Ecuador	—	—	13.6	—	13.6	—
El Salvador	5.5	—	6.1	1.7	11.6	0.1
Guatemala	—	—	8.8	—	3.5	—
Haiti	—	—	—	—	—	—
Honduras	—	—	3.5	—	—	—
Mexico	—	—	13.6	—	10.6	—
Nicaragua	—	—	7.7	0.3	7.7	—
Panama	7.6	0.5	2.8	2.0	10.4	1.2
Paraguay	—	—	2.9	—	—	—
Peru	23.8	—	2.5	4.5	24.8	2.8
Uruguay	2.5	—	8.0	—	2.5	—
Venezuela	32.0	—	20.0	2.8	42.0	—
Central America (Regional)	—	—	2.9	—	...	...
Total Latin America	115.5	0.9	204.9	21.4	223.7	6.4

Country	1962/63	
	Loans authorized	Net disbursements
Argentina	30.0	3.1
Bolivia	10.5	4.3
Brazil	5.9	3.5
Chile	4.9	5.8
Colombia	8.5	2.5
Costa Rica	—	1.9
Dominican Republic	6.5	1.2
Ecuador	9.9	3.8
El Salvador	—	0.1
Guatemala	7.8	—
Haiti	—	0.2
Honduras	5.7	*a*
Mexico	8.0	1.7
Nicaragua	0.2	3.1
Panama	—	—
Paraguay	2.9	4.2
Peru	1.5	—
Uruguay	8.0	12.7
Venezuela	11.0	—
Central America (Regional)	...	...
Total Latin America	121.3	48.1

a Less than $50,000.

Sources: Inter-American Development Bank, *Annual Report,* 1961 and 1962. For fiscal years 1961/62 and 1962/63, Agency for International Development, *U.S. Foreign Assistance,* July 1, 1945—June 30, 1962 (Revised), and unpublished information from AID.

loans. In 1962, however, Brazil did not get any financial resources under Public Law 480, while in the previous years it had obtained almost $60 million. Accordingly, disbursements to Latin America as a whole declined by approximately $45 million.

International Agencies. Total net disbursements on loans from international agencies rose considerably in 1962 (see Table 2–12). This was the second increase in two years; it should be noted that in 1961 subscriptions to financial institutions had more than offset the foreign-exchange receipts on loans account while in 1962 the net balance of loans and subscriptions was positive and much larger than in 1960. At the end of December, 1962, the Inter-American Development Bank's cumulative figures for authorized loans totaled $290 million, while disbursements amounted to only $38 million (see Table 2–12 and 2–13). During 1963, however, the rate of loan utilization accelerated, and by the end of August disbursements on loans eligible for immediate utilization stood at more than 29 per cent. By the same date the IDB's total authorized loans were for the following purposes: industry, 36 per cent; agriculture, 35 per cent; water and sewerage, 12 per cent; electricity and

TABLE 2–12. Latin America: Composition of Official Capital Receipts from International Agencies, 1960–1962

(Millions of dollars)

Item	1960	1961	1962*
Inter-American Development Bank (net disbursements)	—	5.1	32.8
Social Progress Trust Fund[a]	(—)	(0.9)	(21.4)
International Bank for Reconstruction and Development (net disbursements)	28.7	55.1	94.3
International Development Association (net disbursements)	—	0.6	6.0
International Finance Corporation (net disbursements)	12.4	5.2	12.4
Total net disbursements	41.1	66.0	145.5
Subscriptions[b]	−36.0	−76.0	−75.0
Net balance of loans and subscriptions	5.1	−10.0	70.5

[a] Included in the total of Table 2–8.

[b] Subscriptions in foreign exchange only, the most part of which was to the Inter-American Development Bank.

Sources: IDB, *Annual Report*, 1961 and 1962. IMF, *International Financial Statistics*, February, 1963, for IBRD and IFC loans. International Development Association, *Statement of Loans and Credits*, December, 1961, and December, 1962.

TABLE 2-13. Latin America: Loans Authorized and Net Disbursements by the Inter-American Development Bank,[a] 1961-1962

(*Millions of dollars*)

Country	1961		1962	
	Loans authorized	Net disbursements	Loans authorized	Net disbursements
Argentina	29.9	0.2	8.1	4.5
Bolivia	14.5	2.3	2.6	4.9
Brazil	27.4	1.7	35.5	7.1
Chile	18.7	0.3	20.1	3.0
Colombia	13.3	0.1	8.5	2.8
Costa Rica	3.0	—	8.2	0.8
Dominican Republic	—	—	—	—
Ecuador	4.7	—	6.1	0.2
El Salvador	5.8	—	—	0.4
Guatemala	4.7	0.1	—	0.1
Haiti	3.5	—	—	0.3
Honduras	3.7	0.1	6.0	0.9
Mexico	15.2	—	6.8	4.3
Nicaragua	2.2	0.1	—	0.2
Panama	2.9	—	—	—
Paraguay	4.0	—	1.2	1.6
Peru	5.1	—	2.1	1.4
Uruguay	6.3	—	8.1	0.3
Venezuela	9.2	0.2	8.3	—
Total Latin America	174.1	5.1	121.5	32.8

[a] Loans from the Ordinary Capital and Special Fund are included; loans from the Social Progress Trust Fund are not included.

Source: Inter-American Development Bank, *Annual Report*, 1961 and 1962.

transport, 13 per cent; mining, 2 per cent; and reimbursable technical assistance, 2 per cent.

Both authorized loans and effective disbursements by the World Bank [23] expanded regularly during the last three years, the increase being particularly marked in 1962 (see Table 2-14). As in 1961, however, disbursements represented no more than 28 per cent of authorized loans. In relation to total foreign-exchange receipts, the largest amount of liquid funds made available by the World Bank was transferred to Colombia, Ecuador, Mexico, and Peru. In the period 1960-62 almost 97 per cent of

[23] The International Bank for Reconstruction and Development (IBRD) is more commonly known as the World Bank.

TABLE 2–14. Latin America: Loans Authorized and Net Disbursements by the International Bank for Reconstruction and Development, 1960–1962

(Millions of dollars)

	1960		1961		1962	
Country	Loans authorized	Net disbursements	Loans authorized	Net disbursements	Loans authorized	Net disbursements
Argentina	—	—	48.5	—	95.0	17.6
Bolivia	—	—	—	—	—	—
Brazil	—	6.8	—	17.4	—	7.9
Chile	—	4.5	6.0	3.1	—	5.4
Colombia	48.0	7.1	41.5	16.5	50.0	21.9
Costa Rica	2.0	0.6	17.3	1.8	—	4.1
Dominican Republic	—	—	—	—	—	—
Ecuador	—	8.8	—	5.6	—	4.4
El Salvador	3.9	0.5	—	1.2	—	1.1
Guatemala	—	−0.8	—	−1.3	—	−1.3
Haiti	—	0.6	—	0.2	—	−0.2
Honduras	8.8	2.5	—	1.2	—	3.3
Mexico	25.0	1.0	15.0	4.9	160.5	17.4
Nicaragua	12.5	−0.8	—	−0.7	—	0.1
Panama	7.2	—	—	0.7	4.0	2.4
Paraguay	—	−0.4	—	−0.5	—	−0.5
Peru	34.5	−1.9	10.0	5.2	—	9.2
Uruguay	—	0.2	—	—	18.5	−1.0
Venezuela	—	—	45.0	−0.2	—	2.5
Total Latin America	141.9	28.7	183.3	55.1	328.0	94.3

Sources: IMF, *International Financial Statistics*, February, 1959; February, 1960; February, 1961; February, 1962; and February, 1963. For fiscal years 1962 and 1963 see sources for Table 2–10.

total loans authorized by the World Bank were related to the development of transportation and electricity supply. Thus, the experience of recent years indicates that the World Bank continued to deal mainly with projects tending to remedy certain basic deficiencies in Latin America's economic infrastructure.

The International Finance Corporation (IFC) and the International Development Association (IDA), both of which are affiliated with the World Bank, also expanded their activities in their own specific fields. For the time being, however, the scale of such activities is much more limited than in the case of the IBRD (see again Table 2–12). Until now, assistance to private industrial enterprises by the IFC has benefited almost exclusively Latin American countries which are already at a relatively advanced stage of industrialization, such as Argentina, Brazil,

Chile, Colombia, and Mexico. On the other hand, six out of a total of eight loans granted to Latin American countries by the IDA in 1961 and 1962 went to the following countries, which are of relatively small economic size and at a stage of incipient industrialization: Costa Rica, El Salvador, Haiti, Honduras, Nicaragua, and Paraguay. At the end of December, 1962, loans authorized by IFC and IDA reached the cumulative figures of $65 million and $70 million, respectively.

Official Bilateral Contributions from Countries Other Than the United States. The net flow in 1961 of official capital and grants from Japan and OECD countries other than the United States increased considerably over 1960: from $6 million to $93 million [24] (see Table 2-15).

TABLE 2-15. Latin America: Net Flow of Official Capital[a] from Japan and OECD Member Countries, Excluding the United States, 1960-1962

(Millions of dollars)

Country or region	1960	1961	1962
Japan	9	80	—
Federal Republic of Germany	23	30	38
United Kingdom	−26	−1	—
Other OECD Countries, excluding the United States		−16	—
Total	6	93	...

[a] Net grants plus net loans, excluding export credits guaranteed by the governments of the lending countries.

Source: Statistics from the Development Department of the Organisation for Economic Co-operation and Development.

Japan's contribution was mainly responsible for the increase in 1961, accounting, in fact, for the bulk of the total. The net inflow of official capital from West Germany ranked second in importance, while net payments on this account were made to the United Kingdom and other OECD countries for the amortization of Latin American debts. The geographic distribution of total net receipts by destination was uneven, since in 1961 Brazil received over three-fourths of the total (see Table 2-16).

For 1962, the only figure available shows a small increase in West Germany's financial contribution (see again Table 2-15). Indirect evidence, however, makes it appear likely that the flow of capital from Japan declined. This country has been currently engaged in the financing

[24] The figure of $93 million, however, represented only 20 per cent of the financial receipts and donations obtained from the United States Government.

TABLE 2-16. Latin America: Net Flow of Official Capital from Japan and OECD Countries Other than the United States, by Recipient Countries

(Millions of dollars)

Country	1960	1961
Argentina	3.89	21.13
Bolivia	−0.39	0.08
Brazil	1.86	72.77
Central American Republics[a]	0.83	0.30
Chile	7.69	11.62
Colombia	−3.37	—
Ecuador	0.02	0.04
Mexico	3.02	2.64
Paraguay	3.03	0.66
Peru	−0.48	2.41
Uruguay	−0.15	0.23
Venezuela	−2.31	−18.99
Total Latin America	5.92	92.89

[a] Costa Rica, Cuba, Dominican Republic, El Salvador, Guatemala, Haiti, Honduras, Nicaragua, Panama.

Source: Statistics from the Development Department of the Organisation for Economic Co-operation and Development.

of part of the foreign-exchange costs related to the construction of a steelworks in Brazil (Usiminas). In 1961, this venture had been carried out at a quicker pace than before, and by the end of the year Japan had disbursed $75 million out of its original commitment of $100 million. Since the flow of Japanese official capital into Brazil amounted to $56 million in the same year, it would seem realistic to assume that a major part of this had served to finance the Usiminas project. It is uncertain, however, whether the venture is regarded statistically, in a strict sense, as a private direct investment or as an official transaction on loans account, since it involves the intervention of both the Japanese Government and a Japanese private firm. In any case, the disbursements related to the Usiminas project declined in 1962, and, because of their relatively heavy weight in the previous year, it may be presumed that the total flow of official and private capital from Japan has also decreased.

Some Western European governments give indirect aid to developing countries in the form of official guaranties applying to private export credits.[25] It can be anticipated that the credits from West Germany to Latin America were reduced by $90 million between 1961 and 1962.

[25] For a more detailed discussion of these transactions, see the next subsection of this chapter.

In general, the total flow of financial resources from OECD members to all developing countries declined in 1962.[26] According to data compiled by the OECD, this decline has mainly reflected the changes which occurred in the capital movement from Japan and West Germany. In view of the relatively important role played by the two latter countries in Latin America during recent years, such global developments further suggest a weakening in the effective financial aid given to the region by the industrial countries other than the United States. As far as new authorizations in 1962 are concerned, the $150 million loan agreed upon by the Governments of Mexico and France should be singled out; it constitutes the first French official credit granted for long-term development purposes to a Latin American country.

In the period 1960–61, new loans to Latin America authorized by countries with centrally planned economies benefited Cuba only. They reached $357 million, out of a world total of $2,157 million. In the same period, disbursements went to Argentina, Brazil, and Cuba for $27 million, $2 million, and $30 million, respectively.[27] No information is available for 1962.

Private Capital

The United States Contribution. The total flow in 1962 of United States private capital into Latin America amounted to $153 million,[28] whereas the minimum projected amount needed for Alliance purposes has been estimated at $300 million annually.[29] Moreover, even if the IDB's bond issue is added, net foreign-exchange receipts from that source decreased considerably in relation to 1960 and 1961; they had been approximately $500 million in each of those years. The recent decline in the flow of United States private capital affected not only short- and

[26] Total figures are as follows (in millions of dollars):

	Total DAC Countries	United States	Other Countries
1961	7,841	4,246	3,595
1962	7,732	4,242	3,490

Source: OECD.

[27] Source: OECD.

[28] United States balance of payments with Latin America in U.S. Department of Commerce, *Survey of Current Business,* June, 1963. The global figure referred to in the text includes an unknown amount of compensatory capital but excludes the bond issue placed by the Inter-American Development Bank on the United States market. This bond issue certainly raised the total amount of United States resources contributing to the financing of Latin America's development in the near future, but it was not directly and readily available to Latin America in 1962.

[29] See footnote 15, this chapter.

long-term loans but also—and relatively more so—total investment (direct investment plus portfolio securities). Since the latter is by definition an autonomous financial transaction, most probably the amount of noncompensatory funds also declined in 1962.

The fall in total investment at the regional level was due exclusively to certain unfavorable changes in the amount of direct investment (see Table 2–17). And if the balance on the latter account turned from positive to slightly negative, it was mainly because of the developments which occurred in one economic branch in one country: investment in the petroleum sector of Venezuela alone amounted to $167 million, that is, almost equal to the regional figure recorded by total investment in 1961 [30] (see Table 2–18). Only two other countries—Guatemala and Panama—

TABLE 2–17. Latin America: Direct Investments and Transactions in Securities by United States Private Capital, 1960–1962

(Millions of dollars)

Item	1960	1961	1962
Direct investments	95	173	−32
New issues of foreign securities	107	18	27[a]
Redemptions	−20	−9	−5
Transactions in foreign securities	7	13	13
Total	189	195	3

[a] See note for line B on Table 2–7.

Source: U.S. Department of Commerce, *Survey of Current Business*, June, 1963.

registered a negative balance on this account. In the case of Panama, it is possible that for fiscal reasons the outflow of funds has covered some transfer of profits.

Inflow of new liquid funds into the petroleum sector in Argentina ceased almost completely in 1962, after having contributed to a rapid expansion of domestic output in the preceding years. But, on the other hand, United States firms raised their financial contribution to manufacturing industries in such a way that the total amount of new direct investment in Argentina declined only moderately in relation to 1961 and still constituted the highest country figure within Latin America. Since current economic prospects in this country were unsatisfactory, a

[30] See, however, footnote 10, this chapter, for a possible qualification.

TABLE 2-18. Latin America: Net Inflow of United States Private Capital for Direct Investment, 1960-1962

(Millions of dollars)

Country	Total 1960	Total 1961	Total 1962	Mining and smelting 1961	Mining and smelting 1962	Petroleum 1961	Petroleum 1962	Manufacturing 1961	Manufacturing 1962	Other industries 1961	Other industries 1962
Argentina	70	104	94	x	x	52	x	43	73	9	21
Brazil	83	7	14	1	8	16	−15	−2	10	−8	11
Chile	2	xx	13	−14	4	x	x	4	−1	10	10
Colombia	15	−7	21	x	x	−7	26	x	1	x	−6
Dominican Republic	xx	xx	xx	−2	x	1	x	x	x	1	xx
Guatemala	−3	−5	−2	x	x	2	xx	1	x	−8	−2
Honduras	−11	−5	3	−1	x	1	x	—	x	−5	3
Mexico	56	45	30	x	−5	16	16	18	23	11	−4
Panama	30	12	−31	—	—	4	2	2	−2	6	−31
Peru	7	14	14	19	6	−12	7	x	8	7	7
Uruguay	xx	xx	2	—	x	−1	x	xx	xx	1	2
Venezuela	−150	xx	−194	24	x	−44	−167	9	xx	11	−27
Other Countries	−4	8	4	4	−16	4	30	1	1	−1	−11
Total	95	173	−32	31	−3	32	−115	76	113	34	−27

x Included in "Other industries."
xx Less than 500,000 dollars.

Source: U.S. Department of Commerce, Survey of Current Business, August, 1963.

factor partly responsible for the expanded flow of foreign capital into manufacturing might have been the lack of internal liquidity which resulted from official restrictions on bank credit. There was also an increase in direct industrial investment in Peru, as well as in Brazil and Mexico, in spite of the stricter domestic regulations applied to foreign capital in the two latter countries. Thus the long-term prospects offered by relatively large and expanding internal markets apparently continued to play an important role in investment decisions. It is noteworthy, however, that in the last two years the new direct investments made in Brazil by the United States have represented only a small fraction of what they had been during the 1957–60 period ($50 million as an annual average). Moreover, the problem of indemnifying certain recently expropriated foreign-owned public utilities remains unsolved.

In several of the Latin American countries, economic sectors other than manufacturing attracted new direct investments from the United States in 1962. A certain amount of liquid funds on this account went into the petroleum sector in Colombia and into mining and smelting in Chile. The same can be said about direct investments in "other industries"[31] in Argentina, Brazil, Chile, Honduras, Peru, and Uruguay.

For Latin America as a whole, data from the United States balance of payments[32] show a substantial increase in 1962 in the purchases of securities—almost all of them new issues—which would partly offset the decline in direct investment (see again Table 2–17). In 1960, also, the inflow of United States portfolio capital reached $100 million, essentially as a result of a sale of some $75 million worth of Mexican bonds.[33] For 1962, however, United States Treasury statistics on net securities transactions do not show regional figures appreciably higher than those of 1961.[34] While net sales of bonds in the case of Mexico amounted to $13 million against $19 million in 1961, they increased from $6 million to $8 million in Venezuela and from $1 million to $3 million in Panama. Other Latin American countries recorded negative balances on this account; but, in general, net payments for the amortization of bond issues were of small importance, the highest figure for an individual country, Brazil, not having exceeded $4 million. Likewise, net transactions in stocks were of limited importance in 1962, as the main

---

[31] Other industries include trade, banking, public utilities, etc.

[32] See U.S. Department of Commerce, *Survey of Current Business,* June, 1963.

[33] See International Monetary Fund, *Balance of Payments Yearbook,* Vol. 14 (Mexico—footnote to item 12.2 of Table 1).

[34] See U.S. Treasury, *Treasury Bulletin,* July, 1963 (Capital Movements, Section II, Tables 7 and 8).

recipient country, Mexico, received no more than $1.4 million from the sale of domestic shares to United States residents. In fact, the principal factor responsible for the increase in the purchase of securities as shown by the United States balance-of-payments data was the bond issue placed by the Inter-American Development Bank on the United States market.[35] This means that $75 million out of the total of $102 million were not directly transferred to Latin American countries but rather served to increase the IDB's loanable funds. As far as the IDB's loans authorized and actual disbursements in 1962 are concerned, they are part of the movements of official capital which have already been taken into account above (p. 88).

Financial receipts from other United States private sources totaled $149 million in 1962, against $259 million in 1961. Net disbursements on long-term loans declined more than the net inflow of short-term capital. Indeed, long-term banking claims on Latin America declined by $45 million between December, 1961, and December, 1962; that is, a net outflow of funds from the region actually took place on this account.[36] Even though long-term claims on Mexico increased by $23 million, in the case of Brazil and Venezuela they declined by $11 million and $79 million, respectively, in part as a result of amortization payments on private compensatory loans granted in previous years.[37] Since, however, the United States balance of payments shows a net flow of "other long-term capital" to Latin America amounting to $38 million, it appears that in 1962 the region received $87 million from United States private sources other than the banking system.

On the other hand, net movements of short-term domestic capital, such as shown in the United States balance of payments, are almost equal to the net variations in short-term banking claims on Latin America, which are recorded by the *Treasury Bulletin*'s statistics. The corresponding data from these two sources indicate a net inflow of funds into the region amounting to $111 million and $97 million, respectively. Approximately $65 million went to Uruguay and $50 million more to Chile, both

---

[35] See pages 96–99, this chapter. In the balance of payments of the United States published by the *Survey of Current Business*, subscriptions by the U.S. Government to IDB are not entered into the transactions with international institutions, either, but are included in the flow of United States official capital into Latin America.

[36] See *Treasury Bulletin*, various issues.

[37] While disbursement of compensatory loans provides, a posteriori, a temporary remedy for insufficient import capacity, the amortization of such loans produces, a priori, a reduction of that capacity in subsequent years, as it constitutes a current financial obligation of the borrowing country.

of which financed their external deficit mainly through an increase in their liabilities abroad.[38] A substantial part of the credits they have received from United States private banks were certainly aimed at compensatory financing and should therefore, strictly speaking, be excluded from the total flow of *autonomous* capital from United States private sources.

Flow of Private Capital from Western European Countries and Japan. Private export loans constitute the major component of this flow in the case of Latin America. They may or may not be guaranteed by the governments of the exporting countries, and they include the so-called medium-term suppliers credits. In recent years, the guaranteed loans have tended to be distributed more evenly between lenders and borrowers than the direct official contributions from Western Europe and Japan (see Tables 2–19 and 2–20). To some extent, this might be explained by the fact that such financial transactions are closely linked with current developments and trade promotion. On the other hand, between 1960 and 1961 the flow of credits had recorded noticeable changes both in several donor and in some recipient countries, changes that can in part be explained by fluctuations in the rate of delivery—and in the rate of utilization—of the goods imported for investment purposes. Net disbursement to Latin America as a whole, however, declined but very slightly.

It was noted above that in 1962 there occurred a fall in the credits granted by West Germany. This country had previously been the main lending partner of Latin America and had contributed to maintaining the regional total at a steady level in 1961. It is likely, therefore, that the financial resources received by Latin America on this account will show a decrease for 1962.

Incomplete information points to an equally unfavorable change in the amount of private direct investment during the last year. In Brazil, where Western European and Japanese firms had concentrated most of their Latin American ventures in the fifties, total direct foreign investment fell from $147 million in 1961 to $69 million in 1962, notwithstanding a small increase in the inflow of funds from the United States. Besides, direct investment made by West Germany in all Latin American countries went down to $17 million, and it may be that Japanese firms have also reduced their transfer of capital to Latin America.[39] Mexico and Panama, however, might have enjoyed an increase in the flow of

---

[38] See page 112 on compensatory financing.
[39] See page 99, above, for the considerations leading to this conclusion.

TABLE 2-19. Latin America: Private Export Credits Guaranteed by the Governments of the OECD Member Countries, Excluding the United States, 1960-1962

(*Millions of dollars*)

Country	1960	1961	1962
Belgium	5	54	...
France	56	12	...
Germany	71	120	30
Italy	43	−2	...
Japan	6	35	...
United Kingdom	9	−1	...
Others	56	18	...
Total	246	236	...

Source: OECD, *The Flow of Financial Resources to Developing Countries in 1961* (Paris), 14 March 1963; and *Memorandum of Germany to the Development Assistance Committee*, April 10, 1963.

TABLE 2-20. Latin America: Net Flow of Guaranteed Private Export Credits

(*Millions of dollars*)

Country	1960	1961
Argentina	36.61	46.43
Bolivia	−1.56	1.23
Brazil	105.12	70.51
Central America and Caribbean[a]	21.71	18.31
Chile	21.01	7.33
Colombia	−1.76	1.82
Ecuador	−1.27	2.80
Mexico	43.90	43.08
Paraguay	−0.01	−0.22
Peru	−2.48	44.70
Uruguay	15.57	4.38
Venezuela	10.55	−3.65
Total Latin America	237.39	236.72

[a] Costa Rica, Cuba, Dominican Republic, El Salvador, Guatemala, Haiti, Honduras, Nicaragua, Panama.

Source: Development Department of the Organization for Economic Co-operation and Development, May, 1963.

funds recorded on this account. While the United States contribution in Mexico was appreciably smaller in 1962 than in 1961 and turned from positive to negative in Panama,[40] the total amount of direct investment made by all foreign countries remained at the same level in the first country and increased by almost $2 million in the latter.[41]

Movements of Latin American Capital and the Repayment of the External Debt. The net outflow of Latin American capital was of considerable importance in 1962 and probably larger than in 1961. Although there is only indirect and incomplete statistical evidence of such developments, they can be reconciled with the well-known existence of noneconomic explanatory factors, such as internal political instability and the uncertainties of the world situation during the last year. On the other hand, basic economic conditions—especially the increase in exports in many Latin American countries and the continued strength of the industrial sector—apparently would have justified less unfavorable developments in this field.

For Latin America as a whole, the decline in the net inflow of *foreign* capital does not suffice to explain the fall in the total net balance of autonomous financial receipts which results from comparing the respective movements of net current transactions and total compensatory financing[42] (see again Tables 2–5, 2–6, and 2–7). Secondly, private short-term assets of Latin America in United States banks increased by $112 million against $97 million in 1961 (see Table 2–21; if Brazil is excluded from the regional total, the corresponding figures are $165 million and $94 million, respectively). Thirdly, the negative balance of errors and omissions rose from $414 million to $462 million. Conversely, errors and omissions in the United States balance of payments with Latin America increased from $97 million to $150 million. Of course, these figures must not be related exclusively to the unregistered flight of capital. Nevertheless, according to a long-term study made by the United Nations

---

[40] According to the U.S. Balance of Payments published in *Survey of Current Business*, August, 1963. See page 101, above, for a possible qualification.

[41] Available figures on direct investment in Mexico and Panama are as follows:

	1961	1962
	(Millions of dollars)	
Mexico	119	116
Panama	6.2	8.0

Sources: For Mexico, Banco de México, *Informe Anual;* for Panama, national official data on the balance of payments.

[42] As pointed out above, direct data on current transactions and compensatory financing in 1962 are somewhat more complete and reliable than those on noncompensatory capital movements.

TABLE 2-21. Latin America: Short-Term Assets of the Private Sector Reported by Banks in the United States, 1960-1962

(*Millions of dollars*)

Country	1960	1961	1962
Argentina	69	69	108
Bolivia	15	17	18
Brazil	129	132	89
Chile	47	51	83
Colombia	72	71	87
Dominican Republic	24	16	18
El Salvador	19	16	15
Guatemala	17	18	15
Mexico	132	174	197
Panama	103	74	77
Peru	41	50	61
Uruguay	30	29	54
Venezuela	185	234	233
Other Latin American Countries	80	109	117
Total Latin America	963	1,060	1,172

Source: Federal Reserve Board, *Federal Reserve Bulletin* (Washington), April, 1961, 1962, and 1963.

Economic Commission for Latin America (ECLA),[43] the negative errors and omissions are more probably to be found at the level of outflows of private Latin American funds than at that of other external transactions. In particular, short-term assets in United States banks presumably do not account for the most part of such funds, because they enjoy neither the advantage of secrecy nor that of yielding a convenient return. Other financial ventures in the United States and Western Europe may not be so readily accessible, but they do offer one or both of these advantages.

During the last two years, negative errors and omissions in the balance of payments of Mexico were exceptionally large and represented more than half the regional total (see again Table 2-3). While the increase in this negative balance points to an intensification of capital flight, the quite unusual importance of the errors and omissions in absolute terms suggests the possibility of an overvaluation of other transactions (especially of those which are estimated, such as, for example, the tourism receipts). In any event, the recorded outflow of short-term Mexican capital—both from individuals and private banks—reached $49 million, against $26 million in 1961.[44]

[43] See United Nations, *External Financing in the Economic Development of Latin America,* E/CN.12/64a (mimeo), p. 16.
[44] See Banco de México, *Informe Anual,* 1962.

Short-term assets deposited in United States banks by individuals residing in Argentina, Chile, Colombia, and Uruguay increased noticeably in 1962, while they had changed very little in 1961 (see again Table 2–21). In the case of Argentina, moreover, the total outflow may have reached $253 million in the past year.[45]

For Brazil, the national balance-of-payments data as well as the United States Treasury statistics on Brazilian short-term assets record a net flow of private capital into the country. The balance of errors and omissions, however, turned from +$2 million in 1961 to −$137 million in 1962, and the rate of exchange of the cruzeiro on the free market fell by approximately 50 per cent between the two last years. Thus, it is presumed that an increasing amount of Brazilian capital was sent abroad and probably was invested mostly in Western European countries.

On the other hand, in the cases of the Dominican Republic, El Salvador, Guatemala, and Panama, the amount of short-term private assets deposited in United States banks recorded but very small variations, while errors and omissions either did not change at all or declined somewhat. Likewise, the experience of Venezuela in 1962 was relatively favorable, as the net outflow of private capital other than long-term was $69 million smaller than in the previous year. For this country, also, the annual changes in short-term assets in United States banks reflect imperfectly the total net outflow of private domestic capital during the corresponding years.[46]

Apart from the flight of domestic capital, amortization payments on the external debt are another expenditure which currently absorbs a substantial portion of gross foreign-exchange receipts in Latin America as a whole. These payments are taken into account in the net individual figures concerning the different categories of loans analyzed above. There exist, however, some global estimates on amortization and interest payments, which show how heavy was the total servicing of the external

---

[45] According to the review, *Economic Survey* (Buenos Aires), March 5, 1963, amortization payments plus the outflow of short-term capital would have totaled $532 million in Argentina. Since amortization payments alone are estimated at $279 million by the Development Department of OECD, the residual figure for the outflow of short-term private capital is: $532 − $279 = $253 million. This figure may include some margin of error and duplications and constitutes a preliminary estimate.

[46] The figures can be compared as follows:

	1961	1962
	(Millions of dollars)	
Variations in short-term assets in U.S. banks [1]	+ 49	− 1
Total outflow of capital other than long-term [2]	235	166

Sources: 1. *Treasury Bulletin;* 2. Banco Central de Venezuela.

TABLE 2-22. Latin America: Foreign Debt Servicing[a] in Selected Countries in 1962

Country	Total amount in millions of dollars	Percentage value in relation to total capacity to import
Argentina	322	30%
Brazil	399	31%
Chile	107	20%
Colombia	68	14%
Ecuador	16	11%
Mexico	254	17%
Paraguay	4	8%
Peru	48	9%
Uruguay	12	8%
Venezuela	126	10%

[a] Includes interest and amortization payments.

Sources: For all countries, Brazil excepted, Development Department of OECD mainly on the basis of estimates made by the International Monetary Fund. For Brazil, *Boletims da Superintendência da Moeda e Crédito*, 1963.

public debt in several Latin American countries during the last year (see Table 2-22). In this respect, Argentina, Brazil, and Chile found themselves in the most unfavorable situations within the region. On the other hand, it is noteworthy that the financial charge resulting from the servicing of the debt was small not only in Mexico and Peru but also in Uruguay, which for some time has been facing a large deficit on current account.[47]

To avoid an excessive weakening of their capacity to import during the next years, Argentina, Brazil, and Colombia were able to agree with creditor countries upon prolonging the amortization schedules of certain loans. Several refinancing operations have concerned medium-term debts toward Western Europe, the repayment of which contributed to reducing noticeably the net balance on capital account in 1962. At the end of the same year, the so-called Paris Club refinanced half the total debt of $270 million which should have been paid by Argentina in 1963 and 1964. More recently, the Hague Club agreed, in turn, to stagger the maturity dates of Brazil's debt over a ten-year period and up to an amount of $210 million.[48]

[47] See an estimate of external public long-term debts by year and country in, United Nations, *External Financing*, p. 214.
[48] For more details on consolidation loans, see National Foreign Trade Council, *Noticias*, March 27, 1962, for Colombia; November 16, 1962, for Argentina; and July 23, 1963, for Argentina.

COMPENSATORY FINANCING OF THE BALANCE OF PAYMENTS

Compensatory financing in Latin America underwent noticeable changes in 1962, both in its total amount and its structure. As the deficit of recorded external transactions at the regional level increased considerably and the negative balance of unrecorded receipts and payments was somewhat larger than in 1961, compensatory accounts had to provide $261 million more in international means of payment than they had done in the previous year (see Table 2–23). Approximately 55 per cent of Latin America's external deficit was financed through a decline in gross assets of gold and foreign exchange. Another third was accounted for by an increase in liabilities to foreign lenders other than the International Monetary Fund (IMF) and Export-Import Bank of the United

TABLE 2–23. Latin America: International Reserves and Compensatory Balance of Payments Accounts, 1960–1962

(Millions of dollars)

	1959[a]	1960[a]	1961[a]	1962[a]
Official gold and foreign exchange assets	2,759	2,851	2,737	2,254
Gold	(1,590)	(1,359)	(1,390)	(1,185)
Foreign Exchange	(1,169)	(1,492)	(1,347)	(1,069)
Total *tranche* position with IMF	831	1,151	945	1,017
Commercial Banks foreign exchange	356	299	339	362
Total gross monetary reserves	3,946	4,301	4,017	3,616
Annual variation of gross reserves of official and bank gold and foreign exchange		35	−74	−460
Net annual increase (−) of indebtedness to IMF		−82	−260	69
Compensatory loans by the Eximbank		−32	−282	−146
Other compensatory accounts[b] [c]		−728	66	−274
Total compensatory accounts[c]		−807	560	811
Errors and omissions[c]		450	417	483
Total balance of payments[c]		−357	−143	−328

[a] To December 31.

[b] Includes changes in the callable foreign exchange liabilities of official institutions and banks, balance-of-payments credits—except those of the International Monetary Fund and the compensatory loans by the Export-Import Bank of Washington—and variations in the debt by importers.

[c] For greater clarity, the minus sign (−) has been given to compensatory credits that cover a balance-of-payments deficit. However, in accordance with accounting practices for this balance, these changes should have a plus sign. Likewise "errors and omissions" carry a sign opposite to that which appears in the balance of payments.

Sources: IMF, *Balance of Payments Yearbook* and *International Financial Statistics*, July and August, 1963.

States (Eximbank). In contrast, credit granted by the two latter agencies represented in 1961 more than nine-tenths of total compensatory financing for the region as a whole.

The decline in the IMF's contribution to external liquidity in 1962 was not limited to Latin America. Total gross drawings by all member countries amounted to only $584 million, against $2,479 million in the preceding year. Even if the exceptionally large credit of $1,500 million granted to the United Kingdom in 1961 is excluded, the fall in gross drawings between the two last years was no less than $500 million. In the case of Latin America, repayments exceeded drawings for the first time in many years. Thus, for this region alone the net foreign-exchange receipts obtained through transactions with the Fund decreased by $329 million in relation to 1961. Net payments to the IMF were made not only by countries that recorded a surplus in their external payments (Costa Rica, Ecuador, El Salvador, and Mexico) but also by those suffering from serious exchange difficulties, like Argentina, Brazil, and Chile (see Table 2–24). Within the latter group of countries, however, Colombia, Guatemala, and Uruguay received net credits for a substantial amount during 1962. And in the first quarter of 1963 Latin America's transactions with the Fund turned back to positive, as a result of important drawings made by Chile and, once again, by Colombia.

Apart from cutting its disbursements by almost half, the Eximbank did not authorize any new compensatory loans in favor of Latin America in 1962 (see Table 2–25). Compensatory disbursements by the Eximbank (which, like the development loans, are mostly tied in with the financing of United States exports) had been exceptionally important in 1961, and they had benefited a larger number of countries than before. In 1962, along with the decline in the actual transfer of liquid funds, the number of recipient countries in Latin America went down to no more than three. As often in the past, Brazil was the main beneficiary of these loans. Both Mexico and Venezuela, the other recipient countries in 1962, resorted to compensatory credits from the Eximbank for the first time in 1961.

The great decline in Latin America's gold and exchange reserves in 1962 came after two years in which there had been small changes in this compensatory account. Even though the region's external transaction had recorded a large deficit in both 1960 and 1961, its gross assets of international means of payment actually had increased a little in the first year and had decreased by less than $80 million in the latter (see again Table 2–23). It would seem, therefore, that gold and foreign-exchange reserves were resorted to in large amounts in 1962, when compensatory

TABLE 2-24. Latin America: Net Annual Variations in the Debt with the International Monetary Fund, 1960—March, 1963

(Millions of dollars)

Country	1960			1961			1962			January–March, 1963		
	Draw-ings	Repay-ments	Net draw-ings	Draw-ings	Repay-ments	Net draw-ings	Draw-ings	Repay-ments	Net draw-ings	Draw-ings	Repay-ments	Net draw-ings
Argentina	70.0	21.5	48.5	60.0	29.0	31.0	50.0	59.0	−9.0	—	9.0	−9.0
Bolivia	1.0	2.5	−1.5	2.0	4.0	−2.0	3.5	2.3	1.2	1.5	1.0	0.5
Brazil	47.7	—	47.7	60.0	20.0	40.0	—	17.5	−17.5	—	—	—
Chile	—	12.4	−12.4	76.0	16.7	59.3	—	12.7	−12.7	17.5	—	17.5
Colombia	—	15.0	−15.0	65.0	—	65.0	7.5	—	7.5	27.5	—	27.5
Costa Rica	—	—	—	7.5	—	7.5	2.5	6.6	−4.1	6.0	—	6.0
Dominican Republic	9.0	—	9.0	—	—	—	—	—	—	—	—	—
Ecuador	—	—	—	14.0	—	14.0	4.0	6.2	−2.2	—	—	—
El Salvador	13.2	7.5	5.7	8.0	11.2	−3.2	—	8.0	−8.0	—	—	—
Guatemala	—	—	—	—	—	—	5.0	—	5.0	—	—	—
Haiti	—	1.3	−1.3	1.5	2.8	−1.3	3.2	1.3	1.9	0.5	1.0	−0.5
Honduras	5.0	3.8	1.2	2.4	1.2	1.2	5.0	3.7	1.3	—	—	—
Mexico	—	—	—	45.0	—	45.0	—	45.0	−45.0	4.5	4.5	—
Nicaragua	—	—	—	6.0	1.5	4.5	—	—	—	4.5	4.5	4.5
Panama	—	—	—	—	—	—	—	—	—	—	—	—
Paraguay	1.0	0.9	0.1	—	1.6	−1.6	—	1.8	−1.8	—	0.2	−0.2
Peru	—	—	—	—	—	—	—	—	—	—	—	—
Uruguay	—	—	—	—	—	—	15.0	—	15.0	—	—	—
Venezuela	—	—	—	—	—	—	—	—	—	—	—	—
Total Latin America	146.9	64.9	82.0	347.4	88.0	259.4	95.7	164.1	−68.4	57.5	15.7	41.8

Source: IMF, *International Financial Statistics*, May, 1963.

TABLE 2-25. Latin America: Compensatory Loans by the Export-Import Bank of Washington, 1960—March, 1963

(Millions of dollars)

Country	1960			1961			1962			January–March, 1963		
	Authorized	Disbursements	Repayments	Authorized	Disbursements	Repayments	Authorized	Disbursements	Repayments	Authorized	Disbursements	Repayments
Argentina	—	—	9.6	—	—	9.7	—	—	4.8	—	—	—
Brazil	—	3.0	16.0	239.3	110.0	—	—	81.4	—	—	15.8	—
Chile	—	25.0	7.5	17.5	16.7	12.6	—	—	4.3	15.0	7.5	3.0
Colombia	—	—	23.0	19.9	44.9	18.0	—	—	15.6	—	—	—
El Salvador	—	—	—	6.0	6.0	—	—	—	—	—	—	—
Mexico	—	—	—	90.0	75.0	—	—	15.0	—	—	—	—
Nicaragua	—	4.0	—	—	4.0	—	—	—	—	—	—	—
Peru	—	—	15.5	—	—	—	—	—	—	—	—	—
Venezuela	50.0	—	—	25.0	25.0	—	—	50.0	—	—	—	—
Total	50.0	32.0	71.6	397.7	281.6	40.3	—	146.4	24.7	15.0	23.3	3.0

Source: Eximbank, *Statement of Loans and Credits*, December 31, 1960, 1961, 1962, and March 31, 1963.

credits from foreign sources had already been utilized very extensively in previous periods. This regional pattern, however, distorts substantially developments in individual Latin American countries. In the first place, changes in the gross reserves of Argentina, Brazil, and Colombia only accounted for the loss of almost $500 million suffered by Latin America's gross assets in 1962 (see Table 2-26). Secondly, in Brazil, Chile, and Uruguay, the monetary authorities financed the balance-of-payments deficits mainly through an increase in liabilities to external creditors other than the Eximbank and IMF. Thirdly, in 1960 and 1961 several individual countries had experienced large changes in their monetary reserves; but these movements had offset each other to a large extent.

In 1962, Brazil had recourse to the reserves of gold and foreign exchange that the balance-of-payments surplus of the preceding year had made it possible to accumulate. Most of the remaining part of the Brazilian monetary assets, however, are not freely disposable, as they guarantee the repayment of current external debts. Consequently, the Brazilian authorities made additional drawings on loans previously granted by the Eximbank, and they engaged also in costly swap operations [49] (see Table 2-27). But certainly the distinctive feature of the Brazilian experience in 1962 was the postponement of due payments on imports for almost $130 million. Although this step is not without precedent (especially in the mid-fifties), it deserves to be pointed out as a symptom of the liquidity crisis affecting the international transactions of the country.

The fact that the balance-of-payments deficit in Uruguay and Chile was financed almost exclusively through an increase in liabilities did not mean that external illiquidity in these countries was even more acute than in Brazil. Actually, at the end of 1962 gold reserves in Uruguay still were twice as large as the external deficit of the same year; but formal regulations concerning the issue of money prevented them from falling below certain minimum levels. In Chile, the amount of gold and foreign-exchange assets during the past year did not differ substantially from the annual average of the last decade. Since these assets did not account for more than 15 per cent of the current annual value of imports, however, external credits have apparently been preferred as a method of compensation. Chile obtained sufficient quantity of such credits from other sources than the IMF and the Eximbank, and partly through the channel of Chilean private banks.

[49] Through such operations, central banks obtain foreign currency by buying it from private sources at a high rate of interest and with an option of repurchase within a relatively short period.

TABLE 2-26. Latin America: Movement of Compensatory Accounts of the Balance of Payments, 1960–1962

(Millions of dollars)

Country	1960			1961			1962		
	Total compensatory accounts	Gross gold reserves and foreign exchange	Total net balance of other compensatory accounts	Total compensatory accounts	Gross gold reserves and foreign exchange	Total net balance of other compensatory accounts	Total compensatory accounts	Gross gold reserves and foreign exchange	Total net balance of other compensatory accounts
Argentina	+144	+306	−162	−232	−201	−31	−291	−306	15
Bolivia	−2	−5	3	2	—	2	−4	−4	—
Brazil	−411	−10	−401	105	120	−15	−388	−142	−246
Chile	−62	−12	−30	−131	−11	−120	−69	−2	−67
Colombia	−42	−40	−2	−165	−10	−155	−70	−50	−20
Costa Rica	−11	1	−12	−11	4	−15	4	6	−2
Dominican Republic	7	−10	17	−14	−20	6	12	15	−3
Ecuador	−2	−1	−1	−15	1	−16	12	5	7
El Salvador	−22	−10	−12	−7	−9	2	8	−1	9
Guatemala	6	10	−4	−6	2	−8	−17	−5	−12
Haiti	2	1	1	2	1	1	−6	−3	−3
Honduras	−1	−1	—	−3	−1	−2	12	—	12
Mexico	−78	−9	−69	−24	−22	−2	104	17	87
Nicaragua	−4	—	−4	6	4	2	7	4	3
Panama	−6	−5	−1	−7	−4	−3	−1	5	−6
Paraguay	−3	−2	−1	3	1	2	−1	−2	1
Peru	14	20	−6	35	41	−6	13	17	−4
Uruguay	−27	21	−48	−54	−13	−41	−90	—	−90
Venezuela	−309	−159	−150	−44	−16	−28	−45	5	−50
Total, Latin America	−807	95	−902	−560	−133	−427	−810	−441	−369

Source: IMF, *Balance of Payments Yearbook* and *International Financial Statistics.*

TABLE 2–27. Latin America: Movement of Compensatory Accounts of the Balance of Payments in 1962

(Millions of dollars)

Country	Total compensatory accounts	Gross gold reserves and foreign exchange	Net IMF	Gross Eximbank of Washington	U.S. Treasury Department	Swap operations	Deferred import payments	Other liabilities
Argentina	−291	−306	9	—	−17	—	—	23
Bolivia	−4	−4	−1	—	—	—	—	1
Brazil	−388	−142	18	−81	−3	−46	−128	−6
Chile	−69	−2	13	—	—	—	—	−80
Colombia	−70	−50	−8	—	—	—	—	−12
Costa Rica	4	6	4	—	—	—	—	−6
Dominican Republic	12	15	—	—	—	—	—	−3
Ecuador	12	5	2	—	—	—	—	5
El Salvador	8	−1	8	—	—	—	—	1
Guatemala	−17	−5	−5	—	—	—	—	−7
Haiti	−6	−3	−2	—	—	—	—	−1
Honduras	12	—	−1	—	—	—	—	13
Mexico	104	17	45	−15	—	—	—	57
Nicaragua	7	4	—	—	—	—	—	3
Panama	−1	5	—	—	—	—	—	−6
Paraguay	−1	−2	2	—	—	—	—	−1
Peru	13	17	—	—	—	—	—	−4
Uruguay	−90	—	−15	—	—	—	—	−75
Venezuela	−45	5	—	−50	—	—	—	—
Total, Latin America	−810	−441	69	−146	−20	−46	−128	−98

Sources: IMF, *International Financial Statistics*, August, 1963, and *Balance of Payments of Brazil*, 1962. Eximbank, *Statement of Loans and Credits*, December, 1961, and December, 1962. *Economic Survey*, March 13, 1963. Banco Continental, *Newsletter* (Lima), January 21, 1963, and February 21, 1963. Banco Central de Venezuela, *Memoria Anual* (Caracas), 1962.

In 1961, notwithstanding the large deficit of its balance of payments, Colombia had been able to keep its monetary reserves relatively steady and at a level accounting for approximately 30 per cent of the current annual value of its purchases abroad. This situation changed substantially in December, 1962, when Colombia's gold and foreign-exchange assets fell below $100 million for the first time in many years. Although reserves regained somewhat during the first months of 1963, at the end of May they represented only 20 per cent of annual imports. In Argentina, the corresponding proportion between assets and purchases abroad fell even more rapidly, reaching down to 12 per cent at the end of 1962. The country's reserves had increased considerably in 1960. But in 1961, and above all in 1962, the loss in gross assets more than offset the gains of previous years, since Argentina relied very little on other compensatory resources to finance its huge balance-of-payments deficit.

In contrast, some other Latin American countries strengthened their position on compensatory account. In absolute terms, the largest increase in gross assets took place in the Dominican Republic in 1962 and in Peru for the whole period 1960–62. But in relation to the value of imports, improvement in the reserves position was much less conspicuous. While Peru, for example, enjoyed three consecutive balance-of-payments surpluses in 1960, 1961, and 1962, between the beginning and the end of this period the ratio of its reserves to its purchases abroad increased from 18 to 20 per cent only, since the latter also expanded very rapidly.

CHAPTER 3

TOTAL PRODUCTION, CAPITAL FORMATION, AND MONETARY DEVELOPMENT

VARIATIONS IN TOTAL PRODUCT AND CAPITAL FORMATION

Latin America's gross domestic product increased in 1962 by something less than 4 per cent.[1] This figure is comparatively unfavorable with reference to the estimated figure for the preceding year (6.0 per cent) and as against the rate of growth of the area's population. The latter rate has shown an increase during recent years, and it is estimated that during the period to which we are referring—that is, the early part of this decade—it was approximately 2.9 per cent. Thus per capita product increased only slightly in 1964.

In fact, the slow rate of growth of per capita product in 1962 is due primarily to the 3.4 per cent drop in the product of Argentina, a country of considerable weight in the average for the region. In the majority of the other countries, the rate of increase of the product tended to improve with respect to the preceding year, although the product-population relationship also proved negative in some other countries (see Table 3–1). The 1962 figures reveal an improvement over those for 1961 in 13 countries, although in some instances the increase was rather slight. In terms of its contribution to the area's product, Venezuela was the country of greatest influence. There, both agricultural and industrial production increased as much as oil production; and although the services component lagged somewhat behind, product increased by 7 per cent, while during the preceding year it had increased by less than 0.5 per cent. In El Salvador and Guatemala, a more favorable year for agriculture was joined by the industrial expansion stimulated by the economic inte-

[1] Data on Cuba are not available. Calculations are based on the relative weights of the 19 other countries in 1961.

gration of Central America in preventing a repetition of the negative rate obtained by their product in 1961. In 1962, there was a 7.2 per cent increase of product in El Salvador and a 2.0 per cent increase in Guatemala. The same combination of factors permitted Nicaragua to increase its growth rate, while in Honduras the rate of expansion of total production increased despite a slowing of the increase in agricultural output. In Mexico, there was a recovery in agriculture as well as industry; and according to partial information, a similar situation appears to have occurred in Haiti.

Offsetting the changes which took place in the countries just mentioned, the economic growth rate of Brazil and Peru fell sharply. The drop in Brazil occurred primarily in the field of agriculture, in which the increase was merely 1.3 per cent. The total product, which had achieved an increase of 7.7 per cent in 1961, showed an increase of only 4 per cent (approximately) in 1962. Following the same chronological order, the rate for Peru fell from 8.3 per cent to 5.3 per cent. In Peru's case, the lesser rate of increase was general and stemmed from agricultural and fisheries production as well as manufacturing and mining.

In the remaining countries for which information is available, the 1962 rate was greater than that of the preceding year by a slight margin. The growth rate of the manufacturing sector increased in only one of them: Panama. In all the other countries it again diminished. It should be noted in this connection that in several of these countries climatic conditions or the favorable opportunity of the coffee cycle brought about a certain increase in the rate for agricultural production and in part offset the opposite trend which predominated in the remaining economic sectors.

In conclusion, the rate of growth of Latin America's economy, although more positive, is far from being satisfactory, even if Argentina is excluded. Not counting the latter, the product for the 18 remaining countries may be calculated as having increased 5.0 per cent in 1961 and between 4.2 and 4.6 per cent in 1962. On the other hand, Argentina's population increases at an annual rate that is regarded as among the lowest in the area, which means, therefore, that in per capita terms the product of the other countries increased by 1.8 per cent in 1961 instead of 2.4 per cent, and between 1.1 and 1.5 per cent (instead of 0.6 to 1.0 per cent) in 1962. This means a regional deterioration, even without Argentina, despite the fact that conditions improved in most other countries. This phenomenon is accounted for by the great weight exerted by the figures for Brazil in the regional total. At any rate, the general outlook fails to show any changes indicating that in 1962 the tendencies of the past five years were substantially altered. Although the institutional changes initi-

TABLE 3–1. Changes Over the Preceding Year in the Total Agricultural and Manufacturing Gross Product and in Fixed Investments in 1961 and 1962

(Percentages)

Country	Increase of population	Domestic product 1961	Domestic product 1962	Agricultural product[a] 1961	Agricultural product[a] 1962	Industrial product 1961	Industrial product 1962	Fixed investments 1961	Fixed investments 1962
Argentina	1.8	6.8	−3.4	3	1	14	−5	6	0
Bolivia	2.2	4.8	5.0	8	...	5	...	...	...
Brazil	3.2	7.7	3.5–4.5	8	1	11	7	11	5
Chile	2.4	4.4	5.2	−5	−3	5	4	28	14
Colombia	2.3	4.7	5.8	0	5	7	6	7	3
Costa Rica	3.9	2.7	3.0	...	...	...	...	2	...
Dominican Republic	3.5	9.7	...	...	...	...	...	−2	...
Ecuador	3.2	3.4	5.0	6	7	2	2	2	...
El Salvador	3.4	−2.1	7.2	2	13	−2	2	−1	4
Guatemala	3.2	−0.5	2.0	−2	5	0	2	−8	...
Haiti	2.9	−1.6	6.8	...	...	...	...	...	...
Honduras	3.0	3.6	5.7	4	1	3	4	−8	15
Mexico	3.1	3.5	5.0	3	5	4	6	9	4
Nicaragua	3.4	7.9	10.8	8	16	13	22	12	15
Panama	2.8	7.5	8.1	9	4	4	20	23	...
Paraguay	2.5	2.4	...	−2	...	3	...	...	...
Peru	2.6	8.3	5.3	−10	7	9	5	29	15
Uruguay	1.2	2.7	...	12	...	−2	...	3	...
Venezuela	3.1	0.4	7.1	2	11	6	12	−14	7
Latin America	2.9	6.0	3.4–3.8	4	3	9	4	8	5

a Fisheries included.

Sources and Notes: Official sources have been used in the case of Argentina, Chile, Colombia, Costa Rica, Ecuador, El Salvador, Guatemala, Honduras, Mexico, Nicaragua, Panama, Peru, Uruguay, and Venezuela. BOLIVIA, AID Mission; BRAZIL, Conjuntura Econômica y Desenvolvimento e Conjuntura, both February, 1963; as to product, the estimated changes in investments are based upon changes in imports and production of equipment and construction; COLOMBIA, changes in product correspond to an extrapolation of the series worked out by ECLA up to 1960; for COLOMBIA and EL SALVADOR, the changes in investments to the changes in construction and imports of capital goods; HAITI, ECLA/IDB/OAS Mission; NICARAGUA, extrapolation of the product series by the Banco Central de Nicaragua, with the data as to production having been supplied by the same Central Bank; PARAGUAY and the DOMINICAN REPUBLIC, unofficial estimates.

In the case of the averages for Latin America, the following procedures have been used. *Total product*: The national indices have been weighted according to product values for 1961 at prices of that same year. Those values were obtained from Table 121 of United Nations document E/CN-12/659/Add.1. The calculation of the regional average was made on the basis of yardsticks approximating the variations of the product in those countries for which national data are not given; that average is for 19 countries (Cuba excluded) in both years.

Agricultural and industrial product: The available national series (some countries only publish information on National Expenditure and others do not give any breakdown by sectors) were weighted by using values obtained by applying the relation between current values of product and of those sectors to the values described in the preceding paragraph.

Sector averages for Latin America are for countries for which data covering both years are given. It is assumed that including the countries on which information is unavailable would not alter the trend of those averages.

Investments: The method used is the same as that applied for sector averages.

Increase of population: Calculated on the basis of information given in the United Nations, *Monthly Bulletin of Statistics*, July, 1963.

ated during that year may have an important bearing on the future evolution of the great aggregates of Latin America's economy, it would be premature to expect such results by 1962 or 1963.[2]

The changes in the gross formation of fixed capital were equally variable. On the average, those countries for which information is available show in 1962 an increase of approximately 5 per cent, a percentage which is influenced by the Argentine series even more than that of domestic product. In this instance, not only are the figures affected by the greater weight of that country, owing to its high coefficient of investment, according to the national accounts, but also by the smaller number of countries for which information was available for that year. It is therefore quite likely that the more complete regional average may be greater and vary by about 6 per cent, approximately (see Table 3–2). The data needed for a detailed analysis of what happened to fixed investments are not available. However, it should be pointed out that the moderate increase attained in 1962 was influenced to a considerable degree by the comparatively slight variation in fixed investments of the private sector and the difficulty encountered in most countries by the government sector in continuing the large increases undertaken in the immediately preceding years.

Private fixed investments show an increase in almost all those countries for which it has been possible to obtain official data. These increases, however, are generally considerably below the ones shown in relative terms by fixed investment of the public sector. In those countries where the relative contribution to fixed investment by the public sector was high (Chile and Mexico), the average rate of increase of total fixed investment almost quadrupled that of private fixed investment. In those countries in which the public share is small (Honduras and Peru), although public fixed investment increased at even higher rates than in the two countries just mentioned, it succeeded in offsetting only moderately the lower rate of private fixed investment.

The experience of these four countries does not necessarily reflect the situation experienced by the remainder. In fact, most other countries failed to have an equally favorable flow of official capital, nor did the prices or the volume of their exports increase.

Although the incomplete data available show that the government sector was able to increase its investment and thus add to the total formation of capital, this was not so in those cases in which public investments were relatively small or export prices militated against gov-

---

[2] A summary of these undertakings will be found in Chapter 5 of this *Survey*.

TABLE 3–2. Latin America: Fixed Capital Formation by Sectors and the Inflow of Direct Private Investment, 1961 and 1962

Country	1961				1962			
	Fixed capital			Net inflow of direct investment from the United States (in millions of US$)	Fixed capital			Net inflow of direct investment from the United States (in millions of US$)
	(Percentage change over 1960)				(Percentage change over 1961)			
	Total	Private	Public		Total	Private	Public	
Argentina	6	6	6	34	—	−1	1	−10
Bolivia	11	..	..	..	5	..	..	7
Brazil	28	..	..	−76	14	..	23	13
Chile	7	..	−14	−2	3	5	..	28
Colombia	2	..	..	−22	..	..	..	..
Costa Rica	−2	..	..	..	..	..	..	—
Dominican Republic	−2	..	8	—	..	..	..	..
Ecuador	−1	..	8	..	4	..	..	..
El Salvador	−8	−20	..	−2	..	..	..	3
Guatemala	..	..	..	..	..	..	..	..
Haiti	−8	..	..	..	..	..	..	8
Honduras	9	..	..	6	15	..	..	−15
Mexico	12	−1	22	−11	4	3	4	..
Nicaragua	23	27	−12	..	15	6	43	−43
Panama	..	12	102	−18	..	..	..	..
Paraguay	29	..	..	7	15	..	..	—
Peru	3	22	73	—	7	11	20	2
Uruguay	−14	1	12	150	..	..	..	−194
Venezuela	8	..	..	78	5	..	..	−205
Latin America								

Sources: Tables 2–18 and 3–1 of this Survey.

ernment resources. In some countries, there intervened also the fact, already mentioned, that in 1961 there was an upsurge in government investments which could not be repeated readily in 1962.

The changes in private fixed investment in 1962 occurred in response—in addition to the known influence of the capacity to import—to internal factors which vary in importance according to each country. One of the most decisive was the net inflow of direct investments from abroad, which has contributed in recent years to the expansion and diversification of the productive capacity of the manufacturing sector of Latin America. This sector, together with construction, absorbs most of total investment in the Latin American countries.

To a certain extent, the tendency revealed in the Latin American countries in the net inflow of direct investments is reflected in private fixed investment (see again Table 3–2). While it is not claimed that the data are fully comparable or that the number of countries compared is adequate, the contrast between both series suggests that there does exist a tendency whereby contraction of the net inflow of United States investment is accompanied by similar contraction of the rate of increase in the total of private fixed investment. Mexico is the main exception in this case. It had an increase in the inflow of direct investments from different sources, which compensated in part for the situation with regard to United States investment.

Chile and Venezuela are among the countries for which complete data are unavailable and in which apparently there has been a tendency similar to that described in the preceding paragraph. The difficulty of determining accurately the changes in private fixed investments as well as the size of the direct investments from other sources precludes their being included with greater detail in the present analysis, despite their importance.

A factor that has gained in importance with regard to private fixed investments is the slower rate of industrial development prevalent throughout Latin America. This slack is due to long-range factors that became more acute in 1962.[3] Latin America's industrialization calls for continued diversification, for otherwise there can be no coupling of the rapid growth in derived demand with the slow rate of increase of final demand for manufactured consumer goods.

The inflow of direct foreign investment during the 1950's played a dynamic role in that diversification, contributing not only to the financing of imports of capital goods but also to the importation of the correspond-

[3] See OAS/ECLA, *Economic & Social Survey of Latin America, 1961* (Washington, D.C., 1962), and Chapter 4 of the present *Survey*.

ing techniques and systems. It is encouraging, therefore, that despite the decreased totals of direct investments from abroad, those devoted to manufacturing do not seem to have diminished.[4] This fact notwithstanding, the plant capacity installed in certain countries exceeded the demand for the manufactured products. At least in two countries, the contraction of fixed investment in machinery and equipment was attributed to this reason.[5] In two others, this investment was at a considerably lower rate, owing to the necessity of revising in part the implementation of projects for the expansion of manufacturing capacity in order to adapt them to changing demands.[6]

MONETARY DEVELOPMENTS

The monetary setting in Latin America has remained essentially the same for several years now. In 1962 and during the first half of 1963, many countries, in their striving for more rapid economic and social progress, continued to be faced with chronic fiscal disequilibriums and recurrent balance-of-payments difficulties. In keeping with the established pattern, these pressures generally evoked what has now become a fairly uniform policy response in the area: a periodic tightening of the restrictions placed on the use of credit by the private sector of the economy. This policy, applied in an environment of rising costs and prices, has led in more than one instance to the paradox of industry and trade suffering from a serious shortage of funds while money supply was rising at a rapid pace and government deficit spending continued on a large scale.

Inflationary pressures, on the whole, went unabated, and in fact intensified in a number of countries in relation to the situation that had prevailed in 1961. Efforts were made throughout the area to improve existing financial mechanisms, establish new institutions, and perfect techniques that would permit a more efficient channeling of domestic resources into economically productive and socially useful investment. In general, however, the unstable monetary climate and the stopgap nature of the monetary and fiscal measures adopted from day to day to

---

[4] See Chapter 2 of the present *Survey*. There is a possibility, however, that the decline in industrial investments in Brazil by other countries than the United States, Japan, and Western Europe may have brought down the total for the area.

[5] See the *Reports* submitted by the Governments of Honduras and Venezuela to the Special Committee of IA-ECOSOC (Planning and Drafting of Projects) at its July 16 to July 24, 1963 meeting.

[6] See Chapter 4 of the present *Survey*.

relieve economic and social tensions still left relatively little scope for a positive use of financial instruments in furthering long-term development objectives.

Money Supply Trends

The supply of money increased substantially in a large number of countries during the period under review (see Table 3-3). As in 1961, the fastest rate of monetary expansion was recorded in Brazil, where inflationary pressures remained essentially unchecked, at least until recently. But considerable additions to the stock of money were also made in Chile and Colombia, despite the continuing stabilization efforts

TABLE 3-3. Latin America: Percentage Changes in Money Supply, 1957-1963

Country	1957-61 annual average[a]	1961 Dec.	Twelve months ended 1962				1963	
			March	June	Sept.	Dec.	March	June
Argentina	28	11	...	7	4	3	7	11[b]
Bolivia	20	18	18	17	12	12	11	13
Brazil	37	50	45	53	59	63	58	57[b]
Chile	29	13	29	20	25	29	23	46
Colombia	16	24	22	19	14	21	12	...
Costa Rica	4	−3	4	15	24	14	17	21[b]
Dominican Republic	5	1	1	6	−5	11	3	...
Ecuador	5	3	−1	3	11	12	14	15
El Salvador	−3	−4	5	4	6	—	7	6
Guatemala	−1	1	2	−1	−2	4	13	...
Haiti	−3	13	7	8	−3	4	4	2[b]
Honduras	−1	1	4	8	10	14	12	10
Mexico	9	7	6	8	10	13	...	...
Nicaragua	—	3	15	24	24	29	27	19
Panama[c]	5	5	8	4	6	11	15	...
Paraguay	12	27	22	16	5	−2	—	1[b]
Peru	13	19	11	5	4	4	8	...
Uruguay	27	22	8	7	4	1	...	...
Venezuela	6	3	−1	1	−2	−2	−1	4

[a] December-to-December changes.
[b] May.
[c] Demand deposits at private and government banks. No money supply figure is available for Panama, where the bulk of the circulation is in the form of U.S. dollar notes and coin.

Source: International Monetary Fund, *International Financial Statistics*.

carried out by the authorities in these two countries. In the other South American countries—Argentina, Bolivia, Paraguay, Peru, and Uruguay— where more or less formal stabilization programs have been in progress, the growth of the money supply slowed down markedly in 1962 in relation to what it had been in 1961 and earlier. The Central American states, on the other hand, finally emerged from a prolonged period of deflation and generally resumed a course of moderate to rapid monetary expansion in 1962 or the early part of 1963.

Factors of Monetary Expansion

The contribution of the different sectors of the economy to the monetary expansion varied from country to country (see Table 3–4). Foreign operations generated important amounts of liquidity in Ecuador and in some of the Central American countries, where the balance of international payments had become favorable in 1962 after several consecutive years of deficit. The contribution of the foreign sector was also positive in Mexico, Peru, and the Dominican Republic, but in these three countries its impact was overshadowed to a very large extent by the volume of liquidity created through domestic credit operations. On the other hand, in most South American countries, as well as in Haiti and Guatemala, the deficits incurred on external accounts generally led to a considerable absorption of domestic liquidity in 1962. More often than not, however, there were also large fiscal deficits to be financed at the banks in these countries, and bank lending to the private sector was simultaneously making some contribution of its own to the monetary expansion. The net impact on domestic liquidity was therefore always expansionary in some degree, even in the countries faced with the most severe drain of funds on balance-of-payments account.

It is noteworthy that in the countries with favorable balance-of-payments positions, the growth rate in the stock of money and quasi money did not fall below 8 per cent or exceed 16 to 17 per cent in 1962, except in Nicaragua, where the expansionary impact of the external surplus was reinforced by substantial increases in bank lending both to the government and the private sectors. In contrast, in the deficit countries, where domestic credit expansion had to overcome the deflationary impact of a net outflow of funds on foreign account, the increase in money and quasi money tended to far greater extremes. It ranged, in fact, all the way from 2 to 60 per cent during the year, depending on the relative intensity of the pressures brought to bear by each of the different sectors of the economy.

TABLE 3-4. Latin America: Major Factors of Monetary Expansion in 1962

(Changes during the year expressed in percent of total stock of money and quasi money on Dec. 31, 1961)

Country	Banking system's foreign assets[a]	Banking system's net claims on government[b]	Banking system's claims on private sector[c]	Stock of money and quasi money
Countries with balance of payments in equilibrium or surplus				
Costa Rica	9.9	2.2[d]	1.7[d]	13.0
Dominican Republic	1.9	−5.3	15.2	12.4
Ecuador	9.2	0.4	2.1	13.0
El Salvador	5.3	4.0	−3.6	7.7
Honduras	x	8.3	7.1	17.3
Mexico	0.8	−1.7	13.6	11.9
Nicaragua	11.5	10.9	10.5	26.2
Panama	2.9	...	14.7	15.2[e]
Peru[f]	2.6	−3.6	15.1	15.8
Venezuela	— −7.6	—	4.1	1.6
Countries with balance-of-payments deficits				
Argentina	−9.4	8.6	6.8	5.7
Bolivia	−8.5	17.2	5.1	15.1
Brazil	— 26.9	—	37.2	59.9
Chile	— 11.1	—	22.1	35.8
Colombia	−1.6	12.5	12.3	23.6
Guatemala	−7.2	6.7	7.9	8.1
Haiti	−13.7	15.2	1.0	3.0
Paraguay	— −15.6	—	22.7	5.3
Uruguay	— ...	—	15.7	5.9

x Less than 0.05 per cent.

[a] Net of liabilities in the case of Argentina, Bolivia, Chile, Colombia, the Dominican Republic, Ecuador, El Salvador, Haiti, Nicaragua, Paraguay, Uruguay, and Venezuela.

[b] Net of changes in government deposits at the banks, except for Brazil and Uruguay, where gross figures were used. The monetary impact of expenditures out of official counterpart fund balances was also included here for Bolivia and Haiti.

[c] Net of changes in prior deposits for exchange in Brazil and Paraguay.

[d] For Costa Rica, "claims on government" include only those held by the Central Bank; "claims on the private sector" represent all commercial bank credit.

[e] Demand deposits and quasi money only.

[f] Changes between September, 1961, and September, 1962, expressed in per cent of stock of money and quasi money at the end of September, 1961.

Note: This table does not present an exhaustive breakdown of the factors responsible for monetary expansion. For this reason the three components above do not usually add up to the total change in the stock of money and quasi money shown in the right-hand column. The difference represents the net impact of miscellaneous items which

(Continued)

TABLE 3-4. *Continued*

vary from country to country as well as the impact of changes in the banks' capital accounts. It should be noted also that in a number of the Latin American countries the nature of the exchange system and of certain transactions between the Central Bank and the Treasury is such that the monetary effects of foreign transactions are only partly reflected in the data on foreign asset holdings of the banking system, the remainder being felt only through changes in the government accounts. In this table, the foreign and government accounts have been combined in cases where this raises the most serious difficulties.

Source: IMF, International Financial Statistics.

The most striking examples of almost complete divorce between the external-payments position and the evolution of domestic liquidity were offered by some of the larger South American countries—Brazil, Chile, and Colombia. All three have experienced serious balance-of-payments difficulties in most recent years but have simultaneously resorted regularly and extensively to government deficit financing. As bank credit to the private sector also expanded considerably—chiefly to permit the maintenance of current economic activity at rising levels of costs and prices—the domestic monetary expansion, feeding upon itself, proceeded at very rapid rates in 1962 and in the first half of 1963. This was particularly the case in Brazil, where the cumulative inflationary process, virtually unhampered, had already reached considerable intensity in 1961.

A different situation prevailed in the other two major countries affected by large balance-of-payments deficits in 1962; namely, Argentina and Uruguay. In these two countries, domestic monetary expansion not only was slowed in the course of the year but was in fact brought to a near standstill, although some preliminary signs of renewed expansion began to appear in early 1963. The pressure of the fiscal deficit on the banking system was greatly intensified in each case, but in Argentina an offsetting factor was provided by the drastic curbs imposed on bank credit to the private sector. In Uruguay, on the other hand, the balance-of-payment deficit, on both current and capital account, took on such proportions during the year that it absorbed nearly all the liquidity created within the domestic economy by private and government borrowing at the banks.

Monetary trends in most of the remaining countries represented minor variations on the basic theme of domestic credit expansion offsetting to a smaller or greater extent the absorption of funds on foreign sector account. In Bolivia, bank credit to the private sector rose substantially, while important amounts of liquidity were also generated by expenditures made out of the official balances built up in recent years as domestic currency counterpart to United States grant aid. In Guatemala, the monetary impact of the capital outflow and a decline in foreign grants were offset by a compensatory increase in government bank borrowing and accompanied by a moderate increase in credit to the private sector. Haiti, on the other hand, experienced virtually no net monetary expansion, as the impact of the fiscal deficit, financed at the banks and by drawing down counterpart fund balances, did little more than cancel out the deflationary pressures generated in the foreign sector.

It is clear from this brief review that inflationary deficit financing by the government sector was frequently the major factor of monetary expansion in Latin America in 1962. Although the relative importance of public versus private sector borrowing at the banks varies greatly from country to country, outstanding claims on government have shown a tendency to rise significantly faster than credit to the private sector in a large number of countries. This was particularly the case in Argentina, Chile, Colombia, and the Central American countries, where the ratio of government to private sector bank lending jumped sharply in 1962 (see Table 3–5).

There were, however, several notable exceptions to this pattern. In Mexico, Peru, and the Dominican Republic, as mentioned earlier, a fair rate of monetary expansion was achieved on the basis of a brisk increase in credit to the private sector. The operations of the government sector, on the other hand, appear to have led to a net absorption of liquidity in all three countries (see again Table 3–4). Similarly, in Paraguay and Venezuela, after several difficult years, the Treasuries accounts were brought into balance in 1962. This apparently permitted a badly needed acceleration of bank lending to the private sector to proceed in Paraguay without refueling the inflation. The growth of credit to the private sector was much slower in Venezuela, where bank-reserve positions were still in the process of recovering from the huge deficit drains experienced during the 1958–59 flight of capital from the country; but its expansion, at any rate, was not hampered by competitive demands for funds from the government sector. An easing of the fiscal pressure also seems to have conferred relatively greater importance to private sector lending in Bolivia and Guatemala in the first months of 1963.

In Brazil, on the other hand, the banks continued to be under intensive pressure to lend to both the government and the private sector, but the very momentum of the accelerating inflation was bringing private borrowers back into the foreground as the major cause of domestic credit expansion, after several years during which the rapidly growing deficit of the government had taken the lead in this respect.

TABLE 3-5. Latin America: Ratio of Public to Private Sector Credit Extended by the Banking System,[a] 1961–1963

Country	December 1961	December 1962	June 1963
Argentina	.50	.56	.62[d]
Bolivia	4.25	4.09	3.34
Brazil	.71	.66	.68[e]
Chile	.48	.73	.67
Colombia	.23	.32	.32[d]
Costa Rica	[b]	[b]	[b]
Dominican Republic	.92	.68	[c]
Ecuador	.12	.12	.14
El Salvador	.11	.15	.17
Guatemala	.10	.18	.09
Haiti	1.60	1.96	1.89[d]
Honduras	.31	.38	.43
Mexico	.22	.17	...
Nicaragua	.18	.25	.22[d]
Panama	.02	.02[f]	...
Paraguay	.48	.26	.23[d]
Peru	.29	.23[f]	...
Uruguay	.07	.11	...
Venezuela	.14	.04	.06

[a] Credit to the government is net of government deposits at the banks, except for Brazil and Uruguay, for which gross figures were used. Counterpart fund balances were also netted out in the case of Bolivia and Haiti.
[b] Complete breakdown between credit to government and private sector not available.
[c] Not comparable to 1962.
[d] May.
[e] March.
[f] September.
Source: IMF, *International Financial Statistics*.

Balance of Payments and Price Pressures

Balance-of-payments trends continue to loom as a major factor in the determination of Latin American monetary conditions. In fact, the external deficits, because they are so large and recur so frequently, have in many countries assumed an importance that goes far beyond the direct impact they may be allowed to have on the supply of domestic liquidity in any particular year. Over a period of time, the need to correct them, or at least cut them down to a more manageable size, has often been the most important single influence involved in the formulation of overall monetary policies. The fact that, notwithstanding occasional surpluses, virtually all Latin American countries have had a very weak balance-of-payments position in recent years explains the large number of formal monetary stabilization programs that were either in progress or about to be adopted in South and Central America during the period under review. Argentina, Bolivia, and Paraguay, for instance, are still pursuing stabilization policies initiated in 1959, 1956, and 1957, respectively. Chile and Colombia, for their part, have applied stabilizaton programs—with varying degrees of rigor—since the late 1950's and planned to intensify their efforts in 1963. Similarly Uruguay, which did not implement very effectively the program adopted at the end of the last decade, was again taking up its monetary stabilization attempt in 1963. In 1961, stabilization programs had also been undertaken by Ecuador, Costa Rica, and El Salvador in an effort to redress unfavorable balance-of-payments positions and check exchange speculation.

The extent to which the Latin American stabilization policies were able to correct external imbalances in recent years was determined in large part by the *coherence* of the fiscal and monetary measures employed to cut down total effective demand and dampen inflationary pressures in the domestic economy. The record in this respect was analyzed at some length in the preceding issue of this *Survey*.[7] It was pointed out then that generally, with a strong emphasis on credit restriction to the private sector, and at a heavy cost in terms of investment, output, and employment levels, substantial results were often quickly obtained in the form of an improved balance-of-payments position and a new-found confidence in the national currency.

Devaluation of the exchange rate to a more realistic level and direct restrictions on imports had also contributed greatly to the initial successes of most stabilization programs in curbing external deficits. Subsequently, however, as domestic price levels had continued to rise, the new exchange rates for the most part were not allowed to depreciate and had again become substantially overvalued in a number of countries by 1960 or 1961 (see Table 3–6). This undoubtedly contributed to the renewal of import pressures and speculative capital outflows observed in that period in countries whose stabilization policies had initially been rewarded with success. Although the increased import volumes served for a time to ease the renewed inflationary pressures experienced in the domestic economy, large amounts of medium- and short-term foreign debt were accumulated to finance the high import levels, and the exchange rate was supported only at huge costs to official reserves.

[7] See *Economic & Social Survey of Latin America, 1961*, I, 216–17, 225–28.

In 1962, restrictive measures were multiplied to hold down imports and economize foreign exchange in a number of countries, especially Argentina, Chile, and Colombia. Similar pressures were felt in Brazil, where, although no comprehensive monetary stabilization had been undertaken, exchange policy had preserved a certain amount of flexibility through the exchange reforms of early 1961 but had supported increasingly unrealistic rates in the subsequent period of accelerated domestic inflation. Eventually, in each one of these countries in the course of 1962 and in

TABLE 3–6. Latin America: Indices of Exchange Rate and Price Trends after Major 1958–1959 Exchange Rate Adjustments

(December 1959 = 100)

Country	December				
	1959	1960	1961	1962	1963
Argentina					
Cost of living	100	112	168	175	188
Exchange rate	100	99	100	161	167
Bolivia					
Cost of living	100	111	119	123	118[d]
Exchange rate	100	100	100	100	100[d]
Brazil					
Cost of living	100	132	190	305	381[e]
Exchange rate[a]	100	101	156	233	304[e]
Chile					
Cost of living	100	106	116	147	179
Exchange rate	100	100	100	156	175
				230[a]	287[a]
Colombia					
Cost of living	100	107	112	118	157
Exchange rate[b]	100	105	105	141	141
Paraguay					
Cost of living	100	114	150	...	...
Exchange rate	100	103	103	103	103
Peru					
Cost of living	100	103	110	116	120[e]
Exchange rate	100	97	97	97	97[e]
Uruguay					
Cost of living	100	136	151	168	...
Exchange rate[c]	100	99	98	98	148

[a] Controlled free rate.
[b] Principal selling rate.
[c] Rate used in base year was free rate.
[d] March.
[e] May.

Source: IMF, *International Financial Statistics*. Official rates, unless otherwise indicated.

Uruguay in 1963, speculation reached crisis proportions, and a new wave of exchange-rate adjustments, comparable in importance to that of the 1958–59 period, swept away existing parities and in some cases led to major changes in the structure of the exchange markets. The Argentine peso, which had been maintained at the same level for three years after the December, 1958, devaluation, was allowed to fluctuate and depreciated by more than 60 per cent between April and June, 1962 (in terms of number of pesos per dollar). In Brazil, the controlled free-market rate was allowed to depreciate several times in the course of 1962 and once again in April, 1963, so that by May, 1963, the dollar was quoted in that market at nearly twice the cruzeiro value it had had in December, 1961. Chile re-established a dual exchange market in January, 1962, and stopped supporting the official rate in October. Both the free and official rates for the dollar rose sharply in late 1962 and early 1963. In Colombia, the official import rate, which had been supported at 6.70 pesos per dollar since 1960 for fear of the impact its depreciation might have on the cost of living, was finally raised to 9.00 in November, 1962. In Uruguay, the official exchange rate was not devalued until May, 1963. A return to a dual rate system was then anticipated for the near future.

Domestic price and wage pressures, for their part, were largely unabated. In many countries, the rise in the cost of living continued at about the same pace as in 1961 (see Table 3–7), and the resulting claims for commensurate wage increases sent the inflationary spiral on yet another upward round. The exchange rate adjustments, moreover, were not without impact on the price level of the countries concerned. They were probably a major factor in the acceleration of the cost-of-living increases observed in Argentina and Brazil throughout 1962. In Chile and Colombia, the sharp increases in the index around the turn of the year can be attributed to the devaluations of October and November, 1962. Price freezes had to be imposed in some cases to check speculation in essential food items. Particularly drastic measures were called for in Brazil, where poor harvests combined with soaring prices to create acute shortages of staples in some northeastern cities. Concern about the implications of an extremely rapid rise in the cost of living also led the Brazilian Government to re-establish in 1962 an exchange subsidy on imports of wheat, petroleum, and newsprint, which had been eliminated in the course of the 1961 exchange reforms. The abolition of this subsidy, which was one of the objectives of the three-year development plan,[8] was again decreed in January, 1963; but in April, when the

---

[8] See below, p. 185.

TABLE 3-7. Latin America: Percentage Changes in Cost of Living Index, 1957–1963

Country	1957–61 annual average[a]	1961 Dec.	Twelve months ended					
			1962				1963	
			March	June	Sept.	Dec.	March	June
Argentina	42	19	22	27	34	32	36	23
Bolivia	6	7	10	7	5	3	−4	...
Brazil	31	44	46	52	57	62	67	69[b]
Chile	19	10	10	11	12	28	39	46
Colombia	9	5	3	−1	4	5	25	35
Costa Rica	2	—	—	2	5	5	5	4[b]
Dominican Republic	−1	−5	5	11	20	15	3	7
Ecuador	1	3	3	—	4	5	6	7
El Salvador	−1	−4	−2	−1	2	2	2	1
Guatemala	—	3	3	−2	3	−2	...	...
Haiti	−2	3	−1	...	...	...	...	...
Honduras	1	—	1	−1	—	5	5	1
Mexico	6	−2	—	1	2	2	1	1
Nicaragua	—	−2	—	1	−1	—	−2	—
Panama	—	—	—	—	1	—	1	2
Paraguay	15	32	...	...	...	...	...	...
Peru	8	7	7	8	5	5	6	5[b]
Uruguay	27	10	12	9	10	11	8	...
Venezuela	2	1	3	—	−2	−2	...	1[b]

[a] December-to-December changes.
[b] May.
Source: IMF, *International Financial Statistics*.

cruzeiro was devalued to 620 per dollar, the previous rate of 475 was maintained for wheat, petroleum, and newsprint, marking in effect a return to preferential treatment.

Fiscal Pressures

As already noted, the domestic inflationary pressures arose in many countries from the size of the government budget deficit. Although tax reform programs were initiated and tax yields raised in many parts of Latin America in 1962,[9] the impact of these measures was often still too moderate, or came too late in the year, to provide the public sector with resources commensurate with its growing expenditures. The figures

[9] See below, p. 235.

on net government borrowing at the banks give an indication, albeit incomplete, of the gravity of the fiscal situation and, in many countries, of its further deterioration in relation to 1961 (see Table 3-8).

A thorough evaluation of the fiscal situation would, of course, require a more detailed analysis of the structure of government expenditures in the different countries, as the future impact of these expenditures on the economic stability of a country depends to an important extent on the type of expenditure incurred. Considering the limitations as to information, however, the following discussion will limit itself to a partial review of the problem.

TABLE 3-8. Latin America: Percentage Change in Banking System's Net Claims on Government,[a] 1961-1963

Country	1961	1962	1963 First half
Argentina	9	24	11[d]
Bolivia	7	18	−7
Brazil	82	51	8[e]
Chile	75	87	7
Colombia	18	59	2[d]
Costa Rica[b]	73	25	18
Dominican Republic	96	−9	[c]
Ecuador	124	3	15
El Salvador	162	31	5
Guatemala	−4	93	−52
Haiti	11	26	−8[d]
Honduras	2	34	14
Mexico	5	−11	...
Nicaragua	−3	48	−19
Paraguay	20	−33	−2[d]
Peru	−7	−16[f]	...
Uruguay	2	76	...
Venezuela	93	−71	66

[a] Net of changes in government deposits at the banks, except in Brazil and Uruguay, where gross figures were used. Changes in counterpart fund balances were also netted out in the case of Bolivia and Haiti.
[b] Central bank credit only.
[c] Not comparable to 1962 data.
[d] January–May.
[e] January–March.
[f] Twelve months ending September.

Source: IMF, *International Financial Statistics.*

Only in isolated cases were government budgets balanced in 1962. One outstanding example was that of Venezuela, where a rise in oil revenues took place in 1962 and the first months of 1963. Revenue from exchange profits also rose sharply, as a result of a further tightening of exchange control regulations which transferred a large number of nonessential imports to the free market, where dollars could be bought at about 4.5 bolivares, while the Government continued to purchase the bulk of the country's export proceeds at the petroleum rate of 3.09 bolivares per dollar.

Examples of noninflationary financing through the domestic capital market were also rare. Except for Mexico, where government and official entities have continued to finance a large part of their investment needs by borrowing from the nonbank public, what long-term loans were obtained usually came from foreign sources.[10] Bolivia, Paraguay, and some of the Central American countries continued to rely to a considerable extent on United States grant aid. In Peru, where parliamentary delays in tax reform legislation contributed to a deterioration of the budgetary position in 1962, the Government was initially able to draw on accumulated surpluses to finance its deficit and used funds provided by the revaluation of the official gold reserves to cancel part of its debt to the Central Bank. Toward the end of the year, however, a bond issue had to be placed with the banks and the major foreign mining and industrial companies to permit financing of the fiscal deficit.

In the major South American countries, the picture was mostly one of growing budgetary imbalance in 1962, and the year was often spent searching for expedients to postpone government payments and raise additional short-term funds while minimizing, insofar as possible, the impact of the deficit on the over-all monetary expansion.

In Argentina, the fiscal situation took a sharp turn for the worse in 1962, as the difficulties involved in getting at the root causes of the deficit (in particular, the subsidies to the state enterprises) were compounded by the impact of the business depression on the flow of government revenues. Arrears in government payments became common, and suppliers credits increased greatly. A large part of the deficit was financed, both in 1962 and in the first half of 1963, with debt cancellation certificates issued to suppliers and contractors in lieu of payment. In 1962, the Government also floated a special bond issue ("9th of July bonds") with tax exemption and exchange depreciation guaranty clauses, which was also subscribed by state suppliers. In 1963, limitations on Treasury

---

[10] See above, p. 85.

borrowing from the Central Bank were eased by a one-year charter amendment. Moreover, the Government planned to obtain additional funds from the commercial banks, whose cash position had improved in the early months of this year and which are now required to invest a certain proportion of their available resources in government securities.

A stepped-up use of commercial bank resources to finance public expenditures was also made in Chile, where the banks were allowed to include Treasury bills in their required reserves. Colombia, for its part, was considering a measure involving compulsory bank purchases of government bonds up to 5 per cent of demand deposits in the package of emergency powers requested from the legislature to reinforce monetary stabilization in 1963. Large issues of promissory notes had already brought total government borrowing from the Central Bank to record levels at the end of 1962.

A good deal of the potential Brazilian deficit for 1962 was temporarily avoided by delaying a large number of payments to government suppliers and creditors until 1963. A serious financing problem remained, nevertheless, and the Government continued to borrow from the Central Bank on a large scale. At mid-year, the Treasury floated a 150-billion cruzeiro issue of 20-year bonds that the commercial banks were allowed to include in their required reserves. There were also a number of compulsory loans subscribed by income-tax payers through surcharges on their regular income-tax assessments.

Bank Credit to the Private Sector

In countries faced with over-all inflationary pressures and incompressible fiscal deficits, bank credit to the private sector continued to be the major target of restrictive policies. In a number of countries, the rate of growth of total bank credit to the private sector slowed down markedly in 1962. Moreover, even in the countries where the nominal increase was still high, in real terms the change was often insignificant or even negative because of the momentum of the price inflation (see Table 3–9).

This was especially the case in Argentina, where particularly severe restrictions on commercial bank credit and a decline in bank deposits created conditions of acute liquidity shortage which had a considerable impact on the level of economic activity. In Brazil, the rapid growth of bank credit to the private sector was barely enough to keep up with the price increases in the past two or three years, and a slowdown of production became clearly noticeable in the early months of 1963 in many industries—such as the automobile industry—that were especially affected

TABLE 3-9. Latin America: Bank Credit to the Private Sector in 1961 and 1962

Country	Nominal percentage change in credit outstanding		Real percentage change in credit outstanding[a]	
	1961	1962	1961	1962
Argentina	31	9	10	−17
Bolivia	42	22	32	19
Brazil	38	60	−4	—
Chile	27	23	16	−3
Colombia	25	15	19	10
Costa Rica[b]	3	1	3	−3
Dominican Republic	−13	24	−8	6
Ecuador	6	2	3	−2
El Salvador	−4	−3	—	−5
Guatemala	10	11	6	12
Haiti	12	3	8	...
Honduras	7	9	7	4
Mexico	15	20	18	17
Nicaragua	7	8	9	8
Panama	9	11	9	11
Paraguay	12	23	−14	...
Peru	19	22[c]	12	16[c]
Uruguay	17	15	6	3
Venezuela	−1	5	−2	7

[a] Nominal change in bank credit deflated by change in cost-of-living index.
[b] In Costa Rica, the figures are those for total commercial bank credit, which may include some credit to the government.
[c] Twelve months ending September.
Source: IMF, *International Financial Statistics*.

by restrictions to faster credit expansion. Money was also scarce in Bolivia, Chile, and elsewhere. In Uruguay, the lack of liquidity to carry out normal business activities became a major problem.

Changes in commercial bank reserve requirements remained one of the major instruments of monetary policy. In the course of 1962, increases were made in these requirements in a number of countries. In Argentina, increases of 0.25 per cent were made monthly from October, 1962, to May, 1963, though loans for productive investments could be included in the banks' minimum required reserves. The Brazilian authorities raised the required reserves on demand deposits from 14 to 22 per cent in May, 1962, and those on time deposits from 7 to 14 per cent. New increases were decreed in early 1963, with a number of exemptions provided for banks in the north and the northeast as well as banks in some of the central western states and banks engaged in certain priority types of lending. Colombia, for its part, proceeded to a gradual increase in commercial banks' required reserves in the early part of 1962 and has now restored a 100 per cent marginal requirement on deposit increases over the December, 1962, levels.

Marginal reserve requirements were reduced, on the other hand, in Peru, to permit a greater expansion of credit to the private sector in 1962. In January, 1963, to meet anticipated credit needs during the year, the basic requirement, which had remained at 28 per cent since 1961, was raised to 29 per cent and the marginal requirement entirely eliminated, the net effect being a 10 per cent decline in total required reserves. In Uruguay, reserve requirements were temporarily suspended in April, 1962, to ease the credit shortage, but they were re-established a few months later. Reserve requirements were also lowered in Ecuador in the early part of 1962 to offset the effect of the fund shortage which had resulted from the outflow of funds and loss of confidence in the currency in 1961.

Central Bank rediscounting assumed renewed importance in a number of countries where the credit squeeze brought particularly severe hardships on industry and trade. To deal with this problem, emergency rediscount systems were set up in several instances along different lines from those of the usual rediscount mechanisms. In Argentina, the commercial banks' liquidity position was extremely tight during most of 1962, and the reserve deficiencies with the Central Bank substantial. To remedy this, the Banco Industrial was authorized in May, 1962, to rediscount commercial paper of industrial enterprises for the commercial banks up to 20 per cent of each bank's capital and reserves, with 25 per cent of each loan to be used to meet tax payment arrears of the enterprise. Later in the year, further arrangements were devised to enable the banks to provide credit for certain hard-pressed sectors of industry, despite their required reserve deficiencies. A special committee was set up to study the loan position of each bank with reserve shortfalls and to exempt specified credits from the very high penalty rates usually charged for failure to meet the reserve requirements.

In Uruguay, the rediscount ceilings of the commercial banks at the Bank of the Republic had been raised by about 35 per cent at the end of 1961 to provide liquidity for the year-end needs of business and the beginning of a new wool season. Further increases were made in these ceilings in the final months of 1962 to ease the increasingly severe liquidity shortage prevailing in the economy. Finally, in July, 1963, special credits for periods ranging up to five years were made available to industry and agriculture by the Bank of the Republic, to facilitate the repayment of debts incurred in the course of business.

A somewhat similar measure was also recently taken in Brazil. In the early part of 1963, the Government established a temporary fund to help industrial firms recover their liquidity and to provide the working capital that would permit them not to curtail operations.

As would be expected, interest rates were extremely high in many Latin American countries in 1962. They were reportedly running at more than 40 per cent a year in Argentina in the nonbank market, while in Bolivia, for instance, the average effective rate on commercial bank loans ranged between 20 per cent and 25 per cent. Attempts to bring lending rates down and make deposit rates more attractive became an important feature of central banking policy. In Argentina, there was an easing of restrictions and a general increase in rates paid on bank deposits. The Bolivian Central Bank had increased its deposit rates in 1961, and the commercial banks followed suit. In Chile, interest-rate ceilings on commercial bank lending rates were lowered to 12–15 per cent from their previous level of 16.5 per cent. In Peru, a new central banking law also permitted the setting of maximum bank lending rates at 13 per cent in February, 1962. A 16 per cent maximum was established in Uruguay as part of the fiscal and monetary measures accompanying the devaluation of the peso in May, 1963.

Institutional Reforms

The need to perfect instruments of monetary control and develop financial markets on a more adequate scale led to a large number of institutional changes in the past two years. New banking laws were passed in about half a dozen countries and were under study in several others, while various changes were made in the long-term capital markets to stimulate a greater flow of funds into industry and housing construction.

Central Bank legislation was modified in El Salvador and Peru. The Salvadorean Central Bank had been nationalized in 1961 and its credit control powers spelled out. Under the new law which came into force in January, 1962, the bank modified reserve requirements and set commercial bank rediscount ceilings for the first time. In Peru, a new central banking law adopted at the beginning of 1962 redefined the functions of the Central Bank, giving it a more active role to play in the formulation of monetary policy and wider powers to regulate the activity of both bank and nonbank financial institutions. The Peruvian commercial banking law was subsequently modified in July, 1963, to permit an expansion of commercial banking commensurate with the growth of economic activity in the country.

In Nicaragua, the Central Bank was established as an independent entity, separate from the National Bank of Nicaragua, in 1961. Venezuela, for its part, had been given a new central banking law at the end of 1960 to broaden the discount powers of the central banking institution and increase its control over the volume and direction of commercial bank credit. Finance companies became subject to regulation by the monetary authorities in 1961 in Venezuela and in January, 1962, in Argentina.

Major bank reforms were under consideration in several other countries. Bolivia, for instance, was contemplating changes designed to obtain a more satisfactory allocation of credit to the various sectors of the economy, and Costa Rica was considering changes in the banking law to permit greater bank participation in the financing of industrial development. In Brazil, a bank reform bill submitted to the legislature would set up a National Monetary Council and reinforce the powers of the present credit control agency, the Superintendency for Money and Credit (SUMOC). Similarly, the Colombian Government requested in 1963 the power to appoint a special committee which would take over the formulation of monetary policy from the Bank of the Republic, with which it has rested until now.

In Uruguay, steps were taken in May, 1963, to effect a major reorganization of the Bank of the Republic. The Bank would be turned into the sole agency for granting selective credit to industry. Its issue department would be empowered to fix quantitative and qualitative controls on credit extended both by banks and nonbank financial institutions.

Mexico and Nicaragua both passed new General Laws of Credit Institutions in 1962. The Mexican law, among other things, eased regulations on commercial bank export credit activities, created new mechanisms through which medium and small industry could obtain long-term financing from investment banking institutions, and widened the scope for mortgage lending activities by various types of savings institutions. The Nicaraguan law authorized the acceptance of savings accounts from the public by banking institutions and the creation of co-operative savings and loan associations for housing finance.

Other important measures taken in the long-term financing field included the reorganization of official development banks in several countries and the establishment of savings and loan associations in various parts of Latin America. In Colombia, a special fund for medium-term lending to private enterprise began to operate at the Bank of the Republic in June, 1963. In El Salvador, a Capital Market Commission was set up at the end of 1962 to organize, develop, and control the operations in the securities market. The Ecuadorean National Security Commission, for its part, intensified its operations in 1962 and was considering major reforms to permit a better channeling of funds into investment. In 1963, Venezuela announced the establishment of a Fund for the Stabilization of Mortgage Bonds, which would seek to create an active market for bonds issued by the Venezuelan mortgage banks.

CHAPTER 4

THE MANUFACTURING SECTOR[1]

GENERAL DEVELOPMENT OF MANUFACTURING

The general course of the Latin American manufacturing industry in 1962 was less favorable than in several preceding years, at least as far as the growth of over-all production is concerned. In the other aspects of industrial development—primarily intended to set the stage for its future growth—considerable progress continued to be made in a large part of the area. Outstanding among these aspects of organic development are significant progress in projects under way, the gradual completion and integration of industrial processes, the progressive orientation of production toward the potentialities of the regional market, and growing rationalization in the operations of manufacturing enterprises.

The unsatisfactory growth of manufacturing output has been mainly the result of reverses sustained by Argentine industry. In fact, because of the decrease in secondary activities in that country, the manufacturing industry in the region has shown an over-all production increase of only about 4.4 per cent over the preceding year. Excluding the Argentine component from the corresponding regional totals, we obtain a rate of increase of approximately 6.5 per cent, a figure which does not fall so far below the analogous rate of the previous year, which was 7.6 per cent, without Argentina.[2] For purposes of comparison, it may be noted that in the last five years the cumulative rate of growth of industrial production in the area was nearly 7 per cent per annum.

Argentine industry experienced a drop of almost 5.5 per cent in manufacturing production, but as the structure of this sector of the national

---

[1] Although all the data for 1962 in this survey are preliminary, it is well to point out that those of this chapter may be subject to subsequent and quite extensive revisions and must be considered only as indicative of general trends.

[2] In computing these rates, as well as several others which will be given in this chapter, the results of Cuban industrial production, being unknown, have not been taken into account.

economy is fundamentally sound and capable of later development, this phenomenon may be considered as transitory, and it cannot be predicted, of course, at what stage or to what extent it will be overcome.[3] Indications for the next period are not yet sufficiently clear. During the first quarter of 1963, further drops in manufacturing production were noted, although these were at a somewhat lower rate.

Industrial development in the other countries has shown lesser changes with respect to the previous year (see Table 4–1). These changes, of course, have also modified the impact which the respective national industries have had on the growth of the manufacturing product of Latin America as a whole.

Although, in 1962, its rate of growth dropped to less than 10 per cent, after an average growth of about 12 per cent during the four years preceding, Brazilian industry continued to be one of the most dynamic elements in the development of manufacturing in the region. The decline may be explained to a great extent by the general economic difficulties of the year, though this does not eliminate the possibility that it may have had deeper roots. If such were the case, the stimulus of industrial growth in the last seven years would be giving rise to a less intense, but still appreciable, expansion. This change could be connected with the fact that the manufacturing development of the country will be based less and less on the substitution for imports; instead, satisfying the current needs of an expanding internal market, as well as increasing utilization of the possibilities of the regional market, will take on importance.[4]

In turn, Mexican industry has overcome the recessionary forces that had been operating in 1961 and has registered a higher rate of growth than in the preceding year, approximating its former rate of expansion. At the same time, it has been possible to observe signs that efforts to substitute for imports were gradually being intensified with respect to certain industries in which there still seem to be quite extensive potentialities despite the possible effects of the free-trade zone. It is well to mention that in Mexico, just as in Argentina and Brazil, orientation of the industrial sector toward the regional market is becoming more and more perceptible.

---

[3] The industrial recession in Argentina mainly affected the consumer goods industries—current consumer goods and, still more, durable consumer items—and repercussions were felt in several mechanical industries producing parts and equipment; the crisis, coupled with a noticeable lack of liquidity, spread to other sectors also.

[4] Recently there have also been various indications of the interest in Brazilian industrial circles in exporting manufactured articles to areas outside Latin America.

TABLE 4-1. Latin America: Manufacturing Growth, by Country and by Selected Industrial Products, 1957-1962 (Rates of Increase and Weighting)

Country	Rates of growth[a]				Weighting	
	1960	1961	1962*	1957-62	1957	1962
	Growth by country					
Argentina	11.1	13.9	−5.3	2.4	33.7	18.6
Brazil	10.6	11.1	6.9	11.6	30.8	38.4[b]
Chile	−2.3	4.7	4.3	6.0	3.1	2.8
Colombia	5.2	6.8	5.7	5.1	6.6	6.2
Ecuador	5.0	2.1	2.3	2.5	0.7	0.6
Mexico	10.9	3.6	6.4	6.8	15.6	15.7
Peru	15.1	8.7	4.9	7.6	1.6	1.6
Venezuela	−4.0	6.3	11.7	7.2	5.2	5.4
Others[c]	4.2	3.9	4.1	3.6	12.7	10.8
Latin America[c]	8.4	8.8	4.4	6.9	100.0	100.0
	Growth by selected industrial product[d]					
Current consumer goods	4.1	4.1	2.3	3.8		
Cellulose pulps[e]	9.0	10.6	5.6	11.1		
Paper and cardboard[f]	5.0	9.8	5.1	8.1		
Petroleum refining[g]	7.1	6.8	12.3	9.3		
Cement	7.7	5.1	6.6	4.9		
Pig iron	24.3	15.7	7.1	13.1		
Raw steel	14.5	11.3	9.7	11.7		
Finished steel	15.1	11.0	7.4	10.1		
Motor vehicles	...	25.4	12.7	[h]		

[a] Rates given in the first three columns represent increases with respect to the preceding year; coefficients shown in the fourth column are rates of annual growth for the 1957-62 period.

[b] The marked drop in the industrial production of Argentina in 1962 not only caused her manufacturing product to fall in position with relation to the Latin American total but also temporarily raised the weighting for Brazil and the other countries.

[c] Changes in Cuban manufacturing activity, being unknown, are not included.

[d] These data are given by way of illustration and cannot be taken as representative with respect to the total for the sector because the respective weightings are unknown.

[e] For paper and cardboard.

[f] In aggregate.

[g] Including Venezuela.

[h] The corresponding annual rate of 88 per cent does not lend itself to the analysis because a very small initial base is used for the comparison.

Sources: The data for 1957 and a great part of those for 1960 are taken from the ECLA series and are expressed at constant prices. The other basic data come from the following:

Argentina: IA-ECOSOC, *Informe presentado por el Gobierno de la Argentina* (Washington, Pan American Union, 1963) (OEA/Ser. H/X.5, Doc. 11).

Chile and Peru: analogous reports of the respective governments (Docs. 15 and 19).

Brazil: IBGE, Conselho Nacional de Estatística, *Anuário Estatístico do Brasil 1962*, and, for 1962, Estimate of the *Conjuntura Econômica*, February 1963.

(Continued)

TABLE 4-1. *Continued*

Colombia: report presented to the IA-ECOSOC by the Government of Colombia in 1962 (OEA/Ser. H/X.3, Doc. 23) and, for 1962, preliminary data published by *Fortnightly Review*, February 6, 1963.

Mexico: analogous report of the Government (Doc. 32) and, for 1962, Report to the IA-ECOSOC, October, 1963).

Ecuador: *Memoria del Gerente General del Banco Central del Ecuador 1961* and preliminary estimate based on fragmentary national reports for 1962.

Venezuela: Report to the IA-ECOSOC, October, 1963.

The last growth coefficients for Colombia, Chile, and Peru range between 4.3 and 5.7 per cent;[5] only in the case of Peru is there a rather substantial difference between the rates of growth in 1962 and in 1961.

The recent manufacturing development of Peru and Colombia has been achieved with a degree of stability greater than that which prevailed in the Chilean economy that year, and during this period Chile felt various delayed effects of the serious lack of external equilibrium which had become evident toward the end of 1961 and which occasioned severe measures in the beginning of the following year. Still less favorable—according to provisional estimates—was the recent manufacturing development of Ecuador, where industrial growth was quite slow during the five-year period.

At the same time, Venezuelan industry showed a growth of 11.7 per cent. Several intermediate and current consumer-goods industries have recently gathered momentum. Probable contributing factors have been the continuing stimulus of the Government's development policy and the considerable resources of the country for manufacturing development.

Although the trend of Latin American current consumer-goods industries has been unfavorable in 1962—at least as far as the evolution of the respective regional totals is concerned—a large number of those intermediate and mechanical industries on which reports in physical terms are available continue to show considerable dynamism. In certain of the latter branches, production figures, including those for Argentina, show more or less normal development.

Outstanding among the major dynamic branches of manufacturing in the region are petroleum refining and raw steel, with growth rates of between 12.5 and 9.5 per cent.

[5] The high growth rate of manufacturing shown in 1962 by the Chilean index of industrial production has been adjusted downward in the course of official computing of the national product.

The automobile industry and the other mechanical industries—despite the Argentine recession—also made an appreciable contribution to the Latin American manufacturing product (12.7 per cent). In the production of cement, whose expansion had been less vigorous than that of the other intermediate industries during the last five-year period, a higher degree of growth was attained in 1962 than in the previous year; it even exceeded the average annual increase for the five years. Although no up-to-date data are available on the development of chemical industries for the whole region, recent production figures of various nations, especially Mexico and Brazil, indicate a noticeable expansion. Among the normally dynamic industries, the paper industry received a rather weak impetus this year.

Current Consumer-Goods Industries

Current consumer-goods industries—somewhat heterogeneous, but actually traditional manufacturing activities—continued to expand gradually in 1962, although they barely achieved an increase of 2.3 per cent for the region as a whole. Such a low coefficient of growth compares unfavorably even with the cumulative annual rate of 3.8 per cent, which shows the slow growth of these activities throughout the 1957–62 period.[6]

In this connection, it is well to recall that the slow expansion of the traditional industries is due especially to the fact that—at least in the semi-industrialized countries of the region—they no longer have great possibilities of replacing imports. Besides, the great majority of these industries have lacked special stimuli for improving their output or quality with a view to winning new markets, domestic or foreign.[7]

Furthermore, the regional market has not furnished notable incentives in this field, and in the near future it will also probably offer less than to other manufacturing activities.

[6] The figures in this section are for all those manufacturing activities which it is customary to group together under the term "traditional" industries. However, for the practical purposes of the present analysis, the two concepts may be almost identical, since the latter embraces the preponderant part of industries belonging to the former, and only a small fraction of the other industries (for example, the wood and the furniture industries). For more details on the composition of the manufacturing group under consideration, see the definition and explanations given in the *Economic & Social Survey of Latin America, 1961* (Washington, 1962), particularly the note at the bottom of page 388 (Spanish version).

Moreover, the list of branches of industry which make up the traditional group, as considered in this study, also is given in Table 4–2.

[7] The case of certain food branches was, in a way, different. Some, such as sugar processing, have achieved noticeable increases in production upon finding new export possibilities, thanks to special circumstances.

The recent evolution of this manufacturing group, by industrial branches, can be studied only for Argentina, Brazil, Chile, Peru, and Venezuela, utilizing, for this purpose, mainly the respective indices of manufacturing production.[8]

The product of the traditional industries of these five countries represents almost two-thirds of the Latin American product of these manufacturing branches.[9] In 1962, it showed an expansion of 2.6 per cent, in circumstances which the cumulative annual increment for the last five-year period raises to 4.4 per cent [10] (see Table 4–2).

The most remarkable phenomenon of the different activities within the group is the marked decline in the textile industry, attributable not only to the drop in Argentine production but also, in a lesser degree, to a slackening in this activity in Brazil. Moreover, a certain faltering in expansion is to be noted in the subgroups of shoes, clothing, wood, and furniture. As for shoes and clothing, the change is not very pronounced, since these activities only went through a period of stagnation in Argentina and a moderate decline in growth rate in Brazil, which were compensated for to a great extent by the simultaneous increase in development in Peru, Chile, and Venezuela. Similar trends also evidenced themselves in the wood and furniture industries; but in this area the achievements of the latter three countries were not sufficient to compensate fully for the falling off in Brazil and Argentina.

Paper Industry

Latin American production of paper and cardboard showed an increment of 5 per cent in 1962, compared with almost 10 per cent in the year preceding and 5 per cent in 1960 (see Table 4–3). As for cumulative annual expansion during the last five-year period, the industry showed a rate of growth of more than 8 per cent.

In the case of cellulose pulp production—the more retarded item, the production of which, therefore, usually shows a greater dynamism—the recent increment was somewhat over 5.5 per cent; in the two pre-

---

[8] The aggregate of the traditional industries represents at present about 42 per cent of the manufacturing product of all Latin America. Percentages are slightly lower for certain semi-industrialized countries of the region.

In the case of the relatively smaller nations, however, these industries are of great importance both for the totals and percentagewise, their proportion being at times substantially higher.

[9] See note ª, Table 4–2, in order to place these countries in their regional perspective.

[10] It should be remembered that the corresponding rates of growth for all Latin America were 2.3 and 3.8 per cent, respectively.

ceding years it fluctuated between 9 and 10.5 per cent under circumstances which caused the cumulative rate of the last five-year period to rise to 11 per cent.

In 1962, only the production of newsprint maintained the growth rate of the last five-year period (almost 20 per cent), the most notable increases being registered in Brazil and Mexico.

The figures cited show plainly that in the course of 1962 the expansion of Latin American paper production did not attain the growth

TABLE 4–2. Latin America: Growth of the Traditional Industries in Five Selected Countries,[a] 1957–1962

Industrial branches[b]	(Indices: 1957 = 100)				Rates of growth	
	1957	1960	1961	1962*	1961–62	1957–62[c]
Food and drink	100	115	121	125	3.5	4.5
Tobacco	100	115	124	129	3.5	5.1
Textiles	100	123	131	132	1.0	5.6
Shoes and clothing	100	102	118	121	2.5	3.9
Wood and furniture	100	111	115	117	1.8	3.2
Leather and furs	100	99	109	124	13.8[d]	3.2
Total: traditional industries	100	115	122	125	2.0	4.4

[a] Argentina, Brazil, Chile, Peru, and Venezuela. It should be observed that this sampling—selected according to the availability of national indices of manufacturing production—is not sufficiently representative for the whole of Latin America. The rates, at least those relating to the total of the traditional group, are higher than those of the corresponding regional average. Furthermore, the production indices used suffer from certain biases. Nevertheless, it may be assumed that the figures given are at least roughly indicative of recent trends in this field.

[b] The industrial branches to which the data refer represent groupings of the CIIU—Uniform International Industrial Classification of All Economic Activities—or a combination of two groupings.

[c] Rates of cumulative annual growth.

[d] The high rate under this heading is due to the extraordinary character of the Brazilian component. The basic datum—a preliminary estimate taken from the review *Conjuntura Econômica*—is, possibly, an overappraisal of the growth in this branch. It should be pointed out here that various other figures in the indices used also seem to leave a certain amount to be desired in the way of preciseness, but there are reasons for assuming that they counterbalance one another to some degree, at least in the totals of the traditional group.

Sources of basic data: Dirección Nacional de Estadística y Censos, *Boletín Mensual de Estadística* (Buenos Aires), various numbers; Conselho Nacional de Estatística, *Anuário Estatístico do Brasil, 1962;* (Rio de Janeiro), Banco Central de Chile, *Boletín Mensual* (Santiago de Chile), April, 1963; Banco Central de Venezuela, *Memoria Anual* (Caracas), 1957–61; Sociedad Nacional de Industrias, *Industria Peruana* (Lima), April, 1963. Also, for 1962: *Conjuntura Econômica* (Rio de Janeiro), February, 1963, and fragmentary data relative to the production of Chilean, Peruvian, and Venezuelan industry.

TABLE 4–3. Latin America: Production of Cellulose Pulp, Paper, and Cardboard, 1957, 1960, 1961, and 1962

(Thousands of tons)

Country	Paper and cardboard pulp				Paper and cardboard				Newsprint			
	1957	1960	1961	1962*	1957	1960	1961	1962*	1957	1960	1961	1962*
Argentina	71	80	103	102	303	291	370*	363	12	9	9	13
Bolivia	—	—	—	—	1	1	1	1	—	—	—	—
Brazil	258	322*	337	374	468	609*	639	698	49	68*	70	84
Central America[a]	—	—	—	—	1	1	2	2	—	—	—	—
Chile	24	105	122	124	71	120	131	139	20	52	70	75
Colombia	3	9	11	12	40	53	58	61	—	—	—	—
Ecuador	—	—	—	—	1	1	1	1	—	—	—	—
Mexico	167	240	265	273	307	403	423	436	—	14	18	27
Paraguay	—	—	—	—	—	1	1	1	—	—	—	—
Peru	18	30	32	34	37	47	51	54	—	—	—	—
Uruguay	5	6	6	6	30	36	40	41	—	—	—	—
Venezuela	—	—	—	—	19	65*	75*	86*	—	—	—	—
Latin America: Totals	546	792	876	925	1,278	1,632	1,792	1,883	81	143	167	199
Rates of increment for the preceding year		9.0	10.6	5.6		5.0	9.8	5.1		6.0	16.8	19.2
Rates of cumulative annual increment 1957/62				11.1				8.1				19.6

[a] Includes the production of El Salvador and Guatemala.

Sources: For 1957, ECLA/FAO/DOAT Advisory Group on Paper and Cellulose for Latin America (Doc. E/CN. 12/570). For other years: Direct information from the producers of their trade associations and from public organizations. For countries whose production is still low and for which data were not obtained in time, estimates were made on the basis of fragmentary information.

rate of the previous year and that the rate of increment was also lower than that of the last five-year period. The reasons for this decline in expansion during 1962 vary according to the country. While in some cases, mainly that of Argentina, the unfavorable evolution of demand contributed to slow growth or stagnation in production, in the majority of Latin American countries limitations in productive capacity constituted the principal obstacle.

With regard to domestic demand for paper, there do not seem to be any grounds for long-range concern, since consumption normally tends to expand greatly. Thus, while in 1955 regional demand had risen to only 1.8 million tons, in 1965, according to a recent study,[11] it is predicted that consumption will reach 3.5 million, and in 1975, 6.5 million. Furthermore, the progress of projects under way and the new ones that are being drafted afford promising prospects as regards future supply, although complete fulfillment of existing plans and desirable additions thereto will depend to a great extent on the availability of funds for investment, especially foreign exchange. These are not yet assured in various instances.

Argentina. The scant use of the cellulose resources of Argentina in the past and the consequently large volume of imports of this intermediate material and of finished paper led the Government of that country to establish, during the latter half of 1961, a system of tax concessions and facilities in favor of those private industrialists who would be willing to develop their activities along certain lines.[12] Although the general economic evolution of 1962 was not favorable to increase in production during this period, preparation of new plans and the progress thereof seem to demonstrate that this system has constituted an efficacious stimulus, at least from the point of view of future production. In fact, if the plans for expansion of the first five cellulose plants accepted under the scheme, which suppose a total investment of $48 million, were realized, the replacement of imports would be substantially advanced.[13] Subsequently, when the Ledesma project was approved, the number of privileged lumber enterprises rose to six. This industry will use the

[11] ECLA/FAO/BTAO, *Pulp and Paper in Latin America* (New York, 1963).

[12] The benefits granted under this policy are more liberal for those concerns whose programs are integrated with forestation plans, but they are not limited to industries whose activities extend to the extraction of primary wood products. The text of Decree No. 8141, issued in September of that year, may be consulted for further details.

[13] It has been estimated that the consequent gross saving in foreign exchange could run as high as some $30 million per year.

sugar-cane bagasse available in the zone for its integrated paper plant. Meanwhile, a new project has been presented which would also use bagasse and would manufacture various types of paper and cardboard. Finally, it should be mentioned that the Misiones project [14] has passed into one stage of materialization, inasmuch as construction of this plant, of 30,000 tons capacity (in terms of paper), for the production of pulp and kraft paper has been entrusted to an international firm, at a cost of $15 million.

Brazil. Since the mid-fifties, the Brazilian paper industry has met the notably expansive trend in consumption with a fair degree of flexibility. The degree of self-sufficiency in this field has even been steadily increasing. Present indications are that this trend will continue, and it is thought that by 1965 national production could handle 86 per cent of total paper consumption. However, in certain sectors of this industry it will be necessary to continue importing in relatively large quantities. Outstanding among them is that of newsprint, importation of which—though less than in the past—foreseeably will remain for some time at relatively high levels. Thus, according to recent calculations, in 1965, 43 per cent of the total newsprint consumed will still have to be imported.

An important event in the recent expansion was the installation of new equipment at the Monte Alegre (Paraná) newsprint plant. This has increased capacity from 42,000 to 106,000 tons annually. The capacity of the pulp plant recently equipped by this same enterprise runs to 140,000 tons.[15] There are, in addition, several new projects with a good possibility of realization.[16]

Colombia. With the granting of a loan of $1.4 million by the Inter-American Development Bank for the purchase of machinery and equipment, the projected Puerto Isaacs plant (near Cali) in Colombia is now in the preliminary stages of becoming a reality. This new installation would start off with a production of 17,000 tons of wood pulp and subsequently—as of 1966 or a little later—reach 34,000.

---

[14] See OAS/ECLA, *Economic & Social Survey of Latin America, 1961,* Chapter V.

[15] This firm also plans to set up a cellulose plant in the State of Pernambuco. It would use the bagasse found in such ample supply in this sugar-producing zone.

[16] One of the proposed plants would be set up with financial backing from well-known European firms in the field and would produce kraft paper; another would use bamboo, which grows abundantly in the State of Bahia. A third project—and the greatest in scope—has to do with setting up an integrated plant in Montenegro (Rio Grande do Sul) which would use the acacia resources for which the zone is known.

Chile. In southern Chile, preparatory activities for proceeding with expansion of the Laja plant, at an estimated cost of $22.6 million, have continued; it is expected that external financing will be obtained through various international credit organizations. If this project is carried out, the country's cellulose-producing capacity would increase to 140,000 tons. At the same time, a Canadian company is planning construction in Chile of a plant which would produce from 60,000 to 70,000 tons of newsprint, the greater part of which would be earmarked for export to Latin American countries.

Mexico. The recent evolution of the Mexican paper and cellulose industries shows a slackening in growth rate, as compared with preceding years, but there is a prospect that construction potential will open the way for revitalized expansion. Replacement of paper imports has progressed farther in this country than in most of the other producing countries of the region,[17] which also explains why demand has at times been less intense. Moreover, Mexico is one of those countries in which cellulose manufacturing shows the greatest structural changes regarding composition of raw materials used. Among the especially nontraditional materials increasingly used in this country are sugar-cane bagasse, cotton linters, and, recently, wheat straw.

Venezuela. The Venezuelan paper industry has recently gone through a marked expansion with the inauguration of the Maracay plant which, with a capacity of 35,000 tons, will produce writing and wrapping paper, and with the opening of a cardboard factory in the environs of Valencia with a capacity of 26,000 tons annually, which is sufficient to satisfy present demand for this product. At the same time, the largest enterprise in the field has been expanding its paper production capacity from 45,000 to 70,000 tons.

Central America. Although, so far, paper and cardboard production in the Central American Isthmus has been small in quantity and no cellulose is manufactured, it is hoped that the plan for a comparatively important integrated plant will crystallize under the common-market program. It would be carried out in conjunction with a more systematic exploitation of the Honduras timber resources. At the same time, various lesser projects in other countries of the Isthmus are making progress.

---

[17] According to a recent estimate, 85 per cent of needs are now being met locally. This figure, of course, holds true only for the over-all picture, since the margin for replacement in some products is still very great. In particular, local industry contributes only 15 per cent of newsprint consumed.

Chemical Industries

Although over-all data on the recent development of the chemical industries—a very heterogeneous group, in which no one product in particular predominates—are not yet available, the fragmentary information on hand gives reason to presume that expansion here has maintained almost the growth rate of preceding years, the rate this time being in the neighborhood of 10 per cent. Despite such a small variation in the average growth of these industries, greater changes have taken place in their make-up than in the period immediately preceding.

Regarding changes in growth rate by country, the intensive production increases in Mexico and Brazil—16.5 per cent, according to tentative indications—should be pointed out; comparatively significant progress is also to be noted in the case of Venezuela and, to a certain degree, of Peru.

As for the general pattern of expansion and composition by product, the changes which have taken place are quite complex. Mention should be made of the sizable increments shown for various countries in the manufacturing of pharmaceuticals and of fertilizers and their basic ingredients and in processes relating to the obtaining and processing of plastic materials. In the field of relatively new basic materials, the steady development of the petrochemical industries is outstanding and—to a lesser degree—the increasing use of coke by-products. Certain synthesis processes recently introduced have exhibited vigor, as has manufacturing of some materials—such as certain acids and alkalis—the production of which is not so new in the region, but the growing use of which in numerous industries is a corollary of manufacturing development. Thus, for example, Mexican production of sulphuric acid increased 32 per cent in 1962 and that of caustic soda, 17 per cent (see Table 4–4).

The products mentioned also have a prominent place among the items to be manufactured by the plants presently under construction. In addition, comparatively smaller installations are being constructed at various points for the production of insecticides, detergents, explosives, etc., and there is notable interest in the local manufacturing of synthetic rubber.

Brazil. During 1962, the first Latin American synthetic rubber plant was inaugurated in Brazil. It has a capacity of 40,000 tons annually, which can be doubled within a few years. This plant, originally supplied with imported raw materials, has been designated to utilize similar by-products of the Duque de Caxias refinery, located near Rio de Janeiro.

TABLE 4-4. Latin America: Caustic Soda and Sulphuric Acid Production, 1957, 1960, 1961, and 1962

(*Thousands of tons*)

Country	Caustic Soda				Sulphuric Acid			
	1957	1960	1961	1962*	1957	1960	1961	1962*
Argentina	32.6	46.7	53.6	54.9	112	160*	...	...
Brazil	47.0*	80.0	93.0*	102.0	150*	200	...	...
Chile	3.5	6.3	6.2	6.8	45	75	90*	...
Colombia	19.3*	25.0	28.8	29.9	19	26	...	...
Mexico	34.2	65.9	71.3	83.4	182	249	276	339
Peru	1.5	2.8	6.6	7.9	20	38	37	37
Venezuela	0.0	9.7	10.5	14.5	4	7	...	...
Latin America: Total for seven countries*a*	138.1	236.4	270.0	299.4	532	755		
Annual increment rates in relation to preceding year			14.2	10.9				
Cumulative annual increment rate 1957/62				16.7				

a In addition to the seven countries shown in the table, lesser quantities are produced in other Latin American countries, but volumes are not known. ECLA has estimated that, for 1959, sulphuric acid production of the remaining countries—including Cuba—amounted to about 40,000 tons; at the same time, according to an estimate of this Secretariat, caustic soda production in countries other than those listed was very low, probably very slightly over 1,000 tons.

Sources: For MEXICO: Nacional Financiera, *Mercado de Valores*, various numbers, and ECLA, *La Industria Química en America Latina*. PERU: direct information and ECLA, *op. cit.* VENEZUELA: information obtained from the Dirección General de Estadística, and ECLA, *op. cit.* Remaining countries: various national sources and estimates based on fragmentary information.

For processing of the materials required—butadiene and styrene—an adjacent installation is being set up. All of this is part of the country's second petrochemical complex, still in the stages of construction or completion.[18] In addition, there is a synthetic rubber project in the Northeast; this plant, using by-products of the sugar-refining industry, will have a production capacity of 25,000 tons. Toward the end of the year, the construction of new chemical works was begun at Camacari (Bahia); this complex will comprise, first of all, ammonia and urea plants with daily capacities of 200 and 100 tons, respectively. It is also planned to

[18] It should be remembered that the first group of plants of this type was the manufacturing belt around the Cubatão refinery (environs of Santos).

set up installations in this locality for the production of oxygen, carbon dioxide, hydrogen, nitric acid, etc. Among the projects about to be carried out at various points are also three phosphate fertilizer plants (superphosphate) with a combined capacity of almost 300,000 tons.

Mexico. With reference to the Mexican chemical industry, it may be pointed out that, in production value, it ranks second in Latin America, but its long-range growth is more intense than that of any other country of the region. Moreover, it is outstanding because of its many-sided orientation (it is progressing simultaneously in almost all branches of this field)[19] and also because of a policy consistently aimed toward export, along with positive measures for setting up diverse projects on a large scale capable of competing with those of other countries.[20]

In 1962, various plants begun in the country in preceding years were completed. The inauguration of an ammonium anhydride plant in Minatitlán and the virtual completion of another in Salamanca should be pointed out. Toward the end of the year, the first urea plant in the region was set up. Also worthy of mention are three new installations for the production of refrigerating gases, hydrofluoric acid, and carbon tetrachloride, respectively, and two others which will produce organic pigments and synthetic resins. Also, during this same year the range of locally produced pharmaceuticals was increased. Among the projects under construction or in an advanced stage of preparation and deserving of special notice are those coming under a petrochemical program of major proportions which will introduce the production of lampblack, phenol, acetone, methanol, benzene, toluene, ethylene, lead tetraethylene, and various polyesters, as well as synthetic rubber. Investments planned for this development of the petrochemical industry over the next three years amount to almost 2,500 million pesos ($200 million).

Among the other projects under way, a plant with an initial production of 100,000 tons of sodium carbonate is prominent; completion of this project, in addition to making the country self-sufficient for a certain time in this product—since there are also natural sources of supply—will make export possible to the other countries of the region. Finally, mention should be made of the progress in plans for constructing a large

---

[19] Nevertheless, fertilizers are outstanding both as regards production and as regards high growth rate; this fact is connected with the development of an expanded petrochemical program. Mexican chemical products include, among other items, dodecilbenzene, nylon, ammonium, ammonium nitrate, carbon dioxide, etc.

[20] For further details, see: ECLA, *The Chemical Industry in Latin America*, Vol. I, August, 1962 (Doc. E/CN.12/628).

sulphuric acid plant and an installation for the production of citric acid. An installation is also planned for the extraction of sodium sulphate from the Laguna del Rey salt reserves.

Argentina. In Argentina, also, progress continued in various important projects. Near the end of the year, a major chemical center in San Lorenzo (Santa Fe Province) went into its first stage of operation. The recently equipped installations have an annual production capacity of 75,000 tons of sulphuric acid, 14,000 tons of carbon disulphide, 1,000 tons of hydrogen peroxide, and 1,200 tons of phthalic anhydride; in the second stage, they will go on into the manufacturing of ethylene and polyethylene. At the same time, efforts have been made toward solving the pending problems of an important petrochemical complex, construction of which is to begin about the middle of 1963. Its program includes, among other items, synthetic rubber. In connection with the rubber industry, mention should also be made of the groundwork laid by another enterprise for the manufacturing of lampblack. Outstanding among the remaining projects are those having to do with the production of phenol, citric acid, and methyl alcohol. Likewise, it is planned to set up an industrial complex in the southern part of the country for the production of sodium alkalies, as well as chlorine and several of its compounds, including polyvinyl chloride.

It is interesting to observe that for several years these three great countries have been sharing about three-quarters of the chemical production of the region, a proportion which, according to recent ECLA projections, will probably be maintained for several more years.

Colombia. In Colombia, the Mamonal ammonium and nitric acid plant (near Cartagena) was virtually completed toward the end of the year; likewise a fertilizer plant in the same zone, where a great part of its production will be used. In addition, the fertilizer plant of the future Barrancabermeja petrochemical complex has been almost completed; an installation is also planned in this locality for the production of ethylene. Finally, mention should be made of the construction of an insecticide plant, intended to reduce imports of this item by one-half. Among projects recently launched, a second Solvay plant is outstanding; it will be set up near Cartagena, with a sodium carbonate capacity of 320 tons daily; more than half of this quantity will be sold as such, the remainder being reserved for conversion into caustic soda. Moreover, various projects are being promoted for the production of plastics and pharmaceuticals.

Chile. Plans are still under consideration in Chile for setting up a chemical industry center in the south of the country to produce sulphuric acid, fertilizers, and pesticides.

Ecuador, Paraguay. Likewise in the planning stage is the project for a fertilizer-mixing plant in Guayaquil, Ecuador, which would operate on a basis of imported materials. And in Paraguay, construction of an installation for producing plastics is nearing completion.

Peru. During the year, a contract was let for construction of a fertilizer plant in Cuzco, Peru. Preparations are also progressing for the petrochemical project in Los Organos, which is to produce 200 tons of ammonia daily. At the same time, the Callao ammonium plant, which began operations a few years ago, continued to increase its production. In addition, installation of a calcium carbonate plant at Chimbote has virtually been completed. Among projects in preparation are ones for the future production of urea and for increased production of chlorine, hydrochloric acid, etc.

Venezuela. In Venezuela, first-stage construction work has been practically completed for the Morón petrochemical complex, which now comprises fifteen installations and which, within a few months, will begin production of ammonium sulphate, urea, nitric acid, and ammonium nitrate, with a capacity sufficient to meet domestic needs and to export in certain quantities. Expansion of the refining division of this industrial center is expected soon, and so is the beginning of construction work on a plant for the production of explosives. Various other second-stage works will include the manufacture of synthetic rubber and raw materials for detergents. It is planned to complete this stage within about four years. Meanwhile, a lampblack plant has been set up in the environs of Valencia.

Petroleum Refining

The volume of crude oil processed by Latin American refineries in 1962 surpassed that of the preceding year by more than 12 per cent, again registering a high growth rate for the industry after two years of less vigorous expansion (see Table 4–5). The transitory slackening in development for both years was mainly due to a decline in the rate of expansion in Venezuela, a country whose refineries, in terms of capacity, account for almost one-half of the regional installations in this field.[21] Despite two years of moderate growth, the cumulative annual increment for the five-year period on the regional level amounts to 9.3 per cent.

The circumstances contributing to this new surge in Latin American petroleum refining have varied. As for the stimuli of demand, it should be pointed out that, in those countries which produce mainly or exclusively for domestic consumption, not only have the expansionist tendencies peculiar to the demand for petroleum products and by-products continued, but in various instances they have become pronounced. Such tendencies result from rapidly growing needs among conventional consumers of these products and from the continuous entrance of new consumers into the market. Of course, the replacement of imports continued to play a certain role in this expansion; however, the process in general is quite well developed, and in several instances progress in replacement—achieved by putting new installations in operation—merely counterbalanced those periodic increases in imports which had occurred during construction of the new facilities.[22]

Of course, the case of Venezuela is very different, since three-fourths of the refining industry is geared to export; therefore, a significant increase in production supposes improved prospects in the usual foreign markets or the winning of new consumers. Recent expansion was directed to the latter. As for the other exporting countries of the region, it should be pointed out that they sell only marginal quantities of by-products on the foreign market.

Argentina. Recently, the abundant supply of domestic crude oil in Argentina certainly accounted, in part, for the growth in refining operations of that country. An important complementary factor in this increase was the expansion of the Luján de Cuyol (Mendoza Province) installations, with an added capacity of more than one million tons. In addition,

[21] In 1962 the growth rate shown for Venezuelan refining industries was 10.5 per cent; the rates for the remainder of the region, more than 14 per cent. The corresponding coefficients for 1961 were almost 5 and 9 per cent, respectively.

[22] It should also be borne in mind in regard to certain by-products, such as fuel oil, that it may be advisable to cover a certain margin by importing. In fact, domestic demand for the different petroleum by-products does not ordinarily correspond exactly to the proportions in which these by-products are produced in the national processing of crude oil. Local production of a residual product, the need for which is comparatively high, would require additional capacity, calling for large investments, and would suppose export of surplus by-products under not always very favorable terms, since there may also be a surplus in neighboring countries.

TABLE 4–5. Latin America: Petroleum Refining,[a] 1957, 1960, 1961, and 1962

(*Thousands of tons*)

Country	1957	1960	1961	1962
Argentina	10,724	12,303	13,285	15,600
Bolivia	329	305	300	350
Brazil	5,867	8,966	10,426	13,543
Chile	1,006	1,397	1,640	1,970
Colombia	2,444	3,533	3,929	4,193
Ecuador	273	560	560	520
Mexico	11,684	16,023	17,022	16,950[b]
Panama	—	—	—	900[c]
Peru	2,110	2,237	2,242	2,430
Uruguay	1,160	1,389	1,402	1,535
Subtotals[d]	35,597	46,713	50,806	57,991
Rates of increment over the preceding year			8.8	14.1
Rates of cumulative annual increment 1957/1962				10.3
Venezuela	36,745	47,232	49,545	54,746
Rates of increment over the preceding year			4.9	10.5
Rates of cumulative annual increment 1957/1962				8.3
Latin America[d] Totals	72,342	93,945	100,351	112,737
Rates of increment over the preceding year		7.7	6.8	12.3
Rates of cumulative annual increment 1957/1962				9.3

[a] The figures for some countries include natural gasoline. Its production, however, is of minor proportions.

[b] The figures given by Petroleos Mexicanos—which indicate that part of petroleum production which is destined for refining, although this quantity may not be totally refined during the calendar year in which it was taken from the ground—are at some variance with the official figures quoted. They show an increase on the order of 4 per cent for the last year. The data given by this last source, converted into units of weight, show 16.7 and 17.4 million tons for 1961 and 1962, respectively.

[c] Estimate.

[d] Does not include Cuban production, for lack of pertinent data.

Sources: U.S. Department of Interior, Bureau of Mines, *World Petroleum Statistics*, various numbers. For MEXICO: Petroleo Publishing Co., *Petroleo Interamericano*, April, 1963, Dirección General de Estadística, various numbers. VENEZUELA: Dirección General de Estadística, *Boletín Mensual de Estadística* (Caracas), various numbers. The original figures, indicating units of volume, have been converted to tons in accordance with the specific weights set forth in the *Monthly Bulletin of Statistics* of the United Nations.

there were delayed effects of certain expansionist activities begun during preceding periods.

Brazil. In Brazil, the demand for petroleum by-products kept on rising in 1962 as a result of continuing industrial development and the steady growth of the automotive fleet. At the same time, supply was considerably augmented because of the almost full-scale operation of the new Duque de Caxias plant (near Rio de Janeiro), which was set up during the preceding year and has a capacity of more than 4 million tons per year. This additional productive capacity, coupled with better use of certain others, made possible an appreciable replacement of imports in 1962 in spite of increasing consumption, since at the same time the total of imported petroleum products dropped by more than 2 million tons, as compared with the preceding year.

Chile. The half-government-owned Chilean plant of Concón (near Valparaiso), expanded in 1960, considerably increased the utilization of its installed capacity, meeting requirements of the growing demand. Its production exceeded that of the preceding year by more than 20 per cent, a rate surpassed that year only by the expansion in Brazilian refining operations.

Mexico. In 1962, Mexican refineries did not increase the amount of crude processed oil over that of the two preceding years, but the progressive introduction of certain processes made it possible to increase the output of various products of relatively greater value, such as gasoline, kerosene, diesel oil, and gas oil; national output of these products now comes close to meeting domestic demand. Work on new projects has also been advanced.

Venezuela. The fact that Venezuelan refineries increased production in 1962 at a more rapid rate than in the preceding year reflected heavily in Latin American totals. In 1961, the Venezuelan petroleum industry, including the refining sector, had been confronted with the partial loss of certain of its traditional markets. Recently, such difficulties have been largely overcome as a result of the growing European demand for light oils and the gradual entrance of Venezuelan petroleum products in new markets.

Prospects for the refining industries appear even better in 1963 because then the Salamanca and Minatitlán plants will begin operating and thus increase Mexican refining capacity by almost 4.5 million tons a year. In addition, one plant in Bolivia and three in Central America (Guatemala, El Salvador, and Nicaragua) are expected to begin operating. These plants, together with one in Panama, whose first stage was completed in 1962, will add more than one million tons a year to the total capacity of the region.

Finally, projects now under way will bring about a significant increase in the refining capacity of Latin America in subsequent years. By 1965 or not much later, two important Brazilian plants, together with the multiple expansion program planned by Pemex in Mexico and the new Chilean plant in Concepción, are expected to raise the region's capacity by about 10 million tons annually. In addition, consideration is being given to a few relatively small projects in Colombia, Paraguay, the Dominican Republic, and Costa Rica.

The Cement Industry

In 1962, Latin American cement production increased by a little more than 6.5 per cent over the preceding year. This figure is slightly higher than those of the year before and of the last five-year period (see Table 4–6).

It may be noted that regional rates of growth encompass a great many different national coefficients, which not only vary considerably among themselves but also usually fluctuate—sometimes markedly—in consecutive years. Thus, in 1962, the Chilean cement industry registered a growth rate of over 15 per cent and the Mexican and Colombian industries showed rates of approximately 10 per cent, while the figures for Argentina and Venezuela reached levels of only between 1 and 1.5 per cent. But if the percentages for Argentina and Mexico are compared with corresponding data for the preceding year, exactly the opposite trends are noted, for in that year Argentina registered a coefficient of 10 per cent, while Mexico showed production at a standstill. As for Chile and Colombia, it should be pointed out that their cement production, now moving ahead strongly, had shown no signs of growth vitality for several years preceding; on the other hand, the Venezuelan industry had been outstanding in the past for its steady growth.

These facts also seem to point up another characteristic of the course of this industry: the tendency of national growth rates to level off among themselves in the long run, despite the variation in their annual fluctuations. Thus, for the last five-year period, the cumulative rates of Argentina, Chile, Colombia, and Mexico range between 4.5 and 7.0 per cent.

TABLE 4-6. Latin America: Cement Production, 1957, 1960, 1961, and 1962

(Thousands of tons)

Country	1957	1960	1961	1962*
Argentina	2,363	2,641	2,906	2,941
Bolivia	24	39	42	49
Brazil	3,393	4,474	4,709	5,076
Central America[a]	222	269	283*	275
Chile	727	835	883	1,021
Colombia	1,356	1,385	1,567	1,716
Dominican Republic	280	170	207	212
Ecuador	155	201	219	230
Haiti	28	48	44	46
Mexico	2,560	3,089	3,035	3,348
Panama	79	109	114	120
Paraguay	12	14	16	17
Peru	545	600	654	680
Uruguay	417	415	381	402
Venezuela	1,747	1,487	1,513	1,535
Latin America: Totals	13,908	15,776	16,573	17,668
Rates of increase over preceding year		7.7	5.1	6.6
Cumulative annual rates of growth 1957/1962				4.9

[a] Includes El Salvador, Guatemala, Honduras, and Nicaragua; cement is not yet produced in Costa Rica.

Sources: Official statistics and international publications, especially: United Nations, *Statistical Yearbook, 1962*, and *Monthly Bulletin of Statistics,* June, 1963.

Hence, an annual growth of 5 or 6 per cent may be considered quite typical for a group of semi-industrialized countries of the region which, in other aspects, have an appreciable weighting in the Latin American totals.[23]

Besides the marked fluctuations in short-term development of this industry—reflecting the relative instability of the building industry and the fact that in this area the "buffer" of import substitution is practically nonexistent [24]—some attention should also be given to the peculiarity of its long-term rate of growth. In fact, the cumulative five-year rate represents an "intermediate" growth, which differs as much from the

---

[23] Growth of the cement industry over the five years was slightly greater in Brazil and Ecuador and weaker in Peru, Uruguay, etc. The present poor course of this material's production in Venezuela seems to be of a temporary nature.

[24] In general terms. It should be mentioned, however, that toward the middle of 1963 the Peruvian Government withdrew the tariff protection granted this industry, after the latter raised its domestic prices.

growth coefficient of the so-called dynamic industries in the region as from the pattern of traditional manufacturing activities.

In order to account for this behavior of the cement industry, it is necessary to turn to the fact that, despite the sizable substitution achieved in the import area—which constitutes the main difference with respect to the still dynamic industries—it still has, potentially, sufficient new domestic markets. This potential is being progressively exploited through the gradual acquisition of new consumer centers as well as through expanded use of this product in applications more or less novel on the domestic scene. In particular, the completion of various major engineering projects and numerous lesser ones, presently under way throughout the region or planned for the near future, is likely to increase demand for this material. Moreover, intensification of demand for public and private engineering projects can have a more and more stabilizing influence on the development of this industry, compensating somewhat for the erratic incidence of residential construction.[25]

Major expansion of capacity is now in progress in Argentina, Brazil, and Mexico, but the expansion of productive capacity in Chile, Colombia, Peru, and Uruguay is also significant. As for the construction of new installations in Argentina, it is expected that these will cover requirements for the next few years; on the other hand, certain doubts have arisen regarding the ability of the current expansion of Brazil's cement industry to meet the steadily increasing domestic demand.

The Iron and Steel Industry

During 1962, the Latin American iron and steel industry continued to grow at a pace almost as fast as in preceding years. Moreover, in the most important producing countries of the region, its development showed various favorable signs regarding product quality and elasticity of long-term supply, although its short-term availability was not always sufficient; in fact, conditions of relatively ample supply in certain countries alternated with growing shortages in others. So, too, in the rationalization of operations certain progress has been evident, even though in many localities competitive levels have not yet been reached.

The new increase in production resulted almost entirely from the

---

[25] Although the severe economic crisis in Argentina had already had an effect on the course of various important industries at the beginning of the second half of 1962, the cement industry sustained major reverses only in the latter part of the year, and even then it closed the year with a certain advance. This seems ascribable principally to the cushioning effect of the consumption of engineering projects in the petroleum industry.

expansion of existing facilities and the construction of new installations. Originally an even greater expansion had been planned for 1962, but the lack of funds, especially domestic, has delayed completion of certain major projects under construction.

Despite these drawbacks, the manufacture of raw steel in 1962 increased at a rate of almost 10 per cent, slightly lower than that of preceding years (see Table 4-7).

As for the production of finished steels—rolled, wiredrawn, and pressed—the provisional figures available [26] indicate an increase of only about 7.5 per cent for 1962, which is much lower than the increase for the 1957–62 period. However, no symptomatic significance can be attached to this slackening of pace, since it results entirely from the temporary drop in production in Argentine rolling mills, where there is a surplus capacity, without affecting the growth pattern of raw steel manufacturing.

The simultaneous development of pig-iron production should be subject to a somewhat different appraisal. The recent slackening in the growth rate of this item, which fell from 16 per cent in 1961 and 13 per cent for the five-year period to 7 per cent for last year, draws attention. The expansion of cast-iron capacity is characterized by larger production units, and therefore variations in growth are normally more abrupt. In this instance, the circumstances of the year contributed toward a more pronounced fluctuation. In fact, the main reason that more intense growth was registered in pig-iron production than in the other iron and steel operations during the five-year period was the eagerness of various Latin American countries to set up integrated iron and steel mills;[27] this brought on a more or less parallel expansion in the manufacture of steel and cast iron. But as production of the latter item was initially lower, corresponding rates of growth were higher than for steel. Nevertheless, recent problems in financing, more than anything else, delayed completion of certain important integrated projects, for which reason the slackening of pace in this item was more marked than in steel ingots. Actually, the last annual increment in Latin American production of pig iron would be even lower, were it not for the successive installation of electrometallurgical furnaces at the new Venezuelan plant and certain improvements made in the Chilean integrated center.

[26] With respect to the production of raw steel and pig iron, 1962 data are now final for the most part or only subject to relatively minor adjustments; on the other hand, regarding finished steels, a great part of the latest figures are still provisional.

[27] To a certain extent, the setting up of certain new iron-smelting works with charcoal blast furnaces also contributed to this result.

TABLE 4–7. Latin America: Production of Pig Iron, Raw Steel, and Finished Steels in 1957, 1960, 1961 and 1962

Country	Pig iron[a]				Unfinished steel[b]				Finished steel			
	1957	1960	1961	1962*	1957	1960	1961	1962*	1957	1960	1961	1962*
Argentina	34	181	399	396	221	277	442	644	683	773	910	863
Brazil	1,252	1,883	1,977	2,019	1,475	2,282	2,443	2,555	1,838	2,028	2,099	2,349
Central America and Panama[a]	—	—	—	—	...	10[c]	15[c]	16	—	8[c]	12[c]	14
Chile	382	266	296	383	412	448	391	528	305	347	320	411
Colombia	126	176	189	145	127	172	192	157	102	113	134	139
Mexico	429	784	931	967	1,049	1,474	1,682	1,712	380	1,242	1,402	1,429
Peru	—	34	51	38	...	60	76	73	6	43	52	56
Uruguay	—	—	—	—	13	10	9	9	37	33	33	34
Venezuela	—	—	5	173	57	47	71	142	34	51	59	96
Latin America: Totals[d]	2,223	3,324	3,848	4,121	3,545	4,780	5,321	5,836	3,327	4,525	5,021	3,391
Rate of increase over previous year			15.7	7.1			11.3	9.7			11.0	7.4
Rates of cumulative annual growth 1957/1962				13.1				11.7				10.1

[a] In Mexico the figures for pig iron also include porous iron.
[b] This heading also includes raw steel cast in forms smaller than current ingots (billet type) by certain smaller semi-integrated plants.
[c] El Salvador, Guatemala, and Panama.
[d] Latin American totals do not include Cuban production, such data being unavailable.

Sources: Official or international statistics and specialized publications, in particular: *Revista Latinoamericana de Siderurgia*, ILAFA, Santiago de Chile.

In the manufacture of raw steel, the highest increments were achieved in Argentina, Chile, Brazil, and Venezuela. At the same time, for the first time in a long while production remained almost stationary in Mexico and below that of the preceding year in Colombia, a slight drop also being registered for Peru.[28]

In 1961, regional production of 5 million tons of finished steel was supplemented by importing 3 million tons. For 1962, data are not yet complete as to the relation between production and imports, but it may be anticipated that the volume of imports has increased for various countries.

Meanwhile, completion of projects under way and planning for new ones followed a course that was relatively independent of fluctuations in production. The total importance of these projects offers promising prospects for the future production of this industry on the regional level.

Argentina. Despite the serious difficulties encountered by the Argentine economy in 1962 and the depressive effect of large steel imports during the preceding period, progress has been made in standardizing operations at the integrated San Nicolás center where, moreover, development of the so-called "immediate" expansion program has taken place between the first and second stages of construction of this plant. Nevertheless, it has been deemed necessary to postpone the beginning of second-stage operations.[29]

Toward the end of the year, the new semi-integrated plant at Siderca en Campaña (Buenos Aires Province), of 100,000 tons capacity, was

---

[28] In addition to slight variations in percentages for each country in total Latin American steel production, recent changes—especially outfitting of the Venezuelan electrometallurgical plant, as well as various technological transformations effected in the Brazilian industry—also caused steel production to vary according to processes in use. In 1962 about 68 per cent of production was accounted for by Siemens-Martin plants, 25 per cent by electric furnaces, 4 per cent by the Linz-Donawitz process, 2 per cent by Thomas converters, and 1 per cent by the Bessemer process.

[29] With reference to completion of the first stage, in 1962 the mill for hot-rolling sheet steel went into operation, and in the beginning of 1963, that for cold-rolling; only the tin-plate process remains to be begun. As a part of this additional ("immediate") program, the fifth Siemens-Martin furnace was inaugurated at the steelworks. The plan will reach completion with installation of an oxygen plant and certain auxiliary equipment which will soon raise mill capacity to 1.16 million tons per year; this will tend to balance somewhat the capacity of this department with that of the large-scale rolling mill. On the other hand, postponement of the second stage proper precludes the possibility that the plant will reach for 1965 or 1966 the production figure of 2 million tons in steel ingots which had been previously contemplated.

inaugurated. At the same time, first-stage construction work was greatly advanced at Altos Hornos Güemes (Salta Province), whose two furnaces will produce 25,000 tons per year.[30] During the year in question, progress was also made in the planning of other projects, among which is a plant for special steels.

Although these projects will supply some temporary relief as regards supply situation in the near future, it must also be taken for granted that iron and steel shortages in the country will soon again become acute. In fact, recent projections of steel demands in Argentina show an increase in consumption which may rise from 3 million tons of raw steel in 1962 to 3.8 million tons in 1965, 4.4 million in 1967, and 5 million in 1970.

Brazil. An important event in the Brazilian iron and steel industry in 1962 was the lighting of the first blast furnace at the new Usiminas plant[31] in Ipatinga (Minas Gerais). The initial steel-producing capacity of this plant will be 500,000 tons. Capacity will rise to 2 million in the second stage, which will be initiated around 1966. As the completion of several divisions has had to be postponed somewhat in the interval pending introduction of integrated operations, the plant will export pig iron to Japan in exchange for coking coal coming from the United States. Moreover, it will provide Volta Redonda with certain amounts of pig iron and steel and Acesita with coke.[32]

Construction and equipping of Cosipa, another important new plant being erected near São Paulo, has been delayed somewhat longer, although considerable progress has been made in several of its sections. Certain delays also have characterized the transformation of the Vitória ironworks into an integrated center and the construction of the steelworks in the Northeast.[33] At the same time progress has been made through various technological improvements in development of the great Volta Redonda plant, and the integrated Belgo-Mineira and Mannesmann centers have been expanded through new construction work. In conclusion, it is expected that Brazilian steel production, which in 1962 came to 2.5 million tons, may double by 1966 or a little later, a 7-million-ton level being foreseen for 1970. Realization of these goals

---

[30] The first blast furnace was inaugurated at this plant in March, 1963.

[31] For information pertaining to the financing of this plant, see Chapter 2 of the present *Survey*.

[32] It has been estimated that manufacture of chemicals from by-products of coke will double production of this item for the country.

[33] Beginning of partial operations at Cosipa and inauguration of the first-stage steel installations at Vitória are scheduled for the second half of 1963.

would mean almost meeting projected consumption for the second half of this decade, as long as development requirements in this field do not substantially exceed present estimates.[34]

Two interesting features of the recent evolution of the iron and steel industry in this country are the gradual replacement of Siemens-Martins processes by L-D converters (with oxygen injectors) and the increasing regional distribution of the industry.

Colombia. At the Colombian plant in Paz del Rio, a sheet mill with a capacity of 50,000 tons per year went into operation toward the end of 1962. The new development plan for this plant entails raising its steel-producing capacity from 123,000 tons per year to 220,000 or more in the first stage, completion of which is expected by 1965, while in a second state, which will be begun simultaneously but completed at a later time, it is proposed to diversify production to include the manufacture of tin plate, etc.

Iron and steel production in Colombia shows certain trends toward decentralization, inasmuch as this country's two semi-integrated plants now have a combined capacity of slightly more than 50,000 tons and—despite certain considerations to the contrary—new plans are under way for construction of other plants on the Atlantic coast and in the Cauca Valley.

Chile. At the integrated Chilean center of Huachipato, the 500,000-ton mark in ingot production was reached for the first time in 1962. The concern's immediate goal is to increase capacity gradually until a production of 600,000 tons is attained in 1965. This expansion would be effected by an investment of $50 million, partly for replacement of certain equipment and partly for new installations intended to increase productivity.[35]

---

[34] According to statements made by one official of the industry, 500,000 tons of steel per year are needed for the manufacture of automobiles and 100,000 tons for shipbuilding; with reference to canning industry demands, it should be observed that domestic production presently takes care of one-half.

[35] With reference to operation of the blast furnace, changes planned involve injection of petroleum and/or coke gas, strict control of ore size, and setting up a self-fluxing sinter plant, etc. In the steelworks, injection of oxygen into the Siemens-Martin furnaces will be introduced, and the capacity of two of these furnaces will be increased from 100 tons to 200. The rolling mill already has a processing capacity of 600,000 tons per year in ingots, but for optimum output it requires auxiliary installations which will also be set up during this phase of expansion. Shortly after completion of these complementary installations, the remainder of the original plans for expansion is to be carried out, including construction of a second blast furnace and various other works to complement the other stages of production.

Mexico. The temporary standstill in Mexican iron and steel production for 1962 relates to certain phenomena of the economic contraction of the preceding year, resulting in a falling off of apparent steel consumption, which dropped from a level of almost 1,930,000 tons in 1960 to 1,850,000 for 1961.[36] On the other hand, the steady growth of the Mexican iron and steel industry in the past has made it possible to keep reducing the share of imports in this country's apparent consumption, so that the volume of imported items dropped from 40 per cent in 1956 to 30 per cent in 1958 and to 15 per cent in 1961. This reduction in the margin of substitution, which continued downward in 1962 to the 10 per cent level,[37] tended to make producers more cautious in the face of accumulation of stocks. Nevertheless, the domestic steel market seems to be quite expansive on a long-term basis, and construction of new facilities was continued in 1962. Plans of the most important concerns in this field for succeeding years were also maintained. Projects for expansion of the Monclova and Monterrey plants are particularly noteworthy, as are those at Tamsa and two new projects of considerable importance with good prospects of realization.

Peru. Toward the middle of 1962, the owners of the plant at Chimbote, Peru, concluded a contract with a European partner. According to the terms of this agreement the capacity of this integrated center—which had been designed for 60,000 tons and which, owing to certain recent improvements, can now produce about 75,000 tons of raw steel—would be raised within a few years to 350,000 tons, at a cost of $130 million. At present, the country consumes some 200,000 tons, the estimate for 1970 coming to 500,000.

Uruguay. Geological surveys recently carried out in Uruguay have made it possible to estimate that the Valentines iron-ore reserves run to 30 million tons; this amount is sufficient to supply a domestic iron and steel industry over a long period and still leave a surplus for export. Various foreign offers are presently being considered for exploitation of these deposits, and at the same time plans for providing the country with an integrated center have received new impetus.

[36] In 1962 apparent consumption again rose slightly, reaching a level of 1.9 million tons.

[37] In 1962 domestic production met total domestic consumer needs for wire rods, cast-iron pipe, sheet iron, tin plate, and galvanized sheets. Moreover, domestic industry supplied 90 per cent of direct consumption of structural beams; corrugated reinforcements for concrete; spikes; drawn wire; steel for tools, tubing, nails, and staples; hot- and cold-rolled sheets; and hot- and cold-rolled strips.

Venezuela. The new Venezuelan plant at Matanzas, which had gone into operation toward the end of 1961 with the manufacture of seamless tubes, using imported materials, next began producing pig iron, and toward the middle of 1962 it also began to pour steel. Thus, operation of the plant, which will soon be completed with the rolling of beams, began on an integrated basis. The successive putting into operation of the different installations of this plant means a steel-making capacity of 760,000 tons for 1963 and a pig-iron capacity of 700,000 tons. Finished-steel capacity will be 600,000 tons, approximately half of this yearly volume being seamless tubes. Steel-pouring capacity may increase in the coming years, through introduction of certain technological processes, to one million tons, while in the second-stage development of the plant it may reach more than 2 million tons.

For Venezuela, these plans imply not only an early reduction in its sizable steel imports but also, with the passing of time, the possibility of exporting iron and steel in increasingly significant amounts. It is estimated that within about 12 years production in this commercial field could be of a magnitude comparable to that of today's petroleum industry. It should be observed that the government plan for development of the iron and steel industry is closely tied in with the design of a great complex of industrial projects proposed for Venezuelan Guiana.[38]

The Motor Vehicle Industry

During 1962, the automotive industry continued to be one of the most vigorous factors in manufacturing development. However, with the gradual maturing of such operations in the two principal producing countries, the growth rate tended to slacken on the regional plane, falling from the 25 per cent registered for the preceding year—in terms of units produced—to a little over 12.5 per cent.

Of the Latin American production of more than 405,000 automotive vehicles in 1962, 320,000 units were the product of integrated manufacturing systems or of systems on the way to being integrated, the bulk of parts being manufactured locally. The rest were the product of assembly. Of these vehicles, somewhat more than 190,000 were produced in Brazil and slightly less than 130,000 in Argentina [39] (see Table 4–8).

---

[38] Expansion of a semi-integrated plant now able to produce 90,000 tons of steel bars was also completed by 1962.

[39] In Brazil probably more than 93 per cent of component parts are being manufactured locally, and in Argentina, about 65 per cent. Figures in both instances are in terms of value, calculated on an average basis, among the various types of automotive vehicles and for the two halves of the year.

TABLE 4–8. Latin America: Motor Vehicle Production, 1957, 1960, 1961, and 1962[a]

(*Thousands of units*)

	Country and item	1957	1960	1961	1962*
I.	National manufacture[b]				
	Argentina				
	Automobiles and jeeps	12.3	45.1	85.9	91.7
	Trucks	3.0	44.3	50.3	37.4
	Total	15.3	89.4	136.2	129.1
	Brazil				
	Automobiles and jeeps	9.2	57.3	72.7	129.8
	Trucks	20.4	75.7	73.0	61.3
	Total	29.6	135.0	145.7	191.1
II.	Assembly[b]				
	Argentina				
	Automobiles and jeeps	10.0	—	—	—
	Trucks	5.4	—	—	—
	Total	15.4	—	—	—
	Brazil				
	Automobiles and jeeps	—	—	—	—
	Trucks	1.1	—	—	—
	Total	1.1	—	—	—
	Chile				
	Automobiles	—	1.2	3.0	4.5
	Colombia				
	Jeeps	—	—	0.8	2.2
	Mexico				
	Automobiles and jeeps	18.3	31.8	38.6	43.5
	Trucks	22.8	20.5	23.0	21.6
	Total	41.1	52.3	61.6	65.1
	Uruguay				
	Automobiles	—	—	0.0*	0.3
	Venezuela				
	Automobiles and jeeps	8.9	6.4	8.9	8.9
	Trucks	5.9	3.9	2.9	3.5
	Total	14.8	10.3	11.7	12.4
Subtotal I					
Automobiles and jeeps		21.5	102.4	158.6	221.5
Trucks		23.4	120.0	123.3	98.7
Total		72.4	63.8	77.1	84.5

(*Continued*)

TABLE 4-8. *Continued*

(*Thousands of units*)

Country and item	1957	1960	1961	1962*
Subtotal II				
Automobiles and jeeps	37.2	39.4	51.2	59.4
Trucks	35.2	24.4	25.9	25.1
Total	72.4	63.8	77.1	84.5
Latin America				
Automobiles and jeeps	58.7	141.8	209.8	280.9
Trucks	58.6	144.4	149.2	123.8
Total	117.3	286.2	359.0	404.7
Rates of growth in comparison with previous year			25.4	12.8%
Cumulative annual rates of growth for the five-year period 1957–62				28.3%

a Motorcycles, motor scooters, and similar motor vehicles (with fewer than four wheels) are not included.

b The distinction between national manufacture and assembly is based on the criterion adopted in earlier *Economic & Social Surveys of Latin America*, according to which automotive vehicles assembled in a country are considered to be of national manufacture if at least one-third of their weight is made up of locally manufactured components and if—where the domestic contribution does not far exceed such proportions—a plan for gradual increase of that share is being carried out.

Sources: United Nations, *Monthly Bulletin of Statistics*, New York; Conselho Nacional de Estatística, *Anuário Estatístico do Brasil, 1962*, and *Boletim Estatístico* (Rio de Janeiro), October–December, 1962; Dirección General de Estadística, *Boletín Mensual de Estadística* (Caracas), October–November and December, 1962; Dirección General de Estadística, *Revista de Estadística* (Mexico), various numbers for 1962 and 1963; the figures for Chile, Colombia, and Uruguay are based on estimates from fragmentary information.

Moreover, out of the grand total of 405,000 units, 281,000 were automobiles and jeeps and only 124,000, or slightly over 30 per cent, trucks. It should be observed that the percentage of vehicles in this latter category has been gradually falling year after year in the regional totals and, with the exception of Venezuela, in national totals also. Paralleling this trend, ever-increasing emphasis has been placed on satisfying the perceptibly more pressing demand for vehicles for personal use.[40] Hence, production of the latter item increased, even in 1962, by 34 per cent over that of the previous year.

[40] This trend, moreover, corresponds to the distribution of production between the two categories of vehicles in highly developed free-enterprise countries.

The indirect effects of the continuous build-up of the automotive industry continued to constitute, in various ways, stimuli favorable to growth in general. This came about particularly owing to connections with supply industries but also, in some measure, thanks to the support afforded the transportation industries. At the same time, the growth of this activity exerted increasing pressure on insufficient resources and, through the financing of purchase of vehicles, on the limited supply of savings and noninflationary credit sources in general.

Aside from these features general to the evolution of the automotive industry, the state of development and leading problems of the moment naturally show considerable variations among the producing countries.

Brazil. In Brazil, the first-stage development of this branch has now been practically completed with the virtual integration of pertinent producing activities. Nevertheless, the backlog of demand in the automotive field has also been met, for which reason the industry is now faced with the urgent task of adapting its operations to the requirements of current domestic demand and to the needs for more steady export. This presupposes, in both areas, settled costs and prices. According to the results of an official investigation, among the factors of greatest importance in the unsatisfactory evolution of automotive prices are the high degree of remuneration assigned to elements of limited productive value (entrepreneurs, investment capital, highly qualified technicians) and the multiplicity of taxes. Ways of reducing these factors, especially in regard to the problem of taxes on units earmarked for export, are under study. Despite these circumstances, Brazilian exports of vehicles and of parts, in particular, within and without the region, through diverse types of transactions, approached the $10 million level in 1962.

Argentina. Argentina is also engaged in achieving a high degree of integration in its automotive industry, similar to that achieved in Brazil. The plan for gradual replacement of imported parts is, however, only now in its third year of operation and is not expected to be completed until 1965. From the point of view of this objective, the most important events in this field have been the successive installation of new plants for the manufacture of component parts, a process which, despite certain setbacks, has shown undeniable vigor.

The serious crisis through which manufacturing production in the country passed during the second half of 1962—especially in the mechanical industries sector—also affected this activity. Although automotive production did not sustain a reduction of more than 7 per cent in the balance for the whole year, this outcome is due especially to the appreciable increments achieved in the first months of this period.[41]

This crisis also highlighted various problems relating to the operations of this industry, especially in connection with the multiplicity of models manufactured and the capitalization of the respective enterprises, the importing of parts not used in current production, quality control of nationally produced parts, and financing of sales. In accord with present guidelines, it seems probable that, of the 23 assembly enterprises in existence, no more than 10 will be definitively approved. Moreover, urgent measures are planned to assure a more efficient control of imported parts needed during the remaining years of transition, including priority utilization of component parts imported in the recent past for the purpose of building up inventories. At the same time, more complete equipping of the automotive research center maintained by interested industrialists is being expedited with a view to expanding its services both of an advisory nature and for quality control of materials and parts locally produced.

Finally, in matters of sales credits, among other solutions the endeavor is being made to obtain more active co-operation from the foreign parent companies through partial contribution of the necessary funds.

Mexico. Only in recent years has Mexico begun to develop its automotive industry on an integrated basis. Recent laws require that the national content of vehicles be at least 60 per cent, including motors, beginning September, 1964. However, in order to achieve fuller integration, concession of a longer period than in the South American countries is being contemplated. On the eve of liquidating their operations of mere assembly, several foreign firms are trying to maintain themselves in the market by making important investments. Nevertheless, it is felt that in the long run only about eight of them will remain in the field; some of them, of course, representing mergers of two different well-known makes. It is expected that the effect of tax inducements soon to be announced will be considerable; however, at the same time sharp limitations will be introduced on the length of time foreign technicians can be employed. For this and other reasons, it is likely that greater emphasis will be placed on the acceleration of technical training.

In Mexico there is no backlog, accumulated over a period of years, such as that which not long ago characterized the market of several

---

[41] Results for the first quarter of 1963 show a more pronounced drop in the manufacture of automotive vehicles.

South American countries; rather, it is expected that the increase in demand over the next few years will be relatively even-paced.

Chile, Colombia, Venezuela. As for the three remaining countries that produce motor vehicles, it should be noted that assembly plants have been in regular operation for more than a decade in Venezuela and for almost half a decade in the Chilean free port of Arica, while in Colombia this activity has been going on for hardly two years.[42] A common feature of policies of the last three countries in this matter is the manifested desire to achieve gradual integration of their automotive production.

It would seem easier for Colombia and Chile, which are members of LAFTA, to try to organize the manufacture of parts by pooling their resources with those of other nations of that zone. As a matter of fact, certain provisions in this direction have recently been included in their regulations.

Venezuela envisions a somewhat slower pace in future local manufacturing of component parts, but it shows a keen interest in acquiring soon sufficient assembly capacity to be able to forgo all imports of vehicles assembled abroad. Furthermore, specific plans have already been made in the country to begin manufacturing parts in several plants to be constructed during a five-year period in the Valencia area, with local production of certain parts expected to get under way within a year or two. Eventually even motors will be manufactured.

Tractor Production

With respect to the production of tractors in Latin America, it can be said that this industry exists in only two countries at present: Argentina, which has been active for more than a decade, and Brazil, which recently entered into its third year. In 1962, the volume of production in both countries lagged behind expectations [43] (see Table 4–9).

Since the farming techniques employed in vast areas of Latin America are far from efficient, there is, in principle, a great need for mechanization of agriculture. However, general economic conditions and the struc-

---

[42] Small quantities of vehicles are also being assembled in Uruguay, and plans have been made to begin assembly operations soon in Peru.

[43] The relative increase of 20 per cent in this activity for the past year over the previous year is due only to the facts that in Brazil the tractor industry is in the early stage of development and that the basis for comparison is small. Furthermore, two years prior to that the regional total was greater than in 1962, due to the highest levels of this activity reached in Argentina at that time.

TABLE 4-9. Latin America: Tractor Production, 1957, 1960, 1961, and 1962

(*Units*)

Country	1957	1960	1961	1962
Argentina	10,878	20,958	14,730	11,742
Brazil	—	37	1,678	8,077
Latin America	10,878	20,995	16,408	19,819

Sources: For Argentina: *Desarrollo Económico y Social de la Argentina*, Report presented by the Government of Argentina to the Second Annual Meeting of IA-ECOSOC at the Expert Level, 1963, Doc. OEA/Ser.H/X.5 CIES/309; the data for recent years have been taken from various national and international publications. For Brazil: Conselho Nacional de Estatística, *Anuário Estatístico do Brasil 1962* and *Boletim Estatístico*, October and December, 1962.

ture of this productive sector would hardly permit large-scale purchase of such an important piece of farm machinery as long as the prices of locally produced units are not in line with world levels, and especially if it is not possible to keep ample credit systems in operation. The inflationary climate of various nations naturally precludes the extension of credit by private sources; therefore the burden of providing financial assistance in those nations tends for the most part to fall upon the public sector.

Argentina. Argentina now has an annual capacity of assembling 30,000 tractors. In 1960, production had reached 21,000 units, which is substantially greater than the 12,000 or so assembled in 1962. Such a low level of operations in this sector is due in part to the extraordinary conditions of the year under study, but it should be noted that production had begun to drop perceptibly in 1961. Thus, it can be expected that the volume produced will rise again in future years and that progress toward integration of the industry will continue. It should be mentioned that the necessary steps have been taken to secure an important loan from an international financial institution, a considerable part of which will be used to promote farm mechanization. Furthermore, the privileges granted in the past to the importation of internal-combustion engines have been suspended, leaving the local industry to produce them for the manufacture of tractors in accordance with the program for the development of this industry.

Brazil. On the other hand, the increase in Brazilian production was 13 per cent lower than that called for in plans for the industry, due in part to certain delays in getting some new plants under way and also to a more limited demand, which apparently influenced to some extent the lag in the installation of additional units. Furthermore, the already unfavorable demand conditions worsened during the first few months of 1963, at which time production showed a drop from the same period of the preceding year. At any rate, a far-reaching solution to the credit problem is being sought through government intervention, by which means 60 per cent of the cost of each unit is being financed, as well as through the utilization of an inter-American loan in this case.

Mexico. In Mexico, where small quantities of tractors had been assembled in the past, and the industry then suspended, it was recently decided to give full governmental support to firms that produce locally. The purpose of this policy is to substitute imports that fluctuate between 5,000 and 6,000 units per year and eventually to increase farm mechanization, which is inadequate at present. It is estimated that the country will need 220,000 units, instead of the 50,000 that are available now. The integration of this industry will also be carried out gradually. There is now a specific project, with assured financing, for the local manufacture of certain spare parts. In addition, preparations are being made to build one tractor plant soon and possibly a second.

Chile, Colombia, Venezuela. Other plans are under way in these three Latin American countries to intensify their industrialization by promoting their machine industries and the manufacture of motor vehicles.

With respect to the manufacture of tractor parts, a certain degree of co-operation exists among several countries in the center of the free-trade area, but most of the efforts made to date have not produced effective results.

Shipbuilding

The shipbuilding industry is gradually being established in Latin America, although on a relatively large scale it is still restricted to two countries, Argentina and Brazil. To date, only these republics have achieved a marked degree of development.

Brazil. The Brazilian shipbuilding industry, which was established only four years ago, has now reached a yearly capacity of 180,000 deadweight tons (d.w.t.); ships of up to 12,000 d.w.t. are being built; 10,000 workers are employed; and, according to official figures, 60 per cent of the parts are manufactured locally.[44] Whereas in 1961 shipyards in the country were building 17 ships with a total tonnage of approximately 70,000 d.w.t., in early 1962, 21 units were under construction with a total tonnage of 110,000 d.w.t. designed primarily for coastal shipping.

The initial success achieved in the industry leads to the conclusion that current capacity, in addition to improvement by the establishment of two shifts, will expand in the near future. The largest shipyard in the country has initiated an expansion program to utilize its installations for the assembly of ships up to 60,000 d.w.t. It is estimated that a capacity of 300,000 tons would be needed for immediate replacement alone, and a backlog demand still exists. Prospects for exports in the near future are also favorable. Mention should be made of the potential future export capacity of the Brazilian shipbuilding industry resulting from the successful completion of negotiations with Mexico to build five freighters of from 4,500 to 10,500 d.w.t.

Argentina. A rehabilitation plan for the merchant fleet is being carried out in Argentina whereby approximately one-half of the total needs, estimated at one-half million d.w.t., will be met through a 10-year local construction program. Another phase of the program calls for purchases abroad, and meanwhile some secondhand vessels will be purchased. The local phase of the purchase plan involves over 30 units. In May, 1962, the first of three sister ships was launched. These vessels are 8,000 d.w.t. each and are being built by the government-owned shipyard. The aforesaid ocean freighter is the largest vessel ever built at an Argentine shipyard. In addition, in late 1962 a 1,780-ton river-tank vessel was launched, and in early 1963 two tugboats built for the river navigation fleet, which is likewise engaged in a rehabilitation program, were also launched.

Mexico. Mexico is also promoting the expansion of ship installations in Vera Cruz, which were given in concession to a private firm, and it appears that it will also carry out the Mazatlán project, which has the support of a European firm. According to plans, units of increasing tonnage will be built successively, first 3,000-ton vessels and eventually,

---

[44] This percentage indicates the national proportion with respect to ship tonnage. It is estimated that with respect to value, local industry is now contributing over 70 per cent. It is also anticipated that not much later than the end of 1964 nationalization will surpass 95 per cent, as by that time diesel marine engines—which will be produced by then—will be provided entirely by national plants and, moreover, Usiminas would be in a position to deliver thick steel plates for the shipbuilding.

after five or six years, other vessels of from 15,000 to 20,000 tons. Smaller fishing and coast-guard vessels, as well as a few units for export, are now being assembled.

Chile, Colombia, Peru. In Chile and Peru this branch of industry is becoming increasingly important, primarily because locally built units are needed for the expanding fishing industry. Similar plans are now under study in Colombia.

Industrial Machinery and Equipment

Even though a quantification of the recent development of the manufacture of different producers' goods encounters serious methodological and statistical difficulties, particularly in considering its scope for the region as a whole, it may be said that this activity now constitutes an increasingly important segment of the mechanical industries, especially in the three largest and most industrialized countries in the region. The production of machinery and instruments of universal use has been outstanding for many years. Examples are machines, tools, pumps, cranes, and even traveling cranes, as well as diverse components of electrical equipment, including heavy parts. Recently, however, the manufacture of equipment for specific industries has taken on growing importance, such as petroleum, iron and steel, paper, textile, sugar, certain chemical branches, mining in general, and building.

Brazil. In the field of machinery manufacturing, developments in Brazil continue to be outstanding. In 1961, the industry in that country had already met 40 per cent of the domestic demand, and in 1962, according to incomplete data available, there seems to have been continued progress, though at a slightly lower rate. Despite this trend, that branch of manufacturing appears likely to undergo more rapid development in the future. A recent study [45] indicates that it could grow to the point of satisfying approximately 85 per cent of the needs for such machinery.

Mexico. Recent achievements of Mexican industry are also outstanding. Several plants for the production of new types of capital goods have been opened in that country. At the same time it has begun to implement or prepare other projects designed to continue expanding the range

---

[45] ECLA, *The Manufacture of Industrial Machinery and Equipment in Latin America, I, Basic Equipment in Brazil* (New York, 1963).

of equipment produced. In this field, moreover, there appears to be prevalent determination to assure new industries of a competitive position in the future.

Argentina. Notwithstanding the crisis in Argentina, progress continued to be made in various projects. There have been certain delays, which were connected with the simultaneous weakening of the demand for products of several industries in this branch, but which were also partly ascribable to the pronounced lack of liquidity.

CHAPTER 5

THE EXECUTION OF ECONOMIC PROGRAMS UNDER THE ALLIANCE FOR PROGRESS

DEVELOPMENT PLANNING

Economic planning is not a new idea in Latin America; a number of countries have for some time had experience with the formulation and execution of long-term programs for particular sectors or regions.[1] Overall planning has also received attention by a number of Latin American governments. By the time the Charter of Punta del Este was signed, public agencies in Chile, Colombia, Ecuador, and Venezuela, for instance, were engaged in either the actual preparation of national development plans or in laying down the bases for such actions.[2]

Nevertheless, the Charter of Punta del Este signified a new departure in this field. For the first time all member states of the Inter-American System officially endorsed the concept of planning as a vital policy tool for development and, implicitly, as one of the criteria by which national efforts could be evaluated and put into perspective.[3] For the first time, too, the notion that some connection might exist between the quality

[1] Mexico, for example, has for several years had plans covering public investment, private investment, and specific activities in different regions, but coordination of these at the national level is a recent phenomenon. Brazil has had a special Development Bank since 1952 and since 1959 a more comprehensive development agency for the Northeast (SUDENE).

[2] The Corporación de Fomento de la Producción (CORFO) of Chile, created in 1939, had been approaching the aggregate planning stage gradually over a number of years; in Colombia, work on a national development plan was initiated in the latter half of the nineteen-fifties; and in Ecuador, the Junta Nacional de Planificación published in 1958 the *Bases y Directivas para Programar el Desarrollo Económico del Ecuador*. In Venezuela, the Oficina de Coordinacion y Planificación Económica (CORDIPLAN) had been working on a national plan since 1958.

[3] See Charter of Punta del Este, Title 2, Chapter II.

and seriousness of a country's development effort as expressed in its economic plan[4] and the foreign assistance it might be ready to absorb received official endorsement by all member governments.

Viewed in this context, the tasks facing the Latin American governments in 1961, when they subscribed to the principles of the Alliance for Progress, were immense. In most countries, the apparatus of government was not geared to an easy absorption of a centrally designed, coherent economic policy for development; even in those few countries in which enough technically competent personnel could be found to formulate and implement an over-all program, making it operational meant profound changes in the decision-making process, for which time, patience, enthusiasm, and perseverance will continue to be needed.

Progress Achieved in Plan Formulation

It is thus all the more remarkable that by mid-1963 not only had all OAS member states formally created central planning bodies, but an appreciable number had actually either formulated long-term development plans or advanced enough in this direction to expect that by the end of 1964 all but two or three will have finalized such plans. To date Bolivia, Chile, Colombia, Honduras, Mexico, Panama, and Venezuela have submitted plans to the Panel of Experts.[5] The analysis of the first three of these has been completed, and the Panel is well advanced in its evaluation of the Honduran, Mexican, and Venezuelan plans; evaluation of Panama's plan has recently been initiated. The five Central American countries are rapidly advancing in their plan formulations through national programs broadly synchronized on a regional basis with the help of a joint OAS/IDB/ECLA/SIECA (Permanent Secretariat of the General Treaty for Central American Economic Integration)/BCIE (Bank for Central American Economic Integration) mission, which is trying especially to assist in the aspects of national planning that have implications for the regional integration program. Work is also well advanced in a number of other countries[6] (see Table 5-1).

---

[4] Including specific economic and social goals, as well as such sociopolitical changes as land reform and tax reform, which would require strong and well-designed government action and which therefore would have a place in an integral plan, if such a document is indeed considered a government's action program and not merely a statement of desired targets or of past trends projected into the future.

[5] A group of nine high-level experts who, under the mechanisms established by the Charter of Punta del Este, are charged with evaluating national development plans (see Charter of Punta del Este, Title II, Chapter V).

[6] Paraguay, Peru, and Uruguay are receiving the assistance of joint OAS/IDB/ECLA advisory missions in the preparation of their national plans.

The widely differing historical contexts in which planning has arisen in individual countries, and the differing priorities which governments have placed on the various aspects of planning, have resulted in plans in which not only specific targets vary widely but also the length of the planning period, the scope of the sectors covered, the degree of detail regarding specific targets and projects, as well as the institutional and policy instruments to be used for their achievement; in short, the general methods and approaches adopted are by no means uniform (see again Table 5–1). This heterogeneity can be explained partly by the enormous differences among countries in their economic and social conditions and partly by the general lack of experience in successful over-all planning.

In spite of these differences, however, there are also many similarities concerning the specific goals and targets adopted and the methods employed. Regarding the former, a broad framework is given by the Charter of Punta del Este, in which a per capita growth rate of 2.5 per cent is stipulated as the minimum needed to achieve the over-all aims of the Alliance for Progress, and in which a more equitable distribution of income and wealth—particularly of landed property—is part of the central content.[7] Among the tools—other than land and tax reform—to which a commitment also exists are, domestically, an increase in the rate of investment and savings and a reasonable degree of price stability, and in the international sector, the strengthening of the process of regional economic integration and stabilization of basic products prices.

But while the Charter provides a basic framework, it is left to each country to establish its own priorities and to choose the policy tools that seem most appropriate to its own particular circumstances. Even so, there are a number of methodological features common to most of the plans that have been prepared to date. In most cases the general method of planning the organization of resources has been, first, to project the amount of investment necessary to obtain the desired rate of per capita growth in product by applying an estimated capital-output ratio for the economy as a whole, and then to estimate, on the basis of past experience and the expected results of fiscal reform, the amount of private and public savings available, and consequently the net amount of foreign financing necessary.[8] Projections of exports and imports, together with the expected inflow of foreign direct investment, suggest the quantity

---

[7] See Charter of Punta del Este, Title I.

[8] An interesting variation is presented in the Panamanian Plan, in which investment requirements are estimated on the basis of an aggregate production function which permits one to take into account explicitly the expected growth of other inputs, particularly of land and of labor.

TABLE 5-1. Development Plans Prepared or in Preparation

Country	Planning institution and date of creation	Period of plan	Scope[a]	Name of plan
Bolivia	Junta Nacional de Planeamiento (October, 1960)	1962–71	global[b]	Plan de Desarrollo Económico y Social, 1962–71
Brazil	Ministério de Planejamento (1962) Coordenação de Planejamento Nacional (July, 1963)	1963–65	global	Plano Trienal de Desenvolvimiento Económico e Social, 1963–65
Colombia	Consejo Nacional de Política Económica y Planeación (November, 1958)	1961–70	global	Plan General de Desarrollo Económico y Social, 1962–70
Chile	Comité de Programación Económica y Reconstrucción (1961) y Corporación de Fomento (1941)	1961–70	global	Programa Nacional de Desarrollo Económico, 1961–70
Guatemala	Consejo Nacional de Planificación Económica (November, 1954)	1960–64	public investment	Plan de Inversiones Públicas, 1960–64
Honduras	Consejo Nacional de Economía (February, 1955)	1963–64	total investment	Plan Nacional de Inversiones Públicas, 1963–64
Mexico	Dirección de Planeación Nacional (August, 1961) y Comisión Intersecretarial de la Secretaría de la Presidencia y de la Secretaría de Hacienda y Crédito Público (March, 1960)	1962–64	global	Plan de Acción Inmediata, 1962–64
Panama	Dirección General de Planificación y Administración (June, 1959)	1963–70	global	Programa de Desarrollo Económico y Social, 1963–70
Venezuela	Oficina de Coordinación y Planificación Económica (December, 1958)	1963–66	global	Plan de la Nación, 1963–66

TABLE 5-1. Continued

Country	Planning institution and date of creation	Period of plan	Scope[a]	Expected date of termination
In preparation				
Argentina	Grupo del Planeamiento del Consejo Nacional de Desarrollo y Consejo Federal de Inversiones	November 1963-67	global	October, 1963
Costa Rica	Oficina de Planificación	ten years	global	August, 1964
Dominican Republic	Junta Nacional de Planificación y Coordinación (January, 1962)	—	—	—
Ecuador	Junta Nacional de Planificación y Coordinación Económica (May, 1954)	1964-68, 1969-73	global	September, 1963
El Salvador	Consejo de Planificación y Coordinación Económica (April, 1962)	1964-65, 1965-69	total investment, global	September, 1963, July, 1964
Haiti	Conseil Permanent d'Action de Liberation Economique de la République d'Haiti	two years	global	1963
Nicaragua	Oficina Nacional de Coordinación y Planeamiento Económico y Social (December, 1961)	1964-69	global	June, 1964
Paraguay	Secretaría Técnica de Planificación del Desarrollo Económico y Social (April, 1962)	—	—	—[c]
Peru	Instituto Nacional de Planificación (October, 1962)	1964-66, 1962-71	public investment, global	September, 1963, In revision
Uruguay	Comisión de Inversiones y del Desarrollo Económico (January, 1960)	—	—	—[d]

[a] "Global" refers to comprehensive coverage, including sectoral plans as well as aggregate plans and with both the public and private sectors included in total investment.

[b] A two-year investment program is being prepared by Bolivia to implement the over-all plan. See Table 5-2, note b.

[c] On the recommendation of an OAS/IDB/ECLA mission, a diagnosis of the Paraguayan economy and a short-term plan are being prepared.

[d] A diagnosis of the Uruguayan economy, which will serve as a basis for its development plan, has recently been completed by a tripartite mission of OAS/IDB/ECLA.

of new loans needed, to which must be added the amortization and interest costs of such foreign borrowing.

Once the magnitude of the investment program is determined, investment priorities are established according to the needs of each country. Although these often include private investment, the core of the action program is usually public sector investment, leaving the flow of private investment to the voluntary operation of the market mechanism and to the results of general incentive policies. Several countries have included programs of agrarian reform in their national plans; others include special regional programs; and most give some consideration to the problem of unemployment and the need to develop human and natural resources, as well as capital formation. These points, however, are often covered by general qualitative statements, rather than by specific estimates or proposals. Furthermore, based on the experience of the first two years of the Alliance, more emphasis is now being placed on incorporating an inventory of investment projects under way or planned and on including specific projects worked out in sufficient detail to allow prompt action, once financing has been arranged. To date, the dearth of such projects has been a major impediment to prompt and massive development actions by governments and international financing agencies.[9]

Further adjustments of the planning process may be expected in the course of adapting the experience of other countries to Latin America's development needs. For one, the administrative responsibility of planning requires modifications to the traditional operational procedures of arriving at investment decisions; the planning agency should be supplied with sufficient capability and authority to co-ordinate the diverse investment budgets of the ministries, decentralized government agencies, and autonomous regional corporations with the investment plans of private industry, co-ordinating as well the separate request for foreign assistance. To date, the most common arrangement has been to establish the planning agency as an executive organ of the government, authorized to review the ministerial budgets and suggest changes to the cabinet. Mexico is probably the country in which the process of central co-ordination of public investments has advanced farthest; in many other countries as yet only formal arrangements have been made. Costa Rica has solved the problem of defining responsibility by making the planning agency directly responsible for formulating the national budget; in El Salvador, it may revise the budget as presented; and in Guatemala and Panama, special

---

[9] Bolivia, for example, completed in March, 1963, a final draft of a detailed two-year investment plan in response to recommendations by the Committee of Nine that specific investment projects be made ready.

administrative links between the budget bureau and the planning agency are designed to achieve close co-operation. In working out this relationship, some of the countries may also find it useful to expand or alter the representation of different economic sectors in the planning agency's membership. To a large extent, both these immediate tasks and the long-run effectiveness of planning depend on the availability of trained personnel. In the preparation of development plans, as in the success of the development effort as a whole, the problem is as much one of skills and organization as of capital.

Growth Targets: Output, Capital Formation, and the Balance of Payments

The over-all quantitative implications of the various plans differ considerably, ranging, for instance, from a 5.5 per cent annual growth rate in per capita product in Bolivia to rates of 2.5 per cent in Colombia, Honduras, Mexico, and Panama. For this, three main reasons may be adduced, of which the third one is of particular interest because it alone relates to the magnitude of the effort represented by achieving the planned targets. Different target growth rates of total product reflect (1) considerable differences in demographic growth rates, (2) differences in the appraisal of what it is actually possible to achieve from particular increases in inputs, mainly of capital,[10] and (3) differences in the estimates of the amounts of capital that governments expect to be able to mobilize over the planning period.[11] Thus, within a 10-year period Bolivia expects to raise its investment coefficient from a preplan level of 14.7 to 19.6 per cent; Chile, from 13.7 to 21 per cent in eight years; and Colombia from 18.4 to 26.8 per cent in four years [12] (see Table 5–2). Some idea of the size of these programs can be gained by noting that, if the planned investments were distributed equally each year, the eight countries represented in Table 5–2 would alone require foreign investment and credits totaling more than $1.7 billion in 1963 in order to finance an investment program of close to $10 billion.

[10] In other words, differences in the estimated incremental capital-output ratios.
[11] Expressed as a proportion of total product. Thus these differences will be referred to as differences in the investment coefficients.
[12] In the latter two cases mentioned, the Report of the Panel of Experts' Ad Hoc Committees suggests that even greater investment efforts may be possible and desirable. See Nómina de Expertos, *Evaluación del Programa Nacional de Desarrollo Económico y Social de Chile* (October, 1962), p. 109 *et infra*, and *Evaluación del Programa General de Desarrollo Económico y Social de Colombia* (July, 1962), p. 67.

TABLE 5-2. Planned Growth of Gross Domestic Product and the Necessary Investment, Compared with the Magnitudes Realized in 1961 and 1962

Country and period		(1) Gross domestic product—per capita constant prices (% per annum)	(2) Ratio of gross domestic investment to GDP (%)	(3) Total investment of plan period (millions of US$)	(4) Total foreign resources necessary (millions of US$)	(5) Total foreign resources as proportion of total investment (4) − (3) (%)	(6) Net balance of foreign capital as proportion of total investment[a] (%)
Bolivia	1961	2.5	14.7*				
	1962	2.7	...				
	Planned 1962–71	5.5	19.6	1,294[b]	376	29	13
Brazil	1961	4.4	16.3				
	1962	0.3–1.3	16.0				
	Planned 1963–65	3.9	18.2	7,782[c]	1,830	24	7
Chile	1961	2.0	13.7				
	1962	2.7	...				
	Planned 1963–70	3.0	21.0	7,666[d]	1,757	23	14
Colombia	1961	2.3	18.4**				
	1962	3.4	...				
	Planned 1962–65	2.5	26.8	5,832[e]	1,079	18	15
Honduras	1961	0.6	13.5				
	1962	2.7	14.8				
	Planned 1963–64	2.5	20.3	181[f]	71	39	36

Mexico		1961	0.4		15.5**
		1962	1.9		...
	Planned	1962–64	2.3	6,400^a	18.4
Panama		1961	4.6		16.4**
		1962	5.2		19.0***
	Planned	1963–70	2.5	908^b	17.5
Venezuela		1961	−3.6		18.6*
		1962	3.9		...
	Planned	1963–66	4.7	8,415^i	20.3

1,600	25	...	
518	57	53	
1,125	13	2	

* 1958.
** 1960.
*** 1961.

^{a} Total foreign capital inflow less amortization and, in the case of Venezuela, less private capital outflow. See column (5) of Table 5–3.

^{b} Plan Table 21. 1958 prices.

^{c} At the assumed rate of $1.00 = 450 cruzeiros, as implied in Tables 13 and 14 of the plan. See also Social Progress Trust Fund, *Second Annual Report*, 1962, pp. 431–32. 1962 prices.

^{d} At the assumed rate of $1.00 = 1.47 escudos, as applied in the evaluation of the Plan. 1961 prices.

^{e} At the assumed rate of $1.00 = 7.00 pesos, as applied in the evaluation of the Plan. 1961 prices.

^{f} At the current official rate of $1.00 = 2.00 lempiras. Current prices.

^{g} At the current official rate of $1.00 = 12.50 pesos.

^{h} 1961 prices.

^{i} At the official rate of $1.00 = 3.35 bolivares. 1960 prices.

Notes: The Mexican figure refers to GNP.

Guatemala has not been included, as its plan is concerned only with investment by the central government. For the four-year period 1960–64, planned central government investment totals 170.5 million quetzals, 83 million of which correspond to the latter two years, 1962/63 and 1963/64. Of that figure 16 million, or 19 per cent, are expected to be needed in the form of foreign loans.

Sources: See Table 5–1. All data for Chile and Colombia are based on the evaluation of their respective plans by the Panel of Experts, and for Venezuela all data are based on the May, 1963, edition of their Plan. The 1961 and 1962 rates of growth of GDP are from this *Survey*.

TABLE 5–3. Recent and Projected Contribution of Foreign Capital in Seven Countries[a]

(Millions of dollars)

Country and period			(1) Net direct investment	(2) Loans and grants	(3) Total capital inflow (1) + (2)	(4) Amortization of foreign debt	(5) Net capital inflow (3) − (4)	(6) Balance of payments on current account
Bolivia		1958	...	...	...	...	...	−32
	Planned	1963	...	...	80	14	67	−67
		1971	...	...	3	36	−33	33
	Total plan period				376	210	165	−165
Brazil		1961	109	488	597	384	+213	−242
		1962	69	367	436	297	+139	−408
	Planned	1963	100	305	405	465	−60	−203
		1965	110	335	445	355	+90	−159
	Total plan period		310	960	1,270	1,285	−15	−545
Chile		1961	70	394	464	187	267	−265
		1962	55	343	318	202	196	−165
	Planned	1963	30	232	262	95	167	−105
		1965	50	178	228	81	147	−81
	Total plan period		470	1,287	1,757	694	1,063	−570
Colombia		1961	...	...	...	...	−16	−140
		1962	...	...	...	...	54	−121
	Planned	1963	20	252	272	60	212	−212
		1965	20	293	313	51	262	−262
	Total plan period		75	1,004	1,079	228	851	−851

Honduras	1961	−7	9	2	2	—	—
	1962	−4	14	10	2	8	−8
Planned	1963	..	..	32	2	29	−29
	1965	..	..	40	4	36	−36
Total plan period				71	6	65	−65
Panama	1960	..	..	47	12	35	−35
	1961	..	..	35	8	27	−27
Planned	1963	30	20	50[b]	2	48	−48
	1970	56	29	85[b]	8	77	−77
Total plan period		321	197	518[b]	36	482	−482
Venezuela	1960	−182	415	233	255	−22	22
Planned	1963	−193	337	144	85	59	−59
	1966	−173	160	−13	40	−53	53
Total plan period		−727	1,125	398	220[c]	178	−178

[a] Where possible, excluding compensatory capital movements.
[b] At the time of publication of the Plan, Panama estimated an additional 37 million balboas a year, on the average, to be necessary. It is here assumed that this amount is fully supplied by autonomous capital inflows.
[c] Only on those loans contracted by the end of 1962.

Sources: See Table 5–1.
Bolivia: Plan, Table 29.
Brazil: SUMOC, *Boletim*, March, 1963; Plan, Table 9.
Chile: Report to the IA-ECOSOC (CIES/314), July, 1963, and plan evaluation, Table 16.
Colombia: Balance of Payments chapter, this *Survey*, Tables 2–2 and 2–4, Plan evaluation, Tables 22, 23.
Honduras: Plan Table 18 at $1.00 = 2.00 lempiras.
Panama: Report to the IA-ECOSOC (CIES/323); Plan, Table VII.10.
Venezuela: Plan, Table III.7.

In general, a larger proportion of this amount is expected to have to come from grants and credits than from direct investments, although only four of these plans attempt to estimate probable direct investment (see Table 5–3). Of these four, Panama anticipates the largest role for direct investment, which is expected to contribute nearly 40 per cent of total foreign-capital requirements during the plan period; in Brazil and Chile, the proportion is slightly more than one-fourth, and in Colombia, less than one-tenth. Venezuela anticipates a continued net outflow of capital, as will probably be the case also in Honduras in 1963, due to the operations of foreign banana companies.

Of the total requirements of foreign funds, a very high proportion is intended for use in servicing the foreign debt, including part of the debt contracted during the plan period. In Bolivia, Brazil, and Venezuela the amount of foreign capital needed for this purpose exceeds the need for foreign financing of imports of goods and services. Although estimates of the latter are subject, of course, to a much wider margin of error and may in some cases be considerably underestimated, the absolute amounts of amortization costs, which are more easily calculated, would alone require about $675 million in 1963 in the seven countries for which these data are available.[13] To that extent, the figures cited earlier overstate the share of investment resources expected to be supplied from abroad. Excluding Mexico, total investment amounts to about $8 billion and the foreign participation to $1.1 billion, of which amortization costs would absorb $675 million. It may be seen, therefore, that the ambitious investment programs contemplated are intended to be achieved largely through domestic efforts, with domestic savings expected to supply approximately 94 per cent of the over-all needs. In only four of the seven countries under review are foreign resources expected to contribute a larger proportion of total savings than has been the case recently. In all seven, the investment program contemplated for the plan period will call for large increases in domestic savings—so large that they require that the plan contain detailed policies to bring them about. Long-run measures to increase exports are combined with immediate measures to limit the current expenditures of the public sector and to mobilize the savings of the private sector through the expansion of banking facilities and improvement of the capital market and by transferring a larger portion of private resources to the government in taxes; for, while the greater burden continues to fall on the private sector, the increase in

---

[13] The Mexican plan is not available presently for detailed review; references are included where possible.

investment is to occur largely on the initiative of the public sector (see Table 5–4).

Public Savings. Even were the need for greater revenues less insistent and the claim for greater equity less compelling, fiscal policy and administration would be aided by clarifying the tangle of accumulated rate changes and exemptions which comprise much of present tax legislation. The search for additional sources of income provides an impelling incentive, and all seven countries have included in their development plans proposed guidelines for fiscal reform. Yet, despite the unanimous agreement on the need for tax reform, the increase in government expenditure necessary to meet the goals of increased per capita income is not projected to be fully covered by current income during the plan period. Current expenditures of the public sector increase naturally with the extension of services to a growing population, and they are now to be further increased by the per capita expansion of such services as education, public health, and low-cost housing. At the same time, sharp increases in capital expenditures are planned, with public investment growing even faster than total investment. The plans generally express awareness of the need to restrict current expenditures to a minimum by eliminating excess personnel and reducing the subsidies entailed by artificially low rates on public utilities and transportation, and they include estimates of substantial savings to be realized in this respect. Nevertheless, continued deficit financing is implied in plans of this magnitude. For most countries this is an extremely precarious position, as reasonable price stability is a premise of effective development planning.[14] Consequently, it is of great concern that the necessary increase in internal debt be financed in the least inflationary way; that is, that the maximum amount be placed directly in the hands of the private sector.

Private Savings. In some cases, such policies may channel into productive investments private savings not reached by the present banking system or capital market. In the Venezuelan Plan, for example, it is pointed out that the high component of transfers in government capital expenditures is in large part due to the failure of financing institutions to absorb a potentially sufficient supply of savings. Other countries would also benefit by more flexible and more attractive savings institutions, as is witnessed by the recent rapid expansion of savings and loan associations

---

[14] At present inflation is a particularly serious problem in Brazil. A return to price stability there is one of the prime goals of the three-year plan, which includes measures designed to reduce the rate of price increase by half (to 25 per cent) in 1963 and to 10 per cent in the following year.

TABLE 5–4. The Financing of Planned Investment, Compared with Recent Realized Investment

Country	Gross domestic investment			Savings		
	Average annual total (millions of local currency units, constant prices)	Undertaken by Public sector (per cent)	Undertaken by Private sector (per cent)	Gross domestic savings Total Public + Private (per cent of gross domestic investment)		Foreign savings (Balance of payments on current account)
Bolivia[a]						
1958	489	...	...	37	...	63
1962–66	1,040			62	...	38
Planned 1967–71	1,418			106	...	–6
Brazil[a]						
1958	711	...	...	76	...	24
Planned 1963–65	1,167			93	...	7
Chile						
1961	634	53	47	58	...	42
1962	726	57	43	77	...	23
Planned 1963–65	1,034	56	44	86	44	14
Planned 1966–70	1,633	51	49	94	51	6
Colombia						
1959	4,952	23	67	100[b]	24	76
Planned 1962–65	10,206	30	70	85	20	66

Honduras	1961	110	19	81	101	17	86	−3
	1962	127	24	76	95	10	85	5
Planned	1963	168	40	60	65	9	56	35
Planned	1964	195	39	61	63	9	54	37
Panama	1960	72	13	87	51	...	...	49
	1961	92	22	78	71	...	...	29
Planned	1963–70	113	48	52	47	...	...	53
Venezuela	1960	4,917	45	55	102	34	68	−2
Planned	1963–66	7,048	36	64	98	40	58	2

a Investment in billions.
b 1957–60 average.

Sources: See Table 5–1.
Bolivia: 1958 prices, Plan Tables 21, 22, 29 and pp. 110, 111.
Brazil: 1962 prices, Plan Tables X, XI, XIX; 1958 investment converted to 1962 prices by index of wholesale prices excluding coffee. Foreign savings share computed using exchange rate of 450 cruzeiros = $1.00.
Chile: 1961 prices, Report to the IA-ECOSOC (CIES/314), July, 1963 and Tables 5, 12, 13, 16 of plan evaluation.
Colombia: 1961 prices, Plan Tables 1, 4, 33, 55; 1959 data converted to 1961 prices by index of home and import goods prices.
Honduras: Current prices, Plan Tables 18, 38.
Panama: 1961 prices, Report to the IA-ECOSOC (CIES/323), July, 1963, and Plan Tables V–4, VI–1.
Venezuela: 1960 prices, Plan Tables III.2, III.5.

in Latin America. In recognition of this need, Bolivia and Colombia are weighing reorganization of their banking systems to better serve development purposes, and Chile has undertaken, with international assistance, a thorough study of its capital market. Use of these facilities presupposes confidence and interest on the part of the private sector in the development effort, a major prerequisite for the success of the Alliance program.

Foreign Savings. In some countries—Chile and Brazil, for example—private savings are probably adequate, so that in the absence of capital flight they could meet the demand for investment finance.[15] In many other countries, private savings are less elastic, and the persistence of a public deficit makes foreign financing more imperative as the only alternative to monetary expansion. In Colombia, for example, the heavy investment responsibility of the private sector impinges on its ability to save, making it unwise for the Government to resort to internal deficit financing or to tax measures which restrict savings incentives. And in other countries—such as Honduras and Panama—the average propensity to save is so low that further resources from the private sector can be acquired only by increasing the progressivity of the tax structure to absorb some of the great differential in income levels, and by promoting foreign trade, the major source of tax revenues. Thus, Colombia, Honduras, and Panama will rely increasingly on an inflow of foreign savings to finance their planned investment; in Venezuela, the foreign component of savings will remain very low; Bolivia, Brazil, and Chile expect to reduce their dependence on foreign savings through a greater mobilization of domestic resources and by expanding exports.

Export expansion is, of course, a goal shared by all (see Table 5–5), since for the time being the necessary capital goods must be to a large extent imported, even in those countries where import substitution has been under way for some time. Bolivia plans an extensive program of import substitution, especially of processed foods, which is projected to save an estimated $9 million in 1966 and $19 million in 1971. For Brazil, Chile, Colombia, and Venezuela, however, where import substitution has been pursued for a much longer period, it may proceed at a slower rate in the future; for Honduras and possibly Panama it must await an expansion of the market accompanying the progress of Central American economic integration. In general, the plans are moderately optimistic regarding the possibilities of increasing earnings by exporting larger volumes of mineral products, livestock, and a few agricultural com-

---

[15] See, for instance, the Panel of Experts' evaluation on Chile: *Evaluación del Programa . . . de Chile,* p. 162.

modities such as cotton and shellfish, but they do not predict price increases. Expectations about the future of exports to the United States and Japan are more favorable than the projection of future exports to the European Economic Community.

Within the limited opportunities for export expansion, the plans seek maximum diversification. In mineral-exporting countries, agricultural and (in the case of Chile) industrial exports are to increase faster than the traditional exports, while in agricultural countries the mineral-export sector is expected to be more dynamic. But this large category breakdown conceals the extent to which new products enter the export trade; for, in the relatively short period of time covered by these plans, the major effects of diversification will occur within the presently dominant export sector, be it of agricultural or of mineral products. While the same qualification applies to the classification of imports in Table 5–5, the intent to limit imports of goods of final consumption in favor of capital goods is in most cases very clear.

Measures to Reduce Structural Imbalance

Complementary to the goal of export diversification is that of reducing structural imbalance in the domestic economy and correcting the disequilibrium among the economic sectors, both among the different regions of the country and among the employment opportunities of the population.

Gross Domestic Product by Sectors. Within the given increases of total product at a specified annual rate, there is to take place a shift in the composition of output, particularly a marked increase in industrial production as a share of the total, and a sharp rise in some basic services. Industrial production is scheduled to expand at an annual rate of about 11 per cent in Brazil and Venezuela and nearly 10 per cent in Bolivia, compared with annual rates of 6, 8, and 6 per cent, respectively, for agricultural output in these countries (see Table 5–6). In Brazil and Venezuela, the high rates of growth for industry represent a continuation of the direction in which the composition of output has been moving for several years;[16] but for Bolivia the high rate of growth in industrial production projected in the plan will require an effective policy of industrialization. Chile and Colombia also plan rates of growth of industrial production higher than those of primary production or services, but in these two countries the differential is less pronounced.

[16] See OAS/ECLA *Economic & Social Survey of Latin America, 1961* (Washington, D.C., 1962), Chapter V.

TABLE 5-5. Planned Foreign Trade

			Balance of payments on current account (millions of dollars, constant prices)				
Country and period			Exports (f.o.b.)	Imports (f.o.b.)	Balance of trade	Remittances	Balance on current account
			Goods and services				
Bolivia		1958	58	90	...	...	−32
	Planned	1966	111	122	...	...	−11
		1971	195	162	...	...	+33
Planned annual rate of increase							
		1958–71	9.8%	4.6%			
Average annual increase		1953–61[a]	0.8%	0.4%			
Brazil		1962	1,312	1,721	−409	+1	−408
	Planned	1963	1,502	1,705	−203	—	−203
		1965	1,666	1,785	−159	—	−159
Planned annual rate of increase							
		1963–65	5.3%	2.3%			
Average annual increase		1953–61	−0.9%	2.1%			
Chile[b]		1962	575	660	−85	−80	−165
	Planned	1963	630	639	−9	−96	−105
		1965	740	695	+45	−126	−81
Planned annual rate of increase							
		1963–70	5.8%	3.0%			
Average annual increase		1953–61	4.8%	8.4%			
Colombia		1962*	595	716	−121	+1	−120
	Planned	1962	591	699	−108	−44	−152
		1965	699	864	−165	−97	−262
Planned annual rate of increase							
		1962–65	5.8%	7.3%			
Average annual increase		1953–61	−1.5%	2.1%			
Honduras		1962	79	72	...	...	6
	Planned	1963	85	108	−23	−6	−29
		1964	88	118	−30	−6	−36
Planned annual rate of increase							
		1962–64	1.8%	7.0%			
Average annual increase		1953–61	2.0%	1.3%			
Panama[c]		1961	194	224	...	...	−32
	Planned	1963	170	218	...	...	−48
		1970	230	307	...	...	−77
Planned annual rate of increase							
		1963–70	4.4%	5.0%			
Average annual increase		1953–61	9.2%	9.2%			
			Merchandise		Balance	Bal. of services	Bal. on cur. acc.
Venezuela		1960	2,356	1,157	+1,199	−1,177	+22
	Planned	1963	2,713	1,258	+1,455	−1,514	−59
		1966	3,100	1,288	+1,812	−1,759	+53
Planned annual rate of increase							
		1963–66	4.5%	0.8%			
Average annual increase		1953–61	7.1%	6.2%			

Composition of merchandise exports and imports
(per cent of total value)

	Exports				Imports		
Agri-cultural	Min-eral	Indus-trial	Other	Capital goods	Raw materials and fuels	Con-sumer goods	Other
7	82	d	11	37	26	37	—
13	81	6	—	42	31	27	—
19	68	6	7	47	29	25	—
				All Manu-factures		(Food and live animals)	
70	7	...	23	62	22	12	—
70	9	...	21	55	21	13	11
66	11	...	22	50	23	13	14
8	88	4	—	38	28	44	—
5	79	17	—	44	32	21	3
5	74	21	—	45	31	20	3
81	15	...	4	56	37	7	—
71	23	...	6	52	37	11	1
70	24	...	6	56	34	10	1
86	3	1	9	24	33	44	—
86	4	1	10	34	29	37	—
84	4	1	11	36	29	35	—
90	...	...	10	35	11	54	—
89	...	...	11	36	11	53	—
84	...	...	16	39	11	50	—
				Invest-ment goods	Other manu-fact. items	Agri-cultural products	Others
1962: 1	97	d	2	23	62	5	10
2	97	1	—	29	58	3	10
2	96	2	—	42	45	3	10

(Continued)

TABLE 5-5. *Continued*

a The average of annual variations over the period 1953–61.
b The composition of exports is based on 1961 data. Industrial Exports include processed copper.
c The composition of imports is based on 1960 data.
d Less than 0.6 per cent.
Sources: For country sources, see Table 5-1.
Bolivia: Plan Tables 21, 22; 14–17, 28.
Brazil: 1962 data from SUMOC, *Boletim*, March, 1963; 1963–65 data from Plan Tables XIX, XXII, XXIV; Table XXIV was grouped as follows: (*a*) imports of machinery, chemicals, manufactures, and semimanufactures, (*b*) petroleum and metals, (*c*) wheat, which may not correspond exactly to the SUMOC classification used for 1962.
Chile: 1962 data from Report to IA–ECOSOC (CIES/314), October, 1963; 1963–65 Plan, Table 16 and pp. 163, 169, 172, 175; rates of growth in exports and imports 1963–70 pp. 169, 175.
Colombia: 1962, IMF, *Balance of Payments Yearbook*, Vol. 15; 1963–65, Plan Tables 14, 18, 22.
Honduras: Tables 18, 14, 17.
Panama: Report to IA–ECOSOC (CIES/323), October, 1963, Tables VII–10, VII–6, VII–7, VII–4.
Venezuela: Plan Tables II–7, III–11.

TABLE 5-6. Planned Annual Increases in Production, by Sectors, in Five Countries

(Per cent)

Production sector	Bolivia 1958–71	Brazil 1961–65	Chile 1961–70	Colombia 1959–65	Venezuela 1962–66
Average annual increase in:					
Agriculture, forestry	6.3	5.7	5.5	3.5	7.5
Mining	8.5		6.0	6.5	4.4
Industry	9.5	11.2	6.5	6.9	11.3
Manufacturing	8.4	...	6.5	6.4	12.3
Construction	17.4	...	6.9	8.7	8.0
Services	5.0	...	5.1	4.8	6.2
Commerce	5.3	8.2	...	4.7	5.0
Transport, communications	5.5	8.8	...	5.5	7.0
Electricity, gas, water	6.7	...	...	12.5	17.0
Housing property	...	...	2.7	4.5	6.0
Other	3.5	3.0	5.5	2.8	6.0
Government	...	4.8	2.5	5.4	7.0
Other	—	3.5	—	—	—

Sources: See Table 5-1 for list of country sources. Bolivia: Plan Table 25. Brazil: Plan Table XV. Chile: CORFO, version of Plan submitted to Panel of Experts, Table 3. Colombia: Plan Table 2. Venezuela: Plan Table I.1.

Within the general grouping of services, rapid increases are planned in those basic services often referred to as constituting the infrastructure of an economy. The increase in provision of electricity, gas, and water is greater even than the rate of growth of industry in Venezuela and Colombia, and transport and communications are of especial importance in Brazil.

Whereas Bolivia, Chile, and Colombia plan an expansion in mineral production in excess of that in agriculture, in Venezuela this pattern is reversed. Agricultural production is to increase as a share of total product, while the petroleum sector increases at only 4 per cent annually, with total mineral production expanding only slightly faster.

To achieve these output targets, the plans rely on substantial increases in private investment, which continues to be considerably larger than public investment in most of Latin America. The large increases planned in public investment are divided among public works, industrial activities, and social services in the proportions believed most conducive to maximum productivity of all investment, public and private. This criterion does not necessarily conflict with the desire to improve the health and living conditions of the population, since over longer time periods the distinction between economic and social investments has less meaning; nevertheless, the shortage of investment resources does impose a limitation on those projects whose contribution to production is recovered only in the long run. For investment to increase at the planned rate, the major share of projects has to be of the variety which generates an immediate response in rising income from which the further increases in investment may be drawn. Among the four countries which present a sufficiently detailed breakdown of their investment plans, the share of public investment destined for the more specifically social sectors of health, sanitation, education, and housing ranges from 26 to 32 per cent of total planned public investment for Colombia, Honduras and Panama, with the balance of two-thirds to three-fourths allotted to economic investments [17] (see Table 5–7). For Guatemala the corresponding ratios are 16 and 84 per cent. Investment in transport, communications, fuel, and power is to absorb 30 to 52 per cent of total public investment: it ranges from 30 per cent in Panama to more than half of the total in the case of Guatemala and Honduras. In most of these countries, investment in agriculture, manufacturing, and mining is to remain largely the responsibility of private

---

[17] The Mexican plan similarly allots 23 per cent of total public investments to social sectors and 76 per cent to economic activities.

TABLE 5–7. The Distribution of Planned Investment by Sectors

(Per cent)

Sector	Brazil Total investment 1963–65	Chile Public 1963–70	Colombia Public 1963–65	Colombia Private 1963–65	Guatemala Public 1963–64	Honduras Public 1963–64	Panama Public 1963–70	Venezuela Public 1963–66	Venezuela Private 1963–66
Agriculture	8.4	22.0	9.6	16.2	19.1	8.0	8.9	16.9	6.4
Mining	7.6	0.4	1.0	9.9	...[d]	—	...	2.2	16.5
Manufacturing	18.6	7.9	1.0	29.8	...	8.9[f]	5.6	5.4	27.3
Construction	...	25.3	—	—	...	—	13.9	14.0[i]	26.5[i]
Housing	12.4	18.1	13.1	21.2	3.6	4.8[g]	10.1	—	...
Other[a]	...	7.2	—	—	...	—[f]	3.8	—	...
Commerce	...	—	1.6	0.5	...	—	...	0.8	12.5
Transport and communications	29.0	19.8[b]	27.5	15.5	42.4	39.8	22.2	25.2	2.5
Fuel and power	13.7	15.5	16.4	0.7	12.6	12.1	8.1	9.9	2.6
Water supply	...	[c]	8.2	—	2.4	5.9	...	(10.0)[e]	[j]
Health	...	[c]	2.8	2.3	8.1	5.5	9.0		...
Education	...	[c]	8.0	—	2.4	10.1	6.7		...
Urbanization	...	[b]	—	—	...	[g]	...	[i]	[i]
Administration	...	—	10.8	4.0	...	5.0	...	25.5[k]	...
Other	10.3	—	—	—	9.5	—	25.7[h]	—	5.6
Total	100.0	100.0	100.0	100.0	100.0	100.0	100.0	100.0	100.0

a Where not specified, expenditure on construction is included in the investment of the various sectors.

b Transport and communications includes urbanization.

c Not yet available; in preparation. In the IBRD review of the original plan for 1961–70, these items amounted to 8.5 per cent of total gross investment.

d Industrialization of agricultural products is included under agriculture.

e Estimated. See *Sources*.

f "Commerce" is included in manufacturing.

g "Urbanization" is included in housing.

h Not yet programmed.

i "Urbanization" is included in construction.

j "Water supply" is included in fuel and power.

k "Health, education," is included in government.

Sources: Brazil: Plan Table 7; report to IA-ECOSOC, October, 1963. Chile: Plan Table 6. Colombia: Plan Table 13. Guatemala: Plan Table 1; refers only to planned investment of 1962–63 and 1963–64. Honduras: Plan Table 21. Panama: Plan p. 196. Venezuela: Plan Table III.2; public investment in education and health is estimated on the basis of the sectoral programs, deflated from 1962 to 1960 prices by the price index of home and import goods, as given in IMF, *International Financial Statistics*, August, 1963.

investors, supplemented by public investment to the extent of 12 to 17 per cent of the latter's total commitments. In Venezuela, however, where 17 per cent of total public investment is to be devoted to carrying on the Government's agrarian reform program, this share rises to 24 per cent; and in Chile, where more than half of total gross domestic investment is undertaken by the public sector, the proportion is 30 per cent. Again, the largest share—in this case, more than one-fifth of total public investment—will go to agricultural development, as Chile has recently become a net importer of agricultural products.

Regional Disparities. It is a commonplace that regional characteristics —including income levels and resource endowment—vary widely in a country of Brazil's size, but even in a comparatively small country like Panama there are decided differences in resources and productivity in different geographic areas; and regional disparities are perhaps nowhere more pronounced than in Bolivia. In the latter, the problem of floods and erosion in the valleys and of extreme fragmentation of landholdings on the altiplano, together with the pressure of population growth in both areas, has induced the Government to adopt a development strategy which places considerable reliance on a massive relocation of population to the tropical lowland areas of the Oriente. Bolivia's current program of agrarian reform and heavy investments in transport and communications have been devised in large part to encourage colonization of the lowlands. Honduras, too, considers resettlement a necessity; the emergency plan presented by the President of the Republic to complement the public investment program contemplates relocation in agricultural cooperatives of persons living in rural areas where unemployment is most serious. Since 1959, Brazil has succeeded in increasing slightly the share of the Northeast region in total national income, thanks to the creation of a special agency (SUDENE) concerned exclusively with the development of that region and with large investments in Bahia by the state petroleum corporation, Petrobras. The area remains one of great poverty, however, and requires tremendous assistance to attain the rate of growth characteristic of the rest of the nation. The general guidelines of regional planning in Brazil direct the Federal Government to intensify preinvestment activities related to the evaluation and use of natural and human resources, including the offer of financial assistance to state and local governments, which are constitutionally responsible for primary education, and to continue the policy of providing incentives to private investment in the less developed areas. In Venezuela, too, regional planning is in various stages of advancement; the focus of development planning will be on organization of urban services in the metropolitan areas of

Caracas and Maracaibo and the Lago de Valencia region, on agricultural production and small- and medium-scale industry in Los Andes and the Centro-Occidental regions, on intensive agriculture in Majagual, and on hydroelectric power and basic metallurgical industries in Guayana. In Chile and Colombia, regional variations in productivity are closely related to the disparity between urban and rural income levels, which is common in some measure to all countries, but particularly marked in underdeveloped economies.

Employment. One of the most serious obstacles to economic development in Latin America, and perhaps the single most vital factor to its success, is the ability of each country to fully absorb, economically and socially, its human resources. The rate of population growth is high, the rate of growth of the labor force often even higher. In Bolivia, for example, it is estimated that merely in order not to increase unemployment, it would be necessary to create more than a quarter of a million new jobs between 1961 and 1965, and the problem is of similar magnitude elsewhere. In part, the shifting of resources into industrial production noted in these plans was devised in order to provide employment for the migrants from rural to urban areas. The extensive construction programs are labor-intensive and should also aid in creating employment opportunities. The agrarian-reform programs [18] are aimed at the same problem of low productivity, for unemployment and underemployment are equally discouraging to attempts to raise the living standards of the population as rapidly as possible. But all these measures require skills and mobility to a greater degree than is presently characteristic of rural workers. Thus, the bulk of the responsibility for longer-term development still rests with the education programs; only by vigorously developing its underutilized human resources can Latin America hope to enter into a phase of sustained internal growth; and only thus will the region's capacity to absorb foreign financial and technical aid grow with the supply. In this way alone will the present planning efforts increasingly become expressions of concrete governmental actions based on detailed knowledge of the plans and needs of the private sector of the economy.

NATIONAL PROGRAMS OF AGRARIAN REFORM

Since August, 1961, ten countries have passed agrarian reform legislation: Costa Rica and Colombia in 1961; Chile, the Dominican Repub-

[18] See below.

lic, Guatemala, Honduras, Panama, and Peru in 1962; and Paraguay and Nicaragua in 1963. Mexico, Bolivia, and Venezuela previously passed such legislation introducing programs to alter the agrarian structure of their countries; Brazil, Ecuador, El Salvador, and Uruguay have submitted such legislation to their respective legislatures.[19]

The economic and social pressures of antiquated land-tenure systems have long been a recognized problem in Latin America. The exhortation to attend to this very serious situation was summarized at Punta del Este when an important aim of the Alliance was stated to be "replacing the structure of latifundias and minifundias by a just system of property." [20] The coexistence of extremely large land holdings by a small proportion of the rural population and precariously small holdings by the majority of the rural population is characteristic of most of these nations, together with the related problem of large numbers of persons living and working on the land without any legal title of ownership. In agreeing to act to reduce the great inequalities in land ownership, the countries acknowledged a common motive of social justice, seeking a "just system of property." In the lengthy parliamentary discussions that have usually preceded the adoption of such legislation, it has often been claimed that it is equally unjust to substitute a system that would threaten the rights of private property. The resulting legislation represents in each case an attempt to reconcile widely divergent views and aims: a broader distribution of land ownership on the one hand, and the inviolability of private property on the other; a breaking up of the present very large units and the need to provide supplementary services to insure an economically viable system.[21]

---

[19] Two state programs are already in effect in Brazil, in São Paulo and Rio Grande do Sul. In Ecuador, two projects have recently been initiated which deserve mention: a loan of $1,880,000 from AID is to cover 36.5 per cent of the cost of developing 219 mountain villages as part of a five-year rural development program; another AID loan of $2,535,000 is to cover 64 per cent of the cost of relocating 1,600 low-income rural families in northern Ecuador.

[20] The Government of Peru submitted a new agrarian reform bill in August, 1963. Charter of Punta del Este, Title I, point 6.

[21] In most cases the new laws represent the latest step in a series of agrarian reform legislation, but the earlier efforts were generally limited to colonization and did not attempt to deal directly with the system of land tenure. Thus some of the countries not mentioned here also have in effect legislation dealing with land settlement, but only those programs designed as national programs of agrarian reform in accordance with the Charter of Punta del Este are considered in this section. The programs which existed prior to the initiation of the Alliance are considered more briefly than their more recent counterparts and with emphasis on their practical effect rather than on the legislation from which they derive.

The General Pattern of Recent Agrarian Reform Programs

The Legislation. The agrarian reform laws passed since the 1961 Punta del Este Conference are complex pieces of legislation, many of them lengthy and all of them open to differing interpretations on numerous points. The language is often imprecise: different clauses of the same law may be contradictory; and many questions of operating procedure and jurisdiction remain to be worked out in practice.

Any agrarian reform law, however, in seeking to both protect and extend the institution of private property, must incorporate certain basic decisions on method. The least common denominator of such laws includes answers, however imprecise, to the questions of which land is to be affected and which exempted by the program, how this land is to be acquired and prepared for distribution, and what are to be the qualifications and obligations of those receiving title to the land. Within these categories, the dispositions of these particular laws range from terminology so broad that further defining regulations will be necessary, to detailed compilations of exceptions; and implementation will be further complicated by the differing institutional structures as they have evolved in the various countries. In order to present a composite picture of the actions taken recently pertaining to agrarian reform, the summary which follows describes in oversimplified form those characteristics common to most, but not all, of the agrarian reform legislation adopted since the initiation of the Alliance. Later in this chapter (p. 222), the experiences of individual countries are summarized to the extent that the salient discrepancies from the composite picture may be noted.

According to the basic pattern abstracted from the various laws, responsibility for the program is entrusted to a newly created autonomous agrarian reform institute. The duties of the institute include acquiring and distributing land, conducting prior geographical studies, constructing access roads and irrigation canals where necessary, and extending technical and financial aid to the settlers.

The institute or agency entrusted with this program is generally allotted a specific appropriation in the annual budget of the central government and authorized to issue bonds up to a maximum value in local and foreign currency to finance its operations. It is a legal entity directly subordinate to the President, is generally governed by a board of directors, and often maintains local advisory bodies in different areas of the country.

The institute is charged first with preparing and distributing land currently belonging to the state or acquired by the state through voluntary sale of private holdings. When such land is no longer available, it may generally expropriate privately owned land which is idle, poorly exploited, or exploited by third persons. A reserve, generally of 50 to 100 hectares [22] of irrigated lands or the equivalent, is allowed the owner. The purchase price is to be settled by appraisal in each case, taking into account such factors as location, productivity, and recent sale values of similar property, with compensation in currency on terms ranging from five to ten years at an interest rate of about 4 per cent per annum.

There is no limit to the quantity of well-cultivated land which may be held, although most countries reserve the right to expropriate even such land, should it be essential to the regrouping of minifundia or subject to the right of eminent domain as land of "public utility."

Once made ready for occupation, the land must be divided into family farm units of workable area. These units are then distributed to those persons over eighteen who can demonstrate a need for additional land, with preference given those who live in the immediate vicinity and have the largest number of dependents. Selection among the many qualified candidates is left to the institute. Those selected must agree to work the land personally with their families and to fulfill any obligations imposed by the institute with respect to the extent and type of cultivation. The cost of the land plus improvements is to be repaid over a period of 15 to 25 years at low interest rates. Compliance with these regulations entitles the settler to full title; neglect may lead to repossession of the land. Directed colonization projects may also be undertaken, whereby the institute establishes an entire new community, including schools, churches, and other common facilities. A third part of the institute's activities will continue to be the granting of title to land already settled.

In addition to land, the beneficiaries of the agrarian reform laws are promised credit facilities to help in buying equipment and housing, along with technical assistance. Unfortunately, however, while the laws acknowledge the need for expanding such services, in general the language of the law is neither specific nor mandatory in this regard.

Implementation of the Legislation. Approximately half of Latin America's 20 million rural families live a precarious existence on the land. That agriculture alone cannot absorb this number, plus the annual increment in rural population, does not lighten the responsibility of the agrarian reform programs to serve as many as possible as quickly as possible. But difficult problems of organization, time, and finance are being encountered in implementing both phases of the agrarian reform programs: settlement, and the provision of services complementary to the land grant.

---

[22] One hectare equals 2.471 acres.

Settlement on public lands is hindered by the fact that these lands often require clearing, soil studies, and access roads before they are usable, and such preparatory projects are extremely costly as well as time-consuming. Once it becomes necessary to expropriate privately owned lands, the detailed appraisals and negotiations, together with the possibility of a recourse to the courts, postpone settlement [23] and may require large numbers of personnel as well as large amounts of financial resources in order to compensate the owners in currency at an appraised price. Consequently, an agrarian reform program large enough in scope to be effective requires an enormous budgetary allocation which could endanger the monetary stability of the nation.

Nor is the actual distribution of land a simple matter. The specific size of family farm units not only will depend on the size of the family but must take into account as well the geography of different areas, the crops to be cultivated, and the degree of mechanization considered reasonable. Before the technical decisions can be made, however, the general guidelines of agricultural policy must have been well thought out at the national levels, and this requires a degree of comprehensive planning just beginning to be realized in most countries.

Another serious obstacle to the execution of agrarian reform is the current inadequacy of technical and credit assistance available to small agricultural producers. Such services are vital to the new landowners in the same way that they are essential to the development of established farms of the agricultural sector of the economy and to assure rural families a continually rising standard of living. In fact, this particular need was admitted long before the more ambitious project of land reform won acceptance, and it has not yet been met effectively. For the renewed intentions to be more practicable, the effort will have to be more imaginative, and the budget larger, than before. Agricultural extension services and credit availability should be closely associated, encouraging the use of improved techniques by those receiving loan funds. It has been recommended [24] that, in view of the importance of credit assistance in integrating the rural population with the national economy, part of the costs incurred might well be charged to the social investment program, reduc-

---

[23] The Colombian land reform institute, INCORA, reports that in the case of voluntary sale of private lands negotiations may be completed within four months, if there are no complications, whereas an additional five months are necessary before taking possession of an expropriated property. INCORA, *Informe de Actividades en 1962*, p. 83.

[24] See the *Final Report of IA-ECOSOC Special Commission II, on Agricultural Development and Agrarian Reform* (Costa Rica, July, 1963) (OEA/Ser.H/XIII, CIES/Com.II).

ing the burden to be paid by the individual beneficiary. International assistance is helping in this direction by providing loans for credit tied to technical assistance.[25]

The eventual outcome of these programs will depend on the balance of resources between settlement and services; but above all it will depend on the seriousness of those who interpret the laws in administering their application. Competent administrators are essential to the success of any project, but agrarian reform programs in particular will stand or fall with the skill and conviction of those in charge of converting legislation into practice. As mentioned before, the desirability of a wider distribution of landownership has a long history of verbal acceptance in Latin America, expressed in a series of laws dealing with colonization and land reform. But outside of Mexico, Venezuela, and Bolivia, there is only little practical experience in this field,[26] and there still remains a substantial segment of popular opinion opposed to institutional reforms of so basic a nature. Among those who stand to benefit from additional land, the need to change farming methods and possibly to move to a different area has sometimes engendered suspicion of agrarian reform, while those who do not expect to gain more land are indifferent at best and more usually opposed, especially if they foresee part of their own land being sacrificed to carry out the program. The large number of agrarian reform laws passed since initiation of the Alliance is testimony to the compromise achieved between the widespread support of social justice in the abstract and the small but powerful opposition to agrarian reform. Nevertheless, effectively to carry out a mandate which is a compromise requires more skill than to enact a measure which has the decisive support of a large majority.

Aware of the unfavorable connotations to the landowner of the term "expropriation," the laws, in using the term, tend to surround it with assurances of restraint, approaching agrarian reform through the distribution of land rather than through the regulation of tenancy conditions which have in large part created the need for reform. Land cultivated indirectly—that is, by persons other than the owner—is

[25] For example, Colombia recently received three loans totaling $21.5 million from the Agency for International Development for agrarian reform; one of these, of $10 million for 40 years at ¾ per cent interest, will be used to encourage diversification of crops and the use of modern methods of farming and to provide credit tied to technical assistance. In addition, a credit was received by Colombia from the Development Loan Fund of $8 million for agricultural loans not exceeding 17,500 pesos each.

[26] And some of these experiences are so conditioned by particular national factors that their applicability elsewhere may be limited.

generally subject to eventual expropriation, but this is a last resort; meanwhile, exploitation of the land by nonowners, including occasionally even those systems of tenancy which compensate farm labor with limited rights to land use, are free to continue. Some steps have been taken to regulate the length of lease or amount of rent paid, but these are only a beginning, and evasion would not be difficult. Under such conditions, the programs outlined in the agrarian reform laws will accomplish agrarian reform only if, by the efforts of their administrators, costs and delays are kept to a minimum and the technical services are sufficiently decentralized so that the new farms afford a genuine alternative to the present system.

Thus, considering both the high initial costs and the short time these laws have been in effect, it is understandable that the major activity in 1962 consisted in the granting of titles to settlers already occupying land to which they had no legal claim. Organizing the agrarian reform institutes created by the new laws (see Table 5–9) required most of that year, and several of these agencies began operations only in 1963. Consequently the land distributed in 1962 pertained largely to projects formulated prior to the new laws, and this will probably be the case to a similar extent in 1963. More rapid handling of the projects in process is intended, however, as well as the preparation of additional projects. Furthermore, while the land affected in 1962 was for the most part of public ownership, this same procedure of legalizing "invasions" of land is being continually extended to private property. In Peru, for example, the new government has recently announced that it will undertake expropriation of several large estates in the Sierra region to distribute to the Indian peasants who have settled there. Elsewhere, prodding by those who need land is a constant reminder to those entrusted with enforcing the provisions of agrarian reform legislation. To encourage the opening of negotiations on the sale or expropriation of large idle tracts of land, labor organizations will often support selective spontaneous settlements. In the future, co-operation between local representatives of the rural population—such as the labor organizations and the Church—and the central agrarian reform agency should be increasingly valuable in carrying out these programs. It is also clear, however, by comparing in Table 5–9 the goals for 1963 with the number of families owning less than 5 hectares of land, most of whom may be assumed to benefit by inclusion in the agrarian reform program, that if a solution to the problem is to be approached within a decade or so, the dimensions of the annual programs will have to be greatly expanded in each case. This will require a reduction of legal complexities and

TABLE 5–8. Summary of Some Major Features of Agrarian Reform Laws Passed since August, 1961[a]

Country	Month/Year of Law	Land affected[b]	Land exempted[c]	Compensation for expropriated property
Chile Law 15020	11/62	a) Public lands b) Idle or very poorly cultivated private land c) Indirectly cultivated land of legal persons d) Land rented on a lease less than six years e) Minifundia for regrouping f) Latifundia in accordance with a development plan for the region	a) Private land valued at 200 minimum annual salaries of an employee of private business in Santiago plus 20 per dependent, valuation not specified b) Well-cultivated land or rented land of a 6 years or more lease	Price determined in each case, cash 20% down, not less than 10 years at 4%
Colombia Law 135	12/61	a) Private land of more than 2,000 ha. uncultivated 10 yrs. b) Accessible state-owned c) Private property above 100 ha.: uncultivated, inadequately cultivated, indirectly exploited minifundia for regrouping	a) 100 hectares farm land of 200 hectares total excluding steep slopes from "farmland" b) Well-cultivated land	Price negotiated by appraisers; uncultivated land in agrarian bonds, others in cash 20% down, 5–8 years 4–6% interest
Costa Rica Laws 2825 and 3033, 3042	10/61	a) Public lands b) Private land: "Latifundia," uncultivated, indirectly exploited, distributed land on which obligations neglected, farm land used for grazing	To be determined by the Institute, land fulfilling its social function	Not more than fiscal value; bonds or cash at discretion of Institute

Terms of payment by recipient of land	Conditions of land grant	Size of land parcel	Supplementary Services	Special features
To be specified by law; not less than 20 nor more than 30 years	Division of parcel requires authorization	Family Unit[d] one additional unit allowed for each 3 dependents	Credit, technical aid, Social Security, and market facilities	15% of rent receipts must be invested in improvements; special powers to President to regulate salaries, housing norms, imports, education
15 years; principal beginning third year from receipt 2% interest first two years, 4% thereafter; in "directed colonies," 70% plots distributed free; INCORA may rent instead of sell	50% under cultivation in 5 years, 65% in directed colonies; not divisible or transferrable; obey regulations of Institute (INCORA); direct exploitation, (INCORA may buy land plots indirectly exploited)	Family Unit	Credit and technical aid	Advisory committees at departmental and local level; farms of less than 3 hectares legally null
a) Parcels: 25 yrs., beginning 5 yrs. from receipt; repay cost of land, improvements and first year's credit alloted by Institute, discount of 5% per resident dependent. Adjustment in years of poor crops b) Institute may choose to rent to colonists	Direct exploitation; not transferrable or divisible for 15 yrs. and until fully paid, obligations to Institute on cultivation, tax exempt for 5 yrs.	Family Unit; on lands received free by state not more than 10 hectares for crops or 50 for pasture	Credit for one year's crop priority in credit, technical aid	Tax on all land holdings 0.25 to 2.5% taxable value, emphasis on co-operatives, lands of more than 1,000 hectares registered incorrectly transferred to state to extent of uncultivated excess

(Continued)

TABLE 5–8. *(Continued)*

Country	Month/ Year of Law	Land affected[b]	Land exempted[c]	Compensation for expropriated property
Dominican Republic Law 5879	4/62	Lands belonging to and purchased by state	All private property not voluntarily sold or donated	Not applicable
Guatemala Law 1551	10/62	a) Public lands b) Idle private lands on petition	a) Cultivated land b) Rented for at least 5 years with no personal service exacted	Price determined in each case; paid in cash, 5 years at 4%
Honduras Decree 2	9/62	a) Public lands b) Communal lands c) Private lands above 50 ha., uncultivated or idle, indirectly exploited, destined for rural private parcellation and not serving this purpose	50 hectares of irrigated land or equivalent, sufficiently exploited land	Price determined in each case; based on fiscal declaration and recent productivity to be fully paid in cash prior to possession
Nicaragua Decree 797	4/63	a) National lands b) Communal lands c) Lands of National District, municipalities, and state enterprises	500 hectares of first-quality land or equivalent	Valued according to location and potential productivity; terms not specified

Terms of payment by recipient of land	Conditions of land grant	Size of land parcel	Supplementary Services	Special features
Sales contracts to be specified by Institute	Must work land personally; not divisible or transferrable until full title; free of all legal burdens	Family Unit	Housing, credit, technical aid, training	Distribution by raffle
Price determined by Institute; paid 10% down, 20 annual quotas for land, 3 for equipment, no interest; 10% reduction if paid in less than 20 years; public lands may be rented by Institute	Divisible, transferable only with approval of Institute. Direct exploitation	Family Unit not less than 20 hectares	Credit and technical aid	Idle lands taxed 0.75 to 2.50 quetzales per hectare with surcharge of 20%, 40%, 60%, 80% in five years, rent may not exceed 6% crop a year
10 to 20 years, no deposit; no interest on public lands, 3%–4% on land acquired from private owners	Ownership of 1,000 lempiras business capital or 2,000 agricultural from receipt, failure to cultivate 2 years in succession, abandonment of land or family two years, failure to meet housing norms, or resort to indirect exploitation implies loss of title	Not less than 10 nor more than 20 hectares of irrigated land	Credit, technical aid	Farms less than 5 hectares indivisible, payment of rent in kind or labor forbidden, rental must be approved by INA, tax on idle lands 3% tax value year one, to 40% 5 years
Those already settled on and cultivating public or private land free title, otherwise 15–20 years with 2 years of grace at	Work land personally; no renting or tenants; build housing, full cultivation and at least 25% paid qualifies for full title; division or	Family Unit	Credit, technical aid	Free personal services and payment of rent in labor prohibited. Institute to regulate renting and sharecropping

(Continued)

TABLE 5-8. *(Continued)*

Country	Month/Year of Law	Land affected[b]	Land exempted[c]	Compensation for expropriated property
Nicaragua—*(Continued)*		d) Private lands above 500 hectares if: uncultivated or idle two consecutive years, inefficiently exploited, indirectly exploited two consecutive years		
Panama Law 37	9/62	a) Public lands b) Private lands: idle, inadequately cultivated, indirectly exploited	Well exploited	Value established by Agricultural Survey of 1956 or purchase value if purchased after 9/62. Cash or 4% bonds on choice of owner
Paraguay Laws 852, 854	3/63	Land owned or purchased by Institute Private lands on which: a) improvements do not represent 50% of fiscal value of land b) stable population settled c) minifundia	Reserve to be established by law, rationally exploited land (improvements—50% fiscal value)	If not occupied, price is the average of sale price and fiscal valuation in past two years; if occupied, paid average fiscal valuation of last 15 years; cash, 10 yearly installments
Peru Law 14238	11/62	a) Public land b) Lands of legal persons not directly essential c) Private lands: idle deficiently exploited indirectly exploited excessively concentrated in one zone	Reserve to be specified by law for each zone; well-cultivated land	Valued according to productivity

ECONOMIC PROGRAMS UNDER THE ALLIANCE 221

Terms of payment by recipient of land	Conditions of land grant	Size of land parcel	Supplementary Services	Special features
interest not to exceed 5% per year. 5% reduction of total for each child born after receipt of land	transfer requires approval, unembargable; land, equipment exempt from all public charges			
If annual income below 600 balboas, free; otherwise 20 years at 3% with 10 years extension at 6% if necessary. Institute may choose to rent rather than sell	Full cultivation in 5 years if less than 50 hectares, if more than 50 hectares full title when fully exploited, not divisible or transferrable without approval	Family Unit 10 ha. minimum colonization in 50 ha. lots	Credit, technical aid	
Free title to heads of family with 7 minor dependents and to those with 30% disability from Chaco War. Otherwise 15 years; 15% reduction if pay cash	Not embargable or transferrable, may not be rented for 10 years beyond full payment. Must work land personally; build house within 6 months	Varies with type of exploitation from 1/2 to 8,000 hectares	Credit, technical aid	Tenancy contracts to be written; rent not more than 12% fiscal value; crop payment not more than 20% produce; owner not more than 50% profit in joint ventures; tax on latifundia not rationally exploited
Not yet determined	Not yet determined	Family Unit	Credit, technical aid. Legislation to set minimum salary, extend Social Security	Progressive tax on land by area; proceeds for local public works. Legislation to regulate methods of indirect exploitation

(Continued)

TABLE 5-8. (*Continued*)

ᵃ This is only a brief summary of some provisions of these laws to indicate the general directions of action toward agrarian reform; it is by no means complete and therefore not a legally accurate presentation.
ᵇ In case of grave need, other private land may be expropriated on burden of proof of public utility in accordance with the relevant disposition of the respective national Constitutions.
ᶜ Excluding land occupied by buildings, forest reserves, national parks, the shores of rivers and lakes, and land immediately bordering urban concentrations; specific exemptions of this nature are included in the respective laws.
ᵈ The "Family Unit" as used in this table refers to the measure, common to several of these laws but denoted differently, of that quantity of land which is capable of being worked by a settler and his family without additional labor, although help may be obtained during the harvest, and which, given a rational use of available equipment and techniques, will yield a sufficient income to pay off the debt of purchase and provide a progressive improvement in the standard of living of the resident family.

Sources:
Chile: Ley de Reforma Agraria, No. 15020, November, 1962.
Colombia: Ley de Reforma Agraria, No. 135, December, 1961.
Costa Rica: Ley de Tierras y Colonización, No. 2825, October, 1961.
Dominican Republic: Ley de Reforma Agraria, No. 5879, April, 1962.
Guatemala: Ley de Transformación Agraria, No. 1551, October, 1962.
Honduras: Ley de Reforma Agraria, Decree 2, September, 1962.
Nicaragua: Ley de Reforma Agraria, No. 797, April, 1963.
Panama: Código Agrario, Law 37, September, 1962.
Paraguay: Estatuto Agrario, Law 854, March, 1963.
Peru: Bases de la Reforma Agraria, No. 14238, November, 1962.

administrative costs, as well as greater co-operation with those elements of the private sector interested in agrarian reform. Admittedly it will take some time to work out the most efficient procedures for settlement programs and technical and credit assistance programs; and as there is evidence that additional projects are being prepared for implementation in the near future, evaluation of the practical effect of the new laws may be better reserved until the responsible institutes have been operating a full year.

The Experiences of Individual Countries

The individual agrarian reform laws do not, of course, all conform to the same extent to this composite outline. Nor are the present conditions the same in each case. Some of the major features of the different national programs are outlined below, beginning with those agrarian reform programs begun under the Alliance. (See also, Tables 5-8, 5-9.)

Chile. Following the common pattern, Chile's law of November, 1962, aims at higher productivity and a more equitable system of landownership primarily by means of land distribution, beginning with state-owned land and, when necessary, resorting to the expropriation of private land, in excess of 50 hectares, which is idle or very poorly cultivated. Indirectly cultivated land is subject to expropriation when belonging to juridical persons or when rented for a period of less than six years. However, given the order of expropriation, rented land of more than 50 hectares which remains idle is nevertheless liable to expropriation even when the rental contract is of the legal duration. This should reduce somewhat the temptation to evade the effects of the law through simulated rent contracts. The obligation to invest part of the rent receipts in land improvement is raised from 10 to 15 per cent, although enforcement of this provision will continue to be only as effective as in the past. Private land may also be expropriated if it is necessary to the regrouping of minifundia or, under special conditions, if it constitutes a latifundia. With respect to the first, rural land is not to be divided in lots of less than 15 hectares of irrigated land or the equivalent. At the other extreme, "latifundium" is defined as land of single ownership valued at more than 400 times the annual minimum salary of an employee of private business in Santiago. If the prerequisite of a regional development plan is satisfied, latifundia may be expropriated. A reserve allowance of land valued at 200 minimum annual salaries plus 20 for each dependent is authorized by the law. The basis of valuation is apparently to be determined in each case. In addition, the Chilean law grants the President of the Republic extensive supplementary powers to regulate import duties on agricultural materials and to establish norms on agricultural housing, salaries, and co-operatives.

Practical application of the law began in January, 1963. One of the major projects being prepared is the leasing of 53,000 hectares of government land in Magallanes in 937 lots. At present, the cost per family is extraordinarily high, slowing the extension of services to the nearly 300,000 rural families in need of land. The goal for 1963 is to settle 7,000 families, for which approximately $60 million have been budgeted. An extensive aerial photogrammetric and field survey of agricultural lands, undertaken with the aid of a $2.1 million loan from the Inter-American Development Bank as part three of a four-part agricultural survey, is nearing completion and is expected to facilitate greatly all agricultural development programs.

Colombia. In Colombia (agrarian reform law passed in December, 1961), about 90 per cent of agricultural land is devoted to livestock grazing and only a small fraction of government-owned land is readily accessible, so it has been necessary to resort to expropriation of private lands. As a first step, all persons owning rural property in excess of 2,000 hectares must present the title and a description of the land to the Agustin Codazzi Geographical Institute, which will study the economic

TABLE 5-9. Progress in Implementing the Agrarian Reform Legislation Passed since Punta del Este

Country	Agency of agrarian reform	Beginning of operations	Estimated number of families owning less than 5 ha. of rural land
Chile	Corporación de Reforma Agraria	January, 1963	1962: 300,000[a]
Colombia	Instituto Nacional Colombiano de Reforma Agraria	January, 1962	1959: 800,000
Costa Rica	Instituto de Tierras y Colonización	November, 1962[c]	1950: 50,000
Dominican Republic	Instituto Agrario	April, 1962[e]	1960: 225,000
Guatemala	Instituto Nacional de Transformación Agraria	October, 1962[e]	1950: 140,000
Honduras	Instituto Nacional Agrario	September, 1962[e]	1962: 90,000
Nicaragua	Instituto Nacional Agrario	April, 1963[e]	...
Panama	Comisión de Reforma Agraria	March, 1963[e]	60,000
Paraguay	Instituto de Bienestar Rural	March, 1963[e]	...
Peru	Instituto de Reforma Agraria y Colonización	November, 1962[e]	...

Number of families receiving land or title			Budget 1963	Estimated cost per family	Major programs under way
In 1962	First half 1963	Planned total 1963			
	5,860	7,000	60 m.US$	US$7,500	Leasing of 53,000 hectares of public lands in Magallanes in 937 lots
4,324[b]	...	5,000	300 m. pesos authorized	investment of 50,000 ps.	9 projects approved in 1962 will benefit 13,400 families by dividing 44,000 ha. of idle or poorly exploited land and 117,900 ha. by irrigation.
...	...	600[d]	6.6 million colones	...	Plans for distribution of 270,000 ha. to 20,000 squatter families.
738	440	3,000	2 million pesos	550 pesos	Distribution of 100,000 ha. to about 10,000 families; possible hydroelectric development to irrigate 250,000 acres of new land.
20,000		...	...	...	Sebol project in northeast, including a road network; total cost 12.6 m. quetzales.
...	304	...	2 million lempiras	...	Planning to be completed in 1963 on project to settle 6,000 families in Aguan Valley; preliminary studies for National Cadastral Survey.
...	...	...			
...	...	1,200	...	$750[f]	Alanje project to be completed in 1963, Tonosi currently 50% completed and four others 20% completed—total of 110,000 persons to benefit.
25,000	11,253		...	...	Parana River project to divide 42,000 hectares into 1,400 plots has begun; project being studied to develop 10,000 ha. for 2,500 families.
424	1,620	7,000	66 million soles	...	Settlement of 6,460 families in San Lorenzo, 1963 settlement of 2,000 families in Apurimac by 1967–68.

(Continued)

TABLE 5-9. (*Continued*)

ᵃ See Inter-American Development Bank, Social Progress Trust Fund, *Second Annual Report*, 1962.
ᵇ Equals "titles expedited" by INCORA. See INCORA, *Informe*, p. 44.
ᶜ From October, 1961, to October, 1962, the Banco Nacional administered the settlement programs.
ᵈ Refers only to a colonization project in Bataan; other projects are intended but have not yet been quantified.
ᵉ Date of entry into force of law creating the Institute.
ᶠ Weighted average of projected costs of six programs serving 110,000 persons, assuming five persons per family.

Sources:
Chile: Inter-American Development Bank, Social Progress Trust Fund, *Second Annual Report*, 1962; U.S. Department of Agriculture, *Foreign Agriculture*, May 27, 1963; Evaluation of Plan by Committee of Nine; Report to the IA–ECOSOC, July, 1963 (CIES).
Colombia; INCORA, *Informe* and *Boletín Informativo*, various issues; Caja de Crédito Agrario, *Carta Agraria*, various issues. The estimated number of families needing land is the number of farms of less than 5 hectares in 1959 according to the Ministry of Agriculture; the number benefiting in 1962 is the number of "titles expedited" by INCORA as given on p. 44 of the *Informe*. The cost per family settled refers to investment, excluding administrative costs, and is estimated by INCORA (*Informe*, p. 42) to be divided almost evenly between the cost of land and of credit.
Costa Rica: Report to the CIES, July, 1963. The estimated number of families needing additional land corresponds to the number of farms of less than 5 hectares in 1950: see Pan American Union, *La Estructura Agropecuaria de las Naciones Americanas*, 1957.
Dominican Republic: Social Progress Trust Fund, *Second Annual Report*, 1962; "Alliance Weekly Newsletter," August 26, 1963. According to the preliminary results of the 1960 census approximately half of the 450,000 farms consisted of less than one hectare of land.
Guatemala: Social Progress Trust Fund, *Second Annual Report*, 1962. According to the census of 1950, there were 140,000 rural families who did not own land.
Honduras: Social Progress Trust Fund, *Second Annual Report*, 1962; Report to the IA–ECOSOC, July, 1963 (CIES/320–II). The number cited as needing additional land equals the number of farms of less than 5 hectares according to the 1962 census.
Nicaragua: Social Progress Trust Fund, *Second Annual Report*, 1962.
Panama: National development plan; Report to the CIES, July, 1963, (OAS/Ser.H/X5). According to the census of 1960, there were 60,000 rural squatter families.
Paraguay: Social Progress Trust Fund, *Second Annual Report*, 1963.
Peru: Social Progress Trust Fund, *Second Annual Report*, 1963; Report to the IA–ECOSOC (CIES/325).

use of the land; if it has remained uncultivated for 10 years, the owners stand to lose title.[27] When sufficient private holdings are not offered for sale voluntarily, the Colombian National Agrarian Reform Institute

[27] By the end of 1962, 1,238 such reports had been received covering 7.4 million hectares of land, or 25 per cent of the total privately owned rural land. According to the information submitted by the owners, 2.8 million hectares were well exploited, while 4.6 million were not exploited at all. INCORA, *Informe*, 1962, p. 41.

(INCORA) is authorized to expropriate at a negotiated price lands which are uncultivated, inadequately cultivated, or indirectly exploited. In each case, the owner may retain 100 hectares of farm land for his own use, and, except where the object of expropriation is the regrouping of minifundia, he may reserve a further 100 hectares of nonfarm land. Regulations subsequent to the agrarian reform law define more precisely the terms "inadequately cultivated" and "indirectly exploited" and limit the price paid for expropriated land to not more than 30 per cent higher than the value as appraised in the last agricultural survey.[28] In some cases, the settlement programs may represent "directed colonization," whereby INCORA provides schools, churches, and similar community facilities in addition to the land grant; under this system, 70 per cent of the land not necessary for such construction is to be granted free to settlers of scarce resources; the remainder and all other land grants are to be repaid within 15 years of the date of possession. INCORA may, in some cases, however, choose to rent rather than sell the land. In assessing the possibilities for land distribution, INCORA is assisted by advisory committees at the departmental and municipal levels; and in the administration of technical assistance to the settlers, it is supported by an Agricultural-Livestock Institute, created by an agency of INCORA with the financial collaboration of the Ford, Rockefeller, and Kellogg Foundations in July of 1962.

Nine projects were approved in 1962, covering 200,000 hectares which will benefit 15,000 families. Plans for 1963 include the settling of 5,000 families, along with giving assistance to 10,000 families in areas of spontaneous colonization in the form of roads, credit, and land titles. In addition, a project to recover 150,000 hectares of land through irrigation will be initiated in 1963. Despite this ambitious program, the needs remain very great. The uneconomically small size of farms, combined with severe erosion, defines the nature of the problem affecting most of Colombia's rural population. The Ministry of Agriculture stated in 1959 that there were more than 800,000 farms of less than 5 hectares, and it has been generally claimed that a majority of the 1.5 million rural families do not own land. Under such conditions, it is urgent that the program incorporate the maximum number of families at the lowest possible cost. Some financial flexibility is afforded by the stipulation

[28] Several steps were advocated by the Social Agrarian Council (Consejo Social Agrario) in resolutions adopted at its first meeting in April, 1963. These include measures which would abbreviate negotiations between INCORA and proprietors of affected property, define work arrangements in which labor is exchanged for land as labor contracts, and modify local councils to give greater representation to rural labor.

that expropriated land which was unexploited may be paid in agrarian bonds, but a few head of cattle would presumably entitle the owner to a cash indemnity. More valuable provisions are those limiting the price to be paid in cases of expropriation and assuring INCORA a budget of 100 million pesos a year, plus borrowing power of up to one billion pesos over five years.

Costa Rica. Costa Rica's agrarian law of October, 1961, entrusts responsibility for the agrarian reform program to the Banco Nacional; legislation of October, 1962, created the Institute of Lands and Colonization to share this task. Further legislation is promised, regulating the forms of indirect cultivation. Meanwhile, a new tax is imposed on all holdings in excess of 100 hectares, ranging from 0.25 per cent of the value declared for the territorial tax for land 250 hectares or less to 2.5 per cent on excess land of 5,000 hectares and above. Recipients of land are exempt from land taxes for five years.

The law does not make any disposition on poorly cultivated land; it does provide for the expropriation of private land which is not cultivated or which has been indirectly exploited for five years, land distributed to settlers who have failed to comply with the regulations of the institute on land use, and land devoted to grazing which is suitable for crops. Minifundia may be expropriated for regrouping, providing that an adequate land parcel is guaranteed each displaced owner; all lands larger than latifundia are to be automatically expropriated. The term "latifundium" is not defined. Expropriation is to take place only when state land is no longer available and when it is not possible to acquire sufficient land on voluntary sale. Compensation must not exceed the value of the land as declared for tax purposes and will be made in either cash or bonds, at the discretion of the institute. These latter features will permit more extensive purchases than where current value in cash is required. Another distinctive feature of the Costa Rican law is the intended survey of all lands in excess of 1,000 hectares, to determine whether their extension has been correctly reported for the tax rolls; land in excess of the reported area will be inscribed in the name of the institute if it is uncultivated, with the owner allowed to retain 40 per cent of the excess if it is cultivated. There is strong emphasis in the law in favor of the formation of agricultural co-operatives, which are given priority in requests for credit for housing and equipment. Land may be either sold or rented by the institute.

While the problem of land distribution is not as grave in Costa Rica as in some other countries, there are large numbers of squatters without land, and many of the 51,000 farmers who at the time of the 1950 census owned less than 3.5 hectares could use additional land to advantage. Plans for 1963 center on a settlement program in Bataan covering 11,670 hectares and serving 600 families. The estimated budget of ITCO for 1963 is 6.6 million colons, of which 3.8 million will represent capital expenditures.

Dominican Republic. In the Dominican Republic, a major immediate task is the distribution of large areas of land confiscated from the Trujillo family and now held by the Government. To this end the agrarian reform law (April, 1962) outlines succinctly and specifically the responsibility of the Institute of Agrarian Reform. The plots are to be distributed among those needing land by a raffle system, and each recipient is assured both housing and credit. The institute has a budget of 2 million pesos. In order to serve as many as possible of the estimated 225,000 families who, as of 1960, worked farms of less than one hectare, it has cut costs to a minimum (approximately 550 pesos per family).

The program, which began in April of 1963, appears to be moving swiftly, with distribution under way of 100,000 hectares to 10,000 families. At present, another project is being given serious consideration, whereby with large-scale international assistance the Dominican Republic would develop 500,000 hectares of land in an irrigation project similar to the United States Tennessee Valley Authority, with the expectation of thereby doubling the incomes of 250,000 persons.

Guatemala. The Guatemalan law (October, 1962) authorizes the expropriation of private land only insofar as it is left idle and exceeds 50 hectares. Such land is taxed from 0.75 to 2.50 quetzales per hectare, according to five classes of land, with cumulative surcharges of 20 per cent imposed each year for the following four years. Rental contracts must extend five years and imply no personal servitude, but on meeting these two conditions rented land is removed from the effects of the law. In fact, rented land is by definition not idle land, without regard to its state of cultivation.

Given this alternative and the stipulation that expropriated idle land will be paid its current value at 4 per cent interest in five years, the program will be an expensive one if it is to be at all effective. The latest figures available are from the 1950 census, at which time about 140,000 families were landless.

Honduras. In Honduras, according to the law of September, 1962, and subsequent amendments, land which is idle or inadequately cultivated or indirectly exploited fails—by definition of the agrarian reform law—to fulfill its social function and is therefore subject to expropriation. The National Agrarian Institute may, however, rent public land for commercial use and renew such concessions granted formerly; this amendment has helped to quiet protests that the law was intolerant of commercial needs. Land devoted to livestock is adequately exploited if it contains one head of cattle (or five calves) for each 2 hectares or if it is cultivated for forage; farm land is judged according to its yield. All land declared idle or uncultivated is subject to a tax, beginning two years from the date of the law, equal to 3 per cent of the declared value in the first year and rising to 40 per cent in the fifth year. Indirect exploitation of land is permissible only if it represents a sharing of capital and is approved by the National Agrarian Institute; all such contract stipulations which require payment for the land in labor or in kind or which oblige the rentee to sell or purchase at a fixed market specified by the renter are declared null. The expropriation of private property requires prior payment in cash of the full price decided upon by appraisers. The land is to be distributed in parcels of 10 to 20 hectares of irrigated land, or the equivalent, for which payment is made in 10 to 20 years at a rate of interest from zero per cent in the case of national land to 3–4 per cent on private land. The recipient must agree to certain obligations regarding construction of housing, extent of cultivation, and general orderly behavior. The National Agrarian Institute is assured a budget of at least 2 million lempiras per year and is authorized to issue agrarian bonds of 20 years at 4 per cent to finance the compensation of acquired properties.

By mid-1963, provisional title had been granted to approximately 300 families settled on 4,150 hectares. Planning for the settlement of 6,000 families in the Aguan Valley is expected to be completed during 1963. The investment budget for the year is about one million lempiras. Fifty-seven per cent of the 156,000 farms included in the Agricultural Survey of 1962 were of less than 5 hectares and were found to provide an inadequate income.

Nicaragua. The Nicaraguan agrarian reform law of April, 1963, offers free title to 50 hectares to those persons who have been settled on public lands for at least one year prior to the promulgation of the law, with the option to purchase at a price fixed by appraisers any additional area they had under cultivation. The Government also intends to open negotiations with the owners of private land currently worked by squatters in order to transfer title to the latter without charge; the owners will be compensated in bonds or cash in installments. Others in need of land who meet certain standards with respect to age and agricultural experience qualify for family units for which they are to reimburse the Agrarian Institute in 15 to 20 years at interest not exceeding 5 per cent. Payment may be made in produce at market prices, and a deduction of 5 per cent of the total amount is allowed for each child born after occupation of the land parcel. Full title is granted when all obligations have been met, including full cultivation of the land and at least 25 per cent payment. The land parcels are to be formed first on national and communal lands or private land voluntarily sold, then on expropriated private property. Grounds for expropriation are failure to cultivate for two consecutive years or to assume directly the economic risk of cultivation for the same period; inefficient cultivation; or failure to comply with the regulations on natural resources. In each case a reserve of 500 hectares of irrigated land is permitted. Land above this limit may also be expropriated if it prejudices an established nucleus of farmers due to scarcity of land in the area. Free personal services and the payment of rent in labor are prohibited.

The major activity of 1962 was an extension of rural credit through the formation of six new rural credit agencies and the completion of work on basic studies for a project to irrigate 10,000 hectares in the Department of Rivas. According to the census of 1952, close to one-third of the farms in the country were of less than 3.5 hectares.

Panama. In Panama, as in the Dominican Republic, the land to be distributed is for the most part government-owned, although the Agrarian Code of September, 1962, does provide for the expropriation of private holdings in excess of 100 hectares which are idle, poorly cultivated, or indirectly exploited. Compensation is to be made in cash or agrarian bonds, on the choice of the proprietor and at the value determined by the agricultural census of 1956; or, in the case of property acquired after the entry into force of the Code, at the purchase price. Families with an annual income of less than 600 balboas are granted land parcels free; others are given 20 years in which to pay the cost of the land. The institute may also rent land to settlers.

In 1961, the Government presented a five-year plan (1962–66) to settle 4,500 families on 150,000 hectares of idle land. Two projects were ready at that time: Tonosí [29] and Penonomé. The goal for 1963 is to

[29] Tonosí is explicitly excluded from the agrarian program as regulated by the Code; however, according to the development plan this is not an insurmountable problem. A greater problem is to reduce the costs to a feasible level.

distribute 20,000 hectares among 1,200 families, with the help of a $2.9 million loan from the Inter-American Development Bank. According to the 1960 census, there were then about 60,000 landless rural families who lived as nomads, settling on idle property and moving frequently in search of better land.

Paraguay. Laws 852 and 854 of March, 1963, supplement the 1960 legislation on land settlement in Paraguay, replacing earlier measures in this field. The latest laws create the Institute of Rural Welfare to replace the Institute of Agrarian Reform and outline the procedure for land distribution. The institute is in charge of establishing colonies, including all community facilities. Recipients of land will repay the institute in 15 years, although a 15 per cent deduction is granted those who can pay in cash; a 4 per cent interest charge is to form a contingency fund in case of crop failure or public emergency. Title is granted free to fathers with seven or more minor dependents and to those with a 30 per cent disability from the Chaco war.

Colonization may take place on public lands or lands acquired by the institute or may be undertaken by private proprietors with the aid and supervision of the institute. Private establishments of any extension of which the improvements represent 50 per cent of the fiscal value of the land are exempt from expropriation. Land not meeting this condition is considered not rationally exploited, and the institute may encourage the owners to adopt private colonization schemes or to sell to the institute. If necessary, the institute may initiate expropriation proceedings. Land which is not rationally exploited and which exceeds 10,000 hectares in the eastern region of the country or 20,000 hectares in the west, exclusive of forest reserves (the definition of a latifundium), is subject to a progressive tax. The scale of the tax and the maximum limit to landholdings of any one person will be specified in future legislation. Land which has been the site of stable *de facto* settlements for 20 years, or for a shorter period in the event of a social problem, minifundia, and suburban land which is not rationally exploited are also affected by the law, and when the owners are unwilling to sell, the institute may resort to expropriation, paying in cash over 10 years.

The law stipulates that all contracts of rent or share-cropping must be formalized in writing and that rent may not exceed 12 per cent of the fiscal value of the land, nor the proprietor's share of the crops 20 per cent of the total product. Under the system whereby the owner provides land, seed, and tools to third persons who provide labor, the contract must specify the contributions of each and the division of the produce or profit, of which the owner is not entitled to more than half.

From 1956 through 1961 the Institute of Agrarian Reform distributed title to former public lands to 17,000 families, and a further 8,600 families became landowners in 1962. The National Development Bank has initiated a supervised credit program to benefit 4,300 families, and two settlement programs are being prepared along the Paraná River which together will serve approximately 4,000 families.

Peru. In view of the marked disparity in agricultural conditions between the mountainous and coastal areas of Peru, the agrarian reform program there is to be carried out in zones of development. A law of November, 1962, outlined the bases for agrarian reform; but this law may be superseded by a bill submitted to Congress in August, 1963, by the new government. The law of November, 1962, provided for the establishment of family farm units on public land, the land of legal persons not directly essential to their stated purpose, and private lands which were idle, deficiently or indirectly exploited, or excessively concentrated in one zone. It also provided for a progressive tax on land by area, the proceeds of which would be used for local public works, and promised legislation to regulate indirect exploitation of the land and to extend the benefits of minimum wages and social security. Land expropriated was to be valued with reference to its productivity; the precise method of valuation, the reserve allowance, and the obligations and rights of land recipients remained to be specified by implementing legislation. The new bill specifically outlaws all forms of payment in kind or in services for the use of land and declares expropriable in full any rural property worked entirely by persons other than the owner. Land worked in part by nonowners is expropriable to the extent of indirect exploitation. Those proprietors who work their own land are allowed a reserve of 150 hectares of irrigated land or a larger allowance of nonirrigated land, depending on its condition and the area in which it is located. Land belonging to juridical persons is subject to expropriation to the extent that it is not directly essential to the purposes of the possessing organization, whether political, clerical, or business. In the case of both legal and natural persons, the sum of all holdings is considered to constitute one single property, including properties owned by several corporations in which one person or institution holds 40 per cent of the capital stock. Compensation, not to exceed by more than 30 per cent the fiscal value of the land, is to be paid in full in agrarian bonds of 20 years at 5 per cent. These bonds are guaranteed by the state and acceptable in payment of land taxes or as collateral in requests for credit. The recipients of land parcels will repay the price of the land, determined according to its economic capacity over a period of not less than 20 years at 2 per cent interest, with a period of grace to be specified for each zone. They must personally live on and work the land, with the assistance of credit and technical advice.

During 1962, settlement continued on the San Lorenzo project with the distribution of 7,000 hectares in 424 lots; but the most intensive effort is scheduled for the near future. Preparations are being made to settle 4,000 families in the Apurímac region, some 17,000 families are to benefit by the irrigation of 26,000 hectares in Arequipa, and more than a million hectares of mountain land are to be reclaimed by the construction of 14 access roads.

Mexico. Among the countries where agrarian reform legislation was in effect prior to the signing of the Charter of Punta del Este, Mexico has by far the longest experience. The Mexican system of land redistribution, begun during the Revolution of 1910, centers on the *ejido*, or communal land. Over the period 1910–62, approximately 50 million hectares of land have been distributed to more than 3.5 million rural families. Reform of the agrarian code has been approved recently by Congress to increase the availability of land for distribution. A Banco Nacional Ejidal offers a system of agricultural insurance, and the Federal Government has made available a national network of storage facilities and has continued to expand the irrigation system, which now serves one-third of the total cultivated area of the country. In 1962, a new medium- and long-term loan program directed specially to small- and medium-sized farms was begun with the assistance of a $20 million loan from AID. At present, an impressive self-help project is under way in Campeche, where a pioneer group of 500 heads of family is clearing land and constructing living centers as the nucleus of a large-scale resettlement of families from the north.

Bolivia. Bolivia's agrarian reform program, also the product of a revolution, has been in effect since 1953. A new bill, simplifying the procedures established earlier, is expected to be approved in 1963. Reorganization of the Agricultural Bank is also under consideration, as the scarcity of agricultural credit remains a serious problem. During the nine years of existence of the agrarian reform program, 133,000 families have been settled on 4.4 million hectares; 26,000 of these families were settled on 0.9 million hectares in 1962. In addition, 221,000 titles have been turned over, 50,000 of these in 1962. In order to raise the living standards of its population, Bolivia intends a major relocation of rural families from the valleys and altiplano to the fertile eastern lowlands.[30] The single most important project to date, Alto Beni, is part of that plan.

Venezuela. Under Venezuela's exceptionally active program of land distribution, approximately 56,000 families were settled on 1.53 million hectares between the approval of the agrarian reform law in March, 1960, and the close of 1962. The speed of the settlement program has exceeded the flexibility of the financial and technical assistance services, however, hampering the economic effectiveness of the program. To remedy this situation, the Government is currently emphasizing the expansion of agricultural extension services and credit facilities. The number of agricultural extension offices was increased from 124 to 140 in 1962 and is planned to reach 500 by the end of 1966. Agricultural credit also increased substantially in 1962 and is to rise by 25 per cent in 1963. The present goal is to settle a further 100,000 during the period of the national plan, 1963–66. If this can be accomplished, the program will have reached almost all the estimated 180,000 families in need of land. Increasingly rapid extension of technical services will also be necessary, however, if the goal of raising the minimum income of rural workers to at least 80 per cent of that of unskilled industrial laborers is to be met during the plan period.

TAX REFORM

Tax reform is a basic component of the development planning and agrarian reform programs outlined above. In carrying out the greatly increased investment programs and the institutional reforms called for by the Alliance, it has proved necessary to review the yield and incidence of the present tax structure and to reorganize it to serve more effectively as an instrument of economic development. A detailed analysis of advisable tax reforms in Latin America would have to take into account the existing base from which reform is to be undertaken and the special conditions of development in each country; with a generous allowance for simplification, however, it is possible to consider tax policy on the regional level in the general context of development needs.

One obvious need is additional revenue to enable the public sector to carry out its share of the increased investment and to reduce the government deficit. In the past, attempts to prevent government deficits have

[30] See above, the first section of this chapter.

often taken the form of emergency taxes or surcharges on existing taxes to meet an acute financial need. As tax revenues in many countries still derive largely from customs duties and depend to that extent on highly variable external factors, such temporary measures may be revoked and reinstated repeatedly to meet the current needs of the Treasury. The aim of tax reform under the Alliance is to provide for higher tax receipts in such a way that the other goals of tax reform are not prejudiced. The other goals of tax reform can be stated in various ways, but a particularly useful one is the formulation adopted by Special Committee III (Financial and Fiscal Policy and Administration) of the Inter-American Economic and Social Council:

(a) to obtain the resources necessary to finance the planned economic and social development without hampering total investment, including that of the private sector, or causing an unfavorable alteration in the level of prices;

(b) to adjust the tax burden so that it is distributed justly and equitably; this objective will be fulfilled when the tax burden is equal for those in equal circumstances and when the total tax burden is progressive in relation to the economic capability of the taxpayer;

(c) to guarantee effective compliance with fiscal obligations by perfecting the legal system and improving the mechanisms of tax administration;

(d) to adopt an effective and rational policy of fiscal incentives which will serve to channel investments toward activities or areas of high economic and social priority and discourage investment in nonessential activities;

(e) to promote the effective functioning of common markets by harmonizing fiscal systems so as to avoid distortions in the systems of production and commerce in the member countries.[31]

Conforming to these criteria, tax reform measures in 1962 may be reviewed under the following headings: (1) increased tax receipts; (2) more equitable distribution of the tax burden; (3) tax incentives for investment; and (4) improved tax administration, with the latter incorporating objectives (c) and (e).

Increased Tax Receipts

If the public sector is to fulfill its responsibilities under the Alliance, it is indispensable that it be able to obtain the resources necessary to

[31] See *Final Report of Special Committee III* (San José, Costa Rica, July 1963), (CIES/302).

finance the planned economic and social development without incurring any detrimental effect on total investment, public and private, or on the level of prices. The Latin American countries made renewed efforts to meet this objective in 1962, and although budget deficits were not reduced as much as had been hoped, it is believed that with continued efforts, the steps already taken may have some additional delayed effects in future years.

Argentina. In Argentina, a series of measures were introduced in 1962 affecting taxes on income, production, consumption, and foreign trade. A 20 per cent surcharge was imposed on income above a certain level in place of the former tax on extraordinary earnings, to be effective through fiscal year 1964; the deduction of increased assets by industrial and commercial enterprises was limited to 50 per cent of investments made, when these constitute at least 10 per cent of the increase in assets; and the deduction of legal reserves in computing taxable income of corporations was eliminated. Earnings from the sale of securities, when this is a habitual occupation, were excluded from the income tax and made subject instead to a special 1 per cent tax, while the tax on occasional earnings from the sale of land units was raised from 5 to 10 per cent and on earnings from games of chance from 5 to 20 per cent. Other dispositions of the income tax, designed to offer tax relief to lower-income groups and to the livestock industry, are discussed in the following sections. Further revenue-increasing measures included a temporary 5 per cent tax on the production of meat, wool, grains, and oilseeds applicable in 1963. An emergency tax of one peso per liter of gasoline was also imposed, along with the creation of a 5 peso per liter tax on lubricating oils; the latter has subsequently been raised to 10 pesos a liter. Items formerly not subject to a sales tax are now taxed at 3 per cent, but the sales tax on items earlier taxed at 13 per cent has been reduced to 10 per cent for essential products; the sale of items considered luxuries or nonessentials continues to be taxed at 13 per cent. The special sales tax on automobiles has been increased by 50 per cent and a new tax levied on passports. An additional 5 per cent tax on imports, except those declared of high national priority, was also imposed during 1963.

Brazil. In Brazil, new measures introduced in 1962 reinforcing the effects of reforms made the previous year are expected to result in an increase of 150 billion cruzeiros in 1963 revenues. In 1961, the income-tax law was amended, and a state sales tax was introduced in Minas Gerais. More recent measures impose a new tax on earnings from letters of exchange, increase the rates of income tax, and establish a compulsory loan of 20 per cent of the tax on incomes withheld at the source, except income from labor; the former 20 per cent emergency tax was eliminated. At the same time, consumption taxes were altered, with the rates on nonessential items increased. Important revenue gains are expected in the future from the alteration of the tax on electric power from a fixed amount to a rate based on the value of the power consumed and increasing progressively over the next three years, 1963–65; collections on this account are expected to improve 40 per cent by 1965.

Chile. Chile has prepared an extensive program of tax reform. At present, a series of measures is under parliamentary discussion which would restructure the income tax to make it more progressive, introduce a tax on capital gains, modify the tax applicable to gifts and inheritance, provide for periodic re-evaluation of real property, and reform the administrative organization of the Internal Tax Service.

Colombia. The Colombian Government has requested of Parliament extraordinary powers to reorganize completely the decentralized institutes in order to eliminate duplication and rationalize their operations, to reform tax administration (including the administration of taxes by the departments and municipalities), to improve the system of valuing real property, and to reform the system of valuation of intangibles, of setting exemptions, and of determining the rates applied to enterprises which do not distribute profit in the country. Specific tax changes recommended include the establishment of a tax of 3 to 10 per cent on the sale of finished goods, a 20 per cent surcharge on the income tax, a consumption tax on gasoline to be used to finance highway construction, and an import registration fee. A technical assistance mission of the OAS/IDB/ECLA has studied the Colombian tax system and made recommendations on tax reform.

Dominican Republic, Ecuador, Mexico. In the Dominican Republic, Ecuador, and Mexico, one of the most important changes introduced in 1962 was the addition of a global tax on income superimposed on the schedular system. In May, 1962, the Dominican Republic introduced a progressive surcharge ranging from 3 to 40 per cent on personal income; progressive rates of 10 to 38 per cent apply to corporate income. The income tax is expected to contribute one-fifth of all fiscal revenue in 1963, compared to one-tenth in 1961. Ecuador also added to the schedular tax on income from all sources a complementary progressive tax intended to facilitate the eventual transition to a global progressive tax on income. Ecuador is also studying revision of the sales and stamp taxes. In addition to imposing a complementary tax on all income, Mexico in 1962 increased the rates applicable to middle and upper brackets and to rental income, imposed a special 1 per cent tax on income to finance middle and higher education, provided for accelerated depreciation allowances, and established a tax on use and ownership of automobiles. A capital gains tax was initiated in 1962; also a tax on distributable profits which are not reinvested. Tax revenues increased 12 per cent in 1962 over 1961 and are expected to rise by 20 per cent in 1963, with approximately half of these increases credited to the new provisions. Further revision is being considered, especially in the direction of modifying the schedular system of income taxation.

Peru. Numerous tax increases were introduced in Peru in 1962, but most of these were later reduced. A special tax on exports of fish flour, together with the rise in price of the major export products, has contributed additional revenue to reduce the budget deficit, and it is expected that administrative reforms will also contribute to higher tax collections in 1963.

Paraguay, Uruguay, Venezuela. These countries had all made certain reforms in the tax structure in 1961. In 1962, Paraguay, like Argentina, sought to stimulate the livestock industry by offering tax incentives; the income tax on this industry was eliminated, and to replace the loss in revenue a tax was introduced on the sale of cattle or horses. Uruguay introduced a tax on income for the first time in July, 1961, and at the end of that year raised the rate on corporate income from 30 to 50 per cent. Venezuela increased in 1961 the rates of taxation on most types of income and on inheritance taxes, doubling those on corporate income. The Venezuelan four-year development plan for 1963–66 provides for the introduction of taxes on dividends and on land.

Costa Rica. Among the Central American countries, taxes on income, property, inheritance, sales, and consumption have all been considered potential sources of higher tax receipts, with different approaches settled upon by the different countries. Costa Rica has had since 1958 a serious problem of budget deficit, caused in part by the heavy subsidies granted to state enterprises and aggravated by a difficult balance-of-payments situation. Besides the reduction of fiscal revenues originating in the deterioration of export receipts, some other factors have also affected revenues unfavorably. Thus, the industrialization program has also created some difficulty due to the tax exemptions offered as incentives and to the reduced income from imports accompanying the progress of import substitution. New measures to reduce the deficit by raising revenues include the obligation of state banks to pay income and land taxes, a new progressive tax on idle lands graduating with their extension, creation of an Administrative Fiscal Tribunal to handle discrepancies between tax declarations and the dispositions of the law, and improvements of the system of withholding taxes at the source and paying in quarterly installments. Proposals have also been made for a tax on the income of public servants and for other taxes on goods manufactured within the country, the latter to recover some of the loss from reduced imports of these goods.

El Salvador. Following the reform of the income tax in El Salvador in 1961, which made the rate structure more progressive with a range of 2 to 76.5 per cent and which contributed substantially to raising revenues, new measures were introduced in 1962 to improve collections. Reforms are also being contemplated of the tax on inheritance and gifts.[32]

Guatemala. When the Guatemalan income-tax law took effect on July 1, 1963, it marked the first time that all Latin American nations have employed a tax on income. Further amendments are expected to this law, which at present excludes 70 per cent or more of Guatemalan workers through the generous deductions and the gradual increases in rates over broad levels of income.[33] Guatemala has also raised the property tax from 3 to 5 per cent per thousand and provided for the revalution of all property not appraised in the past 15 years to 300 per cent of its last appraised value. A tax has been levied on exports of cotton and some essential oils according to variations in the market price, and the export tax formerly levied on coffee has been lowered.

[32] El Salvador, *Informe Económico Social preparado para la Comisión III del CIES* (June, 1963), p. 14.
[33] *Informe del Segundo Período de Reuniones de la Comisión III* (July, 1963) (OEA/Ser.H/XIII; CIES/Com.III/27 Rev. 2), p. 13; and Banco de Guatemala, *Informe Sobre Finanzas Públicas Correspondiente a los Años 1960 a 1962* (July, 1963), p. 5.

Honduras. Beginning July 1, 1963, Honduras imposed a 20 per cent surcharge on taxable income of 20,000 lempiras or above and introduced a progressive tax on forestry and woodworking industries. The tax on production and sale of carbonated water was increased, and a tax equal to 5 per cent of the sales price was imposed on automobiles formerly excluded from taxation.

Nicaragua. Nicaragua raised the tax on gifts and inheritance and on the transfer of immovable property. The tax on capital was also increased and divided to apply separately to housing and other immovable properties; the former was raised to 0.5 per cent on values not less than 20,000 córdobas in the departments or 30,000 in the capital and the latter to 1 per cent, with a 10,000 córdoba exemption. Certain stamp taxes were also raised and consolidated.

Panama. Panama approved in 1962 a surcharge of 10 per cent on incomes above 1.8 million balboas, an increase from 20 to 40 per cent in the surcharge on income of companies in which more than half of the capital stock is owned by one person or group, and a tax on dividends paid by companies who by virtue of contracts with the state are exempted from income taxes. A land tax was also initiated in 1962, and several consumption taxes were earmarked for specific purposes. Import tariffs were raised by 0.5 per cent, with additional levies on liquor, beer, and automotive vehicles; and the exemption from import taxes formerly granted the autonomous institutions was revoked. The draft of a general tax reform, prepared with the assistance of an OAS/IDB/ECLA Mission, was presented to the National Assembly at the end of 1962.

More Equitable Distribution of the Tax Burden

Among the reform measures listed in the preceding section, there is evident an attempt to alleviate the tax burden on the lower-income groups relative to those better able to contribute to the public sector, and at the same time a concern that private investment not be penalized by heavy taxation.

The tax increases recently imposed in *Argentina*, for example, exempt the lower-income groups by imposing the surcharge only on incomes of 50,000 pesos or more and on capital. At the same time, the family deduction was raised, the basic rate lowered from 9 to 8 per cent, and the sales tax reduced on essential items. *Brazil* also raised the basic family income exemption and restricted increases in consumption taxes to nonessential items. The compulsory loan does not apply to income from personal services.

In *Chile,* the tax on dividends was eliminated in order to diminish double taxation.

Introduction of a tax on income in *Guatemala,* together with the increase of the property tax, and the initiation of a global tax in the *Dominican Republic, Ecuador,* and *Mexico* are also based on consideration of the ability to pay. Mexico also changed the payment of taxes on personal income from a monthly to an annual base, making it conform to the other schedules in this regard and lowering the annual tax charge on those whose incomes may vary widely in different months.

The tax on idle land introduced in *Costa Rica* in 1962 and the initiation of a land tax in *Panama* were also intended to redirect the incidence of the tax away from those of lower income and wealth. In addition, Panama raised the tax on immovable property and applied a surcharge on the income tax which varies from 10 per cent on personal income from personal services to a range of 20 to 40 per cent on the income from capital.

Tax Incentives to Investment

Several of the Latin American countries are presently reviewing the system of incentives to industries or to regions which it is considered desirable to develop, in order to assess their effectiveness in relation to the other objectives of tax reform, such as higher revenues and more equitable distribution of the burden.

Argentina has recently reordered the tax privileges granted for development purposes, and *Chile* has proposed to the National Congress a greater reliance on accelerated depreciation as a stimulus to industries which the development agency, CORFO, designates to be of high priority. *Mexico* offers accelerated depreciation allowances to agricultural, industrial, mining, and construction enterprises and levies a tax on distributable profits not reinvested. *Panama* is also studying a draft of new legislation on incentives, and the members of the Central American Common Market are currently in the process of approving the Agreement on Uniform Central American Incentives. *Brazil* is finding very successful the 50 per cent reduction of income-tax liability to those firms which invest in the Northeast region of the country the amount of the tax saving plus an equal amount from their own capital, with the approval of the Northeast development agency, SUDENE. New measures in *Argentina* and *Paraguay* in 1962 offer special tax reductions to the livestock industry.

Improved Tax Administration

More Efficient Collection. Greater efficiency of collection procedures is essential if the selective emphasis of tax reform—that is, the alleviation of the tax burden on low-income groups and on industries important to the national development—is to be compatible with the primary responsibility of the tax system to produce enough revenues to finance the public sector's responsibility in the development program. But where tax evasion is known to be easy in practice and is widely condoned, to reverse this custom requires strong action. Thus, numerous measures are being enacted or studied to improve the collection of taxes by imposing strict penalties on attempts to evade payment of the full tax liability, as well as by introducing more efficient methods of collecting and accounting.

In *Argentina,* for example, a period of grace was declared, during which previously undeclared income could be registered with the tax authorities without penalty and at a considerably reduced tax rate. Thereafter, certain operations, such as the transfer of real property and of automobiles and qualification for bank credit above specified amounts, are made contingent on the interested persons being registered on the tax rolls. In this way, 450,000 persons disclosed 200 billion pesos in previously undeclared capital, which at the reduced rate brought in 12 billion pesos in taxes, about 9 per cent of total tax revenue collected in 1962. *Peru* and *Uruguay* followed a similar procedure in 1963, reducing rates on tax arrears during a temporary amnesty, after which sanctions were made more strict than before. In Peru, for example, heavy fines of 500 to 500,000 soles and/or two to six months' imprisonment are now the penalties for tax evasion. A national register of taxpayers has also been compiled in Peru.

Mexico has also recently introduced a national register of taxpayers, on which some 3.5 million persons have now been inscribed, from January, 1962, to July, 1963. In addition, Mexico will adopt, beginning in 1962, the practice of individual determination of tax liability, reducing the responsibility of the administration to check these declarations. Electronic computers are used in this task.

Costa Rica and *El Salvador* are now also installing electronic equipment as part of their programs to improve the efficiency of tax collections. In addition, the Costa Rican Government has submitted to the legislature a proposal to deny certain public services to persons who have not declared their income or real estate. In *Honduras,* the Executive is authorized to charge fines for delayed tax payments, and in *Guatemala* the Minister of the Treasury is permitted to take legal action in cases of delayed payment. In *Panama,* too, the process of legal retribution in cases of fraud has been made more effective by eliminating the burden of proving intent to deceive. Additional collection facilities have also been provided by using the offices of the National Bank of Panama throughout the country.

Rationalization of Administrative Methods. Simplification of tax codes and rationalization of administrative methods are also important areas of tax reform, both in themselves and with a view toward regional standardization of tax systems for the purpose of economic integration. In these phases of reform, the adaptability of foreign experience has been particularly useful.

In *Chile,* for example, a complete review of the Tax Service was conducted in late 1962 with the help of United States experts in tax administration, and the results for improved tax collection have been remarkable. Similarly the tax systems of *Argentina, Colombia, Ecuador, Panama, Uruguay,* and the *Central American Republics* have been evaluated by the joint tax missions of the OAS/IDB/ECLA, with recommendations submitted on both structural and administrative reforms.

Tax administration in the *Dominican Republic* is also being studied with the help of the OAS, and consultants from the United States Internal Revenue Service have pronounced the recent reforms in *Honduras* to be outstandingly successful. These reforms are credited with increases of 30 per cent, 25 per cent, and 7 per cent respectively in the collection of export, income, and sales taxes in Honduras in 1962.

Peru and *Ecuador* have created permanent commissions on administrative reform of their respective tax systems. *Argentina, Brazil,* and *Guatemala* already have similar commissions studying comprehensive reform of the tax structure.

In addition, Ecuador has begun a codification of fiscal law and has introduced government-sponsored training courses in public administration. The *El Salvadorean* Government also offers seminars in tax administration, and Chile in 1962 graduated the first class of students from the school of tax administration created in 1961; 375 students, or nearly 50 per cent of the tax administration personnel at the time, completed the course. *Chile* also in 1962 completed for the first time a unified manual of the fiscal code, a project which *Bolivia* and *Ecuador* have since begun, the former with ECLA assistance.

Colombia, Paraguay, and *Uruguay* introduced improved accounting and collection procedures in 1962; *Mexico* initiated a monthly withholding system on wage and salary income; and *Venezuela* initiated the payment of income taxes in the same period in which the income is received.

Further simplification of administrative practices remains one of the objectives of tax reform measures, together with simplifications of the tax measures themselves. For several countries, the distribution of revenues between the central government and its subdivisions also remains problematic. Continued improvements in the area of tax administration are indispensable to meeting the other aims of tax reform, which are together indispensable to fulfilling the over-all goals of the Alliance.

PART II
CHARACTERISTICS AND DEVELOPMENT OF THE CENTRAL AMERICAN PRODUCTIVE STRUCTURE

INTRODUCTION

OBJECTIVES AND PRINCIPAL RESULTS OF THE INVESTIGATION

The effort to achieve the economic integration of Central America, which is motivated by an understanding of current needs and is based on the deep roots of a tradition of community feeling, has been receiving an increasingly more favorable reaction from the nations of this area. This is manifested in the attitude of the government circles themselves, who, following their basic decisions regarding the establishment of a common market, have accelerated the efforts to achieve that objective, at the same time expanding its scope; and in the attitude of private enterprise and the public, who, by their active interest and participation, have added practical content to the process leading to progressive economic union. Despite the serious difficulties that characterize the launching of any undertaking of this kind, many signs in recent developments point to the possibility of a great success.

Such a success, of course, depends on several circumstances. It naturally presupposes a consistent course of action, carried forward not only with the patient dedication of the participants themselves but also with the effective co-operation of the appropriate international organizations and an understanding attitude on the part of those industrialized nations that are in a better position to co-operate in achieving the goals that have been fixed. But, in addition, the joint development must follow, in conformity with the desires of all those concerned, appropriate objective and technical standards. This, in turn, presupposes a better knowledge of the situation and of the possibilities that arise from the new conditions.

This study is a result of the desire of the sponsoring agencies of the American states to help clarify the problem and of the positive co-operation of other organizations that are engaged in making studies in other fields of economic development of this area.

The aim has been to throw some light on three fundamental aspects of the recent *structural developments* and to make certain projections regarding the immediate future, with the emphasis always on the physiognomy of the *combined economy* of Central America.[1] These as-

---

[1] In relation to production, consideration was also given, insofar as possible, to the combined economy of the entire Central American Isthmus parallel to that of traditional Central America. In the latter concept the area of the five Central American States was included, and in the former the Republic of Panama was added.

pects are (1) exports; (2) total production by large sectors, especially industry; and (3) imports and their partial replacement under the integration system.

The immediate aim of the study is to serve as a basis for more thorough up-to-date studies, which would adequately fill the existing lacunae by the use of more recent, more detailed statistics obtained on the spot. However, it has been considered desirable to publish now the results obtained, even though they are incomplete, in order to make them accessible to a greater number of persons interested in the economic development of the Isthmus and to stimulate constructive objectives for later studies.

A few conclusions concerning these studies are set forth below.

Exports. In considering Central American exports and their composition, the study concentrated on recent trends and their probable development in the next five years, in an attempt to ascertain whether or not there are possibilities of a renewed "development outward" and also to throw a little light on the possibilities of financing, with largely internal resources, an accelerated internal development.

It was found, first of all, that—with the exception of the intra-area trade, which has tripled in six years, but which still represents a small percentage of the total—exports of the region have been almost stationary recently. This was due chiefly to the unfavorable development in prices for the principal products. Although certain efforts have been made to diversify this trade, about three-fourths of Central American income from abroad still comes from the export of three commodities: coffee, bananas, and cotton. There are, to be sure, a few other items in the region's trade that have not been so affected by the unfavorable development in foreign markets and that have better prospects for the future; for example, lumber, meat, sugar, and cacao. However, the relative importance of these products is still too small to change decisively the general export trend in the near future.

The projections made in this report [2] suggest that under reasonable assumptions, it may be expected that the stagnation in Central American exports outside the integration area will not continue, but even so the sales of the most important primary products of the region to its tradi-

---

[2] The projections have been made by an extrapolation of the trends observed into the next five years, but other indications of the probable future development of the world market for the basic products in question have also been taken into account. Although the large number of unreliable elements makes it necessary to interpret these results with due caution, it is believed that these projections show roughly what is most likely to occur on the basis of the assumptions established.

tional markets will probably increase only slowly—about 2.7 per cent a year—in the coming five-year period. In particular, the outlook for coffee and bananas does not appear very good, owing to the saturation of the United States market for those products and the present unfavorable conditions for increasing sales of those products in the more dynamic European market, where the preferential treatment accorded to the associated African countries by the European Economic Community prevails. As for cotton, which is a relatively new product in Central America, trade in this product has shown a marked potential for growth, but up to now only Japan has been an expansive market for it. It should also be considered that possible increases in sales of this article will depend almost entirely on the Japanese textile industry, whose present development is characterized by rather uncertain tendencies.

Under these conditions, a definite impetus to accelerate the growth of the Central American export sector could be expected only from significant gains in obtaining new markets for traditional exports and a pronounced development of new or secondary export products, such as lumber, meat, shellfish, soluable coffee, nonferrous metallic minerals, etc.

In any case, the present export outlook makes necessary an intensive development within the area and an increasingly careful diversification of production.[3]

Production. The analysis of the structural aspects of the *total production* of goods and services in the area, especially those referring to *industrial production*, contains more evidence and comments regarding the status of diversification (which, to be sure, is not very advanced) of these economies and the progress made in the process of structural conversion in the last decade. The emphasis is, above all, on the meaning of certain relatively rapid changes that have occurred in the ratios of the large economic sectors. Such dislocations in the production structure are, in general, a natural phenomenon in the course of development. The marked increases in the ratio of certain services and nonimportable elements are quite typical of this stage in the development of economies, while a slow decline in the ratio of the primary sector to total output is the logical result of the advance by the more dynamic sectors. However, in this process in Central America certain special characteristics are worthy of attention.

[3] It should be stated before going further that the diversification proposed, as will be expressed later, does not mean a fragmentation of activities or the establishment of industries that are not able to achieve a certain degree of competitiveness.

First of all, it should be stated that these changes during the ten-year period in question were somewhat greater than those experienced at the same time by most of the countries in other regions in a somewhat similar stage of development.

This fact could be considered as a sign of a more dynamic diversification process. However, this characteristic of Central American development has been, to a large measure, attributable to an insufficient growth of agriculture in the period under examination—and more specifically, during the second five-year period—in relation to the unfavorable trend in farm exports, whose rather unsatisfactory development has been made up only in part by the gains in agriculture for domestic consumption. Actually, the rate of agricultural growth was even less than that of population growth. This endangered the balanced advance of the diversification process, since, during industrialization and the development of services, agriculture should continue to supply these economies with increasing amounts of exchange resources or at least insure the supplying of their increasing demand for food and industrial inputs.

The unfavorable relationship of the sectoral rates of growth also caused a near stagnation of the total output per capita. In fact, the rate of agricultural growth dropped from 3.5 per cent a year during the first part of the decade to about 1.5 per cent in the second half; it should be remembered that in 1960 agricultural activities still represented almost 40 per cent of the total output of Central America. The development of the manufacturing sector, with a rate of growth of 6.5 per cent a year, followed a rather even course throughout the ten-year period but did not make up for the decline in agricultural expansion. The rate of increase of the tertiary activities in the first five years was slightly higher than that of manufacturing industry, but during the second five years it was somewhat lower. In short, the total growth of the Central American economies dropped from almost 5.5 per cent a year in the first five years to 3.5 per cent in the second, with a resulting drop in the rate of increase of per capita output from 2.2 per cent a year to 0.3 per cent.

In examining the possible favorable effects of the shift in the relative position of the various sectors, the impact of this change on the imbalance in sectoral productivity was considered. The progressive industrialization and development of certain services have tended to decrease the marked differences that formerly existed between the productivity of the various segments of the economy, but without remedying these disparities substantially or bringing about a notable reduction in disguised unemployment, which is concentrated in the primary sector. On this point, there are appreciable differences among the various countries of the Isthmus.

The fact that the ten-year transformation of the productive structure has not been motivated by powerful internal forces tending toward diversification is also seen in the course of the *structural development within the manufacturing sector*. Indeed, the composition of industrial output—at least by large groups and branches—showed only slow changes, in contrast to the more striking changes noted in the composition of the total output by broad sectors. In other words, Central American industrial development has not been marked by the usual sharp differences in the growth of the various manufacturing groups.

The traditional industries—which in 1953 represented 85 per cent, and in 1958, 84 per cent, of Central American manufacturing output—showed in this period an annual growth of 5.6 per cent, indicating a greater upward surge than in the more developed economies and than the corresponding average rates for Latin America. This confirms the fact (which is also seen in the low levels of per capita production) that there have been more or less ample opportunities to replace imports in such industries, and it indicates that a continued development of these activities would probably have permitted the countries of the Isthmus to achieve a greater than mere vegetative industrial growth for several more years, even without integration. However, if operating conditions are taken into account, it also appears likely that an attempt to take advantage of such margins for replacement would have led fairly soon to increasing problems in production costs, which, in turn, would have affected incentives for investment, unless an excessive protectionism had been established.

At the same time, the development of a large part of the intermediate industries—which together represented 9 per cent of the sector's output—has been impeded by the rigid restrictions of the economies of scale, and so its over-all growth was only slightly greater than that of the traditional industries, and its rate less than the corresponding average rate for Latin America. Moreover, the intermediate industries of the Isthmus had a rather narrow spread, not only because they lack certain important branches, but also because they consist in several categories of complementary activities of the industries themselves (packing, mixing, repairs, etc.). Nevertheless, it should be stated that several promising initiatives were made in the second half of the period under consideration, and the integration atmosphere has led to the appearance of several projects of major importance.

What has been achieved in the mechanical industries up to now is even less significant; but here, too, there are several initiatives that may be valuable, although they consist for the most part in the assembling of certain appliances.

The integration movement, recently initiated, is expected to have an effect on several characteristics of manufacturing development.

First of all, it is to be hoped that, because of its diverse stimulating effects, it will accelerate the sector's growth, with the first impetus affecting the traditional industries; this will probably be superseded within a few years by the development of the intermediate industries.

Consequently, a certain manufacturing diversification is also likely to occur, chiefly as a result of the establishment of the so-called integration industries, most of which will be intermediate industries.[4] Such new activities would not only benefit from the unification of national markets, which in themselves are very small, but also from the pooling of certain scarce resources.

The establishment of these industries will probably strengthen somewhat, at least temporarily, the monopolistic structure of the Central American industrial market, although measures have been taken to insure reasonable prices. However, at the same time, the expansion of the market for industries for which the scale of operation is not so important will make it possible to increase internal competition, which in turn will promote the gradual rationalization of costs and prices through market forces.

With respect to the problem of costs and prices, it is noted that the potential industrial growth of the developing countries—viewed from the standpoint of demand—is composed of several elements. Although the replacement of imports is at present the most important component, it is also essential to consider the possibilities that may exist in the area of industrial exports and those derived from the simultaneous expansion of the other sectors, including the possible increase in the local market for certain products through the progressive redistribution of income.[5] Progress along these last three lines of industrial expansion is substantially affected by excessively high industrial costs and prices. That is why a process of selection should be applied to manufacturing development, reserving priorities for industries having a solid foundation and promising

---

[4] The integration industries, which, because of their nature, require production on a larger scale, are being established in the various participating countries, where they enjoy certain temporary privileges, for the purpose of supplying the common market. See footnote 1 of this chapter.

[5] In this connection, it is to be noted that higher-income groups show a greater tendency to consume imported articles.

future, and especially for those that can be competitive on the international market.

In making a selection, priority should also be given to those industries that, besides being economically and technically feasible, are capable of exercising a greater stimulating effect through interindustrial linkage forward and backward; that is, their effect of promoting additional industrialization by providing inputs for other industries, or markets for the output of intermediate industries.

Another criterion for selection, which is appropriate to the Central American region, is the possibility of increasing employment, which—in addition to its obvious social implications—would utilize the most abundant resource in the Isthmus and would help increase the value of that resource by practical training.

Attention is given, finally, to the increase in industrial employment and to the structure of employment and capital in the various manufacturing activities. It is shown that in this area there is scarcely any relationship between the productivity of labor by industrial branches and capital intensity. Among the possible reasons for this phenomenon is the prevalence of inadequate utilization of the installed capacity, because it has not been possible to obtain equipment adapted to the requirements of the small Central American national markets; or, in other cases, the shortage of qualified supervisory personnel has prevented operation on three, or at least two, shifts; or else the co-ordination of the operations and the maintenance of the machinery have suffered, owing to a lack of adequate technical skill. It is hoped, owing to certain encouraging signs in the integration process begun, that the strengthening of intra-area trade and common efforts to put production on a technological basis will help solve these problems.

Imports. The final part of the study is devoted to the development of Central American imports, the volume of which depends chiefly on import capacity, and through it, on exports; but the composition of this bears above all the stamp of the production structure, on whose future development the prospects for intra-area import replacement also depend.

Central American imports grew very rapidly in the decade following the war, during which period the volume tripled. In contrast, beginning in the middle fifties, imports were marked by a declining rate of growth and virtual stagnation as a result of the unfavorable export trend, and in three recent years (1958, 1959, and 1961) temporary declines were recorded.

The nature of the changes that occurred simultaneously in the composition of imports varied throughout that period, and there were differences noted also among the various countries. For example, up to 1953 the ratio of intermediate goods to imports in the area increased significantly, while the share of ordinary consumer goods tended to decline. This latter trend was, however, manifested only in the foreign purchases of the three Central American countries having the most advanced industrial development, since the other nations not only maintained, but increased, the ratio of their consumer goods to their imports at the cost of other items. In the second half of the period, the decrease in the volume of manufactured imports subject to replacement tended to extend throughout the area; but even so, the rate of such changes was smaller in the totals. At the same time, there occurred another somewhat significant increase in the share of raw materials.

The inter-area trade continued to be relatively light until 1958, but at that time a definite expansion, at least relatively speaking, began ($20.5 million in 1958; $32.7 million in 1960; and $47 million in 1962).

The growth in the intra-area trade and its undeniably promising outlook has stimulated the industrialization of Central America, which has led, above all, to better utilization of installed equipment and, as stated earlier, has also been an incentive to the establishment of industries. By bringing with it a replacement of imports from outside the area, this trade has increased manufacturing diversification and the strengthening of certain traditional industries, especially textiles and foodstuffs. In its initial stage, this reciprocal trade has encountered several obstacles. These include the tardy accession of two countries; the lack of experience in integration of the agencies called on to put it into effect; and the inexperience of the entrepreneurs in estimating the requirements of the regional market. Nevertheless, such difficulties are being gradually overcome, and co-ordinated development programming and the solution of financing problems are the chief tasks now.

In considering the area as a whole, an important fact is that additional "justified" replacements can be made. Actually, from the standpoint of the integration area, it can be considered that it is a matter of an "overdue" replacement, since it could already have occurred, at least in part, if a common market had already existed in the area. The elimination of this margin presupposes an accelerated growth, chiefly of the manufacturing sector, and the rate at which this process advances depends on prevailing conditions, particularly the volume of investments in the years to come. It has been estimated that an investment of at least $150 million is needed to cover this replacement lag if it is to be done within the next four years. The amount would be considerably higher if the total industrial capacity now being inadequately utilized were not used. It should be noted that this estimate does not include the requirements for a parallel expansion of the infrastructure.

In analyzing the possibilities of the foreign sector, it was not possible to go beyond the export projections already described, although the logical objective was to establish tentatively the future (net) import capacity. Therefore it is not possible to compare the demands of future development with the exchange resources available for that purpose. Nevertheless, the rather narrow margins of possible income from exports indicate in advance that it would be very difficult to purchase the necessary equipment abroad unless rather substantial foreign funds were available for that purpose. Moreover, the present situation also indicates that if foreign loans or additional private foreign investment are tied to high amortization rates or repatriated profits, development, which has been stimulated by an initially favorable atmosphere, could soon be obstructed by the effect of an external imbalance.

THE PROBLEMS OF SMALL COUNTRIES AND THEIR APPLICATION TO THE CENTRAL AMERICAN SITUATION

The circumstances that have, in the past, retarded the economic development of the Central American countries or have tended to channel it in less favorable directions have been most varied. However, if we consider them in rather broad terms, there have been three things in particular that have somewhat determined the direction of the other forces involved.

1. The underdevelopment of the productive resources of the area is so marked that in many fields any gain meant overcoming the initial inertia. To illustrate this point, it is sufficient to refer to the almost complete lack of economic and social infrastructure in vast areas and to the considerable shortage of the other external economies that normally accompany a certain degree of development, including those related to the human element. This situation has prevented access to known or potential natural resources or has impeded their profitable exploitation.[6] Of course, there is also a causal interaction in this situation, since the extremely small economic activity in these areas was also one of the causes of the slowness in establishing basic installations there. Similar

[6] As examples, we could mention the case of Honduran lumber and that of the potential resources in the nearly inaccessible province of Petén, which constitutes one-third of the entire territory of Guatemala.

problems have also hampered several aspects of the manufacturing development and, in the last analysis, the formation of industrial capital and the strengthening of the other factors of production. It should be noted that in recent years there have been certain perceptible indications of improvement in some of the countries of the region in this situation known as the "vicious circle" of the early stages of development.

2. As is widely known, the institutional conditions prevailing in a large part of the Isthmus have been largely responsible for restricting any possible progressive initiatives and decreasing their favorable results. In that connection, mention should be made of the serious problems involved in the existing distribution of wealth, especially in the agricultural sector; the precarious educational and health situation; and the system, which is obsolete in many respects, of socioeconomic incentives that prevail in the community.

3. Finally, reference should be made to the smallness of the countries under study. This factor—in combination with the stage of development of these countries—also appears to have conspired against their more rapid, balanced development. Although the role played by the two abovementioned factors scarcely requires comment today, the third has received little attention.[7] Additional research will have to be devoted to this subject in the future, since the empirical evidence concerning it is far from satisfactory; but certain main points can be established as a hypothesis.

Despite the fact that the problems in connection with economic development involved in the small size of certain countries have not yet been studied very carefully, certain recent events have pointed up their importance. It is reflected especially in the progressive establishment of regional markets, which can be interpreted as an attempt to approach the problem, although at times it has also been the result of political considerations.

In this analysis, it appears sufficient to sum up the conditions considered to be the most frequent disadvantages of those nations that may be classified as "small." It should be noted that ordinarily such a classification is based on the number of inhabitants and, of course, always in a very relative sense. It should also be emphasized that the effects of these disadvantages could be calculated accurately only if all the other circumstances were practically the same in relation to the aspect being considered.

Outstanding among the more general disadvantages of the small coun-

[7] Efforts have been started, however, to analyze the problem seriously. In addition to works by international organizations, see, for example, E. A. G. Robinson, ed., *Economic Consequences of Size of Nations* (New York, 1960).

tries is the fact that their small size does not permit them to utilize properly the economies of scale, which are essential or very beneficial to several industries, especially the intermediate and mechanical industries. For this and other reasons related principally to less variety, on the average, in natural resources, their production structure tends to reveal less diversification than that of the big nations, and their dependence on foreign trade is often greater.[8] Actually—according to certain statistical evidence—not only is their ratio of foreign trade to output usually higher, but also the concentration of exports among the countries of destination.[9] Parallel to this situation, and combined with the fact that the share of their principal products in world trade is often not very high, their negotiating power also tends to be weaker.

Moreover, the burden of certain administrative expenses is often heavier for the small countries. Especially, uneconomic use of their resources, for reasons of security or prestige, can be a heavier burden. At the same time, the need to train and maintain an outstanding intellectual group in a greater variety of specializations, familiar with world progress, may exceed their financial possibilities.

Although disadvantages of this kind tend to be linked with the situation of the small countries that are more or less developed, the problems

---

[8] The greater potential for diversification of the large countries not only helps reduce their vulnerability to external factors but also leads to several domestic advantages. Among the latter should be mentioned the broad play of external economies that usually results from a highly integrated industrial system. The importance of the external economies that can be derived from their specialization is sometimes stressed as a comparable advantage for the small countries. However, the transformation of a system having but one facet into a highly technological one is a very difficult task, and even if it succeeds, it is doubtful that the results will in themselves be comparable to those of the more or less integrated production machinery. As a matter of fact, the kind of specialization that is carried out by the enterprises of a large, diversified economy spontaneously, and chiefly as an internal division of labor, appears in principle to be more conducive to optimum solutions than the "specialization" of a small country, which concept refers rather to the principal course followed by its entire economy, which is adopted in a somewhat compulsory manner and primarily at the precarious level of an international division of labor, while preserving perhaps a high degree of vertical integration at the enterprise level. In any case, the prosperity of such an economy depends largely on the skill of the entrepreneurial group and the government in selecting the specialized activities, and continued success presupposes, in addition, a greater degree of flexibility in order to adjust the direction of the national specialization to the changing conditions of foreign markets.

[9] These differences in the importance and direction of foreign trade appear, of course, only in a comparison of countries at a similar stage of development. For the statistics mentioned, see S. Kuznets in Robinson, *Economic Consequences*, pp. 19–23, and a Summary of the Discussion, *ibid.*, pp. 352–53. In the final section of this *Survey* some of the aspects of Central American exports will be described.

that arise from this fact are much more difficult for those countries that are both small and underdeveloped. Their principal export products, which constitute a significant part of their income, are for the most part primary products subject to considerable fluctuations on the world markets. There is little likelihood that a great variety of natural resources that are easy to exploit and market will be found in their territory, which is usually also very small. At the same time, they have a narrower field of selection of personnel for more complicated tasks, and frequently their capital is insufficient for an undertaking of broader scope. This being the case, a serious error in a project requiring large amounts of scarce resources—for example, a mistake in locating a large hydroelectric plant—can be an irreparable error, because it will probably be a long time before the necessary means to carry out a better-planned project are available.

The case of Latin America illustrates the disadvantageous situation of the small countries in an environment of underdevelopment. Whereas in the economically more advanced areas of Europe certain small nations have overcome the above-mentioned obstacles and have achieved a considerable degree of development, a marked relationship between size and stage of development prevails in Latin America.[10]

As a matter of fact, the three most economically advanced countries in Latin America—Argentina, Brazil, and Mexico—are also the largest in population and area,[11] whereas the nations having the lowest per capita income are almost always among the smallest in population. And although this coincidence is due partly to other factors that are difficult to measure, such as climate, geographic location and configuration, and various ethnic characteristics, the circumstances that surround Latin

---

[10] In speaking of Europe, the examples of Switzerland and Denmark are usually mentioned. However, it should be borne in mind that the economic power of these nations and of others in a similar situation and their solid relations with foreign markets had been formed before World War I; that is, in a period when national boundaries were not such an important barrier in economic events—particularly with respect to the mobility of factors, the monetary system, taxation, and tariff protection—as has been the case in more recent years. However, examples that are more or less comparable, though less striking, are also found in other regions. In such countries, among which New Zealand and Israel are outstanding, it has been a matter of colonization by heavy immigration from the industrialized areas of Europe, accompanied by considerable amounts of capital, foreign exchange, skills, and entrepreneurial experience, at times supplemented by preferential access to large protected markets.

[11] These countries also belonged to the small group of countries whose rate of manufacturing growth between 1957 and 1961 exceeded that of 1950-57. See OAS/ECLA, *Economic & Social Survey of Latin America, 1961,* Graph VI-1.

American development leave little doubt regarding the existence of a causal relationship between national size and economic potential.

In considering the problem of size with respect to Latin America, approaching it from the standpoint of markets, it should be remembered that income levels and the resulting purchasing power of this region are substantially lower than in the industrialized areas. In Western Europe, the per capita output is on an average three and one-half times higher than in Latin America; and in the combined industrialized areas of the world, including the United States, Canada, Australia, New Zealand, and Japan, it is between four and five times higher.[12] Thus, in this region the market absorption capacity of a country with 12 or 15 million inhabitants can be the same as, or less than, that of nations having three, four, or five million inhabitants in the industrialized parts of the world. Suffice it to say that, despite the equality in size of the total market, the structure would be very different.

With respect to Central America, in particular, we should not lose sight of the fact that the population of the countries in this region, when considered separately, ranges between only one and four million inhabitants, an average of slightly more than two million, of which 44 per cent are under fifteen years of age, and that their per capita income is scarcely 40 per cent of that of the five relatively more prosperous nations of Latin America. Therefore their national markets cannot be classified simply as "small," but rather as belonging, even within this category of size, to the extreme cases. In short, no matter how minor the influence of national size on development may be after a certain minimum has been reached, it appears reasonable to consider that, in such definite cases—especially with respect to the inadequacy of the market and of the developed resources that can be combined within it—size has been a rather decisive element in past economic development.

This is also corroborated by the experience in the past few years following the launching of the first plans and government decisions on economic

---

[12] The above-mentioned amounts were estimated on the basis of figures given by P. N. Rosenstein-Rodan. See his "International Aid for Underdeveloped Countries" in *Review of Economics and Statistics,* May, 1961. In this work, figures are given on the per capita output, in dollars, for several countries and areas of the world. The computations are made in two ways, with and without adjustment to impute the greater domestic purchasing power of currency in certain parts of the world. These adjustments do not make the original relationship between the output levels of Latin America and those of Europe vary significantly, but with respect to certain other industrialized areas of the world there are differences of some importance. Thus, in comparing the Latin American per capita output with that of the highly developed regions as a whole, a ratio of approximately 1:5 was obtained without adjustment and about 1:4 with an adjustment.

integration, since in this brief period there has been a very promising current of intra-area trade and at the same time the production of several industries has registered an accelerated growth.

However, in noting such a favorable phenomenon, it should also be remembered that in the Central American countries, economic union implies only the possibility of terminating an extreme situation; but the market of the integrated area, with its 11 million inhabitants today and its 14 million in 1970,[13] will not become similar to that of a large country. In other words, the integrated group will continue to have the characteristics of the rather small economies but will be significantly improved over the past, with levels comparable to those of the medium-type economy of Latin American countries.[14]

[13] If Panama is included, it would have 12 million inhabitants now and something over 15 million by 1970.

[14] In the symposium already cited (See Robinson, *Economic Consequences,* pages 349 ff.), it is suggested that the most "appropriate" dividing line between large countries and small countries is about 15 million inhabitants. It should be pointed out that this statement developed principally from an analysis of the small, economically advanced countries, and no attempt was made to establish a different dividing line for the less advanced countries. The statistics given by Kuznets to demonstrate the existence of a relationship between the size of a country and certain aspects of foreign trade were obtained by a division of about 10 million inhabitants. In this study, the criterion of a population of 15 million was applied as the basis for the classification by size in the computations made for Table I–5, but distinctions were made between countries on the basis of their degree of industrialization.

CHAPTER 6

STRUCTURE, RECENT DEVELOPMENT, AND PROSPECTS OF CENTRAL AMERICAN EXPORTS

Central America's role in the world economy is still largely the traditional one of an underdeveloped area located outside the temperate zone; that is, a supplier of only two or three tropical agricultural commodities to the industrialized countries of Europe, and to the United States. For a long time this trade pattern had provided a valuable stimulus to the region's development. In recent years, however, the relative saturation of the traditional markets for tropical products and the unfavorable trend of prices paid for them have been responsible for a virtual stagnation of Central American export earnings; and while some effort has been made to diversify, excessive dependence on a small number of primary products is likely to remain a serious obstacle to the expansion of exports in the coming years.

These points are illustrated in the present chapter, which seeks to analyze the structure and trend of Central American exports since 1955 and to examine the prospects for the area's major primary product exports in the next five years.

PATTERN AND DEVELOPMENT OF EXPORTS

Outside of intraregional trade, which, though it has tripled, still remains a small percentage of the total, Central American exports virtually stagnated between 1955 and 1961. This was largely a reflection of the unfavorable evolution of prices for two of the area's key exports, coffee and bananas. The sharp export rise experienced in 1962 was solely the result of a large increase in cotton exports, which boosted the export receipts of El Salvador and Nicaragua appreciably but had little or no impact on the rest of the area. Throughout the period, despite the recent appearance of some new export lines, such as meat, shrimp, and soluble coffee, Central America continued to derive the bulk of its export income from coffee, bananas, and cotton. The destination of the coffee and cotton exports underwent some significant shifts, which involved a substantial increase in West Germany's coffee purchases and the emergence of Japan as a major importer of cotton from the area. On balance, however, these shifts did not add up to a marked diversification of the market structure for either product, and Central American exports taken as a whole continued to depend almost exclusively on the United States and Western Europe for their markets.

Currently the total export trade of the five Central American countries amounts to approximately $500 million. The two largest exporters are El Salvador and Guatemala, each of which ships over $100 million of goods annually, while the value of exports from the three remaining countries, Costa Rica, Honduras, and Nicaragua, amounts to some $80 million each (see Table 6–1). Coffee, which represented nearly 60 per cent of all exports from the area in 1955, now accounts for less than half of the total, and the share of bananas has also declined slightly; however, these two products, together with cotton, continue to make up about three-fourths of Central America's exports (see Table 6–2). A few other basic commodities, namely wood, meat, sugar, and cocoa, together now account for about 8 per cent of the total, as against 2 to 4 per cent in 1955–57. The remaining 18 to 20 per cent consists primarily of the growing number of agricultural and manufactured products entering Central American intraregional trade. In trade with the outside world, on the other hand, there are still few other exports, and their value, though rising, is still small. At present their list would include, among

TABLE 6–1. Central American Exports, by Country of Origin, 1955–1962

(Millions of dollars)

Country	1955	1956	1957	1958	1959	1960	1961	1962*
Costa Rica	80.9	67.5	83.4	91.9	76.7	85.8	84.2	85.7
El Salvador	106.9	112.7	138.5	116.0	113.4	116.8	119.1	136.4
Guatemala	107.1	123.3	115.9	107.2	107.5	119.4	115.1	111.6
Honduras	51.5	73.3	64.9	69.8	68.7	63.1	73.0	78.0
Nicaragua	71.9	57.8	64.3	63.8	65.0	56.0	60.6	82.5
Total	418.3	434.6	467.0	448.7	431.3	441.1	452.0	494.2

Source: IMF, *International Financial Statistics*, May, 1963.

TABLE 6–2. Commodity Distribution of Central American Exports, 1955–1962

Commodity	1955	1956	1957	1958	1959	1960	1961	1962*
				(*Millions of dollars*)				
Coffee	243.4	250.0	273.2	247.3	213.5	231.7	210.7	206.2
Bananas	74.9	84.7	80.5	77.3	66.2	69.2	70.7	64.0[a]
Cotton	44.7	46.5	42.1	51.2	59.9	36.9	50.8	84.7[b]
Wood	9.6	8.9	11.7	10.2	12.5	12.8	11.4	...
Meat	—	.1	.1	1.0	5.2	8.6	9.1[c]	...
Sugar	1.8	.6	2.0	2.9	3.8	6.7	8.4[c]	12.0[d]
Cocoa	6.3	3.2	4.3	6.4	7.9	6.3	5.2[e]	5.0[e]
Total major products	380.7	394.0	413.9	396.3	369.0	372.2	366.3	
Other	37.6	40.6	53.1	52.4	62.3	68.9	85.7	
Total exports	418.3	434.6	467.0	448.7	431.3	441.1	452.0	494.2
				(*Per cent of total*)				
Coffee	58	58	59	55	50	53	47	42
Bananas	18	19	17	17	15	16	16	13[a]
Cotton	11	11	9	11	14	8	11	17[b]
Wood	2	2	3	2	3	3	3	...
Meat	—	—	—	—	1	2	2[c]	...
Sugar	—	—	—	1	1	2	2[c]	2[d]
Cocoa	2	1	1	1	2	1	1[e]	1[e]
Total major products	91	91	89	88	86	84	81	...
Other	9	9	11	12	14	16	19	...
Total exports	100	100	100	100	100	100	100	...

— Less than $50,000, or 0.5 per cent.

[a] Does not include small amounts exported from El Salvador and Nicaragua.

[b] Does not include small amounts exported from Costa Rica.

[c] Exports from Guatemala estimated on the basis of U.S. and Central American import data.

[d] Estimated on the basis of U.S. imports.

[e] Estimated on the basis of Costa Rican exports.

Sources: IMF, *International Financial Statistics*, May, 1963, and:
Costa Rica: Dirección General de Estadística y Censos, *Comercio Exterior*, 1955–61.
El Salvador: Dirección General de Estadística y Censos, *Anuario Estadístico*, 1955–61.
Guatemala: Dirección General de Estadística, *Anuario de Comercio Exterior*, 1955–60, and Banco Central de Guatemala, *Boletín Estadístico*, January–February, 1963.
Honduras: Dirección General de Estadística y Censos, *Comercio Exterior*, 1955–61.
Nicaragua: Recaudación General de Aduanas, *Memoria*, 1955–61.

other things, a variety of metals from Honduras and Nicaragua, soluble coffee from El Salvador and Guatemala, and, since 1960, shrimp from El Salvador.

As mentioned above, the continued predominance of coffee and bananas in the Central American export structure was the major factor behind the lackluster performance in 1955–62. During this period, the value of exports of both dropped by 15 per cent (see Table 6–3). In both cases, the declines reflected primarily the fall of prices on the world market. In the case of coffee, the drop in the unit value was so severe that the loss in earnings could not be offset, even with sizable increases in the volume exported. The slow growth of demand for Central American bananas restricted the scope for compensatory volume increases. With cotton, on the other hand, a drastic expansion of the volume exported

TABLE 6–3. Value, Volume, and Unit Value of Central America's Major Primary Product Exports, 1955–1962

(Indices: 1955 = 100)

Export	1955	1956	1957	1958	1959	1960	1961	1962*
Value								
Coffee	100	103	112	102	88	95	87	85
Bananas	100	113	107	103	88	92	94	85
Cotton	100	104	94	115	134	83	114	189
Wood	100	93	122	106	130	133	119	
Meat[a]					100	165	175	
Sugar	100	33	111	161	211	372	467	667
Cocoa	100	51	68	102	125	100	83	79
Volume								
Coffee	100	93	109	122	126	133	132	147
Bananas	100	110	116	113	99	114	113	101
Cotton	100	115	109	136	190	106	141	238
Wood[b]	100	91	117	99	124	128	117	
Meat[a]					100	170	176	
Sugar	100	28	89	136	209	353	395	546
Cocoa	100	68	75	82	121	123	108	88
Unit value								
Coffee	100	110	103	83	69	71	66	58
Bananas	100	103	93	91	89	81	84	85
Cotton	100	90	87	84	71	78	80	81
Wood[b]	100	102	117	118	116	118	119	
Meat[a]					100	97	100	
Sugar	100	120	121	117	100	105	117	119
Cocoa	100	77	90	123	104	82	77	84

[a] For meat, 1959 was used as base year. Exports were insignificant in early years.
[b] For wood, the volume and unit value indices exclude Nicaraguan exports.

Sources: For values, Table 6–2; for volumes, FAO, *Trade Yearbooks* and *Monthly Bulletin of Agricultural Economics and Statistics.* Also, national sources listed in Table 6–2.

TABLE 6-4. Central American Exports, by Destination, 1955-1962

Destination	1955	1956	1957	1958	1959	1960	1961*	1962*
			(Millions of dollars)					
Total exports	418.3	434.6	467.0	448.7	431.3	441.1	452.0	494.2
Central America	13.1	14.7	17.7	21.3	28.7	30.9	37.0	47.3
Total exports outside of Central America	405.2	419.9	449.3	427.4	402.6	410.2	415.0	446.9
United States and Canada	260.9	252.7	260.1	239.7	207.8	218.8	229.6	
Western Europe	113.8	134.4	158.5	146.8	141.8	148.6	129.0	
Japan	16.1	19.4	10.8	25.0	37.6	27.9	41.4	
Other	14.4	13.4	19.9	15.9	15.4	14.9	15.0	
			(Per cent of total exports)					
Central America	3.1	3.4	3.8	4.7	6.7	7.0	8.2	9.6
United States and Canada	62.4	58.1	55.7	53.4	48.2	49.6	50.8	
Western Europe	27.2	30.9	33.9	32.7	32.9	33.7	28.5	
Japan	3.8	4.5	2.3	5.6	8.7	6.3	9.2	
Other	3.5	3.1	4.3	3.6	3.5	3.4	3.3	

Sources: For total exports, IMF, *International Financial Statistics*. For exports by destination, United Nations, *Direction of International Trade*. For Guatemala, the banana customs valuation adjustment, which is given only for total exports, has been prorated to the U.S. and Western Europe components. For Nicaragua, gold exports have been subtracted from both regional and total export figures. The 1962 intraregional trade figure is an estimate from the Secretariat for Economic Integration of Central America, *Carta Informativa*, Anexo Estadístico No. 11.

effectively made up in the 1950's for unfavorable price trends. By 1962, moreover, cotton prices were rising, and the value of exports was nearly double what it had been in 1955. As for the less significant basic product exports from Central America, excepting cocoa, they benefited both from stable or rising prices and expanding volumes. Wood exports rose only moderately; but meat exports, which had hardly existed until 1959, almost doubled in the next two years. Central American sugar exports increased sharply after 1959 as a result of the windfall increase in United States purchases following the exclusion of Cuban sugar from that market.

Throughout the period under review, the heavy specialization of Central America in the export of a few primary commodities has been paralleled by the concentration of its markets (see Table 6-4). The United States, besides providing the largest outlet for Central America's coffee, takes nearly all of its banana, meat, and sugar exports, as well as the greater part of its cocoa. The fall of coffee prices led to a substantial decline in the dollar value of this trade in 1958–59, but in 1961 over one-half of all Central American exports still went to the United States and Canada (the latter importing small amounts of coffee and bananas). Western Europe, which bought increasing amounts of coffee—and some cotton—from Central America, maintained its share of the area's total export trade at about 30 per cent throughout, with West Germany now accounting for the bulk of Central America's European coffee trade and one-third of its total coffee exports, against only 17 per cent in 1955. On the other hand, intraregional exports, though they rose rapidly in this period, still represented less than 10 per cent of the total in 1961, and trade with the rest of Latin America and the Caribbean area countries was almost nonexistent. Japan's share—and Japan came to supplant Western Europe as Central America's major cotton importer—rose to 9 per cent of the total in 1961, solely because of trade in this one commodity.

A more detailed review of the evolution of trade and market distribution of Central America's principal primary product exports in 1955–62 is given in the commodity analyses that follow.

Coffee

Coffee is still by far the most important source of export earnings for Central America. Its share of the total, however, has been declining fairly steadily in recent years and now represents less than half of all export receipts (see Table 6–5). In absolute terms, the annual value of Central American coffee exports has ranged between $200 million and $275 million in the period covered by this study (see Table 6–6). Its abrupt fluctuations had been one of the major factors in the year-to-year changes in total receipts until about 1960; but it has had relatively less impact in the last two or three years, as other export products have risen in importance.

TABLE 6–5. Share of Coffee in Central American Exports Receipts, 1955–1962

(*Per cent*)

Country	1955	1956	1957	1958	1959	1960	1961	1962*
Central America	58	58	59	55	50	53	47	42
Costa Rica	46	50	49	55	52	53	53	55
El Salvador	86	78	79	72	63	66	59	47
Guatemala	70	75	72	73	71	66	60	61
Honduras	21	19	19	16	17	18	13	15
Nicaragua	39	40	44	38	21	34	29	19

Source: IMF, *International Financial Statistics*.

TABLE 6-6. Central American Coffee Exports: Total and by Country of Origin, 1955-1962

Country	1955	1956	1957	1958	1959	1960	1961	1962*
Value				(*Millions of dollars*)				
Total Central America	243.4	250.0	273.2	247.3	213.5	231.7	210.7	206.2
Costa Rica	37.4	33.8	40.6	50.6	40.1	45.4	44.9	46.8
El Salvador	91.5	87.4	109.8	84.1	71.3	76.7	70.2	64.2
Guatemala	75.5	91.9	82.3	77.5	76.3	78.6	69.2	68.3
Honduras	11.1	13.7	12.0	10.9	11.9	11.8	9.0	11.5
Nicaragua	27.9	23.2	28.5	24.2	13.9	19.2	17.4	15.4
Volume				(*Thousands of metric tons*)				
Total Central America	190.3	177.5	207.0	232.4	240.6	253.4	251.1	278.8
Costa Rica	28.3	22.8	29.5	46.2	43.3	46.7	52.0	65.1
El Salvador	71.8	64.5	83.2	80.5	83.0	89.5	86.6	97.5
Guatemala	58.4	61.4	61.8	71.5	82.7	79.9	79.0	80.3
Honduras	8.9	11.9	10.4	11.4	15.3	15.5	12.6	14.5
Nicaragua	22.8	16.9	22.0	22.9	16.3	21.8	20.9	21.4
Unit value				(*Dollars per ton*)				
Total Central America	1,279	1,408	1,320	1,064	887	914	839	740

Sources: For value figures: IMF, *International Financial Statistics*. For volume figures: FAO, *Trade Yearbooks* and *Monthly Bulletin of Agricultural Economics and Statistics*.

At present, coffee brings about $200 million to the region. It is a major export product for each of the five Central American countries. The bulk of the area's coffee exports, however, comes from three major suppliers, Costa Rica, El Salvador, and Guatemala, where coffee earnings account for roughly half of total exports and range between $50 million and $70 million. In Honduras and Nicaragua, on the other hand, coffee brings in only $10 million to $15 million, and, while it still accounts for 15 to 20 per cent of total export receipts, it is topped in one country by bananas and in the other by cotton as a source of foreign exchange.

During the 1955-62 period, the violent price fluctuations that characterized the world coffee market naturally had a strong impact on Central America. After remaining high in 1955-57, the export unit value of Central American coffee fell by approximately one-third between 1957 and 1959. Coffee export receipts dropped sharply as a result. The decline, however, was mostly confined to El Salvador and Nicaragua, where export volumes remained relatively unchanged. In the other three countries, where coffee production had been much expanded in response to the price increases of the early 1950's, large increases in the volume of coffee exported permitted the maintenance of receipts at a relatively steady level (see again Table 6–6). Between 1955 and 1962, the value of Central American coffee exports dropped by 15 per cent, but the volume rose nearly 50 per cent, chiefly as a result of increased shipments from Costa Rica and Guatemala. Costa Rica, in fact, increased its dependence on coffee as a source of foreign exchange in recent years, in contrast to the rest of Central America, where, as mentioned above, the role of coffee has steadily diminished. In El Salvador, in particular, whose dependence on coffee was virtually complete in 1955, the share of coffee in total export receipts was reduced to less than 50 per cent by 1962 (see again Table 6–5).

Central America exports almost all its coffee to the United States and Western Europe. While the United States remains the bigger of the two markets, Europe now stands a close second. Since 1955, Western Europe's share in Central American coffee exports has, in fact, risen sharply (see Table 6–7). In both markets, Central America supplies an equally small share of the total demand for green coffee: approximately 10 per cent. In 1955–61, however, there was a great deal of difference in the behavior of these two markets. In absolute terms, the volume of United States coffee imports from Central America, though it fluctuated widely from

TABLE 6–7. Central American Coffee Exports, by Destination, 1955–1961

Destination	1955	1956	1957	1958	1959	1960	1961
	(Thousands of metric tons)						
United States	133.8	111.3	125.9	137.8	128.4	124.3	130.0
Western Europe	54.4	65.4	78.8	91.9	109.5	121.9	111.7
Other	2.0	0.8	2.3	2.6	2.7	3.5	3.1
Total	190.2	177.5	207.0	232.4	240.6	249.5	244.8
	(Per cent)						
United States	70.3	62.3	60.9	59.3	53.3	49.4	53.1
Western Europe	28.6	36.6	38.1	39.5	45.4	48.7	45.6
Other	1.1	1.1	1.0	1.2	1.3	1.9	1.3
Total	100.0	100.0	100.0	100.0	100.0	100.0	100.0

Sources: 1955–59: FAO, *La Economía Mundial del Café*, 1961. For 1960–61: Pan American Coffee Bureau, *Annual Coffee Statistics*. The data from the Pan American Coffee Bureau differ slightly from that given by the FAO; hence the slight difference between the 1960 and 1961 export volume figures given in this table and those appearing in Table 6–6.

year to year, showed little tendency to expand. Central America merely continued to supply a fairly steady share of a total demand that was rising very slowly. In the European market, on the other hand, not only did total demand grow very rapidly but Central America also managed to secure some improvement in its rather marginal position (see Table 6-8). In practice, what happened is that Western Europe was able to absorb practically all of the increment in Central America's coffee output since 1955.

Within the European market, Central American coffee exports are virtually limited to the European Economic Community (EEC), and within the EEC they have been highly concentrated in one major country, West Germany. The volume of Central American coffee exports to West Germany increased by nearly 150 per cent between 1955 and 1961, while the small sales made to other EEC countries showed almost no change (see Table 6-9). West Germany is, in fact, the only European country where Central American coffee exports are large in absolute terms and have captured a substantial share of the total market: 38 per cent in 1961. Central American coffee holds a fairly important place—about 20 per cent of the market—in a few other countries, such as Austria and Switzerland, but the small size of the over-all market in these countries makes the actual export figures rather marginal (see Table 6-10). This underlines the great importance of the West German market for Central American coffee producers—the only market, in fact, that can be said to have been a dynamic factor in the evolution of Central American coffee exports in the past seven or eight years.

Bananas

Bananas, traditionally the second largest source of export earnings for Central America, declined gradually in importance during the 1955-62 period and in 1962 were surpassed by cotton exports. As a proportion of total export receipts in Central America, bananas represented 18 per cent in 1955 and 19 per cent in 1956, declining in subsequent years to 16 per cent in 1961 and, according to a partial estimate, to 13 per cent in 1962 (see Table 6-11). In Honduras, which is now the largest producer, bananas have accounted for roughly one-half of total exports throughout the period. On the other hand, the relative share of bananas dropped considerably in Costa Rica, which now ranks as the second Central American exporter of the product. In value terms, banana exports have fluctuated within a range of $64 million to $85 million around the average value for the eight-year period of $73 million. In 1961 bananas

TABLE 6–8. Position of Central American Coffee in Major Markets, 1955–1961

(Import volumes in thousands of metric tons)

Market	1955	1956	1957	1958	1959	1960	1961
United States market							
Total coffee imports	1,179	1,275	1,252	1,210	1,390	1,324	1,348
Imports from Central America	134	111	126	138	128	124	130
Central American percentage share	11.4	8.9	10.1	11.4	9.2	9.4	9.6
Western European market							
Total imports	699	763	775	820	920	978	1,071
Imports from Central America	54	65	79	92	110	122	112
Central American percentage share	7.8	8.6	10.2	11.2	11.9	12.5	10.4

Sources: 1955–59; FAO, *La Economía Mundial del Café*, 1961. For 1960–61: Pan American Coffee Bureau, *Annual Coffee Statistics.*

TABLE 6-9. Central American Coffee Exports to Western Europe, by Country of Destination, 1955-1961

(Thousands of metric tons)

Destination	1955	1956	1957	1958	1959	1960	1961
West Germany	32.4	41.8	53.3	68.8	76.9	85.6	77.7
Netherlands	9.9	11.4	9.8	8.2	10.0	11.6	12.1
Belgium-Luxembourg	4.7	3.0	5.0	3.8	5.2	7.1	6.0
Italy	2.3	3.1	4.5	4.6	7.9	6.2	4.3
France	0.4	0.5	0.4	0.1	0.8	0.5	1.6
Total EEC	49.7	59.8	73.0	85.5	99.9	110.9	101.8
Other countries	4.7	5.6	5.8	6.4	9.6	11.0	9.9
Total Western Europe	54.4	65.4	78.8	91.9	109.5	121.9	111.7

Sources: For 1955-59: FAO, *La Economía Mundial del Café*, 1961. For 1960-61, Pan American Coffee Bureau, *Annual Coffee Statistics*.

TABLE 6-10. Share of Central American Coffee in Imports of Major European Countries in 1961

Importing country	Total imports	Imports from Central America	Share of Central America
	(Thousands of metric tons)		*(Per cent)*
West Germany	212	80	38
France	207	1	—
Italy	105	5	4
Sweden	78	6	8
Netherlands	69	5	8
Belgium-Luxembourg	62	4	7
United Kingdom	59	1	1
Denmark	44	—	1
Finland	38	1	3
Switzerland	32	7	20
Norway	27	—	1
Austria	13	3	19

— Less than 500 metric tons, or 0.5 per cent.

Note: The figures in this table, based on European import data, differ slightly from the figures in Table 6-9, which are based on Central American export data.

Source: Pan American Coffee Bureau, *Annual Coffee Statistics*.

TABLE 6-11. Share of Bananas in Central American Export Receipts, 1955–1962

(Per cent)

Country	1955	1956	1957	1958	1959	1960	1961	1962*
Central America	18	19	17	17	15	16	16	13
Costa Rica	41	38	39	29	25	24	25	25
El Salvador	—	—	—	—	—	—	—	—
Guatemala	16	12	13	12	14	17	14	8
Honduras	47	60	52	54	47	45	46	44
Nicaragua	1	—	—	—	—	3	—	—

— Less than 0.5 per cent.
Sources: See Table 6–2.

brought in $71 million in export receipts; preliminary figures indicate $64 million in 1962 (see Table 6–12).

The loss in export receipts in 1962, compared with 1961, is attributable to a sharp drop in volume of bananas exported, which itself was the result of adverse weather conditions in Guatemala. As a consequence of recurring blowdowns and the persistence of Panama disease, the volume of exports has fluctuated widely from year to year; but in the period under review there has been a tendency to increase. In most years the volume has been maintained well above the 1955 level and has contributed toward slowing the decline in export receipts, which may be traced instead to falling export prices. The unit value of banana exports declined steadily from 1955 through 1960 and, despite a slight improvement in 1961–62, remained about 15 per cent lower than in 1955.

More than half the regional banana exports come from Honduras, where the volume of banana exports between 1955 and 1962 increased enough to offset the falling price and to counteract the effect on total value of the declining banana exports from Costa Rica. In that country, the volume of banana exports has been subject to substantial fluctuations and has not yet recovered from the fall in 1959. In Guatemala, the third largest producer, export receipts were relatively stable throughout the period 1955–61 but fell by almost 50 per cent in 1962, causing a loss of $7 million in total regional exports. El Salvador and Nicaragua are not major exporters of bananas.

Canada and the United States both purchase about 40 per cent of their bananas from Central America and together absorb about 90 per cent of the region's banana exports (see Table 6–13). The remainder is largely shipped to Europe: mainly to West Germany, Norway, and Sweden. To date, however, Central America is only a marginal supplier of these markets, and its exports to them are minor in comparison with its dependence on the North American market. As for intraregional trade, it is very small, for all five Central American countries produce bananas in some quantity.

Cotton

Cotton has ranked close to bananas as a source of foreign exchange for Central America in recent years. By 1962, it was bringing in about $85 million, or 17 per cent of total export receipts, as compared to $45 million and 11 per cent of the total in 1955–56 (see Tables 6–14 and 6–15). This remarkable expansion was largely the result of three- and fourfold increases in the value of cotton exports from Guatemala and

TABLE 6–12. Central American Banana Exports: Total and by Country of Origin, 1955–1962

Country	1955	1956	1957	1958	1959	1960	1961	1962*
Value				(*Millions of dollars*)				
Total Central America	74.9	84.7	80.5	77.3	66.2	69.2	70.7	64.0[a]
Costa Rica	33.2	25.7	32.2	26.5	19.1	20.3	20.9	21.1
El Salvador	—	—	—	0.1	0.2	0.2	—	—
Guatemala	17.0	15.0	14.5	13.1	14.7	19.9	16.4	8.5
Honduras	24.3	43.9	33.7	37.6	32.1	28.7	33.3	34.3
Nicaragua	0.4	0.2	0.1	0.1	0.1	1.4	0.1	n.a.
Volume				(*Thousands of metric tons*)				
Total Central America	727.9	798.6	844.7	821.7	722.8	832.6	821.3	736[a]
Costa Rica	329.5	232.8	374.0	301.8	213.4	273.5	230.9	269
El Salvador	—	0.2	0.3	1.4	2.0	2.4	0.5	—
Guatemala	170.6	168.6	129.7	115.8	146.2	190.2	158.5	82
Honduras	220.3	393.6	338.9	401.2	359.6	363.1	430.4	385
Nicaragua	7.5	3.4	1.8	1.5	1.6	3.4	1.0	—
Unit value				(*Dollars per ton*)				
Total Central America	103	106	95	94	92	83	86	87[a]

— Less than US$50,000, or 50 metric tons.

[a] Excluding El Salvador and Nicaragua.

Sources: Value figures: IMF, *International Financial Statistics*, for Costa Rica, Guatemala, and Honduras. For 1955–61, the other value and all volume figures were obtained from the national sources listed in Table 6–2. For 1962, the volume of banana exports from Costa Rica, Guatemala, and Honduras was estimated on the basis of the indices given in *International Financial Statistics*.

TABLE 6-13. Central American Banana Exports, by Destination, 1956-1961

Destination	1956	1957	1958	1959	1960	1961*
	(Thousands of metric tons)					
United States and Canada	716.5	753.4	743.2	626.7	739.9	731.7
Western Europe	76.9	79.7	73.8	82.7	76.9	76.9
Other	5.2	11.6	4.7	13.4	15.8	12.7
Total	798.6	844.7	821.7	722.8	832.6	821.3
	(Per cent)					
United States and Canada	89.7	89.2	90.4	86.7	88.9	89.1
Western Europe	9.6	9.4	9.0	11.4	9.2	9.4
Other	.7	1.4	0.6	1.9	1.9	1.5
Total	100.0	100.0	100.0	100.0	100.0	100.0

Sources: National sources listed in Table 6-2.

TABLE 6-14. Share of Cotton in Central American Export Receipts, 1955-1962

(Per cent)

Country	1955	1956	1957	1958	1959	1960	1961	1962*
Central America	11	11	9	11	14	8	11	17
Costa Rica	—	—	—	—	1	—	1	...
El Salvador	9	16	11	16	20	14	18	26
Guatemala	4	4	4	5	4	5	9	14
Honduras	—	1	1	4	4	1	—	...
Nicaragua	43	41	34	39	45	26	30	38

— Nil or less than 0.5 per cent.

Sources: IMF, *International Financial Statistics;* and:
Costa Rica: Dirección General de Estadística y Censos, *Comercio Exterior.*
Guatemala: Dirección General de Estadística, *Anuario de Comercio Exterior,* and Banco de Guatemala, *Boletín Estadístico.*
Honduras: Dirección General de Estadística y Censos, *Comercio Exterior.*

El Salvador, where the development of cotton cultivation, encouraged as a matter of government policy, effectively made up for the coffee and banana income losses of the period. The pattern was quite different in Nicaragua, however. That country, having developed its cotton exports a few years ahead of the other two major Central American producers, was already highly dependent on this product in the mid-1950's. In 1959, however, fiscal difficulties led the government to withdraw its subsidy to cotton producers. This and falling world prices led to a sharp curtailment of output in the 1959/60 and 1960/61 crops, so that by

1962 Nicaraguan cotton export earnings were just recovering their 1955 level.

The growth of cotton export volumes roughly paralleled that of values in Central America in the 1955–62 period. Cotton prices declined relatively less on the average between those two years than those of other basic exports on the world market. The price of Central American cotton exports dropped gradually in 1955–58 by nearly 30 per cent, but it has been rising since 1959. As a result, and though there were fluctuations during much of the period, by 1962 the Central American cotton producers were able to turn virtually all of their expanded export volumes into rising foreign exchange income.

The major markets for Central American cotton are to be found in the industrialized countries; notably, Japan, West Germany, the United

TABLE 6–15. Volume and Value of Central American Cotton Exports, Total and by Country of Origin, 1955–1962

Country	1955	1956	1957	1958	1959	1960	1961	1962*
Value				(Millions of dollars)				
Total Central America	44.7	46.5	42.1	51.2	59.9	36.9	50.8	84.7[a]
Costa Rica	—	—	—	.3	.9	.1	.4	...
El Salvador	9.1	17.6	15.8	18.1	23.2	15.8	21.3	35.0
Guatemala	4.5	4.9	4.1	5.4	4.0	5.7	10.5	15.4
Honduras	.1	.4	.4	2.6	2.6	.7	.3	3.0[b]
Nicaragua	31.0	23.6	21.8	24.9	29.3	14.7	18.3	31.3
Volume				(Thousands of metric tons)				
Total Central America	63.8	73.5	69.3	86.9	121.1	67.6	90.0	152.0[c]
Costa Rica	—	—	—	.5	1.7	.3	.7	...
El Salvador	12.4	27.9	25.2	29.7	44.0	27.2	35.5	...
Guatemala	6.5	7.8	6.7	9.6	9.7	11.5	20.7	...
Honduras	.9	1.4	1.4	4.4	4.0	1.2	.6[b]	...
Nicaragua	44.0	36.3	36.0	42.7	61.7	27.4	32.5	...
Unit value				(Dollars per ton)				
Total Central America	701	633	608	589	495	546	564	560

... Less $50,000, or 50 tons.
[a] Excluding Costa Rica.
[b] Estimated on the basis of production figures.
[c] Estimated on the basis of 1961–62 production data.

Sources: Values: Same sources as in Table 6–13. Volumes: FAO, *Trade Yearbook* and *Monthly Bulletin of Agricultural Economics and Statistics*. For Guatemala in 1961, Banco de Guatemala, *Boletín Estadístico*.

Kingdom, and the Netherlands. At present, Japan is by far the largest purchaser of Central American cotton, absorbing from two-thirds to three-fourths of the area's exports. The rest goes mostly to Western Europe. This represents a complete reversal of the situation prevailing in 1955, when Western Europe took in the bulk of Central America's cotton exports and Japan bought only one-fourth of the total (see Table 6–16).

TABLE 6–16. Central American Cotton Exports, by Major Markets, 1955–1962[a]

Destination	1954/55	1955/56	1956/57	1957/58	1958/59	1959/60	1960/61	1961/62
(Thousands of metric tons)[b]								
Japan	10	33	14	23	75	41	58	74
West Germany	19	35	9	16	24	6	5	15
United Kingdom	5	9	8	6	15	6	5	7
Netherlands	3	7	3	8	11	2	1	4
(Per cent of total)								
Japan	26	35	22	32	52	67	74	59
West Germany	46	36	13	23	17	10	7	12
United Kingdom	12	10	13	8	10	9	7	5
Netherlands	9	8	6	11	8	3	1	3

[a] Crop year ending in August.
[b] Converted from bales at the rate of 0.21682 metric tons per bale.

Source: International Cotton Advisory Committee, *Cotton—World Statistics* (Washington, D.C.).

In terms of volume, exports to Japan increased about sevenfold between 1954/55 and 1961/62, as Central America benefited both from the rapid growth of the over-all Japanese demand for cotton in 1955–62 and from a substantial improvement in its share of the Japanese market (see Table 6–17). In the major Western European markets, on the other hand, where demand for cotton showed few signs of increase, Central American cotton sales remained more or less stagnant. The Japanese market has thus provided the only outlet for Central America's increased cotton production in recent years. All three major Central American cotton producers are equally dependent on Japan in this respect, and all three have seen the growth of their cotton exports paralleled by an increasing concentration of their sales in one single market (see Table 6–18).

TABLE 6-17. Total Cotton Imports and Share of Central America in Selected Markets, 1955–1962[a]

Country and market	1954/55	1955/56	1956/57	1957/58	1958/59	1959/60	1960/61	1961/62
Total Imports	(Thousands of metric tons)							
Japan	444	517	640	521	550	713	770	619
West Germany	264	278	348	316	266	368	310	282
United Kingdom	322	322	384	314	246	304	249	211
Netherlands	74	73	83	68	69	87	84	74
Share of Central America	(Per cent)							
Japan	2	6	2	4	14	6	8	12
West Germany	7	13	2	5	9	2	2	5
United Kingdom	2	3	2	2	6	2	2	3
Netherlands	5	10	4	11	16	2	1	6

[a] Crop year ending in August.
Source: International Cotton Advisory Committee, Cotton—World Statistics.

TABLE 6-18. Share of Major Markets in Cotton Exports of Major Central American Producers, 1955–1962[a]

(Per cent)

Country and market	1954/55	1955/56	1956/57	1957/58	1958/59	1959/60	1960/61	1961/62
El Salvador								
Japan	42	57	50	59	70	86	91	76
West Germany	8	12	4	12	2	3	6	17
United Kingdom	28	11	5	8	6	4	1	
Netherlands	8	5	4	5	1	—	—	1
Nicaragua								
Japan	24	20	11	12	33	40	57	—
West Germany	24	41	24	28	21	18	18	—
United Kingdom	6	8	20	9	9	17	10	—
Netherlands	23	21	24	25	15	10	6	—
Guatemala[b]								
Japan	—	18	9	16	73	79	80	77

— Nil or less than 0.5 per cent.
[a] Crop year ending in August.
[b] A consistent breakdown of exports by destination is not available on the same basis as for El Salvador and Nicaragua. The figure given here for Guatemalan cotton exports to Japan is based on Japanese import statistics.
Source: International Cotton Advisory Committee, Cotton—World Statistics.

Wood

Since 1955, the value of wood exports has fluctuated annually around an average value of $11 million, reflecting fluctuations of similar proportion in volume; unit value, on the other hand, has remained almost unchanged since 1957, following a rise in that year from the level of 1955–56. In 1961, wood exports accounted for $11.4 million, or 2.6 per cent of total export receipts.

Almost two-thirds of the region's wood exports originate in Honduras; another 20 to 25 per cent come from Nicaragua, with Costa Rica and Guatemala exporting considerably smaller quantities. Wood exports from Honduras showed some increase over the 1955–62 period; exports from the other countries have been stable or declining since 1955 (see Table 6–19).

Although the largest market for Central American wood is the Caribbean area—particularly Venezuela, Jamaica, and Cuba—Central America also exports wood to the United States and to almost every country in Western Europe. There has been a gradual increase in exports to Europe since 1955, and more recently (since 1959) a marked increase in exports to the United States, both shifts taking place at the expense of exports to the Caribbean area, while total exports remained stable (see Table 6–20). In 1961 the share of total wood exports sent to these three areas was approximately 42 per cent to the Caribbean and 25 per cent each to the United States and Western Europe, compared with 58, 19, and 14 per cent in 1955. Intraregional exports, primarily to El Salvador, accounted for less than 10 per cent of the total throughout this period, with a small residual quantity sent to other areas, usually Japan.

Meat

Only Costa Rica, of the five Central American nations, has been an exporter of meat throughout the 1955–62 period; for the region as a whole this is a new export product. Meat exports are still small, only $9 million, or 2 per cent of total exports in 1961, but the rate of increase in recent years has been exceptionally high. The volume exported rose from 14 tons in 1955 to more than 14,000 tons in 1961, with the value increasing from $10,000 to $9 million during the same time (see Table 6–21).

Costa Rica, Guatemala, Honduras, and Nicaragua have all participated in this expansion. Scarcity of land causes El Salvador to remain a net importer. Prior to 1958, Costa Rica was, in effect, the only exporter of

TABLE 6-19. Central American Wood Exports, Total and by Country of Origin, 1955–1962

Country	1955	1956	1957	1958	1959	1960	1961	1962*
Value				(Thousands of dollars)				
Total Central America	9,626	8,925	11,728	10,167	12,454	12,790	11,443	
Costa Rica	195	251	174	153	86	71	144	
El Salvador	—	—	—	—	—	24	6	
Guatemala	500	572	392	435	463	886	876	1,028
Honduras	5,394	4,796	7,810	6,540	8,236	8,217	7,507	7,207
Nicaragua	3,528	3,307	3,352	3,039	3,669	3,592	2,910	
Volume				(Thousands of metric tons)				
Total Central America[a]	168.9	153.3	197.7	167.9	209.4	216.4	197.9	
Costa Rica	7.3	9.6	6.6	4.6	2.1	2.3	3.9	
El Salvador	—	—	—	—	—	1.5	0.2	
Guatemala	11.1[b]	10.3[b]	6.1	7.2	6.9	9.9	11.9[c]	12.9[c]
Honduras	150.5	133.4	185.0	156.1	200.4	202.7	181.9	161.7
Unit Value				(Dollars per ton)				
Total Central America[a]	36.10	36.65	42.37	42.45	41.95	42.50	43.11	

— Less than US$500 or 50 metric tons.
[a] Excluding Nicaragua.
[b] Converted from York tons at the rate of 790 metric tons per York ton (the 1957–58 average).
[c] Metric ton figure estimated on the basis of data in square feet.

Sources: National sources listed in Table 6-2.

TABLE 6–20. Central American Wood Exports, by Destination, 1955–1961

Destination	1955	1956	1957	1958	1959	1960	1961*
	(Thousands of dollars)						
United States and Canada	1,864	1,620	1,431	1,287	1,849	2,283	2,981
Caribbean area[a]	5,558	5,098	7,562	6,453	7,784	6,693	4,745
Western Europe	1,321	1,372	1,745	1,477	1,925	2,823	2,753
Central America	865	784	933	842	823	836	864
Other	9	50	56	110	72	153	104
Total	9,626	8,925	11,728	10,167	12,454	12,790	11,443
	(Per cent)						
United States and Canada	19.4	18.2	12.2	12.7	14.8	17.8	26.1
Caribbean area[a]	57.7	57.1	64.5	63.5	62.5	52.3	41.5
Western Europe	13.7	15.4	14.9	14.5	15.5	22.1	24.1
Central America	9.0	8.8	8.0	8.3	6.6	6.5	7.6
Other	0.1	0.6	0.5	1.1	0.6	1.2	0.9
Total	100.0	100.0	100.0	100.0	100.0	100.0	100.0

Sources: National sources listed in Table 6–2.

[a] Panama, Canal Zone, Mexico, Colombia, Venezuela, Puerto Rico, Cuba, Dominican Republic, British West Indies, Dutch and French Antilles.

TABLE 6-21. Central American Meat Exports, Total and by Country of Origin, 1955–1962

Country	1955	1956	1957	1958	1959	1960	1961	1962
Value				(Thousands of dollars)				
Total Central America	10	53	152	972	5,188	8,591	9,111	
Costa Rica	8	52	147	914	2,892	4,297	2,782	1,839
El Salvador	—	—	5	30	27	7	4	
Guatemala	—	—	—	—	5	205	750[a]	
Honduras	1	—	—	28	458	1,114	1,532	2,926
Nicaragua	1	1	—	—	1,806	2,968	4,043	
Volume				(Metric tons)				
Total Central America	14	72	368	2,014	8,162	13,909	14,348	
Costa Rica	12	71	364	1,934	4,862	7,258	4,849	2,599
El Salvador	—	—	4	25	22	6	5	
Guatemala	—	—	—	—	7	540	971[a]	
Honduras	1	—	—	54	710	1,656	2,381	5,072
Nicaragua	1	1	—	1	2,561	4,449	6,142	
Unit value				(Dollars per ton)				
Total Central America	714	736	413	483	636	618	635	

— Less than $500 or 0.5 metric tons.
[a] Estimated from import data of U.S., El Salvador, and Honduras.

Sources: National sources listed in Table 6–2.

meat. Honduras began exporting in 1958, and Nicaragua and Guatemala followed its example in 1959. The high growth rates of 1959 and 1960 were not maintained in 1961, however, as Nicaragua in mid-1961 found it necessary to prohibit the export of live cattle. This led to a reduction in meat exports from Costa Rica, which had relied heavily on imported Nicaraguan cattle for the expansion of its beef herds. Nicaraguan output, on the other hand, continued to rise rapidly.

At present the United States market absorbs more than 95 per cent of Central American meat exports (see Table 6–22). Intraregional exports have risen but remain small, and exports to other Latin American and Caribbean countries, although also increasing, originate only in Costa Rica and represent less than 3 per cent of total regional exports.

Sugar

Within total regional exports, sugar remains a minor item, contributing approximately $12 million, or 2.5 per cent in 1962. The period 1955–62 was one of rapid increase, however, during which the value of sugar exports rose sixfold. Because of the dominant position of the United States market, where the import price of sugar is tied to the domestic price (historically stable and—until recently—considerably higher than the world price), the unit value of Central American sugar exports has also tended to be relatively stable and above the world price. The total value of Central American exports increased steadily during the 1955–62 period, paralleling a rapid rise in export volume, which was itself largely induced by the availability of the United States market (see Tables 6–23, 6–24, and 6–25).

Prior to 1960, Nicaragua and Costa Rica were the only exporters outside the region. On occasion each sold large quantities of its sugar exports on the world market, Costa Rica shipping more than 50 per cent of its exports to Holland, Jordan, and France in 1955, 1959, and 1960, respectively, and Nicaragua sending more than half its sugar exports to Japan in 1959. But in general the higher-priced United States market was preferred and these overseas contacts were not maintained. Beginning in 1960, when the Cuban share of the United States market was reallocated to other producers, developments in that market became almost the sole factor to affect the trend of Central American sugar exports.

Under the *ad hoc* reallocation of the Cuban share that took place in 1960 and 1961, El Salvador and Guatemala were granted United States import quotas for the first time and the quotas of Costa Rica and Nicaragua were considerably enlarged. The Central American producers

TABLE 6–22. Central American Meat Exports by Destination, 1955–1961

	1955	1956	1957	1958	1959	1960	1961*
				(in metric tons)			
United States and Canada	2	67	363	1,810	7,862	13,439	13,834
Caribbean area and South America	11	4	—	183	271	317	393
Central America	1	1	5	20	29	153	121
Total	14	72	368	2,014	8,162	13,909	14,348
				(in per cent)			
United States and Canada	14.2	93.1	98.6	89.9	96.3	96.6	96.4
Caribbean area and South America	78.6	5.6	—	9.1	3.3	2.3	2.7
Central America	7.1	1.4	1.4	1.0	0.4	1.1	0.8
Total	100.0	100.0	100.0	100.0	100.0	100.0	100.0

— Less than 0.5 metric tons or 0.05 per cent.
Sources: National sources listed in Table 6–2.

TABLE 6–23. Central American Sugar Exports, Total and by Country of Origin, 1955–1962

Country	1955	1956	1957	1958	1959	1960	1961	1962
Value				*(Thousands of dollars)*				
Total Central America	1,819	614	1,963	2,880	3,799	6,690	8,337	11,850
Costa Rica	580	—	104	147	605	1,809	3,132	
El Salvador	293	183	648	1,085	1,001	1,376	1,594	
Guatemala	6	—	198	7	64	67	807	
Honduras	1	2	—	2	15	3	12	
Nicaragua	939	429	1,013	1,639	2,114	3,435	2,834	
Volume				*(Thousands of metric tons)*				
Total Central America	18.5	5.2	16.5	25.1	38.7	65.2	73.0	102.6
Costa Rica	7.0	—	0.9	1.2	6.7	18.8	26.5	
El Salvador	2.4	1.2	5.2	8.5	6.9	10.9	13.9	
Guatemala	0.3	—	1.4	0.1	0.5	0.7	7.0	
Honduras	—	—	—	—	0.2	—	0.3	
Nicaragua	8.8	3.9	9.0	15.4	24.4	34.9	25.3	
Unit value				*(Dollars per ton)*				
Total Central America	98	118	119	115	98	103	115	117

— Less than US$500 or 50 metric tons.
Note: 1961 exports from Guatemala and total exports in 1962 were estimated on the basis of U.S. imports.

Sources: National sources listed in Table 6–2.

TABLE 6-24. Raw Cane Sugar Spot Price, 1955-1963

(U.S. cents per pound)

Period	World market	U.S. market	U.S. quota Premium or discount
1955	3.24	5.95	+1.70 (1955-56 aver.)
1956	3.47	6.09	
1957	5.16	6.25	+0.14
1958	3.50	6.27	+1.91
1959	2.97	6.24	+2.38
1960	3.10	6.30	+2.21
1961	2.91	6.30	+2.45
1962	2.98	6.45	+2.58
1963 (Jan.-May)	7.22	7.98	−0.13 (Jan.-Apr. aver.)

Sources: U.S. Department of Agriculture, *Sugar Reports;* and Merrill, Lynch, Pierce, Fenner and Smith, *Weekly Sugar Letter.*

The 1963 quotations are based on average daily quotations for January-April and an average of Thursday quotations for May.

World market: Prior to 1961, spot price based on No. 4 Contract which was bagged sugar f.a.s. Cuba. Beginning with 1961, spot price under No. 8 Contract, which is also for bagged sugar but f.o.b. and stowed at greater Caribbean ports (including Brazil).

U.S. market: Prior to 1961, spot price for sugar in bags under Contract No. 6 plus 50 cents per pound duty (Cuban). Beginning with 1961, spot price for bulk sugar under Contract No. 7, the terms of which are duty-paid or duty-free.

U.S. quota premium or discount: Net differential between U.S. and world price quotations, once they are reduced to a comparable basis and allowance is made for shipping, U.S. import duties, etc.

TABLE 6-25. Central American Sugar Exports, by Destination, 1955-1962

Destination	1955	1956	1957	1958	1959	1960	1961	1962
(Thousands of metric tons)								
United States and Canada	6.3	3.4	9.9	16.1	15.3	49.1	69.0	102.6[a]
Central America	7.3	1.8	6.6	9.0	7.6	6.4	3.9	—
Other	4.6	—	—	—	15.7	9.8	—	—
Total	18.5	5.2	16.5	25.1	38.7	65.2	73.0	
(Per cent)								
United States and Canada	35.7	65.4	60.0	64.1	39.5	75.3	94.5	
Central America	39.5	—	40.0	35.9	19.6	9.8	5.3	
Other	24.9	34.6	—	—	40.6	15.0	—	
Total	100.0	100.0	100.0	100.0	100.0	100.0	100.0	

— Nil or less than 50 metric tons or 0.05 per cent.

[a] Estimated on the basis of U.S. import data.

Sources: National sources listed in Table 6-2.

were then awarded still larger shares of the United States sugar market in virtue of the new sugar legislation adopted by the United States Congress in 1962. Broadly speaking, the new law incorporated about half of the former Cuban quota into the permanent quotas of other suppliers. The remainder was placed in a "global quota," to be filled with sugar from any foreign supplier on a first-come, first-served basis. Central America benefited on both counts, raising the volume of its 1962 sugar exports to the United States nearly 50 per cent above the already high level reached in 1961.

While permitting the import of larger volumes of sugar from foreign suppliers other than Cuba, the new United States legislation also aimed to reduce the price premium earned by these countries in the United States market in relation to the world sugar price. Sugar coming in under the global quota was to be purchased at a price approximating the world market price. This was to be achieved by collecting a special import levy, fixed from time to time by the United States Department of Agriculture at a level corresponding more or less to the difference between the world and the United States price. Moreover, sugar sold under the exporting countries' individual quotas was also to pay an import fee, which, although much lower than the levy on global quota sugar, was to rise gradually to 30 per cent of this levy by 1964, when the law comes up for review. These two measures would normally have resulted in gradually falling unit values for Central American sugar exports. So far, however, the opposite has happened. The development of a sugar shortage began, in the second half of 1962, to lift the world market price substantially above its depressed level of recent years. The reversal of the United States world market price differential for the time being undermined the United States import levy system, which had been based on it (see Table 6-24). In February, 1963, the import levies were suspended to insure an adequate flow of sugar imports into the United States, and in subsequent months the spot price rose to almost unprecedented heights in both the United States and the world markets, heralding substantial increases in the unit and the total value of Central American sugar exports for the current year.

Cocoa

Cocoa accounts for only about 1 per cent of Central American export receipts. The only important producer is Costa Rica, though small amounts of cocoa beans are also exported by Guatemala and Nicaragua. The total value of Central American cocoa exports has varied from as little as $3 million to as much as $8 million in recent years (see Table

6–26). This is attributable both to large fluctuations in the size of the Costa Rican crop from year to year and to the ups and downs of cocoa prices in the world market. Between 1958 and 1962, for instance, the export unit value of Costa Rican cocoa dropped about one-third. The maintenance of high export volumes first helped slow down the resulting decline in exchange receipts, but by 1961–62 both volume and unit values were relatively depressed. Over the 1955–62 period, cocoa has been an export of irregular importance for Costa Rica, its share ranging from 4 to 10 per cent of the total (see Table 6–27).

Cocoa from Guatemala and Nicaragua is largely consumed locally or exported within the Central American region. The bulk of Costa Rica's cocoa production, on the other hand, is shipped to the outside world. Substantially more than half goes to the United States and about one-fourth to the Canal Zone and Panama (see Table 6–28). Other American importers are Chile and Colombia. The EEC countries, for their part, purchase only a very small amount. This pattern seems to have been rather stable throughout the period under study.

TABLE 6–26. Volume and Value of Central American Cocoa Exports, 1955–1962

Country	1955	1956	1957	1958	1959	1960	1961	1962
	(Millions of dollars)							
Value								
Total Central America	6.3	3.2	4.3	6.4	7.9	6.3	5.2[a]	5.0[a]
Costa Rica	5.9	2.9	4.0	5.9	7.4	5.9	4.8	4.6
Guatemala	.2	.2	.2	.4	.4	.2	...	...
Nicaragua	.2	.1	.1	.1	.1	.2	...	...
	(Thousands of metric tons)							
Volume								
Total Central America	10.2	6.9	7.7	8.4	12.3	12.5	11.0[a]	9.6[a]
Costa Rica	9.7	6.2	7.4	7.7	11.5	11.8	10.2	8.8
Guatemala	.3	.5	.2	.6	.6	.4	...	...
Nicaragua	.2	.2	.1	.1	.2	.3	...	...
	(Dollars per ton)							
Unit value								
Total Central America	618	478	558	762	642	514	473	521

[a] Estimated on the basis of Costa Rican exports only.

Sources: Volume: FAO, *Cocoa Statistics*, January, 1963.
Value: COSTA RICA: IMF, *International Financial Statistics*. GUATEMALA: Dirección General de Estadística, *Anuario de Comercio Exterior*. NICARAGUA: Recaudación General de Aduanas, *Memoria*.

TABLE 6–27. Costa Rican Cocoa Statistics, 1955–1962

Item	1955	1956	1957	1958	1959	1960	1961	1962*
Production[a] (thousands of metric tons)	10.0	7.0	7.4	8.2	11.0	10.7	13.4	9.9
Exports								
Value (millions of dollars)	5.9	2.9	4.0	5.9	7.3	5.9	4.8	4.6
Volume (thousands of metric tons)	9.7	6.2	7.4	7.7	11.5	11.8	10.2	8.8
Unit value (dollars per ton)	613	477	544	768	630	495	467	523
Share of cocoa in total export receipts (per cent)	7	4	5	6	10	7	6	5

[a] Crop year ending in September.
Sources: IMF, *International Financial Statistics*; and FAO, *Cocoa Statistics*.

TABLE 6–28. Costa Rican Cocoa Exports, by Destination in 1961

Destination	Volume (metric tons)	Per cent
United States	5,965	58.4
Canal Zone	1,859	18.2
Panama	644	6.3
Colombia	657	6.4
Chile	341	3.3
EEC	444	4.3
Japan	212	2.1
Others	92	0.9
Total	10,214	100.0

Source: Dirección General de Estadística y Censos, *Comercio Exterior*.

PROSPECTS IN 1963–67 FOR EXPORTS OUTSIDE OF CENTRAL AMERICA

Export projections for an area such as Central America can only be very tentative, even when they cover a time span as short as that between 1962 and 1967. The main reason for this is that Central America earns most of its export income in primary product markets which are per se rather unstable. Because of its small size, moreover, Central America constitutes only a very marginal supplier and therefore cannot hope to influence in any significant way the evolution of the over-all supply and demand. The high degree of concentration of Central American exports in a few major products and its dependence on a few major importing countries also enhance the probability that some unexpected isolated trend or event, which would have only a minor impact on an area endowed with a more balanced export structure, might have a profound effect on the value of its total export earnings. To these permanent factors of uncertainty must be added, for the period under review, two important question marks: that of the impact that the gradual implementation of the European Economic Community's policies will have on the pattern of international trade in tropical products; and that of the trend in international commodity prices, which may now be reaching a turning point in their long postwar downswing and whose future behavior might henceforth reflect a different, and as yet undiscernible, set of basic forces.

Such a combination of factors might be enough to discourage any attempt at forecasting the future trend of Central American exports. Neither does the erratic pattern of these exports in recent years offer much encouragement. A few guiding threads do emerge, however, from the analysis of this pattern in the first part of this chapter and it is possible to extrapolate them in the light of the various, though scanty, clues that are available on future conditions in major commodity markets, future trends and patterns of world demand, and other relevant considerations. Crude as these projections may be, however, they may nevertheless be taken—with a great deal of caution—as a rough indication of what might be expected to happen to Central American exports under a given set of assumptions, which have been chosen as realistically as possible, although necessarily not without some arbitrariness among the various alternatives that appear relatively reasonable at the present time.

Assumptions

Because Central American exports still consist mainly of a few primary products—namely, coffee, cotton, bananas, wood, meat, sugar, and cocoa—the major effort was devoted to an analysis of the export prospects of each one of those products. An *ad hoc* method was adopted in each case. For the two big traditional exports, coffee and bananas, where Central America's productive capacity is ample in relation to demand, the projection of exports is based entirely on the anticipated trend of demand in major markets. The estimates for two other traditional products, sugar and cocoa, rest essentially on expectations concerning eventual marketing arrangements (arrangements affecting only the United States in the case of sugar, but the world market in the case of cocoa). Supply considerations become more directly relevant when coming to projections of the trend of the newer Central American exports. The cotton estimates, for instance, are closely related to expected trends in land acreage and yields, with only crude assumptions about world demand brought into the picture. Finally, in the case of wood and meat exports, for which foreign markets are readily available, the major factor considered is the potential growth of Central American output of these products in the next few years.

The most important assumptions made to arrive at the present projections are those relating to future price trends, the impact of EEC policies on the West German market for Central American coffee, and the evolution of the textile industry in Central America's major cotton market, Japan. In keeping with prevailing market tendencies and current efforts to establish more effective international agreements for some key commodities (coffee and cocoa), fairly stable prices have been assumed for Central America's major exports in the next few years. Cotton prices, for instance, have been postulated to decline by only about 1 per cent a year between 1962 and 1967 and coffee, banana, wood, and meat prices to remain approximately unchanged. Similarly, it is not expected that cocoa prices will go below their present floor (they are more likely to rise if the recent improvement in supply-demand balance persists, as it may, especially if an International Cocoa Agreement actually comes into existence). In sugar, the world market price is expected in the model here employed to come down sharply from its recent peaks, as the transitory factors which have caused them are corrected, but it is assumed to remain substantially above the depressed 1959–62 level. On the other hand, in the United States market, which is more directly relevant for Central America, by 1967 the price of sugar is expected to be brought back down to its 1955–56 level of 5 cents per pound, as the United States is assumed to pursue insofar as possible its policy of narrowing the differential with the world price both before and after the 1964 expiration date of the current Sugar Act.

With regard to the influence of EEC policies on tropical products, it is assumed that there will be little impact on Central America's cocoa and banana exports, in view of the marginal nature of the European market for these two products and in view of the establishment of a duty-free quota for the importation of Central American bananas in West Germany. The case of coffee, however, is expected to be entirely different, and the present projections are based on the assumption of a substantial improvement in the position of African coffee and a substantial deterioration in that of Central America in the important West German market, which may completely stifle the growth of Central American coffee exports to Europe, if it does not actually force some decline in these exports.

Other important assumptions about foreign demand include a fairly steady economic expansion in industrialized countries at something near the current rates (real rise in per capita gross product at about 2 to 2.5 per cent a year in the United States and 4 to 5 per cent a year in most of Western Europe); the continued exclusion of Cuba from the United States sugar market; and the maintenance of a high level of activity in the Japanese cotton textile industry, which has been the major factor behind the growth of Central American cotton exports in recent years. On the whole, however, it was thought prudent not to anticipate the opening up of any major new markets for Central America's basic exports, which will thus, according to these estimates, continue to be highly concentrated in the United States, Western Europe, and Japan.

On the supply side, as mentioned above, no limitations were assumed on Central America's capacity to satisfy forthcoming demands for coffee, bananas, or sugar. In the case of cocoa cultivation, a continuation of the present unsatisfactory state of technique through the next few years is expected to keep Costa Rica's exportable supply well within any ceilings that might be imposed by an eventual International Cocoa Agreement. For cotton, on the other hand, continued strong government encouragement and rapid technological progress are postulated. It is similarly assumed that, in line with recent trends, rapid advances in meat production are feasible. In the development of wood exports, on the other hand, transportation difficulties and the need for investment in new processing facilities are expected to hold back progress somewhat in the near future.

On the basis of these various assumptions, separate projections have been made of the trend of each one of the major primary product exports from Central America to the outside world between 1962 and 1967 (see Table 6–29, column A). Since it has not been possible, however, to avoid considerable arbitrariness in the selection of the assumptions and since a high degree of uncertainty is clearly attached to some of the most crucial choices, it has been decided to make alternative high and low projections under different sets of assumptions for the three most important products, coffee, bananas, and cotton. In the case of coffee, the low estimate is based on the assumption that severe over-

TABLE 6–29. Projected Trend in Value of Central America's Major Primary Product Exports Outside of Integration Area in 1962–1967

Export	Value of exports in 1961* in millions of dollars[a]	A—Preferred projection		Alternative projections			
				B—Low		C—High	
		1967 in millions of dollars	Per cent annual rate of change in 1962–67[b]	1967 in millions of dollars	Per cent annual rate of change in 1962–67	1967 in millions of dollars	Per cent annual rate of change in 1962–67
Coffee	210	205	−0.4	160	−4.2	220	1.2
Bananas	70	78	1.8	70	—	86	3.5
Cotton	51 (85)	85	8.9 (—)	50	−0.3	115	14.5
Wood	11	15	5.3				
Meat	9	25	18.6				
Sugar	8	14	12.2				
Cocoa	5	6	3.1				
Total	364 (398)	428	2.7 (1.7)	340	−1.1	481	4.8

[a] 1962 estimates for cotton exports and total are given in parentheses.
[b] Per cent annual rate of change in 1963–67 given in parentheses for cotton exports and total on the basis of 1962 estimates.

Note: All figures exclude Central American intraregional trade.
Source: A detailed description of the assumptions and methods used to arrive at the projections for each product is presented in p. 296 ff. of this chapter.

production would depress world prices substantially further in the next few years (price declines of 3 to 3.5 per cent a year are postulated) and that Central America would lose a particularly important portion of its West German market as a result of the adoption of the EEC common external tariff. The high projection, on the other hand, is founded on the assumption of a somewhat faster expansion of United States demand for coffee between 1962 and 1967 and the removal of internal taxes on coffee in the EEC countries. For bananas, the derivation of the high and low estimates only involves dropping the assumption of price stability and postulating instead a 10 per cent rise or fall between now and 1967. Finally, in the cotton projections, the crucial factor, as mentioned above, is Japanese demand, which is assumed to grow at a particularly rapid rate to yield the high projection, while a virtual stagnation of this demand and a 2.5 per cent annual drop in cotton prices are incorporated in the low projection. While the "preferred" projections represent what appears to be the best choice at the time of writing, the assumptions embodied in the low and high estimates are far from being ruled out, and the low and high estimates are given here as an illustration of the extent to which actual exports could easily be expected to vary from the "preferred" projection figures by 1967.

Projections

If international commodity prices stabilize, the depression that has affected Central American exports outside the integration area in recent years may be at an end (see Table 6–29). The present projections also suggest, however, that in the next few years the area's major primary product exports to its traditional markets are likely to grow only slowly. Under the "preferred" set of assumptions, export income from these products would increase by about $65 million between 1961 and 1967 (see Table 6–29, column A). This would represent a distinct improvement over the downward trend that prevailed in the preceding six-year period. The average annual rate of growth during the 1962–67 period, however, would amount to only 2.7 per cent. Moreover, as Central American primary product exports are estimated to have increased sharply in 1962, the area, according to this projection, could in fact look forward to only a 1.7 per cent annual rate of growth in these exports for the remainder of the period.

On a product-by-product basis, the present study projects virtually no change in coffee export receipts between now and 1967, a slow growth of banana exports, and moderate annual increases in income from wood and cocoa. Rapid growth would characterize sugar and, above all, meat exports, but the relative importance of these two items is too small for their expansion of itself to have much impact on over-all export trends.

Under these conditions, a really decisive impetus to faster export growth in Central America could come only from further expansion of cotton exports or from significant advances in the conquest of new markets and the development of new and secondary exports. As regards cotton exports, their spectacular growth was the major factor behind the exceptional performance of Central American exports in 1962. Income from this product, however, is more likely to stabilize in the next few years than to continue its upward course, in view of the unfavorable over-all demand-supply situation in the world market and the competition from synthetics. This is what has been assumed in column A of Table 6-29, which shows cotton exports rising at an average annual rate of 8.9 per cent in 1962-67 but undergoing no change in 1963-67. A further large increase in Central American cotton exports in 1963-67, which is embodied in the "high" alternative projection appearing in column C, would easily lift the rate of growth of Central American exports to 5 per cent a year in the next few years. Such increased dependence on cotton exports, however (and presumably on the Japanese market which alone could absorb them), would leave Central America in a precarious position over the longer run unless significant headway is made at the same time in diversifying the area's over-all export pattern by developing minor exports, such as shrimp, soluble coffee, copper, lead, zinc, and simple manufactures (in addition to wood and meat products). The need for such export diversification would, of course, appear all the more pressing if the "low" projection shown in column B should be accepted, since, in that alternative, which embodies in particular the assumption of a continued marked downward trend in coffee prices in the next few years, Central America's export income from major primary products would decline by about 1 per cent a year in the 1962-67 period.

PROJECTION OF THE VALUE OF CENTRAL AMERICA'S MAJOR PRIMARY PRODUCT EXPORTS IN 1967

Coffee

Exports to the United States. Total United States imports of green coffee are expected to rise only slowly. Per capita consumption of coffee is already high (more than 7 kilograms per year) and appears stable.

The income and price elasticities of the demand for coffee are rather low, and it is generally considered that United States consumption will rise only a little faster than population. As a rough approximation, a 2 per cent annual rate of increase in United States coffee consumption could be selected. In this study, an FAO projection of United States coffee imports for 1965 was adopted; this assumes an annual increase of about 2 per cent in real GNP per capita and a price elasticity of -0.29 in the demand for coffee. Assuming, further, that the income elasticity of the demand for coffee ranges between 0.25 and 0.52, the FAO estimates that United States coffee imports in 1965 will range between 1,400 and 1,490 thousand tons if coffee prices fall 30 cents below their 1958 level, and between 1,430 and 1,530 thousand tons if prices drop by 40 per cent.[1] These figures imply an annual rate of growth of 1 to 3 per cent a year in United State coffee demand and yield a range of 1,430 to 1,620 thousand tons as estimated United States coffee imports by 1967 (see Table 6–30). This appears to be in close agreement with a slightly more recent FAO estimate that by 1970–72 North American coffee consumption (that is, United States and Canada) may rise to 1,800 thousand tons if real per capita GNP rises by 2.5 per cent a year and coffee prices continue to fall.[2]

Assuming no drastic change in Central America's share of the United States coffee market, which has fluctuated around 10 per cent for an extended period, it can be estimated, on the basis of the above figures, that Central America's coffee exports to the United States, which amounted to 130,000 tons in 1961, could range between 143,000 and 162,000 tons by 1967.

Within this range, perhaps the best estimate would be based on the low income-elasticity assumption. The two alternative price assumptions yield very similar results, in view of the low price-elasticity assumption adopted at the outset.

Exports to Western Europe. Projections of Central American coffee exports to Western Europe can only be very tentative. European demand for coffee is expected to continue rising at a rapid rate. It is difficult, however, to forecast the extent to which Central American coffee will benefit, in view of the fact that the area's position in most European markets is extremely marginal. In West Germany, where Central American coffee does hold a substantial share of the market, a large element

---

[1] FAO, *La Economía Mundial del Café*, 1961. In terms of 1961 export unit values, the FAO price assumptions imply a 10 to 25 per cent decline for Central American coffee.
[2] FAO, *Agricultural Commodities—Projections for 1970* (Rome, 1962).

TABLE 6-30. Projection of Volume of Central American Coffee Exports to the United States in 1967

Item	Actual exports		Alternative projections for 1967			
			1962–67 price change			
	1960	1961	−10 per cent		−25 per cent	
			Low	High	Low	High
Total U.S. coffee imports (thousands of metric tons)	1,324	1,348	1,430	1,580	1,460	1,620
Share of Central America in U.S. market (per cent)	9	10	10	10	10	10
Volume of Central American coffee exports to U.S. (thousands of metric tons)	124	130	143	158	146	162

Note: The low and high estimates correspond to the alternative income elasticity assumptions of 0.25 and 0.52.

of uncertainty prevails regarding the potential impact of the common external tariff on coffee, the introduction of preference for EEC associated overseas states, and possible modifications in the present regime of high internal taxes on coffee.

On the basis of the above-mentioned FAO projections for 1970, which assume a 3.9 to 4.7 per cent annual increase in real per capita expenditure, a price elasticity of demand for coffee similar to that of the United States, and a somewhat greater income elasticity, EEC total coffee imports can be expected to range roughly between 720,000 and 745,000 metric tons by 1967 if coffee prices fall 30 to 40 per cent from their 1958 level (see Table 6–31, projection 1). This assumes no change in the high internal taxes on coffee that are restricting consumption in Italy, France, and West Germany. Should these taxes be abolished, the FAO calculates on the basis of 1958 imports that EEC imports might rise 43,000 tons.[3] If it can be assumed that at higher import levels the impact of the tax removal would be correspondingly greater, the application of the individual percentage increases to each of the three countries in question yields total EEC import estimates of approximately 780,000 to 805,000 tons for 1967 in the event internal coffee taxes are removed (see Table 6–31, projection 2).

How much of this can be expected to be supplied by Central America will depend almost entirely on what happens in the German market. West Germany currently accounts for roughly one-third of total EEC coffee imports. This is likely to remain approximately unchanged in the

[3] FAO, *Boletín Mensual de Economía y Estadística Agrícolas,* September, 1960.

next few years if all three major coffee markets in the EEC (France, Germany, and Italy) expand at about the same rate between 1962 and 1967 (or, which is more probable, if the Italian market expands somewhat more and the French somewhat less rapidly than the German). On this basis it can be expected that in 1967 West German coffee imports will amount to 240,000 to 248,000 tons if internal taxes are maintained, and 260,000 to 268,000 tons if they are removed. A drop in Central America's share of this market should probably be expected when the full margin of EEC tariff preference is established in favor of associated African producers (by 1966). The anticipated level of the common external tariff (9.6 per cent) might possibly not be high enough per se to offset German preference for the milder Central American coffees over the African ones. However, it must be noted that at present West Germany imposes a high specific duty on coffee. This has the effect of discriminating in favor of higher-quality coffee, for the ad valorem equivalent of this duty is 25 to 50 per cent, depending on the price of the coffee. The adoption of the common external tariff, which is ad

TABLE 6–31. Projection of Volume of Central American Coffee Exports to Western Europe in 1967

(Thousands of metric tons)

Item	Actual exports 1960	1961	Alternative projections for 1967			
			(1)		(2)	
Total EEC coffee imports	617	658	720–745		780–805	
West German coffee imports	197	212	240–248		260–268	
Coffee imports of other EEC countries	420	446	480–497		520–537	
Central American coffee exports to:			(1A)	(1B)	(2A)	(2B)
West Germany	86	78	49	73	53	79
Other EEC countries	25	24	24	24	26	26
Rest of Western Europe	11	10	20	20	20	20
Total Central American Coffee exports to Western Europe	122	112	93	117	99	125

Note: The ranges given for total coffee imports by the EEC countries correspond to the alternative assumption of 3.9 and 4.7 per cent annual increases in real per capita expenditure. The two alternative price assumptions yield very similar results and have therefore not been listed separately. Additional assumptions for projection of Central American coffee exports to the EEC:

EEC internal coffee taxes are maintained and (1A) Central America's share of the West German market drops to 20 per cent; (1B) Central America's share of the West German market drops to 30 per cent.

EEC internal coffee taxes are removed and (2A) Central America's share of the West German market drops to 20 per cent; (2B) Central America's share of the West German market drops to 30 per cent.

valorem, would eliminate this bias, from which Central American coffee has undoubtedly benefited so far at the expense of the cheaper African grades. The removal of internal taxes would have somewhat the same effect, since they are also large and specific, hence weigh more heavily on the lower-priced coffees.

Assuming a drop in Central America's share in the German market from about 40 to only 30 per cent would yield projections of about 73,000 and 79,000 tons as coffee sales to this market in 1967 under our alternative internal tax assumptions (see Table 6–31, projections 1B and 2B). This would represent no major change from current levels and would merely imply that producers outside of Central America would get all the benefit from the anticipated growth of the German market between now and 1967. Conceivably, however, the implementation of the EEC policies affecting coffee might push the share of Central American coffee in the German market down to the 20 per cent level that prevails in countries like Austria and Switzerland. In this case, the projected exports of Central American coffee to West Germany would only be roughly 49,000 or 53,000 tons, which would imply a sharp drop from current levels (see Table 6–31, projections 1A and 2A).

Elsewhere in the EEC area, where Central America supplies only about 5 per cent of total coffee imports, EEC developments are not likely to have much practical impact. In Italy, preferential treatment of the African associated states is expected to work somewhat to the detriment of Latin American coffee producers, but the brunt of the burden is expected to be felt by Brazilian coffee, whose quality is most directly in competition with Africa. In France, tariff preference for African coffee will actually be lessened by the move to the external common tariff, which will be significantly lower than the present duties on Latin American coffee; but this will have little effect in view of the fact that coffee imports from outside the associated states are severely restricted by quotas anyway. For these reasons, it is assumed that Central American coffee imports to the EEC outside of Germany will remain about 5 per cent of total imports and show virtually no change from their current 24,000 to 25,000 ton level.

Outside of the EEC, Central American coffee exports are very small. They doubled from 5,000 to 10,000 tons in 1955–61 and can perhaps be expected to double again to 20,000 tons by 1967, since coffee consumption is also rising rapidly in the rest of Western Europe.

Total Exports. To sum up (see Table 6–32), in terms of volume the projected range for Central American coffee exports in 1967 is wide: 250,000 to 290,000 metric tons if it is assumed that Central America

TABLE 6-32. Summary of Projection of Central American Unroasted Coffee Exports in 1967

Item	Actual exports			Alternative projections for 1967		
	1960	1961	1962*	Low	High	Preferred
Volume (thousands of metric tons)						
Exports to United States	124	130		146	158	146
Exports to Western Europe	122	112		93	125	117
Total exports	253	251	279	250	290	270
Export unit value (dollars per ton)	915	840	740	630[a]	755[b]	755
Value (millions of dollars)	232	211	206	160[a]	220	205

[a] Assuming a 25 per cent decline in prices in 1962–67.
[b] Assuming a 10 per cent decline in prices in 1962–67.

Note: The figures projected for 1967 are for exports outside the Central American Common Market area. The 1960–62 figures given here include intraregional trade in unroasted coffee; the value of this trade was less than $1 million in each of these years.

finds no new major market for its coffee outside of Europe and the United States in the next few years. Within this range, the best single estimate is probably one based on the low assumption for the United States (income elasticity of demand 0.25) and for Western Europe, on the assumption that EEC internal taxes on coffee are maintained but Central America's share in the West German market does not drop below 30 per cent from its present 40 per cent level. This means total exports would reach about 270,000 tons, which represents no major change from present levels and agrees rather closely with the size of the basic quota assigned to the five Central American countries together in the new International Coffee Agreement.[4] On the basis of present production levels in Central America—300,000 tons in the 1961/62 crop year and 325,000 tons forecast for 1962/63—a 270,000-ton export level implies that if attempts are not made to slow the growth of coffee production in some of the Central American producers, the area may be faced with a substantial accumulation of stocks by 1967.

The selection of a price assumption, which has had relatively little impact on the volume projections, becomes crucial when coming to estimate the total value of Central American coffee exports in 1967. A drop in coffee prices by 30 to 40 per cent of their 1958 level—that is, a decline of about 10 to 25 per cent of the 1961 export unit value of Central American coffee—has been incorporated in the volume estimates. The assumption of some continuing decline in coffee prices appears fairly reasonable, since the current situation of overproduction is expected to prevail throughout the world for several more years merely as a result of the plantings undertaken in the mid-1950's before the break in coffee prices. On the other hand, the new coffee agreement should help stabilize prices, but in the immediate future it may be handicapped by the size of the present accumulated coffee stocks. It is difficult, therefore, to determine whether the lower or the higher of the percentage of price reductions that were considered above should be used in computing the value of Central American coffee exports in 1967. Since the price of most types of coffees (excluding African robustas) dropped 5 to 10 per cent in 1962, the assumption of a 10 per cent fall from 1961 would imply virtually no further change by 1967. The alternative hypothesis of a 25 per cent fall in price in 1962–67 would leave room for substantial further price drops after 1962 (at an annual rate of 3 to 3.5 per cent).

Under the more favorable assumptions, there would be no further declines in coffee prices after 1962, and the volume of coffee exports

---

[4] 266,000 metric tons.

would expand to 290,000 tons by 1967. In that case, coffee export receipts would rise to $220 million between now and 1967 (see again Table 6-32). In the eventuality of continued price declines, on the other hand, and of a 250,000-ton export volume, the value of coffee export receipts in Central America would drop sharply in the next few years. But perhaps the best estimate at this time is that by 1967 the price of coffee will have stabilized at about the present level and that the volume of Central American coffee exports will approximate the size of the region's present quota under the new International Coffee Agreement. This would imply an export volume of 270,000 tons, a unit value of something like $755 per ton, and no change in total coffee export receipts over 1962.

Bananas

Export Volume. The general outlook for Central American banana exports depends basically on demand in the major importing countries. A review of these markets suggests that their expansion is not likely to be of such magnitude as to exceed the region's export capability. As the supply in any one year, however, may be greatly affected by disease or poor weather, the estimate of 1967 exports should be considered rather as an attainable average for 1967-68.[5]

Both the United States and Canadian markets, which offer the largest outlets for Central American bananas, have been for some time saturated in terms of per capita consumption. As there is no indication of a change in this situation in the near future, total banana imports in 1967 have been assumed to increase only in response to the growth of population; that is, by an average annual rate of 2 per cent (see Table 6-33). Assuming further that Central America continues to supply the same proportion of these imports, exports to the United States and Canada would also increase 2 per cent a year to 835,000 metric tons by 1967.

Guatemala and Honduras, and to a lesser extent Costa Rica, have also found an outlet for their bananas in Europe. Within the European Economic Community, the French and Italian markets are virtually closed to Latin American bananas and are supplied solely by the African countries associated with the EEC. In view of the 20 per cent tariff to be imposed on banana imports from third countries by 1967, the Benelux market may also be expected to rely increasingly on the African suppliers. West Germany, however, is allowed a duty-free quota for import from third

---

[5] It has also been assumed that while Guatemalan banana production may continue to be relatively depressed, increased production elsewhere will permit the total regional production to increase by the amount projected here.

TABLE 6–33. Projected Trend in Volume of Banana Imports from Central America in Major Markets in 1962–1967

Market	Per capita consumption of bananas in 1961 (kilos)	Projected rate of population increase (per cent)	Projected annual rate of increase of banana imports from Central America in 1962–67 (per cent)
United States	10.1	1.7	⎧ 2.0
Canada	9.0	2.6	⎩
West Germany	8.4	1.3	1.0
Netherlands	5.9	1.2	—
Norway	7.6	0.9	⎧ 4.0
Sweden	5.1	6.6	⎩

Sources: Per capita banana consumption: OAS Group to Prepare a Plan for Action Concerning Banana Exports, *Working Paper* (UP/G.27/6/Add.), January, 1963. Projected rate of population increase: *UN Demographic Yearbook for 1961.*

countries and, as per capita consumption is still rising, there remains room for Latin American exports to Germany to continue. Nevertheless, the restrictive effects of the quota arrangement will undoubtedly be reflected in a relative deterioration of the Latin American export position; as presently calculated, the quota for 1967 is lower than that for 1961. Consequently, although German banana imports have been estimated to rise by between 2.4 and 4 per cent a year in the next few years,[6] Central American exports to Germany are projected to increase by only 1 per cent annually through 1967 (see again Table 6–33).

Aside from occasional exports of small quantities of bananas to other countries, the remainder of Central American banana exports go to Norway and Sweden. Central American exports to this area might be assumed to maintain, but not expand substantially, their share of a market in which per capita consumption remains constant; that is, on the basis of the relatively low rate of population increase in these countries and a decline in per capita consumption of bananas in Sweden between 1955 and 1960,[7] they would rise by only 1 per cent a year. On the other hand, current per capita consumption of bananas is lower than in most other European countries and the United States; and, should the decline noted recently in Sweden have been attributable to temporary factors no longer relevant, imports might increase considerably faster than population in the next few years. A more plausible assumption

[6] See OAS, *The Impact of Trade Restrictions in Europe on the Banana Producing Countries* (Doc. UP/G.27/12, 18 March 1963).

[7] U.S. Department of Agriculture, Foreign Agricultural Service, "Bananas" (FAS—M—128), April, 1962.

would therefore be an increase of 4 per cent a year in Central American exports to these countries. No new important markets are anticipated in these projections of 1967 exports, although Denmark and Japan are two specific possibilities.

Unit Value. While export unit values vary among the Central American republics, depending on the proportions of different varieties of bananas exported, they have shown a similar tendency to decline during the 1950's. Given the saturation of per capita demand in the largest market and the competition of African suppliers for the European market, a rising price is not anticipated in the next few years. Neither does any substantial further price decline appear likely at this time. Central American production is well established; its markets are fairly well defined and its exports closely controlled by a few companies. Although the volume of exports fluctuates widely from year to year, it is doubtful that present United States market prospects will inspire increases in acreage planted to bananas substantial enough to cause a glut. However, if several of the newly independent African nations, encouraged by their prospects in the expanding European market, launch overoptimistic production programs, an over-all excess of supply could force world banana prices still lower. For the present projections, three alternative assumptions have been made regarding the unit value of Central American banana exports in 1967. They are: stability; a 10 per cent decline from the 1961 level; and a 10 per cent increase in export unit value over its 1961 level.

Total Value of Exports. On the basis of the export volume estimates for each major market (derived from Table 6–33), a projected value of banana exports in 1967 is derived for each of the three alternative price assumptions (see Table 6–34). The preferred projection, embodying the

TABLE 6–34. Summary of Projection of Central American Banana Exports in 1967

Item	Annual exports			Alternative projections in 1967		
	1960	1961	1962	Preferred	Low	High
Volume (thousands of metric tons)	833	821	736	910	910	910
Unit value (dollars per ton)	83	86	87	86	77	95
Value (millions of dollars)	69	71	64	78	70	86

Note: The figures projected for 1967 are for exports outside the Central American Common Market area. The 1960–62 figures given here include intraregional trade, whose value was about $1 million in each year.

assumption of price stability, suggests that banana export receipts may rise slightly between now and 1967, and the high estimate based on a price increase shows a more substantial improvement. On the other hand, the low estimate, based on a 10 per cent drop in unit value, implies no change in total value over 1960–61, despite rising export volumes.

Cotton

Exportable Supply. Cotton is a relatively new crop in Central America. Compared with 1948–52, Central American cotton production has grown almost tenfold as a result of a quadrupling of the land area under cultivation and a near doubling of yields per hectare (see Table 6–35). Though yields are now among the highest in the world, they could still rise, and the implementation of various irrigation projects in the major producing countries will tend to increase both the volume and stability of annual output (otherwise subjected to the vagaries of weather conditions). Whether or not the area under cotton cultivation will continue to increase through 1967, however, depends to a large extent on the trend of prices in the world market. As a working hypothesis, it can be assumed that prices will either remain the same or drop only moderately from their present levels. In the long run, cotton prices, which have fallen by more than one-third since their 1950/51 peak, should continue to suffer from the growing competition of synthetic fibers. But drastic declines are not expected, for a substantial widening of the price differentials with synthetics would induce a shift of demand back to cotton.[8]

If prices stabilize at their present level, which have stimulated the most recent spurt in output, Central American cotton acreage can probably be expected to expand by another 25 per cent or so between now and 1967 (see Table 6–35, projection B). A decline in price on the world market, on the other hand, would undoubtedly inhibit such growth, but acreage might remain about unchanged (see Table 6–35, projection A) as long as the price decline was moderate.

In El Salvador, where cotton acreage rose sharply in 1961/62, some cutbacks have been anticipated in the 1962/63 season, and a somewhat lower level of plantings might continue to prevail in subsequent years if prices fall. However, if prices are maintained and markets are available, there is little reason to believe that cotton plantings in a few years' time will be substantially below 80,000 hectares. On the other hand, presumably only rising cotton prices could induce a further extension of the

---

[8] FAO, *Agricultural Commodities—Projections for 1970*, p. II–72.

TABLE 6-35. Central American Cotton Production Statistics, 1955–1963,[a] and Projections for 1967

Country	1948–52 (average)	1954/55	1955/56	1956/57	1957/58	1958/59	1959/60	1960/61	1961/62	1962/63[b]	1966/67 projection[c] (A)	(B)
Production											*(Thousands of metric tons)*	
El Salvador	8	20	30	32	36	39	30	40	56	61	63	72
Guatemala	2	9	10	10	14	16	14	21	31	54	54	72
Honduras	—	—	1	1	3	4	1	1	4	6		
Nicaragua	8	44	35	42	48	47	28	33	55	61	68	90
Total	18	73	76	85	101	106	73	95	146	182	185	234
Area											*(Thousands of hectares)*	
El Salvador	21	30	46	38	40	53	38	51	81		70	80
Guatemala	5	16	21	13	18	28	18	26	46		60	80
Honduras	1	2	2	5	10	8	2	2	...			
Nicaragua	21	86	87	70	61	74	67	61	77		75	100
Total	48	134	156	126	129	163	125	140	204[c]		205	260
Yield											*(Kilos per hectare)*	
El Salvador	360	685	665	834	891	732	786	789	696		900	
Guatemala	300	562	449	772	785	583	791	794	690		900	
Honduras	290	300	390	270	380	440	780	770	...			
Nicaragua	380	511	400	602	778	630	423	534	700		900	
Average	375	545	487	675	785	650	585	680	695[c]		900	
Central America											*(Indices: 1954/55 = 100)*	(A) (B)
Production	25	100	104	116	138	145	100	130	200	249	253	320
Area	36	100	116	94	96	122	93	104	152[c]		153	194
Yield	69	100	89	124	144	119	107	125	128[c]		165	

... Less than 500 tons.
[a] Crop years ending in August.
[b] Estimated on the basis of ginnings within season.
[c] Excluding Honduras.

Note: Projection (B) assumes no drop in price from 1962 level. Projection (A) assumes prices decline up to 10 per cent from 1962 level.

Sources: International Cotton Advisory Committee, *Cotton—World Statistics*, and FAO, *Production Yearbook*.

area devoted to that crop from its 1961/62 high, in view of the over-all shortage of land resources.

There is no shortage of land in Guatemala and Nicaragua, and the governments in both countries are currently making intensive efforts to stimulate cotton production by providing irrigation, roads, and credits as well as technical assistance to cotton farmers. In Guatemala, cotton acreage, which rose from 26,000 hectares in 1960/61 to 46,000 hectares in the following year, has probably reached 60,000 to 65,000 hectares in the 1962/63 crop year. In the light of these increases, it might even be conservative to forecast 80,000 hectares under cotton cultivation in Guatemala by 1967 under the assumption of stable world prices. Falling prices might restrain net increases in planted area after 1962/63, with the bulk of the government effort being devoted to the retirement of less productive lands and their replacement by irrigated or otherwise more suitable plots. In Nicaragua, where cotton cultivation was depressed for several years in a row by bad weather, unfavorable world prices, and credit shortages, the firming world price situation has reportedly induced sharply increased plantings in the past two years. By 1967, cotton acreage might have increased substantially beyond its record extension of the mid-1950's if prices stabilize; but presumably no further gains could be expected in the event of a price decline.

Central American cotton yields, as mentioned above, are among the highest in the world. However, government efforts to introduce irrigation, more advanced cultivation techniques, and better varieties of cotton are likely to result in still higher yield levels in the next few years. Though in Nicaragua yields have lagged behind those of El Salvador and Guatemala in most recent years, the intensity of the effort now reportedly being made in this area may enable it to catch up with the rest of Central America. It is therefore assumed that by 1967 yields will rise everywhere to 900 kilos per hectare, a result which was already achieved by El Salvador during the 1957/58 crop and should therefore not be beyond the reach of any producing country in the region.

On the basis of these assumptions, cotton output in the three major Central American producing countries in 1966/67 can be projected at 185,000 to 234,000 tons, depending on whether prices fall or stabilize between now and then. The size of the allowance that should be made for Honduras depends on whether or not that country can be expected within the next few years to develop cotton cultivation beyond its present small scale. Assuming that it does not, the present projections yield a range of about 190,000 to 240,000 tons for total Central American cotton production by 1967.

How much of this output will be available for export depends on the trend of local consumption. Central American consumption of raw cotton has more or less doubled between 1957 and 1962 to a level of about 15,000 tons a year. The evolution of the textile industry in Central America will determine how fast this growth can continue in the next few years. There is considerable scope for import substitution in the industry. According to a special study by the International Cotton Advisory Committee, however, total fiber consumption in Central America is expected to rise to only about 35,000 tons by 1965 and 44,000 tons by 1970.[9] This would imply that local consumption of raw cotton is not likely to do more than double between now and 1967 to approximately 30,000 tons. Under these circumstances exportable production would amount to 160,000 to 210,000 tons on the basis of our production estimates. Under either price hypothesis, the 1967 figure could thus show a substantial increase over the export volumes of 90,000 tons in 1961 and 135,000 tons in 1962 (see Table 6–36).

World Demand. It is very difficult to say whether demand will be sufficient to absorb such a large volume of exports from Central America in 1967. World demand for cotton is expected to rise only slowly: perhaps at an annual rate of 1 per cent a year in Western Europe and 2 or 2.5 per cent a year in Japan.[10] It might not even rise that fast, in view of the competition from synthetic fibers. On the whole, it seems reasonable to assume that between now and 1967 there will be little change in the level of Central American exports to its traditional markets in Western Europe, where the textile industry is to some extent a depressed sector. This means exports to Western Europe would remain in the 20,000–40,000-ton range, where they have fluctuated in the past three or four years. The crucial question, however, will concern the evolution of the Japanese textile industry, for if its growth is checked as a result of restrictive development in world trade for manufactured cotton textiles, Central America is not likely to find adequate markets for the rising cotton output that has been projected here. On the assumption that Japanese demand for cotton is maintained at high levels, on the other hand, and that Central America continues to improve its relative position on that market, exports to Japan could continue to rise as rapidly as they have in the past. Only this, together with the opening up of new markets elsewhere in the world, could sustain the growth of Central American cotton production at the levels the region will be capable of

[9] International Cotton Advisory Committee, *Prospective Trends in Consumption of Textile Fibers* (Washington, March, 1962) (Doc. 10B XXI), p. 74.
[10] FAO, *Agricultural Commodities—Projections for 1970*, p. III–71.

in the next few years. If this assumption is not acceptable, it should probably be expected that at best exports to Japan can be maintained at their present rate of 60,000 to 70,000 tons, and total exports of cotton at little more than 100,000 tons; in other words, there would be no further expansion (see again Table 6–36).

Value of Exports. The 1967 value projections corresponding to these different sets of alternatives are summarized in Table 6–36. The low projection corresponds to the most pessimistic assumption of virtual stagnation in world demand for Central American cotton and assumes a return of export unit value to its 1959 low. If this should occur, the high cotton export receipts of 1962 would appear as a temporary departure from an otherwise stagnant trend in the value of cotton exports after 1961. The high projection, on the other hand, assumes that the buoyant price situation which has induced the record crops of 1961/62 and 1962/63 will continue to prevail and that demand for cotton will be high, particularly in Japan. Under that hypothesis, Central American cotton export earnings could rise very rapidly in the next few years and top by 35 per cent their 1962 record. Perhaps the most prudent single estimate, however, should be based on the assumption that export unit value will fall somewhat from present levels and that, though markets will be available for Central American cotton in Japan and elsewhere, demand will not be so high as to stimulate much further increases in production after 1962/63. In that case, Central American cotton export receipts can be expected to remain at their present high level, but the next few years would be a period of consolidation rather than one of further advances.

TABLE 6–36. Summary of Projection of Central American Raw Cotton Exports in 1967

	Actual exports			Alternative projection for 1967		
	1960	1961	1962*	Low	High	Preferred
Volume of exports (thousands of metric tons)	68	90	152	100	210	160
Export unit value (dollars per ton)	545	565	560	500	550	525
Total value of exports (millions of dollars)	37	51	85	50	115	85

Note: The figures projected for 1967 are for exports outside the Central American Common Market area. The 1960–62 figures given here include intraregional trade in raw cotton, but the value of this trade was less than $1 million in each year.

Wood

The prospects for increased exports of wood products from Central America are encouraging, but the rate of growth of these exports is likely to be held back by the high demand for wood for local consumption[11] as well as by the diminishing accessibility of coniferous timbers, for which foreign demand is greatest. The wood-processing industry is in the first stages of development and will require considerable planning and investment for expansion. Thus, although the resource is plentiful and demand in the Latin American and Caribbean markets is expected to grow rapidly,[12] the extent to which exports increase during the next five years will depend largely on deliberate government action in that direction.

El Salvador possesses limited quantities of a variety of woods, which it exports to other Central American republics. Costa Rica and Guatemala have considerable resources as yet unexploited. Wood exports from these two countries declined from 1955 to 1959 but increased in 1960 and 1961, although remaining below the levels exported in 1955. Assuming that road construction will permit access to some forest areas previously unexploited and that some technological improvements will take place during the next five years, the volume of wood exports from Costa Rica and Guatemala is assumed to recover the levels of 1955 by 1967. A recent study by FAO and ECLA points out that Honduras, the only major producer of sawn wood in the region, was operating its sawmills at full capacity in 1959 and is unlikely to be able to maintain this peak level in the near future. Nevertheless, Honduras offers the most optimistic

[11] Per capita consumption of sawn wood in Central America exceeds that of all other Latin American countries except Brazil and increased 70 per cent between 1948–51 and 1956–59, faster than in any other subregion of Latin America. Per capita consumption of timber in logs is also among the highest in Latin America, and wood continues to be an important form of fuel through Central America. Boards and sheets of wood are new products to the area, produced only in Guatemala and not yet widely available. Consumption demand for wood in Central America, British Honduras, and Panama has been projected for 1970 in United Nations, ECLA/FAO, *Tendencias y Perspectivas de los Productos Forestales en América Latina* (Santiago de Chile, 1962). The data are as follows:

	1956–59 Actual consumption	1970 Estimated consumption
	(Thousands of cubic meters)	
Sawn	910	1,430
Logs	610	780
Firewood	15,000	18,200
Boards, sheets	14	82

[12] FAO, *Agricultural Commodities—Projections for 1970.*

outlook for wood exports of the Central American countries; numerous studies attest to this potential, and plans have been drafted for a major industrial project destined to speed up the development of the country's forest resources and expand production of both sawn wood and more elaborated products based on this raw material.[13] Assuming that this or a similar project is implemented in the next few years, Honduran wood exports can presumably be expected to continue increasing over the peak levels of 1959–60, although at a much slower rate (5 per cent a year) than that attained in the period 1945–59 (25 per cent +), due to the difficulty of constructing new co-ordinated facilities in a short period of time and to the possible effects of past overextraction in a country where forest resources, although extensive, are already largely (74 per cent)[14] in use.

Nicaragua shares the problem of uneconomic exploitation of forest resources. On the basis of overextraction in the recent past, the FAO/ECLA study mentioned above predicts a decline in wood exports from Nicaragua in the 1960's. The slightly more optimistic viewpoint has been adopted here that the volume of wood exports will be maintained at the average level of 1955–60 through 1967. This presupposes some increase in investment to open new forest areas, as those now accessible are fully in use.

On the assumption that prices will not change, the value of wood exports outside the integration area is estimated at about $15 million in 1967 (see Table 6–37).

Meat

Meat is one of the most promising newer export products of the Central American republics.[15] The market for these exports is at present almost exclusively the United States, with occasional small shipments to South America. As the Central Americans are low-cost producers of this product, there is a good possibility that certain varieties of frozen meats may be sent in the future to Europe and to Japan. But even for the present, the market appears to be ample and the export situation to depend primarily on conditions of supply.

El Salvador has little opportunity to take advantage of this ready market, as pasture land is already fully used. The other four countries

---

[13] ECLA, *El Desarrollo Económico de Honduras,* 1960.
[14] ECLA/FAO, *Tendencias y Perspectivas.*
[15] "Meat" includes beef, veal, pork, and poultry, fresh, chilled, or frozen. As exports outside Central America consist predominantly of beef and veal, the projections are based on estimates of the growth of exports of those products.

TABLE 6–37. Summary of Projection of Central American Wood Exports in 1967

Item	Actual exports 1960	1961	Projection for 1967
Volume			
Nicaragua (millions of board feet)	35.8	27.1	36
Other four countries (thousands of metric tons)	174.4	160.7	233
Unit value			
Nicaragua (dollars per board foot)	0.10	0.11	0.10
Other four countries (dollars per ton)	48.8	48.4	48.5
Value (millions of dollars)	11.47	10.68	15.00

Note: Intraregional exports of wood are excluded both from the 1967 projection and from the 1960–61 figures.

are exporters of meat outside the region, however. With the completion of its first packing plant at the end of 1961, Guatemala increased its prospects for higher meat exports. The outlook is even more favorable in Costa Rica, Honduras, and Nicaragua, where the interest in expansion is prompting the import of pedigreed breeding cattle and extension of pasturage, as well as the construction of new slaughterhouse and packing facilities. Assuming that the recent fall in Costa Rican exports, due to the inability to import Nicaraguan cattle, will be remedied in the next year or two, meat exports from the region may be expected to continue to show a vigorous rate of increase through the 1962–67 period.

The estimates of 1967 beef exports are based on certain rough statistical relationships found to prevail in Central America in recent years concerning the rate of slaughter and average meat content per animal. The size of herd, which in 1961 varied between 1 and 1.6 million head in each of the five countries, is assumed to increase by 4 per cent a year through 1967, the rate of slaughter to rise slightly from the 8 to 10 per cent level of 1960–61 to 11 to 13 per cent in 1967–68, and consumption to increase 4 per cent annually. Although the conditions governing the livestock industry vary among the several countries, projections on an individual basis differ little in result from those obtained by treating the region as a whole. The results for beef exports are summarized in Table 6–38.

Assuming that total meat exports will change in the same proportion, the estimated volume of exports in 1967 is about 40,000 tons. Aside from the crude method of arriving at this figure, the possibility of attaining an export volume of such a magnitude, which implies an annual rate of increase of close to 20 per cent, depends primarily on careful planning of the expansion necessary and on the extent to which domestic consump-

TABLE 6-38. Projected Volume of Central American Exports of Beef in 1967

Item	Actual exports 1960–61 (average)	Projections for 1967–68 (average)
Size of herd (number of heads)	5,600,000	7,100,000
Number of heads slaughtered	570,000[a]	860,000
Consumption (number of heads)	465,000[a]	590,000
Exports (number of heads)	105,000	270,000
Average meat content per animal exported (kg.)	130[b]	140
Volume of beef exports (metric tons)	13,600	37,800

[a] Somewhat higher than usual as a proportion of total slaughter, as Guatemala did not yet have packing facilities in operation, so almost the total slaughter was attributed to consumption.

[b] A weighted average, based on 1960–61 estimates of the volume of exports and estimated boneless equivalent meat content of 92 kg. in Honduras and 135 kg. in Costa Rica, Guatemala, and Nicaragua.

Note: Intraregional exports of meat are excluded both from the projections and the actual figures.

Sources: Size of herd, slaughter, and consumption from: Costa Rica: Banco Central de Costa Rica, *Informe Anual*. Guatemala: Banco de Guatemala, *Boletín Estadístico*. Honduras: United Nations, *Análisis y Proyecciones del Desarrollo Económico, XI: El Desarrollo Económico de Honduras* (E/CN.12/549). Nicaragua: Dirección General de Estadística y Censos *Boletín de Estadísticas;* and FAO, *Production Yearbook, 1961*. Also: ECLA, *La Ganadería en América Latina* (E/CN.12/620), 1961.

tion increases. Demand conditions appear to be highly favorable. A United Nations (FAO) study points out that on the basis of a high and a low income-growth assumption for the economies of Western Europe and the United States, the demand of these countries for meat in 1970 could either absorb all of the estimated world supply at that time or fall slightly short of supply.[16] In the latter case, as the demand for meat is highly elastic with respect to price as well as to income, a moderate price decline would easily clear the market. In either case the outlook for Central American meat exporters is favorable; as relatively low-cost producers of chilled and frozen meats, they may be able to sell at a lower price and also to more distant markets, should their present advantage of proximity to the United States market not be sufficient to absorb increasing supplies in the future.

On the assumption of constant prices (of 1960–61), an export volume of 40,000 tons of meat in 1967–68 would bring in export receipts of $25 million (see Table 6–39).

[16] FAO, *Agricultural Commodities—Projections for 1970.*

Sugar

Central American exports of sugar are directed primarily to the United States market as regulated by the quota system for United States imports of that commodity. Under the present legislation, effective until December 31, 1964, the basic annual quota allocated to the five Central American countries taken together is 72,600 tons. As of early 1963, allocations under the global quota for that year and additional amounts prorated in proportion to the basic quotas or awarded as a result of supply deficiencies in other producing countries totaled 43,300 tons, so that Central America's total allowance for export to the United States during the year reached nearly 116,000 tons and was likely to be increased still further before the end of the year.

A substantial part of this amount corresponds to the reallocation of the Cuban quota. A major assumption in estimating Central America's probable United States quota in 1967 is, therefore, that Cuba will continue to be excluded from the United States market. In addition, it is assumed that while neither total United States sugar consumption nor the share of imports in total consumption is likely to rise considerably, some increase in Central America's allotment is politically feasible as well as consistent with the production conditions in the countries themselves. The 1963 import allocation so far is only moderately higher than actual exports in 1962. On the basis of these assumptions, the 1967 allocation is estimated at 145,000 tons, with the increase expected to accrue largely to El Salvador (which needs a larger foreign market, now that Honduras has become self-sufficient in sugar) and to a lesser extent to Nicaragua, the largest of the Central American sugar exporters.

This is an optimistic estimate, dependent on the assumption that Central American sugar production will continue to show the vigorous in-

TABLE 6-39. Summary of Projection of Central American Meat Exports in 1967

Item	Actual exports 1960	1961*	Projection for 1967
Volume (thousands of metric tons)	13.8	14.2	40.0
Unit value (dollars per ton)	618	638	628
Value (millions of dollars)	8.5	9.1	25.0

Note: Intraregional meat exports are excluded from both the 1967 projection and the 1960-61 figures.

crease which followed the announcement of the 1960 quotas, at which time El Salvador and Guatemala obtained an import allotment for the first time. As stocks are currently low and prices very high, large increases in production are indicated in the next year or two; after that both the volume exported and the destination will depend on the rate at which domestic consumption rises and on the course of prices from their present peaks. Assuming that domestic consumption rises slowly relative to production, the surplus available for export may allow some additional quantities for sale above the United States import quota. Only a small increase in total exports to 155,000 tons is estimated here, although sales on the world market could increase at the expense of sales to the United States if the United States price premium should vanish for any extended period.

The future course of sugar prices is extremely difficult to predict. Historically the United States price has exceeded the world price of sugar by a considerable margin. As mentioned in the analysis of recent trends in sugar exports appearing in the first part of this chapter, the current sugar legislation provides for the elimination of this premium on all sugar imported under the global quota and for its gradual reduction on sugar imported under the individual country's basic quotas; but the import levy system through which this was to be achieved has been temporarily suspended because of the present perturbations in the world sugar market. However, the extraordinarily rapid rise of the world price for sugar in 1963 is attributed to temporary factors, such as the effects of a severe winter on the European beet crop and production cutbacks in some Latin American exporting countries where heavy stock had accumulated. These factors suggest a future decline in price under conditions of expanding supply.

Furthermore, additional sugar-beet acreage is being planned in Europe, and the European Economic Community is expected to be fully self-sufficient in sugar by 1965. Assuming that the world price will have declined from its present peak by 1967, although remaining above the average of the last five years, it should again be below the United States price. If this does occur and the United States renews its policy of reducing the United States market price premium through import fees, the United States price paid to the exporter may be expected to drop below the 1961-62 level. This is what has been assumed here. For the purposes of this projection, the United States price is assumed to have declined 20 per cent below the 1961 level by 1967, and the unit value of exports on the world market is arbitrarily estimated at 3.60 cents per pound, about 25 per cent higher than in 1960.

Under these assumptions, the projected value of Central American sugar exports in 1967 would be $14 million (see Table 6–40).

Cocoa

Costa Rican productivity is low. Cocoa plants are mostly old, and cultivation is done on a small scale by farmers reluctant to adopt modern techniques. Overcoming this resistance could reportedly lead to considerable increases in yields within a very short time (two to three years) and would both improve the quality and stabilize the volume of the Costa Rican cocoa crop. Barring such a development, however, there is no reason to expect substantial increases in the level of Costa Rican cocoa production in the next few years.

TABLE 6–40. Summary of Projection of Central American Sugar Exports in 1967

Item	Actual exports			U.S. quota for 1963	Projection for 1967	
	1960	1961*	1962*			
Volume (thousands of metric tons)	58.9	69.0	101.0	115.9	Exports to U.S.	145.0
					Other	10.0
Unit value (U.S. cents per pound)	4.54	5.23	5.32		Exports to U.S.	4.15
					Other	3.60
Value (millions of dollars)	5.9	8.0	11.8			14.0

Note: Intraregional trade in raw sugar has been excluded from both the 1967 projection and the 1960–62 actual export figures.

Under these circumstances, Costa Rican cocoa exports should not be much affected by the forthcoming International Cocoa Agreement. Whether or not Costa Rica finally comes under the denomination of small producers (for which there will be no export quotas) depends on the selection of 2,000 tons or 10,000 tons annual export maximum as the criterion. But even if the former limit is selected and Costa Rica must be subjected to an export quota, this quota is likely to be ample, in view of the fact that it would apply only to exports of "bulk" cocoa and that one-quarter of Costa Rican exports would be exempt as "fine." Preliminary calculations indicate that, should Costa Rica not be given small-producer status, its basic quota for bulk cocoa is likely to be set at 9,000 to 10,000 tons. Adding fine cocoa exports of about 3,000 tons to this figure, it appears that Costa Rica would be allowed an annual export level of 12,000 to 13,000 tons, which would be quite adequate at the present production rates.

On the demand side, the maintenance of Costa Rican cocoa exports at a level of about 12,000 tons a year merely implies that present markets remain available. There is no reason why this should not be so. United States imports of Costa Rican cocoa have been rather stable in recent years. Prospects are not particularly bright in the Colombian market, but Japanese purchases may grow in importance. The discrimination to be established by the EEC in favor of African suppliers should have little direct impact on Costa Rican exports, in view of the very marginal nature of the European market.

As far as cocoa prices are concerned, they should begin to stabilize, particularly with the help of the minimum price mechanisms contemplated by the draft Cocoa Agreement. While no minimum price has been negotiated yet, there are indications that the price levels that have prevailed in 1962 are considered low by both consuming and producing countries. We can therefore expect that in the next few years prices will at worse be no lower and probably slightly higher. On the assumption that for Costa Rica by 1967 the unit value of cocoa exports is at about its 1960–61 levels, we have a value projection of $5.5 million to $6 million for 12,000 tons, or a little less if export volume should fail to rise even that much from its present depressed level (see Table 6–41).

TABLE 6–41. Summary of Projection of Costa Rican Cocoa Exports in 1967

Item	Actual exports			Projection for 1967
	1960	1961	1962*	
Volume (thousands of metric tons)	11.8	10.2	8.8	12.0
Unit value (dollars per ton)	495	467	523	465–500
Value (million dollars)	5.9	4.8	4.6	5.5–6.0

Note: The 1967 projection is for exports outside the Central American Common Market. The 1960–62 figures may include insignificant amounts of intraregional exports.

CHAPTER 7

PRINCIPAL CHARACTERISTICS AND DEVELOPMENT OF THE CENTRAL AMERICAN PRODUCTIVE STRUCTURE

STRUCTURE OF THE PRODUCTION OF GOODS AND SERVICES

Structure of the Output by Major Sectors of Economic Activity

In order to evaluate properly the range of Central American economic diversification, it must be considered both in global terms—with a view toward appraising the general features of the structural development—and in its more important details, among which those relating to industrialization and foreign trade are especially outstanding.

The purpose of this section is to shed some light on recent trends in current production of goods and services as represented by major sectors of economic activity, with the focus on the changes that have occurred in the sectoral composition of output during the last decade. Variations in the productive structure are, of course, the consequence of the different rates of growth in the several sectors; hence, the analysis will also be extended to the varying progress of sectoral growth and the changing pattern of the forces that determine it.[1]

The most prominent characteristic of the combined productive structure of the five Central American countries lies in the fact that the sector of primary activities, which as early as 1950 was somewhat below half

[1] The problems of the manufacturing structure will be discussed in the two following sections, and the composition of imports, another important indicator of structural changes, will be examined in Chapter 8.

the total product, had dropped by 1960 to levels below 40 per cent [2] (see Table 7-1). It should be noted that the relative position of this sector—which almost entirely represents the agricultural and livestock sector, since the importance of fisheries [3] and mining is small—is slightly outstripped by the position of the tertiary group, consisting of services of all kinds.

When the principal structural characteristics of historic Central America are compared with those of the Central American Isthmus as a whole, it is noted that the proportions do not differ substantially, although the inclusion of Panama, with its special situation resulting from the Canal Zone economy, increases the relative importance of services to some extent and at the same time slightly lowers the position of the primary activities.[4]

With respect to the relative importance of the primary sector of the economy, the highest is found in Honduras, the only country where such activities represented more than half of the total at the beginning of the decade and where they are still not much below that level (see Table 7-2). The lowest proportion for these activities is in Panama, where they account for only one-fourth of output, while in El Salvador, Costa Rica, and Nicaragua they exceed one-third and are almost that high in Guatemala.

On the other hand, the share of the tertiary sector is relatively higher in the output of Panama, although it is likewise marked in the products of Costa Rica and Guatemala.

---

[2] It is appropriate to observe that because of various statistical problems relating to both the national macroeconomic estimates used in the calculations and the effort to consolidate the pertinent data for the entire area, the figures in the table may be regarded only as approximations. Nonetheless, there are reasons to think—and a certain internal consistency of the figures seems to confirm this—that the margins of error are not so great as to distort the essential features of the present structure, and still less the long-range trends shown during the ten years in question. Aside from this, the statistical aspects first mentioned will not be commented upon except in global terms or to point out the reservations that must be kept in mind in interpreting them, and only the latter aspects—with respect to the development time has brought—will be analyzed in greater detail.

[3] According to recent preliminary studies, the prospects of the fishery sector look quite encouraging for the area and apparently will make possible a marked increase in exports in this line as well as an increased domestic supply.

[4] Furthermore, this latter effect is also the consequence of the fact that the agriculture of Panama has no export component of as much importance as those of the other states of the area, and that agricultural output for domestic consumption is usually lower, in terms of value, than that of production for export. While in a number of countries of the Isthmus the share of the export component is around half of the agricultural output, in Panama it is one-third.

TABLE 7-1. Central American Isthmus: Structure of the Combined Output of the Countries of the Area, Excluding and Including Panama, by Sectors of Economic Activity, 1950, 1955, and 1960

(Percentages of the gross domestic product)

Sectors	Central America (historic)[a]			Central American Isthmus[b]		
	1950	1955	1960	1950	1955	1960
Agriculture, stock raising, forestry, hunting, fisheries	45.3	41.9	36.3	42.1	39.9	34.1
Mining (including quarrying)	1.4	1.2	1.2	1.3	1.1	1.1
Subtotal (I): Primary sector	46.7	43.1	37.5	43.4	41.0	35.2
Manufacturing industry	11.7	12.3	14.3	11.5	11.8	13.4
Construction	4.0	4.5	4.2	3.9	4.4	4.5
Electric power, gas, and water	0.5	0.7	0.9	0.7	0.8	1.1
Subtotal (II): Secondary sector	16.2	17.5	19.4	16.1	17.0	19.0
(I+II): Sectors producing goods	62.9	60.6	56.9	59.5	57.1	54.2
Transportation and communications	4.3	4.5	5.2	4.4	4.5	5.2
Commerce	12.2	13.3	12.8	12.0	13.1	12.7
Banking and insurance	2.0	2.3	2.5	2.1	2.3	2.5
Government	5.6	7.6	8.0	5.8	6.6	6.8
Personal services	7.5	7.3	8.6	10.1	10.0	11.6
Income from property	5.4	4.3	5.8	4.8	4.7	6.0
Other services	0.1	0.1	0.2	1.3	0.8	1.0
Subtotal (III): Tertiary sector	37.1	39.4	43.1	40.5	42.0	45.8
Total: Gross Domestic Product	100.0	100.0	100.0	100.0	100.0	100.0

[a] Includes Costa Rica, El Salvador, Guatemala, Honduras, and Nicaragua.
[b] In addition to countries named in Note a, also includes Panama.

Sources: The computations shown in the table were based on figures in the following publications and reports: United Nations, *Yearbook of National Accounts Statistics*, 1957, 1961; United Nations, ECLA, *Boletín Económico de América Latina, Suplemento Estadístico*, 1960, 1961, 1962; *Desarrollo Económico y Social de El Salvador, Desarrollo Económico y Social de Guatemala, Desarrollo Económico y Social de Honduras, Desarrollo Económico y Social de Nicaragua*, and *Desarrollo Económico y Social de Panamá*, reports submitted by the respective Governments to the Inter-American Economic and Social Council in October, 1962 (Docs. Nos. 25, 33, 30, 31, and 22); U.S. Department of Commerce, *Investment in Central America* (1956); direct information from the Central Reserve Bank of El Salvador; the basic data referring to the Guatemalan productive structure for 1950 were estimated on the basis of fragmentary reports, and those for 1955, on the basis of the 1956 productive structure.

In the computations an effort was made to make certain adjustments in the basic figures, mainly for the purpose of eliminating or lessening the conceptual differences that exist in the matter of sectoral classification. For example, it was endeavored to transfer the product of state enterprises, including public utilities and nationalized banking, to the appropriate lines of economic activity; in doing this, recourse was taken to fragmentary information and, in the absence of better indicators, to estimates

(Continued)

TABLE 7-1. (*Continued*)

by analogy. For El Salvador the figures used were for 1959 instead of 1960, since the data prepared by ECLA for that series come up only to 1959, although on the other hand they go back to 1950 and also include 1955. Although the Salvadorean figures on the output of the construction and manufacturing industries and agriculture in 1959 were slightly adjusted in the sense that they indicate the data of the new national series, it is possible that, even so, the proportion shown for construction—which was slightly decreased in the process of the adjustment—may still be somewhat high with respect to the real situation. Constant values were then found for all the amounts, and finally they were converted into dollars of 1950 in order to add them together for the entire area; in making the conversion the method described in ECLA, *Boletín Económico de América Latina* (1956, No. I–2), was used. Possible deficiencies in the parities used may have had some influence on the weighted value, but there are reasons to believe that the proportions in the consolidated structure have not been distorted to any major degree, since the probable errors of weighting have tended to compensate themselves between the more developed and the less developed countries of the area.

With respect to the recent position of the secondary activities, the figures given seem to indicate coefficients for the six countries that range between 15 and 22 per cent. These figures, however, require certain qualifications. The national data used in preparing this table do not refer to identical variants of the concept of gross national product, and this fact particularly affects the relative position of industry. Following the necessary adjustments, the range of variation of these national coefficients is restricted to a spread between 15 and 19 per cent. At the same time, after such adjustments the shares of the manufacturing sector vary only between 10 and 13.5 per cent.[5]

A study of the development that has taken place by sectors reveals a marked decline in the rate of growth in the agricultural sector, which

[5] Although the original data available for Costa Rica, Honduras, and Panama give the output "at factor cost," the data for the other countries give it "at market prices"; that is, they include indirect taxes which are levied mostly on manufactured goods, although they also affect certain tertiary activities. In order to obtain the adjusted sectoral percentages mentioned above, an effort has been made on the basis of the partial information available, especially in the case of El Salvador, to convert the national data that indicated the output "at market prices" to figures that would represent it "at factor cost." This procedure means that the relative position of some sectors decreases as a result of the elimination of the net indirect tax, while the share of the other increases. In the cases considered, the relative position of the entire tertiary sector has scarcely varied, since the decreases in some of its subdivisions—transportation and commerce—were offset by automatic increases in the share of other components of the group. On the other hand, the proportion of the secondary sector, and particularly of the manufacturing industry in the total, decreased, and agriculture's proportion increased by about the same amount. But increases in the share of the agricultural sector are less significant if they are viewed in the light of the earlier shares of this sector, which were characterized by quite high figures.

TABLE 7-2. Central American Isthmus: Structure of the Product, by Major Sectors of Economic Activity of the Six Countries of the Area, Separately, 1950 and 1960[a]

(Percentages of the gross domestic product)

Sector	Costa Rica 1950	Costa Rica 1960	El Salvador 1950	El Salvador 1959	Guatemala 1950	Guatemala 1960	Honduras 1950	Honduras 1960	Nicaragua 1950	Nicaragua 1960	Panama 1950	Panama 1960
Agriculture, stock raising, forestry, hunting, fisheries	45.2	35.8	43.4	37.9	41.2	31.1	55.1	44.1	45.4	37.6	26.9	24.3
Entire primary sector	45.9	36.3	44.1	38.3	42.9	32.8	56.5	45.1	47.8	39.3	27.4	25.0
Manufacturing industry	10.7	11.0	11.4	14.9	14.9	17.3	8.1	12.0	10.1	12.3	10.4	9.6
Entire secondary sector	14.6	15.0	17.1	22.2	19.6	22.2	12.2	16.0	13.2	17.4	15.4	16.9
Tertiary sector	39.5	48.7	38.8	39.5	37.5	45.0	31.3	38.9	39.0	43.3	57.2	58.1
Gross domestic product (Total of the three sectors)	100.0	100.0	100.0	100.0	100.0	100.0	100.0	100.0	100.0	100.0	100.0	100.0

[a] 1950 and 1959 for El Salvador.

Sources: The publications and data mentioned in the reference note and the methodology of Table 7–1. Although the figures cannot be regarded as precise within one decimal point, the decimal points were kept in order not to increase the possibilities of error by rounding the relatively small quantities.

dropped from more than 3.5 per cent per year during the first five years to little more than 1 or 0.5 per cent during the second five years, chiefly because of the less than favorable development of the world market for the area's principal export products (see Table 7–3).

Meanwhile, the growth of the manufacturing sector, with an annual rate of increase of around 6.5 per cent, followed a more or less even course throughout the decade, at least in historic Central America. Since Panama's industrial development was less vigorous during the first five years, the inclusion of its figures somewhat lowers the coefficient for the first period and does not much increase it for the second period.

It is appropriate to point out that the expansion in the secondary sector

TABLE 7–3. Central American Isthmus: Growth Rate of the Various Sectors of Economic Activity in the Consolidated Gross Product of the Area, Excluding and Including Panama, 1950–1955, 1955–1960, and 1950–1960

(*Cumulative annual rates of growth*)

Sector	Central America (historic)			Central American Isthmus		
	1950–55	1955–60	1950–60	1950–55	1955–60	1950–60
Agriculture, stock raising, forestry, hunting, fisheries	3.7	0.6	2.1	4.0	0.8	2.4
Mining (including quarrying)[a]	2.3	2.4	2.3	2.7	3.3	3.0
Subtotal (I): Primary sector	3.7	0.6	2.1	3.9	0.9	2.5
Manufacturing industry	6.3	6.7	6.5	5.7	6.8	6.2
Construction	8.0	2.0	5.0	7.7	4.4	6.0
Electric power, gas, water	8.8	13.3	11.0	7.6	11.0	9.3
Subtotal (II): Secondary sector	6.8	5.8	6.3	6.2	6.4	6.3
Goods-producing segments (I–II)	4.5	2.2	3.4	4.6	2.6	3.6
Transport and communications	6.1	6.5	6.3	5.7	7.0	6.4
Commerce	7.2	2.8	4.9	6.7	3.4	5.5
Banking and insurance	8.1	5.4	6.7	7.3	6.2	6.8
Government	8.3	4.6	6.4	8.1	4.8	6.4
Personal services	4.9	6.8	5.9	4.7	7.2	6.0
Income from property	5.0	9.7	7.3	4.8	9.2	7.0
Other services	14.9[b]	14.3[b]	14.6[b]	−3.9	8.9	2.3
Subtotal (III): Tertiary sector	6.6	5.4	6.0	5.8	5.9	5.9
Total: Gross Domestic Product	5.3	3.5	4.4	5.1	4.1	4.6

[a] Since the share of mining was estimated in some cases on the basis of somewhat uncertain indicators and since small amounts are concerned, it may be that the rates of growth shown are not very exact.

[b] These rates are very high, owing to the fact that they have been computed on the basis of small initial quantities; furthermore, this item refers only to Costa Rica and represents the residual that could not be incorporated into the other sectors.

Source: The basic data indicated in the footnote to Table 7–1 were used.

as a whole was not very different from that shown by manufacturing industry, its most important component. The discrepancies noted are due to the recent less dynamic progress in construction, brought about by the weak growth of total income. The favorable growth rate in the power sector, of 11 and approximately 9.5 per cent, excluding and including Panama, respectively, had little influence on the development of the entire secondary sector, because its weight in the total product is only 1 per cent.

As for the expansion of the tertiary activities, wherein the growth rate was slightly higher during the first five-year period than even the rate shown by manufacturing industry, it is sufficient for the moment to note that during the second five years some of the impetus was lost.

In short, the total growth rate of the Central American economies, both with and without Panama, declined from almost 5.5 per cent per year in the first period to 3.5 per cent in the second, thus giving a growth rate of 4.5 per cent for the entire decade.

With reference to total output, it may be noted that the highest 10-year increase—between 5 and 6 per cent per year—corresponds to Costa Rica, Panama, and Nicaragua, while the lowest occurred in Honduras, where development was at a standstill during the first five years (see Table 7–4). With regard to any increases in the per capita output, attention is called to the fact that the extraordinary population increase in Central America has largely neutralized the effects of the economic expansion. Thus, for the Isthmus as a whole, there was an annual per capita increment of 1.4 per cent in the ten-year period, and for the area without including Panama, 1.2 per cent. For the last five years in particular, it is noted that the rates declined to 0.8 and 0.3 per cent, respectively, having dropped to a negative figure for Nicaragua and remained almost stationary for Costa Rica. Panama was the only country that showed a relatively favorable growth in its per capita product during this second period.

Before attempting to interpret the changes that have taken place in the composition of the Central American output and to evaluate their significance, it is interesting to compare the percentage changes shown in this area with the analogous development of productive structures at the world level. To do this, data for 51 countries [6]—omitting the Central

---

[6] The analysis covers the economic structure of practically all those countries whose output by sectors is given in the latest edition (1961) of the United Nations *Statistical Yearbook,* the chief exception being the countries that have centrally planned economies, since their special characteristics and the fact that they use different macroeconomic concepts preclude comparability of their data.

TABLE 7-4. Central American Isthmus: Growth Rate of the Total Product and Per Capita Growth Rate for the Six Countries of the Area, 1950–1955, 1955–1960, and 1950–1960

(Cumulative annual growth rates)

Country	Annual growth of total product			Annual per capita growth of the product		
	1950–55	1955–60	1950–60	1950–55	1955–60	1950–60
Costa Rica	7.4	4.5	6.0	3.8	0.2	2.0
El Salvador	4.5	3.1	3.8	1.6	1.2	1.4
Guatemala	4.9	4.0	4.4	1.7	0.9	1.3
Honduras	2.3	4.5	3.4	−1.1	0.7	−0.3
Nicaragua	9.3	1.0	5.1	6.4	−2.6	1.8
Panama	4.0	6.8	5.4	1.2	4.2	2.1
Central America (historic)	5.3	3.5	4.4	2.2	0.3	1.2
Central American Isthmus	5.1	4.1	4.6	2.0	0.8	1.4

Sources: The basic data mentioned in the footnote to Table 7–2 were used, as well as the publication of the Inter-American Statistical Institute entitled *América en Cifras, 1960, Estadísticas Demográficas.*

American nations—were classified in seven categories, corresponding to four successive stages of industrial development, and in each category the countries were subdivided into large ones and small ones, except for the very earliest stage.[7]

If what happened in the rest of the world is compared with the changes that took place in the productive structure of Central America, certain interesting conclusions become apparent, despite the limitations of the data. In the first two stages of economic development (categories A and B in Table 7–5), the tertiary sector tends to increase more rapidly than the other two sectors of the economy and even more rapidly than the primary sector.[8] The explanation of this phenomenon is fairly clear. While from its very beginning economic and social development promotes an increase in and diversification of requirements, it is not indispensable that a large part of the goods so required be produced locally, for, at least to the extent of the capacity to import, they can be purchased abroad. However, this solution is scarcely feasible with respect to serv-

[7] For this particular phase of economic development, data have been found for only one populous country, Nigeria, the other nations included in this group having less than 15 million inhabitants.

[8] Actually, this table only shows what the world trend was during the last decade. However, other available figures seem to indicate that similar trends also prevailed in preceding periods. For example, see Colin Clark, *The Conditions of Economic Progress* (London, 1940), or Simon Kuznets, *Aspectos Cuantitativos del Desarrollo Económico* (Mexico, 1959).

ices, and therefore a greater increase in tertiary activities is almost inevitable in this phase of development. An accompanying circumstance is found in the different investment requirements. While the national production of a large part of the new industrial articles, together with the generation of electric power, presupposes relatively sizable fixed investments, this requirement is not tied to an equal extent with the expansion of various tertiary sectors such as (to give prime examples) commerce and general public administration. In turn, various services, whose development usually goes along on a par with an appreciable amount of construction or with other relatively heavy physical investments, are more likely to have the necessary funds available; this customarily occurs in the case of banking and defense. The professional services inevitably require certain investments in human capital; but if longer periods are considered rather than only a few years, the supply of such services can be relatively elastic, although often through various emergency solutions.

The tertiary sector that generally requires larger fixed investments and that frequently fails to obtain them in the first phases of development is transportation; and on top of that situation, numerous regulations frequently curb the natural development of its prices. Therefore the participation of this sector in the gross product does not usually increase much at the beginning; or, to put it in other words, it tends to increase only after a certain degree of industrialization has already been reached.

In the later stages of development—categories C and D in Table 7–5—the total share of services in the gross product does not generally increase so much. Even though it appears to gather new impetus in the highly industrialized stage, a second advance of its relative position is to be seen only in the group of large countries.[9]

As opposed to this fluctuating tendency insofar as the participation of services is concerned, the increases in the relative position of the secondary sector appear to be remarkably constant. In fact, in almost every category of countries, a 3 per cent increase in the ratio of secondary activities in the total product is seen, except for the really underdeveloped coun-

---

[9] A new expansion in the share of the tertiary sector may be attributed to various circumstances, such as, for example, the constantly improving relative remuneration for services in the developed economies and the fact that in many modern societies, flooded with not very costly physical goods, there is a certain tendency to consume increasing volumes—and improved qualities—of specific cultural, health, communications, and recreational services. However, in the case of the larger world powers, especially the United States, the decisive factor in the increased participation of the tertiary sector lies in the extremely high cost of defense.

TABLE 7-5. Central America and the World: Changes in the Structure of the 1950[a]

Sector	A. Underdeveloped countries			B. Less industrialized countries						C. Semi-industrialized countries		
	SMALL AND LARGE			I. SMALL			II. LARGE			I. SMALL		
	1950	1960	Variation	1950	1960	Variation	1950	1960	Variation	1950	1960	Variation
Primary sectors	60	52	−8	41	33	−8	53	46	−7	33	29	4
Secondary sectors	11	13	2	19	21	2	14	17	3	24	27	3
Tertiary sectors	29	35	6	40	46	6	33	37	4	43	44	1
Total	100	100		100	100		100	100		100	100	
Manufacturing sector only	6	7	1	13	15	2	10	12	2	18	20	2

[a] A population of 15 million was the standard used for classification of the countries outside Central America into two size groups. Their classification into industrial development groups was made first according to the share of the manufacturing sector in the total product, ranges of 41–26, 25–14, 13–10, and 9–3% having been set up. Then the original classification was slightly modified in those cases where other indicators of manufacturing development—primarily the per capita national product— were in marked contradiction to the sectoral share. In fact, all the categories include seven countries, except C–I, which covers nine. In cases where the source did not

tries (category A), which includes only African and some Asiatic countries, and for the group of small countries just beginning to industrialize (B–I). In these two latter cases the relative progress of the secondary sector, evidently more difficult than in the later stages, was only 2 per cent.

As for the Central American countries, their structural and various other characteristics place them in the group just mentioned (B–I), and the typical evolutionary forces for this stage do in fact appear to have predominated in the recent structural development of the Isthmus. Nevertheless, it should be noted that their per capita income and certain of their cultural features place them at a slightly higher level than the average of this B–I group.[10] Accordingly, the Central American advance in the field of secondary activities was also somewhat more rapid than

[10] The per capita income in the large countries included in Category B–II, that is, countries relatively less advanced than those of group B–I, is still lower, in average terms, a fact that is also shown by the less developed status of their productive structure.

Product of Selected Countries, Grouped According to Development and Size,

(Percentages of the gross domestic product)

C. Semi-industrialized countries			D. Highly industrialized countries						Central America					
									INCLUDING PANAMA			EXCLUDING PANAMA		
II. LARGE			I. SMALL			II. LARGE								
1950	1960	Variation	1950	1960	Variation	1950	1960	Variation	1950	1960	Variation	1950	1960	Variation
31	29	−2	19	15	−4	19	12	−7	47	37	−10	43	36	−7
23	26	3	40	43	3	39	42	3	16	19	3	16	19	3
46	45	−1	41	42	1	42	46	4	37	43	6	41	46	5
100	100		100	100		100	100		100	100		100	100	
18	20	2	31	33	2	31	33	2	12	14	2	11	13	2

give data for the initial or final reference year, the figures for a year close thereto, or the average for an earlier and later year, equally separated from the reference year, were used. An attempt has been made by the use of such averages to soften, when possible, the effects of extraordinary years. In each category the simple averages of the sectoral shares in the gross national product of each country were calculated, except for Central America, where the sectors and total product were combined for the entire area.

Sources: Table 7–1 and United Nations, *Statistical Yearbook, 1961.*

that of the group in reference.[11] Another fact that may be mentioned is that the growth of transportation in Central America does not seem to have been much below that of the entire tertiary sector, contrary to general experience in this stage of development. Nonetheless, it should be borne in mind that the rates of growth of the transportation sector shown in Table 7–3 were derived for a number of countries from somewhat precarious indicators of the increase in this item.

[11] In view of the significance of increases shown in the relative position of a specific sector, it must always be kept in mind that such increases depend not only on the expansion of the sector concerned but also on the behavior and output of the other sectors. However vigorous the growth of one component element may be, its ratio to the total will not increase if all the other components grow more rapidly. For the same reason a sector may also increase its share in the total with a modest expansion if the growth rate of all the others as a whole is less.

In less developed economies, agricultural output for domestic consumption, and particularly of production for home consumption, is normally very low.

(Footnote continued on page 330)

*Structure of the Economically Active Population
and of Productivity by Sectors*

To complete the picture of the economic structure by large sectors, attention must also be drawn to the distribution of the economically active population among the various sectors of productive activity. Since population censuses were taken in or around 1960 in only three countries of the Isthmus—El Salvador, Honduras, and Panama—recent figures are available for these three countries only, but there are figures for 1950 for all the countries of the area and for the aggregate (see Table 7–6).

It will be noted that the proportion of the population engaged regularly in agricultural activities is in all cases much higher than agriculture's share in total output (see again Tables 7–1 and 7–2). Furthermore, in no case is the population associated with this sector less than half of all the economically active population (the figures here referring to the beginning or to the end of the decade). The coefficients for Panama and Costa Rica are the only ones that do not significantly exceed 50 per cent, those of the other countries ranging around two-thirds.

The participation of the economically active population in manufacturing industry yields figures which, in all the known cases, are rather less than the figures for industry's share in the total output. The sectoral coefficients of Costa Rica, El Salvador, Guatemala, and Nicaragua vary between 11 and 12.5 per cent and those of Honduras and Panama between 6 and 8 per cent. In Central America as a whole, both including and excluding Panama, manufacturing has a coefficient of 10 per cent, while its share in the product is more than 12.5 per cent.

The percentage of population engaged in all the various services in most cases ranges between 17 and 29 per cent, except for Panama, where because of the importance of the sale of services to the Canal Zone, it reaches levels of 37 or 38 per cent, and Honduras, where the coefficient

---

Therefore, despite much greater efficiency in the agricultural component that produces for export, the average output of this sector is usually low. If in this stage of development the relative position of the agricultural sector is high, it is due above all to the small volume of production in the industrial sectors. Therefore, in such economies the relative position of the agricultural sector is not very "resistant" to the possible pressure of the other sectors. As somewhat more vigorous activities, which strictly speaking may not be very strong or very efficient, appear and begin to strengthen themselves, they gain ground relatively easily at the cost of the agricultural sector. Relatively modest industrial investments at this phase, even though possibly more difficult to carry out than larger investments at later stages, may be sufficient to increase the relative position of the secondary sector by various points, at the cost of the "soft" position of agricultural activities of low productivity.

TABLE 7-6. Central American Isthmus: Structure of the Economically Active Population in the Six Countries and in the Area as a Whole, Excluding and Including Panama, 1950–1960 (or 1961)

(Percentages of the total)

Sector	Costa Rica 1950	Costa Rica 1960	El Salvador 1950	El Salvador 1961	Guatemala 1950	Guatemala 1961	Honduras 1950	Honduras 1961	Nicaragua 1950	Nicaragua 1961	Panama 1950	Panama 1960	Central America 1950	Central America 1960[a]	Entire Isthmus[a] 1950	Entire Isthmus[a] 1960
Agriculture	54.7	...	63.1	60.2	68.2	...	83.1	65.8	67.7	...	50.6	51.1	69.1	...	67.5	...
Primary sector	54.9	...	63.4	60.3	68.4	...	83.5	66.1	68.6	...	50.8	51.2	69.4	...	67.9	...
Manufacturing industry	11.0	...	11.4	12.5	11.5	...	5.8	7.7	11.4	...	7.9	7.4	10.1	...	9.9	...
Secondary sector	15.9	...	14.4	16.9	14.3	...	7.0	9.6	14.3	...	12.2	11.0	12.8	...	12.8	...
Tertiary sector	29.2	...	22.2	22.8	17.3	...	9.5	24.3	17.1	...	37.0	37.8	17.8	...	19.4	...

[a] On the basis of data interpolated for the year 1960, in the case of the 1961 censuses. Data received from the Inter-American Statistical Institute, based on the results of the last national censuses for 1960 and 1961.

Sources: United Nations, Demographic Yearbook, 1955, for the year 1950.

for 1950 is exceptionally low.[12] The figures for the area as a whole are 18 per cent and a little over 19 per cent, excluding and including Panama, respectively. It may be deduced that the wide differences noted between the participation of the primary sector in employment and the total output are mainly compensated by the differences in the opposite direction that appear in the shares of the tertiary sector.

Such marked disproportions between the shares of the various economic sectors in output and the corresponding working population emphasize the existence of greater discrepancies in productivity, by sectors, of the labor force.[13] Even with the necessary theoretical reservations, it does not seem out of place, considering the specific conditions of Central America, to relate these phenomena in respect of relative productivity to the high degree of hidden unemployment in the area, which prevails principally in agriculture. There is special justification for this, in view of the open unemployment that appears to exist in various cities of the Isthmus, even though statistics on the matter are scattered. Furthermore, the relationship in this particular case between output and labor also reflects the great importance of coffee production in the agricultural sector of the Isthmus, since the coffee harvest gives employment to a large number of people, most of whom are employed only on a seasonal basis. This does not exclude the possibility that there is an appreciable lack of mechanization in certain other fields in this sector, in which the introduction of more modern methods would substantially increase output.[14]

A brief comparison of the relative sectoral productivities of the various countries reveals, first of all, that the differences between productivity in

---

[12] Although there may be a certain lack of preciseness in relation to the classification of the Honduran data for 1950, there is not much doubt that in terms of order of magnitude the figures approach the real situation.

[13] The term "labor force" is used in this context in a wide sense; that is, it refers to all the economically active population in the various sectors.

[14] It should be recalled that fluctuations in the terms of trade may considerably increase the relative prices of industrial goods, thus augmenting the value of the sectoral products and contributing to the differences between the respective "productivities."

In relation to the concept of the relative sectoral productivities, it should be noted that since their values are figured through the use of data on a sector's output and the labor employed in producing that output and similar data for other sectors, the resultant coefficients may accumulate statistical errors from various sources. Therefore, in this analysis they have been used only in order to compare the sectoral discrepancies within one country with the corresponding discrepancies elsewhere in the area. Likewise it must be noted that in view of the incomplete state of information on the more recent period, only the figures for the year 1950 have been used in the computations.

the agricultural and manufacturing sectors were less pronounced in the case of Costa Rica, El Salvador and Nicaragua and more marked in Guatemala, Honduras, and Panama.[15] On the other hand, with respect to productivity in agriculture and services as a whole, relatively less disproportion was found in Costa Rica, El Salvador, and Panama and more in Guatemala, Honduras, and Nicaragua. Finally, a comparison between manufacturing industry productivity and the tertiary segment shows that although the latter surpassed the former in all cases, the discrepancy was less in Costa Rica, Panama, and El Salvador and more marked in Guatemala, Honduras, and Nicaragua. A summary of the three classifications, made in groups of two, brings out the existence of a more balanced pattern of productivity in Costa Rica and El Salvador, which is obviously related to the relatively greater industrialization of these two countries. On the other hand, the relationships here commented upon do not show the industrial advance of Guatemala, despite its numerous active manufacturing enterprises in various fields. The explanation of this phenomenon is related to certain individual aspects of the country's employment structure, deriving from its ethnic characteristics and especially from the largely nonassimilated way of life of the Indian element.[16]

Finally, in view of what has been said in the preceding paragraphs, it is appropriate to comment on the significance of the continued decline of agriculture's participation in the generation of total product. This is one of the outstanding aspects of the structural transformation that is taking place, and attention should be focused on its scope from a number of angles, taking into account both its possible consequences and its causes.

On the one hand, this process may be regarded as an element of the progressive diversification of production, which is part of the structural

[15] It need scarcely be mentioned that such comparisons cannot be used as elements of judgments as to the greater or lesser absolute efficiency of any given sector in any of the countries concerned. On the other hand, the quantitative relationships may be interpreted as indications, though certainly rough and approximate ones, of the degree of distortion prevailing in the respective economies and, consequently, of the opportunities that exist to increase the total product through a better distribution of the economically active population among the various sectors.

[16] The high relative position in the industry of this country of rural craftsmen, whose productivity is low, even though coexisting with a competent factory element, tends to increase the margin between the relative productivity of industry and of service. At the same time the high proportion of a subsistence rural population, living practically outside the monetary economy, lowers the coefficient of the agricultural sector and helps to widen the differences shown between it, on the one hand, and industry and services, on the other.

transformation implicit in development and which can help to reduce vulnerability to external forces and at the same time ease internal instability. Thus, this process reflects positive factors when it is the consequence of a relatively strong development of the secondary and tertiary segments. The contribution of these sectors to a reduction of hidden unemployment, concentrated especially in the primary segment, certainly merits positive consideration.

However, since agriculture has to provide these developing economies with an increasing volume of foreign exchange resources and insure supplies for constantly increasing food and industrial raw-material requirements, concern may arise with respect to the balanced course of the diversification if—as is the case in Central America—agricultural expansion does not attain a certain minimum, and especially if its rate of growth does not exceed the population growth. One must also take into account the fact that the prevailing impulse in the industrial and service sectors of the area—which in any event is not very pronounced—has not been the only reason for the decreasing share of agriculture in its total product. In fact, in the structural change noted, a large part has been played by the very appreciably worsened situation on the world market for the products of this sector, which, despite noticeable official and private efforts to adapt the structure to the new conditions, has been unable in all cases to attain sufficient flexibility, or at least has not attained it in the short time available.[17]

MANUFACTURING STRUCTURE

Potential of Industrial Growth and its Components

Since the most dynamic element of economic development is normally the growth of manufacturing activities, the potential of development of the industrial sector decisively determines the magnitude of the major changes that are likely to occur in the composition of the total product of the entire economy during the developing stage.

This potential of manufacturing development, in turn, depends not only upon the general availability of resources for industrialization but also upon the internal and external possibilities of this sector to estab-

[17] The present version of this *Survey* will not extend to an analysis of the transformation of the Central American agricultural structure, although reference will be made to certain changes that have occurred in the composition of agricultural and livestock production in relation to certain foreign trade problems.

lish itself in new fields. Its advance toward new areas enables it to expand at a faster rate than what would apply to it if its activities were limited to their original sphere. The most important area for such expansion of the developing manufacturing sector—at any rate, the most generally employed and at times abused area—is the gradual substitution of imports, especially in the beginning stages of industrialization. However, there are also other possible fields for industrial expansion besides mere natural growth, such as judicious recourse to possibilities for export, the additional market that may result from dynamic progress in other sectors (and of the industry itself), and adequate improvement in the distribution of income.

With regard to import substitution, the manufacturing sector's growth potential depends in good measure on its ability to diversify; that is, on its capacity to provide substitutes for imports not only in the field of industries producing ordinary consumer goods—which ordinarily occurs during the first phase of industrialization—but also, if the need arises, in other manufacturing activities. In this respect it need only be recalled that certain industries, especially intermediate and mechanical ones, as a general rule require broader or more developed markets and greater productive factors, which initially are in short supply; but once established on firm and rational bases within an economy, they tend to expand in a sustained form and, through a series of reactions, to give incentive to the expansion of other industries.[18]

Industrial exports, excepting those primary products that are exported after only slight processing, are not usually very significant in the first phases of industrial development, and they have not been so in Latin America. In Central America, aside from the increasing trade among the countries of the area in recent years, such exports to the rest of the world have been practically nil. However, it looks very possible, and in fact desirable, that in the future the impetus of intra-Central American trade will also stimulate interest in the Isthmus in certain lines of manufacture, now only local, that can be exported outside the area, making use of the possible advantages that may result from the lower cost of labor, the availability of certain low-cost raw materials or materials of a specific kind, and certain other differential cost factors. In short, the need to keep open the possibility of future industrial exports, as well as

---

[18] Reference will be made later to the problem of these incentives at the interindustry level, when the elements of the potential of industrial growth are considered from the point of view of supply. For further details concerning the nature and growth of the various branches of industry in Latin America, see OAS/ECLA, *Economic & Social Survey of Latin America, 1961*, Chapter V.

other important considerations that have recently come to be gradually accepted in Latin America, may make it possible to vest Central American protectionism with a kind of selective orientation, without detracting from its effectiveness, in order not to encourage purely anti-economic activities or to distort excessively the cost-price system.

When dynamic expansion in the other sectors is thought of as a factor in the industrial growth potential, the importance of the development of the primary sectors which, in appropriate circumstances, can continue to make great contributions toward increasing income and the internal market, is worth noting. Naturally, beyond a certain point the expansion of these sectors becomes difficult and meets increasingly more rigid limitations, through decreasing returns or other progressively restrictive factors.[19] However, in a large part of the Isthmus, the development of agriculture for internal consumption, encouraged also by the continual improvement of internal transportation, still offers great possibilities for expansion that is free of such barriers.

As mentioned above, the dimensions of the growth capacity of domestic manufacturing are also related to the distribution of income. In fact, a more equitable distribution could increase the market for a great variety of articles and favor the demand for industrial products of local manufacture at the expense of imported products, which are preferred by the more affluent social classes.[20]

Although the last three courses indicated for possible manufacturing expansion do not appear to be very promising for the immediate future, which reaffirms the fact that the replacement of imports is the most important expression of present-day Central American industrialization, consideration of these elements of the industrial growth potential, especially the element of possible future exports, leads to certain judgments which perforce have their effect on an appraisal of past and future development. Keeping those in mind, the structural diversification of manufacturing production, especially when production is limited to a

---

[19] Such is the case with the possible exhaustion of mineral deposits. The situation is similar when it stems from the necessity of voluntarily limiting certain primary exports in order to protect their prices.

[20] Of course, the effect of measures taken to lead to a better distribution is also subject to limitations, and at a certain point, when the average tendency to save decreases, forces contrary to the requirements for greater investment, and hence the requirements of industrialization, may come into play. However, the state may go beyond this critical point in the gradual redistribution, without causing a major drop in savings, by taking up the difference through taxation for purposes of public investment, although it is understood that the effectiveness of this type of intervention also reaches its limits at some point by appreciably reducing the incentive of the entrepreneurial class.

certain number of more or less traditional lines, continues to be a desideratum, highly important but subject to some qualification that will place emphasis on economic efficiency.

Viewed from this angle, the recognized advantages of Central American economic integration stand out in sharp relief.

In the first place, despite the still existing limitations of the integrated market, such a step would make possible the establishment of a series of new industries which could not possibly have been established before in conformity with even a minimum of economic efficiency. Since ultimately free trade within the Isthmus should likewise afford incentive to the aggregate of the primary sector, it may be envisaged that the additional income resulting from this situation will in turn contribute to a widening of the market for industrial goods.

On the other hand, when one considers the possible impact of integration from the supply standpoint, it is evident that the future economic union will significantly expand the field within which limited resources may be pooled in order to undertake activities of greater scope.

Furthermore, beneficial effects can be expected from interindustry relations. In fact, a number of the industries contemplated under the new conditions—especially the intermediate and certain mechanical industries—are capable of exercising "forward and backward linkage effects," [21] or, in other words, of encouraging the creation of or strengthening those industries which are their potential consumers or which may be their principal suppliers. In principle, it may be considered that the greater the size of the economy thus integrated, the better will be the possibility for profitable combinations in the interindustry field, although sometimes—and this must also be kept in mind—it is not so much the size of the economy that counts in that sense but rather the inclusion of certain countries or areas in the integration, which, because of their complementary characteristics, can offer more favorable conditions for establishing such linkage.[22] The gradual complementation of the manufacturing system with interrelated industries will naturally increase the external economies of all of them.

The foreseeable effects of development under these new conditions are, of course, numerous and varied. On the one hand, it can be expected that in the case of industries that can more easily be set up and that are

[21] For the origin of this term, see A. O. Hirschman, *The Strategy of Economic Development* (New Haven, 1958), p. 100.

[22] It is appropriate to remember that the scope of these linkage effects, with all their probable ramifications, also offers certain at least partial elements of judgment for determining priorities among projects according to their social usefulness.

already more or less spread throughout the area—and in which the scales of operation are not so important—skill, and consequently operational efficiency, will increase. On the other hand, it is possible that the establishment of certain new activities that place greater demands on scales of production and limited resources may at least temporarily have the effect of strengthening the monopolistic structure of the industry. Among other effects of integration, it may be expected that the industrialization of the area on very broad bases will have a favorable impact on the present unbalanced situation of productivity among the various sectors; that is, it will alleviate the hidden unemployment situation (localized chiefly in agriculture, although to a lesser extent it is also present in some tertiary sectors), or it will at least prevent the situation from worsening in line with the population growth.

Structure and Development of the Industrial Output

The main purpose of the following analysis is to define the present stage of development of Central American manufacturing production from the standpoint of its structural evolution and to determine the intensity with which this process is currently being carried out. This part of the analysis of the structural changes will be supplemented with a brief study of the growth by lines of industry and by groups thereof and an examination of the development of production by principal manufactured articles.

Data by which the analysis can be brought up to recent years are available only with respect to the manufacture of certain selected articles, since information on the entire structural development of the manufacturing sector beyond the year 1958 is incomplete and of unacceptable quality; in fact, in a number of important aspects it is available, or usable, only up to 1955. For this latter year, the detailed manufacturing structure of Central America as a whole will first be analyzed and, with some consolidation among certain interrelated lines, the structure of the six countries of the area [23] (see Tables 7–7 and 7–8).

[23] It is appropriate to make some comments about the quality of the data used in these tables and to mention the procedures applied to compensate for some of the deficiencies. In very general terms, it would seem that the data available in this respect merit a greater degree of confidence than the macroeconomic figures given in the preceding section, since the manufacturing structures here noted are based primarily on census data (those for Panama are the result of a relatively broad survey) and, except in the case of Guatemala, little estimating is involved. Although the extrapolation of the census data has been carried out with production indices that are subject to a bias that increases with the time involved, this operation has been limited in the present case to "running" the

The lack of diversification in the transformation industries of the area is notable (see Table 7–7). In 1955, as may be seen in the table, 84 per cent of the combined manufacturing product of the integration area, both excluding and including Panama, pertained to the traditional industries, engaged almost exclusively in the production of common consumer goods and their raw materials, excluding the processing of coffee.[24] Within this industrial group, the most important subgroup consists of the preparation of food, beverages, and tobacco, representing approximately half of the total product of the sector; the food industries alone account for close to 27 per cent of the product. The industries producing textiles,

census structure forward or backward for only a few years. However, the census data themselves also suffer from various weaknesses. Along with the usual problems of evaluation, difficulties have been found especially in the matter of coverage and comparability; and although efforts have been made to clear this obstacle as far as possible, the final figures still must be regarded with reservations in some respect. With reference to coverage, an attempt was made to include the handicraft component insofar as data were available. Somewhat sketchy census data were used for El Salvador and slightly adjusted national estimates for Guatemala; coverage for Panama and Honduras, and possibly also for Nicaragua, is not so complete; and for Costa Rica the figures used in certain particular respects—structure and capital intensity—exclude repair shops. Another problem was found in the discrepancies in national censuses with regard to the inclusion of the initial processing of certain agricultural products, especially coffee. The figures on coffee processing, originally included in the census of some countries, were eliminated from the data presented in the interests of comparability and because they were apparently a major source of errors in evaluation. Finally, an attempt was made to moderate the effects of various differences of classification that affected certain interrelated lines in particular, increasing some to the detriment of others. When the data were consolidated at the inter-area level (Table 7–7), the slight deviations of some censuses from the standard classification of the other countries became less important, but in the tabulation of national data (Table 7–8) they would have continued to hinder any easy appreciation of the differences between the countries. Therefore in this table the items that appeared more susceptible to such reciprocal defects were combined among themselves. Certain interrelated items were likewise combined in the subsequent table, since it was considered that the data were not sufficiently comparable in time. All in all, the best structrual data for the area as a whole were those assembled for the year 1955, and it is these that are used in Table 7–7. Similar data for 1960 or some other recent year will be available for Panama and El Salvador possibly during the current year, since their most recent industrial censuses are in the course of being prepared or completed. In Costa Rica, Guatemala, and Nicaragua, new industrial censuses will be taken in 1964.

[24] Also included in this large manufacturing group are the lumber and furniture industries, since both are traditional and they are similar in their behavior. As for coffee processing, it may be observed that in El Salvador in 1956 it represented almost 27.5 per cent of the total value of manufactures, according to the census (which total included the processing of coffee), and a year later in Costa Rica it accounted for 12.5 per cent. It is possible that the Salvadorean figure may be somewhat overvalued.

TABLE 7-7. Central American Isthmus: Consolidated Structure of the Manufacturing Output of the Countries of the Area, Excluding and Including Panama, 1955

(Percentages of the total value added by manufacturing)

CIIU group number	Industrial groups and branches	Central America (historic)	Central American Isthmus
	Traditional industries[a]	83.8	84.0
20	Food	26.5	27.9
21	Beverages	16.4	17.6
22	Tobacco	6.0	5.9
23	Textiles	10.0	8.8
24	Footwear and clothing	17.3	16.0
25	Lumber and cork	4.1	4.1
26	Furniture and accessories	2.1	2.1
29	Hides and skins	1.4	1.6
	Intermediate industries[b]	9.3	9.7
27	Paper, cardboard, and paper products	0.2	0.2
30	Rubber products	0.5	0.4
31	Chemical products	4.3	4.0
32	Petroleum products	—	—
33	Materials made of nonmetallic minerals	4.1	4.9
34	Basically processed metals	0.2	0.2
	Mechanical industries[c]	3.4	3.1
35	Simple metal articles	0.9	0.7
36	Mechanical apparatus and accessories	0.7	0.6
37	Electrical apparatus and accessories	0.3	0.3
38	Transport material	1.5	1.5
	Residual industrial group	3.5	3.2
28	Printing and publishing	2.2	2.1
39	Miscellaneous	1.3	1.1

[a] This group consists almost exclusively of industries engaged in the production of ordinary consumer goods and the pertinent raw materials, although, because of their traditional character and similarity in growth, the lumber and wooden furniture industries are also included here.

[b] The intermediate industries are excluded from the traditional group, but they include the manufacture of certain common consumer goods, especially in certain lines of chemicals which statistically cannot be separated from the groups of intermediate goods.

[c] This group also includes the industries manufacturing simple metallurgical products and the apparatus and equipment repair shops.

Sources: For Costa Rica: General Bureau of Statistics and the Census, *II Censo de Industrias en Costa Rica, 1958*, and publications of the University of Costa Rica (Institute of Economic Research), *El Desarrollo Económico de Costa Rica No. 2, Estudio del Sector Industrial, 1959*.

El Salvador: General Bureau of Statistics and the Census, *Segundo Censo Industrial y Comercial, 1956*.

(Continued)

CENTRAL AMERICA'S PRODUCTIVE STRUCTURE   341

TABLE 7-7. (*Continued*)

Guatemala: Data of the second industrial and commercial census, on the basis of the OAS publication, *Censos y Encuestas Industriales de las Naciones Americanas* (IASI Doc. 3979 Esp.–9/15/59–2600); general results of the third industrial census, adopted from the publication of the General Bureau of Statistics of the Republic of Guatemala, *Guatemala en Cifras, 1960;* and estimates with respect to the handicraft segment of the industry, received directly from national sources and slightly adjusted by the OAS Secretariat.

Honduras: United Nations, *El Desarrollo Económico de Honduras, 1960* (E/CN.12/549)
Nicaragua: Direct information from the Central Bank of Nicaragua.
Panama: OAS (IASI), *op. cit.*

The figures used for Nicaragua are averages of the manufacturing structure in the years 1954, 1955, and 1956; this was done to reduce the effects of some fluctuations between consecutive years. For the same purpose the figures for Honduras were slightly adjusted, taking both earlier and later data into account. In the case of Guatemala, an interpolation between the data for 1953 and 1958 was made. The manufacturing structure of El Salvador, derived from its 1956 census, was weighted for the purpose of consolidating it with the manufacturing product of 1955. The data for Costa Rica for 1955 were obtained by applying the index of production given in the above-mentioned study made by the University to the census data of 1957. The data were consolidated by following the procedure and methodology indicated in the reference notes of Table 7-1.

clothing, leather, and footwear together account for almost 29 per cent of the total, with textiles alone showing 10 per cent. When the Panamanian industries are included in the computation, these last two coefficients drop slightly, to 26 and 9 per cent, respectively. In both cases lumber and wood products amount to 4 per cent and the manufacture of furniture and related products, 2 per cent.

The share of the intermediate industries—excluding those that operate principally for the traditional industries—ranges between 9 and 10 per cent, whether or not Panama is included. This figure contrasts sharply with the participation of approximately 30 per cent attained by this industrial group in the manufacturing product of all Latin America. Of course, in the Latin American structure, the data of the larger and semi-industrialized countries have much weight. In Central America about half of the intermediate group consists of the various chemical industries, especially if the rubber industry is added to them, as it is in the later tables. The production of construction materials of nonmetallic mineral origin has almost as high a share in the total; in fact a larger share, taking the Isthmus as a whole. Cement manufacture is particularly important among these activities, although it does not predominate; the manufacture of bricks, largely on a handicraft basis, and of cement and asbestos-cement products is also of some importance.

It should be noted that the importance of the intermediate industries in the Isthmus is somewhat reduced, not only because of their low volume of production but also because of their poor composition. In fact, not only is their range very incomplete, but various lines shown in this group are really complementary activities connected with other industries. A significant part of the activities classified under the chemical industry belongs more aptly to the "parachemical" industries,[25] and another not insignificant part is concerned with products made on the basis of simple formulas, with packaging, etc. The rubber industries considered here—aside from some plants that manufacture rubber products such as rubber hose, heels, soles, mats, etc.—consist in good part of tire and tube repair shops and some retread shops. In fact, the only tire factory in the region, established some years ago in Guatemala, had not yet begun to operate at the time under consideration.

Neither were there any oil refineries in the Isthmus in 1955, although one is now functioning in Panama, another in Guatemala, a third, recently installed, in El Salvador, and a fourth, likewise recently set up, in Nicaragua.[26] Furthermore, there are some minor semi-integrated iron and steel plants in Panama and El Salvador and some small plants of this kind in Costa Rica, Guatemala, and Nicaragua; but since in the reference period the two steel plants were not yet in operation and the other foundries have very small capacity, the figures shown in the table for basically processed metals are very low in value.[27]

On the other hand, most of the countries of the Isthmus, except Honduras and Costa Rica, were already producing cement in 1955, and later a cement factory was started in Honduras. Furthermore, Guatemala and El Salvador were producing paper in that year, although only in very

---

[25] Under this heading the principal activities included are those producing cleaning materials, toilet goods, candles, paints, matches, and similar items which in large part are consumer goods. See OAS/ECLA, *Economic & Social Survey of Latin America, 1961*.

[26] There is a similar project for Costa Rica and a less definitive plan for Honduras. Although the social usefulness of such dispersion might be open to argument in view of the integration of the Central American economies now under way, it should also be pointed out that the establishment of refineries in all or nearly all the countries of the area is related to the interests of large companies in the matter of distribution, and therefore these companies provide scarce resources. It is also well to note that recent innovations in operational methods have reduced the limits of the economic scales of production in this industry. However, it is debatable whether these small refineries will be able to serve in the future as a basis for additional industrial development, especially petrochemical complexes.

[27] Actually, even in a current table, no very significant coefficients would be shown for this line, since the volumes of production continue to be quite low.

small quantities; although their production has doubled since then, the volume still remains at a low level.[28] Cellulose paste is not yet produced in the area, but it may be noted in this connection that the forest resources of Central America, especially its pine forests, are an important potential source of raw material for the cellulose industry. The greatest problem facing the entire forestry industry of the area is the lack of adequate transportation.[29]

Ranking still lower in significance are the incipient mechanical industries of the Isthmus, in terms of both volume—less than 3.5 per cent of the manufacturing product, as compared with 18 per cent for all of Latin America—and composition. In fact, the most important line in this group is the "transport equipment industry," represented almost entirely by the various motor vehicle repair shops;[30] the product of this line constitutes a little more than 1.5 per cent of the total manufacturing product. Along with this, there are several industries producing relatively simple metal goods, chiefly ironware, nails, containers, and similar items.

In the fourth group, which is a residual group composed of activities difficult to classify elsewhere, the relative position of printing and publishing stands out, representing somewhat more than 2 per cent of the total manufacturing product.

The manufacturing structures of the several countries of the Isthmus do not differ much among themselves in terms of the four principal groups making up the primary subdivision of the manufacturing sector, at least not in respect to the ratios of the traditional group to total manufactures in the six countries (see Table 7–8). Despite this great similarity in regard to the importance of the traditional group as a whole, the industrial lines included in it show greater variability insofar as their relative positions are concerned. This suggests that the uniformly high

---

[28] Along with the small industries producing paper and cardboard in the two countries mentioned, the lines shown in Table 7–7 and subsequent ones also include the manufacture of paper products, such as paper bags, boxes, etc., chiefly from imported materials. This activity is developing also in Costa Rica and Panama.

[29] Furthermore, it should be noted that according to a study made by the ECLA/FAO/DOAT Advisory Group on Paper and Cellulose for Latin America, "the development of the paper and cellulose industry in these countries is closely related to development of the sawmills. Because of the nature of Central American forests, the forestry industry should be regarded as an integrated combination of activities of sawmill and pulp manufacture." (Doc. E/CN.12/570, March, 1961.)

[30] In Costa Rica a plant for the rebuilding of aircraft parts is also functioning. This is a good example of the country's gradual industrialization. Most of the plant's activity is directed toward filling orders from outside the country.

TABLE 7-8. Central American Isthmus: Structure of the Manufacturing Product of the Six Countries of the Area, by Country, 1955

(Percentages of the total value added by manufacturing)

Industrial groups and lines	Costa Rica	El Salvador[a]	Guatemala	Honduras	Nicaragua	Panama[b]
Traditional industries[c]	79.7	79.4	84.0	89.3	89.2	86.0
Food, beverages, tobacco	55.1	55.1	40.7	58.2	48.9	69.2
Textiles and clothing; leather and footwear	15.7	22.0	37.6	19.0	33.5	10.1
Lumber, wooden furniture and accessories	8.8	2.3	5.7	12.1	6.8	6.7
Intermediate industries[d]	9.6	10.2	10.2	4.8	8.0	12.5
Paper, cardboard, paper products	0.5	0.2	0.3	—	—	0.4
Chemical and rubber products	6.2	3.9	5.3	3.9	3.5	1.9
Nonmetallic mineral products	2.9	6.0	4.0	0.9	4.5	10.2
Metals, primary processing	0.0	0.1	0.6	—	0.0	—
Mechanical industries[e]	5.4	5.4	3.0	2.3	0.9	0.7
Simple metal articles	1.2	1.0	1.0	0.3	0.2	—
Mechanical and electrical apparatus	1.0	2.3	0.8	0.5	0.4	—
Transport material	3.2	2.1	1.2	1.5	0.3	—
Residual industrial group	5.3	5.0	2.8	3.6	1.9	0.8
Printing and publishing	3.9	3.0	2.3	2.6	1.8	0.8
Miscellaneous	1.4	2.0	0.5	1.0	0.1	—

[a] 1956.
[b] 1957.
[c] According to the concept indicated in footnote [a] of Table 7-7.
[d] According to the concept indicated in footnote [b] of Table 7-7.
[e] According to the concept indicated in footnote [c] of Table 7-7.
Sources: The basic data listed in the reference note to Table 7-7 were used.

ratio of the group to the national totals of the sector is due primarily to the weakness of the other three groups.[31]

As for the production of food, beverages, and tobacco, the coefficients for Guatemala and Nicaragua are somewhat less than the average for the area, and those for El Salvador, Honduras, and Costa Rica are some-

[31] It is well to point out that within the industrial branches or groups of branches shown in the table there is also a notable geographic variability which in some instances is greater than the variability between the various branches, and, as noted before, the differences in the composition of the various lines of manufacture also lead to discrepancies in the degree of industrialization of the area. This analysis of the structure does not go into such details, but the existence of differences of this type among the six industrial systems stands out on examining the volume of production of selected articles.

what higher; for Panama, very much higher. On the other hand, the relative position of the textile, clothing, leather, and footwear subgroup is relatively prominent in Guatemala and Nicaragua but very low in Panama, where at that time the textile industry was of practically no importance at all. The lumber and furniture industries have a role of some importance in Costa Rica and Honduras, although in the latter country the industry is confined almost exclusively to the primary processing of the lumber.[32]

The share of the intermediate industries is somewhat more variable; the largest is found in Panama and the least in Honduras. The manufacture of chemical and related products is most widely developed in Costa Rica and is of least significance in Panama, while the processing of materials of nonmetallic mineral origin was salient in the 1955 manufacturing structure of Panama and remains in the background in Honduras and Costa Rica.

As for the area's budding mechanical industry, the figures for Costa Rica and El Salvador stand out, relatively speaking, those for Guatemala and Honduras being less, and those for Nicaragua and Panama very low.[33]

The change in the combined manufacturing structure of historic Central America between the years 1953 and 1958 was very reduced [34] (see Table 7-9). The only change worth noting was a slight increase in the participation of the intermediate industries, at the cost of the traditional group. Much of this variation resulted from the increase shown in the industrial processing of nonmetallic minerals, under which the increase in cement manufacture is outstanding.

The rates of growth in the various manufacturing lines during the five-year period concerned (see last column of Table 7-9) confirm the structural changes noted above and at the same time reveal certain

---

[32] There are reasons to presume that in Costa Rica part of the lumber industry was not included in the census. It should be observed in this regard that lumber is a very important element in common construction in Costa Rica. According to the 1949 housing census, almost 70 per cent of urban buildings had wooden walls, as compared with 22 per cent in Honduras. In the other Central American countries the more widely used construction materials are adobe and wattle.

[33] It is possible that the very low figures for Nicaragua stem in part from the use of a more restricted basis in the primary compilation.

[34] Although the probable biases of the industrial production indices used in extrapolating part of the data may have contributed somewhat to the insignificant variations in the figures, there can really be little doubt that the slow transformation reflected therein does portray the actual situation, at least for the five-year period under consideration.

TABLE 7-9. Central America: Consolidated Structure of the Manufacturing Product of the Five Countries, 1953 and 1958; Growth by Groups and Lines of Industry, 1953-1958

(Percentages of the manufacturing product and cumulative annual growth rates)

Industrial groups and lines	Structure of the manufacturing product 1953	1958	Cumulative annual growth 1953-58
Traditional industries[a]	84.9	83.8	5.6
Food, beverages, tobacco	50.0	50.8	6.2
Textiles and clothing; leather and footwear	28.3	26.4	4.2
Lumber, wood furniture and accessories	6.6	6.6	5.7
Intermediate industries[b]	8.2	9.1	8.1
Paper, cardboard, paper products	0.2	0.2	1.0
Chemical and rubber products	4.2	4.8	9.1
Nonmetallic mineral products	3.5	3.9	7.8
Metals, primary processing	0.3	0.2	0.2
Mechanical industries[c]	3.5	3.4	5.2
Simple metal articles	0.6	0.7	7.2
Mechanical and electrical apparatus	1.1	1.1	4.2
Transport material	1.8	1.6	5.1
Residual industrial group	3.4	3.7	7.5
Printing and publishing	2.6	2.8	7.5
Miscellaneous	0.8	0.9	7.5

[a] According to the concept indicated in footnote [a] of Table 7-7.
[b] According to the concept indicated in footnote [b] of Table 7-7.
[c] According to the concept indicated in footnote [c] of Table 7-7.

Sources: The basic data listed in the reference note to Table 7-7 were used.

special features of the industrial situation of the area. The traditional industries showed a growth rate of more than 5.5 per cent per year. This progress is clearly higher than the usual normal growth of such industries, according to what has taken place in many other areas, and it suggests the possibilities for replacement that still exist in such fields. It also reflects the existence of effective incentives for both established enterprises and new investors.

The subgroup in the traditional industry field that showed the greatest relative growth was the processing of food, beverages, and tobacco, similar to the growth noted in that line in all Latin America. In fact, the cumulative annual growth of this activity was over 6 per cent, while the rate of expansion of the combined group of textiles, clothing, leather, and footwear was only slightly over 4 per cent and the combined lumber and furniture industries had a growth rate of less than 6 per cent.

The most intensive growth, more than 8 per cent, was shown by the intermediate industries. However, it must be pointed out that the dynamism of this group was far from surpassing that of the traditional group by the same proportion as occurred in the average for all Latin America. In fact, although at the Latin American regional level the relation between the intensity of expansion of the two industrial groups was 1:2.5, in Central America it was less than 1:1.5. Particularly noteworthy in the increment of the group as a whole was the expansion of its two most important lines; that is, the production of construction materials of nonmetallic mineral origin and of the combined chemical and rubber industries. In the period concerned, the latter showed a very marked quantitative growth—24 per cent—owing to the establishment of a tire factory in Guatemala, but the high coefficient is attributable in large part to the fact that the comparison is made with the very small values shown for the beginning of the period.

Recent Development in the Production of Selected Products and Per Capita Production and Consumption Levels

In order to explain somewhat the industrial development that occurred in the years immediately preceding 1958 and to point up certain details that do not fall within the over-all structural analysis, we shall now attempt to combine the above rates of growth in the various industrial branches with the coefficients of growth recorded in the manufacture of certain important products, taking into account, at the same time, other information available [35] (see Table 7–10).

Wheat flour and sugar are among the food products whose production registered the sharpest rise in the totals for the area in the period 1953–58. According to the figures available for three countries for both products, but especially for flour production, the development continued at a

---

[35] In relating such information to this subject, it should be remembered that the rates of growth considered above are derived from basic data expressed in deflated aggregate values, whereas the coefficients of growth that are going to be studied below are based on data expressing production volumes in physical terms. This may lead to certain minor discrepancies, chiefly in the variations in relative prices. Moreover, it should also be remembered that one of the determining criteria in the selection of the products being considered here was the availability of statistics on that product, in chronological order—and this condition does not necessarily coincide with the importance of the products under consideration—and that in any case the exact weights of these products in the respective production totals are unknown. In view of all these factors, the figures shown cannot be considered to be strictly representative of Central American industrial development, although they do appear to be adequate to illustrate several of the most significant aspects of that development.

TABLE 7-10. Central America: Growth in the Combined Production of Selected Industrial Products between 1953 and 1961

(Cumulative annual rates of growth)

Products	1953–58	1958–60	1958–59	1959–60	1960–61
Wheat flour[a]	14.5	23.0	12.5	33.5	...
Sugar	15.0	11.8	11.4	12.2	8.9
Beer	5.7	−4.5	−5.8	−3.2	...
Cigarettes	2.5	3.6	2.1	5.0	...
Cotton cloth[b]	6.8	18.3	8.0	29.6	...
Cement	15.5	4.0	−2.8	11.2	4.5
Electric power[c]	10.8	9.9[d]	9.9	...	...

[a] There are no data for Costa Rica, since the figures on this item are not very significant.

[b] No data available for Costa Rica and Guatemala.

[c] Concerns the total generation of electric power, including public service and generation of power by companies for their own use. These figures are given as an index of economic activity, although they also include the electricity produced for consumption.

[d] 1958/59.

Sources: Most of the data: United Nations, *Statistical Yearbook*, several numbers, and Pan American Union (IASI), *América en Cifras 1961: 3, Estadísticas Económicas—Producción Industrial*. Certain figures on El Salvador and Guatemala were obtained from national statistical publications and, with respect to El Salvador, from direct information.

healthy rate in the course of the next two years, which are the last ones covered by the information available. It should be noted that the contribution of flour production to the aggregate value of the entire item of foodstuffs is relatively small. In contrast, the contribution of the sugar industries is quite large. Moreover, isolated data show that the processing of milk products and meats, as well as of several canned food products, did not increase markedly in the five-year period under reference or in the next two years, although it was a period of continued development and was favored by the prospect of future demand. From all of this it could be concluded that the rate of growth of foodstuffs, despite the constant contribution of certain items enjoying a very dynamic expansion, did not change substantially in general in Central America between 1958 and 1960.

The increase in the production of beer—which in the five-year period was slightly less than foodstuffs, beverages, and tobacco put together—although probably somewhat higher than beverages alone, suffered a small net decrease in the two following years. The manufacture of cigarettes had been even less dynamic in the preceding period, and this trend has not changed much.[36]

The manufacture of cotton cloth, at least in the three countries covered by the pertinent series, increased at an annual rate of about 7 per cent in the period 1953–58, and in the last two years of the decade the expansion has been accelerated considerably.[37]

In contrast, the production of cement, whose marked expansion of about 15 per cent was definitely higher than that of the other building materials of nonmetallic mineral origin, appears to have lost something of its impetus in the past two years. Such a drop in its rate of growth is related, among other things, to the temporary saturation of the market in several producing countries, although a contributing factor was a simultaneous weakening of the purchasing power in certain countries of Central America.[38] Nevertheless, it should be noted that the prospect for the long-range demand for cement does not appear to be unfavorable, and therefore a new impetus in this branch of production is predicted.

The lumber industry, whose expansion in the past has continued to lag somewhat behind that of the traditional group as a whole, has recently shown signs of a certain revival of vigor. At the same time, fragmentary data indicate an even more marked dynamic trend in furniture manufacturing.

The paper industry, characterized in this area by a rather slow growth, also appears to have gained a certain impetus in recent years, although what is expanding is not the basic paper industries, but rather the processing of paper products, an activity included under this heading.

The information available on the manufacturing volume of these products also permits certain interesting comparisons to be made among the countries of Central America and between them and other areas of the world regarding their respective production levels (see Table 7–11).

Inasmuch as the comparison is made in terms of per capita production, differences in production volumes relating to the influence of the size of population tend to be eliminated. However, the effect of the expansion of areas suitable for certain crops continues to be evidenced in the

---

[36] This does not mean, of course, that this item has not had a somewhat more pronounced growth in terms of value, due to certain increases in the fiscal surcharges applied to it.

[37] In evaluating these increases, we should not lose sight of the fact that, at the same time, the cottage industries and crafts in this industrial activity grew at a slower rate.

[38] In El Salvador, the gradual exhaustion of the ore deposits at the Ajacutla plant has also caused problems, leading to the execution of a new project, soon to be installed, whose equipment will be completed later by the addition of two furnaces from the above-mentioned plant.

industrial processing of those agricultural products. Thus, at least relatively speaking, wheat milling in Guatemala, the activity of sawmills in Honduras, and the processing of sugar in Nicaragua and Costa Rica stand out. Moreover, an increase in manufacturing is apparent in the figures on El Salvador for textile manufacture and especially in the Costa Rican figures for the generation of electricity. The existence of basic paper and steel industries, although in the infant stage, indicates a keen interest in industrialization in El Salvador, Guatemala, and Panama.

A comparison of the figures of Central America or those of the entire Isthmus with those of Latin America as a whole and other areas of the world shows appreciable differences in a large number of the items considered. However, it should also be pointed out that Central American per capita production of sugar is no lower than that of the other areas considered, except Latin America; but even there the coefficients do not differ substantially if the figures for Cuba are omitted from the totals for the region. One item for which the figure for Central American production does not lag much behind Latin America—although it does with respect to the industrialized countries of the world—is the cigarette; and a product in which the Isthmus surpasses the rest of Latin America in production is lumber.

In considering also the coefficients for per capita consumption (see Table 7-12), it can be noted that for certain products of the traditional industries, such as flour and textiles (and certainly this is true also of many other products not included owing to a lack of figures), there continues to be an appreciable margin for substitution, although such margins are much broader in the intermediate industries considered here than in the regular consumer industries.[39]

Finally, both the results of the structural analysis of the Central American manufacturing industry and the rather brief survey of the per capita production and consumption of several important products show that there are still relatively broad margins for substituting imports in the traditional industries and also in the other manufacturing activities that are not very sensitive to scales of operation. Progress in this direction would probably have permitted the countries of the Isthmus to have a greater industrial growth than mere vegetative for several more years, even without integration. However, it also appears likely that the practical utilization of such margins of substitution would also quite soon—

[39] In any case, it should be remembered that a rather significant part of the difference between production and apparent consumption is covered, in the regular consumer items considered, by imports from other countries in the area. More details on this point will be given in the next chapter.

TABLE 7-11. Central America and Other Areas of the World: Per Capita Production of Selected Products, 1960

(Based on figures expressed in physical units)[a]

Countries and areas	Wheat flour	Sugar	Beer	Cigarettes	Cotton cloth	Lumber	Paper and cardboard	Cement	Steel	Electric power[a]
Costa Rica	2.6	51	8	1,023	0.7	93	—	—	0.3*	340
El Salvador	2.5	19	5	327	1.7	1	0.4	33	1.2*	93
Guatemala	13.0	20	4	616	...	10	0.2	31	0.0	67
Honduras	3.3	10	8	533	0.3	141	—	17	—	46
Nicaragua	—	48	2	557	1.4	72	—	22	—	117
Panama	—	24	20	560	...	20	—	104	9.3*	212
Central America (historical)	5.9[c]	25	5	529	1.1[d]	56	0.1[e]	25	0.4[e]	105
Central American Isthmus	5.4[c]	25	7	532	...	53	0.1	32	1.2[f]	114
Latin America	30	73[g]	17	838	2.7	28	9[h]	86[h]	26[h]	422
United States	63	14	59	2,726	9.3	257	167[b]	310	499	5,292
European Common Market	89	28	50	1,055	6.3	78	37	430	361	1,471
European Free Trade Zone	60	21	64	1,813	5.2	112	63[b]	356	256	2,499

[a] The basic data for wheat flour, sugar, cotton cloth, cement, paper products, and steel are given in kilograms; for beer, in liters; cigarettes, in units; and electric power, in kilowatt-hours.

[b] 1959.

[c] The estimate was made by using the production figures of the four producing countries, and the populations of all the nations of this area.

[d] Does not include Guatemala.

[e] Although there are actually only two producing countries, the total population of Central America was taken into account in the estimate.

[f] Although there are only three producing countries, the entire population of the Isthmus was taken into account in making the estimate.

[g] Cuba is included in this figure. If Cuban sugar production were omitted, the per capita coefficient would be 39.

[h] 1961.

Sources: For the Central American Isthmus, those indicated in Table 7-10. In addition, for wheat flour, CEPAL, *Situación de las Actividades Productoras de Trigo y la Industria Elaboradora de Trigo en Centroamérica* (Doc. E/CN.12/CEE/SC.1/78); with respect to lumber: FAO, *Yearbook of Forest Products Statistics 1961*, and ECLA/FAO, *Latin American Timber Trends and Prospects* (Santiago, 1962) (mim.); paper and cardboard: ECLA/FAO/DOAT, Doc. E/CN.12/570; steel: archives of the Economic and Social Study of Latin America 1961; and, population, Pan American Union (IASI), *América en Cifras 1961: 1, Estadísticas Demográficas*. Figures prepared for the other areas of the world: OEA/CEPAL, *Estudio Económico y Social de América Latina 1961*; in addition, with respect to electric power: CEPAL, *Estado Actual y Evolución Reciente de la Industria de la Energía Eléctrica en América Latina* (Doc. E/CN.12/560, 1961). The figures on the per capita production of electric power in Europe have been computed on the basis of United Nations figures, *Statistical Yearbook, 1961*.

TABLE 7-12. Central America and Other Areas of the World: Per Capita Apparent Consumption of Selected Products, 1960

(On the basis of figures expressed in physical units)[a]

Countries and areas	Wheat flour	Sugar	Beer	Cigarettes[b]	Cotton cloth	Lumber[c]	Paper and cardboard[d]	Cement	Raw steel[e]
Costa Rica	29.1	35	8.0	1,042	2.2	158.0	8.6	57	...
El Salvador	10.8	15	5.5	341	(3.3)*	7.5	5.0	39	...
Guatemala	13.4	19	4.5	502	...	10.0	4.5	31	...
Honduras	7.8	14	7.5	539	1.0	81.8	2.2	12	...
Nicaragua	10.2	24	2.9	569	2.5	50.0	3.2	29	...
Panama	19.3	22	19.9	576	...	23.0	9.7	114	...
Central America (historical)	13	21	5.3	536	2.0[f]	44.0	4.4	31	13
Central American Isthmus	14	22	6.6	548	...	42.0	4.9	33	...
Latin America	32	33	17	848	2.8	34.0	13	82	39
United States	61	40	59	2,612	...	274.0	134	320*	500

[a] The figures for wheat flour, sugar, cotton cloth, cement, lumber, and steel are given in kilograms; for beer, in liters; and for cigarettes, in units.
[b] The figures on imports and exports have been converted from tons to units at the rate of one million cigarettes per ton according to a method used by the IASI.
[c] In the conversion of the basic data from cubic meters to kilograms, the conversion rates used were 730 and 520 kilograms per cubic meter for standing broadleaf and evergreen timber, respectively, following a method described by the FAO in *Yearbook of Forest Products Statistics 1961*.
[d] The basic data refer to 1959.
[e] Includes the imported processed steels with their equivalents in raw steel.
[f] Does not include Guatemala.

Sources: For production and population, the same as for Table 7–11. For foreign trade for Latin America: foreign trade yearbooks of the respective countries, except with respect to paper, the source of which was ECLA/FAO/DOAT, Doc. E/CN.12/570; for steel, ECLA, Doc. E/CN.12/CEE/245; and for lumber: FAO, *Yearbook of Forest Products Statistics 1961*. With respect to the United States: United Nations, *Yearbook of International Trade Statistics 1960*.

long before the margins were exhausted—have led to increasing problems in production costs and investment incentives. An increasing protectionism, of course, would have maintained those incentives for some time, but with additional sacrifices in production costs, which would put an increasingly heavy burden on the rest of the community and be detrimental to future manufactured exports.

An attempt to compare the above-mentioned prospects of an individual industrial development in the Central American states with its potentiality for integrated industrial growth, the outlines of which are already perceptible, reveals three promising factors in the picture:

1. A review of the principal industrial plans under consideration suggests that even the partial execution of such plans will bring with it development of the new possibilities for diversification, even though such diversification is on a selective basis.[40]

2. A marked increase can also be noted in the other new enterprises and in the tendency to invest, although in this area there is also a desire to maintain a reasonable cost level.

3. Finally—with respect to the two points above—it can be expected that the rate of growth in the sector will speed up. This may occur especially as the result of an increase in the replacement of manufactured imports from other areas,[41] although the possibility of certain new exports of industrialized products outside the Isthmus is also being considered.[42]

Judging from recent experience, at least a temporary acceleration can be expected, first of all in the field of several traditional industries, such

---

[40] An instrument whose efficacy has not yet been tested is the integration industries, which are "chiefly [certain] plants that produce intermediate goods or capital that must have the whole Central American market for profitable operation" and to which are granted, by special instruments, on the condition that they meet certain requirements, special free-trade treatment for their products within the area and exemption from duties on the importation or local manufacture of the raw materials and semimanufactured products required for their operation for a period of ten years. The conditions the companies must fulfill involve the obligation to meet the standards of quality established by ICAITI (Central American Industrial Research and Technology Institute) and certain commitments regarding prices, system of distribution, and market supply. (For more details, see: ECLA, *Informe de la Octava Reunión del Comité de Cooperación Económica del Istmo Centroamericano* (Doc. E/CN.12/CCE/303 Rev. 1). Up to the present, the treatment has been applied only to the tire industry (Guatemala) and caustic soda (Nicaragua).

[41] A more systematic examination of the problem of substitution, based on an analysis of foreign trade statistics, is presented in the next chapter.

[42] Among the existing and planned industries that will include in their program possible exports even outside the integration area are those of kraft cellulose, plywood, dried-milk products, canned fruits and meats, citric concentrates, instant coffee, chocolate, essential oils, medicinal extracts, certain kinds of jewelry, etc.

as foodstuffs, textiles, lumber, etc., whose impetus is spreading to the branch of pharmaceutical products. And, according to the above-mentioned tentative plans of the integration industries, a more dynamic behavior is to be expected within a few years, particularly in the new sectors of the nontraditional groups. In this connection, mention should be made of the plans to establish an integrated paper industry, using the abundant local long-fiber raw materials; to broaden the range of the chemical industries to include the production of soda, chlorine, insecticides, fertilizers, etc.; to launch the manufacture of glass bottles and a greater variety of ceramic articles; and also to undertake, on a broader scale, the manufacture of basic metal products. Among these, consideration is being given, first of all, to the production of steel rods in larger quantities, and the manufacture of certain other nonflat goods (profile steel and wire) will also be undertaken. In addition, there is a good chance that these new manufacturing activities will soon be complemented by several machine and electrical industries, although several will be only at the assembling level. At the same time, it is expected that the operations in the new refineries will soon be normalized and that there will soon be an expansion in cement production.

Although the information available is not sufficient to permit a projection, on objective bases, of the total industrial development of the integration area with the new activities and those now expanded, it can be stated with some assurance that the execution of most of the above-mentioned projects and of some of those that are today being considered only tentatively could strengthen substantially the development of the intermediate industries in the area, and possibly also that of certain branches of the mechanical industries, thereby increasing appreciably their share of the total sector within the next 15 years.

Industrial Employment and Capital Structure;
Productivity and Capital Intensity

We shall now attempt to examine Central American industrial development from other standpoints, supplementing the study of the structural development of its products with a brief review of certain aspects of employment, productivity, and capital intensity by industrial groups and branches.

Actually, these topics deserve a much more detailed study, because a systematic clarification of such factors could help solve several problems of great importance to the area. For example, undoubtedly the abundance of labor, inadequately utilized, plus the acute shortage of capital resources would seem to call for an industrial policy that is best adapted to such a disparity in the availability of certain factors of production; that is, a policy designed to promote, through tax and other incentives, solutions in the combining of productive resources and the selecting of methods that, while consistent with the other criteria of the development planned, would be the most suitable from the standpoint of maximum joint productivity of existing resources. A course of action to that end would, in turn; presuppose a thorough knowledge of the elements involved.[43] However, the present lack of basic statistics—which are even scarcer or more deficient for employment, and especially capital, than for production—reduces the possibility of research on certain aspects of the situation, which can be only partially clarified.

This being the case, an effort will be made, above all, to ascertain the group of industrial workers for which statistical data are available and whose characteristics can be examined, and then to relate the figures for that group, from the standpoint of comparability, to those of the industrial output analyzed above and to the total economically active population in that sector. Then an attempt will be made to ascertain the over-all growth of the industrial employment in the area, examining the employment structure and linking it to productivity by groups and branches. The fixed capital structure and its intensity by groups and branches will be examined only briefly for two countries, Costa Rica and Honduras. Finally, the problem of the utilization of existing capital in industry will be surveyed.

The figures considered on employment for Costa Rica, El Salvador, Honduras, and Nicaragua apply to all the workers employed in those industrial establishments whose output was studied in preceding sections (especially p. 338). Thus, the two types of figures are, in this respect, comparable for those countries.

The case of Guatemala is different. As a matter of fact, when the characteristics of its industrial output were examined earlier, the census data referring to the manufacturing component of its industry were considered along with an estimate of its home industry sector, which had not been included in the census, while the information available on employment refers only to the "factory" sector. Therefore the figures on Guatemalan industry will be taken up separately and, in those areas

[43] The price system is not a sufficiently reliable index to the relative abundance or shortage of the various factors of production in the different sectors of the economic activity, since, especially with respect to the cost of these factors, it is subject to various effects of distortion. In this connection, it is sufficient to mention the existence of chronic unemployment, both open and hidden, in most of the countries of the Isthmus, and the disequilibrium in the productivity of the various sectors.

where it is desirable to provide a synoptic résumé for all of Central America, only the figures covering the other four countries will be combined.[44]

To interpret correctly the facts given below, it should be remembered that the figures on production and employment in the four countries mentioned are for all the industrial establishments covered by the census and include most of the handicraft sector as far as industrial employment is concerned. These figures, however, do not cover the very small handicraft industries—especially those in rural areas, which include mostly family shops—where self-employment and employment without remuneration are important.

This fact also helps to explain that, although all the workers included in the industrial censuses of the four countries totaled only about 120,000 laborers and white-collar workers, according to the figures projected to 1957,[45] their economically active population in the industrial sector, projected to the same year, totaled about 100,000 more persons. Naturally, the productivity of this additional group—which, moreover, also includes persons who were not employed during the entire year—was very low.[46]

Another point of great interest is the growth in industrial employment in the Central American countries. Unfortunately, the data available permit only a very approximate figure on the subject. Taking into account the incomplete census and other data that are relatively comparable in time, as well as the industrial employment indices of two countries—the last two, with the reservations necessary owing to their fragmentary nature—it can only be estimated that in the period 1953–57 employment in the establishments covered by the census (including that part of the handicraft industry covered by the census) grew at a rate of about 5 per cent a year. The rate of growth was higher in the manufacturing sector of Costa Rica and in the manufacturing segment of the Guatemalan industry, where it rose to about 6 per cent. However, it appears to have been somewhat lower in El Salvador and still lower in Nicaragua and Honduras.

[44] However, the presentation of the statistics on factory employment in Guatemala will be supplemented by a presentation of the output of that same industrial sector of the country to permit a comparison of these two aspects of Guatemalan industry.

[45] Of that total, 51,000 refer to El Salvador, 27,000 to Costa Rica, 22,000 to Nicaragua, and almost 20,000 to Honduras. These figures do not include the employment in coffee processing, with a total of 11,000 persons in El Salvador and 4,300 in Costa Rica; the figures for Honduras and Nicaragua are not known.

[46] Its contribution to the total value added by the manufacturing sector, which is difficult to determine, could scarcely have amounted to 15 per cent in all four countries together.

An average growth of about 5 per cent in industrial employment for the entire area, accompanied by an increase of about 6 per cent in the corresponding output, does not suggest a very rapid structural disruption to the advantage of activities requiring a smaller amount of labor. However, neither does it reveal much progress in productivity, which, as will be seen further on, is not very closely related to the intensity of capital in this area. At any rate, the total productivity in the sector—that is, in industry as a whole, including the segment not covered by the census—has registered a slight additional increase, owing to the gradual decline in the ratio of smaller handicraft establishments. As a matter of fact, there is evidence that the expansion of the latter industries was slower than that of the establishments for which figures were available. Of course, it also means a somewhat slower rate of increase in employment in the industrial sector as a whole.

An even more difficult task is to establish, through comparison, the average productivity in the Central American countries. Such an attempt necessarily is impeded by problems of methodology and information that can be solved only in part. The most serious obstacle until recently had been the lack of a rate of conversion to express in a single unit the manufacturing output of the various countries, in conformity with the price level in each of the countries, being compared. Nevertheless, using the parity figures of a very recent study, certain estimates have been made for the purpose of establishing at least certain categories of volume in this connection.[47]

According to the results of the above-mentioned approximate estimate, it appears that productivity, if the added value per worker, in terms of the purchasing power of currency, is measured, is quite similar in the industries of El Salvador, Honduras, and Nicaragua. In contrast, the average productivity of Costa Rican industry is about 50 per cent higher than that of the other countries mentioned.[48]

One of the structural aspects of industrial employment that deserves attention is the breakdown of employment by large industrial groups and branches and its relationship to the composition of the sector's output. It

[47] The parity figures for the estimates under reference were taken from an ECLA study, *A Measurement of Price Levels and the Purchasing Power of Currencies in Latin America, 1960–62* (Doc. E/CN.12/653). It should be noted that the parities used refer to the purchasing power of currencies in relation to total expenditures and not merely to the price for industrial products.

[48] It may be added, for purposes of comparison, that the average productivity of Chilean industry, in turn, appears to have been 50 per cent higher than Costa Rican—according to the most recent tentative figures—somewhat higher even than the Mexican. It is sufficient to say that such comparisons are lacking in accuracy, owing to the uncertainty of both terms and statistics.

is possible to compare roughly the employment and added value structures for the region as a whole, by countries.[49] Such a comparison brings out similarities and differences in various elements. The differences are especially apparent in the proportions represented by certain industrial branches in the two totals. Nevertheless, there are certain particularities that should be noted even in the large manufacturing groups.

Thus, the percentage of total employment represented by the mechanical industries (5.7 per cent for the four countries as a group) is definitely larger than its share of the output (3.8). This once more points up the fact that the mechanical industries of the area are operated almost exclusively on the handicraft basis, and their output per person is certainly not high.[50] It is not at all surprising that the intermediate industries, in contrast, account for a larger proportion of the aggregate value than of employment. In fact, it is surprising that the difference is not greater.[51] This situation may be partially explained by the fact that most of the intermediate industries in the area have not yet developed the characteristics of such activities in the more industrialized countries; that is, large-scale, more mechanized operation.[52]

The differences between the percentages of employment and output in the various manufacturing branches can be more easily seen from the

[49] With respect to these four countries as a whole, the figures for them being relatively comparable, the last two columns of Table 7–13 permit a comparison; but for a comparison of the various individual structures of these countries, one must also consult the figures in Table 7–8. For Guatemala, see Table 7–14.

[50] In Brazil the opposite has happened, since, according to the most recent statistics, its machine industries account for a larger proportion of the total output than of the total employment.

[51] Whereas, in the four Central American countries as a group, the productivity ratio between the traditional industries and the intermediate group is 1:1.16, in Chile it is 1:1.6, and in Mexico and Brazil, approximately 1:1.8.

[52] The fact that certain intermediate industries should be more mechanized for efficient operation than several other manufacturing activities can be used as an argument against their establishment, but certainly not an unassailable argument, since, in making such a decision, the special conditions of each economy must also be taken into account, and, in the case under consideration, those of the Central American area as a whole. In fact, the establishment of certain industries—especially basic industries intended to stimulate development in the rest of the sector—may be justified from the standpoint of their usefulness to the public, even though their establishment may temporarily increase the average degree of mechanization within the industrial whole instead of increasing to the maximum extent the absorption of labor. But in deciding in favor of industries of this type, it appears in any case to be desirable—without going into theoretical considerations here concerning the various criteria of preference and priority used in evaluating projects—to select one having the technical characteristics that, in addition to satisfying, insofar as possible, the microeconomic principle of profit-making capacity, would insure the greatest possible utilization of available resources for the economy.

CENTRAL AMERICA'S PRODUCTIVE STRUCTURE 359

standpoint of relative productivity, a summary of which gives a synoptic view of a greater number of activities (see Table 7–15).

A comparison of relative productivities [53] in the whole sector (see the first column in Table 7–15) reveals immediately that the branches having the largest production are easily the manufacture of tobacco and beverages. Since this is largely due to the high government monopoly prices and other fiscal surcharges [54] applied to these products, and possibly also to certain foreign profits that can be classed as royalties, these two branches are excluded from the more detailed comparison below, which tends rather to treat the intrinsic elements of the various productivities by branches. Moreover, neither did it seem desirable to include in this comparison the paper, rubber, and basic metal industries of the area, since their employment and output figures are too small to show any significant ratios. On the other hand, it was not necessary to eliminate the data for the first three machine industry headings entirely, although they were very small, since their homogeneity permitted them to be considered as a unit.

If we now compare the remaining 11 headings with each other and with the adjusted average for the sector (see the second column in Table 7–15), we see that they tend to group themselves into three categories. As a matter of fact, three of these branches—the textile, chemical, and nonmetallic mineral industries—stand out because of their relatively high productivity indexes. The miscellaneous industries, printing, and manufacturing of shoes and clothing have an average index, located somewhat above the adjusted average, although below the average for the whole sector. Finally, low indexes of relative productivity characterize the leather and mechanical industries (not including those for transportation equipment), which have very similar coefficients; the lumber, foodstuff, and transportation equipment industries, whose statistics are also very concentrated; and the manufacture of wood furniture and accessories.

Since productivity can be attributed somewhat to greater mechanization and more efficiency, or higher relative prices for the product,[55] it

---

[53] The relative productivity of an industrial branch is its productivity—expressed in the form of an index—with respect to the average productivity of the manufacturing sector.

[54] The basic data are given, in most cases, in terms of the added value at market prices and not of added value at factor cost, which would be more correct for the analysis used here. This is one of the examples of the statistical discrepancies that make the results of this analysis inaccurate.

[55] And, for the reasons given, as a result of the inflated prices for goods under a government monopoly.

TABLE 7-13. Central America: Manufacturing Output and Employment of Four Countries, Total and by Country, 1955 and Other Years near 1955

(Percentages of total industrial employment)[a]

Industrial groups and branches	Employment								Central America (without Guatemala)[b]	
	Costa Rica		El Salvador 1956	Honduras		Nicaragua 1953			Structure of industrial employment 1955	Structure of industrial output 1955
	1953[c]	1957		1953	1957					
I. Traditional industries	(78.3)	77.3	83.4	83.0	82.8	86.7			82.6	83.6
Foodstuffs[d]		41.8	46.6	21.5	27.1	56.0			43.9	27.5
Beverages		3.3	2.9	8.0	6.3	3.5			3.7	20.0
Tobacco		1.1	0.8	1.1	1.0	0.8			0.9	6.6
Textiles		5.0	8.4	3.6	1.3	3.8			5.6	8.0
Clothing		14.8	19.8	14.1	12.9	12.2			16.4	13.8
Lumber and cork		5.2	1.1	31.6	31.1	6.2			7.7	4.9
Furniture and accessories		4.5	2.3	1.5	2.4	1.5			2.6	1.6
Hides and leather		1.6	1.5	1.6	0.7	2.7			1.8	1.2
II. Intermediate industries	(8.4)	8.5	7.6	5.1	7.5	6.6			7.4	8.7
Paper, cardboard, and paper products		0.6	0.2	—	—	—			0.3	0.2
Rubber products		0.9	0.3	0.0	0.0	0.2			0.3	0.6
Chemical products		3.9	2.3	2.3	4.9	3.3			3.0	3.8
Petroleum derivatives		3.1	4.7	2.8	2.6	3.1			3.7	4.1
Basic metals		0.0	0.1	—	—	0.0			0.0	0.0

III. Mechanical industries	(7.0)	8.7	5.2	8.1	6.4	2.3	5.7	3.8
Simple metal products		1.3	1.6	1.0	0.4	0.6	1.2	0.7
Mechanical equipment and accessories		1.1	1.3	2.7	0.3	0.8	1.2	0.9
Electrical equipment and accessories		0.7	0.4	1.3	0.3	0.2	0.5	0.3
Transportation equipment		5.6	1.9	3.1	5.4	0.7	2.8	1.8
IV. Residual industrial group	(6.3)	5.5	3.8	3.8	3.3	4.4	4.3	4.0
Print shops and publishing houses		3.8	2.0	1.1	0.4	2.4	2.0	1.8
Miscellaneous		1.7	1.8	2.7	2.9	2.0	2.3	2.2
Total	100.0	100.0	100.0	100.0	100.0	100.0	100.0	100.0

[a] The figures in the last column of the table, as indicated in the heading, do not represent employment percentages but percentages of the total added value of the industrial sector.

[b] Figures for the employment structure in the factory segment of the Guatemalan manufacturing sector that are not sufficiently comparable with the figures contained here are given in Table 7–14.

[c] The figures for the Costa Rican manufacturing structure in 1953 are estimates based on the industrial employment recorded by the 1957 census, projected in accordance with the ratio of the industrial employment structures of 1957 to that of 1952 in the aforementioned study of the University of Costa Rica. It was necessary to use this procedure owing to various inconsistencies between the employment structure recorded in the 1957 census and that reported, for the same year, in the study. In that connection, account was taken of the fact that the final preparation of the figures in the census came after those figures had been used in making the said study.

[d] The figures under this heading, just as in Tables 7–7, 7–8, and 7–9, do not include the added value for the processing of coffee.

Sources: The basic figures shown in Table 7–7 have been used for the four countries for which figures are given here. The figures in the aforementioned study of the University of Costa Rica have been used as stated in footnote c of this table. In the two countries where figures were available for only one year, the figures for the group of four countries in 1955 were computed by projecting the census figures on the basis of the fluctuation in the corresponding output. Since, in one case, the original figures preceded 1955 and in the other followed 1955, and for other reasons, it was assumed that the resulting bias would not be significant. A linear interpolation was made in the case of the other two countries in order to obtain figures for 1955.

TABLE 7-14. Guatemala: Structure of Employment and Added Value in the Manufacturing Component of the Industrial Sector, 1953 and 1957

(Percentages of total employment and added value for the sector)

	Industrial groups and branches	Employment 1953	Employment 1957	Output 1953	Output 1957
I.	Traditional industries	72.7	70.7	73.0	74.5
	Foodstuffs	18.6	19.7	16.5	17.1
	Beverages	10.1	8.9	20.3	19.5
	Tobacco	3.1	2.3	7.1	13.5
	Textiles	12.8	12.5	9.6	8.4
	Clothing	14.7	13.2	10.1	6.9
	Lumber and cork	7.5	7.2	6.0	4.3
	Furniture and accessories	3.2	4.1	1.9	2.1
	Leather and hides	2.7	2.8	1.5	2.7
II.	Intermediate industries	17.2	15.4	18.7	16.0
	Paper, cardboard, and paper products	0.2	0.5	0.1	0.6
	Rubber products	0.2	1.2	0.1	0.7
	Chemical products	6.7	5.6	9.6[a]	5.7
	Petroleum derivatives	—	—	—	—
	Nonmetallic minerals	7.6	8.0	5.4	8.9
	Basic processing metals	2.5[b]	0.1	3.5[b]	0.0
III.	Mechanical industries	5.7	6.9	3.7	4.0
	Simple metal products	2.5	2.7	1.4	1.2
	Mechanical equipment and accessories	0.5	0.8	0.3	0.5
	Electrical equipment and accessories	0.1	0.5	0.2	0.5
	Transportation equipment	2.6	2.9	1.7	1.8
IV.	Residual industrial group	4.4	7.0	4.6	5.5
	Printing and publishing	0.5	1.1	0.5	4.4
	Miscellaneous	3.9	5.9	4.1	1.1
Total		100.0	100.0	100.0	100.0

[a] The figure for this heading may be somewhat high.

[b] Although the activity in the production of nonferrous metals actually appears to have decreased between the two periods, it may be that the high figure for 1953 is due in part to the inclusion under this heading of part of the respective primary activities.

Sources of the basic data: Industrial censuses of 1953 and 1957 of Guatemala, on the basis of publications referred to in the footnotes to Table 7-7.

would certainly be of considerable interest to determine the possible influence of all these elements on the productivity indexes recorded. However, such an investigation is not possible on the basis of the data now available, and so we shall present below a summary of the scant pertinent information available for two countries of the area.

The data to be given in the table for the fixed renewable capital [56]

[56] The term "fixed renewable capital" in the manufacturing sector or its subdivisions includes buildings and structures, and machinery and equipment, less corresponding depreciation. Land, inventories, and intangibles are not included.

TABLE 7–15. Central America: Structure of the Relative Productivity of Labor in the Combined Manufacturing Sector of Four Countries, 1955[a]

(*Index numbers: average productivity of the manufacturing sector = 100*)

Manufacturing sector	Indexes of the total productivity of the manufacturing sector	Indexes of the productivity of most of the manufacturing sector
I. Traditional industries	101	95
Foodstuffs[c]	63	82
Beverages	563	not included
Tobacco	711	not included
Textiles	144	188
Clothing	84	110
Lumber and cork	64	83
Furniture and accessories	59	77
Hides and leather	68	88
II. Intermediate industries	117	153
Paper, cardboard, and paper products	57	not included
Rubber products	167	not included
Chemical products	127	165
Petroleum derivatives	—	—
Nonmetallic mineral products	112	145
Basic metals	[d]	not included
III. Mechanical industries	65	85
Simple metal products		
Mechanical equipment and accessories	67	87
Electrical equipment and accessories		
Transportation equipment	63	82
IV. Residual industrial group	94	123
Printing and publishing	83	117
Miscellaneous	93	128
Total	100	100[b]

[a] The combined statistics on Costa Rica, El Salvador, Honduras, and Nicaragua are given. The reason for not including the figures on Guatemala in the calculations is stated in footnote 44 of the text. The productivity in the manufacturing sector and its subdivisions has been calculated at the ratio between the statistically recorded values of the output (aggregate value) and of employment (number of persons employed) in the various units. Relative productivity is the productivity of a group or branch, expressed as an index based on the average productivity of the entire industrial sector.

[b] The beverages, tobacco, paper, rubber, and basic metal industries (groups 21, 22, 27, 30, and 34 of the CIIU) are omitted for the reasons indicated in the comments in the text.

[c] The coffee-processing plants are not included.

[d] It could not be calculated because the basic figures, which were very small, lost accuracy when rounded off.

Sources: Those stated in the footnotes to Tables 7–7 and 7–13.

structure of the Costa Rican and Honduran industries—taken from two works on the development of these countries [57] and supplemented with the pertinent estimates—are quite detailed, although, owing to the known difficulties in terms, they may not be very accurate (see Table 7–16).[58] Therefore the figures will be used with the necessary reservations, and even so we shall endeavor only to interpret the aspects that appear to show the existence of one characteristic or another with sufficient distinction.

In comparing the figures for the capital structure of Costa Rican industry with figures for the composition of its output (all this information is shown, along with similar figures for Honduras, in the first five columns of Table 7–16),[59] one is struck by the fact that, with respect to the traditional industries, their proportion of the total capital of the sector is larger than that of output. In contrast, in its intermediate industries, the proportion of total capital is definitely lower than that of output, which, in this case, is due especially to the lack of capitalization of the quasi-chemical industries. The comparable figures for Honduran industry, where the general capitalization level is even lower, do not show such differences in the traditional and intermediate industry groups, although they do show a very low capital intensity for the machine industry group. These differences, as is obvious, are also apparent in the coefficients of capital intensity, or capital-output ratios, by groups or branches shown in the last three columns of Table 7–16.[60]

Although, as already stated, all the fixed capital figures should be interpreted with a certain amount of caution, it appears likely that the coefficients indicating capital intensity in the totals of the two manufac-

---

[57] See the footnotes to Table 7–16.

[58] The same caution is expressed in one of the above-mentioned studies.

[59] The figures available for the capital structure of Costa Rican industry are not fully comparable with the figures in the preceding tables, but comparable figures for output, taken from the same source as the data on capital, are included in Table 7–16. Moreover, these data on output were also used in making the calculations on capital intensity and, along with equally comparable figures on employment, in computing the indexes in Table 7–17. These figures on output differ in various aspects of coverage and valuation from the census figures. Among other differences should be mentioned the fact that they exclude coffee-processing plants, rice-husking mills, and sugar mills, as well as almost all repair shops. They may also contain adjusted values for the headings of beverages and tobacco and figures with more complete coverage for the lumber industries, etc.

[60] "Capital intensity" is the ratio of existing renewable fixed capital in the manufacturing sector or its subdivisions to the added value of the respective production unit. It seemed preferable not to use the term "capital density" here, since this term usually means the ratio of capital to employment.

turing sectors are realistic and have an acceptable degree of approximation. According to those coefficients, the capital-output ratio in the Costa Rican industry as a whole is somewhat less than 2 (and, with respect to its machinery and equipment, somewhat less than 1.5), while in Honduran industry it appears to be nearly unity.

The manufacturing sectors that are most highly capitalized in Costa Rica, in terms of their renewable fixed capital, are the miscellaneous industries, textile and rubber [61] manufacturing, and the manufacture of foodstuffs, paper products, nonmetallic mineral materials, and lumber. In terms of machinery and equipment, the order of the more mechanized industries is quite similar, with the difference that the rubber and paper products industries are above foodstuffs, and the place occupied by lumber is taken by the transportation equipment industries, probably because of the part that the equipment of the airplane parts plant plays in this branch.

In Honduras, the groups whose capital coefficients occupy the first five places are the miscellaneous industries, foodstuffs, textiles, lumber, and nonmetallic minerals. All these are activities that are also among the relatively more capitalized activities in Costa Rica.

Moreover, the manufacture of clothing and shoes, chemical industries, and printing are the chief activities with little fixed capital in Costa Rica. With respect to printing, it should be borne in mind that its output also includes the output of the publishing industry. In point of machinery and equipment, furniture manufacturing, chemistry, and printing occupy the last places. In Honduras, the lowest capitalization characterizes these industries: leather, clothing, beverages, tobacco, transportation equipment and other metallurgical products, as well as furniture manufacturing and the chemical industry, whose coefficients are less than unity.

An interesting fact is the lack of a clear relationship between relative capital intensity and relative productivity by groups and branches (see Table 7–17). It is usually assumed that there is a certain correlation between capital intensity and productivity and that this relationship is maintained when both categories are classified in order or in relationship to their own averages.

It is not possible to give here a complete explanation of the apparent anomaly noted, which is assumed to result merely from statistical errors. However, certain observations on this point may be made.

The importance of the frequency with which equipment is replaced in

---

[61] This industry is relatively diversified in Costa Rica and, among other lines of production, includes the manufacture of foam rubber.

TABLE 7-16. Costa Rica and Honduras: Structure of Existing Fixed Capital and Capital Intensity in the Manufacturing Sector, by Industrial Groups and Branches, 1957[a]

(Percentages of totals for capital/output ratios and structure for industry)

Industrial groups and branches	Structure of existing renewable fixed capital[b]			Output structure		Capital intensity[c]			
	COSTA RICA		HONDURAS[d]	COSTA RICA	HONDURAS[d]	COSTA RICA		HONDURAS	
	Renewable fixed capital (1)	Machinery and equipment (2)	Renewable fixed capital (3)	Value added (4)	Value added (5)	Renewable fixed capital (6)	Machinery and equipment (7)	Renewable fixed capital (8)	
I. Traditional industries	81.2	80.0	83.7	76.6	84.4	1.9	1.4	1.0	
Foodstuffs[e]	31.9	29.6	27.7	23.9	14.5	2.4	1.7	1.9	
Beverages	9.6	10.2	17.1	7.5	31.6	1.9	1.6	0.5	
Tobacco	3.1	3.2	5.2	2.9	9.2	1.3	1.0	0.6	
Textiles	8.3	9.6	14.7	4.7	8.7	3.3	3.0	1.6	
Clothing	5.4	5.9	4.7	12.6	8.4	0.8	0.7	0.5	
Lumber and cork	16.7	15.6	12.7	12.9	9.8	2.2	1.6	1.3	
Furniture and accessories	3.9	3.6	1.1	7.9	1.2	1.8	0.6	0.9	
Hides and leather	2.3	2.3	0.4	4.2	1.0	1.5	1.1	0.4	
II. Intermediate industries	9.7	9.8	6.5	14.0	6.5	1.4	1.1	1.0	
Paper, cardboard, and paper products	0.8	0.9	—	0.7	—	2.2	1.9	—	
Rubber products	1.6	2.0	—	1.2	—	2.4	2.2	—	
Chemical products	4.7	4.8	5.3	9.9	5.6	1.0	0.8	0.9	
Petroleum derivatives	—	—	—	—	—	—	—	—	
Nonmetallic mineral products	2.6	2.1	1.2	2.2	0.9	2.2	1.4	1.3	

III. Mechanical industries[f]	3.4	3.9	3.6	3.7	5.0	1.7	1.5	0.7
Metal products	1.1	1.2	2.4	1.6	3.4	1.5	1.2	0.7
Mechanical equipment and accessories								
Electrical equipment and accessories								
Transportation equipment	2.3	2.7	1.2	2.1	1.6	1.9	1.7	0.7
IV. Residual industrial group	5.7	6.3	6.2	5.7	4.1	1.7	1.4	1.5
Printing and publishing	2.9	3.4	3.7	4.6	3.1	1.0	0.9	1.1
Miscellaneous	2.8	2.9	2.5	1.1	1.0	4.8	3.8	2.4
Total	100.0	100.0	100.0	100.0	100.0	1.8	1.4	1.0

[a] The table also contains the output structure for the two countries under reference with comparable figures for their capital statistics. On the basis of the respective basic data, the capital intensity coefficients contained in the last three columns were calculated. These basic data on output differ somewhat from those of previous tables, for the reasons explained in footnote 1 in this chapter but they are the same as, or comparable with, the figures used in the next table.

[b] This item includes the buildings and structures in addition to machinery and equipment.

[c] The numerator of the ratio represents the renewable fixed capital according to footnote 2; the denominator, the added value.

[d] Statistics for 1956.

[e] The Costa Rican figures do not include coffee-processing plants, rice-husking mills, and sugar mills.

[f] Including the values for basic processing materials, which are very small.

Sources: For COSTA RICA: Publications of the University of Costa Rica (Economic Research Institute); *El Desarrollo Económico de Costa Rica, No. 2, Estudio del Sector Industrial, 1959*. HONDURAS: CEPAL, *El Desarrollo Económico de Honduras*.

TABLE 7-17. Costa Rica and Honduras: Relative Capital Intensity and Relative Productivity, by Industrial Groups and Branches, 1957

(Number indexes: average intensity and productivity in the manufacturing sector = 100)

	Relative capital intensity[a]			Relative productivity	
	COSTA RICA[b]		HONDURAS		
Industrial groups and branches	Renewable fixed capital	Machinery and equipment	Renewable fixed capital	COSTA RICA[b]	HONDURAS[c]
	(1)	(2)	(3)	(4)	(5)
I. Traditional industries	104	103	99	105	101
Foodstuffs[d]	133	124	191	136	52
Beverages	109	115	54	242	184
Tobacco	72	74	57	259	175
Textiles	186	216	168	131	59
Clothing	46	51	56	67	179
Lumber and cork	122	114	129	86	85
Furniture and accessories	47	43	96	65	104
Hides and leather	81	81	36	193	280

II. Intermediate industries	79	80	100	174	100
Paper, cardboard, and paper products	120	141	—	119	—
Rubber products	132	163	—	158	—
Chemical products	57	58	94	284	106
Petroleum derivatives	—	—	—	—	—
Nonmetallic mineral products	124	100	134	52	75
III. Mechanical industries	97	109	73	64	136
Simple metal products	} 84	} 89	} 72	} 54	} 136
Mechanical equipment and accessories					
Electrical equipment and accessories	105	122	77	72	139
Transportation equipment					
IV. Residual industrial groups	93	102	152	112	66
Printing and publishing	57	66	119	103	84
Miscellaneous	270	279	250	66	40
Total	100	100	100	100	100

^a The relative capital intensity of an industrial group or branch is the capital-output ratio within that group, expressed as an index based on the capital-output ratio of the entire manufacturing sector.

^b The basic data used in this table are fully comparable with those of the preceding tables, except Table 7–16. More details are given in footnote 59 in the text.

^c The figures for Costa Rica do not include coffee-processing plants, rice-husking mills, or sugar mills.

^d The figures for this heading, which are very small, are included in the next heading, metallurgical and mechanical industries.

Sources: Those stated in the note to Table 7–13.

several Central American industries should be emphasized. This phenomenon, in addition to explaining at least in part the inadequate effect of capital intensity on productivity in several activities, should be given more attention in view of the high cost of factory installations, part of which are consistently not being adequately utilized. It is true that part of the machinery that is not being sufficiently used is made up of machine units that are not very efficient, although still usable; but similar observations have been made, though to a lesser extent, also in relatively modern plants.

Although there is no over-all information, even by branches, concerning the average degree of utilization of manufacturing equipment in the countries of Central America, the fragmentary data summed up below can throw some light on the situation.[62]

In a survey made in Costa Rica in 1957–58, the conclusion was reached that several of the principal factories for producing foodstuffs could have increased their production between 20 and 25 per cent with the equipment they had without major technical difficulties. In some of the soft-drink plants, installations were found (which, to be sure, were quite old) that were being operated at barely one-third of their capacity.[63] While one large textile factory operated at full capacity, several other plants having equipment of inferior quality were operating with varying degrees of excess capacity. Even more serious was the unused capacity in shoe factories, sometimes amounting to one-fifth of their total potential capacity, and in sawmills. In the latter, a serious obstacle to better utilization of equipment was the seasonal difficulties in transportation. When another briefer survey was made in Costa Rica two years ago, it was again noted that some equipment was far from being adequately utilized.

The report of a consulting firm, which made a direct survey in Guatemala recently, states that only one-fourth of the companies observed operate on more than one shift. Another technical group that went to Nicaragua at almost the same time also found a number of possibilities for increasing the production of several companies in that country by using existing installations.

Among the various reasons for persistent inadequate utilization of the

[62] Sources of such information are: University of Costa Rica, publications of Economic Research Institute; Wolf Management Engineering Co. (for AID), *Costa Rican Industrial Crossroads,* 1961; Barrington and Co. (for the Government of Guatemala and for AID), *Industrial Development of Guatemala,* 1962; International Economic Consultants, Inc., *Incentives to Private Industry in Nicaragua,* 1961.

[63] It should be noted, however, that the brewing industry of the country showed a high degree of utilization of its equipment.

industrial capacity, the following, which appear to be the most important, should be stressed:[64]

1. Certain industries were not able to acquire installations suited to the small Central American markets, especially in the previous period of relative isolation, either because equipment of those sizes are not manufactured or because, owing to certain "indivisibilities," the expectation of possible future expansion made it necessary to purchase much larger units than were desired.

2. There is strong resistance among factory operators to running their plants in three, often even in two, shifts. There are several reasons for this, but one of the chief reasons is the marked shortage of administrative, technical, and supervisory personnel—sometimes the most important bottleneck in industrialization—which makes it necessary for the operator himself to perform all these functions at once, thereby preventing him from delegating his authority so that the operations might be carried on in his absence.

3. In several instances, the equipment could produce a great deal more, even with the same number of hours of operation, if more efficient administrative and technical procedures were applied, but the necessary knowledge and technical skills are not yet sufficiently disseminated.

4. In general, there is also a great lack of knowledge about the operation, maintenance, and repair of machinery. The result is premature deterioration, and the repairs made are often quite temporary, with the resulting loss of time. All of this is aggravated by frequent difficulty in obtaining spare parts locally.

These points show that some of the problems—that is, those relating to the size of the market—can be remedied without great difficulty, at least for those companies that are sufficiently efficient to be able to compete in the other countries of the area, although less "automatically" for those that must make a special effort in order to be on a competitive footing. As a result of the new configuration in Central America, the situation will probably tend to be alleviated, at least partially, with respect to the local supply of certain spare parts. However, other more important difficulties can be solved only by a significant advance in technical and administrative training, and this has also been contemplated within the framework of joint industrialization efforts.

[64] In this discussion no reference is made to the temporary inadequate utilization of equipment owing to accidental causes, strikes and others, much less to equipment existing in name only; that is, installations that are so obsolete or in such disrepair that they are useful only to be held in reserve, in other words, for use for short emergency periods.

CHAPTER 8

EVOLUTION AND STRUCTURE OF CENTRAL AMERICAN IMPORTS AND PROSPECTS FOR INTRA-CENTRAL AMERICAN TRADE

CHANGES IN IMPORT VOLUME

About 1945, the five Central American countries entered upon a period of steady economic development based primarily on heavier foreign demand for their traditional exports and supplemented by a certain measure of diversification in agricultural export commodities for four of the countries and the continuation of manufacturing development initiated in three of them during the first half of the 1940's. Economic development was accompanied by a rapid growth of urban population, which served to diversify the expansion of domestic demand.

Central American production for sale on the domestic markets also grew rapidly, but owing to the difficulties outlined in the Introduction to this study (p. 249), such output was unable to improve its relative share in the satisfaction of domestic demand during most of this period of intensive economic development. With reference to the demand for capital goods, which had been entirely imported in the mid-forties, cement is the only exception to be noted; its production was initiated gradually in four of the countries. The rest of Central American output aimed at internal supply encountered, in the case of foodstuffs, a serious obstacle in the rigidity imposed on agricultural production by deficient landownership systems and the lack of adequate transportation facilities, especially secondary roads between the producing areas and the new or expanding consumer centers.

With the exception of cement and foodstuffs, the manufacturing sector expanded rapidly, outstripping the growth of actual demand for part of its output. Available data on manufacturing structure and growth are insufficient for even an approximate evaluation of the extent to which over-all manufacturing production succeeded in satisfying the demand for manufactured goods. Information on changes in manufacturing and import structures indicates, however, that the latter must not only have increased rapidly but also have adapted to the diversified demand for finished goods created by the rising urban population. Imports must also have supplied the steadily lengthening list of intermediate products called for by manufacturing expansion.

Accordingly, the volume of imports increased at a very high rate. During the ten years prior to 1955, this figure tripled, climbing from $141 million in constant currency in 1945 to $415 million in 1955. This increase was not affected by national differences with regard to manufacturing expansion and, consequently, to the replacement of imports generated by that sector. Thus, for example, in El Salvador and Guatemala, where the increased flow of manufactures was steadiest, imports expanded less than in Nicaragua, and more than in Honduras, both underindustrialized countries. In like manner, imports by Costa Rica, whose manufacturing sector represents the largest share relative to domestic product, expanded somewhat more than those of Honduras, not only during the ten years in question but since as far back as 1937 (see Table 8–1).

Between 1955 and 1957, the rate of expansion for total imports by the region was maintained, but on a less general basis. Nicaragua, whose

TABLE 8–1. Volume of Imports in Central America, Selected Years

(Millions of dollars at 1955 prices)

Year	Costa Rica	El Salvador	Guatemala	Honduras	Nicaragua	Central America
1937	29.8	25.7	44.5	27.9	13.9	127.9
1945	36.8	27.6	34.2	26.7	15.3	140.6
1950	50.0	53.0	82.7	44.8	30.1	260.6
1955	87.5	91.9	103.5	62.0	69.6	414.5
1956	90.7	102.8	130.9	71.8	61.9	458.1
1957	99.2	111.0	147.3	80.2	66.2	503.9
1958	99.8	103.7	146.0	79.2	67.8	496.5
1959	101.1	98.3	139.8	73.7	57.7	470.6
1960	108.0	116.0	138.0	72.0	59.0	494.0
1961	103.0	101.2	137.0	73.0	60.0	474.2

Sources and Notes: Up to 1959, ECLA, *Boletín Económico de América Latina, Suplemento Estadístico,* 1960 and 1961, preliminary projections based on national indexes.

current capacity to import was affected by the decline in international quotations for its export commodities that began in 1956, curtailed its volume of imports by 11 per cent in that same year. In the other countries, the gradual deterioration of these prices was counteracted partly by a greater volume of exports and partly by international loans for public works. Thus, in 1957, Central American imports exceeded the 1955 level by 21 per cent, despite the scant increase in Costa Rican imports.

Since 1958, however, this balancing factor proved, in general, insufficient to offset the increasingly sharper drop in world prices. In that year, imports declined by 7 per cent in El Salvador and to a lesser extent in Guatemala and Honduras. Aggregate imports by the five countries decreased by only 1.5 per cent, however, since Costa Rica and Nicaragua achieved a moderate rise in imports, owing to the greater volume of coffee exported by the former and the reduction in international reserves held by the latter. In 1959, only the first of these two countries showed an increase in import volume; this is partially explained by the rapid development of its meat-freezing industry based on cattle imports. If this item is balanced out by the re-exportation of meat, the volume of Costa Rican imports would then decline in a manner similar to that observed in the other countries.

The stepped-up volume of imports in 1960 largely compensated for the drop of 5.2 per cent in the preceding year, but in 1961 this level was depressed again to almost the 1959 figure.

In short, aggregate import volume has been at a standstill since 1957. The incomplete data available for 1962 indicate a rise that will, at most, only recover the decline of 1961.

CHANGES IN THE COMPOSITION OF IMPORTS

The initial expansion and subsequent contraction of Central American imports in the last ten years have led to moderate changes in their composition. It is difficult to classify the determining factors in order of importance because of their different impact in each of the two five-year periods.

Nevertheless, one of the main factors is the obvious circumstance that the years under study are subsequent to, or a continuation of, a period of maximum structural transformation in Central American imports. That is, in 1953 prior economic development had assured a high level of the ratio of capital and intermediate goods that would attenuate relative changes in the future. This is clearly shown by a comparison of the figures available for 1953, 19 and 32 per cent respectively, with those of 1950, when capital goods amounted to only 16 per cent and intermediate goods to only 22 per cent of import value, calculated at constant prices. Comparatively speaking, consumer goods dropped from 63 per cent in 1945 to 43 per cent in 1950 and to 39 per cent in 1953. The importance of these variations shows that import composition in 1953–62 should not be measured in terms of reduced volume alone but rather by how long-term factors in the Central American economies were accentuated or de-emphasized.

Another factor to be kept in mind, particularly in considering the future activation of long-term factors, is that changes in composition have not always been identical in the five countries. The greater industrial development of Costa Rica, El Salvador, and Guatemala has enabled those countries to cut back imports of consumer goods to a greater extent than the Central American group as a whole; that is, to maintain their relative share of total imports when domestic demand for these goods spiraled. In the other two countries, in contrast, expansion of this demand in 1953–57 brought an increase in the ratio of consumer goods to total imports. In Honduras,[1] for example, this ratio rose from 37 per cent in 1953 to 54 per cent in 1957, thus reducing the decline of this percentage for Central America as a whole.

Finally, the most important factor in the composition of imports during 1958–62 has been the rapid development of reciprocal trade among the five countries. This trade differs sharply as to content from that of import trade with other areas. The percentage of capital goods and fuels, for example, is minimum in reciprocal trade, while the ratio of intermediate goods, in addition to being less than that in trade with other areas, is subject to acute fluctuations that generally respond to climatic variations in the exporting country.

Reciprocal trade has prevented the relative decline that would otherwise have occurred in consumer goods imports following increased balance-of-payments difficulties in 1958. The Treaty of Association signed by El Salvador, Guatemala, and Honduras, and especially the General Treaty of 1960, created the conditions required for reciprocal trade to overcome the limitations imposed by the systems of bilateral treaties on which it was based and to go beyond the mere transactions of unprocessed foodstuffs by which it had been characterized up to that time. Although the volume of such foodstuffs continued to increase, the treaty

---

[1] United Nations, Doc. E/CN.12/549, p. 107.

permitted a substantial increase in the trade of Central American manufactured articles, mostly nondurable goods.

Because of the moderating effect of these three factors, the analysis of changes in the composition of imports is difficult and unsatisfactory when based exclusively on a classification of great aggregates, such as the economic use of the goods; that is, consumption, investment, and industrial processing. Accordingly, this study has preferred to use the *Standard International Classification of Trade* (SICT),[2] which, although it lends itself less readily to possible subdivision of domestic demand, is fully compensated for in this case by the criterion of degree of elaboration. Classification by economic use is employed, however, as a guide for relating the SICT sections to the changes in such demand (see Table 8–2).

Between 1953 and 1957, the expansion of imports was relatively uniform for the various SICT categories. Only beverages and tobacco in Section 1 remained stable, while the growth rates for the other sections were very similar to those obtained for the total index. This situation changed in the next four years, for this time the decline in the total index did not result from a general contraction. In contrast, imports of foodstuffs (Section 0) continued above or level with the 1957 figures.

During the past four years, import composition[3] has varied more rapidly and in greater depth than during the preceding five-year period. Except in the very special case of Section 7 (machinery and automotive equipment), which, because of its direct relation to the investment rate, sharply parallels short-term fluctuations in the Central American economy, changes during the four-year period merely reflect an accentuated continuation of the trends of the previous period. In effect, sections with a high component of goods required by agricultural production or processed by industry maintain their expansion, while those including consumer goods decline in volume, even though these goods do not directly compete with Central American industry.

Generally speaking, the sections analyzed can also be divided into three main groups: (*a*) fuel and equipment, (*b*) items consisting principally of raw materials, and (*c*) manufactures not included in the previous groups.

The essential fact of this classification is that the first two groups, by their very nature, have been far less subject to replacement by domes-

[2] United Nations, *Statistical Papers* (New York, 1958), Series M, No. 10.

[3] An apparent contradiction exists between the dislocation indicated by these trends and the previous statement concerning the gradual nature of changes in import composition. As already noted, SICT is used in order to distinguish in greater detail the changes less clearly indicated by the other classification.

TABLE 8–2. Central America: Indices of Physical Volume of Imports

(1955 = 100)

SICT Description	1953	1954	1955	1956	1957	1958	1959	1960	1961
A. Primarily consumer goods									
0. Foodstuffs	65.2	80.0	100.0	103.8	100.7	110.3	114.0	106.8	100.4
1. Beverages and tobacco	93.0	119.2	100.0	80.6	94.2	106.7	83.1	81.0	73.7
6. Manufactures by materials	94.5	99.7	100.0	112.3	132.9	126.3	118.6	124.0	120.9
8. Other manufactures	85.7	97.0	100.0	111.8	115.0	110.8	113.5	108.4	95.7
B. Primarily capital goods									
7. Machinery and automotive equipment	79.4	87.8	100.0	125.9	128.1	110.4	105.5	110.2	106.8
C. Primarily intermediate goods									
2. Raw materials	65.0	85.5	100.0	109.5	145.0	138.6	86.7	95.8	106.3
3. Fuels	80.2	80.9	100.0	107.3	114.6	127.1	125.7	129.2	133.5
4. Oils and fats	81.7	110.3	100.0	110.3	127.6	120.3	113.1	182.4	183.0
5. Chemical products	65.7	90.6	100.0	106.5	125.1	115.9	114.5	143.2	142.0
Total	83.2	92.0	100.0	110.5	121.6	119.8	113.5	119.2	114.4

Sources and Notes: The total index corresponds to the ECLA estimate based on official data. The partial indices have been calculated using quantum indices for El Salvador, Costa Rica, and Honduras and deflating current values for Guatemala and Nicaragua through unit value indices based on data by products published in the United Nations *Yearbook of International Trade Statistics*, several issues.

tic production than the third group, with reference to the process of import replacement in national terms. As will be noted elsewhere, the distinction between (*b*) and (*c*) is accentuated, when extra-Central American trade is studied exclusively, by the substantial degree of expansion in intraregional trade of the products included under (*c*).

The sections best suited to replacement reduced their share in imports from 41.6 per cent in 1953 to 37.5 per cent in 1961 (see Table 8–3). This percentage is based mainly on imports of intermediate goods and foodstuffs. It should be recognized that not all of the increase in the

TABLE 8–3. Central America: Percentage of Imports by SICT Sections

(Percentages of yearly totals)

SICT Description	1953	1957	1961
A. Fuel and equipment			
3. Fuel	6.6	6.5	8.1
7. Equipment	23.4	25.7	22.8
Subtotal	30.0	32.2	30.9
B. High raw material component			
2/4. Raw materials and noncombustible oils and fats	1.8	2.3	2.4
5. Chemical products	10.5	13.7	16.2
Subtotal	12.3	16.0	18.6
C. Replaceable components			
6. Manufactures by materials	31.6	30.3	29.4
8. Other manufactures	10.0	9.2	8.1
Subtotal	41.6	39.5	37.5

Source: OAS, Department of Economic Affairs, General Studies Unit, calculations based on national statistics.

sections grouped under B is the result of replacement, for an important share of the expansion in chemical products is the result of more widespread use of modern techniques in agriculture.

Foodstuffs (SICT Section 0)

During the ten years covered by the study, food purchases have accounted for about 11 per cent of Central American imports. In other words, as in the case of imports as a whole, food imports have also undergone a period of expansion, followed by a period of stagnation. However, the latter period, already begun in 1955, appeared to break in 1958, continuing on again in 1959. The persistent rise in the volume of imported foodstuffs during 1953–56 can be explained only by the negative effect of excessive rural land concentration, the cumulative investment deficit in the basic sectors, and the lack of marketing mechanisms, among others, which prevented Central American agricultural output from growing and diversifying to keep pace with demand. During that five-year period, the per capita domestic product maintained its former high growth rate and the urban population responsible for the diversification of demand and absorbing most of the imported foodstuffs increased by 5 per cent a year. A study of Honduras illustrates this point.[4] It showed not only a continued increase in the percentage of imported foods consumed by the population but also changes in composition which served to diversify consumption. Thus, the imported items increased their share in food consumption from 7.2 per cent in 1953 to 11.2 per cent in 1957, continuing a long-established trend. Urbanization, which made the least progress in the five Central American countries,[5] led to a relative displacement of traditional foods, since rice and corn consumption rose by only 1.7 and 2.1 per cent a year respectively, as compared to the rate of 3 per cent a year recorded for over-all food consumption. Available information on Costa Rica [6] shows similar trends and leads to the assumption that, with due regard for the differences involved, the situation in Honduras reflected approximately the discrepancy between actual demand and production of foodstuffs in Central America.

The increases registered in 1958 and 1959 were partly the result of the drop in output for consumption in Nicaragua and, to a lesser extent, in El Salvador and Guatemala. However, the importance of this cutback in production was secondary as compared to the rapid development of reciprocal trade in foodstuffs resulting from the treaties already cited and from the Multilateral Treaty of 1958. As a consequence of these agreements, reciprocal trade in these products continued to expand, doubling by 1961 its value in 1957. The lack of variation in imports from all sources indicated by the preceding indexes was due to the fact that the volume of imports from other than Central American sources dropped by 15 per cent between those two years.

These factors have brought about certain modifications in the composition of food imports (see Table 8–4).

[4] United Nations, *Análisis y Proyecciones del Desarrollo Económico, XI: El Desarrollo Económico de Honduras* (Mexico City, December, 1960) (E/CN. 12/549).

[5] ECLA, *Boletín Económico de América Latina,* Vol. 8, No. 1 (Mexico City, 1962).

[6] National University of Costa Rica, *El Desarrollo Económico de Costa Rica* (San José, 1958).

Imports of livestock products (livestock and canned milk) have substantially improved their position within the food group; their 1953 value of $5.6 million doubled to $11.2 million by 1959. The imposition of restrictive quotas on cattle exports by Nicaragua in 1960 was followed by almost total prohibition in 1961, curtailing livestock imports to barely $2.9 million in 1961, one-half of the value recorded in 1959.

With respect to imports of canned milk and cream, their stable value in recent years is due partly to the promotion of dairy cattle production in Guatemala, El Salvador, and Costa Rica. These three countries are making increasing use of stabling, which has signified a steady increase in the consumption of processed fodder.[7] Although there are by-products from the manufacture of oil and milling of grains available for this purpose, the demand for concentrates has exceeded production and led to an increase in the importation of fodder between 1953 and 1960 amounting to 1,000 per cent in terms of volume and 650 per cent in terms of value.

Chemical and Pharmaceutical Products (SICT Section 5)

Central American imports under Section 5 are characterized by almost uninterrupted growth within the period under study. This steady expansion is due to the fact that it includes both raw materials for Central American industry and agriculture, and for finished goods, for which demand is usually unaffected by any decrease in the per capita product, and which, in the case of Central America, are also involved in a relatively recent process of import replacement. Despite the fact that the difficulties entailed in this replacement tend to maintain a high level of consumer goods in this section, the ratio of intermediate goods rose in total value from 51 per cent in 1953 to 58 per cent in 1961 (see Table 8–5). This relative increase is attenuated by the practical difficulty of evaluating quantitatively the component of intermediate goods, in the case of pharmaceutical and toiletry products,[8] and by the high volume of chemical products, classified as basic by two countries, imported by the banana companies at the beginning of the decade, primarily for their campaign to eradicate sigatoka disease.

Import requirements of those companies have decreased as their campaign for plant sanitation has prospered, resulting in the declining curve shown by basic chemical products up to 1959. In 1960, however, the

[7] In Costa Rica, a high percentage was accounted for in 1959 and 1960 by the fattening of cattle for processing and subsequent exportation.

[8] There are reasons to suppose that part of the items classified under 54 and 55 should actually be classified as intermediate goods and that these were the very products that increased rapidly during the period under study.

companies operating in Costa Rica and Honduras were compelled to renew imports of these and other similarly classified products. The rise in imports of basic products in 1960 and 1961 was also the result of the growing demand for these products by industries located in El Salvador and Guatemala. In the first country, this volume doubled between 1957 and 1960, but the increase was even greater in Guatemala because of the demand for lampblack and other chemical inputs for the rubber industry.[9]

Up to 1957, the greater expansion in the importation of intermediate chemical products can be attributed to prepared fertilizers. The available index of unit value shows relatively minor variations; it is accepted as an initial approximation that current values coincide more or less with those calculated at constant prices.[10] It is concluded, therefore, that these imports increased by almost 41 per cent a year between 1953 and 1957, a much higher rate than any of the agricultural production indexes of the five countries. This is, of course, because intensive use of fertilizer has benefited export products. Up to 1953, most imported fertilizer was used in the cultivation of bananas, with a smaller volume earmarked for coffee, cotton, and sugar-cane crops. Since that year, fertilizer for these three crops has absorbed most of the increase in this import item, since both the cultivated area and the yield per hectare have expanded significantly.

The stable level of volume recorded after 1957 corresponds to the reduction in area used for growing cotton and to the fact that the low price for coffee and bananas has to some extent discouraged intensive use of fertilizer. This stability is, to a lesser degree, the result of recent processing of fertilizers in two countries that use products classified here as basic.

In the case of Central American imports, SICT Division 59 (see Table 8–5) includes three types of intermediate products that deserve mention. First are the synthetic plastic materials in primary form [11] whose growth, in terms of both volume and value, has been rapid and is due mainly to the recent date of its technological development and introduction in

---

[9] Although statistical difficulties prevent a numerical demonstration, in recent years the Guatemalan rubber industry has expanded rapidly for both tires and inner tubes and for other articles. As will be noted elsewhere, Guatemala shows a certain degree of specialization in these industrial lines.

[10] Although it is true that the unit price for nitrogen has dropped on the international market in the past three years, the lack of mixers has prevented Central America from taking advantage of this circumstance. Thus, the unit value index reflects the costs of prepared fertilizers.

[11] Also including artificial resins in primary form and unwoven plastic sheets, but excluding rayon and wood pulp.

TABLE 8-4. Central America: Imports of Food Products

(Millions of dollars)

Items	1953	1954	1955	1956	1957	1958	1959	1960	1961
Volume index (1955 = 100)	65.2	80.0	100.0	103.8	100.7	110.3	114.0	106.8	100.4
Livestock	1.9	2.3	2.3	3.0	3.2	3.6	5.9	5.4	2.9
Canned milk and cream	3.7	4.0	4.8	5.2	5.3	5.9	5.3	4.8	5.6
Wheat	1.7	1.7	2.0	2.2	3.3	3.5	4.3	5.8	7.6
Rice	...	1.2	2.2	2.5	1.3	1.9	2.2	0.9	0.7
Corn	0.8	1.7	2.9	4.4	0.4	2.0	2.6	1.3	0.9
Wheat flour	10.2	11.8	13.0	11.0	11.0	12.2	11.0	10.5	10.4
Fruits and vegetables	3.4	4.0	5.3	6.6	5.9	6.0	7.2	7.0	7.8
Sugar	1.0	1.1	1.5	2.8	2.0	2.0	1.6	...	...
Fodder	0.5	0.5	0.7	1.3	1.5	1.8	2.6	3.1	3.0
Margarine and lard	3.6	4.2	5.8	5.0	5.2	6.6	3.4	3.7	3.8
Not classified	11.0	14.0	15.3	13.7	16.0	14.1	14.1	14.6	...
Total	37.8	46.5	56.0	57.7	55.1	59.6	60.7	57.7	55.6

Source: OAS, Department of Economic Affairs, General Studies Unit, calculations based on national statistics.

TABLE 8-5. Central America: Imports of Chemical and Pharmaceutical Products

(Millions of dollars)

	SICT Description	1953	1954	1955	1956	1957	1958	1959	1960	1961
	Volume index (1955 = 100)	65.7	90.6	100.0	106.5	125.1	115.9	114.5	143.2	142.0
	A. Intermediate goods	20.2	25.1	30.5	33.0	39.7	39.3	35.5	46.1	47.1
51/52	Basic chemical products	8.8	6.7	8.3	7.4	8.1	4.9	5.4	10.0	9.3
531/2	Tanning extracts and dyes	0.4	0.2	0.4	0.6	1.3	1.1	1.3	1.0	1.3
56	Chemical fertilizers	3.7	7.5	7.3	10.9	14.6	13.9	12.5	13.5	12.9
59	Other intermediate products	7.3	10.7	14.5	14.1	15.7	19.4	16.3	21.6	23.6
	B. Finished products	19.3	22.6	25.1	25.8	32.4	32.2	32.1	34.7	33.9
533	Paints	3.0	3.7	3.6	4.0	4.2	4.2	3.9	3.9	3.6
54	Pharmaceutical products	11.4	13.2	15.7	15.4	20.5	21.1	20.2	22.6	22.0
55	Toiletry products	4.9	5.7	5.8	6.4	7.7	6.9	8.0	8.2	8.3
5	Total chemical and pharmaceutical products	39.5	47.7	55.6	58.8	72.1	71.5	67.6	80.8	81.0

Source: OAS, Department of Economic Affairs, General Studies Unit, calculations based on national statistics.

Central America. Consequently, it has continued to expand even during the years of greatest import contraction (that is, 1958 and 1959), which suggests an equally intensive growth in the corresponding industries.

The second type of intermediate product in this division is the insecticides, fungicides, and disinfectants, most of which are not confined to domestic use. The volume of these imports shows an average trend toward rapid expansion resulting, as in the case of fertilizer, from their increasing use for export crops. In the last five to six years, their growth has been accentuated by the extent of the damage caused by pests to cotton production in Nicaragua and by the defensive measures adopted by the other producers. This explains why these items have, since 1957, accounted for an unusual share—40 per cent—of Nicaragua's total imports of chemical products, while the maximum figure for the other countries came to only 20 per cent.

The third group of products under SICT Division 59 is a heterogeneous one, including as it does industrial spare parts, sanitation, and other services. Its value fluctuates sharply and shows no well-defined trend.

The foregoing outline stresses the impact of the spread of improved agricultural techniques on import demand for intermediate chemical products. Since no quantitative analysis is possible over several years, by way of simple illustration it has been estimated that, in 1961, 54 per cent of these imports, or a market of $25 million, corresponded to a comparatively limited number of agricultural inputs. It should be emphasized that the number of items is limited because of the prospects of their future production in Central America and, particularly, because of the need for introducing these improved methods in agricultural production for domestic consumption. At present, there are biological laboratories in at least three of the countries, and two have fertilizer mixing plants still operating on a limited scale; therefore it can be noted that there is already a tendency toward replacing imports from other areas.

In mentioning previously the relative ratios of intermediate products and finished goods in the section of chemical and pharmaceutical products, an explanation was given for the diminished importance of the second group. It was also noted that for statistical reasons it was difficult to separate the components of this second group, which, in practice, constitute industrial inputs. Thus, for example, a distinction could be made in the pharmaceutical products between those prepared for retail sale and those imported in bulk. Such a distinction would, however, prove inadequate, since the pharmaceutical products received by the retail merchant in bulk are many and varied. It should be kept in mind that this group of consumer goods includes a component of intermediate products that appears to be on the increase.

Pharmaceutical products contribute to the bulk of imports of chemical consumer goods. Their value increased by 100 per cent between 1953 and 1961, representing an even greater increase in real terms, since the percentage of antibiotics and vitamins, whose international price has declined steadily, has been high and growing.[12] During the last five years, however, these imports have remained comparatively stable; it should also be pointed out that intra-Central American reciprocal trade began to acquire importance in this case.

This latter circumstance is also true for toiletry products and prepared paints, which, for practical reasons, have been defined here as finished goods. The decline since 1957 in the import value of paints has been contained by the expansion of intraregional trade, for by 1961 half of Honduran and Guatemalan imports of this product came from Central America. In the case of toiletry articles, this ratio amounted to approximately 15 per cent, including not only imports by the two countries mentioned but those by El Salvador and Nicaragua as well. In general terms, the value of intraregional trade under this heading can be estimated at slightly over $1.5 million, or 4.5 per cent of imports of finished chemical products.

CHANGES IN SOURCES OF IMPORTS

Over the past decade, fairly substantial changes took place in the sources of Central American imports. Among these, beginning in 1958, mention should be made of the increase in reciprocal trade, the steady, rapid drop in the ratio of imports supplied by the United States, and the rise in the corresponding ratios for Japan and the European Economic Community (see Table 8–6).

Although trade policy—and particularly the series of bilateral treaties [13]

---

[12] Mention should also be made of the lower sale prices offered by European suppliers, whose share of supply has increased relatively more than the North Americans, as a factor operating in the same direction.

[13] These treaties include the following: El Salvador–Nicaragua (1951); El Salvador–Guatemala (1952), amplified in 1957 and 1959; El Salvador–Costa Rica (1954); Guatemala–Costa Rica (1957); and Guatemala–Honduras (1957). It should be noted that some of these treaties had already brought about substantial increases in reciprocal trade; for example, between 1950 and 1957, exports from El Salvador to Nicaragua and Costa Rica multiplied 8 and 4 times, respectively, while Guatemalan imports from Costa Rica and Honduras expanded 100 and 4 times, respectively.

TABLE 8–6. Central America: Origin of Imports

(Percentages of the total)

Country	1950	1953	1954	1955	1956	1957	1958	1959	1960	1961	1962[a]
Latin America	9.0	7.7	8.0	8.0	7.7	7.3	8.6	11.2	11.0	11.7	...
Central America	3.1	3.2	3.6	3.2	2.9	3.2	4.2	6.1	6.4	7.5	11.0
Mexico	3.4	2.1	1.9	2.4	2.1	1.8	2.1	1.7	1.4	1.6	...
Others	2.5	2.4	2.4	2.4	2.7	2.2	2.4	3.4	3.2	2.6	...
North America	73.1	65.8	65.0	64.4	62.7	59.7	57.1	53.2	50.6	48.5	...
United States	70.4	63.9	63.0	62.1	60.8	57.8	55.0	51.0	48.6	46.5	...
Canada	2.7	1.9	2.0	2.3	1.9	1.9	2.0	2.2	2.0	2.0	...
Western Europe	12.0	18.9	20.7	20.5	21.5	23.4	25.0	25.5	27.5	27.6	...
EEC	6.1	12.0	14.2	14.0	14.9	17.4	17.5	17.8	19.8	19.8	...
Germany	2.6	5.7	7.8	7.4	7.4	8.5	9.2	9.1	10.2	9.6	...
Netherlands	0.7	2.4	2.6	2.3	2.6	3.1	3.5	3.4	3.5	4.0	...
Belux	1.2	2.1	1.8	2.1	2.4	3.0	2.2	2.6	2.8	2.9	...
Italy	1.0	1.1	1.1	1.1	1.2	1.4	1.6	1.4	1.6	1.7	...
France	0.6	0.7	0.9	1.1	1.2	1.3	1.0	1.3	1.6	1.5	...
United Kingdom	3.4	4.3	4.2	4.1	4.2	4.2	4.6	4.6	4.4	4.4	...
Japan	0.6	1.7	1.8	2.4	2.9	3.5	3.8	4.9	6.2	6.5	...
Others	5.2	5.9	4.4	4.8	5.4	6.1	5.5	5.3	4.7	5.8	...

[a] Estimated, Department of Economic Affairs, OAS.

Source: United Nations, *Direction of International Trade*, several issues.

that preceded the Multilateral Treaty of 1958 and the General Treaty of 1960—accounts for the recent development of reciprocal trade, in the case of other areas changes in the source of imports have not been the consequence of national discriminatory practices. Except for the "Central American clause," which safeguards concessions among Central American countries, the countries of the region have posed no obstacles to trade by any country with which they maintain normal diplomatic relations. The most notable exception was a minor restriction by Guatemala on imports from countries with which it had a deficit trade balance. Except in the case of countries where trans-shipment of foreign trade is compulsory, such as Switzerland, the Guatemalan restriction has had no effect on the origin of its imports.

The factors that have led to the changes noted in the direction of imports have been related to prevailing conditions in world trade and, to a lesser degree, to structural changes in Central American external demand. Generally speaking, these factors have varied in both number and importance during the past decade. For this reason, they are grouped in the following analysis into general categories, relating, where relevant, strictly Central American factors with those arising from international participation by the highly industrialized countries.

Renewal of Trade with Europe and Japan

In 1938, at least one-third of Central American imports were drawn from the six countries that today make up the European Economic Community, and almost 3 per cent of the total was from Japan. The value of Central American exports to those countries was on approximately the same scale. This trade came to a standstill at the beginning of the 1940's and was not renewed until the end of the same decade.

This renewal was quite rapid, since Central American exports to Europe rose from $62 million in 1948 to $93 million in 1950. Imports, in turn, rose from $37 million to $68 million, respectively, for the same years.[14] In the case of the European Economic Community members, Central American imports increased from $11 million to $32 million and exports from $17 million to $35 million.

However, exports to Europe, and particularly to the Community, were restricted by the balance-of-payments difficulties of the European countries and the fact that the five Central American countries belonged to the dollar area. The latter were therefore obliged to accept trade or

[14] United Nations, *Estudios del Comercio entre América Latina y Europa* (Mexico City, 1953), pp. 30, 31.

payments agreements that entailed a quasi obligation to purchase in Europe when they wanted to increase the volume of their exports. This situation persisted until the mid-1950's, although it became gradually less significant as European balances of payments improved.

With respect to Japan, the renewal of trade was gradual and slow up to 1956. Subsequently, it increased fairly rapidly its relative contribution to Central American imports, to become by 1961 the third most important supplier for the area.

Variations in Prices Paid by Central America

Unit value indices for the exports of highly industrialized countries showed diverse tendencies during the last decade. Especially outstanding was the spectacular improvement shown by the Japanese series, in comparison to the other industrialized countries (see Table 8–7). While the unit values for exports by the United States and the United Kingdom increased by 8 and 12 per cent, respectively, and those of the European Economic Community decreased by 5 per cent in 1961, the Japanese values averaged only slightly more than two-thirds of the same index ten years before.

These changes are only partly explained by fluctuations in the source of purchases for Central American imports. With the exception of Japan, the countries that showed the greatest increase in their sales to Central America were not those whose indexes of unit value of exportation recorded the greatest relative improvement. The maximum expansion of these sales was achieved by Germany, whose prices increased on a

TABLE 8–7. Industrialized Countries: Indices of Unit Values of Exports

(1958 = 100)

Country	1951	1957	1961
United States	95	100	103
EEC	105	103	100
Federal Republic of Germany	96	101	104
Belgium-Luxembourg	121	107	97
France	101	109	96
Italy	123	105	92
Netherlands	108	104	101
United Kingdom	91	101	102
Japan	145	110	105

Source: International Monetary Fund, *International Financial Statistics.*

level with those of the United States; the minimum was registered by Belgium and Italy, where the indexes of unit value of exports dropped by 20 and 25 per cent, respectively.

The disparity in these trends shows the need for a more detailed examination of these prices in order to verify whether the structure of Central American demand for imports can explain the shift to the European Economic Community and Japan. As will be indicated below, the prices of certain industries in these countries have attained a relatively more favorable position than that reflected by the unit value indexes for total exports.

Sectoral Relative Prices

Chemical products and machinery and automotive equipment were among the Central American import items that expanded most rapidly. It should be noted that in both lines the relation of German prices to those of the United States improved throughout the entire period. Between 1950 and 1957, wholesale prices for German chemical products increased by slightly more than half of the United States rate, and while the latter remained almost steady after 1957, German prices declined (see Tables 8–8 and 8–9). The main decline in Central American imports of chemical products from the United States affected those groups in which consumer goods predominate. These, which had expanded by $5.4 million between 1953 and 1957, decreased by $6.5 million in the four following years. In both periods, however, purchases in other zones increased by $7.7 million and $7 million respectively, although if reciprocal trade were excluded, these figures would drop to $7 million in 1953–57 and $4 million in 1957–61. Consequently, a displacement of North American supplies took place during the latter period, due to both greater Central American production and trade and increased purchases in other regions (see Table 8–10).

The situation with regard to machinery is more complex, with a relative advantage for Germany developing only after 1957. Since automotive vehicles are a chief component of this heading—where the relative loss of the United States was greater—it should be noted that, while wholesale prices in the United States increased at the rate of 3.4 per cent a year between 1950 and 1957, those of Germany declined slightly. After 1957, this difference in price variation disappeared, but other additional factors influenced the Central American demand for automobiles, such as heavily rising taxes on gasoline in most of the Isthmus countries, making the European automobiles, which usually burn less fuel, more

TABLE 8-8. Annual Rates of Increase for Wholesale Prices of Selected Groups of Industrial Products in the United States, the Federal Republic of Germany, and Japan, 1950-1961[a]

Product group	1950-57			1957-61		
	United States	Fed. Republic of Germany	Japan[b]	United States	Fed. Republic of Germany	Japan
Machinery, total	4.3	5.0	1.4	3.3	2.0	−3.7
Farm machinery	2.7	7.1	...	2.8	1.5	...
Automotive vehicles	3.4	−0.1	...	0.9	0.8	...
Iron and steel	7.5	9.8	...	0.6	—	...
Chemical products	1.9	1.0	−1.2	−0.1	−1.5	−2.3
Pulp, paper, and paper products	3.6	4.8	...	−0.1	−1.3	...
Paper	4.2	3.0	...	0.5	2.0	...
Textile products	−0.6	−1.0	−6.9	−0.3	−1.9	−1.5
Clothing						
Leather and leather products	−0.7	−2.6	...	2.9	2.0	...
Leather products (footgear)	1.8	0.3	...	2.5	2.4	...
Capital goods, total	...	4.0	...		0.7	0.2
Consumer goods, total	...	0.3	3.2		—	0.7

[a] Due to the different definitions and groupings employed in national statistics, the groups listed here are not fully comparable. However, the differences are not so great as to invalidate the comparisons if they are interpreted as merely indicating general trends.

[b] The period selected was 1951-57 because the value of Japanese exports in 1951 increased by 50 per cent, despite a rise in unit values, which appears to indicate that the rate of reconstruction was still the determining factor in trade.

Source: U.S. Departments of Commerce and Labor, *Business Statistics of the United States* and *Monthly Labor Review;* Statistisches Bundesamt, *Wirtschaft und Statistik;* Japanese Government Planning Agency, *Japanese Economic Statistics.*

TABLE 8-9. Central America: Difference in Import Value of Chemical Products, by Suppliers and Selected Periods

(Millions of dollars)

Chemical product	1953-57		1957-61		1953-61	
	U.S.A.	Others	U.S.A.	Others	U.S.A.	Others
Pharmaceutical products[a]	3.2	5.9	−2.8	4.3	0.4	10.2
Soap and toiletry articles[a]	1.2	1.6	−1.1	1.7	0.1	3.3
Paints[a]	1.0	0.2	−1.6	1.0	−0.6	1.2
Fertilizers	3.3	7.6	−2.0	9.0	−7.9	18.2
Others	7.5	1.1	0.2	9.0	7.7	10.1

[a] The text refers to these three groups in the discussion on consumer goods.

Sources: See Table 8-10. The year 1953 was chosen as the beginning of the period for statistical reasons, since classifications for the preceding years are too heterogeneous.

TABLE 8–10. Central America: Imports by SICT Sections and Selected Sources, 1953, 1957, and 1961

Import		Volume indexes (1953 = 100)		Geographical distribution of imports (Percentages of annual value)								
				Central America			United States			Other areas		
		1957	1961	1953	1957	1961	1953	1957	1961	1953	1957	1961
Food and drink	(0/1)	148	145	16	14	26	58	49	46	26	37	28
Fuel	(3)	144	166	—	—	1	16	21	16	84	79	83
Chemical products	(5)	190	215	2	2	5	67	60	44	31	38	51
Machinery and automotive equipment	(7)	162	135	—	—	1	77	72	61	23	28	38
Other manufactures	(6/8)	139	117	2	2	7	60	55	49	38	43	44
Total		147	137	3.5	3.2	7.5	66.7	59.6	46.4	29.8	37.2	46.1

Notes: The F.O.B. values given for the United States source have been adjusted to C.I.F. by means of the coefficients corresponding to total imports.

Sources: See Table 8–2 for volume indexes. For percentages see Table 8–3 and U.S. Department of Commerce, *Exports by Country of Destination* (Washington, D.C., 1953, 1957, 1961).

desirable. It should also be pointed out that, with reference to farm machinery and tractors, whose relative prices developed much more favorably for the United States, exports to Central America showed no significant differences in comparison with those of other regions (see Table 8–11). In the case of paper, cardboard, and their manufactures, United States sales increased to $7.3 million between 1953 and 1961. Purchases from other zones, primarily Canada and the Scandinavian countries, also increased, by $2.3 million.

TABLE 8–11. Central America: Difference in Import Value of Machinery and Automotive Equipment, According to Origin

(Millions of dollars)

Category	1953–57 U.S.A.	Others	1957–61 U.S.A.	Others	1953–61 U.S.A.	Others
Farm machinery	0.7	0.8	−0.5	−0.9	0.2	−0.1
Tractors	3.9	2.0[a]	−4.1	−1.1[a]	−0.2	0.9[a]
Electric machinery	4.2	5.6	−1.6	1.7	2.6	7.3
Office machinery	−0.2	1.2	−0.2	−0.3	−0.4	0.9
Industrial machinery[b]	11.6	1.4	−6.9	10.5	4.7	11.9
Automobiles	7.7	8.2	−8.2	1.2	−0.5	9.4

[a] Including nonagricultural tractors.
[b] Including die equipment and excavating machinery.
Source: See Tables 8–9 and 8–10.

Import Substitution

With regard to the demand for food and beverages imports (SICT Sections 0 and 1), whose chief extra-Central American component had also been North American, two different factors were at work. Up to approximately 1957, imports from other regions exhibited a greater increase, but after 1958, both these and imports from the United States dropped off as a result of rapidly increasing intraregional trade in these products (see again Table 8–7). Only continued increases in grain exports under Public Law 480 and the greater commercial demand for fodder related to the development of meat exports prevented a far more serious reduction in the North American share of this item.

A similar trend could be observed in certain other light industries [15] that were affected simultaneously by the process of national replacement

---

[15] For statistical reasons, SICT Sections 6 and 8 cannot be presented separately. In the present analysis, however, the chief components of Central American imports of these products are broken down.

and the increase in intra-Central American trade. Thus, for example, imports from the United States of leather and leather products and textiles diminished, but both reciprocal trade and national production by the countries increased [16] (see Table 8-12).

Direction of Investments

Another element in the relative displacement of imports from the United States was the change in investment structure. Although data in this respect are incomplete and at times inconclusive, it appears that

TABLE 8-12. Central America: Difference between 1953-1957 and 1957-1961 in Value Imported from the United States and Other Sources by Chief Components of SICT Sections 6 and 8

(Millions of dollars)

Category	1953-57 U.S.A.	1953-57 From other sources	1957-61 U.S.A.	1957-61 From other sources	1953-61 U.S.A.	1953-61 From other sources
Leather and leather products	0.1	0.8	−0.9	0.5	−0.8	1.3
Nonmetallic mineral products	0.9	2.3	−0.9	0.9	0.0	3.2
Textiles and textiles manufactures	−4.0	12.4	−9.4	10.4	−13.4	22.8
Rubber and rubber manufactures	4.7	0.2	−1.8	2.2	2.9	2.4
Paper and cardboard and their manufactures	2.2	2.0	5.1	0.3	7.3	2.3
Metals and metal manufactures	11.8	13.7	−12.0	3.1	−0.2	16.7

Sources: See Tables 8-9 and 8-10.

since 1958 investments in agriculture have contracted sharply. Because of the existence of large North American agricultural enterprises in Central America, equipment and machinery for this type of investment were in the past supplied primarily by the United States. Although this country, as already noted, was not placed in a disadvantageous position by rising farm machinery prices until 1957, after that date Central American imports of tractors and farm machinery declined from $9.3

[16] However, Costa Rica also sharply stepped up its textile purchases from Japan.

million to $4.6 million, with similar drops for railroad equipment and other nonhighway transportation machinery used by those companies.

At the same time, the increased relative importance of the manufacturing sector in the use of investments during the last five years also appears to have increased the relative importance of Japanese and European investors, with a resulting tendency to acquire industrial equipment in those regions. Thus, between 1957 and 1961, imports of industrial machinery from the United States decreased by slightly less than $7 million, while those from other sources increased by more than $10 million.

INTRA-CENTRAL AMERICAN TRADE

The preceding section has reviewed the growth and structural transformation of foreign demand for the five Central American countries as a whole. Reference was also made to changes in the direction of that trade, placing certain emphasis on the factors that led to displacement of imports from the United States by those from overseas countries and regions. Central American reciprocal trade was mentioned only insofar as it played a significant part in that displacement or as it modified or accentuated trends in the structural change of imports. This treatment is justified mainly because reciprocal trade is still a limited share (10 per cent) of total imports by the five countries. Therefore, in contrast to the size of the remaining imports, its changes in the past are attenuated, and at certain points and periods they become insignificant.

However, it would be a mistake to measure the importance of reciprocal trade in the past or the immediate future solely by the relation between its value and that of total imports. Total volume should increase rapidly and steadily in the next few years if the working hypothesis outlined in this study is realized: a minimum growth of per capita domestic product of 2.5 per cent a year. The growth rate of reciprocal trade will obviously be higher, but, according to the hypothesis, its ratio of total imports will consistently maintain a comparatively low level. It should be kept in mind that with a domestic product increase of 6 per cent annually, the demand for imports from other areas for capital goods, construction materials, and raw materials should grow at an equal or higher rate, without prejudice to a possible substantial rise in overseas purchases of durable consumer goods and fuels. Reciprocal trade, on the other hand, may find itself constrained until such time as Central American production can provide it with raw materials and mechanical products in addition to the farm commodities and manufactured consumer goods that predominate in current trade.

The chief importance of reciprocal trade lies, therefore, in three facts: (a) it has to date made possible the use of productive capacity; (b) it is giving rise to the study or installation of industries operating efficiently in markets with a larger volume than those confined within national boundaries; (c) it has prevented a sharper decline in the importation of consumer goods without unfavorable consequences for balance of payments by the mutual cancellation of balances inherent in such trade.

Generally speaking, it has been difficult to evaluate the first and last of these facts. This is largely the result of the unfavorable prospect presented by the low value of reciprocal trade in comparison to that of total importation or exportation and, to a lesser extent, of statistical problems in relating, on the one hand, productive capacity with exports to Central America and, on the other, consumption to the pressure on external demand. It should be noted, for example, that the increase in exports of vegetables from Guatemala has served to expand the volume of this production, which is cultivated by a great many small and intermediate farmers [17] who do not have easy access to other marketable commodities. This exportation doubled between 1956 and 1960, reaching in the latter year 14 million pounds with an FOB value of 420,000 quetzales, a trade that did not require the heavy supplementary investments in transportation, refrigeration, quality controls, etc., that would have been needed for export to other markets. It is impossible to speculate on what would have happened to the income of these farmers without the Central American market. However, it is nonetheless interesting to point out that in zones where, because of their location, production is utilized solely for the farmers' own consumption or exclusively for the national market, there has been a contraction in horticultural activities.[18]

Another example of how reciprocal trade has led to more efficient use and to expansion of productive capacity is the case of Salvadorean and Guatemalan textile products. According to the Banco Central of El Salvador, the index (based on 1956 = 100) of production for the textile industry increased from 120 in 1957 to 239 in 1961. Production value rose, according to the same source, from 19 million colones in the first year mentioned to 36 million colones in 1961. Consolidating these figures, in order to eliminate the double counting represented by the inclusion of

[17] In the chief producing region, the average area of horticultural farms amounted to 1,000 square varas (0.07 hectares) in 1950.
[18] See Banco de Guatemala, *Informe Económico*, Year IV, No. 7, (Guatemala City, January, 1962).

raw thread and other items used in production, gives an expansion within that period of 13.2 million colones.

The value of textile exports from El Salvador to Central America amounted to 0.2 million colones and 7.4 million colones in 1957 and 1961 respectively. It may be said that one-half of the increased sales by the industry in that period was derived from reciprocal trade [19] or, too, that 25 per cent of the activities of the Salvadorean textile industry in 1961 can be traced directly to the Central American market.

These two examples are not unique for these two countries, and additional ones can also be cited for the remaining countries. However, a wealth of detail is not necessary to illustrate that although the figures for Central American trade are small, they signify a greater impact than those of total trade. It is obvious that the benefits derived by the Guatemalan economy from a sale of 400,000 quetzales divided among two or three thousand small farmers are greater than those resulting from the exportation of an equal value of bananas or coffee. The $3 million in yarn and fabrics exported by El Salvador also have an economic and social impact that can hardly be equaled by the traditional export products.

That is to say, reciprocal trade has become significant because, at a time when factors outside the region were having an unfavorable effect on its economic development, it has provided a market for products for which there was a surplus capacity and, to a certain extent, it has prevented a more serious decline in the Central American economies. This has been achieved with a minimum of additional investments in supplementary services and with greater utilization of previous investments in regional transportation systems.

A brief examination of the composition of reciprocal trade for the region in recent years makes it possible to evaluate easily not only the intensity and continuity of its growth but also the diversification that has led to better use of existing productive capacity (see Table 8–13). The expansion of Sections 0, 5, 6, and 8 in particular are sufficient proof of the direction being taken by effective realization of the 1952 Economic Integration Program.

Nor has the influence of intra-Central American trade on the structure of external demand of the countries in the area received sufficient statistical recognition. The contraction of this demand usually affects first consumer goods; that is, the reducible margin of importation. In

---

[19] The difference between ex-factory and port of export values is unknown but considered to be relatively insignificant.

TABLE 8-13. Central America: Reciprocal[a] C.I.F. Imports, by SICT Sections, 1955–1962

(Millions of dollars)

SICT Section	1955	1956	1957	1958	1959	1960	1961	1962[b]
0 Foodstuffs	6.2	7.0	7.9	9.8	14.4	14.9	14.6	21.5
1 Beverages and tobacco	0.8	0.8	0.8	1.3	1.7	1.1	0.9	0.9
2 Raw materials	1.7	1.8	1.8	1.5	1.6	1.6	2.0	2.3
3 Fuels[c]	0.3	0.1	0.2	0.1	0.1	0.1	0.2	0.2
4 Oils and fats	0.5	0.5	0.8	0.5	0.7	1.6	1.7	1.9
5 Chemical products	0.6	0.8	1.2	1.2	1.9	2.4	3.5	4.5
6 Manufactures by materials	1.2	1.2	1.9	2.4	3.2	6.2	8.1	9.8
7 Machinery and automotive equipment[c]	0.6	0.4	0.4	1.1	1.9	1.5	1.3	1.2
8 Other manufactures	0.8	0.8	1.1	2.3	2.0	3.0	4.4	4.8
Total[d]	12.7	13.4	16.1	20.2	27.5	32.4	36.7	47.0[e]

[a] F.O.B. and C.I.F. values are considered to be equal.
[b] Based on partial data.
[c] Including a small number of re-exported products that it was not possible to exclude.
[d] Excluding SICT Section 9. It exhibits minor differences with other totals given here and in other sources. See Note c.
[e] 50.9 million, if, instead of using data on Guatemalan exports for nine months, the total for twelve months is obtained based on data for imports by the other countries.

Sources and Notes: 1960/62 SIECA (Permanent Secretariat of the General Treaty for Central American Economic Integration); 1955–1959, OAS based on official data of the countries.

cases such as Central America in 1957–61, when such a contraction became necessary because of unfavorable changes in the balance of payments, the decline of these imports led to a shorter supply of goods for consumer units. Although in the long run national production tends to fill this vacuum, initially it calls for greater sacrifice by the low-income urban classes.

Reciprocal trade has maintained the level of food imports and has contained the decrease in other consumer goods (see again Table 8–13). The volume of food trade rose 2.5 times [20] between 1957 and 1961, making it possible for external supplies in the countries importing such goods to maintain their level and to prevent a decline in the already low standards of Central American nutrition.[21] Since 1957, the relative size of increases in other consumer goods have been too high for proper comparison. An example of the percentages that would have to be used is the figure on fabric exports by El Salvador, given in a preceding paragraph, which amounts to 3,700 per cent.

In short, it can be stated that although reciprocal trade could not of itself prevent a decline in consumption, it has at least supplied products that could not have been acquired in other regions without accentuating still further the negative balances of foreign trade in goods.

Finally, it is necessary to analyze the impact of reciprocal trade on the development of new industries: a factor of maximum importance.

Reciprocal trade has passed through three stages. The second corresponds to the period between 1951 and 1957 and the current stage to the last five years. Recent events point to the initiation of a fourth phase, characterized by formation of a common market valid not only for one section but for all the countries of the region.

What is here designated as the first stage actually represents the period of border trade that began in 1838 with the dismembering of the Republic of the United Provinces of Central America. Since then, attempts have been made on various occasions to form political or economic unions, but such initiatives have failed to prosper, owing to the lack of communication facilities between the interested countries. In 1940, only one public service railroad connected Guatemala with El Salvador, and the other facilities were rudimentary except when directly and immediately connected with overseas exportation.

---

[20] Excluding livestock for re-exportation.

[21] Central American rates of morbidity and mortality relating to dietary deficiencies are among the highest in Latin America. Reference: WHO, *Annual Epidemiological and Vital Statistics Reports*.

The status of transportation conditioned trade among these countries, which, except for exchanges between Guatemala and El Salvador favoring the incipient industry of both countries, was restricted to merchandise that did not require developed communication facilities, such as livestock, and to the sale of farm surpluses between neighboring areas of bordering countries. Among these areas, the most important was the border region between El Salvador and Honduras, where traffic was facilitated at the end of the 1940's by development of the highway system of El Salvador [22] and the free trade it maintained with Honduras.[23] These factors contributed to the fact that in 1950 El Salvador's trade with Guatemala and Honduras represented 75 per cent of Central American exports.

It should be noted that the limitations of the road network and the scant diversification achieved by the manufacturing sector did not enable intra-Central American trade to expand to the same degree as that shown by trade among the other Latin American countries in 1940–46. In those years, however, Central American industrialization was initiated, resulting in the installation of plants utilizing national raw materials and some based on the importation of intermediate goods.

In 1945, construction was begun on the Central American segment of the Pan American Highway, designed to link the 17 continental republics. As in the other Latin American countries, the continental goal had to be subordinated to the availability of resources and, naturally, to prior satisfaction of local needs. Thus, at the end of the 1940's the Central American segment was composed of broken national sections unconnected with the Mexican network in the north or the Colombian system in the south.[24]

At the start of the 1950's, reciprocal trade entered upon a new stage by becoming one of the basic instruments in the economic integration policy adopted by the Central American countries. In 1952, the Economic Commission for Latin America (ECLA), at the request of the five Central American governments, convoked the first meeting of the Committee on Economic Co-operation of the Central American Isthmus, established the preceding year. At that meeting, the Committee agreed to initiate a gradual program of economic integration and asked the Secretariat of

---

[22] See United Nations, *El Transporte en el Istmo Centroamericano* (Mexico City, September, 1953).

[23] See SIECA (Permanent Secretariat of the General Treaty for Central American Economic Integration), *Centroamérica y su Mercado Común, Algunos Datos Económicos* (Guatemala City, May, 1962).

[24] The Guatemalan and Mexican networks were connected in the 1960's. Still under study is the section that will cross the Darien region in the south.

ECLA to make a series of studies in this respect. These studies include several directly related to the prospects and possibilities of development offered by reciprocal trade [25] and, among others, one on the deficiencies and required improvements in transportation systems.[26]

For their part, the governments, utilizing these studies, have multiplied their investments in road networks. Such investments not only led to improvements in highway transport at the national level but also aimed at the establishment of a Central American trunk network. Thanks to this effort, in May of 1955 the national systems of Nicaragua and Costa Rica were interconnected, uniting at last the automotive transportation systems of the five countries.[27] Expansion and interconnection of the road network was reflected in the stock of automotive freight vehicles; trucks in circulation tripled between 1950 and 1956, while passenger automobiles increased by only 70 per cent.

In the institutional field, intra-Central American trade received a strong incentive through the bilateral treaties signed as of that period. The prior experience of Central America consisted only of the Free Trade Treaty signed in 1918 by Honduras and El Salvador and the "Central American clause" with which the five republics tacitly complied. The latter made any "most favored nation" concessions agreed upon by any one of the five with countries outside the region extensive to all the Central American countries. In 1951, El Salvador signed a similar treaty with Nicaragua and, at the beginning of 1952, another with Guatemala. In 1954, it completed its system of bilateral agreements by signing one with Costa Rica and revising the old treaty with Honduras. In 1957, free-trade treaties between Guatemala and Costa Rica and between Guatemala and Honduras were also concluded.

The effect of these treaties, improved communication facilities, and increased automotive stock was almost immediate. The value of reciprocal imports rose by 37 per cent between 1950 and 1953, reaching $11.9 million in the latter year. In 1957, this figure rose to $16.9 million, practically doubling the level of the first year mentioned.

Despite these increases, the ratio between reciprocal and total imports

---

[25] See the following ECLA publications: *La Integración Económica de Centroamérica, su Evolución y Perspectivas* (E/CN.12/422); *La Política Tributaria y el Desarrollo Económica en Centroamérica* (E/CN.12/486); *Los Problemas Actuales del Comerico Interlatinoamericano* (E/CN.12/423); and *El Mercado Común Latinoamericano* (E/CN.12/531).

[26] United Nations, *El Transporte en el Istmo Centroamericano*.

[27] The aggregate of trunk highways will amount to 5,162 kilometers, of which 4,485 were serviceable by 1962. In 1959, the total network of the five countries came to 17,000 kilometers firmed or paved.

did not vary significantly and even registered a slight decline. This incapacity to expand in excess of total imports can be explained partly by the insufficient growth of domestic supply. It should be recalled that reciprocal exports include goods that can be used for consumption and are therefore channeled into reciprocal trade only when surpluses are produced or special factors make it necessary.[28] It is not surprising, consequently, that increased trade between the Central American countries was based fundamentally on the foodstuffs required by El Salvador, which up to 1956 was the only country to have concluded bilateral treaties with the other four.

Although the bilateral treaties provided a strong incentive to reciprocal trade, they also gave it a radial direction by which one country served as the center. This direction confined additional trade fundamentally to the products El Salvador needed to buy or had for sale. The other participating countries could not, consequently, make efficient use of the structural unproductive capacity that characterizes underdeveloped countries with a small market.[29] Bilateral conventions signed by Guatemala with Costa Rica and Honduras would unquestionably have led to a more balanced distribution of reciprocal trade. However, in practice they would have superimposed a new radial direction on the former, relegating trade among the other three countries to a marginal position in the Central American market.

In order to remedy this distortion, the Central American governments, at the fifth meeting of the Committee on Economic Co-operation, signed the Multilateral Treaty on Free Trade and Central American Economic Integration. This treaty provided for the establishment of a common market and, as an initial measure, drew up a list of products that, for the purposes of reciprocal trade, should be exempt from import or export duties or other charges by which they are distinguished in each country from national products. An examination of the list, which is in addition to the lists agreed upon bilaterally, shows three groups of products: (a) those already participating in Central American trade,

---

[28] For example, Honduran exports of raw cotton for ginning and subsequent exportation by El Salvador.

[29] It should be recalled at this point that the installation of industries in limited markets and with *ad hoc* protection, as in the case of the Central American countries, occurs as a rule when capacity exceeds possible sales. Part of this surplus capacity results from the limited number of subtypes of products that these installations produce in relation to the greater diversity of such output obtainable from the same equipment. As an illustration, this is the case of looms whose operation can be programmed for various grades or qualities of fabric and whose productive capacity varies, depending on the number of daily shifts.

mainly foodstuffs; (*b*) those produced in one or more countries but not previously exchanged regularly or in significant volume; and (*c*) articles not produced commercially in any Central American country.

Therefore, this treaty was not solely designed to eliminate bilateral distortion of reciprocal trade, for which inclusion of the first two groups would have sufficed. It is the last group of products that lends added importance, since it transforms reciprocal trade into a basic instrument for the development of new industries [30] and also—of prime importance—for the expansion of new subtypes of products by the manufacturing industry. Indirectly, the treaty signified a change in the application of industrial protection laws enacted by the individual countries. Existing systems extended protection to established industries or to those for which specific installation plans were available; that is, they were exercised subsequent to the decisions of the entrepreneurs, whether or not that group had considered the prospects of the Central American market. The lists of the treaty provided the agencies responsible for industrial protection with an essential pattern for channeling investments into the projects best suited to the interests of national economy. This channeling was facilitated by the growing number of applications for protection in all the countries, many of which also solicited the category of Central American industries of integration.

At the seventh meeting of the Committee on Economic Co-operation, held in late 1960, a second treaty was signed: the General Treaty on Central American Economic Integration. This agreement reaffirmed and expanded the stipulations of the Multilateral Treaty, establishing total free trade and co-ordinating these provisions with those agreed upon in establishing the special regulations governing integration industries, transportation, external charges, and other instruments provided for by the Program of Central American Economic Integration in 1952.

The clause of the General Treaty on Integration dealing with transitory special trade regulations is of particular importance for reciprocal trade in the period covered by this study. These regulations led to a broader list of merchandise included in the second and third groups

---

[30] The Multilateral Treaty has been supplemented, among others, by the Agreement on Regulation of Central American Industries of Integration. Such industries are considered to be those that require access to the Central American market in order to operate efficiently.

Note that the 1960 General Treaty overcame an important limitation of the Multilateral Treaty by abolishing the system of lists of products eligible for free-trade status. In their place, it was established that total free trade—except for minor exceptions—was the goal to be reached in a pre-established minimum period by means of general reductions in tariffs with reference to reciprocal trade.

already described and specified the restrictions applicable between pairs of countries in order to prevent unfavorable effects on manufacturing subsectors.

The impact of the General Treaty on Integration can be measured only in a very preliminary manner, since only a short time has elapsed since its ratification. For the time being, it can be stated that it has accentuated the multilateral nature of reciprocal trade as defined by the 1958 treaty.[31] At least, the proportion of this trade corresponding to imports by El Salvador declined to 54 per cent in 1957, to 41 per cent in 1960, and finally to 39 per cent in 1961. This decline has been paralleled by an increase, in 1957 and 1961, of the proportions corresponding to Guatemala from 11 to 25 per cent, respectively, those of Costa Rica from 5 to 11 per cent, and those of Honduras from 15 to 17 per cent. It must be noted that these percentages do not imply a displacement unfavorable to El Salvador, since they are exclusively the result of larger volume participation by the other countries.

The benefits derived by the Central American countries from the gradual and still incomplete [32] application of these two treaties should be measured, first, on the basis of the greater participation by all the countries in reciprocal trade and, second, by the impact these exports have had and will have on the utilization of the industrial capacity of the five countries.

It has been pointed out previously that the initial consequence of the Multilateral Treaty was elimination of the radial trend that had restricted reciprocal trade in previous years. The recent development of reciprocal trade among countries that had formerly traded very little between themselves (Honduras–Nicaragua, Honduras–Costa Rica, Nicaragua–Costa Rica) has been rapid and is beginning to show a certain regularity but is limited by the scant industrial development of Honduras and Nicaragua, which seriously restricts the number of trade products, and by relative withdrawal from the Program of Central American Economic Integration in the case of Costa Rica. These three countries, however, have increased their mutual imports from $1.4 million in 1957 to $2 million in 1961, despite a decrease of $0.5 million in Nicaraguan imports from Costa Rica.

The figure of value traded among these three countries should not be confused with their total participation in reciprocal trade. In 1953, they

---

[31] The expansion of intrazonal trade also continued. Between 1958 and 1960, this sector increased by $12.2 million, while the increase between 1960 and 1962 amounted to between $15 million and $18 million (see Tables 6–7, 1–17).

[32] Costa Rica did not sign the General Treaty until July, 1962.

received 33.3 per cent of intra-Central American imports, a ratio that reached 35.3 per cent in 1961 (see Table 8–14). It is also pertinent to note that the trade of goods with El Salvador and Guatemala has consistently resulted in positive balances that have served to attenuate the unfavorable impact of their deficit balances with the rest of the world in recent years.

These facts are mentioned in order to confine this problem to the prospects offered to Central American trade by the expansion of trade among these three countries and their industrialization. The sole adherence of Costa Rica to the General Treaty in July, 1962,[33] will bring

TABLE 8–14. Central America: Reciprocal Imports, by Groups of Countries and Selected Years

(Millions of dollars)

| | IMPORTS | | | | |
| | Costa Rica, Honduras, and Nicaragua | | El Salvador and Guatemala | | |
Year	Mutual	From El Salvador and Guatemala	From Costa Rica, Honduras, and Nicaragua	Mutual	Total Intra-Central American
1953	0.9	2.8	5.6	2.0	11.4
1957	1.4	4.6	7.0	3.5	16.6
1960	1.3	8.9	10.0	11.1	32.7
1961	2.0	11.2	9.9	14.3	37.9
1962	2.0	15.2	17.1*	16.2*	50.4*

Source: Secretariat for Central American Economic Integration, *Centroamérica y su Mercado*, p. 12.

about a rapid growth of its trade with Honduras and Nicaragua. At the same time, there is already a series of manufacturing projects in these two countries whose capacity has been planned in accordance with the size of the regional market. Their exportable output will consequently expand and diversify, thus helping to correct the radial distortion still present in intra-Central American trade.

In short, it can be said that the last two stages through which intra-Central American trade has passed have resulted in substantial economic benefits for the participating countries. On the one hand, it has made

[33] In November of the same year it signed the protocol required for its admission to the Central American Common Market.

possible the use of agricultural and manufacturing productive capacity which, without the regional market, would have been wasted, owing to the limitations of national demand. On the other hand, it has made possible access by the consumer population to a volume of goods whose purchase abroad would have been smaller without the payments compensation implicit in reciprocal trade. These two points were discussed before examining evolution of that trade.

The task of evaluating the influence of reciprocal trade on industrial development presents serious obstacles. There is a lack of up-to-date statistics that would be required by the optimum system for such evaluation; that is, a framework relating total sales of the sectors to their destination, whether for exportation, additional processing, consumption, or stocks. The approximate equivalent of such a framework has been obtained through studies conducted in Costa Rica, El Salvador, and Honduras by national working groups or joint groups in association with international agencies.[34] Although these studies furnish valuable information, amply utilized in the present study, the most recent is provided by the last of these studies, which corresponds to 1959, a year of little significance for the study of contemporary intra-Central American trade. Since it has been impossible to obtain patterns of this type for a sufficiently recent year, quantitative evaluations are offered, or in their absence qualitative ones, for sectoral production, in discussing statistics on trade classified by sector of origin (see Table 8–15). The gaps and mistakes occasioned by this substitute system can be corrected only in the future with the completion of the study on Central American economic development initiated by a joint group of international, regional, and Central American agencies.

Based on official data on importation by three countries—El Salvador, Guatemala, and Honduras—it is possible to break down the goods according to the industry and sector producing or processing them prior to their entry into intra-Central American trade. This breakdown shows that such trade has, in general, benefited all the sectors (see again Table 8–15). The goods of the primary industries increased in this trade from almost $6 million in 1957 to $9.8 million in 1961, while those of the secondary sectors amounted to $7 million and $20.8 million in the same year, respectively. A comparison of these figures indicates that there has been a substantial increase in the degree of processing of goods

[34] National University of Costa Rica, *El Desarrollo Económico de Costa Rica*, (San José, 1958), and United Nations, *Análisis y Proyecciones del Desarrollo Económico; VII, El Desarrollo Económico de El Salvador* and *XI, El Desarrollo Económico de Honduras* (Mexico City, 1960 and 1961).

TABLE 8-15. Central America: Value of Intra-Central American Imports by El Salvador, Guatemala, and Honduras, by Sectors and Industries of Origin in 1957 and 1961

(Thousands of dollars)

Sectors and industries of origin	1957	1961
I. Primary	5,948.8	9,765.8
a) Agriculture	5,794.8	9,413.6
b) Forestry	98.7	53.6
c) Mining	55.3	298.6
II. Secondary[a]	7,032.1	20,830.7
a) Food	1,875.5	5,620.1
b) Textiles	224.6	3,755.3
c) Footgear, clothing, and other similar items	1,052.2	2,077.0
d) Wood and furniture	978.2	1,588.1
e) Leather and hides	203.3	375.2
f) Paper and cardboard	284.2	596.7
g) Printing	61.0	115.1
h) Rubber	85.7	779.8
1) Tires and tubes	2.8	481.7
i) Chemical products	972.2	3,102.7
1) Paints and dyes	0.8	467.4
2) Toiletries and pharmaceutical products	263.6	1,675.9
j) Mineral products nonmetallic	244.3	1,127.8
1) Cement	213.1	722.5
k) Metallic products (except machinery)	63.4	400.9
Total[a]	12,980.9	30,596.5

[a] Including nonclassified goods.
Source: Official data.

traded, since, because of the greater processing, those of the secondary sector mentioned rose from 54 per cent in 1957 to 68 per cent of the total in 1961.

The significance of these proportions and their increases for Central American trade is even greater when the industrial groups most benefited are examined. Chapter 6 outlined in some detail the structure of the manufacturing sector in these countries, but it is advisable to recall that the Central American manufacturing industries can be divided into those recently established and those initiated in the early 1950's or before. A second division might be based on a technical level, which varies between production methods only barely above the artisan level and the most modern techniques, employing highly productive equipment.

Using these definitions with the latitude required by the statistics, it will be noted that trade in the products of the most recent industries was the most dynamic. Thus, rubber articles increased 9 times in value; toiletry and pharmaceutical products, as well as metallic articles, 6.3

times; and nonmetallic mineral products, excluding cement, 14 times. Among the industries considered for the system of Central American integration industries,[35] the figures (which are minimal, even though they include re-exports in 1957) are too high to be significant as percentages. Trade in tires and inner tubes increased from $3,000 to $482,000 in 1957 and 1961, respectively. For the same years, values for trade in paints and dyes amounted to $800 and $467,000.

With respect to the older industries—here designated as traditional—with only one exception the relative increases are less, although in absolute terms they are the most important. Thus, food products increased between 1953 and 1957 by $3.8 million, equivalent to 200 per cent, and, among others, footgear and clothing expanded by $1 million, or 100 per cent. The exception mentioned is textiles, whose import value in 1957 came to $225,000 and increased 16 times, amounting to $3.8 million in 1961.

It is difficult to attribute a precise significance to these figures for lack of a basis for comparing them quantitatively and in an orderly manner with those of the corresponding output. However, based on the substitutive analysis by sectors and industries of origin, it is possible to arrive at some preliminary conclusions with respect to the effect of reciprocal trade on Central American production.

Unquestionably, this trade has stimulated the industrialization of Central America. In the first place, it has resulted in more efficient use of equipment that was underutilized, due to inherent limitations in the size of the national markets. In some cases, this underutilization was due to simple excess capacity of equipment; in others, such limitations influenced the varieties that existing equipment could produce with a comparatively small additional investment. As a corollary, the differences in this equipment and these additional investments have resulted in a specialization that includes both the industrial groups and the various qualities or other characteristics of the individual articles. Under the influence of this specialization, industrial production has been diversified and has made considerable progress in the replacement of imports from other areas, indicating that in the near future this process will cover about two-thirds of the consumer goods still purchased by Central America.

In the second place, reciprocal trade has also stimulated the introduction of modern techniques in the food industry, whose importance in

---

[35] This refers to the 1958 Agreement on Regulation of Central American Industries of Integration.

the process of economic development needs no explanation.[36] Its development in Central America has been steady, and it has consistently been one of the most vigorous industrial branches with regard to both supply of consumer goods and replacement of imports. It should be noted that the prices paid by consumers in the four countries actively participating in reciprocal trade of food commodities have dropped, while they have increased in Costa Rica and the United States, the chief overseas supplier.

Reciprocal trade has also led to the installation of new industries and to a number of manufacturing projects, most of which can be promptly implemented. Among those recently installed are a tire factory in Guatemala, the only investment to date based on the benefits conceded by the regulations governing Central American industries of integration. The same country also has in operation a number of plants of various sizes producing aluminum, plastic, and rubber articles and processing or packaging pharmaceutical products, all of which are allocating an increasing share of their output to trade with the other countries of Central America. In at least two countries, paint and varnish plants have been installed and are currently operating. In El Salvador, the list of industrial products corresponding to the sample tabulated in 1961 by the General Bureau of Statistics is so diversified that, for all practical purposes, it has no relation to that indicated by the 1956 industrial census.

As will be noted elsewhere, these trends have had different effects on the Central American countries and the main groups of secondary industry.

Reciprocal Food Imports

The coexistence of backward and modern techniques is characteristic of the agricultural sector in underdeveloped countries. Generally speaking, modern methods are more frequently found in export agriculture, while outdated methods are used for domestic consumption crops. Because of this technological factor, it has been observed in much of the underdeveloped world, including many of the Latin American countries, that production for consumption lacks dynamism.

With regard to foodstuffs (see Table 8–16), the increase in this trade is surprising, since primary production in Central America has followed

[36] By the end of the 1950's, the food industry in the United States represented 12 per cent of the value added in manufacturing production, constituting the most important industrial group in that country.

TABLE 8–16. Central America: Intra-Central American Imports by El Salvador, Guatemala, and Honduras, by Food Industry of Origin in 1957 and 1961

(Thousands of dollars and percentages)

Import	1957	1961	Index 1961
	(Thousands of dollars)		(1957 = 100)
1. Meat preparation and curing	17.9	205.1	1,145
2. Dairy products	342.8	417.4	1,220
3. Canned goods, except fish	38.5	314.1	815
4. Milled grains	178.9	542.7	304
5. Sugar and preparations	633.7	339.9	54
6. Sugar confections and chocolate	220.8	944.3	425
7. Miscellaneous	400.8	2,979.7	7,450
Total[a]	1,875.5	5,620.1	300
Total,[a] excluding sugar	1,241.8	5,280.2	425

[a] Including nonclassified industries and marine products.

Source and Notes: See Table 8–15. The standard international classification of all human activities by the United Nations has been the basis for the classification used in this table. The apparent differences are due, on the one hand, to the need for reconciling it with more properly Central American definitions on what constitutes primary production (green coffee, for example) or secondary production and, on the other, to the fact that in the secondary sector subproducts without subsequent processing were assigned to the principal industry.

The comparability between the two years is inexact because of changes in tariff definitions by the countries.

a more or less parallel trend to that of total population and shows a growth of less than the 5 per cent annual estimated expansion of urban population. Furthermore, if consideration is given to the high value of overseas imports, which in the case of El Salvador, Guatemala, and Honduras amounted to $18 million in 1961 [37] for processed foods (that is, in addition to nonprocessed foods), the recent expansion of reciprocal trade in these products is even somewhat contradictory. This contradiction, however, is only apparent. In the first place, in certain areas consumer-oriented agriculture has been technologically improved in recent years, and in addition a series of new crops has been introduced. This is difficult to evaluate on a statistical basis, due to the excessive share of the traditional crops in the total value added by agriculture; their technical improvement is restricted by their greater vulnerability

[37] According to the ECLA estimate, this figure came to $40 million for the five countries in 1960. ECLA, *Estado General y Perspectivas del Programa de Integración Económica del Istmo Centroamericano* (Mexico City, January, 1963).

to the impact of structural changes. Among the most important new products are milk and its by-products, whose production and industrialization have been favored by expansion of the supply of domestic and imported prepared fodder. The same is true for poultry meat [38] and pork, whose dynamism is also concealed by the size of estimated production for on-farm consumption.

In the second place, it should be considered that urban consumers demand processed foods. For example, only insignificant quantities of the $18 million worth imported from overseas by these three countries are used for rural consumption. According to the data presented in the previous section on import composition, this figure runs, depending on the country, between 30 and 70 per cent higher than that for 1953, that is, the market for processed food products is still a broad one in these three countries.

With certain limitations, this broad market area is valid even on the national level, as shown by the recent rise in this production. Although the periods do not cover the same number of years, the indexes of food manufacturing output available indicate during the 1950's annual growth rates of 7.4 per cent in El Salvador, 4.3 per cent in Guatemala, 4.6 per cent in Honduras, 8.8 per cent in Costa Rica, and 12.2 per cent in Nicaragua. The rates for agricultural consumer production, including cottonseed, register comparatively low levels.

This industrialization of farm commodities has been based not only on the growing demand for processed foods but also on the supply of raw materials. Due to the difference between them, there is a certain degree of specialization that is reflected in the trade between these countries. Thus, El Salvador has sharply increased its production and exportation of vegetable oils and oilseed cakes, for which it has had available expanding volumes of domestic cottonseed and the ginning of Honduran cotton. Its milling capacity is also important, and it has been able to expand rapidly its output of flour and bran. In both cases, part of the expansion has resulted from exports to Central America, which in 1961 amounted to 20 per cent of the produced value of oils and 8 per cent of milling.

In Guatemala, the canning industry (except fish) is undergoing a process of initial expansion, having utilized to date only a minimum of the important national potential for the production of fruits and vegetables. Expansion in both the present and the immediate future is based

---

[38] Part of this production is derived from poultry for fattening imported from the United States. Exports from that country to Central America came to almost 3 million head in 1961, in addition to 840,000 eggs for incubation.

on the growing importance of the Central American market to this sector, whose imports from abroad represent approximately 10 times the value of the corresponding Central American trade.

Honduran exports indicate its livestock potential by the fact that its exports of milk and meat by-products expanded. The tonnage of exports of edible vegetable oils prepared for consumption rose by 525 per cent between 1958 and 1961, due to an increase of 50 per cent in the volume allocated to El Salvador and 800 per cent in that sold to Guatemala. It is noted that there is a difference between the Salvadorean product (chiefly oils) and the Honduran (margarines), which points up the specialization existing at the level of the industrial group.

It is difficult to judge the potential role of Costa Rica in this trade. For the time being, the most important products imported by El Salvador, Guatemala, and Nicaragua from Costa Rica are cacao manufactures, including cocoa, candy bars, and other confections.

The foregoing shows that the increase in reciprocal trade of processed foods not only has been favorable to Central American nutrition but also has contributed to the industrialization of agricultural production for consumption demanded by the economic development of these countries. Although in this case it is difficult to judge its importance by the size of manufacturing installations, it has certainly permitted greater development than that offered by the national markets individually and has helped to add value to the subproducts of two main groups.

Reciprocal Textile Imports

Manufacturing output of fabric in Central America received considerable impetus in the early 1940's, when overseas textile products disappeared almost completely from the market. The subsequent renewal of these supplies led to a deterioration in this industry, which was not offset by the subsequent elevation of tariffs. Total Central American textile production declined in varying degrees, depending on the country and the fiber. The most seriously affected sector appeared to be the production of rayon cloth in Guatemala, which, judging by the census data for 1946 and 1953, declined by two-thirds.

Production, particularly of cotton fabrics, recovered rapidly and even exceeded its former level at the initiation of a phase of persistent economic growth that led to expanded domestic demand. It also contributed to the expansion of cotton production, which facilitated the rapid rise in spinning capacity. This increased output, however, was based on a very limited variety of cloth with little or no finish, and it was thus necessary to import in order to satisfy the demand for intermediate and complete finishes.

This division of supply was due to the fact that, although national markets permitted the operation of this industry, they were, on the other hand, insufficient for mass production of medium- and high-quality cloth. Consequently, equipment capacity lacked co-ordination in the different stages of yarn and fabric processing,[39] since it was ample for the production of raw yarn and fabric, insufficient for the intermediate stages, and practically nonexistent for the final finishing processes. A study [40] of the Salvadorean textile industry at the start of the 1950's shows the influence of market size on this bottleneck and the limitations imposed by lack of diversification on replacement of imports.

According to this study, at that time El Salvador lacked machinery to polish yarn or mercerize cloth, while most of the plants also lacked equipment to dye and give other finishes to the intermediate and final goods. Consequently, there existed a situation "prejudicial to the sale of Salvadorean textile products, thus creating a preference for imported products." However, the study found that "it was obvious that the purchase by individual factories of additional equipment" and the costs of operating it were "completely out of proportion" to possible sales.[41] In order to remedy this situation, it suggested the investment of $780,000 in installation of a plant for finished textiles of a scale adequate to serve the entire national textile industry.

This bottleneck in productive capacity was not noticeable in the 1950–57 period, when Salvadorean textile output grew rapidly at the rate of 2.9 per cent annually during the years 1954–57. As in the other countries, this growth was not so much the result of improved technology within the sector as of the concentration of its production on the most popular qualities of cloth. The most important of these was the production of manta (a coarse unbleached cotton), which between the two census years of 1951 and 1956 expanded by 17.3 per cent annually. In addition to manta, most fabric production consisted, even up to 1957, of manta-denim and denim. Dyed and printed cloth in that year accounted for less than 10 per cent of the value of such fabrics.

The difficulties in diversifying this production described above correspond to a period of expansion of the Central American economy and,

---

[39] It should be noted that textile equipment is supplied by countries where this industry normally operates on an integrated basis.

[40] United Nations, *The Textile Industry in El Salvador* (New York, 1954).

[41] *Ibid.*, p. 34.

consequently, of demand for cloth.[42] It would be logical to assume that the economic deterioration after 1956 would have accentuated these problems, as would have the degree of import replacement that had then been achieved through the production of coarse cottons and other popular types of fabric.[43] However, this was not the case. Salvadorean production, which, it will be recalled, had been increasing up to 1957 at the rate of 2.9 per cent a year, began a persistent and rapid expansion that amounted to a cumulative rate of 18.9 per cent between 1957 and 1961. The index corresponding to Guatemala also shows an acceleration, climbing from an average annual increase of 2.2 per cent in 1950–57 to 5.8 per cent between 1957 and 1961. The textile industry for Central America as a whole exhibits the same trend, increasing its production rate from 2.5 per cent in 1950–57 to 8.7 per cent annually in 1957–60.

It would be a mistake to conclude that reciprocal trade was the sole decisive factor in these trends. In the first place, the size of the national markets was larger by virtue of the steady economic development prior to 1957. In Guatemala, El Salvador, and Costa Rica, it had even made possible additional equipment that resulted in a better finished product and, at least in El Salvador, the printing of woven and knitted fabrics. Furthermore, the production of clothing, rubber footwear, and furniture, whose cloth inputs were partly drawn from abroad,[44] continued their rapid growth after 1957 and at the same time increased the percentage of Central American textile inputs.

It is also obvious that the suppression of most restrictions on intra-Central American trade, resulting from the 1958 Multilateral Treaty, created expectations of a broader market and stimulated the additional investments required to improve co-ordination of the stages of production and diversify output. These expectations were fully realized in the two [45] countries where the textile industry had developed most fully and to a lesser extent in the others. Reciprocal trade of textile products increased

[42] A study by the Inter-American Development Bank, *La Industria Textil en América Latina* (Washington, June, 1962), shows a very minor growth in per capita cloth consumption. The figures given are expressed in kilos and consequently indicate only one aspect of textile demand in Central America.

[43] Nicaraguan textile output tripled between 1950 and 1955, declined by 20 per cent in 1956, and has risen slowly and irregularly since then. The drop observed in Honduran textile production is due to a fire in its main plant.

[44] In 1956, for example, the El Salvador census showed an input of imported cloth that came to 80 per cent of total cloth input for clothing and 100 per cent for the other two industries. In 1961, these ratios had declined to 30 per cent and 75 per cent, respectively, on the average.

[45] Excluding Costa Rica, which in 1957 did not participate to the same extent as the others in the Central American market.

from $225,000 in 1957 to $3,755,000 in 1961 in the case of Honduras, Guatemala, and El Salvador; to these figures must be added the increment obtained by the trade of products with thread and cloth inputs, such as the industries mentioned in the preceding paragraph.

In attempting to show the relation between this trade and production, the information on El Salvador is again utilized. Exports of yarn and woven fabrics from that country to Central America in 1957 came to $167,000, a comparatively small figure as related to production for that year. In 1961, following a steady increase, this value came to $2.4 million, at a time when sales by this industry for consumption, manufacture, and export amounted to $7 million. Accepting the small error of comparability between the two values, it follows that one-third of its activity was generated in 1961 by sales to the regional market. Although no information is available on additional investments in textile finishing, it is interesting to note that in 1961 manta represented 33 per cent of all cotton cloth produced, as compared to the 54 per cent recorded by the 1956 census. An important share of these sales consisted of products with a high degree of finish.

Nevertheless, exports by El Salvador were not the only proof of the demand of the Central American market. Guatemalan exports climbed from a minimum figure in 1957 to close to $320,000 in fabrics, chiefly rayon, to which should be added, also in 1961, $170,000 in knitted cotton and rayon fabrics.[46] Honduras is exporting more than $200,000 in ready-made clothing, as compared to only $40,000 in 1957.

One factor that deserves detailed study is the specialization shown by figures on this trade. According to the statistics on foreign trade by El Salvador in 1961 (see Table 8–17), the country imports and exports yarn and cloth, with Guatemala as its main Central American supplier and buyer. There is, however, a considerable difference between the two cases with respect to fiber, type (weight per meter in Table 8–17), and finish. Thus, El Salvador supplied raw cotton thread and received bleached cotton thread and rayon yarn. The differences in type of fabric are also notable. El Salvador exports to Guatemala cotton and synthetic fiber fabrics and receives, in turn, rayon and heavier cotton fabrics.

These differences indicate a specialization based on differences in the degree of utilization of basic equipment capacity (spindles and looms) and on new investments in additional finishing equipment. In the latter case, it indicates that even in an industry such as textiles, where there is a certain parallelism among the five countries, there is a broad enough

---

[46] The Guatemalan figures correspond to imports by El Salvador and Honduras.

TABLE 8-17. El Salvador: Trade in Textile Products with Guatemala, 1961

(*Kilograms*)

Product	Imports	Exports
I. Spinning products		
1. Cotton		
a. raw	—	883,593
b. bleached, dyed or mercerized	3,765	—
2. Rayon	289	—
II. Woven products		
1. Cotton		
a. raw		
less than 80 grams x m^2	14,368	52,864
more than 80 grams x m^2	34,893	2
b. bleached, dyed, mercerized, printed, etc.		
less than 80 grams x m^2	7	385,721
more than 80 grams x m^2	10,757	81,752
more than 50 grams x m^2	7,415	3,011
2. Artificial or synthetic fibers		
a. rayon	38,356	—
b. others	705	3,011

Source: Dirección General de Estadística y Censos, *Anuario Estadístico*, Vol. I, Foreign Trade (San Salvador, 1962).

margin to justify additional investments by Central America as a whole and thus obtain a diversification aimed at accelerating reciprocal trade and replacing overseas textile imports.

PROSPECTS FOR INTER-CENTRAL AMERICAN TRADE

Information currently available and the structural changes likely to occur in the near future restrict any analysis of future prospects of intraregional trade to a very exploratory level. These prospects should be considered in the light of predictable economic development in Central America, the resulting variations in final and derived demand, and the effect of these demands on domestic supply and imports.

Basically, intrazonal trade is a dynamic factor in Central American economic development, for it has brought a new dimension to the scale of industrialization. Existing industrial installations are generally unable to cover the demand of the regional market.[47] In addition, it enables recent and proposed installations to diversify, which is essential—because

---

[47] Practically the only important exception is the wheat-milling industry, whose capacity, partly because of its location and partly because of the institutional barriers that still exist, could duplicate current production and more than satisfy the demand for wheat flour.

of induced expansion in derived demand—to the subsequent pursuit of industrial development.

This new market dimension is, however, very recent, since the Multilateral Trade Treaty dates from 1958 and the General Treaty was only signed in December, 1960. Furthermore, Costa Rica participated in reciprocal trade only on the basis of bilateral treaties up to 1962; consequently, its effect on production and investment has been only partially felt. In view of the difficulties involved in determining the index of macroeconomic reference, this analysis is confined to an exploratory study of the margin of industrialization derived from the new market dimension not yet utilized. In order to project regional trade, it will be necessary to undertake additional studies based on the opportunities offered by future economic growth.

Factors Delaying Reciprocal Trade and the Integration Program

Previous Integration Experience. Although customs tariffs agreements are now in the operational stage, there is no doubt that other institutional aspects are still in a formative and experimental phase.[48] The integration agencies are faced by the need to solve highly important problems, with no precedents to serve as a guide. It is to be expected, therefore, that their effectiveness will continue to increase to the extent that they develop pragmatically a new and suitable methodology. It should be kept in mind that there is a total lack of experience in the economic integration of underdeveloped countries.

Outside of Europe, economic integration experience in the twentieth century that might serve as a pattern for Central America is nonexistent. Furthermore, the industrialization conditions of the six European countries, their advanced level of technology, the massive aid they received from the United States during the 1940's and 1950's, the size of their national domestic markets,[49] and their relative independence in the production of capital goods make comparison with Central America difficult.

This information gap makes it essential to continue and accelerate studies of the Central American economy as a whole, which should focus on both production and the services and regional agencies required to complete the process of economic integration.

---

[48] For example, questions of customs legislation and trade-marks. It should also be noted that trade is closely tied to tax legislation in general.

[49] Note that even the smallest country of the EEC (excepting Luxembourg) has almost the same population and a much larger domestic market than all five Central American countries together.

Although these agencies were provided for and defined in previous years by the Committee on Economic Co-operation of the Central American Isthmus, they have been set up only recently. These include the Permanent Secretariat of the General Treaty on Central American Economic Integration (SIECA), the Central American Committee on Industrial Initiatives, the Central American Chamber of Compensation, and the Central American Bank for Economic Integration, whose effective action has not yet been fully implemented. The last agency commenced operation only in September, 1961. Mention should also be made of the Central American Institute for Industrial Technological Research (ICAITI) and the Central American College of Public Administration (ESAPAC).

New Demands on Managerial Capacity in the Manufacturing Sector. The industrialists of a Latin American country know the absorption capacity of the national market and the competitive activities of other entrepreneurs. This knowledge, largely the result of extended experience, enables them to project their capacity and to regulate their production with an anticipated measure of risk. In the case of Central America, this knowledge has rapidly transcended national boundaries in certain cases, particularly where the industrialists were invited to participate in organization of the bilateral free-trade treaties. Even so, most of this group, either because the size of the enterprise prevented regional-scale operation or because of their lack of managerial ability, were unable to analyze market expansion in their particular case. Even in such industries as textiles, where increased regional sales have been accompanied by a certain degree of specialization, this situation restricts sales to the regional market. Thus, for example, despite the fact that the demand for cotton poplin multiplied approximately 12 times between 1957 and 1961, attaining in the latter year a volume that exceeded optimum plant capacity by 40 per cent, existing or projected companies with finishing equipment will be able to satisfy only approximately one-fifth of this total consumption. This is due in part to the fact that the major share of such consumption corresponds to the derived demand of shirt factories in El Salvador, while direct consumer sales—more easily estimated by the producer—show very little change. This factor will automatically tend to correct itself; but such a correction could be accelerated by means of an advisory agency such as ICAITI, conducting regional market studies, and through a closer relationship between national associations of manufacturing entrepreneurs.

Regional Trade Mechanisms. Reciprocal trade is not properly wholesale by nature and does not follow the same course as traditional foreign trade. Traditional trade possesses a relatively efficient organization by which it links overseas buyers and suppliers with the banking systems, transportation and storage facilities, and wholesale and retail trade. With respect to imports, consumer goods are distributed in each Central American country according to the geographical structure of effective demand and intermediate and capital goods, at the direct request of the producers.

This mechanism is still deficient with regard to intra-Central American trade. Regional marketing of farm commodities is carried out on a rudimentary level that has an unfavorable effect on the volume and form in which these goods enter reciprocal trade. In recent years, it has acquired greater effectiveness with the establishment and expansion of official agencies regulating the production and trade of grain; but the flow of goods from the producer to the wholesaler has been stepped up primarily through massive expansion of the transporter, the most common, but only initially the most efficient, intermediary in Latin America.

Studies are currently being conducted on farm marketing in Central America; those on grain have already been completed in preliminary form.[50] Although these studies and the investments in storage facilities recommended constitute a long step forward, the introduction of modern technology to the trade of other farm commodities is imperative in order to achieve the diversification and increased processing required by the Central American demand for foodstuffs. It should be noted that although the replacement of overseas grain imports has attained quite a satisfactory margin, in 1961 imports of foods that could be produced in Central America were valued at more than $20 million.

With respect to manufacturing products, there was an almost total lack of a Central American marketing mechanism prior to 1957. Since that time, several wholesalers have expanded their operations to other national markets and have helped to improve regional distribution of consumer goods. Most of this distribution continued, however, to depend on direct contacts among producers, on the establishment of sales branches in another country, and, for most of the small and intermediate producers, on agreements with a wholesaler in the country receiving the merchandise. Consequently, there is a lack of relation between the structure of demand and the distribution of Central American production, which occasionally leads to assumed saturation of a Central American

[50] See ECLA, *Comité de Cooperación Económica del Istmo Centroamericano, Progreso de los Estudios sobre Producción y Mercado Integrado de Granos en Centroamérica* (San Salvador, January, 1963) (Doc. E/CN.12/CCE/271).

market in which a volume of the same article as that imported from abroad is often sold.

This factor will tend to correct itself in time, since it depends on the volume and regularity of the transactions. It is presumed that, prior to 1967, it will have acquired an efficiency comparable to that of overseas trade.

Replacement of Overseas Imports and Reciprocal Trade

The chief characteristic of Central American trade is the regional scope it provides for the replacement of overseas imports. This is the basis for expectations of its continued growth and the installation and projections of new manufacturing plants (see Table 8–18). It is also the reason for the pronounced expansion of this trade, together with the corresponding investments, despite the decline in Central American capacity to import.

The process of import replacement has been basic to the economic development of Latin America, for it has led to more intensive industrial

TABLE 8–18. Central America: Manufacturing Plants Recently Completed or under Construction and Planned for 1963[a]

(*Number of installations*)

Industry	Industrial structure in 1958 per cent of value added	Completed or under construction	Planned
Food	26.5	11	3
Textiles and clothing	27.3	1	3
Wood	4.1	—	1
Furniture	2.1	—	1
Paper, cardboard, and their products	0.2	—	3
Rubber products	0.5	2	1
Chemical products	4.3	7	8
Glass and ceramics	...	1	6
Metal manufactures (CIIU 350)	0.9	1	5
Electrical products (CIIU 370)	0.3	3	5
Miscellaneous	1.3	2	2
Total	100.0[b]	28	38

[a] Excluding expansion of existing capacity and industries protected by the agreement on Industries of Integration.

[b] Including other industrial groups.

Source: Unofficial information.

development, based primarily on additions to the market, than was possible to the exporting sectors because of the variable conditions of demand and prices on the international market. Except for isolated cases, economic development has been accompanied by the replacement of imports, a circumstance also observable in the recent past in Central America. It would be reasonable to expect that this process will continue on an individual basis in each country but that its dynamism would be related to market expansion.

In other words, the actual prospects for growth of reciprocal trade are based on the procedure to be adopted and the scope to be achieved by the integration process. If entrepreneurs persist in installing industries that duplicate existing production, some of the advantages offered by the common market with regard to economies of scale will disappear and, in this case, the flow of goods to reciprocal trade will be curtailed. On the other hand, if the integration authorities succeed in preventing the uneconomical duplication of investments, this will lead to the advantages inherent in a larger plant, and the production resulting from replacement of overseas imports will necessarily expand reciprocal trade.

Estimates on the growth of the latter entail, therefore, an analysis of the possibilities of replacing overseas imports.

The 1961 *Estudio Económico de América Latina* [51] summarized the state of that process and classified its phases into the stages of replacement of consumer goods, intermediate goods, and finally capital goods. It stated that a given relation between the size of market and economies of scale corresponds to each of these three stages.

Although this very marked subdivision of the import replacement process is real only if restricted definitions for the three types of goods are accepted, it does permit a description of industrialization based on the import replacement process by stages as a logistic curve that tends to a limit equal in size to the corresponding demand.[52] That is, at any point on the curve, the possibility of replacement at a given time can be evaluated by how much it differs from the limit to which it tends or by measuring imports at that time, which amounts to the same thing.

Undoubtedly, this scheme suffers from a certain degree of simplification; for, on the one hand, the demands that constitute the limits vary in size and, on the other, there are ecological limitations in the case of farm commodities and restrictions imposed by economies of scale on

---

[51] OAS/ECLA, *Estudio Económico de América Latina, 1961* (Washington, D.C., 1962).

[52] This simplification is excessive in the case of capital goods. Here reference is made only to consumer and intermediate goods.

manufactures. It is also true that, in the latter case, the economies of scale affecting the production of intermediate goods can only be utilized once the first stage of import replacement has been completed or shows signs of completion in the foreseeable future.

Despite these observations, the simplified scheme is obviously applicable to the case of Central America, where economic integration has brought about a significant variation in the adjustments made in the past by economies of scale with regard to the replacement process. The former subdivision of the market was the chief obstacle to industrialization, as shown by the increase in reciprocal trade of manufactures in the last five years.

The expansion of such trade has encountered negative factors preventing the growth of both agricultural and manufacturing production in some of the branches where the new scope of the market had eliminated the restrictions on investments previously imposed by economies of scale. It should be noted that there is at present a deferred margin of overseas import replacement composed mainly of farm commodities, consumer and intermediate goods produced by light industries, and construction materials. Following a comparison of the import value of these goods with plant size in other countries (see Annex) it has been estimated that $100 million, or more than one-fifth of overseas imports, correspond to goods whose potential replacement was made possible by the formation of the common market but whose actual replacement has been deferred.

Elimination of this lag would require a step-up in the growth rate of manufactures, which would, of course, depend on the number of years needed to complete the investments required. The magnitude of this rate can be evaluated by the fact that food production at the plant level [53] would have to increase by between 25 and 30 per cent, while textiles and clothing would have to double. In the case of manufacturing groups that are less developed or simply nonexistent in Central America, there would be very high relative additions of particular significance with reference to paper and cardboard, rubber, cement, and finished construction materials.

Although the probability of error may be very high, it is estimated that investments designed to eliminate the deferred margin of replacement would enable the manufacturing growth rate to increase from the current 8 per cent a year to 12 per cent, if a term of five years is allowed for completion of such investments. Even accepting a greater probability of

---

[53] The processing of parchment coffee is omitted in this case.

error, it is difficult to estimate the amount of such investments, since there is little precision with respect to the potential yield of underutilized capacity, another unfavorable consequence of the former subdivision of the market, and to the percentage represented by supplementary additions to equipment. In no case can the estimated initial figure be less than $150 million in fixed equipment used directly for production, a figure which will rise sharply if only part of this underutilized capacity can be used.

One of the reasons for difficulty in determining investment is the possibility of initiating almost simultaneously productions that would supplement the preceding ones. This latent margin of additional replacement is composed of raw materials and intermediate manufactures corresponding primarily to the chemical and base metal industries. The case of rayon illustrates the difference between the former category of replaceable articles and the new one of products whose replacement is subject to increased manufacturing development.

In 1959, Central America imported 700 tons of rayon fiber and yarn and the equivalent of 4,000 tons of raw rayon in fabric and clothing. A plant operating economically and at costs perhaps lower than those on the international market could produce 1,200 tons of acetate and 3,000 tons of viscose.[54] That is to say, deferred replacement (in this case cloth and clothing) and latent replacement (fiber) could be carried out separately or simultaneously, resulting in different estimates of investment and domestic product, despite the fact that consumption of the finished product would not change. The investment required to replace rayon cloth, at the rate of $4,400 per ton of spinning and weaving capacity, may amount to $17.6 million, plus another $6 million for a finishing plant that could also be used to process current output of rayon cloth. The addition of a rayon plant would require a minimum of $11 million more, and the industry as a whole would need a working capital of $7 million.

In other words, either $22 million or $35 million may be invested to supply full production for a consumption whose imports would amount in five years to $40 million. This investment would increase sixfold the production of rayon cloth and, by increasing the domestic supply of textile fibers by one-third, would make it feasible to replace imports of a basic group of chemical products, since rayon production requires cellulose, sulphuric acid, and caustic soda, three products widely used in the manufacturing sector.

[54] See ECLA, Doc. E/CN.12/CEE/245.

It will be noted that future trade expansion, which would hypothetically include two-thirds of the production aimed at reducing the deferred margin of replacement and perhaps one-third to one-half in other cases,[55] depends largely on the continued process of Central American industrialization. Its location is also important, since the flow of goods to such trade will tend to increase with scattered production and to decrease with concentrated production, unless such concentration should reduce the radial trend of trade and thus help to maintain the self-liquidation [56] of current trade balances.

[55] It is assumed here that the producer country would absorb a higher percentage than the average of the other countries and that industries satisfying derived demand would be located preferentially near the purchasers.

[56] Hypothetically, there is a need for an increase in the industrial base in Honduras and Nicaragua over and above the regional average in order to maintain a balanced flow of goods. The replacement of imports in the case of raw foodstuffs that constitute the chief export of these two countries to the region is limited in volume and, save for an improbable increase of its elasticity demand coefficient in the other countries, would not suffice to finance increased purchases of manufactures by Honduras and Nicaragua.

ANNEX. Central America: Overseas and Reciprocal Imports in 1961, in Approximate Relation to Replacement Potential

Sector	1961 Imports (Millions of dollars)		Observations
	Overseas	Reciprocal	
A. Primary sector			
Agriculture	19.1	10.4	Partial replacement only.
Wheat	7.6	—	
Forestry	1.4	0.1	
Mining	4.3	0.3	These imports would increase in the future.
B. Secondary Sector			
1. Existing industries			
Food			
Meat	1.8	0.2	Export industry.
Canned fish	1.2	0.3	Export industry.
Grain milling	7.6	0.7	Underutilized regional capacity.
Bakeries	0.5	0.1	
Sugar	1.4	0.4	Export industry.
Confections	0.9	0.7	
Fats, fodder, and miscellaneous foods	4.4	3.3	
Textiles, footgear, and ready-made clothing			
Woven yarn and fabric	40.8	3.0	More than half are cotton. There are no apparent limitations imposed by economies of scale.
Knitted fabric	2.8	0.9	Same as above.
Apparel	6.1	0.8	
Other clothing	6.9	1.0	Includes hard fibers and wool.
Footgear	1.7	0.8	Underutilized regional capacity.
Wood and furniture			
Sawmills	1.2	1.3	Export industry.
Wood products	0.8	0.3	
Plywood	0.1	0.2	
Furniture	1.5	0.3	
Paper and cardboard products			
Intermediate and consumer goods	9.1		A plant to manufacture cardboard boxes was installed in 1962.
Printing	3.2		Books, magazines, and related products represent only $0.7 million.
Leather and hides			
Tanning plants	2.8		
Articles	1.3		

(Continued)

ANNEX. *Continued*

Sector	1961 Imports Overseas (*Millions of dollars*)	1961 Imports Reciprocal (*Millions of dollars*)	Observations
Rubber			
Tires and tubes	4.6	0.9	A second plant will be installed in Costa Rica.
Rubber articles	2.5		
Chemical products			
Soaps and cleansing preparations	2.4	0.4	Plants under construction or planned in Honduras, El Salvador, and Nicaragua.
Paints	2.1	0.6	Oil plant under construction in Nicaragua.
Fats	0.7	1.4	
2. Industries made possible by regional market			
Food			
Dairy products	6.8	0.4	Overseas imports have decreased as milk production has expanded. Increased replacement requires improved dairy herds.
Dehydrated milk	2.7	—	Construction will be initiated in 1963 on a plant in Nicaragua.
Cheese	0.3		Investment is planned for a cheddar cheese plant.
Preserved fruits and vegetables	3.1	0.4	The average capacity of a canning factory is $1.3 million in sales (1958). Freezing plants sell $0.3 million.
Textiles			
Rayon, intermediate and finished products	8.0		See text.
Chemical products			
Insecticides	14.6	0.6	Construction will start soon on a chlorinated insecticide plant in Nicaragua. Similar projects also exist in El Salvador and Guatemala.

General Note: It is planned to produce caustic soda and chlorine in Nicaragua and sulphuric acid in El Salvador; a sodium sulphate plant is currently under construction in Honduras.

INDEX

Acetone production, 159
Administration: planned investment in, 206
Africa: sugar production, 17; coffee imports, 28; coffee exports, 28, 31, 36, 293, 299; cacao production, 29; cacao exports, 29, 30, 318; coffee production, 36; corn production, 39; corn exports, 45; wool stocks, 55; Rhodesian Selection Trust, 55; copper production, 55, 57; wool exports, 56; copper exports, 58; tin production, 62; total exports to, 70; banana exports, 303
Agency for International Development (AID), 88, 90, 91, 92, 93, 94
Agrarian reform programs, 209–35: in Colombia, 209, 213n, 214n, 216, 223–28; in Chile, 209, 216, 222–23, 224; in Costa Rica, 209, 216, 224, 228; in Dominican Republic, 209, 218, 224, 229; in Peru, 210, 215, 220, 224, 233; in Guatemala, 210, 218, 224, 229; in Honduras, 210, 218, 224, 229–30; in Nicaragua, 210, 218, 224, 230–31; in Panama, 210, 220, 224, 231; in Paraguay, 210, 220, 224, 232; legislation on, 211–222; distribution of land, 212, 213; technical assistance to families, 213; expropriation of land, 213, 215; in Mexico, 234; in Bolivia, 234; in Venezuela, 235
Agriculture: total production in, 122; and tractor production, 179–81; export of products, 203; planned increases in, 204; planned investment in, 206; in Central America, 252, 320, 321, 323, 324, 331. *See also* Agrarian reform programs

Aguan Valley: families settled in, 225, 230
Agustin Codazzi Geographical Institute, 223
Alanje project, 225
Alliance for Progress economic programs, 185–245; development planning, 185–209; growth targets, 191–201; gross domestic product by sectors, 201–8; reducing structural imbalance, 201–9; regional disparities, 208; employment problems, 209; agrarian reform programs, 209–35; tax reform, 235–45. *See also* Agrarian reform programs; Tax reform
Alto Beni project, 235
Altos Hornos Güemes steel plant, 171
Ammonia plants, 158
Ammonium anhydride plants, 159
Ammonium production, 160, 161
Apurimac: families settled in, 225, 234
Arequipa: irrigation in, 234
Argentina: sugar stocks in, 17; sugar exports, 19, 20; sugar production, 20; wheat production, 38; corn production, 39, 42; corn exports, 39, 44; wheat exports, 40; meat exports, 42, 43, 46, 47, 48; corn stocks in, 46; cotton production, 51; cotton exports, 51, 52; wool exports, 54, 56; wool stocks in, 55; lead production, 60; zinc production, 60; petroleum production, 66; exports from, 69; intraregional exports, 73; capacity to import, 76, 78, 79, 81; balance-of-payments position, 79; U.S. grants to, 92; AID loans and net disbursements, 94; Social Progress Trust Fund in, 95; Inter-American Development Bank report, 97; World

427

428 INDEX

Bank loans and disbursements, 98; capital from foreign countries, 100; U.S. private capital in, 103; private export credits, 107; assets in U.S. banks, 109; foreign debt servicing, 111; debt with International Monetary Fund, 114; compensatory loans by Eximbank, 115; compensatory accounts, 117, 118; gold reserves and foreign exchange, 117, 118; fixed investments in, 122; population increase, 122; production in, 122, 146, 148; fixed capital formation in, 125; direct investment from U.S., 125; money supply trends, 128; monetary expansion in, 130; public and private sector bank lending, 133, 138, 141; exchange rate adjustments in, 135; cost of living index, 135, 137; bank reforms in, 144; consumer-goods industries in, 151, 152; paper industry in, 153, 154–55; chemical industry in, 158, 160; petroleum refining in, 162–64; cement production, 166; iron and steel industry, 169, 170–71; motor vehicle production, 175, 177–78; tractor production, 180; shipbuilding in, 182; industrial machinery production, 184; development plans of, 189; tax reform in, 237, 241, 242, 243, 244

Arica automobile assembly plant, 179

Asia: corn production in, 42; corn imports of, 44; total exports to, 70. *See also* China; Japan

Australia: sugar production, 17; wheat production, 38; wheat exports, 40; meat exports, 47, 48; wool consumption, 53; wool stocks in, 55; wool exports, 56; copper production, 57

Austria: banana imports, 24, 26; coffee imports, 32, 273

Automotive industry, 148, 174–79. *See also* Motor vehicle industry

Bahia: investments in, 208

Balance of payments, 74–85, 191–201; and noncompensatory capital movements, 85–111; compensatory financing of, 86, 112–19; countries with surplus, 130; countries with deficits, 130; countries in equilibrium, 130; and price pressures, 133–37

Bananas: prices of, 11, 19, 22; Action Group for, 15, 22; exports of, 19–24; volume of exports, 23; imports of selected countries, 26–27; exports from Central America, 265, 266, 271–75, 276, 294, 303–6

Banco Nacional Ejidal of Mexico, 234

Banks: public and private sector credit from, 133, 138, 140–43; reserve requirements, 141–42; interest rates on lending, 143; institutional reforms 143–45

Barrancabermeja petrochemical complex, 160

Beef: *See* Meat

Beer: Central American production of, 348; per capita production of, 351; per capita consumption of, 352

Belgium: economic activity in, 5, 8; banana imports, 24, 26; coffee imports, 32; meat imports, 46; wool consumption in, 53; copper consumption in, 57; copper imports, 58; tin imports, 63; private export credits, 107; export price variations, 388

Belgo-Mineira steelworks, 171

Benzene production, 159

Bessemer steel process, 170n

Beverages: Central American production of, 340, 344, 346, 348; per capita production of beer, 351; per capita consumption of beer, 352; employment in industry, 360, 362; and capital intensity, 366, 368; reciprocal imports, 397

Bolivia: lead production, 60; zinc production, 60; tin production, 62; tin exports, 63; silver production, 65; petroleum production, 66; intraregional exports, 73; capacity to import, 76, 78, 79, 81; balance-of-payments position, 79; U.S. grants to, 92; AID loans and net disbursements, 94; Social Progress Trust Fund in, 95; Inter-American Development Bank report, 97; World Bank loans and disbursements, 98; capital from foreign countries, 100; private export credits, 107; assets in U.S. banks, 109; debt with International Monetary Fund, 114; gold reserves and foreign exchange, 117, 118; compensatory accounts, 117, 118; fixed investments in, 122; population increase in, 122; production in, 122; fixed capital formation in, 125; direct investments from U.S., 125; money supply trends, 128; monetary expansion in, 130; public and private sector bank lending, 133, 138, 141; exchange rate adjustments in, 135; cost of living index, 135, 137; bank reforms in, 144; paper industry in, 153; petroleum refining in, 163; cement production, 166; development plans of, 186, 188; planned growth of gross domestic product, 192; foreign capital contributions, 194; financing of planned investment, 198; planned foreign trade of, 202; planned increases in production, 204; regional characteristics in, 208; unemployment in, 209; agrarian reform in, 234; tax reform in, 244

Bonds: special issue in Argentina, 139

Brazil: exports to United States, 13; sugar exports, 19, 20, 21; sugar production, 20; banana exports, 23, 26; cacao production, 29; cacao exports, 29, 30; coffee exports, 31, 33, 36, 37; coffee production, 36; corn production, 42; meat exports, 46, 47, 48; cotton production, 50, 51; cotton exports, 51, 52; petroleum production, 66; intraregional exports, 73; capacity to import, 76, 78, 79, 81; balance-of-payments position, 79; U.S. grants to, 92; AID loans and net disbursements, 94; Social Progress Trust Fund in, 95; Inter-American Development Bank report, 97; World Bank loans and disbursements, 98; U.S. private capital in, 103; private export credits, 107; assets in U.S. banks, 109; foreign debt servicing, 111; debt with International Monetary Fund, 114; compensatory loans by Eximbank, 115; compensatory accounts, 117, 118; gold reserves and foreign exchange, 117, 118; fixed investments in, 122; population increase in, 122; production in, 122; fixed capital formation in, 125; direct investments from U.S., 125; money supply trends, 128; monetary expansion in, 130; public and private sector bank lending, 133, 138, 141; exchange rate adjustments in, 135; cost of living index, 135, 137; bank reforms in, 144; manufacturing growth in, 147, 148; consumer-goods industries in, 151, 152; paper industry in, 153, 155; chemical industries in, 157–59; petroleum refining in, 163, 164, 165; cement production, 166; iron and steel industry, 169, 171–72; motor vehicle production, 175, 177; tractor production, 180–81; shipbuilding in, 181–82; industrial machinery production, 183; development plans of, 188; planned growth of gross domestic product, 192; foreign capital contributions, 194; financing of planned investment, 198; planned foreign trade of, 202; planned increases in production, 204; planned investment by sectors, 206; regional characteristics in, 208; tax reform in, 237, 241, 242, 244

Cacao: exports of, 10, 24–25, 29, 30; price of, 11, 24; Action Group for, 15; consumption of, 28; stocks of, 28; production of, 28, 29; imports of selected countries, 30; exports from Central America, 265, 266, 288–90, 294, 317–18; International Cocoa Agreement, 292, 293, 317

Calcium carbonate production, 161

Callao ammonium plant, 161

Camacari chemical works, 158

Cameroon. See Africa

Campeche project, 234

Canada: economic activity in, 4, 5, 6; imports from Latin America, 13; banana imports, 26, 276, 304; coffee imports, 32, 33; wheat production, 38; corn imports, 44; meat exports, 48; copper consumption in, 57; copper production, 57; copper exports, 58; lead production, 60; zinc production, 60; silver production, 65; petroleum production, 66; petroleum exports, 67, 69; total exports to, 70; imports from Central America, 267; wood imports, 282; meat imports, 285; sugar imports, 287

Canal Zone: cocoa imports of, 290

Capital: noncompensatory, 85–111; from United States, 86n, 87, 88–96;

430 INDEX

from loans and grants, 86n, 87, 88–101; total flow of, 87, 108–11; from international agencies, 96–99; foreign contributions of, 99–101, 194–95; private, 101–11, 197; compensatory, 112–19; fixed capital formation, 120–27; target growth rates of, 191–201; private savings, 197; public savings, 197; foreign savings, 200; intensity coefficients in Central America, 364–71

Caracas: urban services in, 209
Carbon disulphide production, 160
Carbon tetrachloride production, 159
Cardboard production. *See* Paper
Caribbean area: wood imports, 282; meat imports, 285
Cartagena: chemical industry in, 160
Caustic soda production, 158, 160
Cellulose production. *See* Paper
Cement industry, 148, 165–67; growth of production, 148, 150; Central American production, 341, 348, 349; per capita production, 351; per capita consumption, 352
Central America: cotton production, 50; intraregional trade, 72, 375, 394–425; Social Progress Trust Fund in, 95; capital from foreign countries, 100; private export credits, 107; paper industry in, 153, 156; cement production, 166; iron and steel industry, 169; development plans of, 186; tax reforms in, 244; exports of, 250–51, 263–318; cotton exports, 251, 263, 265, 266, 275–79, 294, 306–10; production in, 251–55, 319–71; employment in, 255, 354–62; imports of, 255–57, 372–425; problems of small countries, 257–62; coffee exports, 265, 266, 268–71, 272, 273, 294, 296–303; banana exports, 265, 266, 271–75, 276, 294, 303–6; wood exports, 265, 266, 280, 281, 282, 294, 311–12, 313; meat exports, 265, 266, 280–84, 285, 294, 312–14, 315; sugar exports, 265, 266, 284–88, 294, 315–17; cocoa exports, 265, 266, 288–90, 294, 317–18; cotton production, 307; agriculture in, 320, 321, 323, 324, 331; manufacturing in, 321, 323, 324, 331, 334–71; gross domestic product in, 323; capital intensity in, 364–71; reciprocal trade in, 375, 394–425; treaties in, 375, 400; foodstuff imports, 377, 378–80, 382; chemical product imports, 377, 380–85; investments in, 393–94; transportation in, 399; industrialization of, 407. *See also* Exports; Imports; Production
Charter of Punta del Este, 88, 185, 187, 210, 211, 234
Chemical industries, 157–61; in Brazil, 157–59; in Mexico, 158, 159; in Argentina, 158, 160; in Colombia, 158, 160; in Venezuela, 158, 161; in Chile, 158, 161; in Peru, 158, 161; in Paraguay, 161; in Ecuador, 161; Central American output, 340, 344, 346; employment in, 360, 362; and capital intensity, 366, 369; Central American imports, 377, 380–85; import value of products, 390; wholesale prices of products, 390; reciprocal imports, 397
Chile: exports to United States, 13; meat exports, 47; copper production, 55, 57; copper exports, 58; petroleum production, 66; intraregional exports, 73; capacity to import, 76, 78, 79, 81; balance-of-payments position, 79; U.S. grants to, 92; AID loans and net disbursements, 94; Social Progress Trust Fund in, 95; Inter-American Development Bank report, 97; World Bank loans and disbursements, 98; U.S. private capital in, 103; private export credits, 107; assets in U.S. banks, 109; foreign debt servicing, 111; debt with International Monetary Fund, 114; compensatory loans by Eximbank, 115; compensatory accounts, 117, 118; gold reserves and foreign exchange, 117, 118; production in, 122; fixed investments in, 122; population increase in, 122; fixed capital formation in, 125; direct investments from U.S., 125; money supply trends, 128; monetary expansion in, 130; public and private sector bank lending, 133, 138, 141; exchange rate adjustments in, 135; cost of living index, 135, 137; manufacturing growth in, 148, 149; consumer-goods industries in, 151, 152; paper industry in, 153, 156; chemical industry in, 158, 161;

petroleum refining in, 163, 164, 165; cement production, 166; iron and steel industry, 169, 172; motor vehicle production, 175, 179; tractor production, 181; shipbuilding in, 183; development plans of, 185, 186, 188; planned growth of gross domestic product, 192; foreign contributions, 194; financing of planned investment, 198; planned foreign trade of, 202; planned increases in production, 204; planned investment by sectors, 206; regional characteristics in, 209; agrarian reform in, 209, 216, 222–23, 224; tax reform in, 238, 242, 244; cocoa imports, 290

Chimbote: calcium carbonate plant in, 161; steel plant in, 173

China, continental: sugar imports, 19, 21; tin exports, 64; total exports to, 70

Chlorine production, 160, 161

Cigarettes. *See* Tobacco

Citric acid production, 160

Clothing: growth rates in production of, 152; Central American output, 340, 344, 346; employment in industry, 360, 362; and capital intensity, 366, 368; wholesale prices of, 390. *See also* Textiles

Cocoa. *See* Cacao

Coffee: prices of, 10, 11, 25; restrictions on consumption of, 14; International Coffee Agreement, 25, 302; export of, 25–35, 36, 37; stocks of, 31; imports of selected countries, 31, 32, 33; production of, 31, 36; duties on, 32; exports from Central America, 265, 266, 268–71, 272, 273, 294, 296–303

Coke by-products: use of, 157, 171n

Colombia: sugar exports, 20; sugar production, 20; banana exports, 23, 26; cacao production, 29; cacao exports, 29; coffee exports, 31, 33, 36, 37; coffee production, 36; cotton production, 50, 51; cotton exports, 51, 52; petroleum production, 66; petroleum exports, 67, 68, 69; intraregional exports, 73; capacity to import, 76, 78, 79, 81; balance-of-payments position, 79; U. S. grants to, 92; AID loans and net disbursements, 94; Social Progress Trust Fund in, 95; Inter-American Development Bank report, 97; World Bank loans and disbursements, 98; U.S. private capital in, 103; private export credits, 107; assets in U.S. banks, 109; foreign debt servicing, 111; debt with International Monetary Fund, 114; Compensatory loans by Eximbank, 115; compensatory accounts, 117, 118; gold reserves and foreign exchange, 117, 118; fixed investments in, 122; population increase in, 122; production in, 122; direct investments from U.S., 125; fixed capital formation in, 125; money supply trends, 128; monetary expansion in, 130; public and private sector bank lending in, 133, 138, 141; exchange rate adjustments in, 135; cost of living index, 135, 137; bank reforms in, 144; manufacturing growth in, 148, 149; paper industry in, 153, 155; chemical industry in, 158, 160; petroleum refining in, 163, 165; cement production, 166; iron and steel industry, 169, 172; motor vehicle production, 175, 179; tractor production, 181; development plans of, 185, 186, 188; planned growth of gross domestic product, 192; foreign capital contributions, 194; financing of planned investment, 198; planned foreign trade of, 202; planned increases in production, 204; planned investment by sectors, 206; regional characteristics in, 209; agrarian reform in, 209, 213n, 214n, 216, 223–28; National Agrarian Reform Institute (INCORA), 213, 224, 227; tax reform in, 238, 244; cocoa imports, 290

Comisión de Reforma Agraria in Panama, 224

Commerce: planned increases in, 204; planned investment in, 206; in Central America, 321, 324

Communications: planned increases in, 204; planned investment in, 206; in Central America, 321, 324

Compensatory financing, 13, 16, 86, 88, 112–19

Concepción petroleum refinery, 165

Concón petroleum refinery, 164

Congo Republic. *See* Africa
Consejo Social Agrario in Colombia, 227n
Construction: planned increases in, 204; planned investment in, 206; in Central America, 321, 324
Consumer goods, 148, 149, 150–51, 152; imports of, 203; wholesale prices of, 390
Consumption: of cocoa beans, 28; of cotton, 49; of wool, 53; of copper, 57; of tin, 62
Copper: price of, 11, 54; exports of, 54–58, 69; production of, 57; consumption of, 57; imports of selected countries, 58
Corn: price of, 11, 38, exports of, 38–39, 44; production of, 42; imports of selected countries, 44; stocks of, 46
Corporación de Fomento de la Producción (CORFO), 185n
Corporación de Reforma Agraria in Chile, 224
Cosipa steel plant, 171
Cost of living indices, 135, 137
Costa Rica: sugar production, 20; sugar exports, 20, 286; banana exports, 23, 26, 274, 275, 303; cacao production, 29; cacao exports, 29, 289, 290, 317; coffee exports, 31, 33, 36, 37, 268, 269; coffee production, 36; intraregional exports, 73; capacity to import, 76, 78, 79, 81; balance-of-payments position, 79; U.S. grants to, 92; AID loans and net disbursements, 94; Social Progress Trust Fund in, 95; Inter-American Development Bank report, 97; World Bank loans and disbursements, 98; capital from foreign countries, 100; private export credits, 107; debt with International Monetary Fund, 114; gold reserves and foreign exchange, 117, 118; compensatory accounts, 117, 118; production in, 122; fixed investments in, 122; population increase in, 122; direct investments from U.S., 125; fixed capital formation in, 125; money supply trends, 128; monetary expansion in, 130; public and private sector bank lending, 133, 138, 141; cost of living index, 137; bank reforms in, 144; petroleum refining in, 165; development plans of, 189; agrarian reform in, 209, 216, 224, 228; tax reform in, 239, 242, 243; exports from, 264; cotton exports, 276, 277; wood exports, 281, 311; meat exports, 283, 313; productive structure of, 323, 326, 331; industries in, 344; per capita production in, 351; per capita consumption in, 352; employment in, 360; capital intensity in, 366, 368; volume of imports, 373; reciprocal imports, 404

Cotton: price of, 11, 49; stocks of, 49; consumption of, 49, 352; production of, 49, 51, 351; exports of, 49–53, 70; Agreement on International Trade in Cotton Textiles, 50; imports of selected countries, 52; exports from Central America, 251, 263, 265, 266, 275–79, 294, 306–10; production in Central America, 307, 348; world demand for, 309
Credits: compensatory, 13, 16; export, from European governments, 100, 107
Cuba: sugar production, 16–19, 20; sugar exports, 19, 20, 21; exports from, 71; capital from foreign countries, 100; disbursements to, 101; private export credits, 107
Cubatão refinery, 158n
Currency: devaluation of, 80, 82, 83, 134
Cuzco fertilizer plant, 161
Czechoslovakia: coffee imports of, 32

Debt, foreign: servicing of, 110–11
Denmark: coffee imports, 32, 273
Devaluation: of currency, 80, 82, 83; of exchange rate, 134
Development planning, 185–209
Dillon, C. Douglas: speech by, 88n
Direct private investments, 124, 125
Disbursements: on loans from United States, 88–96; on loans from international agencies, 96–99; from foreign countries, 99–101
Dominican Republic: exports to United States, 12; sugar exports, 19, 20, 21; sugar production, 20; banana exports, 23, 26; cacao production, 29; cacao exports, 29, 30; coffee exports, 31, 33, 36, 37; coffee production, 36; intraregional exports, 73; capacity

to import, 76, 78, 79, 81; balance-of-payments position, 79; U.S. grants to, 92; AID loans and net disbursements, 94; Social Progress Trust Fund in, 95; Inter-American Development Bank report, 97; World Bank loans and disbursements, 98; capital from foreign countries, 100; U.S. private capital in, 103; private export credits, 107; assets in U.S. banks, 109; debt with International Monetary Fund, 114; gold reserves and foreign exchange, 117, 118; compensatory accounts, 117, 118; population increase in, 122; fixed investments in, 122; production in, 122; fixed capital formation in, 125; direct investments from U.S., 125; money supply trends, 128; monetary expansion in, 130; public and private sector bank lending, 133, 138, 141; cost of living index, 137; petroleum refining in, 165; cement production, 166; development plans of, 189; agrarian reform in, 209, 218, 224, 229; tax reform in, 238, 242, 244

Duque de Caxias refinery, 157, 164

Duties: on coffee imports, 32

Economic activity: in European Economic Community, 1, 5, 8–9; in United States, 1–4, 5; in industrialized countries, 1–9; in Canada, 4, 5, 6; in Luxembourg, 5; in Belgium, 5, 8; in France, 5, 8; in Italy, 5, 8; in Netherlands, 5, 8; in Germany, 5, 8. *See also* Alliance for Progress economic programs

Economic Commission for Latin America (ECLA), 109, 399

Ecuador: exports to United States, 13; sugar production, 20; sugar exports, 20; banana exports, 23, 26; cacao production, 29; cacao exports, 29, 30; coffee exports, 31, 33, 36, 37; coffee production, 36; petroleum production, 66; intraregional exports, 73; capacity to import, 76, 78, 79, 81; balance-of-payments position, 79; U.S. grants to, 92; AID loans and net disbursements, 94; Social Progress Trust Fund in, 95; Inter-American Development Bank report, 97; World Bank loans and disbursements, 98; capital from foreign countries, 100; private export credits, 107; foreign debt servicing, 111; debt with International Monetary Fund, 114; compensatory accounts, 117, 118; gold reserves and foreign exchange, 117, 118; production in, 122; population increase in, 122; fixed investments in, 122; fixed capital formation in, 125; direct investments from U.S., 125; money supply trends, 128; monetary expansion in, 130; public and private sector bank lending, 133, 138, 141; cost of living index, 137; manufacturing growth in, 148, 149; paper industry, 153; chemical industry, 161; petroleum refining in, 163; cement production, 166; development plans of, 185, 189; tax reform, 238, 242, 244

Education: planned investment in, 206

Egypt: cotton exports of, 50, 52

El Salvador: sugar production, 20; sugar exports, 20, 286, 315; coffee exports, 31, 33, 36, 37, 268, 269; coffee production, 36; cotton production, 51, 307; cotton exports, 51, 52, 276, 277, 279; intraregional exports, 73; capacity to import, 76, 78, 79, 81; balance-of-payments position, 79; U.S. grants to, 92; AID loans and net disbursements, 94; Social Progress Trust Fund in, 95; Inter-American Development Bank report, 97; World Bank loans and disbursements, 98; capital from foreign countries, 100; private export credits, 107; assets in U.S. banks, 109; debt with International Monetary Fund, 114; compensatory loans by Eximbank, 115; gold reserves and foreign exchange, 117, 118; compensatory accounts, 117, 118; fixed investments in, 122; production in, 122; population increase in, 122; fixed capital formation in, 125; direct investments from U.S., 125; money supply trends, 128; monetary expansion in, 130; public and private sector bank lending, 133, 138, 141; cost of living index, 137; Central Bank legislation, 143; paper industry, 153; petroleum refining in, 165; cement production, 166; iron and steel industry, 169; development plans of, 189; tax reform in, 240, 243, 244; exports from, 264; banana exports, 274, 275; wood exports, 281, 311; meat exports, 283; productive structure of, 323, 326, 331; industries in, 344; per capita production in, 351; per capita consumption in, 352; employment in, 360; volume of imports, 373; reciprocal imports, 404

Electric power. *See* Power supply

Employment: problems of, 209; in Central America, 255, 354–62

Ethylene production, 159

Europe, Eastern: sugar production, 17; coffee imports, 32; wheat production, 38; corn production, 42; cotton imports, 52; wool imports, 56; total exports to, 70

Europe, Western: sugar production, 17; coffee imports, 32, 270, 272, 297–300; wheat production, 38; corn production, 42; tin consumption, 62; total exports to, 70; private export credits, 100, 107; private capital from, 106–8; imports from Central America, 251, 267; banana imports, 276; wood imports, 282; cotton imports, 309

European Economic Community (EEC): economic activity in, 1, 5, 8–9; imports from Latin America, 9, 13; discriminatory restrictions by, 14; coffee imports, 14, 32, 33, 271, 273, 298–300; meat imports, 14, 42, 46; sugar imports, 21, 316; banana imports, 22; cacao imports, 30, 290, 318; corn imports, 39, 44; wheat imports, 40; cotton imports, 50, 52; wool imports, 54, 56; exports to, 70, 71; future of exports to, 201; imports from Central America, 251; Central American imports from, 387; export price variations, 388

European Free Trade Association: imports from Latin America, 9, 13; sugar imports, 21; cacao imports, 30; coffee imports, 32, 33; wheat imports, 40; corn imports, 44; cotton imports, 50, 52; wool imports, 56; total exports to, 70; per capita production in, 351

Exchange rate adjustments, 135

Export-Import Bank of Washington (EXIMBANK), 88, 90, 93, 112–13, 115, 116, 118

Exports: Latin American, 1–73; to United States, 9, 12; to European Free Trade Association, 9, 13; to European Economic Community, 9, 13; stabilization of receipts, 10; prices of products, 10, 11; of sugar, 10, 16–19, 20, 21, 69; of cacao, 10, 24–25, 29, 30; of coffee, 10, 25–35, 36, 37; of wool, 10, 53–54 of silver, 10, 64–65; of petroleum, 10, 65–68, 69, 70, 71; international market for products, 10–68; of foodstuffs, 13; to Canada, 13; of bananas, 19–24; of wheat, 35–38, 40; of corn, 38–39; of meat, 39–48, 70; of cotton, 49–53, 70; of copper, 54–58, 69; of zinc, 58–60, 61, 70; of lead, 58–60, 61, 70; of tin, 61–64; total exports, 68–73; principal regions of destination, 70; of fishery products, 70; intraregional, in Latin America, 73; credits from European governments, 100, 107; expansion goals, 200–1, 202; diversification in, 201; from El Salvador, 264; from Costa Rica, 264; from Honduras, 264; from Guatemala, 264; from Nicaragua, 264; price fluctuations in selected countries, 388
—Central American, 250–51, 263–318: cotton, 251, 263, 265, 266, 275–79, 294, 306–10; volume of, 266; value of, 266; of bananas, 265, 266, 271–75, 276, 294, 303–6; of coffee, 265, 266, 268–71, 272, 273, 294, 296–303; of wood, 265, 266, 280, 281, 282, 294, 311–12, 313; of meat, 265, 266, 280–84, 285, 294, 312–14, 315; of cocoa, 265, 266, 288–290, 294, 317–18; of sugar, 265, 266, 284–88, 294, 315–17; destination of, 267; prospects in 1963–67, 290–96; projection of value in 1967, 296–318

Expropriation of land, 213, 215

Fertilizers: production of, 157, 160, 161; Central American imports, 383; import value of, 390

Financing of planned investment, 198

Finland: coffee imports of, 273

Fiscal pressures, 137–40

Fishery products: exports of, 70

Fixed capital formation, 120–27

Foodstuffs: export of, 13; growth rate

in, 152; Central American output, 340, 344, 346; employment in industry, 360, 362; and capital intensity, 366, 368; Central American imports of, 377, 378–80, 382; reciprocal imports of, 397, 408–11
Ford Foundation, 227
Foreign Assistance Act: grants under, 91
Foreign capital contributions, 194–95
Foreign debt servicing, 110–11
Foreign exchange reserves, 112, 113, 117, 118
Foreign savings, 200
Foreign trade: plans for, 202–4
France: economic activity in, 5, 8; banana imports, 15, 24, 26; coffee imports, 32, 58; wheat exports, 41; corn exports, 44; meat imports, 46; wool consumption in, 53; copper consumption in, 57; tin consumption in, 62; tin imports, 63; credit granted by, 101; private export credits, 107; coffee imports, 273, 298, 299; export price variations, 388
Fur products: growth rate in, 152
Furniture. *See* Wood

Germany: economic activity in, 5, 8; banana imports, 19, 26, 304; coffee imports, 28, 32, 273, 297, 299; meat imports, 46; wool consumption in, 53; copper consumption in, 57; copper imports, 58; tin consumption in, 62; tin imports, 63; capital from, 99, 101; private export credits, 107; cotton imports, 278; 279 export price variations, 388, 390
Ghana. *See* Africa
Gold reserves, 112, 113, 117, 118
Grants. *See* Loans and grants
Gross domestic product, 122: planned growth of, 192; planned increases by sectors, 201–8; in Central America, 323
Guatemala: sugar production, 20; sugar exports, 20, 286, 316; banana exports, 23, 27, 274, 275, 303; coffee exports, 31, 33, 36, 37, 268, 269; coffee production, 36; cotton exports, 51, 276, 277, 279; cotton production, 51, 307; intraregional exports, 73; capacity to import, 76, 78, 79, 81; balance-of-payments position, 79; U.S. grants to, 92; AID loans and net disbursements, 94; Social Progress Trust Fund in, 95; Inter-American Development Bank report, 97; World Bank loans and disbursements, 98; capital from foreign countries, 100; U.S. private capital in, 103; private export credits, 107; assets in U.S. banks, 109; debt with International Monetary Fund, 114; compensatory accounts, 117, 118; gold reserves and foreign exchange, 117, 118; production in, 122; population increase in, 122; fixed investments in, 122; fixed capital formation in, 125; direct investments from U.S., 125; money supply trends, 128; monetary expansion in, 130; public and private sector bank lending, 133, 138, 141; cost of living index, 137; paper industry, 153; petroleum refining in, 165; cement production, 166; iron and steel industry, 169; development plans of, 188; planned investment growth, 193; planned investment by sectors, 206; agrarian reform in, 210, 218, 224, 229; tax reform in, 240, 242, 243, 244; exports from, 264; wood exports, 281, 311; meat exports, 283, 311; cocoa exports, 289; productive structure of, 323, 326, 331; industries in, 344; per capita production in, 351; per capita consumption in, 352; employment in, 362; volume of imports, 373; reciprocal imports in, 404
Guayana: industries in, 209
Guayaquil fertilizer plant, 161

Hague Club, 111
Haiti: sugar exports, 20; sugar production, 20; coffee exports, 31, 33, 36, 37; coffee production, 36; intraregional exports, 73; capacity to import, 76, 78, 79, 81; balance-of-payments position, 79; U.S. grants to, 92; AID loans and net disbursements, 94; Social Progress Trust Fund in, 95; Inter-American Development Bank report, 97; World Bank loans and disbursements, 98; capital from foreign countries, 100; private export

credits, 107; debt with International Monetary Fund, 114; compensatory accounts, 117, 118; gold reserves and foreign exchange, 117, 118; fixed investments in, 122; production in, 122; population increase in, 122; fixed capital formation in, 125; direct investments from U.S., 125; money supply trends, 128; monetary expansion in, 130; public and private sector bank lending, 133, 138, 141; cost of living index, 137; cement production, 166; development plans of, 189
Health programs: planned investment in, 206
Honduras: banana exports, 23, 27, 274, 275, 303; coffee exports, 31, 33, 36, 37, 268, 269; coffee production, 36; intraregional exports, 73; capacity to import, 76, 78, 79, 81; balance-of-payments position, 79; U.S. grants to, 92; AID loans and net disbursements, 94; Social Progress Trust Fund in, 95; Inter-American Development Bank report, 97; World Bank loans and disbursements, 98; capital from foreign countries, 100, 195; U.S. private capital in, 103; private export credits, 107; debt with International Monetary Fund, 114; compensatory accounts, 117, 118; gold reserves and foreign exchange, 117, 118; production in, 122; population increase in, 122; fixed investments in, 122; direct investments from U.S., 125; fixed capital formation in, 125; money supply trends, 128; monetary expansion in, 130; public and private sector bank lending, 133, 138, 141; cost of living index, 137; cement production, 166; development plans of, 186, 188; planned growth of gross domestic product, 192; financing of planned investment, 199; planned foreign trade of, 202; planned investment by sectors, 206; regional characteristics in, 208; agrarian reform in, 210, 218, 224, 229–30; tax reform in, 241, 243, 244; wood supply in, 257n, 311; exports from, 264; cotton exports, 276, 277; wood exports, 281; meat exports, 283, 313; sugar exports, 286, 315; cotton production, 307; productive structure of, 323, 326, 331; industries in, 344; per capita production in, 351; per capita consumption in, 352; employment in, 360; capital intensity in, 366, 368; volume of imports, 373; reciprocal imports, 404
Huachipato ingot production, 172
Hungary: coffee imports of, 32
Hydrochloric acid production, 161
Hydrofluoric acid production, 159
Hydrogen peroxide production, 160

Imports: of industrialized areas, 9; world imports of coffee, 32, 33; total capacity for, 74–85; and balance of payments, 74–85; expansion goals, 200, 202; replacement of overseas imports, 419–23. *See also* Reciprocal trade
—Central American, 255–57, 372–425: volume of, 372–74, 377; intraregional trade, 375, 394–425; foodstuffs, 377, 378–80, 382; chemical products, 377, 380–85; sources of, 385–94; trade with Europe and Japan, 387–88; price variations, 388; sectoral relative prices, 389–92; import substitution, 392
Indonesia: tin production in, 62
Industrial production, 122. *See also* Manufacturing; Production
Industrialization of Central America, 407
Industrialized countries: economic activity in, 1–9
Insecticides: production of, 160, 161
Institute of Rural Welfare in Paraguay, 224, 232
Instituto Agrario in Dominican Republic, 224
Instituto de Bienestar Rural in Paraguay, 224, 232
Instituto Nacional Agrario in Honduras, 224, 230
Instituto Nacional Agrario in Nicaragua, 224, 231
Instituto Nacional Colombiano de Reforma Agraria (INCORA), 213, 224, 227
Instituto Nacional de Transformación Agraria in Guatemala, 224
Instituto de Reforma Agraria y Colonización in Peru, 224
Instituto de Tierras y Colonización in Costa Rica (ITCO), 224, 229

Integration industries, 254
Inter-American Development Bank (IDB), 92, 96, 97, 105, 155, 223, 232
Inter-American Economic and Social Council: stabilization of export receipts, 10–13; Committee on Basic Products, 13–14, 15; Meat Action Group, 14, 42; and restrictions on coffee consumption, 14; Group of Experts on Sugar, 15; Cacao Action Group, 15; Banana Action Group, 15, 22
Interest rates on bank lending, 143
International Bank for Reconstruction and Development (World Bank), 96, 97n, 98
International Cacao Agreement, 15, 25
International Cocoa Agreement, 292, 293, 317
International Coffee Agreement, 25, 302
International Cotton Advisory Committee, 309
International Development Association, 96, 98
International Finance Corporation, 96, 98
International Lead and Zinc Study Group, 59, 60
International Monetary Fund (IMF), 13, 16, 112–13, 114, 116, 118
International Tin Council, 62, 64
International Wheat Agreement, 35
International Wool Study Group, 54
Investments: fixed, 122; private, 124, 125; direct, 124, 125; and planned growth of gross domestic product, 192; foreign capital contributions, 194–95; financing of, 198; distribution by sectors, 206; tax incentives to, 242; in Central America, 393–94
Ireland: meat exports of, 47, 48
Iron and steel industry, 148, 167–74: growth rate of, 148, 149; in Argentina, 169, 170–71; in Brazil, 169, 171–72; in Chile, 169, 172; in Colombia, 169, 172; in Peru, 169, 173; in Mexico, 169, 173; in Venezuela, 169, 174; per capita production of steel, 351; per capita consumption of steel, 352; wholesale prices of steel, 390
Italy: economic activity in, 5, 8; banana imports, 15, 24, 26; coffee imports, 32, 273, 298, 299; meat imports, 43, 46; wool consumption in, 53; copper imports, 55, 58; copper consumption in, 57; tin consumption in, 62; tin imports, 63; private export credits, 107; export price variations, 388
Ivory Coast. *See* Africa

Japan: sugar imports, 21; coffee imports, 32; corn imports, 39, 44; wheat imports, 40; cotton imports, 50, 52, 278, 279, 309; wool consumption in, 53; wool imports, 54; copper imports, 55, 58; tin imports, 63; total exports to, 70; capital from, 99, 100, 101, 106–8; private export credits, 107; future of exports to, 201; imports from Central America, 251, 267; cocoa imports, 290, 318; Central American imports from, 387; export price variations, 388, 390

Kellogg Foundation, 227

Lago de Valencia region: urban services in, 209
Laguna del Rey salt reserves, 160
Laja newsprint plant, 156
Lamb exports. *See* Meat
Lampblack production, 159, 160, 161
Land-tenure systems, 210
Latifundias: structure of, 210
Latin American Free Trade Association (LAFTA), 71, 72, 179
Lead: price of, 11, 58; exports of, 58–60, 61, 70; stocks of, 59; International Lead and Zinc Study Group, 59, 60; production of, 60
Lead tetraethylene production, 159
Leather products: growth rate in, 152; Central American output, 340, 344, 346; employment in industry, 360, 362; and capital intensity, 366, 368; wholesale prices of, 390
Ledesma project, 154
Legislation for agrarian reform, 211–22
Linz-Donauwitz steel process, 170n, 172
Loans and grants: from United States,

86n, 87, 88–96; from international agencies, 96–99
Los Andes: agriculture and industry in, 209
Los Organos petrochemical project, 161
Luján de Cuyol petroleum refinery, 162
Lumber. *See* Wood
Luxembourg: economic activity in, 5; coffee imports, 32, 273; meat imports, 46; export price variations, 388

Machinery, industrial, 183–84: wholesale prices of, 390; import value of, 392; reciprocal imports, 397
Magallanes: land leases in, 223, 225
Majagual: agriculture in, 209
Malaya: tin production, 62; tin imports, 63
Mamonal ammonium and nitric acid plant, 160
Mannesmann steelworks, 171
Manufacturing: general development of, 146–84; growth of output, 148; consumer-goods, 148, 149, 150–51; petroleum refining, 148, 161–65; cement industry, 148, 165–67; iron and steel industry, 148, 167–74; motor vehicle industry, 148, 174–79; paper industry, 151–56; chemical industries, 157–61; tractor production, 179–81; shipbuilding, 181–83; industrial machinery and equipment, 183–84; exports of products, 203; planned increases in, 204; planned investment in, 206; in Central America, 253, 321, 323, 324, 331, 334–71; integration industries, 254
Maracaibo: urban services in, 209
Maracay paper plant, 156
Matanzas steel plant, 174
Mazatlán project, 182
Meat: price of, 11, 39; Action Group for, 14, 42; exports of, 39–48, 70; imports of selected countries, 46, 47, 48; exports from Central America, 265, 266, 280–84, 285, 294, 312–14, 315
Mechanical industries in Central America, 340, 344, 346: employment in, 361, 362; and capital intensity, 367, 369
Metal products: employment in industry, 361, 362; and capital intensity, 367, 369

Methanol production, 159
Mexico: sugar stocks in, 17; sugar exports, 19, 20, 21; sugar production, 20; cacao exports, 29; cacao production, 29; coffee exports, 31, 34, 36, 37; coffee production, 36; corn production, 42; meat exports, 43, 48; cotton production, 50, 51; cotton exports, 51, 52; copper production, 57; copper exports, 58; lead exports, 60; lead production, 60; zinc production, 60; zinc exports, 61; lead exports, 61; silver production, 65; petroleum production, 66; petroleum exports, 67, 68, 69; exports from, 69, 70; intraregional exports, 73; capacity to import, 76, 78, 79, 81; balance-of-payments position, 79; U.S. grants to, 92; AID loans and net disbursements, 94; Social Progress Trust Fund in, 95; Inter-American Development Bank report, 97; World Bank loans and disbursements, 98; capital from foreign countries, 100; U.S. private capital in, 103; private export credits, 107; assets in U.S. banks, 109; foreign debt servicing, 111; debt with International Monetary Fund, 114; compensatory loans by Eximbank, 115; compensatory accounts, 117, 118; gold reserves and foreign exchange, 117, 118; production in, 122; fixed investments in, 122; population in, 122; fixed capital formation in, 125; direct investments from U.S., 125; money supply trends, 128; monetary expansion in, 130; public and private sector bank lending, 133, 138, 141; cost of living index, 137; bank reforms in, 144; manufacturing growth in, 147, 148; paper industry in, 153, 156; chemical industry in, 158, 159; petroleum refining in, 163, 164, 165; cement production, 166; iron and steel industry, 169, 173; motor vehicle production, 175, 178; tractor production, 181; shipbuilding in, 182; industrial machinery production, 183; development plans of, 186, 188; planned growth of gross domestic product, 193; agrarian reform in, 234; tax reform in, 238, 242, 243, 244
Middle East: petroleum production and exports in, 69

Minatitlán: ammonium anhydride plant in, 159; petroleum refinery in, 164
Minifundias: structure of, 210
Mining: export of minerals, 203; planned increases in, 204; planned investment in, 206; in Central America, 321, 324, 340, 344, 346
Misiones project, 155
Monclova steel plant, 173
Monetary developments, 127–45; money supply trends, 128–29; expansion factors, 129–33; balance-of-payments trends, 130, 133–37; fiscal pressures, 137–40; bank credit to private sector, 140–43; institutional reforms, 143–45
Monte Alegre newsprint plant, 155
Monterrey steel plant, 173
Morón petrochemical complex, 161
Motor vehicle industry, 148, 174–79: growth rate of, 148, 150; in Brazil, 175, 177; in Argentina, 175, 177–78; in Mexico, 175, 178; in Chile, 175, 179; in Venezuela, 175, 179; in Colombia, 175, 179; import value of, 390; wholesale prices of, 390; reciprocal imports, 397

National Agrarian Institute of Honduras, 224, 230
National Agrarian Institute of Nicaragua, 224, 231
National Agrarian Reform Institute of Colombia (INCORA), 213, 224, 227
National Cadastral Survey, 225
Netherlands: economic activity in, 5, 8; banana imports, 24, 26, 304; coffee imports, 32, 273; meat imports, 46; wool consumption in, 53; copper consumption in, 57; copper imports, 58; tin imports, 63; cotton imports, 278, 279; export price variations, 388
New Zealand: meat exports, 47, 48; wool stocks in, 55; wool exports, 56
Newsprint. *See* Paper; Printing and publishing
Nicaragua: sugar production, 20; sugar exports, 20, 21, 286, 315; coffee exports, 31, 34, 36, 37, 268, 269; coffee production, 36; cotton production, 51, 307; cotton exports, 51, 52, 276, 277, 279; intraregional exports, 73; capacity to import, 76, 78, 79, 81; balance-of-payments position, 79; U.S. grants to, 92; AID loans and net disbursements, 94; Social Progress Trust Fund in, 95; Inter-American Development Bank report, 97; World Bank loans and disbursements, 98; capital from foreign countries, 100; private export credits, 107; debt with International Monetary Fund, 114; compensatory loans by Eximbank, 115; gold reserves and foreign exchange, 117, 118; compensatory accounts, 117, 118; fixed investments in, 122; population increase in, 122; production in, 122; fixed capital formation in, 125; direct investments from U.S., 125; money supply trends, 128; monetary expansion in, 130; public and private sector bank lending, 133, 138, 141; cost of living index, 137; Central Bank legislation, 144; petroleum refining in, 165; cement production, 166; development plans of, 189; agrarian reform in, 210, 218, 224, 230–31; tax reform in, 241; exports from, 264; banana exports, 274, 275; wood exports, 281, 312, 313; meat exports, 283, 313; cocoa exports, 289; productive structure of, 323, 326, 331; industries in, 344; per capita production in, 351; per capita consumption in, 352; employment in, 360; volume of imports, 373; reciprocal imports, 404
Nigeria. *See* Africa
Nitric acid production, 160
Noncompensatory capital movements, 85–111
Northeast development agency (SUDENE), 185n, 208, 242
Norway: coffee imports, 32, 273; banana imports, 304

Oficina de Coordinacion y Planificación Económica (CORDIPLAN), 185n
Oil, crude: production of, 161–65
Organisation for Economic Co-operation and Development, 99–101
Oriente: population relocation in, 208
Output: target growth rates of, 191–201
Pakistan: cotton exports from, 50, 52
Panama: banana exports, 23, 27; coffee exports, 31; intraregional exports, 73;

capacity to import, 76, 78, 79, 81; balance-of-payments position, 79; U.S. grants to, 92; AID loans and net disbursements, 94; Social Progress Trust Fund in, 95; Inter-American Development Bank report, 97; World Bank loans and disbursements, 98; capital from foreign countries, 100, 195; U.S. private capital in, 103; private exports credits, 107; assets in U.S. banks, 109; debt with International Monetary Fund, 114; compensatory accounts, 117, 118; gold reserves and foreign exchange, 117, 118; population increase in, 122; fixed investments in, 122; production in, 122; fixed capital formation in, 125; direct investments from U.S., 125; money supply trends, 128; monetary expansion in, 130; public and private sector bank lending, 133, 141; cost of living index, 137; petroleum refining in, 163, 165; cement production, 166; iron and steel industry, 169; development plans of, 186, 187n, 188; planned growth of gross domestic product, 193; financing of planned investment, 199; planned foreign trade of, 202; planned investment by sectors, 296; regional characteristics in, 208; agrarian reform in, 210, 220, 224, 231; tax reform in, 241, 242, 244; cocoa imports, 290; productive structure of, 323, 326, 331; industries in, 344; per capita production in, 351; per capita consumption in, 352

Paper industry: growth rate of, 148, 150; activities in, 148, 151–56; in Argentina, 153, 154–55; in Colombia, 153, 155; in Brazil, 153, 155; in Chile, 153, 156; in Central America, 153, 156, 340, 344, 346, 349; in Mexico, 153, 156; in Venezuela, 153, 156; per capita production, 351; per capita consumption of paper, 352; employment in industry, 360, 362; and capital intensity, 366, 369; wholesale prices, 390

Paraguay: meat exports, 47, 48; cotton production, 51; cotton exports, 51; intraregional exports, 73; capacity to import, 76, 78, 79, 81; balance-of-payments position, 79; U.S. grants to, 92; AID loans and net disbursements, 94; Social Progress Trust Fund in, 95; Inter-American Development Bank report, 97; World Bank loans and disbursements, 98; capital from foreign countries, 100; private export credits, 107; foreign debt servicing, 111; debt with International Monetary Fund, 114; gold reserves and foreign exchange, 117, 118; compensatory accounts, 117, 118; production in, 122; fixed investments in, 122; population increase in, 122; direct investments from U.S., 125; fixed capital formation in, 125; money supply trends, 128; monetary expansion in, 130; public and private sector bank lending, 133, 138, 141; exchange rate adjustments in, 135; cost of living index, 135, 137; paper industry in, 153; chemical industry in, 161; petroleum refining in, 165; cement production, 166; development plans of, 189; agrarian reform in, 210, 220, 224, 232; tax reform in, 239, 242, 244

Paraná River project, 225, 233

Paris Club, 111

Payments: balance of, 74–85. *See also* Balance of Payments

Paz del Rio steel plant, 172

Pemex expansion program, 165

Penonomé project, 231

Peru: exports to United States, 13; sugar stocks in, 17; sugar exports, 19, 20, 21; sugar production, 20; coffee exports, 31, 34, 36; coffee production, 36; cotton production, 51; cotton exports, 51, 52; copper production, 55, 57; copper exports, 58; lead production, 60; zinc production, 60; lead exports, 60, 61; zinc exports, 61; silver production, 65; petroleum production, 66; petroleum exports, 67, 68; exports from, 69, 70; intraregional exports, 73; capacity to import, 76, 78, 79, 81; balance-of-payments position, 79; U.S. grants to 92; AID loans and net disbursements, 94; Social Progress Trust Fund in, 95; Inter-American Development Bank report, 97; World Bank loans and disbursements, 98; capital from foreign countries, 100; U.S. private capital in, 103; private export credits, 107; assets in U.S. banks, 109;

foreign debt servicing, 111; debt with International Monetary Fund, 114; compensatory loans by Eximbank, 115; compensatory accounts, 117, 118; gold reserves and foreign exchange, 117, 118; production in, 122; population increase in, 122; fixed investments in, 122; fixed capital formation in, 125; direct investments from U.S., 125; money supply trends, 128; monetary expansion in, 130; public and private sector bank lending, 133, 138, 141; exchange rate adjustments in, 135; cost of living index, 135, 137; Central Bank legislation, 143; manufacturing growth in, 148, 149; consumer-goods industries in, 151, 152; paper industry in, 153; chemical industry in, 158, 161; petroleum refining in, 163; cement production, 166; iron and steel industry, 169, 173; automotive industry in, 179n; shipbuilding in, 183; development plans of, 189; agrarian reform in, 210, 215, 220, 224, 233; tax reform in, 239, 243, 244

Petrobas: investments by, 208

Petroleum: price of, 10, 11, 65; exports of, 65–68, 69, 70, 71; production of, 66; subsidy on imports of, 136; growth rate in industry, 148, 149; Central American output, 340; employment in industry, 360, 362; and capital intensity, 366, 369

—refining industries, 148, 161–65: in Argentina, 162–64; in Venezuela, 162, 163, 164; in Brazil, 163, 164, 165; in Mexico, 163, 164, 165; in Chile, 163, 164, 165

Pharmaceuticals: production of, 157; Central American imports, 377, 380–85

Phenol production, 159, 160

Philippines: sugar production in, 17

Phthalic anhydride production, 160

Plastics: production of, 160, 161

Poland: coffee imports of, 32

Population: relation to production, 122; relocation of, 208

Portugal: coffee imports of, 32

Power supplies: planned increases in, 204; planned investment in, 206; in Central America, 321, 324, 348; per capita production of, 351

Price pressures, and balance-of-payments, 133–37

Prices: of silver, 10, 11, 64, 70; of export products, 10, 11, 388; of sugar, 18, 287; of bananas, 19, 22; of coffee, 25; of wheat, 35; of corn, 38; of meat, 39; of cotton, 49; of wool, 53; of copper, 54; of lead, 58; of zinc, 58; of tin, 61; of petroleum, 65

Printing and publishing: subsidy on imports of newsprint, 136; in Central America, 340, 344, 346; employment in, 361, 362; and capital intensity, 367–69

Private capital: from United States, 101–6; from Western Europe and Japan, 106–8

Private investments, 124, 125

Private savings, 197

Production: of sugar, 17, 20; of cacao beans, 28, 29; of coffee, 31, 36; of wheat, 38; of corn, 42; of cotton, 49, 51; of copper, 57; of zinc, 60; of lead, 60; of tin, 62 of silver, 65; of petroleum, 66; variations in total product, 120–27; gross domestic product, 122; industrial, 122; population related to, 122; agricultural, 122; planned increases in, 204. *See also* Gross domestic product

—in Central America, 251–55, 319–71: of cotton, 307; current production of goods and services, 319–34; manufacturing structure, 334–71; growth in production of selected products, 348; per capita production of products, 351; per capita consumption, 352; employment and capital structure, 354–62; and capital intensity, 364–71

Public Law 480, 88, 90, 91, 92, 93, 96, 392

Public savings, 197

Publishing. *See* Printing and publishing

Puerto Isaacs newsprint plant, 155

Punta del Este Charter, 88, 185, 187, 210, 211, 234

Quotas: for sugar exports, 18–19, 288, 315; for coffee exports, 25, 302; for lead exports, 59; for zinc exports, 59

Reciprocal trade in Central America, 375, 394–425: countries participating in, 404; food imports, 408–11; tex-

tile imports, 411–15; factors delaying, 416–17; and replacement of overseas imports, 419–23
Refineries: petroleum, 148, 161–65
Refrigerating gases: production of, 159
Regional disparities, 208
Reserves: gold and foreign exchange, 112, 113, 117, 118
Resettlement of population, 208
Rhodesia. *See* Africa
Rivas Department, 231
Rockefeller Foundation, 227
Rubber products: manufacture of synthetic rubber, 157, 159, 160; Central American output, 340, 344, 346; employment in industry, 360, 362; and capital intensity, 366, 369
Russia. *See* Soviet Union

Salamanca: ammonium anhydride plant in, 159; petroleum refinery in, 164
San Lorenzo: chemical center in, 160; project in, 225, 234
San Nicolás steel plant, 170
Savings: private, 197; public, 197; foreign, 200
Securities transactions, 104
Shipbuilding, 181–83
Siderca en Campaña steel plant, 170
Siemens-Martin steel plants, 170n, 172
Silver: price of, 10, 11, 64, 70; exports of, 64–65; production of, 65
Social Agrarian Council, 227
Social Progress Trust Fund, 88, 90, 92, 95, 96
Sodium carbonate production, 159, 160
Soviet Union: sugar production, 17; cacao imports, 30; coffee imports, 32, 33; wheat production, 38; wheat exports, 41; corn production, 42; cotton imports, 52; wool imports, 54, 56; lead exports, 60; zinc exports, 60; tin imports and exports, 64; petroleum production, 66; petroleum exports, 67; total exports to, 70
Spain: meat imports of, 42
Standard International Classification of Trade (SICT), 376
Steel. *See* Iron and steel industry
Stocks: of sugar, 18; of cacao beans, 28; of coffee, 31; of wheat, 38; of corn, 46; of cotton, 49; of wool, 55; of lead, 59; of zinc, 59

Subsidies: governmental, 136
Sudan: cotton exports from, 52
SUDENE agency, 185n, 208, 242
Sugar: export of, 10, 16–19, 20, 21, 69; price of, 11, 16, 18; Group of Experts on, 15; production of, 16, 17, 20, 348; U.S. legislation on, 18; stocks of, 18; import quotas of, 18–19; imports of selected countries, 21; exports from Central America, 265, 266, 284–88, 294, 315–17; Central American production of, 348; per capita production of, 351; per capita consumption of, 352; Central American imports, 382
Sulphuric acid production, 158, 160, 161
Superintendency for Money and Credit (SUMOC), 144
Sweden: coffee imports, 32, 273; wool consumption in, 53; copper consumption in, 57; copper imports, 58; banana imports, 304
Switzerland: banana imports, 24, 26; coffee imports, 32, 273; copper consumption in, 57
Syria: cotton exports from, 52

Taiwan: sugar production in, 17
Tamsa steel plant, 173
Tax reform, 235–45: increased receipts, 236–41; in Argentina, 237, 241, 242, 243, 244; in Brazil, 237, 241, 242, 244; in Chile, 238, 242, 244; in Mexico, 238, 242, 243, 244; in Dominican Republic, 238, 242, 244; in Ecuador, 238, 242, 244; in Colombia, 238, 244; in Costa Rica, 239, 242, 243; in Paraguay, 239, 242, 244; in Peru, 239, 243, 244; in Uruguay, 239, 243, 244; in Venezuela, 239, 244; in Guatemala, 240, 242, 243, 244; in El Salvador, 240, 243, 244; in Nicaragua, 241; equitable distribution of tax burden, 241–42; in Panama, 241, 242, 244; in Honduras, 241, 243, 244; investment incentives, 242; improved administration, 243–45; collection procedures, 243–45; in Bolivia, 244; in Central America, 244; and fiscal pressures, 137
Textiles: growth rates in, 152; Central American output, 340, 344, 346, 348;

INDEX 443

cotton cloth production, 348, 351; per capita consumption of cotton cloth, 352; employment in industry, 360, 362; and capital intensity, 366, 368; wholesale prices of, 390; reciprocal imports, 411–15. *See also* Wool

Thailand: corn production, 39; corn exports, 45; tin production, 62

Thomas converters in steel production, 170n

Tin: price of, 11, 61; exports of, 61–64; consumption of, 62; production of, 62; International Tin Council, 62, 64; imports of selected countries, 63; Soviet Union exports and imports, 64

Tobacco: growth rates in, 152; Central American output, 340, 344, 346, 348; per capita production of cigarettes, 351; per capita consumption of cigarettes, 352; employment in industry, 360, 362; and capital intensity, 366, 368; reciprocal imports, 397

Toluene production, 159

Tonosí project, 225, 231

Tractor production, 179–81

Transportation: planned increases in, 204; planned investment in, 206; in Central America, 321, 324; and trade among countries, 399

Treaties in Central America, 375, 400–3

Turkey: cotton exports from, 52

United Kingdom: economic activity in, 4–8; meat imports, 14, 42, 43, 47; banana imports, 15, 24, 26; coffee imports, 32, 273; wool consumption in, 53; wool imports, 54; copper consumption in, 57; copper imports, 58; lead stocks in, 59; zinc stocks in, 59; tin stocks in, 62; tin consumption in, 62; tin imports, 63; capital from, 99; private export credits, 107; cotton imports, 278, 279; export price variations, 388

United Nations Commission on International Commodity Trade, 13

United States: economic activity in, 1–4, 5; imports from Latin America, 9, 12; sugar imports, 17, 21, 287, 315; sugar legislation, 18; sugar prices in, 18; banana imports, 22, 26, 276, 304; coffee imports, 28, 31, 32, 33, 270, 272, 296–97, 298, 301; cacao imports, 30, 290, 318, wheat production, 38; corn production, 39, 42; wheat exports, 40; meat imports, 43, 48, 285, 312; corn exports, 44; corn stocks in, 46; cotton stocks in, 49; cotton exports, 50; cotton imports, 50, 52; wool consumption in, 53; wool imports, 54, 56; copper production, 55, 57; copper consumption in, 57; copper exports, 58; copper imports, 58; lead stocks in, 59; lead imports, 59; zinc stocks in, 59; zinc imports, 59; zinc production, 60; lead production, 60; tin stocks in, 62; tin consumption, 62; tin imports, 63; silver production, 65; petroleum production, 66; petroleum imports, 67, 69; petroleum exports, 69; total exports to, 70; loans and grants from, 86n, 87, 88–96; private capital in Latin America, 101–6; Latin American assets in banks, 109; direct investments from, 125, 126; future of exports to, 201; imports from Central America, 251, 267; wood imports, 282; per capita production in, 351; per capita consumption in, 352; export price variations, 388, 390, 392

Urbanization: planned investment in, 206

Urea production, 158, 161

Uruguay: meat exports, 42, 43, 46, 47, 48; wool exports, 54, 56; wool stocks in, 55; intraregional exports, 73; capacity to import, 76, 78, 79, 81; balance-of-payments position, 79; U.S. grants to, 92; AID loans and net disbursements, 94; Social Progress Trust Fund in, 95; Inter-American Development Bank report, 97; World Bank loans and disbursements, 98; capital from foreign countries, 100; U.S. private capital in, 103; private export credits, 107; assets in U.S. banks, 109; foreign debt servicing, 111; debt with International Monetary Fund, 114; gold reserves and foreign exchange, 117, 118; compensatory accounts, 117, 118, production in, 122; population increase in, 122; fixed investments in, 122; direct investments from U.S., 125; fixed capital formation in, 125; money supply trends, 128; monetary expansion in, 130; public and private sector bank lending, 133, 138, 141; exchange rate adjustments in, 135; cost of living index, 135, 137; bank reforms in, 144; paper industry in, 153; petroleum refining in, 163; cement production, 166; iron and steel industry, 169, 173; motor vehicle production, 175, 179n; development plans of, 189; tax reform in, 239, 243, 244

Usiminas: project in, 100; steel plant in, 171, 182n

Valencia automotive industry, 179
Valentines iron-ore reserves, 173
Venezuela: exports to United States, 13; cacao production, 29; cacao exports, 29, 30; coffee exports, 31, 34, 36; coffee production, 36; petroleum production, 66; petroleum exports, 67, 68, 69, 71; exports from, 69; intraregional exports, 73; capacity to import, 76, 78, 79, 81; balance-of-payments position, 79; U.S. grants to, 92; AID loans and net disbursements, 94; Social Progress Trust Fund in, 95; Inter-American Development Bank report, 97; World Bank loans and disbursements, 98; capital from foreign countries, 100; U.S. private capital in, 103; private export credits, 107; assets in U.S. banks, 109; foreign debt servicing, 111; debt with International Monetary Fund, 114; compensatory loans by Eximbank, 115; gold reserves and foreign exchange, 117, 118; compensatory accounts, 117, 118; production in, 122; fixed investments in, 122; population increase in, 122; fixed capital formation in, 125; direct investments from U.S., 125; money supply trends, 128; monetary expansion in, 130; public and private sector bank lending, 133, 138, 141; cost of living index, 137; Central Bank legislation, 144; manufactring growth in, 148, 149; consumer-goods industries in, 151, 152; paper industry in, 153, 156; chemical industry in, 158, 161; petroleum refining in, 162, 163, 164; cement production, 166; iron and steel industry, 169, 174; motor vehicle production, 175, 179; tractor production, 181; development plans of, 185, 186, 188; foreign capital contributions, 195; financing of planned investment, 199; planned foreign trade of, 202; planned increases in production, 204; planned investment by sectors, 206; regional characteristics in, 208; agrarian reform in, 235; tax reform in, 239, 244

Vera Cruz ship installations, 182
Vitória ironworks, 171
Volta Redonda steel plant, 171

Wage increases: effects of, 136
Water supply: planned investment in, 206
Wheat: price of, 11, 35; International Agreement, 35; export of, 35–38, 40; stocks of, 38; production of, 38; imports of selected countries, 40; subsidy on imports of, 136
Wheat flour: Central American production of, 348; per capita production of, 351; per capita consumption of, 352; Central American imports, 382
Wood: growth rates in production of furniture, 152; exports from Central America, 265, 266, 280, 281, 282, 294, 311–12, 313; lumber output of Central America, 340, 344, 346, 349; per capita production of lumber, 351; employment in lumber industry, 360, 362; and capital intensity, 366, 368
Wool: export of, 10, 53–54, 56; price of, 11, 53; consumption of, 53; International Wool Study Group, 54; stocks of, 55; imports of selected countries, 56
World Bank, 96, 97n, 98

Yugoslavia: wheat production, 38; corn exports, 39, 44

Zinc: price of, 11, 58; exports of, 58–60, 61, 70; stocks of, 59; International Lead and Zinc Study Group, 59, 60; production of, 60

ECONOMIC SURVEY OF LATIN AMERICA, 1962

designer—Edward D. King
typesetter—Monotype Composition Company
typefaces—Baskerville, Engravers Roman
printer—Universal Lithographers, Inc.
paper—Perkins and Squire SM
binder—Moore & Co.
cover material—Columbia Riverside Linen